D0553815

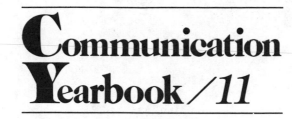

Communication Yearbook /11

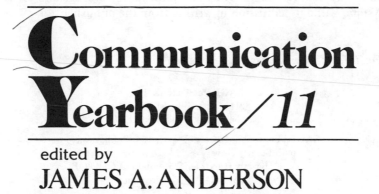

Communication Yearbook/11

edited by
JAMES A. ANDERSON

 Published Annually for the
International Communication
Association

SAGE PUBLICATIONS
The Publishers of Professional Social Science
Newbury Park   Beverly Hills   London   New Delhi

For information address:

SAGE Publications, Inc.
2111 West Hillcrest Drive
Newbury Park, California 91320

SAGE Publications Inc.   SAGE Publications Ltd.
275 South Beverly Drive   28 Banner Street
Beverly Hills   London EC1Y 8QE
California 90212   England

SAGE PUBLICATIONS India Pvt. Ltd.
M-32 Market
Greater Kailash I
New Delhi 110 048 India

Printed in the United States of America

Library of Congress: 76-45943
ISBN 0-8039-3138-7

FIRST PRINTING 1988

CONTENTS

THE INTERNATIONAL COMMUNICATION ASSOCIATION

The *Communication Yearbook* series is sponsored by the International Communication Association, one of several major scholarly organizations in the communication field. It is composed of 2,500 communication scholars, teachers, and practitioners.

Throughout its 38-year history, the Association has been particularly important to those in the field of communication who have sought a forum where the behavioral science perspective was predominant. The International Communication Association has also been attractive to a number of individuals from a variety of disciplines who hold communication to be central to work within their primary fields of endeavor. The Association has been an important stimulant to the infusion of behavioral concepts in communication study and teaching, and has played a significant role in defining a broadened set of boundaries of the discipline as a whole.

The International Communication Association is a pluralist organization composed of ten subdivisions: Information Systems, Interpersonal Communication, Mass Communication, Organizational Communication, Intercultural and Development Communication, Political Communication, Instructional and Developmental Communication, Health Communication, Philosophy of Communication, and Human Communication Technology.

In addition to *Communication Yearbook*, the Association publishes *Human Communication Research*, the *ICA Newsletter*, and *ICA Directory*, and is affiliated with the *Journal of Communication*. Several divisions also publish newsletters and occasional papers.

PREFACE

This preface introduces a new series in the history of the *Communication Yearbook*. As readers know, the previous series featured commissioned overviews along with selected papers from the previous International Communication Association convention. Experience showed the combination often to be awkward. It was decided to split commissioned works from the convention papers, the former to remain the contents of the *Yearbook* and the latter to be published in a *Proceedings*. But the radical change is not in this split: The radical change is in the set of principles that govern the purposes of the *Yearbook,* the nature of the articles commissioned, and their critical analysis in following commentaries.

PRINCIPLES

There has been much criticism, some of it justified, of professional academics writing only to other professional academics and then only to those of their own kind. There has developed in communication and other disciplines a "boutiques of inquiry" mentality. Articles are written in coded language about issues empowered by members with the righteousness of incised perspectives. In spite of my frank language, there is clear value in such articles for some of the work that must be done in this and every field of inquiry. There is other work to be done, however. That work involves finding the connections that constitute the structure most of us call communication. The first principle of this series, then, is to seek articles that, while written from the working perspective of the authors, have something to say to the field at large. It is time that the deconstructive rot of ferment begins to come together as a wine of some promise.

The second overarching principle is that the *Yearbook* is no longer to be read as an encyclopedia. Rather, readers should profit in ideas and insights from reading the whole work. The principle of connections provided the underlying themes, and authors committed themselves to achieving a quality of accessibility.

The final principle—to represent many different working perspectives—follows from the first two. Pluralism seems to be a dominant figure in most visions of the future of academic inquiry. Pluralism need not be divisive; it can be enlightening and energizing. The mechanics of accomplishing this representation extend beyond a given volume. A *Yearbook* editor's term is three years, which allows some flexibility in developing differing emphases across those volumes. This volume develops themes in media, conversation analysis, criticism, phenomenology, persuasion, methodology, and opinion formation. Following volumes will pursue themes in power, friendship, technology, the self and other, life stages, intercultural relations, media and politics, confrontation, and contextualism, among other topics.

CHARACTER OF THE MONOGRAPHS

Some explanation needs to be given about the character of the major works presented in this volume. Authors have written what are often called open texts. Such texts provide space for the reader to participate in the development of the monograph themes. In practical terms, authors have achieved this openness by the deliberate reflexive analysis of a line of argument, by the explicit recognition of their perspective, and by the acceptance of other concerns, along with other methods, that can be brought to bear on the issue. It is expected that readers will take complementary or contrary positions in much the same way that the commentators who follow each monograph have. The opportunity to do so is neither a violation of one's own faith nor an error on the part of the author.

COMMENTARIES

A Utah colleague, Doug Birkhead, has commented that we have given a sub rosa character to the great bulk of the critical work done in this field. Most of that work is done in anonymous critiques of unidentified manuscripts within the review process. For Professor Birkhead and others, criticism ought to be a regular public activity in which the principles of evaluation are owned and the consequences of their application can themselves be evaluated.

The monographs that appear in this *Yearbook* were first selected as proposals through a review process involving the editor and content specialists. Once the proposals were selected, the editor's work was to support the authors in their efforts to accomplish what was proposed within *Yearbook* guidelines. Authors redrafted their articles for clarity, precision, and development, as we all must. Articles have not been redrafted—as is often the case—to close off avenues of critical analysis.

Commentators for each monograph were proposed by the author(s) and selected by the editor specifically to explore those avenues as they appeared in the themes developed within the monograph. Each commentator was asked to express his or her own position and then to pursue the analysis from that position.

Commentators are neither friends nor enemies. Their purpose is to enlarge our understanding of the monograph by giving us another place to stand and view the work. They do not address questions of fault and error, but rather what can be seen from where.

LOOKING FOR CONNECTIONS

There are any number of themes that inevitably connect work within this discipline—those of text, action, process, meaning, context, and power, for example. Space for this preface precludes more than the hasty analysis of just one of these themes. In my opinion, the special significance of even a hasty analysis is that the discipline of communication is found in these and other themes rather than in their particular expression in organizations, media, or relationships of various kinds. A particular benefit of the *Yearbook* is that it features many working perspectives that can function to provide a view of communication themes across them.

As an example of what can be done, let us consider one of the unresolved, in fact growing, tensions in communication theory—the relative status of text versus action in the explanation of communication processes. Traditional communication theory gives primary status to the text, a term indicating any bounded content. The facts of the text, indeed, explain the effects of exposure to the text. The last two decades have seen other theories—in interaction analysis, contingency theories, uses and gratifications, and accommodation theory—that shift the emphasis to the act of reception or, more complexly, to the social action of interpretation. Here, the text becomes the raw material from which a number of accounts can be given.

The perspectives of text and action and the tension between them is well represented in this volume. The three opening chapters, on the concept of the active audience, envelop us immediately in the controversy. Biocca stands firmly on the side of text—exposure inevitably leads to primary effects in attention and retention. Lindlof privileges action, detailing three levels of social context that engage interpretation. And Gunter champions the middle ground, working differential effects across differentially situated individuals.

The end-points comparison of Biocca and Lindlof shows a substantive degree of incommensurability in their arguments. Biocca constitutes the individual as a decontextualized entity and as the place where effects occur. Lindlof, on the other hand, makes the social action claim that individuals (as opposed to physical bodies) appear only *in situ* and effects occur only in a referenced context. Much of the active-passive audience argument hinges on these differing definitions of the individual.

Altheide and Snow's article on media formats uses the individual as the locus of effects and grants no space to social action. The characteristics of media formats are sufficient to explain certain qualities of a society's view of reality. Gumpert, in his following commentary, calls this claim into question, pointing out that media are not unidimensional, but present multiple and conflicting formats, and their audiences are active agents in the interaction with content.

Zimmerman resolves the tension between text and action by arguing that the qualities (including, presumably, coherence) of a text—in his case a conversation—are the achievements of the co-constructors. The text is the product of action; analysis of a text informs us of the premises of its creating action. Meaning is a local production encountered at the point where the text is engaged (by the co-constructors, by the analyst, and so on).

This position is remarkably different from Biocca or Altheide and Snow, in which meaning is clearly distributed across members of the audience. In Zimmerman's conversation analysis, the regularities appearing in conversational texts are the conventions of performing conversations, not those of meaning. For Biocca, Altheide and Snow, and similar text-effects analyses, the regularities in media texts are pressed as conventions of meaning. The contrary position in media is taken by Meehan in her commentary on Deming's television criticism article. Meehan argues that the characteristics of television texts can best be understood as the consequences of the forces of the marketplace on the community of practitioners.

The arguments of Zimmerman, Meehan, and other text-as-product perspectives suggest that meaning making itself is a practice. By extension, we can conclude that the analysis of the characteristics of meaning will inform us of the premises of its creating action—interpretation. This is clearly the position taken by Lindlof and by Pilotta et al.; it is the underlying presumption of Pacanowsky and is contained in the call for future research in opinion formation by Edelstein. These four, in their own ways, locate interpretation as a social action within some community of intellect.

There is a strong connection in Altheide and Snow's notions of cognitive formatting and the theoretical bases of Rogers and Dearing's use of agenda theory (described below). Both posit a reality-interpreting cognitive entity (structure? text? operator?) in their respective constructs of agenda and format. There is a long history of the use of such entities in human behavior theory, beginning with instincts and moving through motivations, cognitive maps, values, attitudes, and now to uses and gratifications, cultural stories, schemata, opinion agenda, and formats. In their typical description, these cognitive entities are the result of the interaction between the individual and the set of forces encountered in the social/physical environment. Each individual, then, is the product of this interaction. In this manner, these entities locate society inside the head of each person. The purpose of such entities is always the same: to "create" the individual as the smallest unit in the analysis of human behavior. Because each individual is a microcosm of society, the analyst can discover societal effects from individual behavior.

A much different approach is taken by Lindlof, Pilotta et al., Pacanowsky, and Edelstein. In their separate ways, they argue for the incompleteness of the individual, that human behavior is always co-oriented, and most often appears in mutually supervised performances. In these four, one will not find the individual as the smallest unit of analysis, but rather the social organization.

Certainly, Lindlof and Pilotta et al. provide the strongest statements of this position. It is, however, with Edelstein in comparison with the review work of Rogers and Dearing that the implications for communication research of this position become clear. Both Edelstein and Rogers and Dearing work the field of opinion formation. In staying close to the historical perspective of agenda research, Rogers and Dearing use an exposure model in which an opinion agenda is created in the individual through exposure to mediated content. The individual so inoculated produces the behavioral effects of agenda setting. With this model, agenda researchers have been able to "read" the media for a list of important issues and "read" society by collecting the rankings of these issues from individuals. The survey protocol is an objectified context that stands for all other possible contexts, thereby precluding the analysis of other contextualized rankings. In short, the agenda effect stops with Lippmann's pictures of the mind drawn as the media would have them.

Edelstein reviews research that takes or can be reanalyzed through what he calls a "communication model." This model involves some ingredient of social action to complete the opinion formation effect. In this model, media exposure is neither necessary nor sufficient for any effect but is presumed to be an ordinary activity of mediated societies that potentiates a number of opinion-sensitive outcomes. The outcomes that occur with particular individuals depend not on the qualities of media exposure but on the conditions in which opinion-based behaviors are evoked. Powerful "communication effects" can be shown from this perspective where only "limited behavioral effects" were seen before.

Both Kreps and Reardon adopt a similar position for at least part of their separate analyses of communication in health care. They explore the different social constructions of disease and health and the performances of wellness and illness. Message effectiveness is seen dependent on these social contexts. The problem faced in the design of persuasion strategies relevant to prevention and to treatment compliance is how to insinuate appropriate texts into the social action contexts of abuse and therapy. (My presumption is that just saying no—or yes—is not enough.) What is clearly missing for the solution to this problem is both a theoretical understanding and the empirical analysis of social action and its performances.

Each of the two works of criticism in this volume, while firmly planted in the text, takes a separate, liberating turn toward action. Deming's major effort is to claim space within the world of criticism for the analysis of television on its own grounds. While pointing out the legitimate differences in significance, she compares the television critic's struggle for autonomy with that of feminism. In her concluding consideration of what a television-centered television criticism would look like, she eschews the traditional critic's move to find audience meanings in the careful examination of the characteristics of the medium's content. Rather, that careful examination should point to the openings in the text where the "auditors" can practice their invention.

Cheney and Tompkins's work is exactly a set of methods for the careful examination of content. They claim that in the analysis of communication often the only facts the analyst has are those of the text. One's facts are as they are made, in this case in Burkean analysis. Cheney and Tompkins do not make Deming's move to the audience. They choose to explore the intent of the author, thus using the facts of the text to inform us of the achievement of that intent. This effort has a correspondence with Zimmerman, with a notable difference in sociological scale. Cheney and Tompkins explore the achievements of the author(s) of a text; Zimmerman explores the achievements of a society within a textual form.

At least two threads of interest have appeared as this analysis has begun to disentangle the text-versus-action dialectic: It is clear that theorists who use the text as the container for the agents of behavioral effects and those who find effects in social action require particular and different definitions of the individual. It is also clear that the text is a genuine resource for those who study action when considered as an archive of achievements or as the materiel of that action.

INTERESTING METAPHORS

Prefaces have a certain character of a travelogue, as the tourist who has been there before gets to highlight the points of his or her own interest. All of the articles have not-to-be-missed features. Ones that particularly intrigued me are listed here.

The Audience of Biocca, Gunter, Lindlof, Altheide and Snow, and Deming

From the aggregated, discrete elements of Biocca to the community of intellect represented in Lindlof, and from the auditor as nearly victim in Altheide and Snow to Deming's inventive practices, the concept of the audience reveals itself in many forms. Biocca sees the audience as that set of individuals caught in the vortex of the sociological, psychological, and semiotic influences encountered in the text. This audience is a unitary concept—a view that could easily be seen from the standpoint of Altheide and Snow. For Gunter, audiences are created by the shared characteristics that vary across different levels of perceptiveness and discrimination. There are, therefore, functional audiences differentiated by age, class, gender, and the like. Lindlof's and Deming's audiences appear in the processes of communal membership. For Deming, individuals practice their interpretive perceptiveness (or lack of it) of a common text from within those memberships. But Lindlof's formulation may not require the individual commonly to attend a text to be an audience member. It may be enough that the community practices attendance. Given this variety, is there an audience? Certainly, the traditional audience occupying a common space and participating in a common activity has disappeared.

Health Care

Gary Kreps and Kathleen Kelley Reardon, in their separate works, pursue the deconstruction of the notion of health care. Health care not only delivers goods and services for the management of illness (and increasingly wellness), it also delivers what Kreps calls "a dark and mysterious mysticism," what Reardon calls the "stigma" of diagnosis, and the political economy of medicine. When viewed from the perspective of the health care practitioner, the proper health care message must accomplish all of these tasks. That health care message, then, must define illness and wellness in a manner that privileges the practitioner (consult your doctor), maintains his or her control of proprietary information, creates the motivating fear of illness, and justifies the expense and effort of the cure.

Empowering the Premises of Action

The two pieces on organizational communication in this volume are each founded on separate metaphors that can be profitably used to enhance our understanding of both. Pilotta et al. extend the work of Niklas Luhmann by offering the organization as a communication medium through which the premises of action are transmitted. Members act out the proper order of things each day. Pacanowsky crafts a morality tale of the empowerment of autonomy and creativity from his ethnographic study of W. L. Gore and Associates. On the one hand, Pacanowsky's ethnographic study provides the empirical expression of the theory contained in Pilotta et al. On the other, Pilotta et al. demonstrate that all organizations are empowering and that empowerment is morally neutral although performances are not. We may have applauded W. L. Gore and Associates or not, depending on the value we place on creativity and autonomy, but in terms of empowerment, Gore is behaving only as an organization must.

Achievements

Don Zimmerman's presentation of the notion of achievements (a concept also implicit in the work of Cheney and Tompkins) seems to provide an illuminating metaphor for the ethnographer and a complementary one for the cultural studies scholar and the rational structuralist. For example, the organization ethnographer is often at a loss to account for the structural products of the processes of organizing. Recognizing them as the politically embedded, historicized achievements of the members permits the ready integration of these material elements into the social action narrative. The benefit to the cultural studies scholar is in the enhancement of the pivotal notions of class or gender and of the powerful relational concept of hegemony. For those who rest on postmodern justifications, there is some relief from what can be a despairing perspective. Finally, the rational structuralist who considers the force of the invisible hand of the market or organization on those under its influence is offered an explanation of how those market forces develop and are maintained. As can be seen, this metaphor struck a responsive chord.

Computers and Cognitive Entities

I believe that the computer as a metaphor for cognitive processing has also resonated through the discipline well. At the moment, we seem to be deeply involved in the problems of insisting on some form of local constructionism or interpretation in the analysis of textual meaning and yet wanting that process to be consistent across the sites of interpretation. Altheide and Snow show us one solution: the positing of common cognitive structures—in their case formats—that direct that interpretation. Altheide and Snow argue that information is formatted by its mode of presentation and that those formats are "taken in" to become cognitive screens of reality.

In reading Altheide and Snow and other works using cognitive entities, there is a sense that one attraction of these theoretical concepts comes from their affinity with the computer metaphor of the mind. Interpretation is directed by mental software in which formats (schemata, maps, scripts, and so on) are "coded," "stored," "retrieved," "edited," "dumped," all operations in good, solid computer talk. There is a potential problem in all this, as the von Neumann architecture of the computers most of us work with does not correspond well with what is currently claimed about the structure of the brain or the operation of the mind. Multidimensional topography that describes the perspective from a site of interpretation seems a more likely metaphor.

Public Opinion as
Political Empowerment

Edelstein and Rogers and Dearing are quite right in their agreement that the materiality of public opinion is nothing more or less than its measurement. Both Edelstein and Rogers and Dearing provide us with good insights into the problems of the concept of public opinion. This concept seems best fitted to an earlier age, when people read the broadsheets, talked in the square, and then moved to the town hall to vote their opinions. What does public opinion mean, however, in a society composed of many publics, most members of which have little access to the political processes? There is a suspicion that agenda-setting is a method and public opinion the product of just talk. That is, the media provide us with the common ground upon which we can conduct a conversation or reply to a questionnaire about government. Does the talk anticipate decision making or is it its own end?

If we are to hold that public opinion is a set of shared concepts from which individuals act in consort, then Edelstein's call for the study of the interpersonal communication processes by which this sharing is accomplished and that action emanates is central. If, on the other hand, we are governed by political elites who exploit the concept of public opinion to justify their own ends, then the line of reasoning in Rogers and Dearing comes more to the fore. In either case, we are best served, as Rogers and Dearing tartly observe, by better theorizing than by yet another empirical study.

If I have done my job in this preface, your appetite has been whetted for the themes of communication that are layered through all of these works. My recommendation is, of course, that you read the whole book. As we each pursue our own professional specializations, it is important to come back to the realization that we are all studying communication. You'll find it well presented here.

ACKNOWLEDGMENTS

Such success as an editor may have is first and foremost in the hands of the authors that appear in the volume. My greatest thanks go to the authors and commentators, who worked hard against difficult deadlines to produce the original works that appear here.

I would also like to thank my reviewers, Stephen Acker, Dennis Alexander, Richard Rieke, Felipe Korzenny, Susan Tyler Eastman, Don Faules, Robert Boiko, Mary Strine, Douglas Birkhead, David Eason, and the several dozen colleagues who advised me on individual works.

The work of the *Yearbook*'s editorial associates, Gina Gregg and Alexis Olds, as well as the contribution of staff and scarce resources by the University of Utah Department of Communication made this publication possible.

Finally, I would like to thank the International Communication Association's Executive and Publication committees for their support and counsel in crafting the editorial direction of the *Yearbook*.

—*James A. Anderson*
Salt Lake City, Utah

SECTION 1

THE MASS MEDIA AUDIENCE: PERCEPTIVE, INTERPRETIVE, OR NOT

1 The Perceptive Audience

BARRIE GUNTER
Independent Broadcasting Authority, London

Arguing the claim that the content of television does not predict its effects, Gunter examines the portrayal of violence and of the sexes in objective and subjective terms. He demonstrates that objective content analytic methods do not correspond to the perceptions of children and adults in these content areas. He concludes that both children and adults actively interpret content rather than passively being cultivated by it.

THIS chapter will examine how audiences cognitively respond to and make sense of television programs for themselves. Television viewing will be conceived of as a cognitively active phenomenon during which audiences interpret and make judgments about programs on the basis of their understanding about certain rules of television format and content and through comparisons of what they see on the screen with what they may know, through more direct experience, about the world in which they live.

Traditional models of television effects have tended to underplay the significance of cognitive mediating processes. And even those perspectives—such as uses and gratifications—that do emphasize the concept of the "active" media consumer in the context of discussions about media effects lack sophistication at both conceptual and methodological levels to reveal the complexity and measure the significance of cognitive psychological interpretive mechanisms and processes.

It will be argued, and demonstrated through reference to appropriate research findings, that comprehension and judgmental processes affect perceptions of what is seen on the television screen and cognitively mediate any impact television might have on viewers' attitudes, beliefs, values, and actions. In other words, television does not simply act on passive viewers; rather, they act on it.

CONTENT AND INFERRED IMPACT

Recent research, for example, has shown that television viewers, young and old, are selectively perceptive and judgmental in their responses to programs

Correspondence and requests for reprints: Barrie Gunter, Independent Broadcasting Authority, 70 Brompton Rd., London, SW31EY, UK.

Communication Yearbook 11, pp. 22-50

(Gunter, 1985; Wober & Gunter, in press). The ways viewers perceive and evaluate characters and events on television do not always match descriptive incident counts or the meanings inferred from them by researchers. Taking the perspective of this position, this chapter will consider the problem of content analysis and inferred impact, a comparison of subjective and objective accounts of content, the relationship between audience perceptions and TV effects, and the implications of these three for our research agenda.

According to one effects model—cultivation analysis—television, principally through its fictional portrayals, may often distort social reality and convey warped messages or impressions about society to viewers (Gerbner & Gross, 1976; Gross & Morgan, 1985). "Messages" as such are usually identified and defined through content analysis, in which a priori coding frames are employed to classify the content of programs and to provide "objective" counts of objects and events portrayed in them.

At the level of content assessment, this model posits the manner in which television portrays people, institutions, and events in a distorted, stereotyped fashion and may condition beliefs among individuals who consume a heavy diet of the programs that are consonant with its own content profiles. In other words, frequent viewers, who are taken typically to be individuals for whom television is the primary source of information about the world, learn lessons from watching television that produce distorted perceptions of social reality. According to two of the proponents, "The basic hypothesis of cultivation analysis is that the more time one spends living in the world of television, the more likely one is to report conceptions of social reality that can be traced to television portrayals" (Gross & Morgan, 1985, p. 226).

The model itself describes the impact of television as composed of several stages. The first stage is to elaborate, descriptively, the nature and form of television content—to describe its features and to identify its stereotypes or aspects of reality that are distorted.

The analysis of television content, via descriptive study of what is shown in programs, has revealed that the world of television does not mirror precisely the world of reality. Television presents a stereotyped worldview in its entertainment content. Ordinary, everyday reality is not conceived to be what viewers would usually find entertaining; exaggerations of reality or fantastic situations are what turn viewers on.

Researchers who use content analysis, however, often go beyond the simple provisions of descriptions of what happens on screen to make inferences about the meanings conveyed by various patterns of television portrayals to the watching audience. Extended meanings are typically "read" into programs by the researchers themselves, who assume that the same meanings are perceived and then absorbed unchanged by viewers. Seldom, though, are these assumptions verified in terms of direct audience responses to programs.

The content analysis of television programming is typically carried out by trained two-person monitoring teams. A great deal of emphasis is placed on reliability of coding: Monitors are put through a rigorous month-long training exercise to ensure that they catalogue specified properties of programs in the same way (Signorielli, 1985). It is vital that there is strong agreement across monitors in the way a coding frame is applied. And only when there is sufficient level of agreement can the monitoring exercise be seen to have worked properly.

The technique is designed to reflect "what large communities absorb over long periods of time" (Signorielli, 1985, p. 241). But the underlying assumption throughout all this research is that the patterns of portrayed events, institutions, and descriptive fashion carry the same meanings for audiences as those that are inferred from this analysis by the researchers. This assumption, however, may give rise to inaccurate assessments of the particular aspects of television programs that have meaning or value for viewers and of what precisely the nature of that meaning might be. At this point, it might be useful to provide some illustrations of the kind of objective, description accounts of television content being referred to here. There are many areas of programming that have come under scrutiny in this way, but the arguments being put in this chapter can be elaborated succinctly with reference to two areas in particular—the portrayal of violence and the portrayal of the sex roles on television.

Measurement of TV Violence

The common method of measuring violence on television is to count the number of times particular kinds of incidents occur over a sample of programs. Perhaps the most extensive analysis of television violence has been carried out by Gerbner (1972) and his colleagues. Using a technique called "message system analysis," these investigators have monitored samples of prime-time and weekend, daytime television put out for all major U.S. networks every year since 1967. During this time, this analysis has come to be regarded by some as the definitive measure of the nature and extent of violence on network television.

For coding purposes a simple normative definition of violence is employed: "The overt expression of physical force against self or other compelling action against one's will on pain of being hurt or killed, or actually hurting or killing" (Gerbner, 1972, p. 31). Using this definition to guide them, coders record such features as the frequency and nature of violent acts, the perpetrators and victims of violence, and the temporal and spatial settings in which the acts occur. From certain combinations of these measures, a Violence Profile is derived that purports to represent an objective and meaningful indicator of the amount of violence portrayed in television drama.

The overall picture of the world of television drama revealed by message system analysis is that it is a violent one. For example, Gerbner, Gross, Signorielli, Morgan, and Jackson-Beeck (1979) reported that since monitoring first began in 1967-68, an average of 80% of programs contained violence and 60% of major characters were involved in violence. The average rate of violent episodes was 7.5 per hour, and in weekend, daytime children's programs, violent episodes averaged almost 18 per hour. Indeed, programs directed at children typically scored high on most measures of violence except for killing; cartoons, in particular, consistently exceeded all other categories of programs, including adult adventure action and cross-detective shows.

According to Gerbner and his colleagues, the portrayal of violence on television drama programming demonstrates a pattern of unequal relative risks among characters of different sex, age, and socioeconomic and ethnic groups, in which certain character types are victimized consistently more often than others. Between 1967 and 1979, for example, Gerbner et al. (1979) observed that victims of violence outnumbered perpetrators, but the relative levels of victimization varied, being greater for some types of characters than for others. Men were much more likely than women to become involved in violence of some kind on television, but once involved they were much less likely than their female counterparts to be victims.

Risks of victimization in the world of network television drama were high among children and adolescents and unmarried women and were especially high for elderly women. "Good" male characters, frequently featured as heroes in action-adventure series, were much more likely to be killers than killed. "Good" female characters, on the other hand, were much more likely to be fatally hurt than were "bad" female characters, even though the former were less often involved in violent episodes. Regardless of the character type involved in violence, though, all such episodes are given equal weightings of seriousness in this content analysis. As we will see, however, television scenes depicting violence perpetrated or suffered by different types of characters are not always judged as equally serious by viewers.

Portrayal of the Sexes on TV

Objective content analysis has been applied extensively to assess the way the sexes are depicted on television. Some reference was made to differential portrayals of men and women in television drama by the Gerbner group in their study of television violence. Other researchers have investigated in more detail the different attributes that television emphasizes for men and women. The overriding concern is that television portrayals of the sexes are highly stereotyped and may cultivate sex-stereotyped beliefs among viewers who are regularly exposed to them (Gunter, 1986).

Two principal features of sex stereotyping have been identified. First, there is a gross underrepresentation of women in many prime-time programs in terms of actual numbers of appearances on screen, especially in major roles, relative to the presence of men. One writer has referred to this phenomenon as the "symbolic annihilation of women" by television (Tuchman, 1978). Second, even when women do appear, they tend to be portrayed only in a very narrow range of roles. In television's fictional life, women tend to be most often found in the home, and much less often at work. Television has also been accused of portraying women as incompetent, especially when they appear in anything other than marital or familial roles. According to some writers, this is reflected particularly in the extent to which female characters on prime-time television are depicted in the receiving end of violent attacks (Gerbner, 1972; Gerbner & Gross, 1976; Signorielli, 1984). Thus Tuchman (1978) has argued that television plots symbolically denigrate women, so that even when they are portrayed in leading roles and outside the home, they are surrounded and continually rescued by male colleagues.

The serious implications of the apparent tendency toward sex-role stereotyping on television lies with the possible impact this content may have on the public's beliefs about men and women. The greatest concern is for the effects on young children at the stage when they are just beginning to learn sex-appropriate attitudes and behaviors.

Analyses of television content since the 1950s have consistently reported that less than one-third of all characters in prime-time television drama on networks in the United States are female (Gerbner & Gross, 1976; Head, 1954; Miller & Reeves, 1976; Tedesco, 1974). Analysis of the types of roles allocated to female characters has indicated stereotyping in terms of the social roles of women and with respect to the personality points predominantly characterizing them. Television has been accused of projecting an image of women as homemakers whose lives revolve around romantic affairs, marriage, and familial activities. Women tend only rarely to be shown as gainfully employed outside the home and as having any real ambitions to be professionally successful (De Fleur, 1964; Downing, 1974; Seggar & Wheeler, 1973). They also tend to be depicted as emotional, passive, and dependent on men for help with personal and professional problems; men tend to be shown as more powerful, more competent, and generally superior (Lemon, 1978; Turner, 1974).

All this evidence, however, has resulted from content analysis; that is, objective counts of occurrences of different female role-types as programs. In the absence of direct measures of audience response, the influence of stereotyped sex-role portrayals can only be inferred. We need to know whether individuals encode the messages implicit in television content profiles and incorporate them into their existing belief systems concerning the sexes. Studies with children and adolescents have indicated the existence of statistical relationships between amount of viewing and traditional beliefs about the role of women (Beuf, 1974; Frueh & McGhee, 1975; McGhee & Frueh, 1980; Morgan, 1982), with youngsters who watch a great deal of television tending to hold more traditional sex-role beliefs than those who view relatively little television. Further studies with children have shown, however, that responses to questions about sex-roles vary according to the nature of television portrayals to which youngsters are exposed. Viewing women in nontraditional roles, for instance, can lead to a reduction in sex-role stereotyping (Atkin & Miller, 1986; Pingree, 1978).

OBJECTIVE AND SUBJECTIVE
ACCOUNTS OF TELEVISION CONTENT

Two sets of comparisons will be made in this section. First we will examine audiences' perceptions of how things are depicted on television (subjective descriptions) and compare them with content analytic accounts (objective descriptions). A further comparison will be made between audiences' perceptions of how certain social entities are depicted on television and how they appear to be in real life. In so doing, we will find that research indicates that viewers do not always read the same meanings into television as do researchers. In regard to many social groups, objects, institutions, and events, viewers' perceptions of how these things are in the real world are different from perceptions of how they are portrayed on television. Audiences often exhibit a level of sophistication in the judgments they make about television content. This sophistication is often underestimated or not taken sufficiently into account by some research models intent on demonstrating cognitive and behavioral effects of the medium.

Some writers have envisaged a process of influence in which greater amounts of TV viewing can produce biased or distorted beliefs about the world that are consistent with TV's stereotyped portrayals (Gerbner & Gross, 1976; Gerbner et al., 1978, 1979).

These "cultivation" effects are measured by comparing the beliefs of heavy and light TV viewing to indicate associations between particular types of opinion and levels of TV watching. This model embodies many problematical assumptions about caused relationships between what is shown on TV and the formation of particular patterns of social perceptions, beliefs, and opinions among viewers about the world in which they live (Wober & Gunter, in press).

One such assumption is that "messages" inferred from program content profiles concerning various social groups are recognized and encoded by audiences, who assimilate them into their existing knowledge structures. It is also assumed that more frequent viewers will be more strongly influenced by TV's messages than will less frequent viewers purely as a function of greater volume of exposure to them. However, measures of the *amount* of viewing may not be valid and sufficient indicators of TV effects, because TV content and viewers' preferences for that content vary considerably, and two heavy viewers who watch totally different kinds of programs may hold two quite disparate sets of beliefs as a result.

In comparison with straightforward descriptive content analysis, relatively little research has been done on how viewers perceive TV's images of social groups and phenomena. Content analyses, from which inferences about TV effects are often made, may actually be poor indicators of audience perceptions (Ceulemans & Fauconnier, 1979; Perloff, Brown, & Miller, 1982).

For instance, traditional procedures for the measurement of violence on TV do not normally take into account what viewers themselves perceive to be violent. Typically, the violence of a program is assessed in terms of the number of incidents it contains that match what the researchers themselves decide is violent.

Although this procedure provides reliable codings of specific kinds of incidents, these codings may have relevance only for the original coders and may lack any real meaning for the general viewing public untutored in this coding methodology. From these simple frequency counts, Gerbner and his colleagues, for example, have derived more complex assumptions of the ways in which units of content occur together on TV to form recurring profiles that represent messages about the structure and dynamics of contemporary society (Gerbner, Gross, Morgan, & Signorielli, 1980). No evidence is provided, however, to show whether or not these so-called messages are actually perceived and learned by viewers.

Problems arise when generalizing from statements about or descriptions of television content and the symbolic messages carried by that content to how the content is perceived and understood by the audience. It is necessary to establish the degree of equivalence between the meanings attributed to programs by trained coders and the meanings attributed to them by ordinary viewers. To what extent do the images and messages defined by content analysis share the same universe of meanings as the perceptions of viewers? With incidents such as shootings or fights, it may be relatively easy to achieve correspondence between program structures defined a priori by a system of content coding and audience perceptions of content. But it may be less easy to accurately infer meaningful messages concerning norms or relationships unless direct information is obtained from the viewers (Gunter, 1981, 1985).

Although it may be impossible to define exactly what the audience in general means by "violence," there is evidence to suggest that viewers' perceptions do not accord strongly with objective counts of program incidents. Research has shown that structures such as those monitored in message system analysis are not always perceived by ordinary viewers as salient attributes of programs. For example, a content analysis of British television output, using a fixed definition of violence, showed that the rate of violent incidents per hour was four times as great for cartoon shows as for any other type of program (Halloran & Croll, 1972), while a study of the audience's perceptions of television violence indicated that cartoons were not ruled as particularly violent (Howitt & Cumberbatch, 1974).

Even in films with human characters, violent scenes may not appear as important aspects of content, and viewers may often fail to mention violence in discussions about films containing violent action shortly after viewing unless specifically asked about such content. In a field study conducted by audience researchers at the British Broadcasting Corporation (1972), viewers were asked to fill out a questionnaire about specific programs shortly after they had been broadcast, in which reactions to violence and other aspects of program content were probed. It was found that perceptions of programs as *violent* did not depend on the actual number of violent incidents. Nor was there any strong relationship between perceiving a program as violent and verbally reported emotional arousal. Assessment of violence as unjustified, however, was associated with negative evaluations of the program. Most respondents also claimed that "realism" was an essential element in their perceptions of televised violence, with violent real-life events reported on news bulletins or shown in documentaries generally rated as more violent than violence portrayed in fictional settings. Although this study can be regarded as little more than exploratory, it nevertheless indicates that viewers' personal assessments of television programs are determined by many different content factors, of which violence is only one, and by no means the most important.

Adults' Perceptions of TV Violence

Recent research has revealed that adults and children alike are capable of highly refined judgments about television violence. Viewers have their own scales for deciding the seriousness of incidents and their opinions do not always agree with researchers' categorizations of violence (Gunter, 1985; Van der Voort, 1986).

Instead of deciding in advance what violence is—or is not—these researchers allowed viewers themselves to decide about the seriousness of violence contained in various functional television portrayals. Gunter (1985) reported 12 experimental studies in which groups of people were shown scenes taken from British crime series, westerns, science fiction series, and cartoons. Viewers were invited to make a variety of personal judgments about each scene along a set of qualitative rating scales. Scenes were shown singly or in pairs for comparative judgment. Variations in perceptions of the scenes were examined in relation to a number of things—the types of programs the scenes came from, the types of weapons or instruments of violence that were used, the physical setting of the action, and the degree of observable harm the violence caused to victims in each scene. The results indicated that viewers may be significantly influenced in their personal opinions about television violence by many different attributes of television portrayals.

For example, familiarity of surroundings is one of the most powerful factors influencing viewers' perceptions of television violence (Gunter, 1985; Gunter & Furnham, 1984). The closer to home the violence is portrayed as being in terms of place and time, the more serious it is judged to be. Thus it was found that violence in British crime series was generally rated as more violent than similar portrayals on U.S. series of the same type. Portrayals of "violent" behavior in cartoons or science fiction programs, however, were seen as essentially nonviolent.

Perceptions of television violence were also found to vary significantly with a number of other characteristics of television portrayals. The kinds of fictional characters who inflict the violence, how the violence is inflicted, and how much harm is done to those on the receiving end all emerged as important mediators of viewers' opinions about television violence.

Some of the results, however—paradoxical opinions about violence perpetrated by law enforcers and by criminals, or by men and by women— were markedly different, depending on the types of programs from which they came. With extracts from British crime series, for instance, viewers were most concerned about violence inflicted by men upon women; while in scenes from American series, they were concerned more by women being violent to men (Gunter & Furnham, 1985). In an American context, violence performed by criminals was perceived in more serious terms than that used by law enforcers (usually the police); while in British settings, it was law enforcer violence that viewers were more troubled by (Gunter, 1985).

One can only speculate at this stage as to the reasons why these differences in opinion occur. One answer may lie in the societal norms regarding the use of violence. Traditionally, society approves of some forms of violence under certain circumstances, and disapproves of others. For example, violence used by police officers to uphold the law, or that used by private citizens in self-defense against an attacker are, within certain limits, permissible. Under these circumstances, however, the use of violence must not far outweigh the magnitude of the behavior of the lawbreaker or attacker. Where the force used to repel an attacker is much greater than that justified by initial provocation, violent retaliation will not be found so acceptable.

Children's Perceptions of TV Violence

Van der Voort (1986) conducted a study of children's perceptions of TV violence at three schools in Holland. In all, 314 children were shown full-length episodes of eight television scenes. The episodes varied from realistic crime drama (*Starsky and Hutch* and *Charlie's Angels*) to adventure series (*Dick Turpin* and *The Incredible Hulk*) and fantasy cartoons (*Scooby Doo, Tom and Jerry, Popeye,* and *Pink Panther*). Immediately after showing each program, a postexposure questionnaire was filled in measuring 10 perception variables: (1) readiness to see violence, (2) approval of violent actions seen in the program, (3) enjoyment of the violence seen, (4) evaluation of the program, (5) emotional responsiveness, (6) absorption in the program, (7) detachment while watching, (8) identification with the program's chief characters, (9) perceived reality of the program, and (10) comprehension and retention of program content.

Van der Voort investigated whether programs perceived to be realistic were also more absorbing for children who would thereby respond to them with more emotion and less detachment than they showed toward programs perceived to be more fantastic. Results showed that law enforcement programs as well as children's adventure programs were rated as realistic. Thus *Starsky and Hutch* and *Charlie's Angels* were perceived to be realistic, while *The Incredible Hulk, Dick Turpin,* and cartoons were seen as fantastic. Realistic programs were watched with more involvement, more emotion, and less detachment. The two crime drama series mentioned above were regarded as containing the most violence of any of the programs the children were shown.

Van der Voort found, in fact, that judgments of the amount of violence programs contain by 9- to 12-year-olds differ little from those of adults. He makes the important point, however, that

> children's violence ratings do differ from those of content analysts who analyze the amount of violence a program contains by means of the systematic observation of programs recorded on videotape. Programs that are extremely violent according to "objective" content analysis can be seen by children as hardly containing any violence. (p. 329)

Thus, although content analyses have identified cartoons as being among the most violent of television programs in terms of numbers of objectively identified incidents per hour or per show (Gerbner, 1972; Gerbner & Gross, 1976), such programs tend to be seen by children as containing hardly any violence at all.

On the basis of the above findings with both adults and children, it is clear that viewers classify program content differently from the descriptive analysis of research frameworks that employ narrow definitions of violence. Although objective cataloging of incidents in programs has the useful function of providing reliable counts of how often certain categories of items occur, the relevance or meaning of those items for the audience can be properly ascertained only through the perceptions of viewers themselves. There would be some merit in recommending a subjective approach rather than a purely objective one in the analysis at least of televised violence because this perspective enables one to identify the programs that viewers themselves take most seriously. A subjective approach can outline ways in which differential weights of seriousness can be applied to programs. This approach will lend more confidence that the classification of programs is at least based on criteria that are significant to viewers.

Sex-Role Perceptions

People tend to ascribe certain personality attributes as well as behaviors to men and women. For example, traits such as nurturance, dependence, and passivity are typically classified as feminine, while dominance and aggression are generally considered as masculine (Bem, 1974; Rosenkrantz, Vogel, Bee, Broverman, & Broverman, 1968). Analyses of TV content profiles have indicated that TV portrayals tend to emphasize certain of these sex-typed characteristics in men and women (Butler & Paisley, 1980; Tuchman, Daniels, & Benet, 1978). What evidence is there though that traits emphasized on TV are also the ones most salient to viewers?

Children's Perceptions of TV Sex-Role Portrayals

There is evidence that children prefer TV characters of their own sex (Joy, Kimball, & Zabrock, 1977; Maccoby & Wilson, 1957). Children may also selectively attend to same-sex characters on TV and interpret sex-role images or themes in programs according to what they already know about sex-roles. One researcher has found that when 4- to 9-year-old children were questioned about sex-stereotyped TV material, they exhibited a ready ability to elaborate upon scenes in ways dependent on existing understanding about sex roles (Durkin, 1984). Children would explain, for example, that hypothetical fathers—not actually seen in a program—were "out at work," while mothers not seen were "washing the dishes." These youngsters were able to account for a range of male and female TV portrayals in this way.

Young viewers, even when not especially primed, tend to perceive sex-type attributes in TV characters (Mayes & Valentine, 1979). When not given explicit instructions to attend to particular characters or behaviors, children may still tend to focus more attention on same-sex characters than on opposite-sex characters (Sprafkin & Liebert, 1978).

More recent research has indicated that male characters on the screen may often attract greater attention from young viewers of both sexes than do female characters. Evaluations of female characters may be especially harsh and recall of their actions may be particularly poor among female members of the audience. In one study, when groups of 8- to 11-year-old girls and boys were shown one of two versions of a newscast, one read by a female newscaster and the other by a male newscaster, differences in levels of recall were associated with sex of newscaster and sex of the respondent. Girls remembered significantly less from the female newscaster than from the male, while boys exhibited no similar effect (Tan, Randy, Huff, & Miles, 1980). The researchers suggest that while boys may have considered the role of TV newscasting as appropriate for both men and women, girls may not have perceived it as appropriate for their own sex. Girls may therefore have paid less attention to the news when it was read by a female newscaster. Since this study was done, however, female newscasters and reporters have become far more commonplace both on network and local news broadcasts in the United States and United Kingdom. The acceptability of women professionals anchoring the news may well have increased significantly during this time. It could be interesting to conduct a follow-up study to find out whether children's perceptions and memory of television news when read by male or female newscasters are different now from nearly 10 years ago.

Evidence has also emerged that preexisting sex stereotypes among young viewers may distort their perceptions and memories for TV portrayals. Children shown a videotape of a male nurse and female doctor afterward tended to identify the doctor as having been the male character and the nurse having been the female character. Only the oldest children (aged 12 years) tended to give correct identifications (Drabman et al., 1982).

In another study, Williams, La Rose, and Frost (1981) showed teenage boys and girls program segments from a TV series aimed at counterstereotyping. The principal male character was portrayed as a man who could mix strength and leadership with gentleness and supportiveness. Another teenaged female character was shown as someone who not only possessed the usual feminine qualities but also as a person who could assume leadership and take risks in ways normally associated with only males. Afterwards, young viewers were asked questions about the program and the characters.

Opinions about what they saw varied both as a function of the sex of the child and in relation to the sex of the TV character in question. Boys' evaluations of male and female characters on TV indicated that the more they saw the male character in a stereotyped way, the more they liked him, whereas the more counterstereotyped a female character was perceived to be, the more boys liked her. The children had relatively strong factual comprehension of the TV programs, but their comprehension of the sex-role objectives of the programs was lower than hoped for. Similarly, the desires to imitate the counterstereotyped characters' behaviors were mixed and, in some respects, inconsistent.

Williams et al. found, overall, a selective bias in perceptions of the program materials, such that stereotyped males and nonstereotyped females seemed to be better liked and better remembered. This finding is consistent with the notion that children may pay greater attention to masculine-type behaviors, whether performed by male or female characters on the screen. On the other hand, attention to male characters behaving in a nonstereotypic fashion apparently is much weaker and may be the most difficult example of behavior of all to get across.

Another explanation, however, could be that the behaviors of stereotypic and nonstereotypic characters are registered equally well, but the child tends to report only that which is more actively classified as "sex-appropriate." It is only possible to surmise about the internal cognitive processes operating here on the basis of this study; clearly, a more detailed investigation is called for.

Adults' Perceptions of TV Sex-Role Portrayals

Research on adults' perceptions of the sexes on television has investigated awareness of the relative presence of males and females on the screen and subjective ratings of the personality traits of males and females in television programs and advertisements. These studies have revealed that viewers' subjective perceptions of the characteristics of males and females on television do not always correspond with the personality profiles of the sexes inferred from traditional, objective content analysis research.

The profile from content analyses. To facilitate the comparison between traditional content analyses and subjective-perception profiles of the way the sexes are shown on television, results from a few studies of the former type will first be presented. Scheibe (1979) had 14 male and female viewers rate a sample of television commercials using adjectival scales designed to measure the personality characteristics of the men and women depicted in them. Some confirmation of attributes identified by earlier objective content analyses emerged. For example, female characters in the commercials were perceived as more concerned about the appearance of their home and as more dependent on the opposite sex than were male characters. However, there were differences in perceptions of characters appearing in prime-time and daytime commercials. In general, female characters were perceived as less able spouses, less mature, more foolish, and less successful than male characters, but in daytime commercials the situation reversed: Women were seen in a more positive light than were men on similar dimensions. Scheibe concluded that, with respect to personality traits, male characters are portrayed as negatively as female characters. The real difference comes with the time of day when the commercial is shown.

Sharits and Lammers (1983) asked male and female business school students to give their opinions about male and female personalities portrayed in over 100 television advertisements. Females in the commercials were rated more favorably than were men on many attributes. Females were perceived to be portrayed as better spouses and parents, more mature, more attractive, more interesting, and more modern than males. Little difference was found in the perceptions of male and female judges. One final interesting observation, however, was that men seem increasingly to be filling sex-object roles in television advertisements.

In a study of the perceived personality traits of male and female characters in dramatic television programs, Peevers (1979) recruited six judges to evaluate the principal males and females in selected television dramas using Bem's Sex-Role Inventory. Bem's work on psychological androgyny (1974, 1975, 1976) has presented an alternative to traditional sex-role stereotypes. Instead of conceiving of an individual as primarily masculine or feminine, as though these characteristics existed along a continuum, the concept of androgyny allows consideration of an individual in terms of the degree to which she or he possesses both kinds of qualities. To Bem, the androgynous person is mentally healthy, able to act competently in situations requiring traditional male characteristics and also in those in which traditional female characteristics are adaptive.

Peevers reported two studies conducted one year apart. In the first of these, results indicated that 85% of all male characters were classified in highly masculine terms, while only 44% of all ratings for females fell in the feminine range. In addition, 28% of female characters' sex-role scores were in the masculine range, compared with only 4% of male characters who had opposite sex scores. More than twice as many female characters scored in the androgynous range as did male characters (28% versus 11%). The second study replicated the first and indicated that males were perceived as being more stereotypical than females, thus presenting a contrast to the generally held notion that it is females who are highly and consistently stereotyped by the media.

Peevers's study indicated that the traditional male role is highly valued; so valued that it is overdramatized in TV programs. The sex-role scores of many male characters were so extremely masculine that they could hardly be achieved by real people. The "supermasculine," nonhuman portrayal of the male role abounded on the TV screen, presenting a continuing picture of an unattainable but supposedly desirable role model.

Analysis of the female role portrayal, on the other hand, revealed that it was more diversified, more flexible, and more human in the sense that female characters' sex-role scores fell within the limits attainable by real people. According to Peevers, these results dramatically illustrated the acceptance of greater flexibility in the female role in our society. Deviations by female characters in the direction of masculine qualities were acceptable because those qualities are valued. Conversely, male deviations from the male role remained highly unacceptable.

Viewers' perceptions. Viewers' perceptions of the sex role or sex traits of television characters, however, may depend upon the way they perceive themselves. Goff, Goff, and Lehrer (1980) explored young adults' perceptions of the qualities of five well-known female characters on U.S. television using the Bem Sex-Role Inventory and also looked at how these perceptions were related to viewers' self-ratings on the same scale. Self-perceptions turned out to have stronger associations with character perceptions than did the actual sex of respondents.

Androgynous respondents were likely to perceive television characters in androgynous terms, too. Respondents who saw themselves in masculine terms, however, perceived television characters to be more feminine, while more feminine-rated respondents perceived the characters in more masculine terms. These results provide evidence that non-sex-typed (androgynous) viewers have a less polarized impression of the personalities of television characters that are largely consonant with their perceptions of themselves.

Perceptions of the sexes on TV and in everyday life. Recent British research has attempted to shed more light not only on how the sexes are seen by viewers on television, but also on how these television perceptions differ from the way in which the sexes are seen in everyday life (Gunter, 1986). Respondents received viewing diaries listing all programs broadcast on the four main U.K. television channels during each week in which they gave appreciation scores for all programs seen, thus providing a record of their viewing for the week. An attached questionnaire listed 10 propositions about women and then equivalent propositions about men and asked respondents to say how often each proposition was true of men or of women "as they appear on television." On the reverse side of the sheet, the same propositions were presented and respondents were asked to repeat the exercise but for men and women "as they actually are in real life." The propositions were designed to reflect traits identified by previous content analysis research as typical features of female and male portrayals on television.

There were a number of noteworthy differences between perceptions of how the sexes appeared on television and perceptions of the way they were seen in real life. Respondents thought that women most especially, but also men, were shown on television as likely to get on well if they were good-looking. And this was believed more often to apply to success in the world of television than in real life. Women respondents were less likely than men to say that women in real life needed to be good-looking to succeed. Both sexes, however, thought that television underplayed males' needs to be gentle and affectionate compared with what they considered was true in real life.

With regard to traditionally "masculine" attributes, the general perception across respondents was that such characteristics apply more to men than to women and to a similar extent both on television and in real life. Once again, though, there were differences of opinion in connection with certain attributes. Women respondents were more likely than were men respondents to say that women in real life might be interested in politics. This difference was reflected in perceptions of the portrayal of women's interest in politics on television.

Men respondents were generally less androgynous in their perceptions of the sexes than were women respondents. Thus men were less likely than women to link feminine characteristics with men or masculine characteristics with women. However, both men and women respondents made this distinction more strongly with respect to television portrayals of the sexes than for their perceptions of the way the sexes are in real life. This is an important distinction on the part of television viewers. If perceivers can and do recognize that television portrayal differs from real-life nature, and people are in contact with the latter, there is no need for them to infer that television portrayal is an accurate picture of real life. In short, if people recognize television as different, this recognition may insulate them from the "short-circuits" of perception that are implied in the "cultivation effects" theory.

Implications

The description of sex-role portrayals on television as highly stereotyped is not consistently reinforced by the perceptions of viewers. Furthermore, the characteristics identified as typical of female or male portrayals on television by content analyses are not necessarily the ones that turn out to be the most salient to the audience. Although audience perceptions of the sexes on television do not exhibit a consistent pattern throughout, one significant finding is that viewers do not seem passively to absorb everything they see on television. Perceptions of characters and behaviors appear to be mediated by preexisting dispositions. Thus boys often pay more attention to male characters than to female characters, while girls pay relatively more attention to females than do boys, although they may still be attracted to some male characters more than they are to most female characters on the screen.

On the question of whether viewers perceive sex-role portrayals as sexist or not, as content analysis research has indicated they are, again the findings reveal a level of sophistication among members of the audience that is so often underestimated. On some attributes, audience perceptions reinforce the content descriptions of the way women and men are shown; on other attributes, the two kinds of judgments do not match. One thing that has emerged from recent audience research, however, is that even if television's sex-role portrayals are seen on some dimensions as stereotyped, beliefs about the sexes in real life may be quite different.

AUDIENCE PERCEPTIONS
AND TELEVISION EFFECTS

This section will examine the extent to which TV influences audiences' social attitudes, beliefs, values, and certain notions. It will emphasize the important role of cognitive or perceptual mediators in controlling such impact. In particular, two aspects of comprehension of TV content have emerged as important mediators of relationships between viewing patterns and social perceptions. The first concerns the ability of viewers to distinguish reality from fantasy content on the small screen. This ability may depend partly on real-life experiences with the same objects or behaviors as are shown on TV, and against which TV representations can be compared, and partly on knowledge about different categories and functions of programs (e.g., news and drama), which can guide viewers' decisions as to whether or not to believe all that they see on the screen. The second concerns the ability to follow storylines effectively and to be able to identify how different plot elements link together to form a coherent story.

We have seen already that children as well as adult viewers can and do distinguish between different types of television portrayals in such areas of content as violence and sex-role depictions. Furthermore, viewers differentiate between TV depictions of social entities and phenomena and how they know them to be in real life. These are important distinctions that can often work to limit the impact of television portrayals on sociocultural beliefs. In this section, we take a look at research evidence that has emerged fairly recently, which demonstrates how significant this mediating process can be.

Perceptions of Crime and Law Enforcement

In the longstanding concern about the portrayal of violence on TV, much early emphasis was placed on the potential impact of observing violent behavior that could be imitated by viewers, especially by the young and impressionable who are more prone to copy the actions of attractive, violent protagonists. More recently the emergence of the enculturation perspective has led to a shift away from the way in which isolated portrayals of violence may change the behavioral conduct of individuals in the audience to a more holistic consideration of the meanings conveyed to mass audiences about criminal and violent propensities in society by recurring patterns of victimization portrayed in programs. Through its repeated portrayal of violence, some researchers have argued that TV cultivated distorted perceptions of the incidence of crime and violence in the real world. Such effects are predicted to be most strong among those people who watch a great deal of TV and who may therefore acquire a great deal of their knowledge about the world from it. Empirical demonstrations of this relationship have been derived from survey data, which indicate that people claiming to be heavy viewers of TV exhibit different patterns of beliefs about social violence from light viewers of TV (Gerbner et al., 1978, 1979, 1980).

For example, Gerbner et al. (1979) examined fear of walking in the city in their own neighborhood at night among a sample of New Jersey schoolchildren and individuals interviewed in two national surveys in the United States. Comparing the responses of those people who claimed to watch TV for four hours or more each day and those who claimed to view for fewer than two hours, Gerbner and his colleagues found that more frequent viewers in all samples were consistently more fearful than were less frequent viewers.

Reanalysis of Gerbner's data by other American researchers failed to reproduce his results and has revealed problems with the original methodology (Hirsch, 1980; Hughes, 1980). Although response was made to these critiques (Gerbner, Gross, Morgan, & Signorielli, 1981), some doubts remain. Apart from methodological arguments, however, the theoretical position of the cultivation perspective has not been universally accepted by mass communication researchers. An alternative view proposed by Zillmann (1980), for example, postulates that, if anything, the effects of viewing crime drama on television should be the opposite to that indicated by the Gerbner group. Because there is little reason to expect people to view material producing aversive states such as fear, and because television crime drama invariably features the triumph of justice—the bad guys are usually caught and punished in the end—individuals who watch these programs should find comfort and reassurance through them.

Support for this position is provided by Gunter and Wober (1983), who found a positive relationship between beliefs in a just world and exposure to television crime drama programming. This finding suggests that crime drama may not simply convey images of social dangers but also of social justice, where wrongdoers are eventually caught and punished. It also leaves open the possibility, however, that those who believe in a just world seek to support these beliefs by more frequent exposure to crime drama on television.

Recent research has indicated that, regardless of the direction of causality inferred from correlational links between television viewing and perceptions of crime, demonstration of the nature and significance of television's contribution to these anxieties and beliefs requires a more sophisticated model of influence than that put forward. Increasing recognition has been given to three additional elements that represent important enhancements to the original cultivation effects model: First, judgments about crime can have different frames of reference. Tyler has made a distinction between two kinds of judgments people make about crime (1980, 1984; Tyler & Cook, 1984): (a) judgments at the *societal* level, which refer to general beliefs about the frequency of crime in the community at large; and (b) *personal* judgments, which refer to beliefs about personal vulnerability to crime and one's own estimated risk of being victimized. Tyler (1980) found that these two levels of judgment were not related to each other on all aspects. He also found that societal-level judgments, but not personal-level judgments, were related to media experiences. Estimates of personal risk were primarily determined by direct, personal experience with crime (Tyler, 1980; Tyler & Cook, 1984).

Second, at either one of these two levels, the perceived likelihood of other-or self-involvement in crime or the concern about such involvement are situation specific and may not be the same from one setting to the next. Tamborini, Zillmann, and Bryant (1984), for example, demonstrated that fear of crime is not a unidimensional construct. As well as the distinction between personal level and societal level, fear of crime in urban areas was found to differ from fear of crime in rural areas.

Third, relationships between levels of exposure to television and perceptions of crime may be content specific. In other words, any influence of television on beliefs about crime may depend on how much informationally relevant programs (i.e., those with crime-related content) are watched. Weaver and Wakshlag (1986) found that among individuals with direct experience of crime, concern about personal safety was positively correlated with the amount of crime-related programming watched. Viewing of programs that did not have crime themes was not linked with anxieties about personal involvement in crime. Among those individuals without direct experience of crime, there was a negative association between crime viewing and concern for future personal security. Thus the authoritative effects of TV—if indeed that is what we have some evidence for here—may be specifically located in areas of programming that have perceived informational relevance to the domain of social experience within which such effects are being measured.

Further evidence has been provided by Elliott and Slater (1980), who investigated relationships between viewing of law enforcement programs and perceptions that various crime drama programs were realistic. These relationships were examined for three different groups of adolescents. One group had had no direct experience with law enforcement agencies. Another group had had such contact in a positive way, through formal classes in law enforcement or sponsorship through school supplied by such agencies. A third group had had negative contact with law enforcement agencies because they had violated the law and been arrested, convicted, and either incarcerated or put on probation.

It was found that students with positive law endorsement experience perceived crime drama programs (e.g., *Charlie's Angels, Baretta, Rockford Files, Hawaii Five-O*) in least realistic terms. The negative direct experience group, on the other hand, saw four of six crime programs as more realistic than either the limited or positive direct experience groups. The authors accept that their data cannot determine for sure whether more frequent viewing leads to more perceived realism or whether they are watched because they are seen as realistic. Some sort of reciprocal relationship is likely.

In a subsequent study, the same authors again used three groups divided according to degree and nature of direct contact with law enforcement agencies as above (Slater & Elliott, 1982). Total television viewing and crime drama viewing were measured, along with perceptions of the degree of realism for each of six law enforcement programs on television at the time (*Baretta, Charlie's Angels, Hawaii Five-O, Rockford Files, Starsky and Hutch, Quincy*). A number of questions were posed about societal safety and law enforcement processes and activity and two possible answers were supplied—an accurate answer and an exaggerated answer—for respondents to choose from.

Multiple regression analyses revealed for the image of societal safety that negative direct experience, amount of viewing of law enforcement programs, and perceived realism of law enforcement programs were significant predictors. Young people whose experience with the police had resulted in some form of detention were less likely than the other students to see their environment as safe. Greater law enforcement viewing was associated with greater perceived safety, while greater perceived realism of law enforcement programs predicted greater perceived danger. Understanding of law enforcement processes was positively associated with positive and negative direct experience with law enforcement and negatively with greater perceived realism of crime programs. Negative direct experience and perceived program realism were positively related to acceptance of television portrayals of police behavior.

The evidence suggests that of the viewing/reality variables, the most important predictor variable is perceived law enforcement program realism, a variable generally excluded from cultivation analysis studies. This variable consistently emerged as a significant predictor of social reality perceptions. It could be that if a program is perceived as realistic, viewing it alone may be sufficient to influence social beliefs, quite apart from any or all other viewing. Gross viewing measures alone may therefore be wholly insufficient for the prediction of the nature of television cultivation effects.

Potter (1986) examined the effects on relationships between amount of television exposure and estimates of real-world violence of controls for perceived reality of TV content. He examined three types of reality perception: first, the "magic window" conception of TV, which reflects the degree to which a viewer believes TV content is an attractive, accurate representation of actual life. TV is a magic window that presents a beautiful picture of the world. People who score low on this dimension think of TV content as a highly stylized form of communication that presents fantastic settings and characters who are very different from those in real life. Second is the "instruction" conception of TV, which sees television as an instrument that augments and expands their direct experiences. People at one end of this scale believe that TV programming, even if it is fictional in nature, presents useful moral lessons that help them work through problems vicariously and learn how to cope. At the other extreme are people who believe that the fictional situations on TV programs are so unusual and distorted that they can see no usefulness in drawing parallels to their own lives. Therefore, they do not expect to learn anything of importance from TV. Third is the "identity" conception of TV, which reflects the degree of anomaly the viewer perceives between TV characters and situations and the people and situations experienced in real life. It is the degree to which viewers feel that TV characters could fit into their real everyday lives.

In the presence of demographic controls there was no evidence of a relationship between frequency of TV viewing and perceptions of victimization rates. Individuals who scored high on magic window reality exhibited the instruction effect, while the low group exhibited a reverse effect. Consequently, higher amounts of viewing were associated with lower extremes of victimization. When individuals were grouped according to their scores in the instruction and identity discussions, the instruction effect was generally among those in the low groups.

Storyline Comprehension and Cultivation Effects

The impact of television on children's beliefs about social reality may also be mediated by their ability to follow the storyline of a television drama. The cultivation perspective has all too often focused on gross learning responses to total television watching, when, in fact, the psychological impact of television can vary across different types of television content and across different types of viewers. While television viewing may be demonstrated to bear a linear relationship with certain social beliefs, the relationship may be curvilinear or nonexistent with other conceptions of social reality.

It is logical to assume that the extent to which "lessons" are learned from television and the nature of that learning will depend, among other things, on the way individuals watch television and are able to comprehend the content before them on the screen. Research has shown that the ability to remember facts from television programs and to draw inferences that go beyond the explicit content in programs improve with age through early and middle childhood. Findings indicate that children younger than eight have great difficulty keeping track of the order and relationships between events in a plot separated in time, but are able to follow them when they occur close to each other (Collins, 1973, 1979).

More recently, Collins has pointed out that drawing implications is a crucial skill for adultlike understanding of typical television plots. He points out that much of what is crucial to plot comprehension never appears or is not stated explicitly; rather, while it may be quite definitely and intentionally implied by the producer, the information has to be inferred by the receiver. Research has shown that children do *less well* with implicit than explicit content, although performance does improve with age (Collins, 1981).

Pingree (1983) conducted a study with fifth, sixth, and seventh graders in Wisconsin. The children answered questions about viewing habits and social reality beliefs. Two weeks later they watched an edited television program and were asked questions about the content of the program. They were then divided on the basis of scores on the latter exercise into low and high inference makers. Social reality questions dealt with prevalence of violence and criminal behavior, beliefs about family life and marriage, interpersonal mistrust, and sex roles.

Total television viewing was related to beliefs about working women and violence. Greater amounts of television viewing were associated with believing that women should not work outside the home and with television-biased estimates of the amount and nature of violence in the world.

Pingree also looked at relationships between viewing different categories of programming and social reality beliefs. More significant relationships emerged from this analysis. The pattern was quite complex, however, with different areas of content relating in different ways to specific beliefs.

The main focus of this study, however, was on differences between low and high inference makers. And what emerged from this comparison was that associations between viewing and beliefs were much stronger among low inference makers than among high inference makers. The correlations between television viewing and belief came largely from those children who did less well at drawing inferences, even when grade, sex, and achievement scores were controlled. Also of note was the finding that beliefs of the high-inference group appeared to be more integrated than those of the low-inference group. Children who put together separate facts to infer the implicit content of a particular television show also seemed to put together and integrate their beliefs into some sort of system. Yet their viewing and their beliefs were not related.

Pingree suggests that what she labels as inference-making abilities is tapping the activity with which people watch television. Those who are less "active" when viewing may be more influenced by what they see. It seems that inference making and activity are linked. Pingree found, for example, that respondents who agreed with the statement "When I watch a TV show, I like to relax my mind and just listen and watch" tended to do less well at drawing inferences from the program shown to them. She suggests that low involvement/activity might lead to larger social reality effects because filtering and evaluating mechanisms are deactivated and all bits of information have equal probabilities of retention—analogous to young children, who cannot filter out the incidentals and concentrate on what is central to the plot. Although an interesting possibility, this study does not provide any direct evidence on the cognitive processes mediating these social reality effects of television.

Perceptions of Sex-Roles

Further evidence on the importance of television versus real-world distinctions in mitigating the cognitive and social effects of television viewing derives from research on television and sex-role stereotyping. Investigations of television's effects on children's and adult's perceptions in this domain have tended to fall into two categories. First, there are surveys that attempt to establish correlational linkages between the amount of time spent watching television and the degree to which viewers hold certain sex-typed attitudes and beliefs. Second, there have always been attempts under laboratory conditions to manipulate sex-role perceptions of viewers experimentally through controlled exposure to particular kinds of television programs or portrayals.

Gerbner and Signorielli (1979) examined patterns of television viewing among adults and correlated them with answers to a series of questions measuring sex-stereotyped attitudes. They reported positive relationships between amount of viewing and beliefs that women should stay at home and that a woman should not work if her husband can support her. These findings were explained in terms of a television influence upon sex-role attitudes. This interpretation must be treated with caution, however, since more than one explanation would be consistent with the data. Does television viewing cause sex-stereotyped attitudes, or do these relationships indicate that people with such attitudes watch more television than people with less sex-stereotyped attitudes?

Volgy and Schwartz (1980) reported higher levels of sex-stereotyping among adults heavily exposed to television entertainment programs, although doubts have been cast on their results in view of the flimsy measures employed (see Hawkins & Pingree, 1982). Two years later, Rose, Anderson, and Wisocki (1982) reported finding a significant relationship among college students between how they described themselves on an inventory designed to measure sex typing and the amount of television they said they watched. Amount of sex stereotyping in self-descriptions was positively correlated with amount of claimed viewing of programs that had been previously rated by the researchers as strongly stereotyped in their portrayals of the sexes.

Other American researchers have suggested that the nature of television's influence on beliefs about women and men varies across different population subgroups. The relationship between television viewing and sex stereotyping may not be a straightforward linear one in the same direction across all viewers whereby sexism grows stronger with heavier viewing. Instead, there is evidence to suggest that television-sexism relationships work in opposite ways across different population subgroups. According to one line of argument, television cultivates a common level of sexist orientation, causing those who are less stereotyped or traditional in their beliefs about women's roles to become more so, and those who are strongly sexist in their beliefs to become less so (Gerbner & Signorielli, 1979).

British research has produced less conclusive evidence of systematic relationships between television viewing and beliefs about the sexes. Gunter and Wober (1982) reported a study that was concerned not simply with relationships between total television viewing and beliefs about women and men, but also with the way these perceptions were associated with particular patterns of program watching. Since different programs portray women and men in different ways, do individuals who watch a great deal of one type of program hold different beliefs about each sex from individuals who watch more of another type of program? And if such patterns or relationships do exist between program preferences and beliefs, are they to be interpreted as evidence of selective viewing or specific television influences? A further question investigated by this research related to the assumption by some writers that television cultivates sex stereotyping as audiences assimilate traditionalist messages about the nature and roles of the sexes, conveyed explicitly or implicitly by programs. But, as we have already seen, viewers' subjective perceptions of male and female television portrayals may differ from the character profiles painted by objective content analysis. Two important comparisons, largely missed by most researchers, are whether viewer's perceptions of the sexes as seen on television are the same as their perceptions of the sexes in real life and whether both sets of perceptions relate in similar ways to patterns and preferences of television viewing.

In the Gunter and Wober study, diary measures of television viewing were related to questionnaire responses concerning the way women were seen on television and in real life. The questionnaire was in three parts. In the first place, respondents were asked to say how true or untrue it was that women on television in daily life serials (soap operas), in situation comedies, or in advertisements are portrayed as "not being interested in politics," "wanting at sometime to be mothers," "quarrelsome with other women," "very interested in jobs and careers," "very keen on romantic affairs with men," "depending on men to help them out of trouble," and "more likely to get on if attractive." In the second part, respondents were required to say how true or untrue each of these items was of women in real life. In the final part, slightly reworded versions of these items were presented concerning the way women *ought* to lead their lives. These items were chosen to reflect common characterizations or roles portrayed by women on television that had been previously identified by content analysis studies, and that supposedly functioned to cultivate sexist stereotypes among viewers (see Butler & Paisley, 1980; Lemon, 1978; Tuchman, 1978).

Content analysis studies have, over the years, identified a number of prominent images of women on television and inferred that, through regular viewing of these, stereotyped beliefs about women are cultivated among the general public. The results from the present study afforded the opportunity to examine actual public perceptions of female portrayals on television *and* to see whether or not these perceptions correspond with the "images" of women defined through content analysis.

In serious drama, content studies have indicated that women are portrayed mainly in domestic, familial roles, and much less often, in professional, career-oriented roles. Women are often shown as preoccupied with romance and as dependent on men to help them whenever they get into trouble, especially outside the home (Lemon, 1978; Seggar & Wheeler, 1973; Tuchman, 1978). Perceptions of women on television serials obtained from viewers by Gunter and Wober (1982), however, did not indicate strong tendencies for viewers to see women as wanting to be mothers, preoccupied with romance, or depending on men when in trouble. Viewers' subjective perceptions on these attributes did not coincide with the "images" of television women identified by objective content analysis. Agreement between viewers' perceptions and objectively coded qualities of women did occur on the item concerning women shown as interested in jobs and careers.

There was no consistent evidence across attributes of relative differences in perceptions of women on television by light and heavy viewers of action-adventure programs that corresponded with inferences about the cultivation of stereotyped beliefs derived from content analysis. Heavy viewers of TV action-adventure actually perceived women in television serials as more independent of men rather than as less independent, as would be predicted by content analysis. There was no marked relationship between amount of action-adventure viewing and perceptions of television women as wanting to be mothers and settled with a family, even though content analyses have often indicated that this is the way women are shown (Tedesco, 1974; Tuchman, 1978). Heavy action-adventure viewers were less likely than light viewers of these programs to perceive women on television as career-oriented, and, on this one item, audience perceptions actually corresponded with content analytic descriptions of the way women are portrayed (see Butler & Paisley, 1980).

Two other important questions are whether viewing behavior relates to perceptions of women in real life, and whether real-life perceptions are consistent with television perceptions of women. Gunter and Wober's study found that beliefs about women being interested in careers, being keen on romance, being dependent on men when in trouble, and needing to be attractive to be successful were each related to action-adventure viewing for television and real-life perceptions. But how consistent in direction were these relationships?

Heavy action-adventure viewers perceived women on television serials as not interested in jobs and careers more than did light action-adventure viewers and also believed that this is the way women *are* and *should be* in real life. In addition, heavy action-drama viewers perceived women less as keen on romance on television and in reality and believed that they should not be preoccupied by sexual relations with men in everyday life. There was an inverse relationship between amount of serious action-adventure viewing and the belief that attractiveness was an essential feature for television women to be successful and that women relied heavily on their attractiveness to make progress in life. Heavy action-adventure viewers also tended to believe, more than did light viewers, that women should not be judged on looks alone. Finally, heavy action-adventure viewers perceived women as dependent on men in television serials or in real life less than did light viewers and believed more that women should be self-reliant. Clearly, there is consistency in the beliefs held about women as they are depicted on the television screen in certain programs and as they appear in real life, although these beliefs do not always match the images of women on television identified by objective content analysis.

CONCLUSIONS

Interest in the influence of TV on public consumptions of social reality has generated a great deal of research in the past 10 years in which a holistic view of TV's effects has come to the forefront. The real power of TV to shape the public outlook on the world is believed to lie in its symbolic representation of sociocultural norms and values, which through regular and cumulative exposure become absorbed into the psyches of viewers. The social beliefs that TV supposedly cultivates, however, are described by some writers as distorted or stereotyped representations of social reality. This claim may be true. The problem raised in this chapter is with the way in which researchers have often chosen to identify and elaborate how TV distorts or stereotypes aspects of reality. Messages and meanings have commonly been inferred to reside within TV content, which may not be as apparent or as relevant to audience members as researchers assume.

This chapter does not wholly dismiss content analysis as a useful method through which to assess the character of people, objects, and events portrayed on television. In order to measure in detail what television programs contain, there must of necessity be some system of classifying and cataloging the contents of programs. The doubts raised here are over the efficacy of traditional content analysis to express the meanings that audiences really apprehend from programs. The call is for analytical frameworks in the future to incorporate the cognitive interpretations and affective evaluations viewers themselves place on television content if they are to get at what programs really mean for audiences.

By all means, let us continue to count violent incidents in programs to produce television violence profiles. But the definitions of violence and of what constitute relatively more or less serious or disturbing violent acts on screen should be determined or at least guided by audience opinions. It may be perfectly possible, and quite reasonable, to decide to produce quantitative measures of objectively definable and identifiable incidents—such as, for example, the use of firearms—without recourse to the audience. One could count the number of times somebody pulls a gun and fires it, and this counting could produce reliable results across several different monitors. But it would be wrong to assume that all such incidents have the same meaning for, are perceived in the same way by, or generate the same level of emotional response from viewers. The meaning of the event will be affected by the type of program in which it occurs, the character(s) involved, the reason for its occurrence within the storyline, its consequences for those involved, and perhaps by other factors, too. Definitional frameworks or systems of classification based on audience research can not only be readily applied to produce television content profiles, but they are also likely to yield indicators that more accurately represent or reflect the ways in which viewers respond to programs.

Comparisons between the descriptive character of TV programming deriving from objective content analysis and the perceived character of TV from the subjective point of view of the audience do not always match up. Since viewers' perceptual evaluations and cognitive interpretations of TV content have been found to mediate its impact upon them, these perceptual and cognitive factors need to be built into models of program content assessment if the latter are to provide ecologically valid foundations on which to build authoritative effects research. Cultivation effects researchers correctly recognize the inherent complexity of the world of television, but they are wrong to assume that the significant messages and meanings conveyed by TV can be identified without reference to the content perceptions of the audience. The audience is perceptive and its members are highly discriminating in their cognitive responses to TV content. And those cognitive discriminations can actively determine what viewers learn from TV and how much they allow it to influence their outlook on society.

REFERENCES

Atkin, C., & Miller, M. M. (1986, April). *Experimental effects of television advertising on children*. Paper presented at the meeting of the International Communication Association, Chicago.

Bem, S. (1974). The measurement of psychological androgyny. *Journal of Consulting and Clinical Psychology, 52*, 155-162.

Bem, S. (1975). Sex role adaptability: One consequence of psychological androgyny. *Journal of Personality and Social Psychology, 31*, 634-643.

Bem, S. (1976). Probing the promise of androgyny. In A. Kaplan & J. Bean (Eds.), *Beyond sex-role stereotypes: Reading towards a psychology of androgyny*. Boston: Little, Brown.

Beuf, F. A. (1974). Doctor, lawyer, household drudge. *Journal of Communication, 24*, 110-118.

British Broadcasting Corporation. (1972). *Violence on television: Programme content and viewer perceptions*. London: Author.

Butler, M., & Paisley, W. (1980). *Women and the mass media*. New York: Human Sciences Press.

Ceulemans, M., & Fauconnier, G. (1979). *Mass media: The image, role and social conditions of women* (Report no. 84). Paris: UNESCO.

Collins, W. A. (1973). Effect of temporal separation between motivation, aggression and consequences: A developmental study. *Developmental Psychology, 8*, 215-221.

Collins, W. A. (1979). Children's comprehension of television content. In E. Wartella (Ed.), *Children communicating: Media and development of thought, speech, understanding* (pp. 21-52). Newbury Park, CA: Sage.

Collins, W. A. (1981). Recent advances in research on cognitive processing television viewing. *Journal of Broadcasting, 25*, 327-334.

DeFleur, M. (1964). Occupation roles as portrayal on television. *Public Opinion Quarterly, 28*, 57-74.

Downing, M. (1974). Heroine of the daytime serial. *Journal of Communication, 24*, 130-139.

Drabman, R. S., Robertson, S. J., Patterson, J. N., Jarvie, G. J., Hammer, D., & Cordua, G. (1981). Children's perceptions of media-portrayed sex roles. *Sex Roles, 12*, 379-389.

Durkin, K. (1984). Children's accounts of sex-role stereotypes on television. *Communication Research, 11*, 341-362.

Elliott, W. R., & Slater, D. (1980). Exposure, experience, and perceived TV reality for adolescents. *Journalism Quarterly, 57*, 409-414, 431.

Frueh, T., & McGhee, P. E. (1975). Traditional sex-role development and amount of time spent watching television. *Development Psychology, 11*, 109.

Gerbner, G. (1972). Violence in television drama: Trends and symbolic functions. In G. A. Comstock & E. A. Rubinstein (Eds.), *Television and social behavior, Vol. 1: Content and control.* Washington, DC: Government Printing Office.

Gerbner, G., & Gross, L. (1976). Living with television: The violence profile. *Journal of Communication, 26*, 173-199.

Gerbner, G., Gross, L., Jackson-Beeck, M., Jeffries-Fox, S., & Signorielli, N. (1978). Cultural indicators: Violence profile No. 9. *Journal of Communication, 28*, 176-207.

Gerbner, G., Gross, L., Morgan, M., & Signorielli, N. (1980). The main streaming of America: Violence profile No. 11. *Journal of Communication, 30*, 10-29.

Gerbner, G., Gross, L., Morgan, M., & Signorielli, N. (1981). A viewer's journey into the scary world of Paul Hirsh. *Communication Research, 8*, 39-72.

Gerbner, G., Gross, L., Signorielli, N., Morgan, M., & Jackson-Beeck, M. (1979). The demonstration of power: Violence profile No. 10. *Journal of Communication, 29*, 177-196.

Gerbner, G., & Signorielli, N. (1979, October 29). *Women and minorities in television drama, 1969-1978* (Research report). Annenburg School of Communications (Philadelphia) in collaboration with the Screen Actors Guild, AFL-CIO.

Goff, D. H., Goff, L. D., & Lehrer, S. K. (1980). Sex role portrayals of selected female television characters. *Journal of Broadcasting, 24*, 467-475.

Gross, L., & Morgan, M. (1985). Television and enculturation. In J. R. Dominick & J. E. Fletcher (Eds.), *Broadcasting research methods.* Boston: Allyn & Bacon.

Gunter, B. (1981). Measuring television violence: A review and suggestions for a new analytical perspective. *Current Psychological Reviews, 1*, 91-112.

Gunter, B. (1985). *Dimensions of television violence.* Aldershot, England: Gower.

Gunter, B. (1986). *Television and sex role stereotyping.* London: IBA and John Libbey.

Gunter, B., & Furnham, A. (1984). Perceptions of television violence: Effects of programme genre and physical form of violence. *British Journal of Social Psychology, 23*, 155-184.

Gunter, B., & Wober, M. (1982). Television viewing and perceptions of women on TV and in real life. *Current Psychological Research, 2*, 277-288.

Gunter, B., & Wober, M. (1983). Television viewing and public trust. *British Journal of Social Psychology, 22*, 174-176.

Halloran, J. D., & Croll, P. (1972). Television programmes in Great Britain. In G. A. Comstock & E. A. Rubinstein (Eds.), *Television and social behavior. Vol. 1: Content and control* (pp. 415-492). Washington, DC: Government Printing Office.

Hawkins, R., & Pingree, S. (1982). Television influence on social reality. In D. Pearl, L. Bouthilet, & J. Lazar (Eds.), *Television and behavior: In ten years of scientific progress and implications for the eighties.* Rockville, MD: National Institute of Mental Health.

Head, H. (1954). Content analysis of television drama programmes. *Quarterly of Film, Radio, Television, 9*, 175-194.

Hirsch, P. (1980). The "scary" world of the non-viewer and other anomalies: A reanalysis of Gerbner et al.'s findings on cultivation analysis: Part 1. *Communication Research, 1*, 403-456.

Howitt, D., & Cumberbatch, G. (1974). Audience perceptions of violent television content. *Communication Research, 1*, 204-227.

Hughes, M. (1980). The fruits of cultivation analysis: A re-examination of the effects of television in fear of victimization, alienation and approval of violence. *Public Opinion Quarterly, 44*, 287-302.

Joy, L., Kimball, M., & Zabrock, M. (1977, June). *Television exposure and children's aggressive behavior*. Paper presented at the meeting of the Canadian Psychological Association, Vancouver.

Lemon, J. (1978). Women and blacks on prime-time television. *Journal of Communication, 27*, 70-74.

Maccoby, E. E., & Wilson, W. C. (1957). Identification and observational learning from films. *Journal of Abnormal and Social Psychology, 55*, 76-87.

Mayes, S. L., & Valentine, K. B. (1979). Sex role stereotyping in Saturday morning cartoon shows. *Journal of Broadcasting, 23*, 41-50.

McGhee, P., & Freuh, T. (1980). Television viewing and the learning of sex-role stereotypes. *Sex Roles, 27*, 179-188.

Miller, M., & Reeves, B. (1976). Dramatic TV content and children's sex-role stereotyping. *Journal of Broadcasting, 20*, 35-50.

Morgan, M. (1982). Television and adolescents' sex role stereotypes: A longitudinal study. *Journal of Personality and Social Psychology, 55*, 76-87.

Peevers, B. H. (1979). Androgyny on the TV screen? An analysis of sex role portrayals. *Sex Roles, 5*, 797-809.

Perloff, R., Brown, J., & Miller, M. (1982). Mass media and sex-typing: Research perspectives and policy implications. *International Journal of Women's Studies, 5*, 265-273.

Pingree, S. (1978). The effect of nonsexist television commercials and perceptions of reality on children's attitudes about women. *Psychology of Women Quarterly, 2*, 262-276.

Pingree, S. (1983). Children's cognitive processing in constructing social reality. *Journalism Quarterly, 60*, 415-422.

Potter, W. J. (1986). Perceived reality and the cultivation hypothesis. *Journal of Broadcasting and Electronic Media, 30*, 159-174.

Rosencrantz, P., Vogel, S., Bee, H., Broverman, I., & Broverman, D. (1968). Sex role stereotypes and self-concepts in college students. *Journal of Consulting and Clinical Psychology, 32*, 287-295.

Schiebe, C. (1979). Sex roles in TV commercials. *Journal of Advertising Research, 19*, 23-28.

Seggar, J., & Wheeler, P. (1973). World of work on TV: Ethnic and sex representation in TV drama. *Journal of Broadcasting, 11*, 201-214.

Sharits, N., & Lammers, B. H. (1983). Perceived attributes of models in prime-time and daytime television commercials: A person perception approach. *Journal of Marketing Research, 20*, 64-73.

Signorielli, N. (1984). The demography of the television world. In G. Melischek, K. E., Rosengren, & J. Stappers (Eds.), *Cultural Indicators: An International Symposium*. Vienna: Austrian Academy of Sciences.

Signorielli, N. (1985). The measurement of violence in television programming: Violence indices. In J. R. Dominick & J. E. Fletcher (Eds.), *Broadcasting research methods*. Boston: Allyn & Bacon.

Slater, D., & Elliott, W. R. (1982). Television's influence on social reality. *Quarterly Journal of Speech, 68*, 69-79.

Sprafkin, M., & Liebert, R. M. (1978). Sex-typing and children's preferences. In G. Tuchman, A. Daniels, & I. Benet (Eds.), *Hearth and home: Images of women in the mass media* (pp. 288-339). New York: Oxford University Press.

Tamborini, R., Zillmann, D., & Bryant, J. (1984). Fear and victimization: Exposure to television and perceptions of crime and fear. In R. N. Bostrum (Ed.), *Communication Yearbook, 8,* 492-513. Newbury Park, CA: Sage.

Tan, A., Randy, J., Huff, C., & Miles, J. (1980). Children's reactions to male and female newscasters' effectiveness and believability. *Quarterly Journal of Speech, 66,* 201-215.

Tedesco, N. (1974). Patterns in prime-time. *Journal of Communication, 74,* 119-124.

Tuchman, G. (1978). The symbolic annihilation of women by the mass media. In G. Tuchman, A. Daniels, & J. Benet (Eds.), *Hearth and home: Images of women in the mass media.* New York: Oxford University Press.

Tuchman, G., Daniels, A., & Benet, J. (Eds.). (1978). *Hearth and home: Images of women in the mass media.* New York: Oxford University Press.

Turner, M. E. (1974). Sex-role attitudes and fear of success in relation to achievement behavior in women. *Dissertation Abstracts International, 3*(5-13), 2451-2452.

Tyler, T. R. (1980). The impact of directly and indirectly experienced events: The origin of crime-related judgements and behaviors. *Journal of Personality and Social Psychology, 39,* 13-28.

Tyler, T. R. (1984). Assessing the risk of crime victimization: The integration of personal victimization and socially transmitted information. *Journal of Social Issues, 40,* 27-38.

Tyler, T. R., Cook, F. L. (1984). The mass media and judgements of risk: Distinguishing impact on personal and societal level judgements. *Journal of Personality and Social Psychology, 47,* 693-708.

Van der Voort, T.H.A. (1986). *Television violence: A child's eye view.* Amsterdam, Holland: Elsevier Science.

Volgy, J. J., & Schwartz, J. E. (1980). TV entertainment programming and socio-political attitudes. *Journalism Quarterly, 57,* 150-155.

Weaver, J., & Wakshlag, J. (1986). Perceived vulnerability to crime, criminal victimization experience, and television viewing. *Journal of Broadcasting and Electronic Media, 30,* 141-158.

Williams, F., La Rose, R., & Frost, F. (1981). *Children, television and sex-role stereotyping.* New York: Praeger.

Wober, M., & Gunter, B. (in press). *Television and social control.* Aldershot, England: Gower.

Zillmann, D. (1980). Anatomy of suspense. In P. Tannenbaum (Ed.), *The entertainment function of television.* Hillsdale, NJ: Lawrence Erlbaum.

2 Opposing Conceptions of the Audience: The Active and Passive Hemispheres of Mass Communication Theory

FRANK A. BIOCCA
University of North Carolina, Chapel Hill

Working the definitions, ideologies, and implications of the concepts of active and passive audiences, Biocca uses the research literature to demonstrate that the active audience position is overextended and often trivial. He removes the locus of control from both the media and the individual and places it in the center of physiological, psychological, social, and semiotic structures.

A T the very center of mass communication research there lies a fundamental dichotomy, a split between opposite conceptions of the mass communication process and its audience. In one of its many forms, it permeates a number of theoretical and methodological debates.

Over the last 40 years of theory and research, a kind of theoretical tug-of-war has emerged. On one end of the rope we find the *active audience*: individualistic, "impervious to influence," rational, and selective. On the other end, we have the *passive audience*: conformist, gullible, anomic, vulnerable, victims. Huffing and tugging at each end is an assorted lot of key media theorists championing their perception of the social reality.

Mass communication theory's simultaneous embrace of both conceptions frames many of the questions we ask about the sociopolitical role of the media, the audience member's cognitions of self and "reality," as well as the moment-to-moment cognitive processes by which the individual decodes media content and form. What are the limits of individual intellectual freedom in the face of the institutions for the dissemination of information and

AUTHOR'S NOTE: I would like to acknowledge Jay Blumler, Mark Levy, Jack McLeod, Joe Capella, and Gary D. Gaddy for their open-minded review and critique of an earlier draft.

Correspondence and requests for reprints: Frank A. Biocca, Center for Research in Journalism and Mass Communication, School of Journalism, University of North Carolina, Chapel Hill, NC 27514.

Communication Yearbook 11, pp. 51-80

ideology? Are these institutions vehicles for social conformism or bearers of liberating knowledge?

Such questions call out for a theoretical analysis of the fundamental epistemological assumptions that guide, and sometimes mislead, our research on the nature of the mass media and their audiences. Because of the central importance of this amorphous active-passive dichotomy in mass communication theory, this chapter will:

(1) establish and analyze the theoretical components of the concepts of *activity* and of the "active audience";
(2) trace the intellectual origins of the original concept of audience *passivity* and vulnerability and the "reaction" it engendered;
(3) critique the implications of the concept of audience activity for cognitive and social theory and research; and, finally,
(4) make some proposals for the clarification and, it is hoped, the advancement of research in this area.

WHAT IS AUDIENCE "ACTIVITY"?

For the uses and gratifications "paradigm," the concept of the active audience is a key player on a sometimes disorganized chess board of theories, beliefs, and conceits. Theorists in this paradigm insist that this "most basic tenet" (Swanson, 1979, p. 41) of *audience* activity "is important" (Rouner, 1984, p. 173), "constitutes one of the essential underpinnings of the approach" (Palmgreen, 1984), and is "fundamental to the study of mass communication effects in general, and central to the uses and gratifications approach in particular" (Levy, 1983, p. 109). For some observers, active audience theory may itself be "a new dominant paradigm in effects research" (Hawkins & Pingree, 1982, 1986). Even among some of the critics of uses and gratifications, the concept of audience activity constitutes "a decided gain over the psychological assumptions underpinning the older research tradition" (Carey & Kreiling, 1974), which "we should applaud" (Swanson, 1979, p. 41).

One of the strengths and, simultaneously, one of the weaknesses of the construct is its "extraordinary range of meanings" (Blumler, 1979, p. 13). It is both cognitive and sociostructural, normative and objective, socially variable yet innate. The various qualitative forms of the concept exist within a temporal dimension as well. Like media consumption behavior, activity is said to exist prior to media use ("preactivity"), during media use ("duractivity"), and following media use ("postactivity") (Blumler, 1979; Levy, 1983; Levy & Windahl, 1984a, 1984b).

It has become clear that this literature has given birth to a protean and infinitely malleable meta-construct that is "undeniably complex and multi-dimensional" (Palmgreen, Wenner, & Rosengren, 1985). Each facet purports to define an intangible and relative process called "activity." Even though the concept has been used extensively in much mass communication theory and research for over a decade, one still finds theorists who dodge an adequate theoretical exposition of the term *activity*, apologizing, for example, that "the concept of activity is not easily defined" (Rubin, 1986, p. 293). Before examining the whole, let us first dissect the parts in search of an underlying structure. What follows is an attempt faithfully to structure descriptors used in the definitions and research into the concept of activity (Blumler, 1979; Levy & Windahl, 1984a, 1985; Palmgreen, Wenner, & Rosengren, 1985; Rubin, 1984).

- *Audience activity as "selectivity":*

Grounded in the theories of selective attention, perception, and retention (Klapper, 1960), audience activity is portrayed as the funneling process of media, program, and content selection (Heeter, D'Allessio, Greenberg, & McVoy, 1983). In the uses and gratifications literature, the term *selectivity* is most often used to denote selective exposure (Levy, 1983, p. 110). But there has been a recent attempt to expand the concept into the areas of selective perception and selective retention (recall) (Levy & Windahl, 1985).

- *Audience activity as "utilitarianism":*

In an extension of the concept of selectivity, theorists using this facet of the concept emphasize the *utility* of the process of choice. The audience member is the embodiment of the self-interested consumer. Beyond mere selectivity, which in some cases implies a certain defensiveness on the part of the audience, the utilitarian version of the concept suggests a certain level of rational choice in the satisfaction of clear individual needs and motives (Dervin, 1980; Katz, Blumler, & Gurevitch, 1974; Levy, 1983; Palmgreen, 1984; Palmgreen & Rayburn, 1985).

- *Audience activity as "intentionality":*

It is in this form that the concept emphasizes the more cognitive dimensions of activity. Intentionality points to schematic processing and structuring of incoming information (Fiske & Kinder, 1980; Garramone, 1983; Planalp & Hewes, 1979; Swanson, 1979). Media consumption and attention are said to be schema driven. Patterns of consumption and memory bear the clear imprint of the audience member's motivation, personality, and individual cognitive processing structure (McGuire, 1974; Wenner, 1985).

- *Audience activity as "involvement":*

According to Hawkins and Pingree (1986), "cognitive effort" has become the focus of methodological and theoretical debate. Levy (1983) uses the label "involvement" to characterize both the level of "affective arousal" and a level of cognitive organization and information structuring. The same activity term is further used to label behavioral manifestations of active "involvement," such as parasocial interaction (e.g., "talking back" to the television).

• *Audience activity as "imperviousness to influence":*

Though the phrase "imperviousness to influence" is identified with Bauer (1964a), this facet of "activity" can be cited as the sociopolitical "bottom line" of the concept. It clearly is for many writers part of the underlying "effect" of activity on the process of mass communication. For other writers, "impervious to influence" functions as a kind of goal of activity by reference to the degree to which the audience limits, influences, and controls the effects of media.

This activity is sometimes portrayed as subversive of communicator goals and intentions. Using examples of failed information campaigns drawn from the body of limited effects research, Dervin (1980) has joined with others in extending this dimension of the concept into a phenomenological individualism emphasizing idiosyncratic decodings of "information."

Though this typology of the forms of the concept reveals the breadth of its use, it is clear that the various facets of the concept are not orthogonal (see Rosengren, 1985). They overlap, some potentially consuming the others. Each has emerged piecemeal after the concept, according to active audience theorists, was accepted as an "article of faith" (Blumler, 1979; Palmgreen et al., 1985).

What also seems to be missing is the unknown core of the concept. Rosengren (1985) notes that it is "paradoxical that one of the central concepts of a research tradition should have remained unexamined for such a long time" (p. 276). Levy and Windahl (1985) echo his concern: "Despite its centrality to mass communication theory, however, the notion of audience activity has received little conceptual development or direct study" (p. 110; see also Windahl, 1981; Rubin, 1986).

Why has the concept of activity remained unexamined? The fact that the theorists of the active audience have called it an "article of faith" reveals a sense of ideological commitment. (Here using ideology as the basic intellectual structure underlying one's thinking.) This ideological commitment is laced with liberal democratic ideals of individual rationality, independence, and "self-possession."

The source of the active audience stance can be surmised from the independence cry resonating from the notion of "imperviousness to influence." To understand and fully analyze the concept of active audience and the research agenda it has engendered, we must appreciate its intellectual origins.

BAUER'S INDEPENDENCE CRY, "IMPERVIOUSNESS TO INFLUENCE"

The creator of the phrases "imperviousness to influence" and the "obstinate audience," which later became euphemistically translated to the "active audience," is the social psychologist Raymond Bauer (1963, 1964a, 1964b; Bauer & Bauer, 1960). Bauer (1964b) is almost universally cited among uses and gratifications theorists and critics as the author of this declaration of audience independence (Blumler, 1979; Blumler, Gurevitch, & Katz, 1985; Carey & Kreiling, 1974; Dervin, 1980; Elliott, 1974; Levy, 1983; Levy & Windahl, 1984a, 1985; McGuire, 1974; McLeod & Becker, 1974, 1981; McQuail, 1983; McQuail & Gurevitch, 1974; Palmgreen, 1984; Pingree & Hawkins, 1982; Weibull, 1985; Wenner, 1985). For these theorists, Bauer's article is a milestone in a purported "paradigm shift" from "administrative" approaches to more receiver-oriented research perspectives.

Bauer's mission is clearly signaled in the first paragraphs of his article. He quotes Isidor Chein (1962):

> The opening sentence of *Ethical Standards of Psychologists* is that "the psychologist is committed to a belief in the dignity and worth of the individual human being." . . . But what kind of dignity can we attribute to a robot? (p. 31)

Bauer was decrying the temperament of a decade when Skinnerians held court in psychology departments and the Cassandras of mass culture theory bickered and warned that mass media had brought Pavlovian conformism into the home via TV. Mass communication theorists joined with like-minded colleagues in psychology and sociology to rescue the abstract individual. In this classic article, the media, led by advertising and social scientific institutions, are pitted against the individual armed only with his or her good sense and "obstinate" psyche.

Framed within almost mythic terms, Bauer puts forward a version of the passive and active dichotomy. A model of "one-way influence" (the passive audience), which Bauer associates with an odd alliance of exploitative communicators and mass culture critics, is pitted against a model that is couched in the language of the marketplace, a "transactional model." Here "exchanges are equitable" and "each party expect(s) to get his money's worth" (pp. 319, 320).

Bauer was attempting to retrieve not only the individual but the *image* of the individual, which lies at the heart of classic liberal democracy: the ideal independent citizen who is rational, self-determining, and freely pursuing life, liberty, and property. This model of the individual was threatened by social critics who pointed out that in a society where mass production and mass-produced consensus were king and queen, democracy was illegitimate.

It is clear in this article that Bauer's primary impetus for the "active audience" model is a moral one. He writes, "The issue is not . . . the *findings* of social science. . . . The real issue is whether our social model of man—the model we use for running society—and our scientific model or models—the one we use for running subjects—should be identical" (p. 319).

THE SPECTER OF THE "PASSIVE" AUDIENCE

The tone of urgency in this early version of the debate revealed that the active audience theorists implicitly shared a belief in the possibility of the fully realized passive audience model—the Orwellian specter of a truly "mass society." Often depicted in terms of the extreme stereotype of mass society theorists (Durkheim, 1893/1964; LeBon, 1893; Reisman, 1950), the passive audience is grey, uniform, anomic, faceless, gullible, and defenseless against the power of the propagandist. This sociological myth is in some ways a pastiche of images generated by the media themselves. Mass-disseminated images are retrieved of masses screaming in unison at 1930s Nuremberg rallies, farmers running out of their homes during Orson Welles's "War of the Worlds," millions of faceless consumers salivating for the mass-produced good life. These are referents for the labels and stereotypes of mass entertainment and public opinion surveys. In the recent literature, an audience researcher acknowledges and perpetuates the myth of the passive audience with her characterization of a "global priesthood" with "non-selective" and "habitual" viewing habits (Rouner, 1984, p. 168). The mass waits vulnerable and irrational.

For the contemporaries of Bauer who subscribed to the passive audience image, the mass production of messages presented a certain illusion (Anders, 1957). Everywhere, the TV image and the newspaper page were exactly the same. Everywhere, there was a similarity of form. The exact same physical image could be seen in the subway, in the newspaper, in the home. From this illusion came the leap claiming that the exact same physical message produced its exact likeness in the consciousness of the audience. The result seemed equally obvious. The mass production process had evolved into the assembly line of the mind (Van den Haag, 1957).

The theory of the passive audience was not merely a phase in the history of mass communication theory. It lives on in many of our assumptions and fears about the effects of mass communication. "Cultivation" theory (Gerbner, Gross, Morgan, & Signorielli, 1980, 1986) is one of the inheritors of the passive audience tradition. Gerbner et al. (1986) write:

> People are born into a symbolic environment with television as its main-stream. . . . Television viewing is both a shaper and stable part of certain lifestyles and outlooks. It links the individual to a larger if synthetic world, a world of television's own making. . . . The content shapes and promotes . . . dominates their sources of information, continued exposure to its messages is likely to reiterate, confirm, and nourish (i.e., cultivate) their values and perspectives. (pp. 23ff.)

The notion of the "passive" audience has evolved a great deal in this newer "mainstreamed" model. But in it we find the spirit of the "passive audience" tradition, the fear of the rise of mass society, now a gray and slow-moving "mainstream."

In the course of the development of mass communication theory, there were a number of possible reactions to the specter of mass society. The strident if sometimes hollow claims of radical individualism visible in the "alternative" culture of the 1960s were one response. Another approach was to question the validity of certain notions of "mass society." For active theorists, this often involved denying the ascendancy of the *mass* in mass communication. Blumler (1979), a leading exponent of uses and gratifications theory, notes that this school has "always been strongly opposed to mass audience terminology as a way of labelling the collectivities that watch TV shows, attend movies, and read magazines and newspapers in their millions" (p. 21). The confusion and disappointment in mass communication research (Berelson, 1959; Klapper, 1960), born of the inability to find and measure convincing evidence of mass "hypodermic" effects, facilitated the use of the new "active audience" as a rallying cry.

But who was this "active" audience member and what would be evidence of activity? The active audience member began to take on characteristics of the classical liberal democratic citizen. In Bauer's formulation emphasizing the "transaction," there was an emphasis on choice. This choice was anchored in and ensured by an independent, even obstinate, citizen. Freedom of choice and the exercise of that choice was a sign of "audience activity" and, in another sphere, the health of the body politic.

But the new active audience left something to be desired. The active "individual" was a modern citizen-consumer patrolling the periphery of his or her consciousness with a vigilant consumerism. This was not the citizen of Rousseau or Jefferson. This was a shopkeeper's citizen. Freedom and consumerism had been integrally joined in the American psyche. The famous Nixon-Kruschev "kitchen debate" had been carried out in the home of this new ideal citizen. The "freedom of choice" was a consumerist cornucopia of choices. What could be more appropriate in a mass culture typified by mass consumption than to glorify choice—the mere act of selecting a mass media product—as the hallmark of individualism and activism. Freedom was achieved by denying the effectiveness of mass communication and mass culture and by multiplying the number of choices. With the statistical explosion of probabilities and choices, how could mass culture take hold? The very consumption that the passive audience theorist so feared was turned on its head. Bauer's triumphant shout announced that the passive audience was "liberated."

In succeeding articles, declarations of the death of the passive audience were to become an academic ritual (for examples of a widespread phenomenon, see Berlo, 1977; McLeod & Becker, 1981; Palmgreen, 1984). For some, the pursuit of the active audience became an imperative. It became, in the words of Bauer (1964b), "the model which ought to be inferred from the research" (p. 319). In research that followed, attempts have been made to turn the "ought" into an "empirical reality." But it will be argued that the agenda at the base of the commitment to what Blumler (1979) has called an "article of faith" has led to many oversights, theoretical difficulties, and tortuous reasoning as the concept has expanded into a system of research.

IN SEARCH OF THE
OVERALL MEANING OF ACTIVITY

From the previous section we can see why the concept of audience activity is often defined through the negation of its antagonist, the passive audience. In the new expansive universe of the active audience, is it possible to be inactive or passive?

As the reader will recall, we find among the main tenets of the activity theory the concepts of utility, intentionality, and selectivity (Blumler, 1979), as well as involvement (Levy, 1979). But as we look closer at the concepts, a number of troubling questions emerge. Could it be that the *mythic* passive audience is being opposed by an *empty shadow* we call the "active audience"?

Looking at the basic concept of utility, a problem immediately reveals itself. Blumler's (1979) definition of utility, "mass communication has uses for people" (p. 13), defines use—any use whatsoever—as an indicator of activity. It restates what is seemingly obvious at the risk of being trivial. We must ask if it is likely for the uses and gratifications researcher ever to get the response from subjects that they "use" the mass media, because it has absolutely *no use* for them. Defined in this way, can this "activity" fail to dominate over its more passive antagonist of "un-use"?

Similar questions emerge when looking at intentionality. Intentionality is defined by Blumler as "media consumption . . . directed by prior motivation" (1979, p. 14). Again, should we be surprised that our audience members rarely respond that they read newspapers, listen to the radio, or watch television for "absolutely no reason at all." Self-report methodology by its very nature and structure invites the respondent to give meaning to his or her behavior. The very act of responding is an invitation to rationalize one's behavior, to create attitudinal "causes" for one's actions. If the existence of "passivity" is to be defined by self-reports of unmotivated behavior, should we be surprised by its absence?

The concepts of selectivity and involvement lead us to even more troubling questions. The process of selectivity, the sheer act of choice, is used as an indicator of activity. But it is almost *impossible* for the audience member to use the media without "choosing" to do so or, at least, selecting a medium. An audience member scanning a newspaper will inevitably be activated to choose some content. Indeed, it is a rare audience member who will turn to any medium and randomly select some content. Should we be surprised, given how the odds are stacked theoretically, when research results (Barwise, Ehrenberg, & Goathardt, 1982) "reveal" that the audience "does not seem so passive. Viewers do not just pick a program at random" (p. 27).

According to some measures of activity, haphazard flicking of the dial or surveying the offerings would turn the audience member into a member of the "active audience" (Levy & Windahl, 1984a, 1984b, 1985). In this case, we could have the paradoxical result that the highly selective audience member who watches only a specific program will appear "less active" than the less selective "channel hopper."

The concepts of activity and selectivity are supposed to be properties of individuals, but we are informed by Levy and Windahl (1985) that a major component of selectivity is a property of the *medium*:

> The selection of media sources, and thus audience activity of this type, is constrained by the number of possible choices the audience member has at his or her disposal. . . . developments in communication technology that provide audience members with a greatly expanded repertoire of choices are resulting in increased levels of selectivity. (p. 26)

Levy and Windahl seem to be saying that by merely giving our "active audience" member more choices, we make him or her more active. But this claim says little about our audience member. The more we expand the statistical probabilities and scatter of choices, the more "seemingly" individualistic the choices become. Can conformism in mass culture be sabotaged by merely offering a "greater selection" of media products? To use an example from another realm, Do more brands of blue jeans equal less conformism?

And finally, we must ask one last disturbing question: If "involvement" is defined as *some* level of "cognitive or affective arousal" (Levy & Windahl, 1984a) or the use of schema to process media content, then what—short of brain death—would render an individual a member of the passive audience?

From these few questions about the basic components of the concept of activity, we can see that the pliable facets of the term seem to make the concept virtually *unfalsifiable*. It is, by definition, nearly impossible for the audience not to be active.

INTERNALIZED FREEDOM AND
THE INEVITABLE RETREAT
INTO COGNITIVE ACTIVITY

Each new communication technology (movies, television, computers, satellite broadcasting) and each potential psychological refinement by advertisers and propagandists ("subliminal techniques," physiological monitoring, etc.) activates public alarm over potential loss of cognitive independence. The history of mass communication effects research can be seen as a response to perceived threats to the sanctity of the individual and this realm of inner freedom and self-determination. (For movies, see Payne Fund Studies, Lowery & DeFleur, 1983; for comics, see Wertham, 1954; for television, see Surgeon General, 1971, and Gerbner, 1980; for ideological stampeding, see Noelle-Neumann, 1974; for mass psychotic behavior, see Phillips, 1980.)

Since much of the underpinnings of our social system lie anchored in Enlightenment notions of reason (Cassirer, 1951), it is no wonder that potential threats to this philosophy, and the claims to self-determination that it upholds, have been met with desperate resistance. The irrational philosophies of humankind popular at the beginning of this century and the seeming susceptibility of the public to media-disseminated propaganda provoked alarm among media and social theorists (Lasswell, 1927; Lippman, 1965) while offering opportunities for others (Bernays, 1965). Ever since Luther's pamphlet, *Freedom of a Christian* (1952), both freedom and self-determination have been anchored by an inner freedom, control over the realm of one's thoughts (Marcuse, 1972). The rational, self-determined individual is the sine qua non of the philosophy of liberal democracy and possessive individualism (MacPherson, 1962).

If the concept of audience activity is to maintain its theoretical link to the concept of "imperviousness to influence," then the cognitive, as opposed to the behavioral area, represents the "final frontier." For Swanson (1979) "cognitive activity is . . . an important, perhaps definitive, part of the study of 'what people do with media'" (p. 41). Though uses and gratifications theorists acknowledge the importance of psychological research from within their paradigm (Rouner, 1984), they also sadly acknowledge a "scarcity of empirical investigations of psychological origins" (Palmgreen, 1985) of needs, motivations, and cognitive processes.

When describing the audience activity as information processing, active audience theorists point out that individuals have varying levels of attention (Anderson & Lorch, 1983; Levy, 1983) and involvement (Levy, 1983; Levy & Windahl, 1984a, 1984b). Theorists characterize media use as intentional, goal-directed, and motivated behavior (Katz et al., 1974; McQuail, Blumler, & Brown, 1972; Rosengren, 1974). Individuals "construct meanings" in accordance with motivations and schema (Delia, 1974; Levy, 1983; Swanson, 1979). They are also active by becoming cognitively or affectively aroused (Levy, 1983; Levy & Windahl, 1984a, 1984b), which might be manifested as parasocial behavior (Levy, 1977, 1983).

A researcher describes the specific meaning of these terms by describing "active television viewing" as viewing that "goes beyond mere exposure and might involve critical or analytical processing of information . . . " where viewers "may think about aspects of character and plot," which they "do . . . immediately or later" (Rouner, 1984, p. 170-171). The same writer goes so far as to imply innate bases for "activity" such as "IQ" (p. 170). Such sketchy outlines often define the cognitive dimensions of "audience activity."

Given such descriptions, if activity is to be defined simply by the fact that audience members process information, use schema, and, in effect, "think" while using a medium, then obviously audience activity must be granted. This designation of activity renders the concept not only obvious, but unfalsifiable, while failing to distinguish any significant differences between the processing of media information and the cognitive processing of any other human experience. If simple processing equals activity, then the motto of the active audience theorist should be, "I think, therefore I am active."

The debate over the cognitive activity of the active/passive audience does not rotate on the point of whether the audience "thinks" and processes information or on typologies of motivational theory (McGuire, 1974). Rather, the question turns on whether the audience has active control over the structure of the information process and whether the individual is best described not as passive but as reactive to the structure and content of the media. Anderson and Lorch (1983) demarcate the battleground clearly when they state that "the active theory puts control of viewing directly within the viewer (rather) than with the television set" (p. 9). This crucial and somewhat political point is echoed by uses and gratification theorists who argue that the audience member "bend(s) programs, articles, films, and songs to his own purposes" (Blumler, 1979, p. 202), leading McLeod and Becker (1981) to observe that "audience members in the real world exercise considerable freedom in their use of the mass media" (p. 71).

Anderson and Lorch (1983) peg the debate over the active or passive audience on the key issue of the processing of formal properties of the medium, specifically TV. Their question is whether the formal properties of the medium guide or "control" processing of content leading individuals to react to the medium, or whether the initiative lies with the active individual who uses "strategies" to manipulate media content.

Using an ingenious experimental manipulation involving altered versions of the *Sesame Street* program, Anderson and Lorch do show that attention among children is related to comprehension. They claim further to have isolated various formal features, namely "cues for attention," that are used within active viewing strategies by children as markers of interesting content. Anderson and Lorch's work clearly deflates the excessively passive caricatures of the audience peddled by popular writers (Mander, 1978; Winn, 1977). Mander, for example, writes that the viewer has "no cognition, no discernment, no notations upon the experience [s/he] is having" . . . "the viewer is little more than a vessel of reception."

But what are we to make of these findings in the debate over the active, passive, or reactive audience? Anderson and Lorch (1983) in a rather polemical article feel they cannot eliminate the claims for automatic viewing processes as their own research shows a process of "attentional inertia" that maintains viewing (or nonviewing) "across breaks in comprehension and changes in content" (p. 9). This finding at the very least shows that the cognitive processing is not as vigilant as one might suppose from the theoretical claims.

Furthermore, even Anderson and Lorch's "attentional cues" are the result of a process of media training, or what might be called "media socialization." These provide guides to cognitive processing that are taken up by the individual. It is important to note that the internalization of attentional cues comes *after* a thorough initiation into the terrain of television's forms and conventions. Levy and Windahl (1984a), who purport to offer a "model of audience activity and gratifications" (p. 58), ignore this highly reactive process and acknowledge that their "model does not currently deal with processes of or socialization to media consumption nor with the creation of new patterns of media use" (p. 58). If a laboratory rat learns to press the right bars "actively" to receive some pleasant electronic stimulus, where does the locus of control stand, with the cognitive maneuverings of the laboratory rat or with the reinforcer?

The children's minds that Anderson and Lorch describe are still minds in which the medium retains a great deal of initiative and, lest we forget, minds "strategically active" but also strategically inducted into a world in which all experience is prefabricated. We cannot assume that because there is evidence of processing, including strategic processing, that the viewer indeed "exercises considerable freedom."

"ACTIVE" AND "PASSIVE":
A SPLIT BETWEEN CONSCIOUS
AND PRECONSCIOUS PROCESSES?

To some degree, the split between the active and passive audience is reflected in the very processes of the mind. From the perspective of cognitive research, the battle between the active and the reactive/passive conceptions of the viewer can be recast in terms of the conscious versus the preconscious processing. In parallel terminology, it may be cast as the relative dominance of strategic, attentive processing versus early preattentive and automatic processing. The viewer-media nexus from this perspective also touches on the issue of intentional versus nonintentional absorption of information.

Much active audience theory is moved by the undercurrents of seventeenth-century Cartesian rationalism and individualism that is so much a part of our intellectual culture. There is a tendency to identify cognition with that section of the information processing that is consciousness and open to introspection. This same tendency is found in phenomenologically oriented critical theorists who, in the words of Husserl, owe a great deal to the "Cartesian overthrow," which placed the conscious mind and one's self-constitution of that conscious mind at the center of the lifeworld and of science (Husserl, 1973). This preservation of the sanctity of the conscious mind is crucial to a defense of stronger versions of the active audience concepts.

The very definition of the active audience as it is found in the communication literature implies a vigilant, self-directed, rationalistic consciousness aware of its needs and motivations, bending media materials in pursuit of these motivations and in the maintenance of cognitive independence. Hawkins and Pingree (1985), following a suggestion by Salomon (1979), point to "cognitive effort" and "mindful and deep processing" as a purely conscious or "nonautomatic mental elaboration." If a significant part of the processing occurs outside the conscious mind or preconsciously, if the preconscious cognitive processing is strongly affected by media forms and structures, and if memory reflects as much the preconscious and unconscious processes as the conscious ones, then the active audience member would be ruler over a highly reduced territory.

This conclusion points to the interesting realm of preconscious processing. Here we find that the medium, its semiotic/syntactic forms, and other environmental variables interact with early preattentive, preconscious, and automatic cognitive processes. Lachman, Lachman, and Butterfield (1979), in an excellent review of the information processing literature, point out the following:

> It is the exception and not the rule when thinking is conscious; but by its very nature, conscious thought seems the only sort. It is not the only sort; it is the minority. . . . There are many forms of life whose information processing is accomplished entirely without benefit of consciousness. Unconscious processing is phylogenetically prior and constitutes the product of millions of years of evolution. Conscious processing is in its evolutionary infancy. (p. 298)

One such unconscious process that has been studied in relation to television viewing is the orienting reflex (Kimmel, Van Olst, & Orlebeke, 1979). Reeves et al. (1984, 1986) used a continuous electroencephalogram measure (EEG) of alpha waves to study the involuntary orienting response to movement and edits in television commercials. Subjects were instructed simply to watch regular television programming including commercials in as naturalistic a setting as possible. Alpha waves have been shown to be negatively correlated with mental effort and attention. Reeves et al. found that these purely formal characteristics of the medium forced the viewers to cognitively *react* to communicator controllable, formal features. It was further found that data-drive decreases in alpha waves were positively correlated with learning as measured by immediate and delayed recall measures. Reeves et al. provide evidence of significant cognitive processes that seem clearly to influence and possibly even to bypass the processing strategies of the viewer. Furthermore, these stimulus-driven orientation responses lead to the successful transfer of information into memory.

The EEG measures call into question Anderson and Lorch's (1983) contention that such movements are merely cues for comprehensibility since the orienting reflex can be triggered by sudden incomprehensible and primitive stimuli such as random light or sound bursts. The response is clearly stimulus driven, reactive, largely involuntary, and manipulatable by the communicator. These findings clearly support a theory of reactive processing of television in which the final semantic residue of a specific media experience involves a kind of cortical dialogue between the formal features and content of the medium and the "frames" (Minsky, 1975) or schemata (Rumelhart, 1978) of the audience member. Stimulus-driven, nonintentional processes clearly influence memory. While the resulting memory trace is not absolutely determined as to content, the processing guidance provided by the formal features of the medium significantly outline the majority of audience decodings.

Let us look a little more closely at the concept of passive and active processes in cognition. The perceptual and cognitive experience of our proverbial television veiwer is the *product* of wonderfully complex and subtle preconscious processes that translate the noise and light of TV into a phrase of meaning in the endless chatter of social communication. This patterning, construction, and identification of meaning is not so much "passive" as sensitive and "reactive" (as demonstrated by Reeves et al., 1984) to the shifts in the stimuli of the environment including the media environment.

How is one to maintain the standard view of the active member with its echoes of the nineteenth-century image of a rationalistic and self-willed individual? To maintain such a view of the active audience member would require a defense of the sanctity of the conscious realm and would require one to lay claim to strong control over the realms of *meaning* of the television message and *memory* for the message. But, as we will see, this position may be a difficult one to hold, given what is increasingly known about the structures of human cognition.

While conscious thought may be active in that it directs attention and prepares the organism for action (Turvey, 1977), one of the functions of consciousness and attention may be to inhibit the less focused semantic associations of the preconscious processing (Marcel, 1983b, p. 283; Posner & Snyder, 1975). A number of studies suggest that the preconscious processing of meaning may be carried out automatically to a high level whether this analysis is followed or not followed by conscious selection and identification (Allport et al., 1985; Carr, McCauley, Sperber, & Parmlee, 1982; Marcel, 1983a, 1983b; McCauley, Parmlee, Sperber, & Carr, 1980; Philpott & Wilding, 1979). Methodologically most of these studies try to demonstrate semantic priming effects for unreported and undetectable stimuli such as words or overlapping drawings in which one drawing is not identified. For example, in a typical experiment studying the stages of processing and the structure of semantic memory, a word such as *tree* or *wrist* is presented below detection to assess the degree to which it facilitates the processing and influences the specific meaning of a polysemous related word such as *palm* (Marcel, 1983a).

Evidence is found for what seems to be spreading semantic activation of networks of meaning of a word in the process of identification and selection of a particular meaning. Meaning may not be the exclusive domain or even predominant domain of the conscious mind. The content of consciousness is the product of these earlier preconscious processes. As we will see below, these more reactive processes can influence meaning, behavior, and memory. Because these studies suggest that much high-level processing may occur offstage, this finding has potentially disturbing, philosophical consequences for our notion of the self-possessed, rationalistic citizen-subject.

There has been continued controversy over the structure and effects of preconscious processing (Dixon, 1971, 1981) with challenges on theoretical or methodological grounds (Cheesman & Merikle, 1984; Hollender, 1985; Johnston & Dark, 1986). Nonetheless, the question for many is not so much whether there is some semantic analysis at the preconscious level but how much of semantic analysis is carried out at that level.

In a study designed to develop new techniques for studying film and television structure (Biocca, Neuwirth, Oshagan, Pan, & Richards, 1987; Reeves et al., 1986) researchers found evidence for the same kind of preconscious priming effects. Based on this finding and the psychological evidence, we can claim that the meaning of a television message, while constructed *within* the individual viewer and therefore by the viewer, may be largely constructed outside of consciousness. Conscious experience and thought appears to be one of the later stages in a hierarchy of cognitive processes that monitor the overflowing perceptual environment (Marcel, 1983b; Marr, 1981). Ancillary preconscious processes regulate the flow of information, assemble it, and connect it to the prodigious information stored in interconnected networks of meaning in long-term memory. These preconscious processes shape the television stimulus before conscious and attentional processes and may mitigate goal-motivated processes. Meaning in television may be the final product of a complex interaction of message form and content, contextual and situational factors, as well as the semiotic competence of the viewer, sociopsychological construction of the viewers' semantic associations, and, finally, idiosyncratic processing dispositions (Biocca et al., 1987).

There is also the startling evidence from work on split brain patients (Gazzaniga, 1985) in which stimuli in the form of two stories are each presented separately to one of the two hemispheres. The stories were visually flashed to the separate hemi-retina of each eye. The hemi-retinas (left and right) of each eye are connected to the contralateral hemisphere (left hemi-retinas to the right hemisphere and vice versa). The split brain patients had to recall the story with a verbal report. Verbal activity is predominantly controlled by the left hemisphere. When the story was recalled, it contained the left hemisphere's "version" of the story as well as information "seeping in" from the remaining connections to right hemisphere. This "seeping" was evidenced by suppositions and inferences built into the recalled story. The recalled version furnished by the verbally dominant left hemisphere provided coherent but incorrect rationalizations for its linguistic behavior, which included information whose origins in the speaking left hemisphere could not identify. To one of the key figures in this research area, neuropsychologist Gazzaniga, the findings suggest a modular mind in which consciousness is an inference-making (rationalistic), action-oriented processor that does not have direct access to information from other modules that govern behavior.

The processing of mass media such as television by members of the "audience" may involve a set of bottom-up processes absorbing information from the environment, categorizing, and structuring with high capacity, perceptual, and cognitive routines. These early processes, which are *not open* to introspection by the conscious mind, nonetheless create meaning and influence the disposition of the subject while leaving behind long-term memory traces.

On the other hand, there is also evidence of active processes associated with consciousness, that *definitely* influence the structure of preconscious cognitive routines (Marcel, 1983a, 1983b) by influencing the selection of semantic "models" the viewer will use while processing and interpreting the television stimulus. These processing "agendas" (I hesitate to call them schemata because of problems with the schema concept) may be based on moment-to-moment changes, differing goals, and long-term dispositional states. They may indeed inhibit certain semantic associations and be the source of "oppositional readings" of the television message. These oppositional readings are *not guaranteed.* As the persuasion literature reveals, the communicator may take a "peripheral," indirect message strategy specifically intended to minimize "conscious elaboration" of the message and the generation of oppositional counterarguments (Cacioppo & Petty, 1986; Moore & Hutchinson, 1986; Petty & Cacioppo, 1981).

Information processing, though it may be relatively unengaged, can display astounding persistence. Shepard's (1967) now classic series of experiments on the tremendous capacity of the mind for pictorial recognition memory, even in states of low motivation and "activity," is an excellent example of such processes. When we consider the fact that these processes are *actively exploited* by communicators such as advertisers (Krugman, 1977), the claim of cognitive "independence," based on schematic processing alone, appears exaggerated. Regardless of the well-established theory that information is schema driven and these schemata provide "anticipatory frameworks" for decoding, Neisser (1976), who is invariably cited whenever the word *schema* is used, acknowledges the significance of the stimulus- (data-) driven aspect of the information-acquisition process. *Learning would be impossible without it.*

SOCIAL ORIGINS OF
ACTIVITY AND THE "LOCUS OF CONTROL"

As we peer inside the mind of the audience member, it may be that we will find the two hemispheres of activity and passivity along with more complicated sets of processes. Our ideal active audience member, as defined by the active audience theorist, seems upon reflection to be burdened by the baggage of our seventeenth-century ideal of the rational, self-willed, and self-determined individual.

To Jean Paul Sartre (1960/1976) the question of the activity or passivity of the individual in face of the media seemed reasonably clear:

> When I listen to a broadcast, the relation between the broadcaster and myself is not a human one: in effect, I am passive in relation to what is being said, to the political commentary on the news, etc. This passivity, is an activity which develops on every level and over many years, can to *some extent* be resisted: I can write, protest, approve, congratulate, threaten, etc. But it must be noted that these activities will carry weight only if a majority (or a considerable minority) of listeners who do not know me do likewise. (p. 271)

Sartre's simple discussion brings up the political question of *control* to which we will also add the scientific question of *cause*. Both are different faces of the same issue.

The question of the source of activity or the "locus of control" lies at the heart of the active versus passive audience debate. Locus of control can be defined as the place or agent wherein resides the major determining or causal force of the content and orientation of the audience member's cognitions and behavior. Does this locus of control lie in the social origins of motivations, in some psychological force, in the formal structure of the medium itself, in the myriad content and the persuasive ("great"?) communicator, or does it reside in the individual? If the concept of "activity" is to have the political teeth alluded to by Sartre or even if the concept is to have psychological strength, this question must be answered. This is the question addressed in this section.

For the early mass society theorist, the locus of control lay with the manipulators of the mass media, while for the more demographic and class-oriented traditions (Lazarsfeld, Berelson, & Gaudet, 1948), the locus of control lay in common and predictable experiences and socialization influences that cut along class or demographic lines. In other tradition (McLuhan, 1962, 1964), the locus of control lay with the medium itself, its formal features, and its powerful organization of experience. There are certainly other stances than these and countless combinations and permutations. The truth may indeed lie in a well-integrated combination of these.

The active audience construct has gravitated to assertions that posit most of the locus of control within the individual. When this position has been forcefully asserted, it has often been cast as exaggeration wherein the individual is militantly self-determined. Dervin (1980), using tenuous metaphorical references to physical theories of relativity, sketches a theory of phenomenological subjectivism that sometimes teeters on the abyss of solipsism. McLeod and Becker (1974) have observed, "Perhaps the approach does depict the audience as too powerful if it can be inferred that almost any need can induce any media behavior, which, in turn, provides any gratification" (p. 80).

It is rarely an all-or-nothing proposition. More often the active audience theorist retains the locus of control within the individual but acknowledges the influence of social and psychological forces. Palmgreen (1984) states that the "meaning of the media-related needs and requirements of individuals springs from their location in and interaction with the social environment" (p. 25). In Levy and Windahl's (1984a) attempt at a balance, they argue that while individuals are "conditioned by social and psychological structures" and constrained "by available communications, individuals choose what communication settings they will enter." *But* this decision is "motivated by goals and uses that are self-defined" (pp. 51-52). What we have is often an attempt to maintain the sanctity of the individual including rhetorical statements regarding individual freedom as much of the causal force shifts to vaguely specified antecedent social and psychological forces.

McGuire (1974) admits "that external circumstances play a large part in determining one's media exposure," but nonetheless asserts that this "does not rule out the possibility that personal needs are also a factor" (p. 168). Though work is accumulating in the area, Palmgreen (1984) acknowledges there is a "scarcity" of empirical investigations of the psychological origins" of media uses gratifications while adding in a thorough review that "in most of these investigations the social origins of gratifications are not the primary focus of study" (p. 26). While mentioning the importance of these factors, which obviously influence the locus of control and the direction of preponderant influence, uses and gratification and active audience theorists state that they have paid "less attention" to social and psychological origins and that "social and environmental circumstances that lead people to turn to the mass media are . . . little understood" (Katz et al., 1974, p. 24, 26). These theorists add that there is "no general theoretical framework which systematically links gratification to their social origins" (Levy, 1978; Palmgreen, 1984, p. 28).

What, then, of the claims of "imperviousness to influence" of the audience and the stronger definitions of activity that so animated the early stirrings of the active audience in Bauer's writings? How much real, fully exercised control lies in the hands of the audience member? In the classic terminology of Sartrean existential philosophy, are the audience members oriented *for themselves* or *for the other*? To put it another way, is the individual "active" for himself or herself or "active" as an agent of social structures and forces? If the individual's relation to the media and media content is largely determined by social or sociopsychological imperatives, some of which may be *media generated*, then are the claims of "freedom of choice," "self-definition," and "cognitive independence" rhetorical exaggerations? Has a commitment to a free and independent individual cast too optimistic a light on the socially buffeted audience member? These questions are important because they address the larger question of freedom and determinism of which the communication theory's active-passive audience debate is an instantiation.

If the audience member is not as much in control of the process, as implied by active audience theorists, what we may have, then, is a largely amorphous vessel within which swirls the influence of larger forces. The individual becomes the vortex in a whirling pattern of physiological, psychological, social, and semiotic structures.

At this point, the somewhat humonistic question of the locus of control turns to the rather scientific question of causality. If we are to have an adequate explanation and understanding of the meeting of audience member and the medium, we have to obtain a sense of the true causes of media behavior and of the intellectual or cognitive framework of the viewer. Blumler (1979) informs his reader that these individual "orientations" . . . covary with numerous other communication relevant factors such as (a) people's circumstances and roles, (b) their personality dispositions and capacities, (c) their actual patterns of mass media consumption, and (d) ultimately, the process of effects itself" (p. 202). Note that his (a) and (b) factors can be listed as *causes* of these "orientations" and that (c) and to a lesser degree (d) are *effects* of these orientations.

The more deeply active audience theorists look inside these "active individuals" who "bend the media" to their uses, the more these theorists find that their active audience members are transparent. Motivations or "orientations" are mentioned, but these notions tend to fade in reference to social and psychological origins of these "causes." In the very act of trying to rescue the individual from the rhetoric of mass society, the active audience theorist inevitably delivers him or her once again to the tossings of social forces. The admitted antagonism (Blumler, 1979) of the active audience theorist to mass audience terminology leads him or her to avoid dissolving the causal force of the individual agent into antecedent social and sociopsychological variables. The individual consciousness and body are definitely the *locus of action* but not necessarily the *locus of control*.

TOWARD A MORE MODEST APPRAISAL OF ACTIVITY

Does all the discussion over the activity of the audience merely boil down to a general statement that the individual or individual intentionality is a mediating variable? Or is it a phenomenological exploration of the meaning of media, media use, and media content to the individual—a Copernican shift that places the audience member's motivations at the center of a research universe?

But how far can we go with this concept beyond phenomenologically tinged descriptions of the experience of the media as "lived"? For Carey and Kreiling (1974) and Swanson (1979), this concept is valid enough, liberating individual action from the functionalist or system-oriented strings sought by puppeteer social scientists. In this "action/motivational" perspective (McQuail & Gurevitch, 1974), external explanatory frames are cast off and the audience member himself or herself validates the language of experience. This subjective experience of the media and one's action with the media are indeed a highly desirable source of study. But its aggregation as data in the spirit of functionalist hubris does not necessarily define an "objective" reality. With all the statistical manipulations of these self-reports, the active audience researcher cannot really declare that such constitute the whole of the interaction between media and audience. As Carey and Kreiling (1974) so aptly point out:

> In any universe of discourse persons construct legitimations that make their own normative patterns of behavior appear right and reasonable, and social scientists often conspire with such communities to heighten the plausibility of their activities. (p. 230)

If, as the individual constructs his or her reality and the content of semantic memory, a team of social structures, media structures, and physiological structures stand "actively" beside, handing to the individual the bricks and mortar of that self-construction, then what are we to make of this product? If the fully anchored causes of the "activity" of the audience are ignored or cannot be adequately specified other than individually self-reported causes or motivations, then what kind of science can we build other than a phenomenological inventory of meanings, rationalizations, and, sometimes, false consciousness?

One fall-back position is to argue for some variant of the transactional model (McLeod & Becker, 1974, 1979; Schramm, 1983) heralded by Bauer (1964a). In Bauer's formulation that model was couched in the language of the marketplace with references to "hard bargains," "contracts," and one's "money's worth." The analogy conveniently implied an equitable exchange between equals, "at least most of the time." The analogy was an attractive one because it made the media-audience transaction fit so neatly into the logic of American socioeconomics. It hailed the "sovereign consumer" in the communications marketplace. But, as Schramm (1983) notes, the transaction is just as often "inequitable." Just as Galbraith (1968) and others have largely exploded the business myth of the independent "sovereign consumer," the "hard-bargaining" active audience member may be more myth than substance. The audience member has power, rarely as an isolated "active individual," but, as Sartre observed above, more often as part of an active group (see also Habermas, 1983). The individual, indeed, acts and chooses, but within an ideological structure whose raison d'être is economic accumulation or sociopolitical advocacy presented as information or entertainment.

For some theorists, the active audience concept may almost be a mystical entity with some of the causal power once ascribed to similar ideological fulcrums such as the "soul," "reason," "the will," "the ego." These are all centers of activity and self-direction. The active-passive debate could be freed of the need to establish the center of the communication universe: the individual, the medium, or the culture. Unfortunately, the communication universe already bedeviled with complexity becomes more so when such relativity abandons a search for a solid center.

In this decentered universe, a number of competing and interacting points of "activity" would probably need to be incorporated. The fact that mass communication theory frequently returns to some form of the active-passive audience dichotomy reflects an attempt by mass communication theorists to come to grips with fundamental interactions among the audience, the media, and communicators. At present, active audience theory may obscure important relationships by overemphasizing the role of the audience and failing to incorporate key factors fully.

The following are suggested as possible ways of reformulating certain aspects of theorizing on the active audience:

(1) *Abandon the metaconstruct of the "active audience."* It is clear from our discussion that the metaconstruct of audience activity attempts to cover too many phenomena with the fuzzy entity called "activity." Theorists who work with the concept admit that it is "undeniably complex and multidimensional" (Palmgreen et al., 1985) and that there is "no reason" to anticipate an "exhaustive" and possibly adequate definition. Rather, the concept floats on a bed of cultural connotations that cannot be fully defined, let alone really measured.

There seem to be two versions of the active audience concept, a strong one and a weak one. The strong one emphasizes the autonomy of the audience, its self-determination, and, at the very least, an obstinacy bordering on "imperviousness to influence." This emphasis is part of the origin of the concept and the form often implied in social and psychological theories. The weak form merely points to motivational and behavioral phenomena such as selectivity and utility. This emphasis is the "activity" that is most often measured and offered as "proof" of a global concept of activity.

The conclusion that the metaconstruct should be abandoned is emerging within the uses and gratifications tradition itself. In an interesting and bold article, Blumler et al. (1985) call for a "rejection of audience imperialism . . . the audience member is not an unconstructed master of his or her cultural faith" (p. 259). At the very least this suggests abandoning the strong version of audience activity.

This retreat leaves us with the weak version. Because the weak version attempts to bask in the grand connotations of independence emanating from the strong version, it is suggested that it be abandoned also. In its place, the various subcomponents of "activity," selectivity, utility, involvement, and so on should be treated as *separate* concepts. The sometimes humble claims that each concept can make should not be merged to imply the more sweeping claims of the strong version of activity.

(2) *Theoretically define and measure the communicator's objectives, strategies, and perceptions of the audience.* Part of the dichotomization of the active and passive audience grows out of a shifting sense of who best achieves their objectives in the mass communication encounter, the audience or the communicator. This concern deals with the issue of the primary "locus of control" over the flow and use of information in the process of communication. This question is considered at the level of interpersonal communication. It should be incorporated into the study of audience activity, if we are to pretend to make any definitive statements on the level of audience independence, the equity or lack of equity in the "transaction," and the existence or nonexistence of "imperviousness to influence." This investigation may require not looking at generalized media use, but at specific messages in specific contexts as has been suggested by McLeod and Becker (1981).

If audience decisions are based on prior motivations, how does the communicator use audience motivations and goals to assure the success of his or her message and the audience research is clearly built on this strategy (Bettman, 1986; Cacioppo & Petty, 1986; Greenwald & Leavitt, 1986; Moore & Hutchinson, 1986). Game theory could be used in this kind of analysis. What happens when the goals of the communicator and the audience member match or conflict in a variety of ways? What situations lead to goal conflict? How and what kind of oppositional readings are possible when they are in conflict, and how are oppositional readings limited?

(3) *Incorporate a theory of the text into the analysis of activity.* In the hands of some theorists, concepts of utility and selectivity tend to reify media and information by overly stressing their instrumentality. It is easy to see media and information as objects or tools pulled to satisfy some need or social purpose outside the context of the medium-viewer interaction. But when the viewer uses the form of a medium as a gratification (Smith, 1986), the viewing is labeled "ritualistic" and therefore passive (Rubin, 1984, 1985). It becomes difficult when perceiving the audience in this way to see the *process* of the creation and unfolding of meaning that occurs when an audience member utilizes or thinks *within* a medium and a set of codes. Explanations will always tend to point outside the ongoing process of media-audience interaction.

Recently, some active audience theorists have rediscovered the text and the power of the message itself (Blumler et al., 1985). Analysis of the structure of the text allows the researcher to ask, To what degree is the message and the codes it uses open or closed (Eco, 1979, 1984)? Thus this is a potentially rich area. An unflaggingly rigorous semiotic theory combined with the theories and methods of cognitive psychology could allow researchers to tap a dimension where media, cognition, and sociocultural variables meet simultaneously in the semantic and syntactic structure of the message and its codes. Recently, some researchers have attempted to develop a technique for studying the *process* of *moment-to-moment* interaction of the audience member with film or television program (Biocca et al., 1987). It is hoped that these researchers can use such a technique to tease out the influence of the structural properties of media on the developing semantic *path* of meaning from other influences such as audience motivation, procedural and semantic knowledge, context, as well as more traditional demographic variables.

Is audience "obstinacy" a purposeful, oppositional bending of the message and its codes or simply a lack of familiarity with the code? To what degree is the success or failure of a message based on its content (attitudinal disposition or behavioral request) or the form (use of codes, specific encoding, perceived source)? To what degree do the codes encircle the audience and the communicator and define the parameters of active and passive decoding?

(4) *Include the psychological role of the medium and, specifically, its formal structures in moment-to-moment information processing.* To what degree is audience activity or passivity (behavioral or cognitive) influenced by media socialization and habituation to the formal features of the medium itself? It is clear that the notion of activity will be dependent on the development of research on the relative influence of strategically driven processing as well as automatic processing on information gain and the organization of that information in memory. The work of Salomon (1979) offers a good model for tracing how the medium itself—its specific formal features and the structure of its symbol systems—influence the processing of information. We cannot talk about activity of the audience without understanding the "active" role of the medium itself. What kind of information does the medium favor and make more salient? For example, it is clear that different kinds of information are favored by linguistic and pictorial media (Paivio, 1971).

(5) *Define the role of media socialization and habituation.* Related to the role of the medium is the need to understand and to incorporate in any discussion of the audience the process of media socialization. Specifically, we could better understand the indoctrination of the audience into the structural and symbolic forms of the media, and the creation of development of patterns of media consumption. Media socialization can be studied at a variety of levels:

(1) Media socialization at the level of ontogenetic and epigenetic development concerns the work on the development of children's perception and use of the media (Wartella, 1979a, 1979b) and can provide some insight into the cognitive skills that are required, favored, and developed by a particular medium.

(2) Media socialization of specific audiences such as cohort groups, "interpretive communities," "taste cultures," and other social strata investigates the impact, indoctrination, habituation, and relative influence of a medium and its contents over time. Smaller social currents caused by the differential introduction of new media, differential use, and differential susceptibility to effects can be teased out (see Wober, 1983, for an attempt to

capture this kind of information). This level of analysis is well developed in uses and gratification theory as well as in industry audience research. Motivational and demographic characteristics of media use have been addressed by a number of researchers. What is being suggested is not an analysis of the audience characteristics at this level, or the uses and gratifications of new technologies (Williams et al., 1985), but an analysis of the medium as an "active" agent.

The goal is to create a context to assess where the initiative lies in the process of media selection (Zillmann & Bryant, 1985) and moment-to-moment information processing. Specifically, how much of the initiative lies with the medium due to past socialization, or medium specific access to hard wired (genetic) automatic responses (i.e., the orienting response) or soft wired (learned) responses to media specific characteristics (i.e., pace of film cuts). This interaction is a critical and interesting one. It has been pursued in experiments and can be analyzed with surveys as Wober (1983) has tried, as well as searching historically for evidence of perceptual shifts (Biocca, 1986, in press-a, in press-b).

(3) Media socialization at the cultural level, in some ways, was the grand question the media-centered (McQuail, 1985) theories suggested, though not fully answered, by writers like Innis (1950) and McLuhan (1962, 1964). Understanding the "use" of media for cultures (large audiences?) from this vantage point can be regained by studying the media socialization within cultures and significant subcultures over longer time spans (Eisenstein, 1979) or cross-culturally. The influence of the form is of course by no means fixed or independent but is to some degree channeled by existing cultural traditions, the influence of other "media traditions," and by the sociopolitical and professional organization of media institutions.

These few suggestions arise primarily from cognitive and semiotic perspectives because active audience theory, especially within the "uses and gratifications" theory, already addresses many of the traditional sociological questions. Factoring in all these variables is certainly not easy, but it is necessary if we are to answer the larger question posed by the active-passive audience debate. But with all factors combined, it is questionable whether we can really speak clearly of "activity" as a property just of individuals or audiences, or even primarily of individuals or audiences. With so many antecedent causes and interactions, "activity" seems like an inappropriate label for a host of phenomena.

In this more relative universe that is proposed, individuals do not so much act as react and interact within humanly created constellations of social and cognitive structures. The question of initiative at any point in time artificially isolates a moment in the communication process. Given the philosophical foundations of Western society, it is understandably difficult to cede any ground regarding the sanctity and power of the individual, the temple of rationalism. Our vision is often clouded by our desire to see self-determined and self-reliant individuals.

Without subscribing to the possibility of an ideology-free science, we can observe that it has often been easier to change one's scientific model to match one's desired social model, than to ask society to change to fit that same desired social model. The origin of the active audience construct was an overreaction. It was overreaction bred of disillusionment. Mass communicators had to explain the lack of clear mass media effects and, in some cases, their lack of success as manipulators. But this disillusionment was simply an intractable reality interfering with social engineering fantasies of the social sciences.

The goal of the active audience theorists is to free people from the undue influence of the media by showing how they *already* are free. A side effect was to suggest freeing the social sciences of the "duty" to protect us from ourselves. But though it was originally devised to show how the individual was free from communicator manipulation, the active audience concept may have come full circle. According to Levy and Windahl (1984a), who used activity as a variable rather than a simple declaration, the "active audience" may be "*more affected*" by the media. The thesis is dialectically transformed into its antithesis. Bauer's (1964a) "imperviousness to influence" evaporates.

We can see that the concept of active audience defined as cognitive independence, personal freedom, and imperviousness to influence appears strangely to be both bloated and seemingly anemic and thin. By attempting to cover everything the audience member does, it ends up specifying little and excluding nothing. Every twitch, every thought, every choice—both mindful and mindless—is recorded as evidence of "activity." In some extreme formulations of the active-passive audience dichotomy, only a corpse propped in front of a television set could be registered as a member of the much scorned "passive audience." But our audience is made of real human beings throbbing with life in a society that—thankfully—has not yet reached a point of psychic and social closure, a state of total determinism. Should we be surprised when, as social scientists, we behold perception, choice, reflection, and even selection? And if in the shopping isles of media fare our active citizen chooses his or her banalities in pink, blue, or red boxes, should we pronounce them free, active, and "impervious to influence"?

REFERENCES

Anders, G. (1957). The phantom world of TV. In B. Rosenberg & D. M. White (Eds.), *Mass culture: The popular arts in America* (pp. 358-367). New York: Free Press.

Anderson, D. R., & Lorch, E. P. (1983). Looking at television: Action or reaction. In J. Bryant & D. R. Anderson (Eds.), *Children's understanding of television* (pp. 1-33). Hillsdale, NJ: Lawrence Erlbaum.

Barwise, T. P., Ehrenberg, A. S., & Goodhardt, G. J. (1982). Glued to the box: Patterns of TV repetitive-viewing. *Journal of Communication, 32*, 22-29.

Bauer, R. A. (1963). The initiative of the audience. *Journal of Advertising Research, 3*, 2-7.

Bauer, R. A. (1964a). The communicator and his audience. In L. Dexter & D. M. White (Eds.), *People, society, & mass communications*. New York: Free Press.

Bauer, R. A. (1964b). The obstinate audience. *American Psychologist, 19*, 319-328.

Bauer, R. A., & Bauer, A. (1960). America, 'Mass society,' and mass media. *Journal of Social Issues, 16*, 3-66.

Berelson, B. (1959). The state of communication research. *Public Opinion Quarterly, 23*, 1-6.

Berlo, D. K. (1977). Communication as process: Review and commentary. In B. D. Rubin (Ed.), *Communication Yearbook 1* (pp. 11-27). New Brunswick, NJ: Transaction Books.

Bernays, E. L. (1965). *Biography of an idea: Memoirs of a public relations counsel.* New York: Simon & Schuster.

Bettman, J. R. (1986). Consumer psychology. *Annual Review of Psychology, 37*, 257-289.

Biocca, F., Neuwirth, K., Oshagan, H., Pan, Z., & Richards, J. (1987). *Prime-and-probe methodology: An experimental technique for studying film and television.* Paper presented at the meeting of the International Communication Association, Montreal.

Biocca, F. A. (1986). Sampling from the museum of forms: Photography and visual thinking in the rise of modern statistics. In M. McLaughlin (Ed.), *Communication yearbook 10.* Newbury Park, CA: Sage.

Biocca, F. A. (in press-a). Media and perceptual shifts: Early radio, music, and indoctrination through sound. *Journal of Popular Culture.*

Biocca, F. A. (in press-b). The pursuit of sound: Radio, perception, and the composer in the early twentieth century. *Media, Culture, and Society.*

Blumler, J. (1979). The role of theory in uses and gratifications studies. *Communication Research, 6*, 9-36.

Blumler, J. G. (1985). The social character of media gratifications. In K. E. Rosengren, L. A. Wenner, & P. Palmgreen (Eds.), *Media gratifications research: Current perspectives* (pp. 41-59). Newbury Park, CA: Sage.

Blumler, J. G., Gurevitch, M., & Katz, E. (1985). Reaching out: A future for gratifications research. In K. E. Rosengren, L. A. Wenner, & P. Palmgreen (Eds.), *Media gratifications research: Current perspectives* (pp. 255-273). Newbury Park, CA: Sage.

Cacioppo, J. T., & Petty R. E. (1986). Central and peripheral routes to persuasion: The role of message repetition. In L. Alwit & A. A. Mitchell (Eds.), *Psychological processes and advertising effects.* Hillsdale, NJ: Lawrence Erlbaum.

Carey, J., & Kreiling, A. (1974). Popular culture and uses and gratifications: Notes towards an accommodation. In J. Blumler & E. Katz (Eds.), *The uses of mass communications: Current perspectives on gratifications research* (pp. 225-248). Newbury Park, CA: Sage.

Carr, T. H., McCauley, C., Sperber, R. D., & Parmlee, C. M. (1982). Words, pictures, and priming: On semantic activation, conscious identification, and automaticity of information processing. *Journal of Experimental Psychology: Human Perception and Performance, 8*, 757-777.

Cassirer, E. (1951). *The philosophy of the enlightenment.* Princeton, NJ: Princeton University Press.

Chein, I. (1962). The image of man. *Journal of Social Issues, 18*, 36-54.

Cheesman, J., & Merikle, P. (1984). Priming with and without awareness. *Perception and Psychophysics, 36*, 387-395.

Delia, J. (1974). Constructivism and the study of human communication. *Quarterly Journal of Speech, 63*, 66-83.

Dervin, B. (1980). Communication gaps and inequities: Moving toward a reconceptualization. In B. Dervin & M. J. Voight (Eds.), *Progress in communication sciences* (Vol. 2). New York: Ablex.

Dixon, N. F. (1971). *Subliminal perception: The nature of the controversy.* London: McGraw-Hill.

Dixon, N. F. (1981). *Preconscious processing.* Chichester: John Wiley.

Durkheim, E. (1963). *Suicide: A study in sociology.* Englewood Cliffs, NJ: Prentice-Hall. (Originally published in 1871.)

Eco, U. (1979). *The role of the reader: Explorations in the semiotics of texts.* Bloomington: Indiana University Press.

Eco, U. (1983). *Semiotics and the philosophy of language.* Bloomington: Indiana University Press.

Eisenstein, E. (1979). *The printing press as an agent of change and cultural transformation in early modern Europe* (Vols. 1 and 2). New York: Cambridge University Press.

Elliot, P. (1974). Uses and gratifications research: A critique and a sociological alternative. In J. Blumler & E. Katz (Eds.), *The uses of mass communications: Current perspectives on gratifications research* (pp. 249-269). Newbury Park, CA: Sage.

Fiske, S. T., & Kinder, D. (1980). Involvement, expertise, and schema use: Evidence from political cognition. In J. Cantor & J. F. Kihlstrom (Eds.), *Personality, cognition, and social interaction* (pp. 171-187). Hillsdale, NJ: Lawrence Erlbaum.

Galbraith, J. K. (1968). *The new industrial state.* Harmondsworth, England: Penguin.

Garramone, G. M. (1983). Issues versus image orientation and effects of political advertising. *Communication Research, 10,* 59-76.

Gazzaniga, M. S. (1985). *The social brain: Discovering the networks of the mind.* New York: Basic Books.

Gerbner, G., Gross, L., Morgan, M., & Signorielli, N. (1980). The mainstreaming of America: Violence profile no. 11. *Journal of Communication, 30,* 10-29.

Gerbner, G., Gross, L., Morgan, M., & Signorielli, N. (1986). Living with television: The dynamics of the cultivation process. In J. Bryant & D. Zillman (Eds.), *Perspectives on media effects* (pp. 17-39). Hillsdale, NJ: Lawrence Erlbaum.

Greenwald, A. G., & Leavitt, C. (1986). Cognitive theory and audience involvement. In L. Alwit & A. A. Mitchell (Eds.), *Psychological processes and advertising effects.* Hillsdale, NJ: Lawrence Erlbaum.

Habermas, J. (1983). *Theory of communicative action. Vol. 1: Reason and rationalization in society.* Boston: Beacon.

Hawkins, R. P., & Pingree, S. (1982). Television influence on the construction of social reality. In D. Pearl, L. Bouthilet, & J. Lazar (Eds.), *Television and behavior: Ten years of scientific progress and implications for the eighties.* (Vol. 2, pp. 224-227). Washington, DC: Government Printing Office.

Hawkins, R. P., & Pingree, S. (1986). Activity in the effects of television on children. In J. Bryant & D. Zillman (Eds.), *Perspectives on media effects.* Hillsdale, NJ: Lawrence Erlbaum.

Heeter, C., D'Allessio, D., Greenberg, B. S., & McVoy, D. S. (1983, May). *Cable viewing.* Paper presented at the meeting of the International Communication Association, Dallas, TX.

Hollender, D. (1986). Semantic activation without conscious identification in ichotic listening, parafoveal vision, and visual masking: A survey and appraisal. *Behavioral and Brain Science, 9,* 1-23.

Hoveland, C., Lumisdane, A., & Sheffield, F. (1949). *Experiments on mass communications.* Princeton, NJ: Princeton University Press.

Husserl, E. (1973). *Cartesian meditations.* The Hague: Martinus Nijhoff.

Innis, H. (1950). *Empire and communications.* Oxford: Clarendon.

Johnston, W. A., & Dark, V. J. (1986). Selective attention. *Annual Review of Psychology, 37,* 43-75.

Katz, E., Blumler, J., & Gurevitch, M. (1974). Utilization of mass communication by the individual. In J. Blumler & E. Katz (Eds.), *The uses of mass communications: Current perspectives on gratifications research* (pp. 19-35). Newbury Park, CA: Sage.

Kimmel, H. D., Van Olst, E. H., & Orelbeke, J. F. (Eds.). (1979). *The orienting reflex in humans.* Hillsdale, NJ: Lawrence Erlbaum.

Klapper, J. T. (1960). *The effects of mass communication.* New York: Free Press.

Krugman, H. E. (1977). Memory without recall: Exposure with perception. *Journal of Advertising Research, 17,* 7-11.

LaBerge, D., & Samuels, S. J. (1974). Toward a theory of automatic information processing in reading. *Cognitive Psychology, 6,* 293-323.

Lachman, R., Lachman, J. L., & Butterfield, E. C. (1979). *Cognitive psychology and information processing.* Hillsdale, NJ: Lawrence Erlbaum.

Lasswell, H. D. (1927). *Propaganda technique in the world war.* New York: Knopf.

Lazarsfeld, P. F., Berelson, B., & Gaudet, H. (1948). *The people's choice.* New York: Columbia University Press.

LeBon, G. (1893). *The crowd: A study of the popular mind.* London: Ernest Benn.

Levy, M. (1978). The audience experience with television news. *Journalism Monographs, 55.*

Levy, M. (1983). Conceptualizing and measuring aspects of audience "activity." *Journalism Quarterly, 60,* 109-115.

Levy, M., & Windahl, S. (1984a). Audience activity and gratifications: A conceptual clarification and exploration. *Communication Research, 11,* 51-78.

Levy, M., & Windahl, S. (1984b, May). *Audience activity: A conceptual survey and research agenda.* Paper presented at the meeting of the International Communication Association, San Francisco.

Levy, M., & Windahl, S. (1985). The concept of audience activity. In K. E. Rosengren, L. A. Wenner, & P. Palmgreen (Eds.), *Media gratifications research: Current perspectives* (pp. 109-122). Newbury Park, CA: Sage.

Lippman, W. (1965). *Public opinion.* New York: Free Press.

Locke, J. (1952). *An essay concerning human understanding. Vol. 35: Great Books of the western world.* Chicago: Encyclopedia Britannica. (Original work published in 1694)

Lowery, S., & DeFleur, M. L. (1983). *Milestones in mass communications research.* New York: Longman.

Luther, M. (1952). *Reformation writings of Martin Luther* (Vol. 1). London: Allen & Unwin.

MacPherson, C. B. (1962). *The political theory of possessive individualism.* London: Oxford University Press.

Mander, J. (1978). *Four arguments for the elimination of television.* New York: Morrow.

Marcel, A. J. (1983a). Conscious and unconscious perception: An approach to the relations between phenomenal experience and perceptual processes. *Cognitive Psychology, 15,* 238-300.

Marcel, A. J. (1983b). Conscious and unconscious perception: An approach to the relations between phenomenal experience and perceptual processes. *Cognitive Psychology, 15,* 238-300.

Marcuse, H. (1972). A study on authority. In H. Marcuse, *Studies in critical philosophy.* Boston: Beacon Press.

McCauley, C., Parmlee, C. M., Sperber, R. D., & Carr, T. H. (1980). Early extraction of meaning from pictures and its relation to conscious identification. *Journal of Experimental Psychology: Human Perception and Performance, 6,* 265-276.

McGuire, W. (1974). Psychological motives and communication gratification. In J. Blumler & E. Katz (Eds.), *The uses of mass communications: Current perspectives on gratifications research* (pp. 167-196). Newbury Park, CA: Sage.

McLeod, J., & Becker, L. (1974). Testing the validity of gratification measures through political effects analysis. In J. Blumler & E. Katz (Eds.), *The uses of mass communications: Current perspectives on gratifications research* (pp. 137-167). Newbury Park, CA: Sage.

McLeod, J., & Becker, L. (1981). The uses and gratifications approach. In D. Nimmo & K. R. Sanders (Eds.), *Handbook of political communication* (pp. 67-100). Newbury Park, CA: Sage.

McLuhan, M. (1962). *The Gutenberg galaxy.* New York: Signet.

McLuhan, M. (1964). *Understanding media: The extensions of man.* New York: Signet.

McQuail, D. (1983). *Mass communication theory.* Newbury Park, CA: Sage.

McQuail, D., Blumler, J. G., & Brown, J. (1972). The television audience: A revised perspective. In D. McQuail (Ed.), *Sociology of mass communication* (pp. 135-165). Harmondsworth, England: Penguin.

McQuail, D., & Gurevitch, M. (1974). Explaining audience behavior: Three approaches considered. In J. Blumler & E. Katz (Eds.), *The uses of mass communications: Current perspectives on gratifications research* (pp. 287-302). Newbury Park, CA: Sage.

Moore, D. L., & Hutchinson, J. W. (1986). The influence of affective reaction in advertising: Direct and indirect mechanisms of attitude change. In L. Alwit & A. A. Mitchell (Eds.), *Psychological processes and advertising effects.* Hillsdale, NJ: Lawrence Erlbaum.

Minsky, M. L. (1975). A framework for representing knowledge. In P. Winston (Ed.), *The psychology of computer vision.* New York: McGraw-Hill.

Neisser, U. (1976). *Cognition and reality.* San Francisco: W. H. Freeman.

Neisser, U., & Becklen, R. (1975). Selective looking: Attending to visually specified events. *Cognitive Psychology, 7,* 480-494.

Noelle-Neumann, E. (1974). The spiral of silence: A theory of public opinion. *Journal of Communication, 24,* 43-51.

Palmgreen, P. (1984). The uses and gratifications approach: A theoretical perspective. In R. N. Bostrom (Ed.), *Communication yearbook* (Vol. 8, pp. 20-55). Newbury Park, CA: Sage.

Palmgreen, P., & Rayburn, J. D. (1985). An expectancy approach to media gratifications. In K. E. Rosengren, L. A. Wenner, & P. Palmgreen (Eds.), *Media gratifications research: Current perspectives* (pp. 61-72). Newbury Park, CA: Sage.

Palmgreen, P., Wenner, L. A., & Rosengren, K. R. (1985). Uses and gratifications research: The past ten years. In K. E. Rosengren, L. A. Wenner, & P. Palmgreen (Eds.), *Media gratifications research: Current perspectives* (pp. 11-37). Newbury Park, CA: Sage.

Petty, R. E., & Cacioppo, J. T. (1981). *Attitudes and persuasion: Classic and contemporary approaches.* Dubuque, IA: W. C. Brown.

Philips, D. P. (1980). Airplane accidents, murder, and the mass media: Towards a theory of imitation and suggestion. *Social Forces, 58,* 1001-1024.

Philpott, A., & Wilding, J. (1979). Semantic interference from subliminal stimuli in a dichoptic viewing situation. *British Journal of Psychology, 70,* 559-563.

Pingree, S., & Hawkins, R. P. (1982). What children do with television: Implications for communications research. In B. Dervin & M. Voight (Eds.), *Progress in communication sciences* (Vol. 3, pp. 225-244). New York: Ablex.

Planalp, S., & Hewes, D. (1979). A cognitive approach to communication theory: Cogito ergo dico? In M. Burgoon (Ed.), *Communication yearbook 5* (pp. 49-78). New York: Transaction.

Posner, M. I., & Snyder, C.R.R. (1975). Attention and cognitive control. In R. L. Solso (Ed.), *Information processing and cognition: The Loyola symposium.* Hillsdale, NJ: Lawrence Erlbaum.

Reeves, B., Biocca, F., Neuwirth, K., Oshagan, H., Pan, Z., & Richards, J. (1986, September). *Effects of supra vs. subthreshold picture primes on emotional attributions about people on television.* Paper presented at the meeting of the Association for Consumer Research, Toronto.

Reeves, B., Thorson, E., Rothschild, M. L., McDonald, D., Hirsch, J., & Goldstein, R. (1984, May). *Attention to television: Intrastimulus effects of movement and scene change on alpha variation over time.* Paper presented at the meeting of the International Communication Association, San Francisco.

Reeves, B., Thorson, E., Schleuder, J. (1986). Attention to television: Psychological theories and chronometric measures. In J. Bryant & D. Zillman (Eds.), *Perspectives on media effects.* Hillsdale, NJ: Lawrence Erlbaum.

Reisman, D. (1950). *The lonely crowd.* New Haven, CT: Yale University Press.

Rosengren, K. (1974). Uses and gratifications: A paradigm outlined. In J. Blumler & E. Katz, *The uses of mass communications: Current perspectives on gratifications research* (pp. 269-286). Newbury Park, CA: Sage.

Rosengren, K. E. (1985). Growth of a research tradition: Some concluding remarks. In K. E. Rosengren, L. A. Wenner, & P. Palmgreen (Eds.), *Media gratifications research: Current perspectives* (pp. 275-285). Newbury Park, CA: Sage.

Rouner, D. (1984). Active television viewing and the cultivation hypothesis. *Journalism Quarterly, 61,* 168-173.

Rovet, J. (1976). Can audio-visual media teach children mental skills. *Research in Education, 11,* 126. (Ms. no. 122 827)

Rubin, A. M. (1984). Ritualized and instrumental television viewing. *Journal of Communication, 34*, 67-78.

Rubin, A. M. (1985). Media gratifications throught the life cycle.. In K. E. Rosengren, L. A. Wenner, & P. Palmgreen (Eds.), *Media gratifications research: Current perspectives* (pp. 195-208). Newbury Park, CA: Sage.

Rubin, A. M. (1986). Uses, gratifications, and media effects research. In J. Bryant & D. Zillman (Eds.), *Perspectives on media effects* (pp. 281-302). Hillsdale, NJ: Lawrence Erlbaum.

Rumelhart, D. E. (1978). The building blocks of cognition. In R. Sprio, B. Bruce, & W. Brewer (Eds.), *Theoretical issues in reading comprehension.* Hillsdale, NJ: Lawrence Erlbaum.

Salomon, G. (1979). *Interaction of media, cognition, and learning.* San Francisco: Jossey-Bass.

Sartre, J. P. (1976). *Critique of dialectical reason.* London: NLB. (Original work published 1960)

Schramm, W. (1983). The unique perspective of communication: A retrospective view. *Journal of Communication, 33*, 6-17.

Shepard, R. N. (1967). Recognition memory for words, sentences, and pictures. *Journal of Verbal Learning and Verbal Behavior, 6*, 156-163.

Singer, J. (1980). The power and limitations of television: A cognitive-affective analysis. In P. H. Tannenbaum (Ed.), *The entertainment functions of television* (pp. 31-59). Hillsdale, NJ: Lawrence Erlbaum.

Skinner, B. (1971). *Beyond freedom and dignity.* New York: Knopf.

Smith, R. (1986). Television addiction. In J. Bryant & D. Zillman (Eds.), *Perspective on media effects* (pp. 109-128). Hillsdale, NJ: Lawrence Erlbaum.

Swanson, D. (1979). Political communication research and the uses and gratifications model: A critique. *Communication Research, 6*, 37-53.

Turvey, M. T. (1977). Preliminaries to a theory of action with reference to vision. In R. Shaw & J. Bransford (Eds.), *Perceiving, acting and knowing: Toward an ecological psychology.* Hillsdale, NJ: Lawrence Erlbaum.

U.S. Surgeon General's Scientific Advisory Committee on Television and Social Behavior. (1972). *Television and growing up: The impact of televised violence.* Washington, DC: Government Printing Office.

Van den Haag, E. (1957). Of happiness and despair we have no measure. In B. Rosenberg & D. M. White (Eds.), *Mass culture: The popular arts in America* (pp. 504-536). New York: Free Press.

Wartella, E. (1979a). Children and television: The development of the child's understanding of the medium. In C. Wilhoit & H. de Bock (Eds.), *Mass communication review yearbook* (Vol. 1, pp. 516-554). Newbury Park, CA: Sage.

Wartella, E. (Ed.). (1979b). *Children communicating: Media development of thought speech, and understanding.* Newbury Park, CA: Sage.

Wenner, L. A. (1985). Transaction and media gratifications research. In K. E. Rosengren, L. A. Wenner, & P. Palmgreen (Eds.), *Media gratifications research: Current perspectives* (pp. 73-94). Newbury Park, CA: Sage.

Wertham, F. (1954). *Seduction of the innocent.* New York: Holt, Rinehart.

Williams, F., Phillips, A. F., & Lum, P. (1985). Gratifications associated with new communications technologies. In K. E. Rosengren, L. A. Wenner, & P. Palmgreen (Eds.), *Media gratifications research: Current perspectives* (pp. 241-252). Newbury Park, CA: Sage.

Winn, M. (1977). *The plug-in drug.* New York: Viking.

Wober, M. (1983). *Broadcast media and sensotypes: A search for the latter and their links with the former.* London: Independent Broadcasting Authority.

Zillman, D., & Bryant, J. (1985). Affect, mood and emotion as determinants of selective exposure. In D. Zillman & J. Bryant (Eds.), *Selective exposure to communication* (pp. 157-190). Hillsdale, NJ: Lawrence Erlbaum.

3 Media Audiences as Interpretive Communities

THOMAS R. LINDLOF
University of Kentucky

An interpretive community is the site of the socially coordinated practices that raise the premises of interpretation for the content of media. Locating himself between the extremes of presented and constructed meaning, Lindlof places the horizon of interpretation at the boundaries of community membership. Reworking the concept of genre, he shows genres of content to be achievements of the interpreting community, genres of interpretation to develop across memberships, and introduces the notion of genres of social action to account for the multiple referents of mediated communication activity.

T HE introduction of interpretive perspectives in the communications field has prompted some to look anew at the relationship between the practices of research methodology and the practices by which persons organize and account for their communicative activity. Not far from the surface of such discussions often lies the issue of the locus of control of behavior. With particular regard to the media audience, concerns are raised about seeming disjunctions between reception and usage, and behavior and meaning. It has become nearly axiomatic for mass communication scholars to assume an interpreting activity on the part of media users. The status of the literal expressions of that activity in theory development, however, remains a matter of some disagreement. In a similar vein, the typical practice of studying media audiences as aggregates of individual attributes may belie the socially contingent nature of much mediated communication activity. Finally, there exists ongoing dissidence as to whether it is possible (or desirable) to carry out media effects research without accounting for the ever expanding and interacting frames of meaning that "subjects" generate in their encounters with mediated content.

Taking these issues as a programmatic point of departure, an alternative approach has been emerging that posits most media use as situation specific, oriented to social tasks, and evolving out of participation in *interpretive communities*. In the place of conceiving and operationalizing the media

Correspondence and requests for reprints: Thomas R. Lindlof, Department of Telecommunications, University of Kentucky, Lexington, KY 40506.

Communication Yearbook 11, pp. 81-107

audience as an aggregate phenomenon, there springs a concern with how media are accommodated within the working assumptions of social groups for the purposes of constituting and controlling the meanings of their activities. On the one hand, the often private, diffuse, and improvised conditions of media reception allow for the possibility of idiosyncratic uptakes of message evaluation. Yet most kinds of mediated content imply some type of social action (and, indeed, media discourses are implemented with great tenacity in marketing, political, and other decisional contexts), which in turn impels users toward common interests and common coding schemes.

An interpretive community construct resolves these apparent contradictory tendencies. This construct proposes that meanings of mediated communication events arise in those spheres of life in which social action requires the pragmatic application of media technology or content. The individual's actual reception of mediated content represents a social performance mandated by the role structure operative in the reception setting. It is misleading, however, to regard the reception moment as the site of meaning generation. Reception-derived meanings are more accurately a residual of those coherent processes of social action and interpretation in which intersubjective agreements about media textuality, called *virtual texts* here, play a major part. The virtual text is not a gloss on any "real" meaning of mediated content or act of usage. Rather, it operates as the conceptual ground by which members locate the coherence of their media-related practices and utterances. In its canonical version, the virtual text is recognized by members as the authoritative interpretation of mediated communication events. *Personal competence* in such communities is indexed in the ability to artfully interpret, and in many cases utilize in social interaction, the core mediated content or artifacts specific to the community.

These communities are sometimes considered "subcultures" in that their members' sodality consists of a shared commitment to certain inflections on the behavioral norms and ideologies of the dominant social order. It is the stance of this article that, while interpretive communities often form as oppositional entities in extraordinary circumstances, it is far more common for a group to negotiate via selective usage of mediated content the terms of its relationship to legitimized interests. Thus the criterial features of any interpretive community consist in the modes, meaning constructs, and frequency of its internal messaging in using media technologies and content.

This conceptualization of the audience is explicitly hermeneutic in that the behavioral expressions of competency in one community observe a local coherence that may well be partly incommensurable with other communities. In other words, our ability to know an interpretive community, its idioms and rules of discourse, is not necessarily enhanced by knowing how they correspond to external benchmarks of interpretation or usage. The agenda implied in this conceptualization would seem to require close study and explanation of those discourse situations that affect media-based meanings. The term *audience*, implying a dutifully attentive spectatorship, may come to be seen as irrelevant for this purpose. As new communication media continue to be developed, marketed, and adopted (albeit in uneven socioeconomic and lifestyle distributions), "correct" end-user behavior may come to be defined by the repertoire of knowledge and skills the user chooses to apply on self-selected occasions. The implications of these considerations for the conduct and applications of media audience research are potentially great.

This chapter proposes to develop a language for describing interpretive communities of mediated communication. This effort entails a first approximation at defining the properties of the interpretive community phenomenon, some prominent types of such communities, and the kinds of mediated communication practices that can and do occur.

The entry point for this development will be an examination of how the semiotic function is dealt with in media audience research. This brief excursion will result in a more precise reading on where the interpretive paradigm is likely to make its contribution.

Fortunately, developing a language for discussing interpretive communities does not call for an entire array of new terminologies. The article will draw upon those concepts from the fields of social phenomenology, reader-response criticism, and communications, which provide a useful lexicon for studying the *in situ* sense-making activities of natural media use groups. Application of the interpretive paradigm to media research is also assisted by the work of those in cultural studies who have explicated the polysemic character of mass communication codes (Carey, 1975; Fiske, 1986; Hall, 1980; Newcomb, 1984), as well as the work of media ethnographers who have been documenting situated media use practices (Lindlof, 1987c). Although the accretion of field studies of media audiences may be slow in building, many in the communication research community have been receptive to the potential of this perspective (Newcomb & Hirsch, 1984; Rogers & Chaffee, 1983; Wartella, 1987). The development of a language for productively exploiting the interpretive audience metaphor builds on all these efforts.

CONCEPTIONS OF "MEANING" IN MEDIA AUDIENCE RESEARCH

This section reviews the ways in which meaning, understood here as "the import of any signification" (O'Sullivan, Hartley, Saunders, & Fiske, 1983, p. 132), is practically treated in typical media research paradigms. Since discussions of "the meaning of meaning" often founder in either didactics or equivocation, this one has a rather narrow purpose: to locate where the semiotics of audience activity fits as a research subject in the field of mass communication. Research assumptions about person-media encounters can be broadly grouped according to whether the production of meaning is seen as controlled by objective elements of content and the agencies that design it (presented meaning), or as controlled by persons who engage in mediated communication (constructed meaning). In the discussion that follows, these two conceptions, and their implications for studying acts of audience interpretation, will be examined in both their pure and more elaborated forms.

Presented Meaning

The presented meaning argument is consistent with the objectivist philosophy of science, which holds that "there is or must be some permanent, ahistorical matrix or framework to which we can ultimately appeal in determining the nature of rationality, knowledge, truth, reality, goodness, or rightness" (Bernstein, 1985, p. 8). That is, meaning is located in the ways that content is patterned and intended by its designers, and represents referents in an ordered world external to the mediated content. In practical terms, content is organized into self-evident categories; some categories that are well known and sanctioned in the mass communication field include horror, pornographic, violent, credible, realistic, fantasy, prosocial, and stereotyped content. The research interest is in what persons "get out of" the content (in terms of recall, evaluation, or cognitive-affective gratifications), or how persons' behaviors or attitudes are influenced by exposure to the content. The fact that a category, such as violence, may be conceptually and operationally defined differently by different investigators does not alter the premise that meaning can be located at the level of a general category and that all instances of that content can be referenced through the membership rules of the category.

One should note that this line of argument removes the issue of meaning attribution from contention by objectifying it as an artifact (or, better still from the objectivist perspective, an epiphenomenon) of the world. As such, the presented meaning of any sample of mediated content can be fully decontextualized for research purposes. Moreover, presented meaning is "transparent" because investigator, confederates, subjects, reviewers, and readers of the research are all presumed to know what is meant by a category such as violence. Even when violence is defined in some detail through demonstrations of exemplars for either subjects or content coders, it is assumed that whatever variations in meaning that do exist can be controlled *with respect to the operational definition*. In the end, there is *a* meaning that goes with the content.

Investigators have more recently been interested in research models that discriminate different modes of perception or usage among audience members for particular content categories. For example, one recent review proposes that social reality conceptions derived from television exposures are conditioned by individual information processing abilities as well as socially contingent structures and experiences (Hawkins & Pingree, 1982). Another synoptic review presents a uses and dependency model that relates audience members' active selections of mediated and interpersonal information sources to a complex array of individual needs and motives, social requirements, and media and societal systems (Rubin & Windahl, 1986). In these formulations and many others, the requirement that meaning is wholly content controlled is relaxed. It is expected that indicators of specified constructs will vary as a function of such social and person variables as comprehension and inferential ability, developmental state, social reference groups, and affinity for particular communication channels. Not only is the meaning of a communication act not entirely presented in content, but it is possible that the constructs of interest (e.g., what counts as reality/fantasy at different age levels) may change as a result of interpreting how persons "negotiate" some species of content.

Persons *cannot* negotiate or argue, however, for either the terms on which mediated communication acts are presupposed (content as operationally defined, behavior prescribed as response options), or their own a priori meaning constructions. Additionally, "content" as the stable and predominant focus of inquiry is generally taken for granted. It may be that such research encourages subjects to commit the fundamental attribution error (Sherman & Corty, 1984), except that it is their *own* behavior toward which they are encouraged to overestimate dispositional causes. Despite the interest in studying variations in meaning attribution, most studies continue a presented meaning bias regarding the operation of audience member expectations in their protocols.

There is another kind of presented meaning that is radically different from the ones discussed thus far. This perspective posits at least one level of meaning that is systematically organized "beneath" a more overt and conventionally acceptable level. These deeper logics operate at psychological or ideological levels and may motivate behavior in ways that serve the interests of content designers. Moreover, this type of meaning is often thought to exert its intended effects with greatest efficacy if persons approach a media encounter assuming a conventional or transparent meaning.

This type of presented meaning is characterized by structuralist and psychoanalytic approaches to the media reception process. There are significant differences, however, between the two approaches, which I will mention only briefly. The structuralist explanation of a *hegemonic* presented meaning (Gitlin, 1982; Hall, 1982) presumes that professional media codes are used to develop certain content strategies that directly or indirectly serve the political and economic interests of the dominant social order. These strategies foster acceptance by audience members of the distribution of power and resources in society and thus render the performance of critique either less likely or impotent. The psychoanalytic explanation of *sublimated* presented meaning focuses on the ways the mediated content allows acceptable and collective modes of subjectively enacting psychologically conflicted themes (Freud, 1961; Kaminsky & Mahan, 1985). In contrast to the structuralist approach, the genesis of these themes is found at the level of child development in the family content. The social and political themes detected in popular cultures are actually concatenations of earlier, more primal conflicts between self and social demands.

Both approaches assume that while content is structured meaningfully at deep levels, the person consciously experiences a simpler, more rationalized understanding. This assumption may explain why both have been used more as positions from which to conduct critical analysis of content and institutions than for empirical study of audiences. Not only is it methodologically problematic to gain access to the ideologically biased response embedded in conventionalized expressions, but such close textual interpretations also require the investigator to accept rather uncritically the foundations of the approach.

Constructed Meaning

Meaning that is person controlled is created out of an entire range of sources: the person's ongoing needs, beliefs, and attitudes; social affiliations and reference groups; cultural memberships; language use; the resources and artifacts available in the settings of human activity. Central to constructed meaning is the idea that significance comes into being *in the articulation of a specific person-medium encounter* (which may occur after the media reception event that precipitates it), but only within the terms of a form of social reality. As with the proverbial tree-falling-in-the-forest question, there is no meaning in *I Love Lucy* if there is no interpreting person to articulate it. A trope that is used to characterize *Lucy* serves both descriptive and performative functions and in so doing proposes a version of a given life world (Goodman, 1984). The trope is an act carried out in a specific social situation that is undertaken for reasons that have to do with communicative roles salient to the person. Constructed meaning is therefore fully contextualized in the actual procedures utilized by a person for interpreting and making known to others the act of media use.

The constructed meaning perspective is sometimes construed as claiming that every person's idiosyncratic history of socialization—that is, the biography of specific events that have been encountered—results in unique and *indeterminate* configuration of response to each instance of using mediated content. It is important to examine what is mistaken about this argument in order to distinguish clearly the social constructionist premise on which interpretive communities are based. The indeterminacy argument represents the mirror image of presented meaning. The presented meaning approach assumes that content attributes can be assessed universally by appeal to objectified membership rules of certain categories, and that persons' responses to instantiations of those categories (whether they have any history of exposure to them or not) reflects the potential of that mediated content for affecting attitudes or behavior. Indeterminacy, for its part, assumes that every person possesses a unique repertoire of both experience and competence. It follows from this argument that none of these instances can be compared by a common metric with any other. There is no basis for comparing responses to the "same" mediated content. Each person's construction is incommensurable.

At this point, one could reasonably ask of the indeterminate meaning adherent, if meaning is constructed by persons by means of unique meaning matrices, why is there so much consensus about what elements make up, say, a realistic cop show? One answer, an empirical one, is that there is actually a great deal of variation once an effort is undertaken to inventory from a variety of persons the actual expressions and attendant meanings about this subject. Another, more principled answer is that the existence of agreement on a conceptual category indicates a high frequency of communication on the subject, exposure to the same types of verbal and nonverbal performance, and enactments in roughly similar media use situations for the persons that are sampled. From the socially constructed meaning approach, then, consensus does not advance the warrant for objectified reality. It only indicates trace evidence for widespread social practices that have culminated in a relatively high degree of intersubjective agreement. A full accounting of such agreements as they are revealed in socially coordinated practice would result in a cultural level of explanation that is not reducible to primitive psychological or physiological terms. *This is the level at which an interpretive community construct can be proposed.* Although mediated content is certainly an indispensable component in the explanation of an interpretational act, its epistemological status must be located in the pragmatics of usage endemic to particular groups of interlocuters.

On the other hand, following Chomsky, every person will improvise utterances that had never been previously perceived and learned due to possibly innate generative mechanisms. This capacity neither permits an indeterminacy evaluation of how meaning is assigned nor disallows the idea that linguistic (and media use) competence is exercised through social-contextual knowledge. In other words, an improvised utterance can only be invented and understood by others against a ground of conventionalized meaning.

Acceptance of the constructed meaning assumption does not entail rejecting the importance of attributing intention to content designers. One can, in fact, identify a strain of constructed meaning that purposely *subverts* the purposes or beliefs attributed to its designers and distributors. This subcategory follows the general precept that meaning is person controlled in the social action context. However, it also moves beyond the sort of constructed meaning implied in our root definition above in which the person is seen as naive to all but his or her own horizon of purposes for making sense of content (the "natural attitude," as phenomenologists would have it).

In subverting meaning, an imputed intention of the designers and distributors of the mediated content forms a thesis against which the person constructs an antithesis. The resulting synthesis completes a dialectic of meaning that expresses a particular form of life—in effect, a subculture. The accuracy of the intention imputed by the subculture member to the content designer/distributor is not at issue. Rather, the subversion of the content's intended meaning stands as a statement that asserts the correctness of the form of life displayed in such related areas of membership as work, politics, dress, and language use. The coherence and stability of the subculture's roles for membership ultimately depend on the maintenance of this dialectical relationship. Cooptation of such a group's self-image by subtly changing aspects of content signifiers (see Gitlin, 1980) is one strategy by which a media institution may destabilize the dialectic.

Punkers' deliberate development of their own forms of music performance (Lull, 1987), black audience members' construals of the way their own ethnic group is portrayed (Blum, 1964), police officers' ironic and self-conscious use of television portrayals of law enforcement (Pacanowsky & Anderson, 1982)—these documented cases underline the commonness with which otherwise unremarkable mass messages are construed by subculture members with particular reference to their own ambiguous or special positions in society. More strikingly, the practices of subverting meaning find purposeful application in everyday situations. Because their daily lives may be problematic, the "unusual" interpretations constructed from content by members may be directed to some very immediate goals: releasing tension, confirming group solidarity, serving notice to others about the boundary of their own group, and so on.

The dialectic involved in subversion of meaning turns the analysis of hegemony from a static presented meaning presumption to a lively interest in the different ways that audience members "see" patterns, motives, conflicts, or convergences of interest in mediated content.

INTERPRETATION AND COMMUNITY

We have seen that a constructed meaning approach to media audiences becomes viable once we abandon the position that situated encounters with media produce indeterminate meanings. Thus we avoid the solipsistic position that only the experiencing self can report privileged data regarding the import of a communicative event. The goal of developing systematic knowledge of how audiences are naturally constituted must begin with an explanation of how interpretation of mediated content operates as an intersubjective phenomenon. The first of several disciplines to which we appeal for theoretical grounding is that of *social phenomenology*.

Charles Taylor (1977) has argued that the aim of a science of interpretation is to make coherent sense of ensembles of human behavior that appear to other humans as "actions" by virtue of having been motivated by intentions. What is called the construction of social reality (Anderson, 1987; Berger & Luckmann, 1967) is the continual process of producing and perceiving behavior in ways that appear commonsensical and rational. In some form or other, social phenomenology examines "how it is that members [of a culture] produce and sustain the *sense* that they act in a shared, orderly world, in which actions are concerted in stable, repetitive ways that are recognizable and reportable" (Wilson, 1970, p. 78). The object of social scientific study therefore is the person's "natural attitude" (Leiter, 1980)—that is, the cultural glosses on objects and relations that are unquestioningly used in everyday perception. As Schutz perceptively observed, a person's credulity in his or her own categories of experience is based on assumptions about a preexisting social world and the mutuality of perspective. Accepting the culturally given categories of experience as objective is key to the performance of social roles. Upon entering another culture, where behavioral signifiers mean different things (Schutz, 1944), the natural attitude may suffer disorientation from the lack of a way to translate newly encountered interpretive systems. To a great degree, then, the illusion of objectivity for what are in essence arbitrary social conventions is a necessary one for achieving desired identities for the self (Goffman, 1959; McCall & Simmons, 1978; Rosaldo, 1984).

Social phenomenologists are typically interested in identifying the nature of the skills involved in achieving a situational identity. They attempt to understand the interpretive procedures (Cicourel, 1974) or logic-in-use (Hawes, 1977) of persons: that is, metacommunicative rules that allow persons to know which speech acts, vocabularies, or other kinds of "communication work" are appropriate in particular social contexts. For the purpose of this chapter's discussion, the term *practice* will be used to designate the kinds of activities that involve a media technology or mediated content for accomplishing a socially intelligible goal. Cross-cultural researchers Scribner and Cole (1981) have described practice as

> a recurrent, goal-directed sequence of activities using a particular technology and particular systems of knowledge. We use the term "skills" to refer to the coordinated sets of actions involved in applying this knowledge in particular settings. A practice, then, consists of three components: technology, knowledge, and skills. (p. 236)

For these authors, technology refers to the implements, artifacts, and symbol system by which a specific set of skills can be performed in the service of socially intelligible goals. In their study of schooled and unschooled literacy in a region of Liberia, they found that an indigenous script had persisted (despite the introductions of Arabic and English) because of its perceived usefulness in such affairs as record keeping, letter writing, and personal diaries. There was an apparent accommodation of the script and the categories of experience that its use encompassed to the ongoing interests of those people.

Similarly, as Taylor (1977) points out with regard to different concepts of "bargaining" that exist between Japan and the United States, a vocabulary that is not grounded in actual social practice will not have sense for members.

Yet those social practices that do in fact order the world for members are constituted by how they are signified in vocabularies and instances of usage. This mutual dependence of intentional act and symbol system underlines for Taylor the central role of intersubjectivity in communication:

> Common meanings are the basis of community. Intersubjective meaning gives a people a common language to talk about social reality and a common understanding of certain norms, but only with common meanings does this common reference world contain significant common actions, celebrations, and feelings. These are objects in the world that everybody shares. This is what makes community. (p. 122)

It is only through alignment with a particular community, with its language forms and social practices for validating membership, that a person can understand *how* an object or event means for another. What seems to be a behavior pattern that is enacted uniformly—for example, literacy (Scribner & Cole, 1981; Szwed, 1981) or television viewing—may in fact be a practice that is woven into the other significant practices that make up the everyday life of a community.

The idea of communication activity as constituted in community relationships has traditionally been the focus of sociolinguistic research of the "speech community." That disciplinary interest concerns the manner in which linguistic phenomena are represented in sociohistoric contexts and undergo change as a function of geographic and social movement (Gumperz, 1968; Hymes, 1972). With the traditional study of the grammatical rules of dialects and their diffusion, the communication field has incorporated an emphasis on the ontology of performances (Stewart & Philipsen, 1984). Research and theory focusing on the communication rules governing interactional regularities in discourse (Cushman, 1977; Philipsen, 1975; Shimanoff, 1980; Sigman, 1980) has the potential for reconstructing the tacit intersubjective understandings of media use. The approach portrays interlocuters as knowledgeable and creative in their utilization of situational resources for communication acts. Although the conceptual work of relating the operation of rules of media use situations is still in development (Lull, 1982), research has already appeared that articulates the rule-bound character of media use, particularly as it invokes *setting* as an organizing principle (Lemish, 1982; Lindlof & Traudt, 1983; Wolf, Meyer, & White, 1982). It is uncertain, though, how rulelike statements can elucidate the expansive interpretational practices of mediated communication.

A promising approach to studying community-based social practices of media has recently emerged from an unexpected direction. A variant of the deconstructionist movement in literary studies, *reader-response criticism* has sought to reject the autonomy of the text in favor of how multiple texts (derived from one work) are constituted, or "concretized," in the readings of multiple readers (Mailloux, 1982). The most applicable of the reader-response models to the case of electronic media systems—represented by Jonathan Culler (1975), Umberto Eco (1979), and especially Stanley Fish (1980)—argues that

> reading . . . is a complicated semiotic and fundamentally social process that varies both in place and in time. . . . [D]ifferent readers read differently because they belong to what are known as various interpretive communities, each of which acts upon print differently and for different purposes." (Radway, 1984a, p. 53)

Formerly associated with a phenomenological emphasis on the singular interaction of reader and text, Stanley Fish has since become a prime exponent of an *interpretive community* conception of reading, "which studies the underlying systems that determine the production of textual meaning and in which the individual reader and the constraining text lose their independent status" (Mailloux, 1982, pp. 22-23). In the introductory essay to his volume *Is There a Text in This Class?* Fish (1980) describes his intellectual movement from refuting the authority of authorial intention in the process of criticism (a "subject-object dichotomy") to recognizing constitutive interpretive strategies that exist *prior* to the text. Moreover, those strategies

> proceed not from [the reader] but from the interpretive community of which he [sic] is a member; they are, in effect, community property, and insofar as they at once enable and limit the operations of his consciousness, he is [community property] too. . . . [T]he claims of objectivity and subjectivity can no longer be debated because the authorizing agency, the center of interpretive authority, is at once both and neither. An interpretive community is not objective because as a bundle of interests, of particular purposes and goals, its perspective is interested rather than neutral; but by the very same reasoning, the meanings and texts produced by an interpretive community are not subjective because they do not proceed from an isolated individual but from a public and conventional point of view. (p. 14)

Fish's early working method consisted of utilizing a reified "informed reader" (that is, an ideal type conversant in literary genre and history) to generate a "*temporal* flow of the reading experience" (see pp. 22-67). Although helpful in depicting some types of reader-assisted information required for the author to achieve rhetorical effects, his method is obviously limited to the analyst's identification of preexisting modes of interpretation. Such models of potential competence are not dissimilar to those proposed by semiologists of electronic media, in which potentially divergent audience "readings" (or "aberrant" decodings) can be posited only with respect to a preferred reading that is imputed to content designers (Fry & Fry, 1985; Hall, 1980; Streeter, 1986). The study by Radway (1984b) of the world of romance readers, however, relying primarily on focus group and individual interviews, did seek to describe the discursive strategies employed by readers of a popular albeit stigmatized genre. The specific contribution of her research was to take advantage of the interpretive community theory to position the *enactment* of romance reading in the daily needs and concerns of the Smithton women.

"Community" therefore refers to commonalities of purpose and practice, even though members of a community need not be symmetrical or homophilic in their power or knowledge roles. (As Fine, 1983, makes clear in his study of fantasy gamers, potential members must give up claim to distinctions based on age, educational level, or other status markers upon entering the symbolic subculture. There, a different set of interpersonal relations, based on game competence, applies.) A community is not a merely ad hoc entity as in a "lifestyle enclave" (see Bellah, Madsen, Sullivan, Swidler, & Tipton, 1985). While members may use material accoutrements for social signaling purposes, consumption patterns do not of themselves define the community. The basis for membership in the interpretive community may vary (e.g., in terms of differential access and the complexity of symbolic codes involved), but the system of meanings it represents is sufficiently robust and extensive in its moral applicability or social instrumentality as to interpenetrate many diverse life pursuits. Mediated communication practices "create" communities in ways that differ substantially from other forms of social affiliation. Although not intended as a taxonomy, the propositions that follow bring those differences into relief and suggest the range of properties that can be expected.[1]

PROPERTIES OF THE
INTERPRETIVE COMMUNITY

Fine and Kleinman's (1979) recent reconceptualization of the "subculture" construct from the interactionist perspective concluded that subcultures are distinguished by the nature of their information interlocks with the larger population, the weak ties of their members, and the members' generally high level of identification with internal norms. They state that the construct can be considered "*a gloss for communication* that occurs within interlocking groups and for knowledge and behaviors shared by these groups" (emphasis added; p. 9).

Interpretive communities of media usage operate similarly in that their prime referents are not formal organizations, kinship structures, or any other natural collectivity. Rather, they come into being with the typically ritualistic or rule-governed enactment of communicative events whose sense for the interlocuters is located in the sharing of media technologies, content or software, codes, and occasions. Thus an interpretive community operates in a *virtual* form such that objectified social categories like occupation, socio-economic or social class position, and social group affiliations are not coextensive with the media usage processes that characterize an interpretive community (Pask & Curran, 1982; Pylyshyn, 1980). In other words, the concrete referents of an interpretive community are easily elided because they actually consist of ongoing, situated communication. For example, there is some indication that the usages of media found in prison can be explained by inmates' perceptions of the exigencies of being incarcerated, and that a prison "houses" distinctive styles of using media for convivial or disengagement purposes (Lindlof, 1986, 1987a).

Similarly, the users group of a computer bulletin board is an interpretive community existing through shared commitments to standardized protocols, speech acts, and other conventions that are sensical only with respect to the virtual social form. Each user's primary group ties to family may become temporarily insignificant, or take on a different but routine inflection, when the person logs on and converses through the network (Lindlof, 1987b).

In effect, each interpretive community functions as a sort of overlay of information structure on the structures of kinship and social organization. The linkages that facilitate information throughput in an interpretive community may or may not correspond to the linkages that structurally define social units. But it is likely that kinship and social organizations partly function as stable relational areas where the "seams" of otherwise enclosed interpretive worlds may become engaged in discourse (Radway, 1986). The most common case of multiple interpretive community overlays is represented in the family. A number of interpretive communities may be nested within the bonds of familial intimacy, such as a mother-daughter dyad bound by practices of storytelling, book reading, doll and puppet play, television viewing, and audio-cassette playing. The overlays may also be partial, as with the commitments to popular music textuality and praxis that allow an adolescent to form peer group associations outside the household. Although the older child is a member of the social category called a family, he or she may also be a member of a social network that claims music-based media as a central component of its group life (Christenson, DeBenedittis, & Lindlof, 1985; Larson & Kubey, 1983; Lull, 1985). The differential utilization of communication media, texts, and interpretive codes is based not only on economic advantage, information search skills, and willingness to adopt innovations, but also the extent to which the bundled elements of mediated communication are perceived to be accessible to and exploitable by the group norms and meaning systems with which one has experience.

In postulating the properties of the interpretive community construct, it is necessary to grasp the concept of *genre* in its manifold sense of content, interpretation, and social action. Genres of content will be offered as achievements of the interpreting community. Genres of interpretation will be shown to operate as the intersubjective meanings specific to the community, the *virtual texts*, that exert a certain historical gravity in stabilizing, directing, focusing, elaborating, and coordinating the activity of mediated communication. Genres of social action will be proposed as accounting for at least part of the proliferation of *referents* in social life that form the basis of mediated communicative activity.

GENRES OF CONTENT

It is evident that a commonality underlying a great many interpretive communities—indeed, that which appears to possess face validity for their existence—is the usage of specific genres of mediated content. Genre, for popular culture critics and researchers, has been variously regarded as "order" (Kaminsky & Mahan, 1985), as systems of formal and thematic conventions (Gronbeck, 1984; Thorburn, 1981), and as a "typological construction" for sorting texts by examining the variety between relative to the variety within categories (Rothenbuhler, 1986b). Attalah (1984) treats genres as discourses *about* such conflicted realities as sexuality and class—a definition that avoids, as he sees it, the tautological confounding of genre with a priori content categories.

As a classification device, generic content can be effective in locating functional interpretive communities since the analyst can, in a sense, triangulate interpretations converging from several different sectors of the empirical world. Generic conventions might therefore be conceived as an intersecting set of cognitive coordinates for many "actors" with disparate interests in the same artifact. For example, Radway (1984) solves the problem of knowing where to begin locating the romance-reading constituency by applying "the publishing industry's own understanding of the book-buying public" (p. 54). That is, the marketing category of romance confirmed the existence of a "loose conglomerate" of readers who have certain social needs, literacy skills, and interpretive procedures for operating on that kind of content. Although Radway expresses reservations about relying on self-selected readers, it is clear that the romance scenarios limned by the readers produce a complex, sophisticated, and, finally, surprising projection of feminine strength in the service of a patriarchal status quo (as one interpretation of the data, at least).

Genre appears to work well in the case of Radway's romance readers for several reasons that are instructive for evaluating its ontology in general. First, a genre of content implies some lengthy history of cultural development in which thematic variations are adopted and discarded, refinements of production technique and aesthetic occur, and the surrounding cultural imperatives mix with the current instances of genre always to give the form a contemporary look or feel (no matter that the genre may have a period setting, as with Westerns). Just as a genre cannot consist of one television program (implying no family resemblences or antecedents), a genre cannot die precipitously or be willed out of existence. A genre can, however, expand to assimilate deviant or outlier forms and thus acquire a modified identity. A genre can also transpose its core narrative properties and implicit ideology from one set of signifiers to another (e.g., the transposition of the Western to a new space drama type). These permutations require the active participation of the principal actors in interpretive communities whose discourse enriches the constitutive properties of genre with the only significance it has—a process that will be elucidated later in this essay.

This cultural freight that the genre carries allows the researcher to engage in the sort of "thick description" from multiple texts that Geertz (1973) has advocated. Observations and accounts can take on differently accented meanings by being supplemented with analysis of original programs, critical commentary, and other artifacts. In non-Western nations, certain dramatic genres may in fact be created and developed with the goal of fostering specific kinds of development-oriented discourses in local usage communities (Rodgers, 1986); other genres, such as the telenovela, become indigenous for manifestly commercial reasons (Straubhaar, 1984). The significance of these changes in interaction between genre and interpretive community demand multiple data sources.

Finally, genres suggest regencrative processes at work in the culture writ large and small. Not only do the learned codes of a long-lived genre acculturate succeeding generations in its particularized way of seeing the world (Hobson, 1982; Traudt & Lont, 1987), but also, as interpretive community members move through time, the recycling of generic material may revive old forms of media use practices for present purposes (Corry, 1986; O'Connor, 1983).

The obverse function may also be more common than is usually apparent: using the perceived conventions of a genre as the basis for moral argument in established interpretive communities (Liebes, 1984). Here one would expect to find a virtual text that incorporates some critique of other interpretive communities. Genre knowledge and enjoyment of specific generic content is not necessarily confined to those who seek its most conventional or quintessential elements. On that premise, one could even view the product development of media industries as driven *not* by consumption trends, whose meaning is seldom clear, but rather by the vigor of specific genre discourses found in interpretive communities, of which media consumption is a residual effect (see Turow, 1984). The "cultural forum" (Newcomb & Hirsch, 1984) through which content-designing entities and audience members engage in negotiation over symbolic forms is at best inexpertly managed. When the dialogue is most direct, it is typically over methods for fine-tuning the categorical representation of marginalized groups (Montgomery, 1986; Turow, 1984). Yet it is also likely that the widespread messaging of highly interested interpretive communities can eventually affect the ratings and circulation audit mechanisms, which in turn drive most aspects of media product development. Since those who most influence consumer decisions may also be the most selective and therefore the most competent in their information seeking (Katz & Lazarsfeld, 1955), there is reason to open investigation into the group dynamics of the audience interpretation process. The notion that genre is an achievement of the interpreting community therefore requires an examination of two additional senses of genre: as interpretation and as social action.

GENRES OF INTERPRETATION

From the previous section, it is apparent that content genres may act as an organizing principle for audience activity. Yet the analysis suggests that the interpretive work performed by audience members—not in the aggregate, but in modes of interaction—empowers the content genre's attributes with their significance. This suggests that interpretive communities share common codes, or intersubjective agreements, that are instantiated in ordinary acts of media content selection, decoding, and application. The origins of those semiotic commonalities might best be accommodated in a theory of genres of interpretation, which could explain how persons "stylize" their media-based accounts in interaction. A lucid presentation of how genre is constituted by speech activity and how genre in turn facilitates the production of individual utterances, can be found in the work of language theorist Mikhail Bakhtin (1986).

Bakhtin argues that literary language is the (temporarily stable) product of a complex historical process of assimilating stylistic changes that occur at the level of utterances in social life. There is an extremely wide-ranging system of generic styles for formulating utterances in everyday life—for example, bookish speech, scientific speech, journalistic-commentarial speech, official-business speech, table conversation, intimate dialogue, and so on. Genres, as "relatively stable and normative forms of the utterances," not only structure speech acts in comprehensible forms, but also permit creative manipulation of their constituent utterances. Thus, even though there is a standardization implied in genre, individual stylistics emerge in usage.

Bakhtin's conceptualization of the utterance is fundamental to his overall view of speech genres. Unlike the sentence unit, which as an abstract construction has no communicative significance, the utterance can be generated only in speech flow. The utterance is characterized by its "finalization" (the interlocuters jointly recognize when an utterance has ended) and by the fact that its production implies a response. The utterance is also a profoundly historical phenomenon in that its sense, placement, and capacity for change emerges from the knowledge that current interlocuters have of its past usages. The speech genre is, in effect, the way that we come to understand and use individual utterances as modes of interpretation:

> When we select words in the process of constructing an utterance, we by no means always take them from the system of language in their neutral, *dictionary* form. We usually take them from *other utterances*, and mainly from utterances that are kindred to ours in genre, that is, in theme, composition, or style. Consequently, we choose words according to their generic specifications. . . . In the genre the word acquires a typical expression. Genres correspond to typical situations of speech communication, typical themes, and, consequently, also to particular contacts between the *meanings* of words and actual concrete reality under certain typical circumstances. . . . This typical expression (and the

typical intonation that corresponds to it) does not have the force of compulsoriness that language forms have. The generic normative quality is freer. (Bakhtin, 1986, p. 87)

The extreme heterogeneity of speech genres in everyday life, and their plasticity in use, makes them available for absorption into *secondary (complex) speech genres*. These secondary genres—artistic, scientific, political, and other highly developed and complex cultural communications—incorporate the concrete utterances of everyday life, but only by conventionalizing and/or formalizing them. Bakhtin further notes that in any epoch, there will be certain dominant primary and secondary genres.

With respect to genres of mediated communication, one is faced with a somewhat different set of circumstances. Most television programming is heavily laden with primary speech genres (e.g., the parasocial interaction phenomenon draws systematically on colloquial forms of address). Yet the television program qua secondary speech genre reformulates that material in highly stylized performances that offer possibilities for innovative utterances and visual/aural accoutrements in everyday life. The success of an utterance synthesized in the media presentation (ostensibly a secondary genre) may actually be indexed in whether it is adopted as a feature of existing primary genres by the audience. Thus in order for a given work of popular culture to function effectively as a standardized marketing entity, it must be amenable to the terms already in use by a community of interpreters; its utility declines in direct relation to its potential as *private* fantasy (Dayan, 1986).

How do we understand these media-based terms of agreement that constitute a community of interpreters? One way is simply to understand how they construct the "text"—whether that text is a class of television programs, a cult film, a computer bulletin board, a cable channel, or some other content referent. This manner of examining genres of interpretation consists in assessing how individual utterances, historically situated in a long series of usages, exhibit dimensions of intersubjective agreement.

As Bruner (1986) explains this hypothesized process, a reader reads a work of fiction by generating his or her own version. That version is a *virtual text*: a narrative in its own right, expressing the reader's own construction of generic conventions, but also consisting of idiosyncratic associations and construals of the act itself (i.e., demand characteristics). Bruner's technique for eliciting readers' virtual texts is to ask for a retelling of a short narrative. The reader's historical consciousness is revealed in the retelling. The new narrative that emerges is "like" the story in some respects, but in the final analysis acts as a conversation between the reader and the literary tradition as instanced in the story.

Although Bruner only suggests that his subject's interpretive activity can be "rated" in terms of its cultural appropriateness, the strong implication is that the presuppositions for narrative-making derive from experience in a community of interpreters who read in similar ways. Certainly, television viewers approach their self-selected viewing occasions with certain presuppositions. Morley's study (1980) of how samples of news programs are "read" by British viewers chosen from educational and occupational groups has come to be regarded as a model study of audience semiotic activity. He undertook the focus group interviews with the expectation of finding construals of content varying in terms of social class indicators of the groups. The discovery of some anomalous configurations of decoding—for example, that groups with similar class positions (shop stewards, apprentices, and black students) inflected the preferred readings differently—forced Morley to seek an explanation in the structure of the discourses they habitually engage in. Using the terms under discussion here, the virtual texts that resulted from his exegesis of group interviews showed good within-group consistency (suggesting canonical versions were operative; see below), but the pattern of cross-group inconsistencies suggested that the primary genres utilized for interpreting television portrayals were not coextensive with British social class categories.

The most probable virtual text that emerges from analysis of an interpretive community's mediated communication represents its *canonical version*. The canonical version authoritatively indexes the levels of reader or interactional competence deemed desirable or appropriate by the community. In a very practical sense, the competence of any individual member's virtual text (as performed in specific utterances and social acts) is granted by the community as a whole by reference to its canonical version. It may not be uncommon for a canonical interpretation of an event to be inextricably tied to other aspects of the way that members of the community practice the media reception event, as in the televised Olympics (e.g., Rothenbuhler, 1986a). It should also be noted that not even the community acts autonomously, since there are competencies existing in other social formations, embodied in discursive practices (e.g., the public school's stance on "appropriate" amounts and kinds of television viewing), that impinge on or somehow affect the argumentation within the community concerning the values of its own practices. Although there is the risk of reifying a mentalistic phenomenon, the virtual text concept is useful for making clear the genres of interpretation that appear to underlie many communities of viewers, readers, listeners, or users of specific media content.

It bears repeating that meaning systems, as the researcher-exegete formulates them, cannot be objectified apart from how meaning is expressed by members of an interpretive community. Identification of a virtual text can be accomplished through a variety of research processes ranging from the controlled focus group to the retelling methods characteristic of folklore to the ethnographic case study. The accounts resulting from any of these processes represent the residual of significance obtained from the site of mediated communication. The researcher's attempt to bring conceptual coherence to the account produces a representation of the community's virtual text, in both its canonical and individually deviant forms—that is, a translation in the researcher's native scientific language of the idiomatic enactments of using and interpreting media in a particular culture. The success of this endeavor rests in no small part in the ability to gain insight into the genres of social action of the interpretive community: those concrete, observable practices that constitute generic interpretations and enable coordination among them, particularly in the development of a canonical text.

GENRES OF SOCIAL ACTION

It should be apparent by now that utterance regularities and other behavioral skeins do not simply facilitate, but actually constitute the genres of interpretation discussed above. (Remember that coordinated social action as a *requirement* of media interpretation is necessary if the presented meaning approach is rejected.) Following Bakhtin again, the elements of a speech genre—theme, composition, style—also appear in media-based social action, for instance, achieving camaraderie by using a comedy character's "signature" comic line at a moment of delicate timing. In so doing, interpretive communities may single out bits of content behavior that are particularly useful in the relational sense. Continued emphasis on and elaborations of that content in arenas of everyday life may have the effect of elevating it to genre status (as an utterance in its own right), especially if the community's canonical text is widely shared. The community's adaptation of that content becomes a specialized performance, attuned to a time and place known by competent members; if the enactments become extensive enough, content designers themselves may learn to incorporate the content with greater self-consciousness regarding its artistry and effects.

In some situations, the interpretive work of a community may not be directed toward a specific "text," in the sense of a delimited content type, but instead with reference to enduring communication problematics. The two broad ones that are examined here—developmental relationships and social-situational exigencies—do not exhaust the possibilities for social action genres but do cover some prominent forms in Western cultures.

Developmental Relationship

An interpretive community's referent may be grounded in the multimodal discourses of acculturation. The communicative asymmetry of such mentor-apprentice communities is evident in the practical efforts of parents explaining the contradictions and discrepancies of the television world (Messaris, 1987). This community's development probably begins in infancy when television is framed as a field of trackable, imitatable objects, and the vocalizing of parents signifies important information (Lemish, 1987). The implicit task of much of the early interaction between parents and children has to do with the development of an adequate category system, particularly if the variance or contradictory relationship of categories "is a matter of current social consequence" (Messaris & Sarett, 1981, p. 231).

One of those variant categories is clearly that of realism (Gross, 1985). Investigations of developmental differences in certain media-based skills suggest that the child's knowledge of plot conventions and character representations has consequences for the nature of categories of realism that are articulated (Dorr, 1983). By middle childhood, the child is able to objectify simple narratives and "discount" some of the techniques of artifice that are used (Freidson, 1953). Older children also demonstrate more flexible mental schemas for comprehending subtle or idiosyncratic story elements (Collins, 1982). They possess the more complex cognitive organization required for discerning character motivation and for relating narrative events in terms of a unified whole, as tested by recall measures of comprehension. The linkage between these abilities and a "more adequate" way of conceptualizing television reality may in turn be related to the child's developing understanding of the contextual demands of the viewer role.

Nelson Goodman's (1976, pp. 37-38) contention that frames of reference regarding realism are taken for granted when they are our own (rather than an alien culture's) is important for understanding how persons become proficient in developing television realism concepts. In effect, children's statements regarding their confusions over the realism of characters and program conventions may be evidence that, with age, they are increasingly held responsible for shifting their meaning assignment activity toward adult frames of reference. Children's early conceptions of television realism, therefore, may not be deficient *for the purposes of being a child* until their increasing interdependence with adult mentors for purposive action demands the development of new interpretive procedures.

While most of the developmental communities involve the child in the role of apprentice, there is intriguing evidence that in many families children acculturate their parents in the use of certain interactive media technologies (Ferrari, Klingzing, Paris, Morris, & Eyman, 1985; Tinnell, 1985). Developmental communities of adult actors may also be discerned where the specific referents are processes of recruitment and role socialization in institutions (Lindlof, 1987a; Sigman, 1982) or organizations (Kling & Gerson, 1977).

Social-Situational Exigency

The concept of social-situational exigency covers those environmental and sociohistorical conditions that elicit a coordinated syndrome of mediated communication activity. Wagner's (1981) metaphor of culture-as-invention applies to the development of interpretive communities in response to the needs of social situations. The virtual social forms that derive from situations, organizations, or group norms are overdetermined by invention. That is to say, there are a great many "formats" in personal, professional, and public relationships that may serve as the occasion for a trope, gesture, or role-play generated from mediated content.

Conversely, a more specialized media outlet or content form, not widely known, can be exploited expansively to generate holistic settings for social conduct. Because material from a highly specialized secondary media genre may not be so widely known as to have standard formats waiting for it (e.g., the community of those cognizant of the Ingmar Bergman filmic style and theme), its chief usage will be for collectivizing like-minded others. The individual and joint creativity exercised in engaging media resources by reference to exigencies therefore operates in one of two ways: (1) highly conventionalized content is used to mediate social individuation, *to segment action*; or (2) highly differentiated or nonconventional mediated content is used to engender collectivities, *to create joint action*.

An instance of the first can be seen in the appropriation of highly conventionalized portrayals from broadcast television entertainment as methods for managing or commenting on relationships. Lull (1980) cites from his naturalistic research a number of highly situational applications. He argues that television can punctuate or reduce uncertainty in conversation; facilitate social learning by children; and serve as the target of correction by viewers seeking a competency evaluation from others. Bryce and Leichter (1983) find that "the use of television as a source of information differs from its referential use [often by children, either in requests for purchases or in play] in that in the former it is called up as an authority outside the interaction" (p. 320). In much greater detail, Morley's (1986) recent study of 16 British families finds that gender-related differentiations of husband-wife roles underlie such media-related action as program selection, attention behavior, use of the VCR, and remote-control technologies. Much like romance readers, the wives in this study report "solo viewing"—particularly of content that is labeled "feminine"—as a pleasure, apparently associated with some guilt, that can be enjoyed only when there are no others present in the household.

Television's broad circulation of imagery, token expressions, and easily mocked-up content forms is directly responsible for its efficacy in segmenting action in everyday life. *The competence of the interpretation is defined in social interaction*: specifically, at those times when actual engagement of media resources occurs, for applying the media nickname, volunteering a "public opinion," selecting the article of clothing for purchase, telling the joke, and so on. However, as the Morley study suggests, there may be some very important distinctions between competence displayed during "reception" (exposure to mediated content) and "usage" (the actual engagement of media lore in constructing or aligning intentional behavior). A home environment dominated by male needs may present one set of demands for female viewing competence, while female usage competence outside the home—deriving from the same viewing experience—may well involve a very different inflection. The same content may be used in entirely different speech genres, and perhaps in entirely different ideologies as well.

The second way in which an interpretive community is referenced by social-situational exigencies concerns the utilization of differentiated material for collectivizing situations, or for creating joint action. The consumption of specialized, deviant, or abstruse communications media or mediated content will tend to drive collectivizing activity. Subcultures and interest groups form. Specialized language codes, artifacts, and even merchandising schemes join the effort. Turkle's (1984) description of computing subcultures amply demonstrates their tendency to construct rather self-contained symbolic worlds around particular technologies or even programming interests. At the same time, the release of computing terminology into general circulation fuels the first process, that of utilizing widely known material to segment or individuate action. Clearly there is much to learn about how the usage of media technology is interdependent with social needs.

CONCLUSION

This chapter has presented some perspectives on how media audiences can be considered as a certain kind of community—one that exists through shared assumptions about and social practices of mediated communication. The interpretive community construct is not meant to replace or even improve upon the many other productive research areas that investigate media uses and effects. In fact, there are a great many questions, particularly those that seek to explain and verify determinate causes of media exposure and use for which an interpretive perspective is quite ill-suited to address. As Anderson (1987) has observed, it is far from obvious just what the contribution of interpretive research, particularly as it is pursued through naturalistic inquiry, is supposed to be and what it means in answering enduring questions about the nature and impact of communication technology.

What is evident is the ascending curve of interest in alternative research approaches that are based in roughly the same camp; these approaches partake in a semiotic interest in human activity and are marked by a reluctance to accept what I have referred to as a presented meaning presumption in examining communicative events. To some in the communication research community, this direction represents a retreat (or, more seriously, a devolution) toward either collections of mere descriptions of local behavior at best, or an undisciplined phenomenology of audience introspections at worst. Certainly there is little prospect in making significant gains toward covering laws of communication with this perspective. Yet, even without the powerful incentive of achieving generalizability, there continues to be active experimentation with the forms and techniques of interpretation. Geertz's (1983) remark on the semiotic turn in the social sciences can also be said about the communications field: "The woods are full of eager interpreters" (p. 21).

I would submit that the interest in investigating the natural forms of audience activity and meaning construction has much to do with the perceived need to make contact with another culture, and then make good explanations of thoughts and actions *through the process of translation*. In short, it is the processual act of translation that counts, and in many ways that is its own justification.

Consider that nearly all of the intact "audience" groups discussed in this chapter predate the entry of the researcher on the scene and will likely persist for some time after the researcher departs. Consider that most of the members of these groups will think of themselves first as members of families, members of a cell block, members of a computer club, and so on. If they think of themselves as an "audience member" at all, it is likely to be because they have been confronted with the category and have decided in a reflective moment that perhaps it "*could* be one of my roles."

Consider that each member has a history with each of those other members. They are considered to be competent in some areas, not in others; or thoughtful, skilled, quick, or slow. In other words, there is a repertoire of descriptors that are not colorless, but are invested with significance because the mobilization of actions within the group demand certain kinds of moral reasoning.

Under these conditions, the researcher must rather quickly come to terms with this new set of circumstances and find ways to describe these symbolic alignments. Because contemporary societies with advanced media systems are shot through with diverse and coexisting interpretive communities (in which arguments regarding the legitimacy of the canonical virtual text of the "other" is frequently the norm), the task of locating the essence of an interpretive community could be called daunting. As the information coming in is sorted and managed, the researcher's own descriptors for signifying action may be subject to dramatic change. What is seen initially as a naive scene becomes problematic, contradictory, messy, or threatening. The tendency to relativize will often follow on the heels of such culture shocks, but such relativization also assumes a detached position for the researcher. The claim of detachment is not simply impossible; it is misleading to the participants and users of the research. As Wagner (1981) comments: "[The researcher] will 'participate' in the subject culture, not in the way a native does, but as someone who is simultaneously enveloped in his own world of meanings, *and these meanings will also participate*" (p. 8). The contribution of these efforts is not in claims to an objective truth, but rather in the ability of its translations to be useful to both science and the communities that it documents.

NOTE

1. A caveat must be attached to this discussion. The terms that are presented do not represent the kind of "experience-near" concepts, or folk classifications, that characterize an emic approach to cultural analysis. The terms, some of which are adapted from the preceding review, should be understood for what they are intended to do: provide a provisional, first-cut prolegomenon for the theories that will come into being as studies of media-based cultures are completed.

REFERENCES

Anderson, J. A. (1987). *Communication research: Methods and issues*. New York: McGraw-Hill.
Attalah, P. (1984). The unworthy discourse: Situation comedy in television. In W. D. Rowland, Jr., & B. Watkins (Eds.), *Interpreting television* (pp. 222-249). Newbury Park, CA: Sage.
Austin, B. A. (1981). Portrait of a cult film audience: *The Rocky Horror Picture Show. Journal of Communication, 31*(2), 43-54.
Bakhtin, M. (1986). The problem of speech genres. In C. Emerson & M. Holquist (Eds.), *Speech genres and other late essays* (V. W. McGee, Trans.) (pp. 60-102). Austin: University of Texas Press.
Bellah, R. N., Madsen, R., Sullivan, W. M., Swidler, A., & Tipton, S. M. (1985). *Habits of the heart*. Berkeley: University of California Press.
Berger, P. L., & Luckmann, T. (1967). *The social construction of reality*. Garden City, NY: Doubleday.
Bernstein, B. (1975). *Class, codes and control*. New York: Schocken.
Bernstein, R. J. (1985). *Beyond objectivism and relativism: Science, hermeneutics, and praxis*. Philadelphia: University of Pennsylvania Press.
Blum, A. F. (1964). Lower-class Negro television spectators: The concept of pseudo-jovial scepticism. In A. B. Shostak (Ed.), *Blue collar world* (pp. 437-443). Englewood, NJ: Prentice-Hall.
Bruner, J. (1986). *Actual minds, possible worlds*. Cambridge, MA: Harvard University Press.
Bryce, J. W., & Leichter, H. J. (1983). The family and television: Forms of mediation. *Journal of Family Issues, 4*, 309-328.
Carey, J. (1975). Communication and culture. *Communication Research, 2*, 173-191.
Christenson, P. G., DeBenedittis, P., & Lindlof, T. R. (1985). Children's use of audio media. *Communication Research, 12*, 327-343.
Cicourel, A. (1974). *Cognitive sociology*. New York: Free Press.
Collins, W. A. (1982). Cognitive processing in television viewing. In D. Pearl, L. Bouthilet, & J. Lazar (Eds.), *Television and Behavior: Ten years of scientific progress and implications for the eighties* (pp. 9-23). Rockville, MD: National Institute of Mental Health.
Corry, J. (1986, August 3). Why some old shows never fade. *New York Times*, p. 25.
Culler, J. (1975). *Structuralist poetics*. Ithaca, NY: Cornell University Press.
Cushman, D. (1977). The rules perspective as a theoretical basis for the study of human communication. *Communication Quarterly, 25*, 30-45.
Dayan, D. (1986). Review essay: Copyrighted subcultures. *American Journal of Sociology, 91*(5), 1219-1228.
Dorr, A. (1983). No shortcuts to reality. In J. Bryant & D. Anderson (Eds.), *Children's understanding of television: Research on attention and comprehension* (pp. 199-200). New York: Academic Press.
Eco, U. (1979). *The role of the reader*. Bloomington, IN: University of Indiana Press.
Ferrari, M., Klinzing, D. G., Paris, C. L., Morris, S. K., & Eyman, A. P. (1985). Home computers: Implications for children and families. *Marriage & Family Review, 8*(1/2), 41-58.
Fine, G. A. (1983). *Shared fantasy: Role-playing games as social worlds*. Chicago: University of Chicago Press.
Fine, G. A., & Kleinman, S. (1979). Rethinking subculture: An interactionist analysis. *American Journal of Sociology, 85*, 1-20.
Fish, S. (1980). *Is there a text in this class?* Cambridge, MA: Harvard University Press.
Fiske, J. (1986). Television and popular culture: Reflections on British and Australian critical practice. *Critical Studies in Mass Communication, 3*, 200-216.
Freidson, E. (1953). Adult discount: An aspect of children's changing taste. *Child Development, 24*, 39-49.
Freud, S. (1961). *Civilization and its discontents*. New York: W. W. Norton.

Fry, D. L., & Fry, V. H. (1985). Elements of a semiotic model for the study of mass communication. In M. McLaughlin (Ed.), *Communication yearbook 9.* Newbury Park, CA: Sage.

Geertz, C. (1973). Thick description: Toward an interpretive theory of culture. In *The interpretation of cultures* (pp. 3-30). New York: Basic Books.

Geertz, C. (1983). Blurred genres: The refiguration of social thought. In *Local knowledge* (pp. 19-35). New York: Basic Books.

Gitlin, T. (1980). *The whole world is watching.* Berkeley: University of California Press.

Gitlin, T. (1982). Prime time ideology: The hegemonic process in television entertainment. In H. Newcomb (Ed.), *Television: The critical view* (3rd. ed., pp. 426-454). New York: Oxford University Press.

Goffman, E. (1959). *The presentation of self in everyday life.* Garden City, NY: Doubleday-Anchor.

Goodman, N. (1976). *Languages of art: An approach to a theory of symbols.* Indianapolis: Hackett.

Goodman, N. (1984). *Of mind and other matters.* Cambridge, MA: Harvard University Press.

Gronbeck, B. E. (1984). *Writing television criticism.* Chicago: Science Research Associates.

Gross, L. (1985). Life vs. art: The interpretation of visual narratives. *Studies in Visual Communication, 11*(4), 2-11.

Gumperz, J. J. (1968). The speech community. In D. L. Sills (Ed.), *International encyclopedia of the social sciences* (Vol. 9, pp. 381-386). New York: Macmillan.

Hall, S. (1980). Encoding/decoding. In S. Hall, D. Hobson, A. Lowe, & P. Willis (Eds.), *Culture, media, language* (pp. 128-138). London: Hutchinson.

Hall, S. (1982). The rediscovery of "ideology": Return of the repressed in media studies. In M. Gurevitch, T. Bennett, & J. Woollacott (Eds.), *Culture, society and the media* (pp. 56-90). New York: Methuen.

Hawes, L. (1977). Toward a hermeneutic phenomenology of communication. *Communication Quarterly, 25*, 30-41.

Hawkins, R. P., & Pingree, S. (1982). Television's influence on social reality. In D. Pearl, L. Bouthilet, & J. Lazar (Eds.), *Television and behavior: Ten years of scientific progress and implications for the eighties* (pp. 224-247). Rockville, MD: National Institute of Mental Health.

Hobson, D. (1982). *Crossroads: The drama of a soap opera.* London: Methuen.

Hymes, D. (1972). Models of the interaction of language and social life. In J. J. Gumperz, & D. Hymes (Eds.), *Directions in sociolinguistics* (pp. 35-71). New York: Holt, Rinehart & Winston.

Kaminsky, S. M., & Mahan, J. H. (1985). *American television genres.* Chicago: Nelson-Hall.

Katz, E., & Lazarsfeld, P. (1955). *Personal influence.* New York: Free Press.

Kling, R., & Gerson, E. M. (1977). The social dynamics of technical innovation in the computing world. *Symbolic Interaction, 1*, 132-146.

Larson, R., & Kubey, R. (1983). Television and music: Contrasting media in adolescent life. *Youth and Society, 15*, 13-32.

Leiter, K. (1980). *A primer on ethnomethodology.* New York: Oxford University Press.

Lemish, D. (1982). The rules of television viewing in public places. *Journal of Broadcasting, 26*, 757-781.

Lemish, D. (1985). Soap opera viewing in college: A naturalistic inquiry. *Journal of Broadcasting & Electronic Media, 29*, 275-293.

Lemish, D. (1987). Viewers in diapers: The early development of television viewing. In T. R. Lindlof (Ed.), *Natural audiences* (pp. 33-57). Norwood, NJ: Ablex.

Liebes, T. (1984). Ethnocentrism: Israelis of Moroccan ethnicity negotiate the meaning of "Dallas." *Studies in Visual Communication, 10*(3), 46-72.

Lindlof, T. R. (1986). Social and structural constraints of media use in incarceration. *Journal of Broadcasting & Electronic Media, 30*, 341-355.

Lindlof, T. R. (1987a). Ideology and pragmatics of media access in prison. In T. R. Lindlof (Ed.), *Natural audiences* (pp. 175-197). Norwood, NJ: Ablex.

Lindlof, T. R. (1987b, April). *Modes of accommodation of new media technologies by families.* Paper presented at the meeting of the Central States Speech Association, St. Louis, MO.

Lindlof, T. R. (Ed.). (1987c). *Natural audiences: Qualitative research of media uses and effects.* Norwood, NJ: Ablex.

Lindlof, T. R., & Traudt, P. J. (1983). Mediated communication in families: New theoretical directions. In M. S. Mander (Ed.), *Communications in transition* (pp. 260-278). New York: Praeger.

Lull, J. (1980). The social uses of television. *Human Communication Research, 6,* 197-209.

Lull, J. (1982). A rules approach to the study of television and society. *Human Communication Research, 8,* 3-16.

Lull, J. (1985). On the communicative properties of music. *Communication Research, 12,* 363-372.

Lull, J. (1987). Thrashing in the pit: An ethnography of San Francisco punk subculture. In T. Lindlof (Ed.), *Natural audiences* (pp. 225-252). Norwood, NJ: Ablex.

Mailloux, S. (1982). *Interpretive conventions.* Ithaca, NY: Cornell University Press.

McCall, G. J., & Simmons, J. L. (1978). *Identities and interactions.* New York: Free Press.

Messaris, P. (1987). Mothers' comments to their children about the relationship between television and reality. In T. R. Lindlof (Ed.), *Natural audiences* (pp. 95-108). Norwood, NJ: Ablex.

Messaris, P., & Sarett, C. (1981). On the consequences of television-related parent-child interaction. *Human Communication Research, 7,* 226-244.

Montgomery, K. (1986). The political struggle for prime time. In S. J. Ball-Rokeach & M. G. Cantor (Eds.), *Media, audience, and social structure* (pp. 189-199). Newbury Park, CA: Sage.

Morley, D. (1980). *The "Nationwide" audience: Structure and decoding.* London: British Film Institute.

Morley, D. (1986). *Family television: Cultural power and domestic leisure.* London: Comedia.

Newcomb, H. M. (1984). On the dialogic aspects of mass communication. *Critical Studies in Mass Communication, 1,* 34-50.

Newcomb, H. M., & Hirsch, P. M. (1984). Television as a cultural forum: Implications for research. In W. D. Rowland, Jr., & B. Watkins (Eds.), *Interpreting television* (pp. 58-73). Newbury Park, CA: Sage.

O'Connor, J. J. (1983, July 19). Where time stands still. *New York Times,* p. 25a.

O'Sullivan, T., Hartley, J., Saunders, D., & Fiske, J. (1983). *Key concepts in communication.* London: Methuen.

Pacanowsky, M., & Anderson, J. A. (1982). Cop talk and media use. *Journal of Broadcasting, 26,* 741-756.

Pask, G., & Curran, S. (1982). *Micro man: Computers and the evolution of consciousness.* New York: Macmillan.

Philipsen, G. (1975). Speaking "like a man" in Teamsterville: Culture patterns of role enactment in an urban neighborhood. *Quarterly Journal of Speech, 62,* 15-25.

Pylyshyn, Z. W. (1980). Computation and cognition: Issues in the foundations of cognitive science. *Behavioral and Brain Sciences, 3,* 111-132.

Radway, J. A. (1984a). Interpretive communities and variable literacies: The functions of romance reading. *Dedalus, 113,* 49-73.

Radway, J. A. (1984b). *Reading the romance: Women, patriarchy, and popular literature.* Chapel Hill: University of North Carolina Press.

Radway, J. A. (1986). Identifying ideological seams: Mass culture, analytical method, and political practice. *Communication, 9,* 93-123.

Rice, G. E. (1980). On cultural schemata. *American Ethnologist, 7,* 152-171.

Rodgers, S. (1986). Blank tape cassette kinship: Constructing kinship through the Indonesian national mass media. *American Ethnologist, 13,* 23-42.

Rogers, E. M., & Chaffee, S. H. (1983). Communications as an academic discipline: A dialogue. *Journal of Communication, 3*(3), 18-30.

Rosaldo, M. Z. (1984). Toward an anthropology of self and feeling. In R. A. Shweder & R. A. LeVine (Eds.), *Culture theory: Essays on mind, self, and emotion* (pp. 137-157). New York: Cambridge University Press.

Rothenbuhler, E. W. (1986a, May). *Media events and social solidarity: An updated report on the living room celebration of the Olympic Games.* Paper presented at the meeting of the International Communication Association, Chicago.

Rothenbuhler, E. W. (1986b, May). *The saliency of genre in identifications of television programs: Comparing college students and television critics.* Paper presented at the meeting of the International Communication Association, Chicago.

Rubin, A. M., & Windahl, S. (1986). The uses and dependency model of mass communication. *Critical Studies in Mass Communication, 3*, 184-199.

Schutz, A. (1944). The stranger. *American Journal of Sociology, 49*(6), 499-507.

Scribner, S., & Cole, M. (1981). *The psychology of literacy.* Cambridge, MA: Harvard University Press.

Sherman, S. J., & Corty, E. (1984). Cognitive heuristics. In R. S. Wyer, Jr., & T. K. Srull (Eds.), *Handbook of social cognition* (Vol. 1, pp. 189-286). Hillsdale, NJ: Lawrence Erlbaum.

Shimanoff, S. (1980). *Communication rules.* Newbury Park, CA: Sage.

Sigman, S. (1980). On communication rules from a social perspective. *Human Communication Research, 7*, 37-51.

Sigman, S. (1982). *Why ethnographers of communication do ethnography: Issues in observational methodology.* Paper presented at the meeting of the Speech Communication Association, Louisville.

Stewart, J., & Philipsen, G. (1984). Communication as situated accomplishment: The cases of hermeneutics and ethnography. In B. Dervin & M. J. Voigt (Eds.), *Progress in communication sciences* (Vol. 5, pp. 179-217). Norwood, NJ: Ablex.

Straubhaar, J. D. (1984). Brazilian television: The decline of American influence. *Communication Research, 11*, 221-240.

Streeter, T. (1986, May). *Polysemy, plurality, and media studies.* Paper presented at the meeting of the International Communication Association, Chicago.

Szwed, J. F. (1981). The ethnography of literacy. In M. F. Whiteman (Ed.), *Writing: The nature, development, and teaching of written communication.* Hillsdale, NJ: Lawrence Erlbaum.

Taylor, C. (1977). Interpretation and the sciences of man. In F. R. Dallmayr & T. A. McCarthy (Eds.), *Understanding and social inquiry* (pp. 101-131). Notre Dame, IN: University of Notre Dame Press.

Thorburn, D. (1981). Television melodrama. In R. P. Adler (Ed.), *Understanding television* (pp. 73-90). New York: Praeger.

Tinnell, C. S. (1985). An ethnographic look at personal computers in the family setting. *Marriage & Family Review, 8*(1/2), 59-70.

Traudt, P. J., & Lont, C. M. (1987). Media-logic-in-use: The family as locus of study. In T. R. Lindlof (Ed.), *Natural audiences* (pp. 139-160). Norwood, NJ: Ablex.

Turkle, S. (1984). *The second self: Computers and the human spirit.* New York: Simon & Schuster.

Turow, J. (1984). *Media industries.* New York: Longman.

Wagner, R. (1981). *The invention of culture* (rev. ed.). Chicago: University of Chicago Press.

Wartella, E. (1987). Commentary on qualitative research and children's mediated communication. In T. R. Lindlof (Ed.), *Natural audiences: Qualitative research of media uses and effects* (pp. 109-118). Norwood, NJ: Ablex.

Wilson, T. P. (1970). Normative and interpretive paradigms in sociology. In J. D. Douglas (Ed.), *Understanding everyday life* (pp. 57-79). Chicago: Aldine.

Wolf, M. A., Meyer, T. P., & White, C. (1982). A rules-based study of television's role in the construction of social reality. *Journal of Broadcasting, 26*, 813-829.

Finding the Limits of Audience Activity

BARRIE GUNTER
Independent Broadcasting Authority, London

S INCE the earliest days of mass communication research, a fundamental theoretical division has existed that reflects two antagonistic sets of assumptions about the way individuals interact with mass media. Arguments over whether audiences are essentially *active* or *passive* have been central to discussion about the role and impact of mass media. Each notion has gained prominence at different times throughout the history of mass communication research.

The *passive* audience embodies a concept of audience members as being individuals who rarely use media with any real sense of purpose or reason, who absorb unquestioningly anything the media present, and who may be changed psychologically, socially, or culturally by the media. The notion of the *active* audience conceives of audience members as being selective in their media behavior, as being cognitively and affectively involved in the media content being consumed, and as being able to limit purposefully the extent to which media influences impinge upon them. Today, the *active* audience concept is in the ascendancy. More and more mass media researchers are arriving at the opinion that audiences use and respond to media content actively rather than passively.

THE ACTIVE-PASSIVE
DICHOTOMY IN BIOCCA

But how realistic and meaningful is the distinction between the active and the passive audience? What does this distinction itself mean? To answer questions such as these we need to consider definitions of activity (versus

Correspondence and requests for reprints: Barrie Gunter, Independent Broadcasting Authority, 70 Brompton Rd., London, SW31EY, UK.

Communication Yearbook 11, pp. 108-126

passivity). Does the dichotomy refer to different classes of audience members—for example, "active" versus "passive" media consumers? Does it refer, in a broader theoretical sense, to an assumption about the way media predominantly are used and responded to by all individuals? In other words, does all media consumption involve an element of "activity"? It is probably nearer the truth to assume that media usage can be both active and passive. Furthermore, it is not a dichotomy of media consumers as much as a distinction between styles of media use that can be exhibited by the same individuals on different occasions and in connection with different media or types of media content.

In his essay "Opposing Conceptions of the Audience: The Active and Passive Hemispheres of Mass Communication Theory," Biocca examines both active and passive concepts. Focusing mostly on the former, he attempts to identify different ways in which theorists and researchers have conceptualized and operationally defined "activity." What becomes clear from this analysis is that activity has been used in all ways, with reference to how audiences approach and use media, to the functions media may serve for them, to their responses to media content, and to changes that may occur in the individuals themselves following exposure to media.

In this commentary, I wish to reexamine the notions of audience activity highlighted by Biocca and, where appropriate, expand upon the remarks he makes, particularly in the light of recent media and media research developments. The latter largely reinforce the notion of the active audience.

FIVE AREAS OF ACTIVITY

Biocca offers five definitions that derive from research into audience activity. These are:

(1) audience activity as "selectivity"
(2) audience activity as "utilitarianism"
(3) audience activity as "intentionality"
(4) audience activity as "involvement"
(5) audience activity as "imperviousness to influence"

These five areas are not conceived to be orthogonal. Many of them overlap and in practice may actively interact with each other or exhibit varying degrees of interdependency. They serve to illustrate the variety of ways in which different researchers have investigated how audiences can be active as they approach media, while using media and following media use. The scheme also indicates that definitions of activity have seldom been properly attempted by media researchers. It is an abstract and complex concept that, despite its theoretical popularity, has lacked a thorough, systematic definitional analysis.

Selectivity

Let us take a look at what these five areas make reference to. First, the notion of selectivity refers to activity involved in making a choice about using media. A number of different types of decisions may be important here. To begin with, a media consumer must make a decision to use a particular medium. The chosen medium may be preferred at a particular time over other activities, some of which might be media related. Thus a person may decide to watch television in preference to reading, listening to music on records or tapes, listening to the radio, or model building and doing domestic chores. That may be the limit of the act of selectivity, however. Once engaged in watching, the individual may not care about which particular programs are on and becomes, therefore, "passive" in accepting whatever is on. The selective act was to decide to watch television per se, but beyond that the viewer entered a "passive" mode of watching.

Of course, selectivity processes may not end with the decision simply to watch some television. The individual may continue to watch only if there is something being shown that he or she wants to see. The decision to view in the first place may have been guided by the knowledge that a particular well-liked program was about to be shown. Hence, the act of selectivity in this context goes beyond simply wanting to use the medium and embodies a desire to watch a particular offering on that medium.

Selectivity, as an explanatory concept, can be used to denote even more precise involvement with media content. The examples just discussed refer to behavioral selectivity toward television. The viewer chooses to watch television rather than do something else, or chooses to watch certain programs. But selectivity on the part of an active audience can also occur at a cognitive level. While watching a program, the viewer may selectively pay more attention to some parts of it than to others. In consequence, some parts of the program may be better remembered than others afterwards. Selective perception and selective retention of media content signify two examples of cognitive audience activity. Such processes may occur automatically. Viewers, for example, may selectively choose to watch certain programs and selectively filter from them particular ingredients, because these materials contain information that they need to know. There is some evidence that selective exposure to mass communications may be determined by the need to obtain particular kinds of information (Mendelsohn, 1983) or to have certain personal beliefs reinforced (Gunter & Wober, 1983) or to bring about changes to unpleasant mood states (Boyanowsky, 1977; Zillmann & Bryant, 1985). Meanwhile, selective perception and memory of program content may be produced by preexisting beliefs and stereotypes. In other words, individuals may actively process media content, selectively distorting it, sometimes without realizing what they are doing, so that it is more consistent with stereotyped beliefs they hold about the world (Drabman et al., 1982; Williams, La Rose, & Frost, 1981).

Utilitarianism

Second, activity as "utilitarianism" suggests that not only are individuals selective in their use of media, but also that media content is selectively chosen for the purpose of satisfying particular needs and motives (Katz, Blumler, & Gurevitch, 1974; Palmgreen & Rayburn, 1982; Rubin, 1981, 1983). Within the uses and gratifications perspective, different investigators have identified long lists of reasons people give for using media. We have seen above that audiences may selectively retain information for which they have a particular need or that has special significance for them. The idea that individuals utilize media in the current sense, however, assumes that selection for special reasons occurs in advance, and not once exposure is under way.

Some researchers have found that different clusters of claimed gratifications obtained—for example, television—are related in different ways to different preferred areas of programming (Rubin, 1979). Although this type of audience activity analysis can be useful, it is not without its problems, conceptually and methodologically. The endorsement of simple statements that express reasons for media use, for instance, probably only scratches the surface and does not provide a proper measure of the underlying psychological antecedents of selective exposure to media. Another point is that gratifications statements often tend to make reference only to the medium as a whole. In other words, "I watch TV to learn about the world," "I watch TV to relax," and so on refer to reasons for watching television per se. But television schedules contain a wide variety of different kinds of programs. Each of these gratifications may apply as reasons for watching a number of particular program types, while with regard to other types they may not be relevant. Researchers' attempts to get at "activity" in television viewing have often failed to probe deeply enough, therefore, to give a proper idea of the nature and degree of that activity across different viewing fare.

Intentionality

Third, we come to the notion of activity as "intentionality." Biocca outlines two examples of what this means. The intentionality concept assumes that media use is selective and is driven by prior needs and motives. These motives may stem from particular personality characteristics of individuals. Individuals may be driven to watch programs that reinforce certain beliefs they hold. In a similar vein, there is some evidence that individuals with particular attitudinal or behavioral dispositions may in the longer term tend to move toward certain types of media content. Individuals of an aggressive nature, for example, have been found to exhibit preferences for violent media content (Atkin, Greenberg, Korzenny, & McDermott, 1979; Gunter, 1985).

At the cognitive level, the processing of information from media and the degree of continuous attention paid to media content may be driven by existing cognitive structures. Individuals develop idiosyncratic frames of reference into which new knowledge is slotted. Information is not stored in a haphazard fashion but is moulded to fit comfortably within existing knowledge structures. Research on memory for broadcast news has revealed that the extent of general knowledge about public affairs or of background knowledge about particular news topics are among the most powerful predictors of remembering news reports on television or radio news bulletins (Berry, 1983; Findahl & Hoijer, 1975; also see Gunter, 1987b). Individuals will pay attention to media content that they can understand and readily absorb into memory; attention may wane when comprehension is poor, however. Attention to a mass communication, according to some recent writers, is driven actively by comprehension. As viewers monitor a television program, they are more likely to continue paying at least some attention to it if they can understand its contents (Anderson & Lorch, 1983).

Involvement

Fourth, there is the idea of audience activity as "involvement." Involvement can occur at any of several distinct levels—cognitive, affective, and behavioral. Cognitive effort may be invested in following a storyline when watching a televised drama, taking in information from television news broadcasts, and in making judgments about the content of programs (e.g., whether to believe what is shown).

Affectively, the extent to which audiences get involved with television programs may depend on how much viewers identify with television characters and empathize with or "feel for" them in the predicaments in which they are portrayed. Audience involvement with television drama characters and other personalities on the screen may manifest itself behaviorally in parasocial interaction. Both young viewers (Greenberg, 1974) and older viewers (Rubin & Rubin, 1982) have indicated companionship as an important function of television. Viewers are not simply emotionally involved with or attached to television people, they may also engage in private conversations with them, perhaps by making remarks about the appearance of the person on screen, or by actually talking to that person, possibly agreeing or disagreeing with something he or she might have said or done. This activity has come to light with particular clarity in recent observational research in which viewers were monitored by video cameras housed in a special television cabinet while they watched television in their own homes (Collett & Lamb, 1986; Svennevig, 1987; Svennevig & Wynberg, 1986).

Identification with television personalities may occur for a variety of reasons and to varying degrees among different viewers. The extent to which it occurs may depend significantly on the viewer's own personality and social circumstances. Even individuals who enjoy the regular real-life companionship of relatives, friends, and workmates show the capacity, cognitively and affectively, to get deeply involved with events or issues in the news or with the storylines and characters in fictional dramas. For some, their involvement may last only for the duration of the program, however, whereas for others, the gratifications provided by the vicarious companionship of a television character may extend beyond the viewing situation. Thus although both kinds of viewer may become "involved" in programs, their reasons for doing so and certain aspects of the cognitive and affective mechanisms underlying that type of audience "activity" may be different in each case.

Imperviousness to Influence

Fifth, we come to the notion of audience activity as "imperviousness to influence." On the evidence of failed information campaigns and inconclusive findings from studies of the impact of mass media on social behavior, some writers have concluded that mass communications are relatively ineffective at influencing the way people think, feel, and behave, at least in any long-term sense (e.g., Klapper, 1960). There are limits to the effects of mass media on mass publics, partly due to the fact that individuals are by and large not susceptible to media influences. With regard to television, for example, we know that audiences do not accept everything they see in programs (see Wober & Gunter, 1987). Much of what is seen may be quickly forgotten (Gunter, 1987b), and hence, for that reason alone, is unlikely to have any further influence. Even when programs are remembered, the things they show may be classified by viewers as irrelevant to their own concerns. Character portrayals may be thought to provide inappropriate role models of social conduct, relationships between characters may be judged as lacking realism, and events depicted in many programs may be perceived as unlikely to occur in everyday life as viewers themselves know it (see Gunter, 1986, 1987a).

The enjoyment of television in a lighthearted, superficial sense as a source of amusement, relaxation, or temporary distraction may be accompanied by a more "active" judgmental process through which much of what is taken in from the small screen is dismissed or rejected as something not to be taken seriously. Although not discussed to any great extent by Biocca, the crux of the notion of imperviousness to influence as an aspect or type of audience activity lies with the active-interpretive process that often characterizes an audience member's interaction with a mass medium. Limits on the impact that televison can have are placed by viewers themselves, by their motivations for watching in the first place, and by cognitive judgments made about programs and what they contain while viewing. Viewers can distinguish different genres or types of programs (Gunter, 1985; Van der Voort, 1986) and reactions to programs can depend significantly on how they have been categorized or labeled. Viewers also make comparisons between people, events, and relationships depicted on television and their experiences with similar entities and phenomena in real life (Gunter, 1986, 1987a). It is through the labeling of much of what is seen on television as distant from or irrelevant to real life that the influence of the media can be actively limited by viewers themselves (Potter, 1986). Greater ability to comprehend television storylines is related to whether significant connections occur between patterns of television viewing and distorted beliefs about the real world. Higher comprehension levels tend to weaken television's influence (Pingree, 1983).

Perhaps nobody is wholly impervious to the influences of television. We have all at some time learned something new from television or had our emotions stretched by sad and distressing or amusing and uplifting programs. But the suggestions made by some critics that television is a major developmental force in our lives, which is misused and which is having a largely negative impact, is a gross overstatement. Much of the responsibility for how much television affects audiences lies with the activity level of viewers themselves, both in the way they use and respond to television transmissions.

RECOMMENDATIONS AND POSSIBILITIES

Biocca ends by making a number of recommendations concerning "possible ways of reformulating certain aspects of theorizing on the active audience" (p. 71). His first recommendation is to "abandon the metaconstruct of the 'active audience'" (p. 71). The argument here is that activity is too broad a concept, which has been ill-defined and used to cover too many things. Biocca identifies two versions of the active audience concept—a strong version and a weak version. The strong form refers to the notion of the imperviousness of the audience to media influence. The audience is conceived as being self-determining in its use of media and in how it reacts to media content. The weak form does not dismiss the possibility of media influences, but indicates that audiences have a freedom of choice when using mass media. They can select from among available media and media contents those they wish to consume and this they may do in the service of particular needs, gratifications, and goals. Biocca favors rejection of the strong form and acceptance of the weak form with its notions of selectivity, utility, intentionality, and involvement, which in turn reflect a degree of autonomy and responsibility on the part of audience members, through which the nature and extent of media impact can be limited.

This choice would seem to be justified on the evidence presented in our earlier discussion that audiences are often selective and instrumental in the way they use media, and in the way they process, accept, and react to media content, but not all the time. And while audiences can and do exhibit varying degrees of personal control over their use of media and are capable of shaping and limiting media influences, media content can nevertheless have social, cultural, and psychological effects on media consumers.

The second recommendation is to "theoretically define and measure the communicator's objectives, strategies, and perceptions of the audience" (p. 72). Essentially, this recommendation is for the attainment of a closer match between the communicator's aims and the audience's needs. In practical terms, it is a call for more effective audience research that can be fed back to media professionals both to indicate the success of communications they have put out and to provide information to guide the production of effective future communications.

Mention is made of the effectiveness of research as such within the sphere of advertising. There are other areas, however, in which specialist audience research can prove to be useful; in particular, the production of informational (e.g., news and current affairs) and educational television programs may gain significantly from careful research. With regard to television news, for example, research has revealed that audiences frequently exhibit poor comprehension and memory of the news from television broadcasts. The news is forgotten rapidly within a short time of the broadcast. This may be a function of passivity on the part of viewers whose attention and cognitive involvement are at a low level while the news is on. It has been found, however, that even relatively attentive and interested viewers can have problems taking in the information from television newscasts with any degree of success (Berry, 1983; Katz, Adoni, & Parness, 1977; Neuman, 1976). The reasons for this difficulty may be found in the way the news is presented (Gunter, Berry, & Clifford, 1982). Many of the techniques and routines of news production are geared to enabling news editors efficiently to pull together diverse news stories into coherent, flowing programs and meet tight deadlines every day. The design of the finished product is governed, however, by aesthetic concerns relating to what a good program should be like and by naive psychologizing on the part of news professionals about the news needs and cognitive information processing capabilities of their viewers (Gunter, 1983a). Unfortunately, misconceptions about the audience abound (Robinson & Sahin, 1984) that result in presentation styles that, although designed and believed to enhance audience comprehension of the news, actually impede it. Recently, several researchers, working independently, have concluded that news production could be improved and that research into how audiences cognitively process the news from television broadcasts could show the way (Gunter, 1987b; Robinson & Levy, 1986).

It has become clear that in areas of specialist broadcasting, where productions are designed to have a certain kind of impact, carefully planned audience research can play a useful part in guiding production strategy so as to enhance the effectiveness of programs in achieving their intended objectives. Although this type of research is often regarded with some suspicion by those professionals working on the production side, early results have indicated that media audience research may have a useful contribution to make in areas such as news or educational broadcasting, where audience activity (e.g., cognitive information processing) is a crucial variable. Acceptance by the communicators that audiences are active in a cognitive sense is not enough. They need to know in more precise terms about the nature of this activity and how to build programs whose structures and presentation styles cater to it.

A further recommendation is to "incorporate a theory of the text into the analysis of activity" (p. 72). The knowledge that a viewer likes to watch particular television programs, for example, because they are perceived to bring certain (broadly verbalized and defined) gratifications actually reveals little about the way in which viewers interpret the meanings conveyed by programs that are the most significant for them. Biocca indicates that semiological analysis enables detailed examination and assessment of the values and social message carried by programs. Having used such techniques to classify and elaborate on the nature of what a program contains, cognitive psychology can supply theoretical and empirical frameworks within which audience absorption of the meaning of a program can be empirically investigated. By breaking down, operationally, the discourses of television programs into semantic and syntactic components, it may be possible to investigate the different psychological levels at which viewers cognitively process programs. This marriage of semiological and empirical audience analysis would seem to hold some promise.

A fourth recommendation is to "include the psychological role of the medium and, specifically, its formal structures in moment-to-moment information processing" (p. 73). A medium such as television is characterized by not only its content but also its grammar—a set of formal features that lend structure to the content and also carry meanings of their own that have to be accurately interpreted by audiences if they are properly to understand the program. The grammar of television is learned by viewers through experience, although some people are better "readers" of the medium than others. The significance of the formal features or grammar of television for information processing from (educational) programs has been demonstrated by Salomon (1979). Research elsewhere with television news programming has indicated how both the text structures (Findahl & Hoijer, 1985; Larsen, 1981) and visual format features (Davies, Berry, & Clifford, 1985) can influence learning.

Understanding the grammar of television, for instance, can enhance comprehension and learning of its content. Through the natural course of everyday viewing experience, children become familiar with the formal features of television, at least to some extent. This learning is indicated by research that reveals better comprehension of program storylines among older children than among younger ones. But "television literacy," or the competence to read the grammar of the medium, can also be formally taught. Some early attempts at this have shown that enhanced literacy can give rise to better retention of television news and better comprehension of television drama (Kelley, Gunter, & Kelley, 1985). Biocca correctly observes that the psychological role of the formal features of media is an important area for future study.

Finally, Biocca points to the need to "define the role of media socialization and habituation" (p. 73) into the discussion about the audience's interaction with media. This work could be done at several different levels of analysis, which would include (1) investigation of the development of children's perception, understanding and use of media; (2) concern for media socialization among particular groups within the audience to address their motives for watching and also the way in which various personality characteristics have a bearing on media use; and (3) study of media socialization within and among cultures and significant subcultures over long time spans.

All these recommendations for areas of future investigation by mass communications researchers are worthy of consideration. However, they do cover a broad spectrum, and we are left with a plethora of possibilities. A more systematic taxonomy of types of activity is needed. Furthermore, it might be most useful to develop this classification within a single conceptual reference frame. Since we are concerned principally with aspects of audience "psychological" activity—cognitive, affective, and behavioral processes—a psychological or social-psychological perspective could prove most appropriate.

THE AUDIENCE AND LINDLOF

Practically all of us who watch television also belong to various social, occupational/professional, or public groups. We may live in a family houschold or one that we share with friends. Even if we live alone, we may nevertheless regularly come into contact with a variety of other "communities" in which we regularly interact with others. This may be at a place of work, through organized group activities outside work, and through social gatherings with friends and acquaintances.

These various "community" or group activities constitute the sociocultural environment in which we live and learn. Learning is important. Groups survive largely because their memberships adhere to certain norms, rules, and codes of conduct that in part define the identity of the group as an entity; more important, they ensure that individual members work together collectively, even though that may mean suspending or suppressing selfish wishes. The needs and objectives of the group have to be put first, if it and its members are to survive.

Successful groups are built on clearly defined rule structures that are accepted, understood, and conformed to by the membership. To a great extent, this claim applies whether the group we are concerned about is the family, school, place of work, social club, or the society at large. The values and norms we learn through our interactions with and membership in different groups color our outlook on the world including our use of media and the way we interpret and respond to media content. Certainly, the interpretations audiences place on media output will be affected by their experiences in the broader sociocultural milieu.

In his essay, "Media Audiences as Interpretive Communities," Lindlof presents a thesis that conceives of audiences as active in their uses of and responses to mass media. The utilization of media and the interpretations placed upon media contents are seen as being determined significantly, though not exclusively, by a variety of sociocultural factors characterizing media audiences and whose rule or normative-value-driven influences shape the way media consumers "read" the media and the messages they convey. Lindlof offers a perspective for the assessment of audiences' interpretations of media that is founded in critical or semiological analysis of media content. It is not intended that this approach should replace other research perspectives, but rather that it could usefully supplement them, conceptually and method-ologically, to enhance our understanding of how audience functions as actively interpretive media-consuming communities.

The essay typifies many that approach the study of media-audience interaction from a semiological direction in being heavily laden with jargon and opaque prose. There is a certain irony in the fact that an approach that attempts to formulate an analytical framework designed to improve our understanding of how audiences read mass communications is still so difficult to read. Nevertheless, Lindlof does have some points to make: some reinforced by empirical studies of how audiences consume and interpret mass communications, others not.

IDENTIFYING HOW AUDIENCES INTERPRET MEDIA

Lindlof begins his discussion of the ways in which audiences interpret media content by offering two conceptions of meaning in media: (1) *presented* meaning and (2) *constructed* meaning. The first refers to assessing the nature of media content and the second is concerned with the interpretations audiences place on media content.

Presented Meaning

The study of presented meaning normally involves analysis of media content. The aim of this study is to identify and elaborate content profiles: to catalogue objects, characters, events, and relationships, and the contexts in which all these are situated. The research interest may be in what people "get out" of content, in terms of what they remember and understand of it, what they feel about it, or the gratifications that they obtained from it, but typically, the analysis of presented meaning in the sense referred to here has no basis in or direct correspondence with audience response to media content. Usually, "meanings" are "read" into content by analysts who make the assumption that the same meanings are relevant to, salient for, and absorbed by audience members. The fact is that audiences often place different interpretations on media content from communication theorists or semiologists.

Lindlof makes mention, by way of example, that "a category, such as violence, may be conceptually and operationally defined differently by different investigators [but this] does not alter the premise that meaning can be located at the level of a general category and that all instances of that content can be referenced through the membership rules of the category" (p. 84). Thus violence as a general concept of category can be given a definition for operational purposes, with an agreement being reached by experimenters, coders, and other participants that this is the definition they will all work with. This is an artificial constraint, but one that is necessary to achieve the research objectives. Coders, for example, must be in agreement about what it is they are meant to be recording when assessing the content of programs. If not, different coders would probably produce different accounts of what programs contain. In this sort of analysis, violence is decontextualized, and individual differences among participants in the research, regarding perceptions or judgments about violence, are suspended. Under normal circumstances, these individuals, in common with ordinary audience members, would probably disagree about the content of television programs. They would be likely to employ personal definitions of what is meant by violence or stereotyping and so forth, and their appraisals of programs would give rise to diverging descriptive accounts of what each program is like.

Recently, researchers have begun to lay stress on the importance of the perceptions of audience members in classifying television program content. Viewers discriminate, for example, between different forms of violence on television (Gunter, 1985; Van der Voort, 1986). Audience responses to programs may depend on their motives for watching, personal psychological characteristics, or factors relating to their social background and group affiliations. Developmental factors also are important since they are connected with how well viewers can understand programs and draw inferences from them. This empirical perspective introduces the idea that the meaning of media content is not contained solely within the content, but derives from the interpretations individuals place on it. Such interpretations are affected by existing knowledge structures and frames of reference into which new media content is fitted and made sense of by audience members.

The analysis of media content for its dominant structures and patterns is an important exercise that may be essential to any proper analysis of the meanings assimilated by audiences from the media. Content analysis, using a priori coding frames, can be a useful technique, but inferences and assumptions about how audiences interpret media content can properly be made only through audience research. That is, audience members must be investigated themselves for the meanings they gain from media content.

Constructed Meaning

This perspective holds that meanings of content conveyed by mass communication are person controlled through interpretation. A television program, for example, means what a viewer interprets it to mean. And viewers' interpretations of programs depend on existing needs, beliefs, attitudes, social affiliations, reference groups, cultural memberships, and so on.

Thus constructed meaning holds that each individual places a unique "reading" on media output. Despite the fact that individuals differ in their responses to television, there can nevertheless often be considerable agreement across viewers about television programs. Different individuals are able to identify and agree on the elements that characterize particular program genres (Frost, 1969; Haldane, 1970). Common viewing experiences may produce this agreement. But agreement may exist only at fairly superficial levels. More detailed probing for the meanings taken from programs may reveal considerable individual differences in interpretation and inference making even with those programs about whose category membership there is superficially a general consensus of judgment (Furnham & Gunter, 1985; Gunter, 1985; Gunter & Furnham, 1986).

INTERPRETATION AND COMMUNITY

We have already recognized that individuals live in a social world that is rule based and shared with others. People who live in a particular community have certain accepted ways of behaving, which stem from shared values, beliefs, attitudes, and codes defining modes of conduct that are appropriate under different social circumstances. The idea of community is grounded in and in part defined by the dominant styles of communication. Rules of communication are shared by individuals who constitute a community. The rules of the group of community can affect how individuals use mass media. Research has shown that media use does have a rule-bound character (Hedinsson, 1981; Lemish, 1982; Lindlof & Traudt, 1982).

Lindlof points out that semiology has aroused much interest in understanding how ideological codes of media users produce particular "readings" of mediated content. Audiences are assumed to be actively interpretive when interacting with media content. There is growing empirical evidence to indicate that this assumption is true (Anderson, 1979; Anderson & Lorch, 1983; Huston & Wright, 1983). Unfortunately, in semiology, which lacks any actual empirical investigation of audiences themselves, "meanings" are usually read into media content on behalf of audience members by the researchers. And, as we have noted already, this mode of interpretation may bear little or no relevance to the judgments audiences make about media content.

Further, although audiences may be interpretive communities, there is a danger in placing too much emphasis on assessing the meaning of media at this level. It tends to play down the significance of individual differences in use of or response to the media. Sure enough, individuals who have common reference groups may share certain value systems that produce commonalities in their ways of thinking about certain subjects or in their modes of behaving in particular situations. But not all individuals think and behave in the same way. The perspective offered to us by Lindlof does not seem to allow for individual variations, which can often be highly significant and pronounced.

PROPERTIES OF INTERPRETIVE COMMUNITIES

In some cases, empirical studies have been conducted to verify the patterns of media use and interpretation for individuals inferred from semiological-style analyses. These studies have helped to show that interpretive communities do not always follow standard demographic structures, such as social class, occupational status, or social group affiliation. Within families, for instance, there may be "a number of interpretive communities nested within the bonds of familial intimacy, such as a mother-daughter dyad bound by practices of storytelling, book reading, doll and puppet play, television viewing, and audio-cassette playing" (p. 93). Older children in the household may be part of a social network that claims music-based media as a central component of its group life. Hence, it may be important to look beyond standard parameters of classifying individuals to discover the sociocultural reference groups that have the most significant mediating impact on media interpretations.

Lindlof identifies two categories of properties of the interpretive community, which he classes *virtual texts* and *referents*. Virtual texts refer to the way in which individuals produce subjective meanings for media communications. According to some writers (for example, Bruner, 1986), readers generate their own versions of a work of fiction; they place their own constructions on passages of prose or other media content. Individuals structure stories according to existing knowledge systems or schemata housed within their memories. They interpret content media according to existing frames of reference that are built upon background knowledge about the subject matter or more generally about the language in which it is written or spoken.

Schemata are representative of an "active" audience and have been studied in relation to learning from mass communications. Empirical research grounded in cognitive psychology has indicated that learning from media narratives can be significantly influenced by the way information is structured and elaborated. Where the structure of a narrative communication is consonant with the structures of existing schemata applied by audience members when processing the new information it contains, comprehension is enhanced. When there is structural or systematic dissonance between these two, learning may be impaired (Findahl & Hoijer, 1985; Larsen, 1981; Thorndyke, 1979).

REFERENTS

Lindlof introduces three kinds of referent: (1) genre, (2) developmental, and (3) social-situational. Each one indicates different ways in which audiences behave as interpretive media consumers. A genre refers to a particular category of media content, such as a type of television program, which follows certain thematic conventions. Genres can attain varying levels of popularity and for different reasons. Some genres achieve success for commercial reasons (e.g., telenovelas), others because they serve a useful purpose in the community (e.g., provision of local news or of educational programming). A genre may offer a particular reflection on the world. Certain genres may go out of fashion, but then, at appropriate times, are revived to become popular once again, in the presence of special audience demands or needs.

Lindlof discusses the importance of the development of comprehension abilities through the early years of life in the foundation of skills used by interpretive audiences. This development, he says, "probably begins in infancy when television is framed as a field of trackable, imitatable objects, and the vocalizing of parents signifies important information" (p. 99). In other words, television viewing begins in early childhood and provides youngsters with a constant flow of ideas for behavioral examples, which might be absorbed and copied by them. However, parents who talk to their children about the things they see on television can play a significant role in mediating any influences television might have on their youngsters. Through increased viewing experiences, children—who initially have difficulty following dramatic storylines in many television programs—develop cognitive abilities to understand television more fully. They come to make finer discriminations between realism and fantasy programming, for instance (e.g., Dorr, 1980), and they develop cognitive frames of reference or "schemata," which enable them more effectively to comprehend television storylines (e.g., Collins, 1979).

As they grow older, children's perceptions of and vicarious relationships with television characters also change (Reeves, 1979). Throughout this developmental process, the child's family plays a signficant part. Different families have different styles of bringing up their children and these socialization practices styles of control may be reflected in the media usage habits of children and in the way they respond to media content (Hedinsson, 1981; also see Gunter & Svennevig, 1987).

Finally, the social-situational exigency "covers those environmental and sociohistorical conditions that elicit a coordinated syndrome of mediated communication ability" (p. 99). This syndrome refers to the norms and established codes of practice found within groups, organizations, and social situations in which individuals interact with each other. In personal, professional, and public relationships, there are established forms of conduct that are accepted by the majority as the proper way to behave in those conditions.

Lindlof identifies two ways in which this class of referents operates: "(1) highly conventionalized content is used to mediate social individuation, *to segment action*; or (2) highly differentiated or nonconventional mediated content is used to engender collectivities" (p. 101). In plainer English it seems, from examples given by Lindlof, that the first of these refers to instances where television may be used as a source of conversation or a yardstick to test out the accuracy of others' beliefs or "competencies."

Lindlof also refers to the "utilization of differentiated material for collectivizing situations, or for creating joint actions." He continues, "The consumption of specialized, deviant, or abstruse communications media or mediated content will tend to drive collectivizing activity. Subcultures and interest groups form"(pp. 101-102). By this, he presumably means that television, for example, may broadcast a special interest program that brings together individuals who have an interest in that particular subject matter, so that through this shared media experience they become as a group for a while. Subcultures, with their own style of dress, speech, and behavior, may also seek to have their identity reinforced through particular programs such as those broadcasting special types of music.

Special subgroups may indeed have special interests. These interests may be catered to by special television programs. In Britain, the new Fourth Channel was introduced to cater principally to minority group viewing interests. In practice, although minority groups may show some tendency to switch on to programs broadcast especially for them, these groups also exhibit the broader viewing likes and dislikes of the mass audience. At the same time, minority interest programs may attract people who are merely casual viewers. When examining the role of media to effect the development of new subcultures or to strengthen the identity of ones that already exist, it may be important to differentiate between media and the relative capacities of different forms of mass communication to operate in this way.

CONCLUDING REMARKS

Lindlof's chapter attempts to identify some perspectives on how media audiences can be considered as a particular kind of community, whose identity is defined by shared assumptions about and styles of using the media. He offers the concept of the "interpretive community" as a supplement to other ideas about the ways audiences use and respond to media in the hope that it will provide a new research angle to complement other research perspectives.

He is right to invite us to consider alternative perspectives—and, indeed, approaches that cause us to take a closer look at the construction of different kinds of media content, the structures and profiles that characterize them, and the meanings they convey to audiences. All of these considerations could lead to research developments that could enhance our understanding of the nature and extent of media influences. For example, semiological approaches may initially seem to offer valuable instruments for the analysis of media content at a descriptive level (and to some extent in practice may do so), but whether they can usefully go beyond that description to provide valid indicators of the meanings of media content for audiences is highly questionable. As we noted earlier, this approach typically has little or no systematic contact with the audience, and the "meanings" interpreted from media content are read into it by respondents of the perspective without any effort being made to find out if the same meanings exist for audience members.

The complex symbolism and arrays of social and cultural messages identified through semiological styles of media content analysis are often ingenious and may indeed provide valuable insights into what the media are communicating to audiences. But, in the end, if valid statements are to be made about what audiences learn from the media or how they are influenced by media—cognitively, affectively, or behaviorally—these effects must be measured among audience members themselves. They cannot be inferred through guesswork, no matter how detailed or sophisticated the media content assessment happens to be.

REFERENCES

Anderson, D. R. (1979). *Active and passive processes in children's television viewing.* Paper presented at the annual meeting of the American Psychological Association, New York.

Anderson, D. R., & Lorch, E. P. (1983). Looking at television: Action or reaction? In J. Bryant & D. Anderson (Eds.), *Children's understanding of television: Research on attention and comprehension* (pp. 1-33). New York: Academic Press.

Atkin, C., Greenberg, B., Korzenny, F., & McDermott, S. (1979). Selective exposure to televised violence. *Journal of Broadcasting, 23,* 5-13.

Berry, C. (1983). Learning from television news: A critique of the research. *Journal of Broadcasting, 27,* 359-370.

Boyanowsky, E. O. (1977). Film preferences under conditions of trust: Whetting the appetite for violence, information or excitement? *Communication Research, 4,* 33-45.

Bruner, J. (1986). *Actual minds, possible worlds.* Cambridge, MA: Harvard University Press.

Collett, P., & Lamb, R. (1986). *Watching people watching television.* Report to the Independent Broadcasting Authority, Great Britain.

Collins, W. A. (1979). Children's comprehension of television content. In E. Wartella (Ed.), *Children communicating: Media and development of thought, speech, understanding* (pp. 21-52). Newbury Park, CA: Sage.

Davies, M., Berry, C., & Clifford, B. (1985). Unkindest acts? Some effects of picture editing on recall of television news information. *Journal of Educational Television, 11,* 85-98.

Drabman, R. S., Robertson, S. J., Patterson, J. N., Jarvie, G. J., Hammer, D., & Cordua, G. (1981). Children's perceptions of media-portrayed sex roles. *Sex Roles, 12,* 379-389.

Dorr, A. (1980). When I was a child I thought as a child. In S. B. Whitney & R. P. Abeles (Eds.), *Television and social behavior: Beyond violence and children* (pp. 191-230). Hillsdale, NJ: Lawrence Erlbaum.

Findahl, O., & Hoijer, B. (1975). *Man as a receiver of information: On knowledge, social privilege, and the news* (Department Rep.). Stockholm: Sveriges Radio Audience and Programme Research Department.

Findahl, O., & Hoijer, B. (1985). Some characteristics of news memory and comprehension. *Journal of Broadcasting and Electronic Media, 29,* 379-396.

Frost, W.A.K. (1969). The development of a technique for TV program assessment. *Journal of the Market Research Society, 11,* 25-44.

Furnham, A., & Gunter, B. (1985). Sex, presentation mode and memory for violent and non-violent news. *Journal of Educational Television, 11,* 99-105.

Greenberg, B. S. (1974). Gratifications of television viewing and their correlates for British children. In J. Blumler & E. Katz (Eds.), *The uses of mass communications: Current perspectives on gratifications research* (pp. 71-92). Newbury Park, CA: Sage.

Gunter, B. (1983a). Do aggressive people prefer violent television? *Bulletin of the British Psychological Society, 36*, 166-168.

Gunter, B. (1983b). Forgetting the news. In E. Warbetter, D. C. Whitney, & S. Windahl (Eds.), *Mass communication review yearbook* (Vol. 4, pp. 165-172). Newbury Park, CA: Sage.

Gunter, B. (1985). *Dimensions of television violence.* Aldershot, England: Gower.

Gunter, B. (1986). *Television and sex role stereotyping.* London: IBA & John Libbey.

Gunter, B. (1987a). *Television and the fear of crime.* London: IBA & John Libbey.

Gunter, B. (1987b). *Poor reception: Misunderstanding and forgetting broadcast news.* Hillsdale, NJ: Lawrence Erlbaum.

Gunter, B., Berry, C., & Clifford, B. (1982). Remembering broadcast news: The implications of experimental research for production technique. *Human Learning, 1*, 13-29.

Gunter, B., & Furnham, A. (1986). Sex and personality differences in recall of violent and non-violent news from three presentation modalities. *Personality and Individual Differences, 7*, 829-837.

Gunter, B., & Svennevig, M. (1987). *Behind and in front of the screen: Television's involvement with family life.* London: IBA & John Libbey.

Gunter, B., & Wober, M. (1983). Television viewing and public trust. *British Journal of Social Psychology, 22*, 174-176.

Haldane, I. R. (1970). Can attitudes be quantified? Measuring television audience reactions by multivariate analysis techniques. *Proceedings of the Market Research Society Thirteenth Annual Conference,* Brighton, England.

Hedinsson, E. (1981). *TV, family and society: The social origins and effects of adolescents' TV use.* Stockholm, Almqvist & Witisell International.

Huston, A., & Wright, J. C. (1983). Children's processing of television: The informative functions of formal features. In J. Bryant & D. Anderson (Eds.), *Children's understanding of television: Research on attention and comprehension* (pp. 35-68). New York: Academic Press.

Katz, E., Adoni, H., & Parness, P. (1977). Remembering the news: What the picture adds to recall. *Journalism Quarterly, 54*, 231-239.

Katz, E., Blumler, J., & Gurevitch, M. (1974). Utilization of mass communication by the individual. In J. Blumler & E. Katz (Eds.), *The uses of mass communications: Current perspectives on gratifications research* (pp. 19-35). Newbury Park, CA: Sage.

Kelley, P., Gunter, B., & Kelley, C. (1985). Teaching television in the classroom: Results of a preliminary study. *Journal of Educational Television, 11*, 57-63.

Klapper, J. T. (1960). *The effects of mass communication.* New York: Free Press.

Larsen, S. F. (1981). *Knowledge updating: Three papers on news memory, background knowledge and test processing.* University of Aarhus, Institute of Psychology (Psychological Reports, Vol. 6, No. 4).

Lemish, D. (1982). The rules of television viewing in public places. *Journal of Broadcasting, 26*, 757-781.

Lindlof, T. R., & Traudt, P. J. (1982). Mediated communication in families: New theoretical directions. In M. S. Mander (Ed.), *Communications in transition* (pp. 260-278). New York: Pineger.

Mendelsohn, H. (1983, May). *Using the mass media for crime prevention.* Paper presented at the annual convention of the American Association for Public Opinion Research, Bush Hill Falls, PA.

Neuman, W. R. (1976). Patterns of recall among television news viewers. *Public Opinion Quarterly, 40*, 115-123.

Palmgreen, P., & Rayburn, J. D. (1982). Gratifications sought and media exposure: An expectancy value model. *Communication Research, 9*, 561-580.

Pingree, S. (1983). Children's cognitive processing in constructing social reality. *Journalism Quarterly, 60*, 415-422.

Potter, W. J. (1986). Perceived reality and the . . . hypothesis. *Journal of Broadcasting and Electronic Media, 30*, 159-174.

Reeves, B. (1979). Children's understanding of television people. In E. Wartella (Ed.), *Children's communicating: Media and development of thought, speech, understanding* (pp. 115-155). Newbury Park, CA: Sage.

Robinson, J. P., & Levy, M. R. (1986). *The main source: Learning from television news.* Newbury Park, CA: Sage.

Robinson, J. P., & Sahin, H. (1984). *Audience comprehension of television news: Results from some exploratory research.* London: British Broadcasting Corporation, Broadcasting Research Department.

Rubin, A. M. (1979). Television use by children and adolescents. *Human Communication Research, 5*, 109-120.

Rubin, A. M. (1981). An examination of television viewing motivations. *Communication Research, 8*, 141-165.

Rubin, A. M. (1983). Television uses and gratifications: The interaction of viewing patterns and motivations. *Journal of Broadcasting, 27*, 37-51.

Rubin, A. M., & Rubin, R. B. (1982). Older persons' TV viewing patterns and motivations. *Communication Research, 9*, 287-313.

Salomon, G. (1979). Shape, not only content: How media symbols partake in the development of abilities. In E. Wartella (Ed.), *Children communicating: Media and development of thought, speech, understanding* (pp. 53-82). Newbury Park, CA: Sage.

Svennevig, M. (1987). *The viewer viewed.* Paper presented to ESOMAR Seminar on Research for Broadcasting Decision-making, ESOMAR, Amsterdam.

Svennevig, M., & Wynberg, R. (1986, May). Viewing is viewing is viewing . . . or is it? A broader approach to television research. *Admap*, pp. 267-274.

Thorndyke, P. W. (1979). Knowledge organisation from newspaper stories. *Discourse Processes, 2*, 95-112.

Van der Voort, T.H.A. (1986). *Television violence: A child's eye view.* Amsterdam: Elsevier.

Williams, F., La Rose, R., & Frost, F. (1981). *Children, television and sex role stereotyping.* New York: Praeger.

Wober, M., & Gunter, B. (1987). *Television and social control.* Aldershot, England: Gower.

Zillmann, D., & Bryant, J. (1985). Affect, mood, and emotion as determinants of selective exposure. In D. Zillmann & J. Bryant (Eds.), *Selective exposure to communication* (pp. 157-190). Hillsdale, NJ: Lawrence Erlbaum.

The Breakdown of the "Canonical Audience"

FRANK A. BIOCCA
University of North Carolina, Chapel Hill

L INDLOF'S and Gunter's articles bring together intellectual trends that are symptomatic of a larger phenomenon. What we can see before us is the progressive breakdown of the "canonical audience." I am not referring here to a breakdown of a specific gathering of media users. What is occurring is a breakdown of the *referent* for the word *audience* in the communication research from both the humanities and the social sciences. Our earlier notions of the mass media audience rested on the extrapolations from and idealizations of physical gatherings, the theater audience, the audience at the political rally, the street-running mob. This primordial audience we can call the "physical audience." The canonical audience, the theoretical entity at the center of much mass communication theory, was modeled upon this physical audience of the theater, the meeting, the mob. Borrowing from common notions of mob psychology, the canonical audience came to be perceived as responsive, pliable, and even "passive."

Beginning with the newspaper and accelerated by the arrival of broadcast media, this physical audience was dispersed into separate cubicles—the living room. By the 1950s, Reisman (1950) would write about the new social formation, which he called the "lonely crowd." For a while this lonely crowd still mimicked the older, more cohesive, physical audience. In early network radio there was frequent reference to the "live" studio audience. Applauding in the background, laughing, participating, they reminded the mass media user of his or her role. The form suggested that the isolated audience member was still part of the physical presence, still in touch with an actual physical community that laughed and reacted in unison.

In the early days of television, the audience was again ritually enacted. The camera was frequently turned toward the "studio audience," reminding the distant viewer of his or her role. Others like oneself were there in the crowd;

Correspondence and requests for reprints: Frank A. Biocca, Center for Research in Journalism and Mass Communication, School of Journalism, University of North Carolina, Chapel Hill, NC 27514.

Communication Yearbook 11, pp. 127-132

the viewer belonged to a community of viewers. When the *Today* show first aired, this audience became more like the TV viewer. The audience, standing on a New York street outside the NBC studios, viewed the program through a window, a plate glass very much like the TV screen itself. Every morning the camera ritually turned toward them. The community of viewers was affirmed, and TV viewers were authenticated in their role.

While some programs still retain a studio audience, the canonical audience, which the studio audience represented, a conceptual "community of viewers" has been disintegrating. On many programs, echoes of the older physical audience remain only in the peals of the laugh track. These ripples of contagious laughter are a throwback to the unifying crowd experience of the theater audience. But this crowd experience also included a far less humorous "audience," the one chillingly unified in films of the infamous Nuremberg rally. The laugh track instructs the viewers on how to be a member of the television audience, the aggregate so meticulously monitored by the Nielsen corporation. It is perhaps symbolic of the disintegration of this older concept of the audience that the voices laughing uproariously on the laugh track machines of network television have been dead and silent for many years.

As the older audience concept began to fragment, new ways of describing the special interaction of the medium and the reader/viewer/user began to emerge. The concept of the *interpretive community* advanced by Lindlof reflects a number of these developments. Lindlof points out problems associated with studying the aggregate audience, normally probed and stratified by mass communication's survey research. In the audience profiles that emerge either from discriminant or factorial analyses, the actual experience of the medium is lost, as well as the social and situational contingency of the experience. In the older physical audience of the theater and the mob, these two elements were automatically integrated. Socially self-selected and situationaly united by a common physical environment and purpose, be it a "pleasant evening" or political agitation, the physical audience member was surrounded by his or her role. He or she was immediately instructed and socialized into that role by the very reaction of the mass of fellow audience members. The canonical interpretation of the message was guided by the applause, boos, and laughter of the crowd. The concept of the interpretive community and its description by the media ethnographer recaptures part of the texture of the physical audience while questioning the interaction of the reader/viewer/user and the medium.

THE "TRANSFER OF MEANING": WHERE DOES MEANING RESIDE?

Both Lindlof's and Gunter's arguments regarding the interaction of the medium and the audience circle this fundamental question. The reef of meaning has accelerated the breakup of the canonical audience. For example,

Lindlof concludes that there is an "ascending curve of interest in alternative research approaches . . . [which] partake in a semiotic interest . . . and . . . a reluctance to accept what I have referred to as presented meaning" (p. 102). Two larger trends have influenced the changing notion of audience. The "structuralist and semiotics wave" that swept through the humanities and social sciences in the 1960s and the 1970s thrust the question of interpretation into the foreground. The ferment over meaning had until then been bottled up in more esoteric philosophical and linguistic debates.

Lindlof's reformulated audience is built around norms, rules, and logics of interpretation. The emphasis on the text and the moment of semiosis shifts attention away from the author/communicator and the "authorial text" to a problematic interaction between the text and the reader. Concern regarding the author's intent and the ability of the reader to "decipher" the author/director/actor's message correctly begins to dissolve when the text/film/program is seen as a relatively autonomous cultural product that is forever reconstituted fresh and anew in the mind of each individual reader/decoder.

The "moment of semiosis," those critical milliseconds of processing where meaning is retrieved and constructed, has become a focus of study. Spurred by psychology's inquiry into the time course of cognitive processing and the structure of semantic memory, a powerful research program is under way in the social sciences and it is fed by the socioeconomic demands for a functional "artificial intelligence."

QUESTIONS OF METHOD

The contrast between the text and the process of decoding is to a large degree the central point of Gunter's article. Research claims resting on traditional content analysis have unreliable predictive value. As Gunter points out, there is a gap between "content" and actual as opposed to "inferred impact." It is a point worth noting, considering the fact that linguistics, even before Chomsky, abandoned attempts to measure meaning strictly from operations conducted on surface lexemes. This measurement had been attempted by linguists influenced by the early communication theory known as information theory. Content analysis is still anchored in the notion of a relatively stable, self-evident, and objective meaning, an approach that is similarly questioned in much of Lindlof's analysis.

But the problem with content analysis is not just a question of limitations of the method—which are many—but the inappropriate use of the method. Content analysis was intended to give the researcher insight into the social production of the message, insight into organization pressures and agendas (Holsti, 1969; Lasswell, Leites, & Associates, 1949). Growing out of the analysis of propaganda broadcasts before and during World War I, the method was well suited to the task. It was well suited to detect biases in the encoding of a message.

In cultivation theory, content analysis is used to support theoretical statements about the decoding process. It is here that many problems enter and the weaknesses of the method become most apparent. When Gunter contrasts objective and subjective measurement strategies of television content, he is contrasting a decoder-based theory of meaning with a message-based theory that locates much of meaning in the text. The many mediating "variables" found in the processing strategies of the audience member, active in constructing meaning, suggest not only a more complicated process but shifts that analysis to the cognitive processes of the audience member.

At the opposite extreme but equally erroneous is the position that Lindlof labels "constructed meaning," for which I will use the term *constructionism*. Beginning with the readily granted notion that "individuals" with "idiosyncratic histories" decode messages in "unique meaning matrices," constructionism argues, for an extremely relativistic notion of subjective meaning. As Lindlof explains, "Each person's construction is incommensurable." This position is used to shake loose the power of the semiotic code and social meaning as well as claims for an objective, self-evident and presented meaning. Shared meaning, when it exists, becomes mere "trace evidence" of social practices. Given the amazing coordination of communication and action constituting modern society, it is unlikely that the powerful engine for social communication can be dismissed as a mere trace element in a unique individual's consciousness. This position never manages to escape solipsism sucessfully. Furthermore, this position's formulations of cognitive processing and individuality are often anchored in phenomenological theories. As I point out in my own article, there are significant limitations in basing one's theories predominantly on conscious and introspective processes.

The ethnographic or "social phenomenological" study of the interpretive community offers potentially interesting and valuable insights into some key factors in the interpretive processes of the audience. The method can allow the researcher to observe the development and use of genres and interpretive rituals in a naturalistic setting. Many of the nuances involved in the use of the media can be observed. Members of the community act as interpreters and informants. Skilled collection of observational data can reconstruct, to some degree, the ideational universe in which a medium, a program, and other cultural artifacts truly live.

As Lindlof points out, it is important to assess how a programming "genre" becomes recognized and how it is influenced by a cultural grouping's definition of semiotic "competence." The analysis of the genre from the audience's viewpoint and not from the creator/producer's viewpoint can firmly anchor decoding conventions and nets of meaning within an integrated social context. One can observe how media and information are used. In a general way, this analysis is also the ambition of uses and gratification theory. What has been lacking in the latter is a strong theoretical model of the communication process to guide and explain findings. Methodologically, another problem has been the reliance on survey methodology to attempt to reconstruct the audience's intellectual and social environment. There is some doubt that the integration of media use, conventions of decoding, and constructions of social reality can easily be deciphered primarily or predominantly from the traditional survey techniques.

On the other hand, as Lindlof himself points out, naturalistic, hermeneutic, and ethnographic approaches represent real problems in satisfying basic research goals such as generalizability. Arguments for the generalizability of results must often rest on implicit assumptions or explicit assertions that the microcultural process under study is somehow representative or typical of more widespread groups or processes. While the method of detailed "thick description" of a small social unit can provide rich and intuitively elegant data, there is genuine difficulty in observing the effect of larger social and extended time units on the immediate process being described. This is a kind of question that historical and survey researchers seem best equipped to answer.

"Naturalistic" method is by no means free of the procrustean distortions of technique and procedure when it must translate subtle social interaction, visual phenomena, and internal motivations into preexisting academic terminology and frames. Translation into verbal as opposed to statistical "languages" still places great distance between the community of investigators and the actual event/community at the center of a particular report. Mediation is inescapable. This is, no doubt, why the issue of *reflexivity*—the reflexive awareness of a researcher's observational activity as well as the effect of observation on phenomena—is such an issue among cultural anthropologists studying symbolic and communication behavior (Myerhoff & Ruby, 1982; Rabinow, 1982). Having stripped away the rhetoric of objective "data" that animates some of our more philosophically naive research traditions (though not some of the more recent strains of the philosophy of science), it is inevitable that issues of reflexivity would come to the fore.

This leads us to another question: What is the degree to which cultural-level explanations can be reduced to primitive psychological or physiological terms? The argument against reduction is clearly evident in the work of the anthropologist Geertz (1973, pp. 145ff., 216ff.) and is argued elegantly by the philosopher Taylor (1964, 1980). Lindlof mentions the objection in his article. Clearly, simple reduction of cultural-based arguments is not possible. Having said this, the typical writer begins to ignore evidence from these areas. Psychological and physiological processes can definitely act as constraints on the range of explanation and behavior at higher levels of analysis. Our model of audience and of media as "lived" must clearly cut across all these levels, including media stimulus as a physiological process in the decoding audience member. If meaning is a process pulsing through the audience member, then neurons will be just as relevant as reference groups.

I sometimes fear that the attack on the objectivity of social scientific methods is often confused with an attack on quantification. The number is portrayed as something foreign, inhuman, a product of some distant machine culture. There are few things that are more human—defined as essential and unique products of the human mind—than the concept and use of numbers. The concept of number exists nowhere else other than in the human mind. Like language, it is used to model the phenomena we all experience. It is exasperating when those who claim to study and embrace language fail to see numbers as simply another language, another means of making a statement. Like all statements, it has only the relative claim to truth and validity found in any other human utterances. But there is little doubt that for *some* statements and relations, there are few other languages that may be more precise or articulate. Even though we commonly observe the naive empiricist smugly flaunting a table of numbers in the same manner that a preacher waves his bible, this misuse should not lessen their value any more than it makes them unimpeachable. Unfortunately, the "data" never "speak for themselves," be they "naturalistic" or "numerical."

REFERENCES

Geertz, C. (1973). Thick descriptions: Toward an interpretive theory of culture. In *The interpretation of cultures*. New York: Basic Books.

Holsti, O. (1969). *Content analysis for the social sciences and humanities*. Reading, MA: Addison-Wesley.

Lasswell, H. D., Leites, N., & associates (1949). *Language of politics: Studies in quantitative semantics*. Cambridge, MA: MIT Press.

Meyerhoff, B., & Ruby, J. (1982). Introduction. In J. Ruby (Ed.), *A crack in the mirror: Reflexive perspectives in anthropology* (pp. 1-38). Philadelphia: University of Pennsylvania Press.

Rabinow, P. (1982). Masked I go forward: Reflections on the modern subject. In J. Ruby (Ed.), *A crack in the mirror: Reflexive perspectives in anthropology* (pp. 173-186). Philadelphia: University of Pennsylvania Press.

Reisman, D. (1950). *The lonely crowd*. New Haven, CT: Yale University Press.

Taylor, C. (1964). *The explanation of behavior*. New York: Humanities Press.

Taylor, C. (1980). Understanding in human science. *Review of Metaphysics, 34*, 25-38.

The Practice of
Attendance and the
Forms of the Audience

THOMAS R. LINDLOF
University of Kentucky

S EVERAL years ago, Salomon and Cohen (1978) proposed that television viewing is not a behavior, but rather a group of constructs whose actual employment in measurement depends on the conceptual interests at hand. The authors argued that the meanings of television viewing in a given study "are derived from theoretical conceptions of what it is in television that may have one or another effect when viewed" (p. 266).

The televiewing-as-construct idea opened to view some assumptions that were (and often still are) taken for granted. Since the article's publication, a variety of cognitive, affective, and socially contingent components of message reception have been identified that appear to explain behavioral outcomes more satisfactorily. Certainly, the three chapters presented here bear witness to some of the fundamental rethinking of the media reception process that has been under way for some time now.

However, a basic ambivalence about the status of the *individual* in mediated communication processes emerges in these chapters. How much does the audience member know about his or her reasons for using media, and how in fact do we treat those reports? What do we do with the expressions, verbal and nonverbal, emitted by real audience members? Is the individual's assessment of the dimensions of television content an act that relates meaningfully to cognitive process, or is it a social performance to be evaluated primarily in that light? Is the individual an autonomous "user"? Is there an audience made up of aggregate exposures for a message, or is the audience constituted of social categories with differential needs, preferences, and perceptual capacities, or is our audience language itself all wrong, perhaps to

Correspondence and requests for reprints: Thomas R. Lindlof, Department of Telecommunications, University of Kentucky, Lexington, KY 40506.

Communication Yearbook 11, pp. 133-145

be replaced by concepts and indicators based in types of social action? I would further argue that this ambivalence is not unique to the three authors, but is characteristic of much of the research conducted in the area of media audiences. Salomon and Cohen's constructs provide little guidance, since they position the individual's perceptions of content at the center of the television effects universe.

What is interesting about the chapters by Biocca and Gunter, when they are directly compared, is that both are concerned with how the individual is structured for operating in mediated communication environments. But the concern is approached and expressed very differently by the authors. Gunter treats the issue of differential social perceptions of media content domains, while Biocca is concerned with some longstanding assumptions regarding media user activeness. These differences should become manifest in the two commentary sections that follow, particularly as they are interpreted through the position developed in my own chapter—which was also written with the status of the individual as a background issue.

WHO IS COMPETENT TO
PRACTICE TELEVISION VIEWING?

At first blush, the absurdity of this question—implying some sort of "meritocracy" for gaining access to the television medium—might seem to call for a reappraisal of this author's intentions. The question is intended, however, to call attention to some central issues, conceptual and methodological, that Gunter raises concerning how audience members perceive social behavior portrayals on television. Specifically, Gunter posits a "sophistication" of individual response to television portrayals that belies seeming consistencies in the content itself. My comments are mostly directed to assumptions regarding the sources of and skills involved in sophistication in mediated communication.

Gunter's research agenda—explaining how social perceptions interact with mediated content—is arguably one of the most complex in all of mass communications. First, one reason for this complexity is simply the large number of spurious factors that can account for variances in what are often statistically significant but substantively small effects. Although some spurious factors have been identified (and research artifacts could be included here), few are amenable to satisfactory measurement or control. The many spurious factors that have likely not yet been identified may remain so if verification continues to operate as the near-exclusive mechanism for theory development.

Second, as Lindlof and Meyer (1987) have remarked, a "big effect" is seldom the outcome of a singularly big cause, but rather of a cumulative sequence of multitudinous "small causes" that interact over an extended period of time. An individual's endorsement of a social perception statement may be associated with media use and media perception variables. But it may also index the cumulative effect of responses to many messages—some mediated, some not—that systematically reinforce each other. The large aggregate effect can therefore be seen as a summary destination representing varying intensities for different individuals, reached by many different routes. Conversely, the processes by which an effect is attenuated in the course of normal social interaction are probably quite common, but seldom studied. As we grant the importance of the questions Gunter raises, we need also to recognize the magnitude of difficulty involved in defining the appearance of these phenomena, not to mention developing causal models of their occurrence.

A final point to be made about the complexity of the processes under Gunter's examination concerns the question of how much autonomy to attribute to content and format characteristics of the message. Consistent measurements of content are, of course, warranted by the supposition of some autonomy of the message. That is, exhaustive and mutually exclusive category systems can be devised for a given class of messages; these category systems provide a means for systematically describing content, as well as a basis for understanding audience responses to those descriptions. Yet many would argue that the procedures of content analysis reify the autonomy of the message. This is Gunter's most telling criticism of much of the cultivation analysis literature, and the point of departure for constructing his own position.

To summarize Gunter's review, cultivation analysis is fundamentally flawed by having built its arguments on an assumption that audience members perceive television in the same terms as the content categories of the message system analysis phase of the Annenberg program. Although the application of a priori coding schemes to content samples may yield reliable patterns of particular attributes over time, their relationship to viewer-generated categories applied to similar content samples is problematic. Gunter cites the results of several studies that were designed to elicit viewer perceptions of such ostensible content characteristics as violence and sex-role-typed social information. It is demonstrated that viewers may rate certain kinds of violence as low in importance, while other kinds rate higher. For example, "familiarity of surroundings" differentiates British viewers' perceptions of seriousness of violent acts regarding American and British television series. Gunter also reviews evidence that would disabuse us of the notion that heavier consumption of television is associated in some linear fashion with more "traditional" or "sexist" perceptions of gender roles. Rather, selective biases operate among particular "population subgroups" that inflect interpretations of both television portrayals and their real-world counterparts in directions other from those implied by content analysis. For example, his research program has revealed that heavy viewers of action-adventure content perceive female characters as more independent of men rather than as less independent and also as less interested in romance.

Gunter's conclusion regarding the lack of efficacy of content analysis for predicting audience perceptions aligns with my own discussion of how the audience semiotic is assumed in certain media research paradigms. Using my language, Gunter would reject the "presented meaning" assumption, and instead seek to learn how audience members go about the purpose and activity of assigning meaning to mediated content. My reading of the climate of opinion in the mass communication research community is that most scholars would readily concede that audience perception cannot be directly inferred from content analysis results. This part of Gunter's thesis, it is safe to say, is not controversial.

In rejecting content analyses as perceptual benchmarks, however, Gunter proposes certain cognitive mediators in the meaning assignment process about which there may be more substantive debate. Two mediators that he posits as central to this process are realism discernment and story comprehension. There are differences between my conception and Gunter's concerning how and why audience members engage in meaning assignment—particularly with regard to realism judgments—which will in turn inform the discussion regarding the individual.

Realism discernment—or, alternatively, perceptions of television reality— is conceived as a highly active audience process in which a portrayal is assessed by criteria located in the viewer's direct experiences or societal-level distributions of the content referent. The cultivation analysis perspective proposes that systemic content distortions alter the social perceptions of the heavier-viewing respondent in directions indicated by the content characteristics under study. This perspective can afford to dismiss the actual exposure regimens of respondents for two reasons.

First, the message system analysis purports to show that content distortions are pervasive and rather uniformly distributed in entertainment programming. Second, the cultivation analysis program advances the notion that viewers do not exhibit content selectivity, but are instead ritualistically engaged with the medium. For both of these reasons, measures of gross viewing amounts are seen as adequate for discriminating the effects of exposure. (Some claim, however, that the viability of the cultivation hypothesis is not dependent on these assumptions.) For Gunter, this line of logic ignores the experiential frameworks of individual viewers who are actively engaged in discerning the accuracy of the televised representations of such referents as sex role. Reality perceptions are proposed as one of the principal means by which individual viewers' experiential frameworks are applied in construing mediated content.

For the interpretive community conceptualization of the audience, realism becomes a research subject only in the actions of persons for whom such conceptions—those relating to veridicality, accuracy, representativeness—are pragmatically relevant. Its utility, as a way of knowing the world, seems to derive from its capacity for creating a comprehensive nomological system. In other words, acculturation partly involves learning *how to name* different orders of reality. Concurrent with that learning, we come to know how realism operates as a basis for verifying the moral dimensions of our behavioral acts. Those displays that are judged realistic are generally taken for granted as such and do not become problematic until competing versions (competing for legitimacy, competing as qualitatively different alternatives) come to the fore.

The question, for the interpretivist, is not how realistic specific media portrayals are for population subgroups, but rather how and in what sociohistorical situations do particular individuals jointly refer to realism in social action. We would be justified in putting the concept "realism" in scare-quotes in this way since its signification among social collectivities shifts as a function of its precise usages for naming. It may be that realism, as segregated from other "nonrational" modes of cognition, is a profoundly Western conception. If that is the case, then part of our attention should focus on realism as a cultural construct.

Perhaps there is a more fundamental question that can focus this discussion of the nature of realism discernment: Who *is* the sophisticated viewer? The one who can effectively distinguish the fictional artifice and/or the social distortions seemingly endemic to the television medium? The one who is best able to maximize the complex dramatic possibilities of a program by employing an ideal story comprehension capacity, and thereby be able to recount character motivations, enabling conditions, consequences of acts, and higher-level inferences? The one who is capable of explicating many different orders of interpretation from one particular media "text"? Or, perhaps, those cognoscenti who can tell the true hidden agenda of content designers and distributors?

As with the prior discussion of realism, my own understanding of sophistication is in reference to media use competencies that are sensical only as culturally variant constructs. Like the criticisms that intelligence tests are either culturally biased or represent limited domains of ability, the case for a global definition of television viewing competence runs into similarly contentious queries: competence for whom, under what conditions, and for what purposes? Aptitude testing, of course, is predicated on linguistic, logico-mathematical, and other reasoning abilities that relate to economically valued skills repertoires in society. The practical value of the tests lies in their capacity to discriminate individuals in terms of skills that are functional for certain institutional roles. The practical value of similar criteria of media use competency has yet to be determined.

One would be wrong in saying, however, that there are no sophisticated viewers or that no standards of viewing competence exist. For the active audience proponents that Biocca critiques, competence consists of a rational self-analysis of needs and the most efficient means of gratifying them. For Gunter, self-analysis is also required, but in conjunction with knowledge of the many dimensions by which television portrayals deviate from known reality criteria. These accomplishments by the individual undoubtedly occur in certain situations.

Everyday competency in the use of media is rarely subject to evaluation by an expert examining board. It is equally improbable that the individual can establish an isolable standard of competency by fiat, without having to display those acts that support the competency claim to public inspection. Rather, media-use competency standards are established and maintained by a "jury of one's peers." They arise in the contexts of social action in which knowledge and characteristic uses of mediated content are normative features. The sophistication involved in "troping" with the experiential and format frames that the media routinely circulate—employing mediated content in interaction and discourse—would seem to be of a higher order than the rather didactic expectations of perceived reality criteria. Moreover, the bias operating in such criteria against the acceptability of fantasy engagement with content would seem to rule out the serious study of a number of practical applications of the viewing experience. For example, Radway's romance readers engage themselves deeply in their chosen textual material, but show no apparent signs of misunderstanding the stylized narrative devices and characters for the way the world really is. The romance reader's competence—notably indexed in the abilities to distinguish different levels of romance novel quality and to make the reading activity fit in the interstices of family life—originate in the intersubjective agreements by which her feminine roles are recognized by others. Constant attention to the romance form's deviations from normative male and female behavior would clearly be dysfunctional for her purposes. Debate within and between interpretive communities about what is of importance in a domain of popular culture is typically a salutary activity, but not efforts at a final arbitration.

In conclusion, Gunter has offered compelling reasons for rejecting simplistic formulations of the relationships between content, selective exposure, and social perceptions. As he correctly points out, content analysis remains highly useful as a data source of broad patterns of mostly manifest content characteristics. But its value as a source of hypotheses of audience perceptions and behavior is extremely limited. The need to develop models of message response that more closely approximate the processual complexity of actual audience activity is clearly and convincingly stated.

However, treating a priori reality variables as a general mediator of televised social information may be as potentially misleading as the application of a priori content codings if our intent is to understand the meaning assignment process of committed media users. Current research practices aggregate normative realism perception values of individuals drawn from population subgroups. The assumption is that each individual possesses a set of values on some realism endorsement measure that are common to the subgroup of which the individual is a categorical member. There is no evidence of ecological validity for any such common metric within or across subgroups. Moreover, there is seldom an adequate justification offered for the different reality perceptions that reside in such diverse subgroups as women, Britishers, racial minorities, or children. Ipsative research procedures might be better suited for studying individual perception, although other procedures would be required for investigating the social processes of reality concept formation. While story comprehension as perceptual mediator was not examined here, one could pose similar questions about it. Does story comprehension represent an idealized and possibly culturally variant model of sophisticated viewing, and in what social-contextual conditions is it functional? The question—Who is the sophisticated viewer?—is one that should logically begin in the venues where viewers consensually define competence and its demonstrations.

WHAT FORMS SHOULD
WE MAKE OF THE AUDIENCE?

It is taken for granted that whenever researchers undertake to study a media audience for any reason, they are investigating an entity that exists "out there," to be located empirically and subjected to research operations.

Simultaneously, we use a veritable profusion of terms in our professional writings and utterances to refer to that which an audience does. While I prefer to speak here of a media reception process, there will be differences of opinion and usage regarding what lexeme might best replace *reception*. Among the terms on the (probably incomplete) menu are: *attendance, exposure, consumption, selection, usage, interpretation, decoding, transaction*, and *negotiation*. The difficulty, at least for those monists who wish for a metatheoretical Esperanto, is that the terms are hardly synonymous. Some of the terms imply activity, others passivity. Some imply choice behavior, while others imply that there are modes of understanding. In some way, each term represents a site for congregating particular research problems, literature, methodology, applications, and pedagogy.

The point of this exercise is that each researcher, singly but also as a subscriber to a shared view, creates the audience through his or her research language and associated research tools. The data and claims will obediently conform to the manner by which such language engages the everyday life of which media are a part. In a manner of speaking, the audience waits only for the one who seeks it.

In the spirit of this way of looking at things, Biocca has produced an irreverent critique of the concept of the "active audience." He has explored the historical antecedents and ideological commitments that, inadvertently or not, shaped an entire generation of research efforts of audience uses of media. Notably, he provides almost no assessment of the actual empirical result of this substantial body of work. Rather, Biocca fixes on the rhetoric of audience activity as found in the seminal as well as more recent theoretical statements. This rhetoric is then turned back on the warrants and methodologies utilized in investigating audience activity in order to question the value of the claims generated by the enterprise in toto. The boldness of the critique is indexed in the emptiness he finds in concepts that others find meaningful. His move is analogous to the agnostic who regards sacred vestments as mere clothes that are used in rituals of the faithful.

There is much of value in this evaluation. The idea that the individual's motivations constitute the locus of control for mediated communication— here the self-actualizing media consumer—has tended to obscure much about engagement with media that is either routinized in its operation or constituted by social agreement. In other words, there is a lot going on in mediated communication that is never clearly reported to the individual, either by the environment or by his or her own central nervous system.

The model of the fully awake television viewer—selective, utilitarian, intentional, involved, and impervious to influence—is seen by Biocca as having been necessitated by a desire to counter the concept of media determinism. The"specter of mass society," as well as several empirical failures to support direct effects, led to a reconsideration of the role of individual differences in information-seeking behavior. The new argument proposed that if media campaigns failed to produce massive and uniform impacts, then there must be some psychological analogue of message "filters" operating among audience members that are in turn determined by differential motivational sets. It was apparently a short step from that analysis to the proposition that the selection and processing of mediated content had to proceed through actively conscious evaluation. Assertions of activity in the audience, according to Biocca, rapidly assumed the eminence of ideology. The famous dictum that media do not do things to us, but rather we do things with the media, may perhaps possess an inherent attractiveness for scholars in a political culture where individual self-determination is the article of faith. The author is, therefore, willing to entertain the idea that some active audience proponents were guided, or misguided, by beliefs that had little to do with a scientific attitude toward the audience.

Apart from the claim of its highly charged ideological origins, one other problem impeding understanding of audience activity is simply that such diverse phenomena as choice behavior, social action, intentionality, and cognitive effort among others have been conflated. That is, in the effort to extend the explanatory reach of activity to all levels of audience phenomena, large inventories and typologies of motivations, needs, and gratifications have been developed that inappropriately mix a host of concepts under a common rubric. In the process, whatever clear signification "activity" once had is now clouded.

A related problem concerns the low threshholds for conceptualizing and recording audience activity. Biocca questions the value of the selectivity concept since it is seen simply to reference choosing behavior, which he claims is impossible not to do at some minimal level. And at a decisive point later in the chapter, he asks, "Does . . . locus of control lie in the social origins of motivations, in some psychological force, in the formal structure of the medium itself, in the myriad content and the persuasive ('great'?) communicator, or does it reside in the individual?" (p. 67). All of those possibilities except the last do not require a provision for conscious control by the audience member. Indeed, the active audience position is faulted for its exclusive reliance on self-reports of the conscious individual. Since any self-report indicates *some* self-monitoring, such an unusually low threshold for indexing activity produces findings (particularly as expressed in the uses and gratifications literature) that are unfalsifiable and therefore of little scientific value.

As part of his mission for depolarizing the activity-passivity "force field" that is alleged to have aligned mass communication debate for so long, Biocca proposes that it is not necessary to deny the activeness of the organism and its ideation. But, it is necessary to consider all the forms through which cortical activity operates: unconscious, preconscious, and conscious. Drawing on recent neurological and cognitive psychological work, the author begins a conceptualization of the human actor as operating consciously—in terms of self-monitored computational acts—on a limited range of perceptual information that arrives only after it has been processed at many levels below awareness. Although the unconscious (as a sort of staging area for conscious thought) has been a feature of psychological discussion for nearly 100 years, the preconscious is relatively new. Biocca is not entirely clear in his description of it, but the preconscious apparently functions in a modular way to alert the organism to changes in the environment of a highly specific nature. The preconscious also prepares the organism for and executes particularized responses not under review by the centers of consciousness. (A discussion of the implications of the modularity thesis for information processing theory can be found in Fodor, 1983.) The orienting reflex is one preconscious response to visual/auditory stimuli. Other kinds of visual analysis, driven by salient features of the target, are also carried out preconsciously prior to admittance to the conscious. Therefore, the preconscious achieves efficiencies for the organism by maintaining perceptual vigilance and early response mobilization.

A few preliminary experiments involving priming techniques and brain activity monitoring are discussed in regard to the role of the preconscious in responses to television. Most of Biocca's case, however, is built on reinterpretations of extant "active audience" research concepts. Thus he notes that debate has recently shifted away from the audience passivity thesis, and toward the question of whether viewers behaviorally *react* to changes in the television stimulus field, or instead utilize schematic representations of television content structures (based largely on the organization of formal features of content) that efficiently allocate attention from other activities. The major body of research centering on this issue, including that produced by Daniel Anderson and his associates (e.g., Anderson & Lorch, 1983), indicates that the mature child viewer is more likely to direct attention to the television when the stimulus is moderately complex in order to make optimal use of existing knowledge schemas. Younger children, on the other hand, are less efficient in their attentional behavior due to incomplete schematic representations. Biocca notes that the evidence of extended looks by the child across content feature boundaries—called "attentional inertia"—could be viewed as a stimulus-driven process (although Anderson and Lorch interpret it as a sense-making effort by the child). He goes on to suggest that even the seemingly purposive pattern of attending to informative "cues" of the program are actually patterns of habituation. Current models of top-down schema processing, he states later, exaggerate the independence of the human actor from information inhering in the stimulus.

In assessing the overall effort, Biocca's presentation offers a hardy corrective to some widespread and perhaps unfounded assumptions about the media audience. It is obviously too early to foreclose the possibility that many of the levels of media use, from physiological response to larger-scale social action, operate outside the autonomous and conscious gaze of the individual. In point of fact, there are as many indications of the highly routinized character of media use as the active and purposeful. He may be less succinct in the final section of the chapter, where the agenda for future research casts a very expansive net over some new and not-so-new paradigms. The following comments, stimulated by the Biocca essay, suggest directions for thinking about the role of the individual and about research metaphors in mediated communication.

What Can We Learn from the Audience Member's Self-Report?

We can answer this question with "quite a lot and not very much." Obviously there is a need to investigate conscious processing without having to resort to self-reports, especially in order to avoid the confounding of the two in reference to activeness. I would argue that in tandem with that thrust, there is an equally compelling need to investigate the conditions under which the self-report itself is produced. The self-report is a special form of oral discourse, elicited and codified by the researcher. My own predilection is to enlarge the object of study in order specifically to understand self-report as discourse as well as a behavior contingent on internal cognitive organization and process. Despite some anecdotal and peripheral information that can be gleaned from studies conducted for other purposes, we know almost nothing about the conditions of mediated communication that either facilitate or inhibit accurate self-reports of past behavior patterns, ongoing motivational states, or the content of thought. Since uses and gratifications and many other research domains depend on these reports' accuracy, it is essential to know as much as possible about how they are produced.

In the sense that most audience members can provide, in response to appropriate questioning and probing techniques, detailed accounts in their own vernacular of how mediated content and the circumstances of media-use mean to them, many useful data *can* be obtained. First, there is the account's referential content, which allows us both informant data and experiential data that are often privileged to the reporting individual. That person's unique vantage is partly a function of the specific sorts of social interactions that occur over time. But also, the researcher's reconstruction of the first-order constructs by which the individual orients to mediated communication events is subsidized by the way that those constructs are expressed in interaction. Ironically, the individual may not be aware of those surplus meanings. This in itself is a matter of some theoretical interest. However, the individual's lack of awareness of all modalities involved in verbalization does not invalidate the value of the self-report, as long as the researcher is, in fact, motivated and equipped to account for those highly sensitive indications of sociolinguistic variation in the speech performance situation (Briggs, 1986).

In the sense that every individual functions in a pre-Copernican relationship to the world—in that all our knowlege is fundamentally informed by axes extending from our physical position in the world, as well as our positions relating to predecessors and successors in the historical world (see Schutz, 1932/1967)—the self-report *must* also be inaccurate. Despite the best efforts of agencies with social engineering objectives, the individual has his or her own reasons not to aspire to "lay scientist" standards of logical argument and evidential sufficiency. If we ask, for instance, the individual to provide *analyses* of his or her typical motives for mediated content choices, we should not be surprised to receive explanation instead. This shift poses major problems for any research protocol that turns critically on obtaining analytic reports from the individual.

Can we dispense altogether with the individual's discourse, self-reports included, and go about the business of obtaining the ever elusive veridical and uncontaminated response by other means? Probably not, if it is understood that (a) discourse is the major constituent element of human activity, and (b) discourse (and the categories of meaning to which it is bound) inevitably affects behavioral productions.

The Relationship of the
Conscious to the Other Black Boxes

Much of Biocca's analysis concerns decomposing the individual into those components of cognition that are conscious and those that are not. Moreover, it is suggested that the greater and the most critical part is not conscious. The active audience is therefore a myth. The individual is not only physiologically constituted to attend consciously to very limited decision-making domains, but is also the end product of a media socialization process that inculcates a set of natural-appearing media formats, content styles, and related attitudes.

A question arises as to the relative importance we impute to those processes that are conscious vis-à-vis those that are automatic, modular, and/or stimulus driven. Let us say that we were able to determine in moment-to-moment observation of multiple indicators of cognition, that 90% of normal televiewing is characterized by relatively nondirected thought routines. The other 10% may be attributed to directed thought in which higher arousal and activated propositional networks are indicated. Could we then make the claim that television viewing is an activity in which conscious thought and its concomitant products of directed scanning and evaluation play a minor part? I think not. It would be necessary to consider whether the 10% that is conscious consists of moments that are invoked at vital junctures in the viewing session. Is conscious processing necessitated by failures in the default values in the routines of unconscious or preconscious processing for adequately analyzing the stimulus features (if the argot of artificial intelligence may be permitted here)? It may also be that those elements of the stimulus that are perceived in the preconscious mode have an influence on the nature of the cognitions reported during viewing, or in retrospective reports. While the idea that the individual's conscious reporting system is mostly quiet during viewing is intriguing, it would be useful to know how particular moments of conscious evaluation influence succeeding nondirected or "automatic" routines in real time.

From the interpretive position developed in my chapter, a certain degree of nonconscious cognition is also necessary at the cultural level. Routinization, in the form of ritual interactions, is highly functional for discharging role-related acts (Langer, 1978). A variety of consciously executed tactics may be ultimately designed to allow certain processes or contents that are unconscious to remain so. The verbal slip, explained from either Freudian or information-processing perspectives, exemplifies the imperfection of those tactics. The verbal slip, however, cannot exactly be critiqued as a failure of interactional competence. The utilization of social action genres of mediated communication *can* be critiqued simply because conscious purpose is assumed. Part of the research interest must include those scenes where the individual assimilates the conventions for participating in genres. In such scenes, the individual may be acting unaware of the learning process that is being engaged. For example, children's strategies for attending strategically to television or other media may be culturally variant. Is it feasible to investigate how individual information processing ability is shaped by the kinds of interactional expectations that lead to communicative competence?

Controlling Our Metaphors

One could argue that the active audience concept's primary purpose (and one that might be recognized by most of its proponents) is that of a metaphor for organizing thought about communication. The use of a metaphorical framework for understanding a theoretical problem does not in itself constitute the blind adoption of an ideology. For example, it has been proposed that a "dependency" metaphor is effective for understanding how functional alternatives, communication channel affinity, need for ambiguity reduction, and other factors determine whether television is used by individuals for broadly ritualistic or instrumental purposes (Rubin & Windahl, 1986). The metaphor has utility, even though we do not need to take it as a literal description. A richly described analogue for an empirical phenomenon can have great value for focusing conceptual efforts. Perhaps a greater awareness of the potential seductiveness of metaphors for misdirecting research activities is one message from Biocca's essay that can be applied beyond concerns with the active audience.

REFERENCES

Anderson, D.R. & Lorch, E. (1983). Looking at television: Action or reaction? In J. Bryont & D. R. Anderson (Eds.), *Children's understanding television: Research on attention and comprehension* (pp. 1-33). New York: Academic Press.

Briggs, C. L. (1986). *Learning how to ask: A sociolinguistic appraisal of the role of the interview in social science research.* Cambridge: Cambridge University Press.

Fodor, J. A. (1983). *The modularity of mind.* Cambridge, MA: MIT Press.

Langer, E. (1978). Rethinking the role of thought in social interaction. In J. Harvey, W. Ickes, & R. Kidd (Eds.), *New directions in attribution research* (Vol. 2). Hillsdale, NJ: Lawrence Erlbaum.

Lindlof, T. R., & Meyer, T. P. (1987). Mediated communication as ways of seeing, acting, and constructing culture: The tools and foundations of qualitative research. In T. R. Lindlof (Ed.), *Natural audiences: Qualitative research of media uses and effects* (pp. 1-30). Norwood, NJ: Ablex.

Rubin, A. M., & Windahl, S. (1986). The uses and dependency model of mass communication. *Critical Studies in Mass Communication, 3,* 184-199.

Salomon, G., & Cohen, A. (1978). On the meaning and validity of television viewing. *Human Communication Research, 4,* 265-270.

Schutz, A. (1967). *The phenomenology of the social world* (G. Walsh & F. Lehnert, Trans.). Evanston, IL: Northwestern University Press. (Original work published 1932)

SECTION 2

TELEVISION CRITICISM: FORMATS AND FEMINISM

4 For Television-Centered Television Criticism: Lessons from Feminism

CAREN J. DEMING
University of Arizona

This article extracts from feminist texts an analysis of subordination to reflect on the state of television criticism in the hegemony of literary elitists. Examining television criticism itself, the issues of bardic traps, empiricist criteria, corporate authorship, and viewer autonomy are discussed. The liberation of television criticism from its literary and film heritage is seen in the recognition of the oppositional potential of television's melodramatic form.

We can now understand why there should be so many common features in the indictments drawn up against woman, from the Greeks to our times. Her condition has remained the same through superficial changes, and it is this condition that determines what is called the "character" of woman: she "revels in immanence," she is contrary, she is prudent and petty, she has no sense of fact or accuracy, she lacks morality, she is contemptibly utilitarian, she is false, theatrical, self-seeking, and so on. There is an element of truth in all this. But we must only note that the varieties of behavior reported are not dictated to woman by her hormones nor predetermined in the structure of the female brain: they are shaped as in a mold by her situation.

—Simone de Beauvoir, *The Second Sex*

No influx of talented directors or writers can offset the technical limits of the medium itself. No matter who is in control, the medium remains confined to its cold, narrow culverts of hyperactive information. Nothing and no one can change this, nor can anyone change how television's technical limits confine awareness. As the person who gazes at streams becomes streamlike, so as we

AUTHOR'S NOTE: Portions of this essay were delivered at the Iowa Symposium and Conference on Television Criticism, 1985, the Michigan State University International Conference on Television Drama, 1986, and the annual meetings of the International Communication Association, 1986. I thank Bruce Gronbeck for his suggestions on drafts of this chapter.

Correspondence and requests for reprints: Caren J. Deming, Department of Media Arts, University of Arizona, Tucson, AZ 85721.

Communication Yearbook 11, pp. 148-176

watch television we inexorably evolve into creatures whose bodies and minds become television-like.

—Jerry Mander, *Four Arguments for the Elimination of Television*

The history of women's art is a history of exclusion and confinement dating to the emergence of partriarchy. When men wrested economic and political power from women, it was logical that they also would appropriate fantasy and creativity; for women's stories were incomprehensible and fearsome. The Greeks excluded women (and slaves) from attendance (as either actors or audience) at their tragedies ostensibly because the presence of either inferior group threatened to debase the ethical and aesthetic character of the drama. Christa Wolf (1986) summarizes the interrelated developments that brought women and their goddesses under male control:

> This whole earthy-fruitful hodgepodge, this undisciplined tendency to merge and change into each other, this thing which it was hard to put a name to, this throng of women, mothers and goddesses which it was hard to classify and to count, was brought under control, along with the right of male inheritance and private property, after what appear to have been long, difficult centuries, which now are described as dark and have been forgotten. (p. 100)

Out of the public sphere—until the present century, really—women and their art were relegated to the domestic and the decorative, the sensual and the trivial.

As a case in point, women writers long were demeaned for being preoccupied with domestic problems and the emotions attending them. Such "frivolous" themes condemned stories about them to "hopeless mediocrity." The overwhelming need for liberation from such thinking was voiced by Beauvoir (1952/1977):

> How could one expect [woman] to show audacity, ardor, disinterestedness, grandeur? These qualities appear only when a free being strikes forward through an open future, emerging far beyond all given actuality. Woman is shut up in a kitchen or in a boudoir, and astonishment is expressed that her horizon is limited. Her wings are clipped, and it is found deplorable that she cannot fly. Let but the future be opened to her, and she will no longer be compelled to linger in the present. (p. 352)

Some 25 years earlier, Virginia Woolf (1929) saw independence as the prime necessity if an inchoate women's literature was to flourish. She implored young women "to earn money and have a room of your own, . . . to live in the presence of reality" (p. 114). She saw the woman writer as a looking glass "possessing the magic and delicious power of reflecting the figure of man at twice its natural size" (p. 35). Lacking the self-confidence to explore their own experience intellectually or artistically, women writers were distracted by criticism of their moral vision and accompanying values; and, with few exceptions, they altered their values "in deference to the opinion of others" (1929, p. 77). Woolf saw the lack of integrity as "the flaw in the centre that had rotted [their novels]." She marveled at the courage it must have taken Jane Austen, Emily Bronte, and George Eliot to have written "as women write" (p. 78).

Contemporary feminist critics locate the problem in the inherent androcentricity of dominant artistic forms and the inability of those forms to convey an experience that women recognize as congruent with their own. Rachel DuPlessis (1985) links the problem in narrative to gender simply and powerfully: "All forms of dominant narrative, but especially romance, are tropes for the sex-gender system as a whole" (p. 43). In her note to that statement, DuPlessis defines the sex-gender system as

> a linked chain of institutions such as the sexual division of labor in production and in the socialization of children, valorized heterosexuality and the constraint of female sexuality, marriage and kinship, sexual object choice and desire, gender asymmetry and polarization. (p. 209)

The sex-gender system works to subjugate women, as it has throughout the history of Western civilization, through the double jeopardy of containment and ridicule.

The connection between the problem posed for all women by the dominant androcentric ideology and the specific problems that ideology poses for artists and writers was made early by Woolf and others. Contemporary feminist critics identify the relationship between narrative and ideology as explicitly hegemonic, circumscribing the creation and interpretation processes. Drawing upon Althusser, DuPlessis (1985) rests her study of the romance

> on the proposition that narrative structures and subjects are like working apparatuses of ideology, factories for the "natural" and "fantastic" meanings by which we live. Here are produced and disseminated the assumptions, the conflicts, the patterns that create fictional boundaries for experience. Indeed narrative may function on a small scale the way ideology functions on a large scale—as a "system of representations by which we imagine the world as it is." (p. 3; quoting Althusser, 1977)

The absence of represented female experience and vision in dominant narrative forms thus conspires with the sex-gender system at large to maintain the marginal status of women, their ideas, and their art. As Bovenschen (1986) acknowledges:

> Women's absence from the hallowed chambers to which they were denied entry is now presented as evidence of their extraordinary lack of ability. The recourse

to nature for the substantiation of uniquely "sexual" characteristics postulated *a priori* certitude and guaranteed agreement. (p. 28)

The first principle of feminist criticism is the subversion of that tautology.

Elaine Showalter (1977) identifies three phases of development in women's writing under patriarchy:

> First, there is a prolonged phase of *imitation* of the prevailing modes of the dominant tradition, and *internalization* of its standards of art and its views on social roles. Second, there is a phase of *protest* against these standards and values, and *advocacy* of minority rights and values, including a demand for autonomy. Finally, there is a phase of self-discovery, a turning inward freed from some of the dependency of opposition, a search for identity. An appropriate terminology for women writers is to call these stages *Feminine, Feminist* and *Female*. (as quoted in Moi, 1985, p. 56)

As later writers have pointed out, Showalter's stages do not occur in a discrete chronology. Rather, any women's writing is likely to manifest more than one stage of development. The ambivalence of most women's texts makes Showalter's stages useful conceptually, if inadequate to categorizing women's writings. That ambivalence is a strategy for surviving "the transitional space between the *no longer* and the *not yet* without going mad" (Weigel, 1986, p. 73), a reaction to the tension between the longing for an authentic mode of expression and the forces suppressing that expression.

Despite the controversy over Showalter's formulation, feminist critics agree that the pursuit of authentic expressions of women's experience is central. Showalter's "female" stage more commonly is referred to by Anglo-American writers as "woman centered" in order to avoid association with biological determinism (see Moi, 1985, p. 51). A woman-centered analysis, therefore, acknowledges gender as socially constructed while presupposing "the centrality, normality, and value of women's experience and women's culture" (Eisenstein, 1983, p. xviii).

For critics, a woman-centered analysis is one that is "thoroughly genderized," to use Gisela Ecker's phrase. This means that the gender of both artist and critic, "including their relations to gender-values in their institutions and within the theories they apply," must be taken into account (Ecker, 1986, p. 22). Implicit in the feminist critical agenda, then, is the utopian myth of woman as authentic (not second) sex, woman seeing and experiencing herself as autonomous (not deviant) and complete (not lacking male traits) (see Weigel, 1986, p. 79).

Encouraged by the work of Woolf and (now) long lines of feminist critics, novelists, and poets, women have found the courage to write the stuff of women as women write. The result is a vast women's literature whose development parallels the incremental recognition of the validity of a distinct woman's vision in a wide range of disciplines.

What have women's history and the history of women's literature to do with television criticism? Although I would not trivialize the problems of women and women artists by suggesting that the problems of television and television critics are equivalent, certain comparisons are valid. My eventual purpose in exploring those comparisons is to articulate some lessons television critics might learn from feminist writers, who turned so much negative force to energy for good by discovering and then promulgating the merits of their own thoughts and expressions. Ultimately, I will advance the thesis that feminist modes of thinking may be applied productively to television. Specifically, I will suggest that feminist epistemology and ethics provide a way out of television criticism's predicament, a predicament born of traditional literary modes of critical thinking, traditional ways of thinking about television, and some realities in the role of television in American life.

Before we turn to the subject of television, however, a few words about terminology are in order. In this essay, *feminism* refers to "an analysis of women's subordination for the purpose of figuring out how to change it" (Eisenstein, 1983, p. xii, citing Gordon, 1979, p. 107n). Feminist criticism is by definition overtly political whether or not specific critical works also include a program of action for effecting change. *Feminine* is a term eschewed by many feminists because of its association with socially and culturally prescribed behaviors that subordinate women. To this writer, *feminine* is not necessarily pejorative. I use the term to refer to behaviors and attitudes commonly adopted by women, most of which are socially constructed, and some small (although undefinable) parts of which may be related to biology. Obviously, a feminine way of thinking or behaving is not necessarily feminist; however, it may not necessarily be entirely regressive, either. My point is to have use of the word as an adjectival form of *female*. This usage acknowledges the extensive influence of patriarchy on the construction of gender but stops short of throwing out the baby with the bathwater. Feminist writers need access to a fuller, not a narrower, lexicon than other writers have at their disposal; and redefining and reclaiming terms are as appropriate to the feminist agenda as coining new ones.

THE PREDICAMENT OF TELEVISION CRITICISM

That writing television criticism still is regarded in some quarters to be a futile, if not deadly, exercise is not news to communication scholars. Like the pots and potsherds of women novelists, television is too prosaic and mundane to engender valuable thoughts. The subject is so unworthy, in fact, that some academicians find themselves in the delicate position of uttering high-sounding statements about the meaning of television in one breath and adamantly denying they watch the cursed thing in the next. It was inevitable that the wet blanket thrown by literary elitists upon the study of all popular culture phenomena would extend to the critical study of television.

As history would have it, however, television was born in the heyday of scientism. Like the introduction of pool to River City, the introduction of television to the American home spelled trouble. The American love affair with its "idiot box" was a social problem. Thus the critical study of television (at least in America) was not merely irrelevant (as was the study of comic books or popular westerns), but it was entirely inappropriate. As its social and psychological effects were what we had to "discover," the tools of the social scientist were most appropriate for understanding the impact of television. Anyone foolish enough to look upon television as art, by any definition, was in double jeopardy.

To this day, aesthetically oriented analyses of television and television programs are easy targets. One must acknowledge that some critical work is merely descriptive and even that some critics are starstruck. As Beauvoir (1952/1977) said of women's faults, "There is an element of truth in all this" (p. 343). Even critics who are properly skeptical, however, and even those who surpass description to advance arguments (see Brockreide, 1974) are vulnerable if they find admirable qualities in television.

The Reality Criterion

One reason for this state of affairs is related to the historical dominance of the idea that television is a social problem. In the light of television's ubiquity, popularity, and power as an information medium, it seemed natural to use social reality criteria for judging it. Seen from within, however, the medium was driven by economic and, yes, artistic values, as well as by social values. Thus it was also natural that television would be found wanting in social realism, at best an ambiguous mirror (see Loevenger, 1968/1978), at worst a cheap and distorting reflector.

Ien Ang (1985) has identified two major flaws in the use of what she calls "empiricist realism" as a criterion for evaluating television programs, in this case, *Dallas*. First, no text can be a direct, immediate reproduction or reflection of an "outside world," the problematical nature of such a concept notwithstanding. Second, Ang found that Dutch fans of *Dallas* experience the series as realistic in some ways, even though they recognize that it is not empirically realistic. In other words, Ang's fans experience genuineness of characterization and effect in *Dallas* even though they are well aware of the fiction's constructedness.

Feminist literary critics also have rejected the social reality criterion. Moi's (1985) critique starts from the failure of demands for faithful reproduction of a world outside the fictive to consider the constructed nature of any reality. Her critique proceeds to the inability of "extreme reflectionism" to "accommodate notions of formal and generic constraints on textual production, since to acknowledge such constraints is equivalent to accepting the inherent impossibility of ever achieving a total reproduction of reality in fiction" (p. 46).

Using any empiricist concept of reality as a criterion for evaluating fictions also runs headlong into a clash with the feminist demand for the portrayal of positive role models. In 1970, I was asked—not unsympathetically—how feminists could argue for more realistic portrayals of women and, at the same time, for more positive role models in an arena such as government. In a film about the U.S. Senate (which at the time had no women members), would I want realism or role models? It is not surprising that so many women novelists have opted to write fantasy and science fiction, in which modes they are free to posit worlds unfettered by the reality criterion. More to the point, some feminist film critics use the term *corrective realism* (see Kramarae & Treichler, 1985, p. 163) to describe portrayals suited to the role-modeling agenda. The awkwardness of an attempt to unite such contradictory notions in a critical principle underlines the point that the reality criterion is critically and politically a dead end.

Focusing attention on the fictive nature, or constructedness, of so-called reality programs (news, documentary, talk, games) yields a more productive line of inquiry than demanding empirical realism from television fictions. Popular fictions, even preliterate ones, always have claimed to tell "the true story" of "what really happened." In retrospect, such claims mark the mythic overtones of the narrative. Instead of "How realistic is television?" critics need to ask, "Whose fictions are these? What culture(s) do they serve?" Framing the issues surrounding realism this way leads not to a dead end but to a higher level of analysis—more sophisticated models of balance and fairness, as well as of the audience's interpretive behavior. The critic's conception of the television audience was affected by other factors, which I will take up shortly.

The Bardic Trap

Of course, not all television critics succumbed to the reality criterion's inevitable condemnation of the medium. However, even critics who could see a positive role for television fettered it with circumscribed expectations. Fiske and Hartley's (1978) notion of *bardic television* illustrates this point. Characterizing television as a bard, those authors see its role as:

(1) To *articulate* the main lines of the established cultural consensus about the nature of reality.
(2) To *implicate* the individual members of the culture into its dominant value-systems.
(3) To *celebrate,* explain, interpret and justify the doings of the culture's individual representatives in the world out-there.
(4) To *assure* the culture at large of its practical adequacy in the world by affirming and confirming its ideologies/mythologies in active engagement with the practical and potentially unpredictable world.
(5) To *expose,* conversely, any practical inadequacies in the culture's sense of itself which might result from changed conditions in the world out-there, or from pressure within the culture for a reorientation in favour of a new ideological stance.

(6) To *convince* the audience that their status and identity as individuals is guaranteed by the culture as a whole.

(7) To *transmit* by these means a sense of cultural membership. (p. 88)

Fiske and Hartley's list of functions is more comprehensive and more positively cast than most descriptions that preceded it. Yet, at least two implications of the bardic view of television are problematical. First, as the authors state,"these seven functions are performed *in all message sequences of the television discourse"* (p. 89, emphasis added). I do not wish to quibble over the accuracy of that statement—though I suppose one could—but rather to point out its implication that television is, by definition, monolithic and centrist. It is functionally antiliterate and, just like a woman, generically mediocre. Invoking Barthes, Fiske and Hartley (1978) compare bardic television to the ethnographic society's "mediator, shaman or relator whose 'performance'—the mastery of the narrative code—may possibly be admired but never his 'genius'" (p. 86, quoting Barthes, 1977). By precluding genius from being found on television, Fiske and Hartley have set a "bardic trap" for the television critic.

A second reason for the view that anyone who praises television must be an inferior critic is television's proclivity for melodrama. For good reason, as I will argue later, the marriage of television and melodrama is a natural one. To those who take the narrow view of melodrama, however, all those cop shows and soap operas are just so much evidence of television's depravity.

A third, and related, reason that critics are predisposed to negative criticism of television is the existential paralysis that derives from the absence of an appropriate artistic and critical tradition. Woolf (1929) described what she saw as the greatest difficulty facing early nineteenth-century women novelists:

> They had no tradition behind them, or one so short and partial that it was of little help. For we think back through our mothers if we are women. It is useless to go to the great men writers for help, however much one may go to them for pleasure. Lamb, Browne, Thackeray, Newman, Sterne, Dickens, DeQuincey—whoever it may be—never helped a woman yet, though she may have learnt a few tricks of them and adapted them to her use. (p. 79)

Television's lack of place in the critical canon stunted the early growth of television criticism. I am not referring here merely to the paucity of places to publish critical essays on television or of secure places in which the academic could practice television criticism. The problem runs deeper than that.

The Missing Auteur

Television is a medium that cannot be read in the strictly literary sense. The bardic voice, as Fiske and Hartley (1978) assert, is oral as opposed to literate. It easily avoids the "vast and wide-ranging . . . cultural repertoire not appropriate to transmission by television" (p. 86). This is a profound insight that is not without truth. However, it has a profoundly deleterious impact on the validity of television criticism as an endeavor as well. Based on a vision of the individual author's seeking individualized expression in an idiosyncratic text, literacy by definition devalues the expressions of the collective, and by implication, a medium preoccupied with such expressions.

So far, this discussion reiterates the idea of the bardic trap. The point I wish to make here is that the conception of the artist as a lone individual is inappropriate to a medium in which artifacts are produced by groups under the direct control of powerful economic institutions. The preoccupation with literacy and its standards of value (including the preference for individualized characters over stereotypes, see Seiter, in press) forestalls the attempt to develop standards appropriate to a collaborative art. Unlike film critics, who could salvage a remnant of literary tradition in auteurism, television critics have not found true auteurs, the efforts of Newcomb and Alley (1983) notwithstanding.

Most television programs get made only with the approval of powerful gatekeepers within the networks and production companies that service them. Television production is simply too expensive to be done speculatively. Once in production, programs evolve with the contributions of actors and technical staff. In series production, time constraints are so severe that programs are always polished to a limited perfection. Network censors, who must approve every moment broadcast by a network, have the power to delete the most carefully crafted scene on the basis of an "objectionable" word or image.

Ultimately, as Fiske and Hartley's notion of bardic television implies, the "author" of most television programs is the culture *as perceived by television's gatekeepers*. Critics need to develop and to apply standards derived from an understanding of the contingencies under which programs are produced. Such standards would recognize the influence of the culture at large as well as the culture of the industry and the particular organization from which a program emerges. Individual achievements should not be overvalued by ignoring the cultural context, nor should they be undervalued by insisting that only idiosyncratic works are significant.

The Problem of Closure

In addition to the practical problems created by applying aesthetic criteria inappropriate to the works under study, dedication to traditional literary standards presupposes the completeness of the "text" and, by implication, the passivity of the "reader." As Moi (1985) argues, the traditional humanism underlying the demand for unity and idiosyncrasy is part of patriarchal ideology and is

> constructed on the model of the self-contained powerful phallus. Gloriously autonomous, it banishes from itself all conflict, contradiction and ambiguity. In this humanist ideology the self is the *sole author* of history and of the literary

text: the humanist creator is potent, phallic and male—God in relation to his world, the author in relation to his text. History or the text become[s] nothing but the "expression" of this unique individual: all art becomes autobiography, a mere window on to the self and the world, with no reality of its own. The text is reduced to a passive, "feminine" reflection of an unproblematically "given," "masculine" world or self. (p. 8)

Aesthetic standards derived from such a conception of art and artists inevitably generate negative judgments of works created in an atmosphere of compromise, as well as those created by women.

These standards also interpose themselves between television critics and their subject by valorizing closure in the conceptualization of narrative (see Chatman, 1978, pp. 21-22). Television's preference for serial and series forms demands a kind of analysis different from that appropriate to the novel or poem. In one sense, the problem is to define the unit of analysis apropos of a particular critical question. Those who have been quick to pronounce a "discontinuous" (see Ang, 1985, p. 27) or "indeterminate" (see Allen, 1985, pp. 76-77) television "text" shallow and monolithic most often are those (unlike Ang and Allen) whose narrow definition of that text precludes any other judgment. In another sense, however, the problem is to define narrative in a fashion that depends less on traditional ideas of closure and adequately takes into account television's ongoing nature.

Viewer Autonomy

Finally, the traditional dominance of textuality and the autonomous author conspired with the social reality criterion to cloud the role of the audience in making meaning from programs. Despite overwhelming empirical evidence that the "hypodermic" theory of mass communication grossly underestimates the autonomy of the viewer (see Schramm & Roberts, 1971, pp. 8-10), critics have been slow to abandon the theory in fact. The assumption that watching television makes one "television-like" (see Altheide & Snow, 1987; Mander, 1978) undergirds much of what has been written. Whether the issue is violence, role modeling, agenda-setting, or attitude formation, television critics often leave simplistic assumptions of effects unstated even when whole arguments depend upon them. When stated, assumptions about effects rarely have been qualified carefully enough. The result is criticism that unravels all too easily.

Television criticism needs to be informed by more sophisticated views of the televisual text and the audiences for television programs. Fortunately, much groundwork has been laid by advocates of readership theories, poststructuralist and deconstructive theories (the varied descendants of semiotics), and their Marxist cousins. However, little direct application or extension of these approaches to American television has occurred. It remains for television critics to advance and refine these theories in relation to the medium they know best.

To summarize, the maturation of television criticism has been impeded by devalued status in the academy born of cultural elitism, by the dominance of empiricism (and especially behaviorism) coincident with the rise of television, by the resultant precedence of a social reality criterion of judgment, by the lack of a critical tradition generative of appropriate aesthetic criteria, and simplistic views of television production and reception. In the face of odds so great as these—not to mention the fact that the medium has existed as a mass phenomenon for less than a generation—the current immaturity of television criticism is more natural than astonishing.

LIBERATING TELEVISION CRITICISM

If the foregoing description of the "problem" of television criticism is at all accurate, the discipline indeed is in need of liberation. It must be liberated from limitations imposed by critics themselves as well as from those imposed by tradition and circumstance. It is here that the experience of women and the struggle for emancipation by women artists is most instructive. As they began stripping away the elements of "women's condition" in society on the way to self-discovery, that effort produced a burgeoning women's culture—literature, art, and science. The keys to that development are increased recognition that gender is socially, culturally, and politically constructed (and thereby susceptible to opposition) and increased confidence in women's own experience and vision.

Similarly, the keys to a powerful new generation of television criticism are increased recognition of the cultural, political, and economic constructedness of television programs of all types (including commercials and continuity) and exposition of the ways in which television is susceptible to opposition and development. Critics have an important role to play in that development.

Feminist writers have politicized not only criticism but artistic creation itself. Their subversion of established critical judgments abets the growth of a new television criticism. With Beauvoir as avatar, feminists have exposed the constricting biologism that has kept women in "their place." The lesson for television critics is that "TV biologism" must be rooted out and criticism politicized along more constructive lines. If more critics were to assume, as some clearly do, that television and, more important, television viewing, are not by nature depraved, more good television criticism would be written. Beyond that, if "television-centeredness" became a tenet of critical practice, a new world of discovery would be at hand. By "television-centered" I mean criticism grounded in thorough understanding and appreciation for the cultural, economic, and political milieu that frames the construction of televisual messages *and* specific, detailed analysis of the aesthetics (selection and arrangement of visual and temporal elements) of television programs with an eye toward identifying potential for change.

Repetition as Virtue

The following paragraphs constitute an agenda, no doubt incomplete, for achieving a more productive, television-centered television criticism. First, we need to recognize that the mundaneness and repetitiveness of television are necessary to its functioning. If we understand and accept the mythic and ritualistic functions of television, we can see its conventionality as the affirmation of an implicit dominant ontology (a term used by Feibleman, 1946) essential to popular forms. Repetition may thus be seen as something like having to be pregnant—with the tedium, discomfort, pain—as a prerequisite to giving birth. Critics, such as Fiske and Hartley, who have adopted such a view of television (if not the imagery) have found fertile ground to till.

If we are to avoid the bardic trap, however, it is not enough to see television as "empty" ritual. We must understand that originality cannot exist without repetition. Repetition is the background (a set of occurrences) that makes originality (one event) visible. As Edward Said (1983) puts it, "Originality is the difference between primordial vacancy and temporal, sustained repetition" (p. 133). In any medium of expression the redundant moments outnumber the original ones, as artistic production is a complicated process of "conquering and reclaiming, appropriating and formulating, as well as forgetting and subverting" (Ecker, 1986, p. 47). The obligation of the critic is to understand television's redundancy in such a way as to remain sensitive to its potential for originality, even for genius. To achieve an appreciation for the figure-ground relationship of originality-redundancy, critics must situate themselves between an analytical system and culture and, above all, close to the subject, as Said (1983) suggests:

> The inevitable trajectory of critical consciousness is to arrive at some acute sense of what political, social, and human values are entailed in the reading, production, and transmission of every text. To stand between culture and system is therefore to stand *close to*—closeness itself having a particular value for me—a concrete reality about which political, moral, and social judgements have to be made and, if not only made, then exposed and demystified. (p. 26)

If an "anthropological" view of television is to advance criticism (and I think it can), the critic must adopt the anthropologist's habit of going to the field, recorder in hand, to observe phenomena in their particularity.

As feminist researchers discovered the near impossibility (and political undesirability) of delineating uniquely feminine language (Moi, 1985, pp. 153-173) or aesthetic conventions (Ecker, 1986, p. 48), they began to advocate the close scrutiny of individual texts as those texts relate to ideology, psychology, politics, and other texts (see Moi, 1985, pp. 155-156, citing Volosiňov, 1929, and Kristeva, 1980). Television criticism, too, would benefit from a greater emphasis on individual programs, series, and even episodes.

Working out from the particular (rather than applying ready-formed analytical systems) gets critics closer to the subject *before* deciding which analytical systems with what limitations are appropriate. Psychoanalytic and semiotic analyses of television, for example, easily become exercises in the use of arcane terminology devised for literary analysis when they emphasize the *system* of analysis at the expense of greater understanding of the *object* of analysis. The danger in not having a large body of television-centered analysis to work from is production of criticism that, at best, is able to see only the most obviously repetitive features, missing the rest, and that, at worst, misunderstands those same repetitive features.

Moreover, repetition is not always tedious. Ang's (1985, pp. 64-66) analysis of letters from *Dallas* viewers reveals that they derive pleasure from recognizing familiar patterns of behavior common to popular forms. Further, the letters reveal that such conventions are not taken by these viewers to be referential but rather to be metaphors for problems and stresses of modern life. Speaking of Sue Ellen Ewing's alcoholism, for example, Ang asserts that "such a metaphor derives its strength from a *lack* of originality and uniqueness: precisely because it constantly recurs in all sorts of popular narratives, it takes on for viewers a direct comprehensibility and recognizability" (p. 65). It is this sort of insight that is likely to be "missed by the intellectual who only watches a soap opera now and then with a mistrustful attitude and seeks to evaluate the narrative only on the basis of its literary value" (pp.65-66).

Critics always need to be vigilant for condemnations resulting from failure to comprehend either the detail or the context of particular works. The lesson of feminism here is clear: male critics, failing to comprehend women's creativity, also failed to recognize that failure as a shortcoming of their criticism. Instead, they projected the shortcoming onto women and called it the "eternal feminine mystique" (Ecker, 1986, p. 38). Only through careful work by analysts intimate with the subject was the mystique dispelled.

The Incomplete Text

In addition to appreciating television's fondness for repetition, a second, related task is to look upon television programs as inherently incomplete, or heteronomous, texts rather than as autonomous causers of effects.[1] This move is a logical approach to textuality in a medium in which "authorship" is dispersed across collaborative teams and institutions. A "deconstructive" stance toward textuality argues that "the meaning of a text is diverse, multiple, unstable" (Batsleer, Davies, O'Rourke, & Weedon, 1985, p. 112) and finally produced by a "reader." The text manifests a "system of reconstruction-inviting structures" (Rimmon-Kenon, 1983, p. 119) that sometimes are referred to as constituting an "implied reader" (see Chatman, 1978).

The implied reader, as a manifestation of the text, is discrete from real audience members, whose highly variable responses to television have been demonstrated in the empirical literature. Out of respect for the variability in their sense making, *auditors* is preferable to *viewers* (a term implying too much passivity) and to *readers* (for obvious reasons) when referring to television's audience. Auditors, in sum, are actively involved in listening (sound dominates picture in television), examining, checking, and adjusting content to suit their experiences of the world.

The auditing process is not arbitrary. If it were, there would be no basis for linking audience responses to texts at all. However, the research of Ang (1985), Modleski (1982), and Radway (1984), for example, demonstrates that the matter of audience response to popular media is far more complex and variable than usually has been recognized. Recent feminist inquiry on this topic raises the issue of why women attend to books or films or television programs that are alien to women's experience or that even are misogynist. Gertrud Koch (1986), whose article is titled "Why Women Go to Men's Films," poses the likelihood of a film "subhistory" not entirely dictated by the male gaze, which gives minimal scope to female projections (p. 115). Such a hypothesis opens the inquiry not only into why women use "male" media, but also to why any auditor uses any medium or program and, as important, what auditors do in the "reading" process. There is little certainty about these matters either in the empirical literature or in the critical literature.

Film scholars, Koch among them, assert that television is an impoverished medium, far less able than film to provide interpretive opportunities. Literary critics, of course, made the same assertion about films until television came along to free film to be art. There is no reason television critics should accept this judgment. The history of film criticism and recent audience research argue for just the opposite stance. Television-centered criticism, together with what we may now call audience-centered criticism, promises to show us the openings in texts that auditors use to transform those texts to suit their various purposes.

An added advantage of the attitude toward textuality expressed above, which by now should be obvious, is its amenability to interaction with the analytical schemata of empirical research. For example, critics may find useful the research into the parasocial relationships that television auditors build with television personalities. Piccirillo (1986) employs the concept of *parasocial closure* to argue for the utility of a critical perspective that takes everyday televisual experience into account in analyzing television as art. Ang (1985) uses *Dallas* fans' and foes' own accounts of pleasures derived from auditing the series as a basis for her reinterpretation of the text. Tentative and limited in scope as such efforts are, they point in a promising direction.

Only barely tapped is the enormous potential for insight generated by the critic's willingness to engage with the empiricist's growing data on such topics as the physiology and psychology of perception (the ultimate locus of aesthetics), demographics, and attention direction, as well as qualitative data from ethnographic studies. To suggest that empiricists too might benefit from interaction with critics working along these lines is not immodest. With some practice, the deconstructive critic would be well-suited to teasing out the implicit assumptions in a set of questions or responses.

So much for modesty. The critic is well advised to be extremely wary of taking existing data about audiences at face value—that is, without first deconstructing the research that produced them. Marketing and demographic studies are notorious for employing assumptions biased in terms of gender, class, and race. As Koch (1986) observed of that administrative research:

> Flicking through these studies is like looking at a nineteenth-century atlas. They are spotted with blank patches, unexplored areas, which nevertheless already bear the names of the colonisers: the routes are known; who owns what has already been agreed. (p. 112)

Although Koch's analogy may be extreme if extended to academic research, female respondents have appeared as mystifying deviants often enough for vigilance to be appropriate there, too.

The Invitation to Interpret

There are other gains more intrinsic to criticism to be made by thinking of the televisual text as incomplete. Though not noted for the production of Brechtian, or "interrogatory," texts (see Belsey, 1980, p. 129) that highlight contradictions, television nonetheless produces programs that invite rather than discourage interpretation. *All in the Family* and *Hill Street Blues* are examples that readily come to mind. However, the greatest critical advantage occurs when we approach the more typical television text, the slick, hermetically sealed narratives that vituperative critics have discarded as hopelessly consumerist.

As Frank Kermode so graciously has pointed out, even the most well-formed narratives have their "secrets," even though they do not advertise them. Narrative secrets are those elements of plot that "form associations of their own, nonsequential, secret invitations to interpretation rather than appeals to a consensus" (Kermode, 1981, p. 89). What we make of the text, then, depends on how we attend to it:

> In reading according to restricted codes we disregard as noise what, if read differently, patiently, would make another and rarer kind of sense. And the text, almost with "cynicism," tells us what is there, confident that we shall ignore it. (p. 96)

Thinking of all texts as to some degree incomplete, if even cynically so, challenges the critic to action; for some secrets of the text may not be manifest in the text.

The Critic's Invention

It is the television critic's job—perhaps in concert with the audience researcher and surely in concert with the audience—to identify the unspoken or unenacted in a text. Whether we call this work decentering, deconstructing, or simply thinking critically, it is the critic's responsibility, regardless of the pretensions of the text: "The critic is responsible to a degree for articulating those voices dominated, displaced, or silenced by the textuality of texts" (Said, 1983, p. 53). As Belsey (1980) acknowledges, the responsible critic is, then, "frankly inventive":

> In producing knowledge of the text criticism actively transforms what is given. As a scientific practice it is not a process of recognition but work to produce meaning. No longer the accomplice of ideology, no longer parasitic on an already given literary text, criticism constructs its object, produces the work. In consequence the author loses all authority over the work. (p. 138)

The heteronomous televisual text (whose "author," ironically, we failed to find) enjoins critics to exercise their interpretive freedom, as auditors have done all along.

Acknowledging the creativity of the critical endeavor enhances rather than obviates the critic's obligation to be systematic in approaching texts. No matter how systematic the analysis, however, the inventive elements of criticism are certain to distress the scientistic empiricist. I would argue nonetheless that television critics have not been inventive enough, and not just in Said's sense. That is, they have not been able or willing to spend much effort imagining how concepts of empirical research might be adapted to the critical project; nor have many been willing to look as patiently at television as literary critics have looked at literature. As a result, few of television's "secrets" have been revealed.

Series Television

Appreciating the value of repetition and accepting the incompleteness of the televisual text pave the way for achieving a third task in the liberation of television criticism. That task is to turn attention away from literary criticism's traditional emphasis on narrative closure in favor of something that fits televisual discourse better. Series television is resistant to narrative resolution. Ellis (1982) suggests that the news update is a more proper fictive model than the well-made story for series television:

> The TV [*sic*] series repeats a problematic. It therefore provides no resolution of the problematic at the end of each episode, nor, often, even at the end of the run of the series. . . . Fundamentally, the series implies the form of the dilemma rather than that of resolution and closure. This perhaps is the central contribution that broadcast TV has made to the long history of narrative forms and narrativised perception of the world. (p. 154)

Although television resolves particular incidents, the underlying problematic of the series must remain. Here, then, is television's genetic link to melodrama, a form that expunges particular villains but does not offer redemption.

Adding the notion that auditors establish ongoing parasocial relationships with television personalities, who shamelessly trample the borders between representation and presentation, it becomes clear that new conceptions of narrative and of closure are in order.

Melodrama is a natural focus for rethinking television narratives. That idea is not entirely new (see, for example, Thorburn, 1982; Ang, 1985). The purpose of the second half of this essay is to incorporate implications of recent feminist research into that critical agenda. Specifically, this analysis is intended to demonstrate the potential for liberating television criticism through the application of feminist principles by exploring the particular case of television melodrama.

TELEVISION MELODRAMA

Two contemporary works of feminist literary criticism provide insight into the problems posed by the romance genre to women writers and readers: Rachel DuPlessis's *Writing Beyond the Ending* (1985) and Janice Radway's *Reading the Romance* (1984). DuPlessis analyzes the works of several twentieth-century writers selected for their "critical approach to the production and maintenance of gender categories" and subsequent reworkings of the romance plot and related narrative conventions so as to make "alternative statements about gender and its institutions" (p. x). The techniques for reworking the romance are what DuPlessis refers to as "writing beyond the ending."

Where DuPlessis's focus is writers of so-called serious fiction, Radway tackles the contemporary popular romance. Radway's analysis includes a historical survey of popular publishing and ethnographically oriented work among a group of romance fans. Her discussion of genre thus incorporates elements of text, institutional forces, and readership.

Against the background provided by the insightful treatments of the romance by DuPlessis and Radway, my purpose is to explore television melodrama to identify some points at which melodrama seems especially vulnerable to oppositional readings by audiences and critics and to form-breaking reworkings by television creators. My thesis is that by its very definition television melodrama is amenable to feminist opposition and, by implication, other types of opposition as well. After discussion of key elements of the melodramatic form, I will apply those ideas to soap operas and prime-time crime dramas for purposes of illustration. My purpose is not to devise an analytical system that works in all varieties of television melodrama. Rather, it is to show that the form is more open than the romance and therefore hegemonically more "leaky" than the hermetically sealed romance.[2] Recognition of melodrama's oppositional potential thus is central to the liberation of television criticism.

Like the popular romance, which Radway (1984) characterizes as "a myth in the guise of the truly possible" (p. 207), melodrama shrouds its mythic structure in topicality. Unlike the romance, however, melodrama is at its heart a modern form, an artistic response to the shattering of myth and loss of tragic vision, which Peter Brooks (1976) traces to the French Revolution. It is a response to "a world in which the traditional imperatives of truth and ethics have been violently thrown into question, yet where the promulgation of truth and ethics, their instauration as a way of life, is of immediate, daily, political concern" (p. 15). Having abandoned the likelihood of the absolute triumph of virtue, melodrama rehearses the confrontation with its enemies (clearly labeled as villains), expunging them over and over again. The drama "represents both the urge toward resacralization and the impossibility of conceiving sacralization other than in personal terms" (Brooks, 1976, p. 16).

According to Brooks (1976), melodrama is a theatrical substratum found in works of low art (those that attempt little, risk little, and are therefore conventional and un-self-conscious) as well as high (ambitious works whose conception and mode of representation constitute "the very process of reaching a fundamental drama of the moral life and finding terms to express it"; p. 12). Melodrama polarizes good and evil and shows them operating as real forces in the world. It uses "heightened dramatic utterance and gesture" to demonstrate the moral drama in ordinary, private life. It assumes that "the quotidian life, properly viewed, will live up to the expectations of the moral imagination." Finally, it posits good and evil as moral feelings, thus asserting that emotion is the realm of morality (p. 54).

Melodrama thus resists evaluation according to empiricist conceptions of realism (see Ang, 1985, pp. 35-37). Its realm is affect. As Ang points out about *Dallas*, melodrama evokes what Raymond Williams has called a "structure of feeling" (quoted in Ang, 1985, p. 45). More precisely, what Ang's viewers recognize is an authentically tragic structure of feeling, "tragic because of the idea that happiness can never last for ever [as it can in romance] but, quite the contrary is precarious" (p. 46). Melodrama's tragic universe is not that of "great suffering," the traditional domain of romance and patriarchal heroes, but of "what is usually not acknowledged as tragic at all and for that reason is so difficult to communicate, . . . the ordinary pain of living of ordinary people in the modern welfare state" (Ang, 1985, p. 80). To Ang, the melodramatic imagination (Brooks's term) is a normal aspect of modern life, a way of seeing ordinary suffering as special and meaningful. Watching melodramas—with their extravagant feelings and incidents at the expense of characterization—is therefore not compensation for or escape from the reality of daily life but a dimension of it (p. 83).

Melodrama's emphasis on affiliation, as opposed to individualism (its preference for moral order over glorification of the individual hero), not to mention its fascination with quotidia, points to the form's attraction to feminine conceptions of morality. As Carol Gilligan (1982) has demonstrated, women conceive of morality as a construct quite different from the construct formed by men. While men tend to see moral problems as the result of conflicting *rights*, women tend to see moral problems as arising from conflicting *responsibilities*:

In this conception, the moral problem arises from conflicting responsibilities rather than from competing rights and requires for its resolution a mode of thinking that is contextual and narrative rather than formal and abstract. This conception of morality as concerned with the activity of care centers moral development [upon] the understanding of responsibility and relationships, just as the conception of morality as fairness ties moral development to the understanding of rights and rules. (p. 19)

In the light of these gender differences, it is no wonder that daytime melodrama—with its endless talk of relationships and responsibilities—is attractive to so many women viewers and despised by so many men. More important, however, placing Gilligan's conception of morality next to Brooks's conception of melodrama as representing the urge toward resacralization in terms of personal responsibility and emotion suggests a link between the two that may help to explain why both women and melodrama have been despised categorically as primitive or trivial. Furthermore, in the restoration of melodrama as a valid form, we may valorize feminine moral thought as distinct from that of males.

Moreover, melodrama came to television gendered, with contrasting female-oriented and male-oriented species already evolved. Early nightime melodramas—most notably crime dramas and westerns—inherited radio's penchant for adolescent fictions. There, white-hatted heroes fought black-hatted villains, and women were kept at a distance. Wives and potential wives, if not anathema, were as irrelevant to the Lone Ranger and Joe Friday as to Kojak and the A-Team.

Daytime Melodrama

Yet television also inherited the soap opera, a species of melodrama that from its inception was peopled by women and—as often as not—produced by women for a predominantly female audience. Despite recent forays into terrorism and thievery of ancient artifacts, the primary concern of soaps is affiliation: familial, romantic, and social (see Allen, 1985, p. 74). Compared to popular romance—whose affiliative goal is the heroine's developed "self-in-relation" to one whose principal preoccupation is elsewhere in the world (Radway, 1984, p. 139)—the soap opera is preoccupied with the web of relations within a community whose members (predominantly white, middle-class professionals) bear similar characteristics and talk to each other a lot.

In addition, as Allen (1985, pp. 63, 76-77) points out in an intriguing discussion of the relative indeterminacy of the soap opera text, the form depends more heavily than less open forms on the auditor's creative participation: "The soap opera privileges that ever-changing moment [when] the reader comes to the text once again" after an absence as short as a commercial break or as long as several years. Drawing heavily from Modleski (1982), Allen (1985) contrasts the formal characteristics of the soap opera to those of the male-oriented narrative. The dominant form favors action over dialogue and ruthlessly reduces indeterminacies in order to arrive at a single moment of closure, solution, and knowledge. The soap opera makes the consequences of actions more important than action itself, introduces complications at every opportunity, and denies the desire for ultimate control by assuming its own immortality. In the male narrative dialogue is motored by plot and serves to explain, clarify, and simplify. In the soap opera, dialogue increases indeterminacy and retards resolution. (p. 92)

Thus the moment of narrative closure[3] in soap operas is more like a pause for breath. Closure in a soap always threatens to come unstuck, as indeed it sometimes does.

This is not to say that soap operas do not serve the sex-gender system; they are intensely conservative. However, unlike the romance's polar outcomes for the heroine—euphoric (marriage) or dysphoric (death) (see DuPlessis, 1985)—soap operas' outcomes are layered with potentialities for further development. In soaps, neither marriage nor death is final. Resistance to narrative closure provides an opening for speculation by auditors, as well as by creators, as to how the case itself may be reopened. That opening is not insignificant. Like an unsealed letter, soap operas' unsealed narratives may be easier to open than we might have suspected.

Next to its focus on female characters, the soap opera's preoccupation with process (as reflected in its resistance to closure and emphasis on the personal ramifications of actions) may explain more than any other factor the form's attraction to female audiences. In a sense, soaps' creators are always "writing beyond the ending," DuPlessis's term for a group of techniques subversive of the finality of narrative closure in the romance. Finally, soap operas may be the best of a bad deal for female television auditors. Like Radway's subjects, who view their romance-reading as a mild form of protest to a system they cannot change, soap opera fans may be getting from daytime melodrama the best that television has to offer them. More important, auditors of soap operas may be finding *in the form* something resonant with their experience as women. Even though the predictability of traditional romantic closure has an important compensatory function, Radway's (1984, p. 65) readers describe their fascination with the process of bringing heroine and hero together (which varies from novel to novel). The soap opera's preoccupation with developing (and dissolving) relationships, for better or for worse, is a female-oriented narrative convention.

This is not to say that the convention is unique to television or to soap operas. Every narrative faces a paradox: It must ensure that it will be understood (and so employs familiar, intelligible conventions) and it must delay comprehension "so as to ensure its own survival. To this end, it will introduce unfamiliar elements, it will multiply difficulties of one kind or another . . . , or simply delay the presentation of expected, interesting items" (Rimmon-Kenon, 1983, pp. 122-123). Soap operas exploit this paradox, some critics would say, to excess. Rather than to dwell on matters of taste, however, the point is to understand in meticulous detail the operation of the text in the televisual context (television-centered analysis) and to discover with equal sophistication what auditors do with the textual invitations and secrets identified (audience-centered analysis). This is a tall order because what we don't know about soap operas from these perspectives is far greater than what we know.

Prime-Time Melodramas

Prime-time melodramas would seem to speak less ably than daytime melodramas to women's experience. Nonetheless, they too provide evidence that melodrama is a leakier form than romance. This claim is especially true of television melodrama by virtue of the fact that television dramas are performed. Thorburn (1976/1982) has called attention to the sophistication of television acting, in which the required obedience to formulaic plots and characterization challenges the performer "to recover from within himself and from his broadly stereotyped assignment nuances of gesture, inflection, and movement that will at least hint at individual or idiosyncratic qualities" (pp. 533-535). Thorburn's masculine pronouns suggest (as do his exclusively male illustrations) that his point refers to male performers.

Although it is true that prime-time melodramas have been male territory traditionally, some contemporary crime dramas explicitly explore the gender differences that come to light when women invade that turf. Even such phallocentric series as *Policewoman* and *Charlie's Angels* contained moments when female actors were able to use their performances (if not often the script) to enter what Edwin Ardener (see DuPlessis, 1985, p. 41) called "the zone of difference," that tiny space created by the mismatch of dominant visions with muted ones. In contemporary series such as *Cagney and Lacey* and *Hill Street Blues*, the zone of difference remains small (dominant vision still prevails); but the zone of difference is entered more often and much less covertly than was the case in the past.

The very presence of female protagonists in crime dramas affords writers and actors opportunities to "break the sentence," to use Woolf's term for writing (or speaking) with rhythm, pace, flow, and expression that are authentically and unmutedly female (see DuPlessis, 1985, pp. 32-33). Even though the context of dialogue may be unquestionably male, the performer may inject a female voice or glance that indicates, however subtly, that she is unafraid of making gender an issue. With series longevity, relationships between characters can take on increasing significance. Judine Mayerle (1987) has demonstrated how characterization has assumed ascendancy over traditional generic elements of crime drama through the history of *Cagney and Lacey*. The series' increasing concern for Cagney and Lacey's relationship to each other and for the effects of their work on their personal lives and families is an instance of what Charlotte Brunsdon (1983) has observed as characteristic of soap operas: that they "[*colonize*] the public masculine sphere, representing it from the point of view of the personal" (p. 78).

Such a narrative strategy suggests that "breaking the sequence," Woolf's term for rupturing the expected order of events in a narrative to break their hegemonic inevitability (DuPlessis, 1985, pp. 34-46, *passim*), also is possible in television. Here the movement of television drama away from narrative closure and toward an emphasis on process (in some cases, the experimentation with high melodrama) is extremely significant. Moving the site of struggle away from *action* in the streets toward *conversation* in the precinct house or even the boudoir or delivery room moves it in the direction of the mind, where all things are possible.

Summarizing the achievements of novelists in this arena, DuPlessis (1985) notes that consciousness is the ultimate battleground for the attack on persistent gender-linked and gender-producing institutions, including dominant narrative:

> To change ideas about the world, and to depict such a change, it is logical that narrative, as a site of ideology, should focus on mind, as a site of ideology. These quests of consciousness have, moreover, as their major action the changing of seeing, perceiving, and understanding for characters. (p. 197)

Although clearly not feminist, some television melodramas demonstrate the movement toward interiority, movement that implies the possibility of making gender an issue within the form, if not feminizing it.

As I have attempted to demonstrate elsewhere (Deming, 1985), *Hill Street Blues* is high melodrama, an open form preoccupied with the search for a means to express the urgency and the difficulty of restoring moral order in a society run amok. Under the influence of the soap opera, perhaps, *Hill Street Blues* dwells on process, questioning the rightness of traditional definitions of morality and justice on a regular basis.

Although not formally as open to interpretation as *Hill Street Blues*, other prime-time series show a willingness to explore the zone of difference. In addition to *Cagney and Lacey* and *Hill Street Blues*, series such as *Remington Steele* and *Moonlighting* show women taking care of themselves in the male domain of crime fighting and, at least occasionally, calling attention to gender differences. The very premise of *Remington Steele* makes a feminist grimace, but the fact that Laura Holt has to pretend that she is not the owner of a detective agency in order to have a successful business in a male-dominated society makes gender an issue. The premise opens the crime show to the manifestation of opposition within the form or oppositional interpretations by auditors. *Magnum, P.I.*, as analyzed by Sandy Flitterman (1984), problematizes cultural constructions of masculinity, constructions that normally are totally naturalized in crime melodramas. By taking the zone of difference to the streets, such series turn those streets to liminal space.

In addition, melodrama's proclivity for exaggerated emotional intensity and extreme character portrayals makes the form amenable to denaturalization. Thorburn (1976/1982) indicates that when melodrama's reassuring conclusions and moral allegorizing are viewed as conventions, these recurring features of melodrama can be perceived as the *enabling conditions* for an encounter with forbidden or deeply disturbing materials: not an escape into blindness or easy reassurance, but an instrument for seeing. And from this angle, melodrama becomes a peculiarly significant public forum, complicated and immensely enriched because its discourse is aesthetic and broadly popular: a forum or arena in which traditional ways of feeling and thinking are brought into continuous, strained relation with powerful intuitions of change and contingency. (p. 532)

Melodramatic conventions thus mark the form's artifice, in contrast to more transparent narratives. When carried to the extreme—as in *Hill Street Blues*'s violent mood shifts, thick narrative texture, frequent and obvious use of ellipsis, self-conscious shooting style—opaqueness of form calls the auditor's attention to aesthetic manipulation. *Moonlighting*'s characters address the auditor directly, allude to famous films, and explicitly imitate film characters to similar effect. Such devices employed in the narrative serve to invite interpretation rather than to discourage it.

Although soap operas do not indulge in such obvious stratagems for stimulating auditors' critical faculties, regular use of dream or memory sequences (complete with soft focus and filtered voices) and other easily recognizable conventions mark the artifice of that form, too. On this point, I differ with Allen's (1985) position that soap operas' adaptation of the Hollywood realist narrative results in "austere" transparency. Rather, the very heavy-handedness of the soap opera style is a formal given that announces the entry into the liminal realm, which, in the case of melodrama, is the realm of relationships and emotion given privilege over action. This aesthetic precept of melodrama, of which auditors are aware, renders any remnant of the debate over melodrama's lack of realism irrelevant. Ang (1985) comments that it is viewers' awareness of the constructedness of *Dallas* that grants them the distance to indulge in the excessive emotions aroused in the melodrama.

Finally, melodrama also lends itself to another strategy used by Woolf to break narrative rigidity in the romance, the collective protagonist. Novelists have seized upon multiple protagonists and multiple narrators in opposition to the characteristic masculine tradition in narrative, the detached, "objective" narrator (Weigel, 1986) or the unitary progress of the romantic hero. These strategies blur the edges of characters' personalities, opening them to interpretation. The strategies represent a formal assertion that alternatives to the dominant paradigm exist even when (as is usually the case) the voices of opposition ultimately do not prevail.

The community of characters traditional in soap operas and now commonplace in prime-time melodrama allows for paradigmatic complexity, as Allen (1985) has pointed out. Although most voices of the protagonist chorus speak in the language of dominant ideology (Woolf's "inheritors"), some member or other will always function as an outsider and thereby as critic of that ideology. For Woolf, the technique allows "inheritor and critic to coexist in one narrative space" (DuPlessis, 1985, p. 174). Some television narratives, such as *Hills Street Blues* and *St. Elsewhere* (not to mention *The A-Team*), cast misfit-critics in a prominent and sympathetic light. Collaborative art that it is, television is created under constant pressure to routinize storytelling technique. The group protagonist is one means by which variants may be incorporated so that the tyranny of formula is never complete.

In concluding this review of the points at which television melodrama is amenable to the voicing of sentiments in opposition to dominant, male-gendered ideology—notably its ability to privilege process over action, to resist narrative closure, to make artifice opaque, and to utilize effectively the collective protagonist—it is appropriate to offer a qualification. Despite the capacity of the narrative to incorporate opposition, the pressures to silence it are enormous. I would be the last to suggest that the ideological force of television narrative should be understimated. Nevertheless, the very presence of even brief moments of resistance we can see manifested in the form is encouraging. Each time a female character speaks in her own voice, enacts even part of a story her way, attention is called to the need to recognize the all-important difference in her experience. As long as the difference is manifested at all, it serves as a reminder that Radway (1984) is correct when she states in the conclusion to her study of romances and their readers that the ideological power of cultural forms "is not yet all-pervasive, totally vigilant, or complete" (p. 222). Television melodrama, as startling as the idea may seem, is a locus of potential opposition to dominant constructions of gender in the popular arts.

CONCLUSION

The foregoing discussion of television melodrama uses feminist criticism and recent works of television criticism in an attempt to demonstrate the utility of television-centered analysis. The approach acknowledges the creative potential of auditors and creators. Most important, it acknowledges the creative potential of television criticism. Television-centered criticism is the opposite of parasitic because it actively mediates between textuality and social realities. The remaining paragraphs of this essay explore some implications of the assumptions basic to this analysis.

The first implication is that no critic can afford to ignore the political ramifications of the act of writing criticism. This principle stems from the Lacanian notion that art is a privileged realm of culture in the sense that it is an area where gaps in the existing symbolic order are likely to occur. If television art (with its public, popular, commercial, collaborative nature) is less privileged in Lacan's sense than other art, then television critics have greater responsibility to identify the lacunae in television's hegemony. Critics can understand and acknowledge the exploitation, however feeble appearing, of openings for opposition by creators and by auditors. Critics can provide a bridge between creator and auditor that encourages the liberation of both.

And critics can point to openings, thereby helping to create them, as yet unexploited by creators or auditors.

This is not to say that television critics should become preoccupied with proving that television is "art" by definitions developed for use in the analysis of other media. Just as the idea that women, given the opportunity, can be "as good as" men is dishonest (see Ecker, 1986), so is the idea that television can be "as good as" high art, patronizing and debilitating. As feminists see women's difference as an opportunity for creativity and not as a deficit, so should television critics be willing to seek out new, television-centered standards.

It follows that the television critic should be cautious when tempted to apply existing analytical systems to televisual phenomena. Like feminists, television critics cannot afford to be ignorant of current theories if they are to be allowed to practice criticism in the academy. However, as Ecker (1986) points out, "There is only a very fine line between committed criticism and academic conformism (p. 36). Critics need to be aware of the potential of existing theories to undermine development of different aesthetic forms. Television-centered criticism assumes, then, a healthy distrust of conceptual and methodological tools generated for other arts.

Moreover, canonizing works and forms should be placed low on the television critic's agenda if not eschewed altogether. Developing a television canon is extremely difficult in the light of television's youth and vitality. The target moves awfully fast for accurate critical aim. Literature and art critics have taught us that canons change with time anyway. Television critics should not be afraid to suspend judgments contributive to the establishment of critical hierarchies. For good political reason, television critics ought not to imitate their literary cousins, whose practice has in some ways inhibited rather than fostered the creative growth of literary art.

Janet Batsleer et al. (1985) provide a critique of the "consensus" of liberal literary criticism, whose values are intelligence, distinction, discrimination, evaluation, and judgment. These authors point out that canons are derived from these values, "not from any intrinsic properties [of works] but from the fact that [these values] necessitate a continuous process of comparative placing and opposition" (p. 29). Criticism thus elevates the normal process of discrimination engaged in by readers to the status of "transcendent ethical value." As feminists question whether they should be trying to bring the concerns of women to any already constituted body of work or to develop a practice that transforms criticism itself (see Batsleer et al., 1985), so should television critics question the impulse toward critical orthodoxy. The danger to television criticism is appropriation of its practice by old and inappropriate methods with their crippling assumptions.

Television critics should not be too eager to abet the progress of such a takeover. I do not mean to imply here that the literary and film critics now finding television a tempting subject of study should be told to mind their own business. Rather, television critics should lead the way by doing the primary research necessary to produce television criticism characterized by vitality and integrity.

At minimum, television critics need to understand televisual aesthetics as they are applied, to understand the implications of production processes (as opposed to emphasizing standards of judgments developed for finished works created by individuals), to understand the role of compromise and the impact of institutional and regulatory restraints, and to understand the role of affiliative themes and serial forms in shaping television discourse. Furthermore, television critics need to recognize and to document the variety of forms that constitutes the televisual text. This effort requires a willingness sometimes to study programs or series or commercials one at a time, starting with their concrete particularity. It means resisting, or at least suspending, the manly inclination to argue deductively from principles assumed to apply to all television equally. It also means being open to the possibility that televisual texts may be palimpsests, manifesting opposition under a glossy surface of consumerist or patriarchal values.

In short, I am advocating criticism that is unquestionably programmatic, the aim of which is to increase the political, economic, cultural, aesthetic understanding, appreciation, and critique of television. However, I am at the same time advocating criticism in which the absence of critical orthodoxy is a virtue, criticism that does not replace an old literary or filmic canon with a new television one. Rather, we need to amass detailed analytical work on television programs and the industries that produce them to use as the springboard to more general theoretical work. Without that work in hand, our arguments will continue to be more moral and ethical than intellectual in the best sense.

In closing, it is appropriate to comment upon the audience for television-centered television criticism. To whom should it be addressed? First, television critics should write for one another in order to develop a body of knowledge worthy of anyone else's attention. That is, we need to write criticism that, like traditional literary criticism, assumes a reader who is "educated, responsive to the text, [and] attentive" in order to advance our own knowledge agenda. However, this reader is not necessarily the "masculine [reader who is assumed to be] in command of and fully engaged by the high culture of the Anglo-American elite" typical of literary criticism (see Batsleer et al., p. 142). Television critics arise from a variety of backgrounds, a fortunate situation that inhibits the development of canonical hierarchies and requires the utmost precision and specificity in the application of terminologies and analytical methods.

Television critics also should write for more general audiences. As a group, television critics perhaps are most aware of the need for the general population to understand the social and cultural power of a medium so ubiquitous as television. The criticism that appears in the press and popular periodicals is scattered and mostly superficial, and media literacy is not yet a common goal of public school curricula in America, although it is elsewhere. If not writing for the popular press themselves, academic critics should be teaching courses required of journalism majors, at the very least, and advocating the inclusion of critical approaches to television in general education.

Finally, critics should work to cultivate an audience for television criticism among television's creators and gatekeepers. Unlike literature, a field in which creation and criticism are allied occupations, television writing and production reside in a universe far removed from criticism. Unlike drama and art critics, however, television critics are not regarded with hostility, either. They more often are thought of as benignly ignorant, a situation that could change if more television-centered criticism were written. The audience of practitioners and regulators is important if critics do not wish to abandon the utopian goal of having significant influence on television itself someday.

For those critics who hope that by their efforts television will go away, let me pose one last parallel to feminism. As Lenk (1986) suggests, the feminist agenda requires women to develop a new relationship to other women, an objective that sometimes requires women to neglect their relationship to men. The liberation of television criticism requires critics to develop a new relationship to television (what I am calling television-centeredness). Developing that relationship calls for ignoring some predispositions and suspending some old habits, healthy academic exercises undertaken to produce television criticism that is both wise and salutory.

NOTES

1. "The philosophical influence behind most reader-oriented approaches is phenomenology.... While autonomous objects have immanent (i.e., indwelling, inherent) properties only, heteronomous ones are characterized by a combination of immanent properties and properties attributed to them by consciousness. Thus heteronomous objects do not have a full existence without the participation of consciousness, without the activation of a subject-object relationship" (Rimmon-Kenon, 1983, p. 118).

2. The concept of hegemony developed by Gramsci (1971) is central to cultural studies, where it refers to the ability of dominant classes to exercise social and cultural leadership (as opposed to coercion) to maintain economic, political, and cultural leadership. "Hegemony naturalizes what is historically a class ideology, and renders it into the form of common sense" (O'Sullivan, Hartley, Saunders, & Fiske, 1983, pp. 102-104). Hegemony is never complete; it is always "leaky." The potential for opposition always exists because conflicts of interest between dominant classes and subordinate classes exist, and because there are voices to introduce opposition into the symbolic order. Art is seen as a privileged area, in which gaps in the symbolic order are most likely to occur (Ecker, 1986); critical analysis is a site where gaps are identified and moments of opposition described.

3. DuPlessis (1985) identifies the moment of narrative closure as one place where transindividual assumptions and values are most clearly visible, and where the word convention is found resonating between its literary and social meanings.

REFERENCES

Allen, R. C. (1985). Speaking of soap operas. Chapel Hill: University of North Carolina Press.
Altheide, D. L., & Snow, R. P. (1987). Toward a theory of mediation. In J. A. Anderson (Ed.), Communication Yearbook (Vol. 11). Newbury Park, CA: Sage.

Althusser, L. (1977). *For Marx* (B. Brewster, Trans.). London: New Left Books.

Ang, I. (1985). *Watching Dallas.* London: Methuen. (Original work published 1982 as *Het geval Dallas,* Amsterdam: Uitgeverij SUA)

Barthes, R. (1977). *Image-music-text.* London: Fontana.

Batsleer, J., Davies, T., O'Rourke, R., & Weeddon, C. (1985). *Rewriting English: Cultural politics of gender and class.* London: Methuen.

Belsey, C. (1980). *Critical practice.* London: Methuen.

Bovenschen, S. (1986). "Is there a feminine aesthetic?" (B. Weckmuller, Trans.). In G. Ecker (Ed.), *Feminist aesthetics* (H. Anderson, Trans., pp. 23-50). Boston: Beacon.

Brockreide, W. (1974). Rhetorical criticism as argument. *Quarterly Journal of Speech, 60,* 165-174.

Brooks, P. (1976). *The melodramatic imagination: Balzac, Henry James, melodrama, and the mode of excess.* New Haven, CT: Yale University Press.

Brunsdon, C. (1983). *Crossroads*: Notes on soap opera. In E. A. Kaplan (Ed.), *Regarding television: Critical approaches—An anthology* (pp. 76-83). Frederick, MD: University Publications of America.

Chatman, S. (1978). *Story and discourse: Narrative structure in fiction and film.* Ithaca, NY: Cornell University Press.

Culler, J. (1982). *On deconstruction: Theory and criticism after structuralism.* Ithaca, NY: Cornell University Press.

de Beauvoir, S. (1977). *The second sex* (H. M. Parshley, Trans.). Excerpted in R. Agonito (Ed.), *History of ideas on women: A source book* (pp. 343-360). New York: G. P. Putnam's Sons. (Original work published 1952)

Deming, C. J. (1985) *Hill Street Blues* as narrative. *Critical Studies in Mass Communication, 2,* 1-22.

DuPlessis, R. B. (1985). *Writing beyond the ending: Narrative strategies of twentieth-century women writers.* Bloomington: Indiana University Press.

Ecker, G. (Ed.). (1986). *Feminist aesthetics* (H. Anderson, Trans.). Boston: Beacon.

Eisenstein, H. (1983). *Contemporary feminist thought.* Boston: G. K. Hall.

Ellis, J. (1982). *Visible fictions: Cinema, television, video.* London: Routledge & Kegan Paul.

Feibleman, J. K. (1946). *The theory of human culture.* New York: Duell, Sloan, & Pearce.

Fiske, J., & Hartley, J. (1978). *Reading television.* London: Methuen.

Flitterman, S. (1984). *Thighs and whiskers: The fascination of Magnum P. I.* Paper presented at the meeting of the British Film Institute's International Conference on Television Studies, London.

Gilligan, C. (1982). *In a different voice: Psychological theory and women's development.* Cambridge, MA: Harvard University Press.

Gordon, L. (1979). The struggle for reproductive freedom: Three stages of feminism. In Z. R. Eisenstein (Ed.), *Capitalist patriarchy and the case for socialist feminism.* New York: Monthly Review Press.

Gramsci, A. (1971). *Prison notebooks.* London: Lawrence & Wishart.

Kermode, F. (1981). Secrets and narrative sequence. In W.J.T. Mitchell (Ed.), *On narrative* (pp. 79-97). Chicago: University of Chicago Press.

Koch, G. (1986). Why women go to men's films. In G. Ecker (Ed.), *Feminist aesthetics* (H. Anderson, Trans., pp. 108-119). Boston: Beacon.

Kramarae, C., & Treichler, P. A. (1985). *A feminist dictionary.* Boston: Pandora.

Kristeva, J. (1980). *Desire in language: A semiotic approach to literature and art* (L. S. Roudiez, Ed., A. Jardine, T. Gora, & L. Roudiez, Trans.). Oxford: Basil Blackwell.

Lenk, E. (1986). The self-reflecting woman. In G. Ecker (Ed.), *Feminist aesthetics* (H. Anderson, Trans., pp. 51-58). Boston: Beacon.

Loevenger, L. (1978). The ambiguous mirror: The reflective-projective theory of broadcasting. In F. Voelker & L. Voelker (Eds.), *Mass media: Forces in our society* (pp. 424-440). San Francisco: Harcourt Brace Jovanovich. (Reprinted from *Journal of Broadcasting,* 1968, *12,* 97-116)

Mander, J. (1982). *Four arguments for the elimination of television*. New York: William Morrow.

Mander, J. (1978). Character shaping genre in *Cagney and Lacey. Journal of Broadcasting and Electronic Media, 31*, 131-151.

Modleski, T. (1982). *Loving with a vengeance: Mass-produced fantasies for women*. London: Methuen.

Moi, T. (1985). *Sexual/textual politics: Feminist literary theory*. London: Methuen.

Newcomb, H., & Alley, R. S. (1983). *The producer's medium: Conversations with creators of American TV*. New York: Oxford University Press.

O'Sullivan, T., Hartley, J., Saunders, D., & Fiske, J. (1983). *Key concepts in communication*. London: Methuen.

Piccirillo, M. S. (1986). On the authenticity of televisual experience: A critical exploration of para-social closure. *Critical Studies in Mass Communication, 3*, 337-355.

Radway, J. A. (1984). *Reading the romance: Women, patriarchy, and popular literature*. Chapel Hill: University of North Carolina Press.

Rimmon-Kenon, S. (1983). *Narrative fiction: Contemporary poetics*. London: Methuen.

Said, E. W. (1983). *The world, the text, and the critic*. Cambridge, MA: Harvard University Press.

Schramm, W., & Roberts, D. F. (Eds.). (1971). *The process and effects of mass communication* (rev. ed.). Urbana: University of Illinois Press.

Seiter, E. (in press). Stereotypes: Notes on research and pedagogy. *Journal of Communication.*

Showalter, E. (1977). *A literature of their own: British women novelists from Bronte to Lessing*. Princeton, NJ: Princeton University Press.

Thorburn, D. (1982). Television melodrama. In H. Newcomb (Ed.), *Television: The critical view* (3rd ed., pp. 529-546). New York: Oxford University Press. (Original work published 1976)

Volosiňov, V. N. (1973). *Marxism and the philosophy of language* (L. Matejka & I. R. Titunik, Trans.). New York: Seminar. (Original work published 1929)

Weigel, S. (1986). Double focus: On the history of women's writing. In G. Ecker (Ed.), *Feminist aesthetics* (H. Anderson, Trans., pp. 59-80). Boston: Beacon.

Wolf, C. (1986). A letter about unequivocal and ambiguous meaning, definiteness and indefiniteness; about ancient conditions and new view-scopes; about objectivity. In G. Ecker (Ed.), *Feminist aesthetics* (H. Anderson, Trans., pp. 95-107). Boston: Beacon.

Woolf, V. (1929). *A room of one's own*. New York: Harcourt, Brace & World.

Frames and Centers:
The "Problem" of
Television Criticism

ROBERT C. ALLEN
University of North Carolina, Chapel Hill

THE organizing question asked by Caren Deming's thoughtful and provocative essay is, "What might television criticism learn from feminist scholarship?" The answer she gives is, not surprisingly: "Quite a bit!" She is quite correct, it seems to me, to see a useful analogy between feminist scholars and television critics and between the denigrated status traditionally assigned women's writing and that suffered by popular television. Furthermore, the relationship between feminist scholarship and television criticism is more than merely analogous: Since the mid-nineteenth century, women have been the primary consumers of popular literature in the United States, and, since the early days of network radio, they have also been the primary audience sought for many types of popular broadcast programming.

Deming's point, however, is not just that television criticism might learn a few useful lessons from the experience of feminist scholars. Rather, she sees feminist scholarship's intellectual "liberation" of gender issues to be a model that might inspire a parallel emancipation of television criticism from enslavement within outmoded conceptual and methodological paradigms. The crusading tone of the latter half of the essay follows from an analysis of the current state of television criticism that finds it in dire need of radical reform. To suggest that a "new" television criticism must above all be "television centered" is concomitantly to imply that, to this point at least, much of television criticism has been decentered, off the mark, deflected away from its proper goals and object of inquiry.

It may well be that the field of television criticism has taken so long aborning that its advent will precede by only a few years the technological

Correspondence and requests for reprints: Robert C. Allen, Department of Radio, Television, and Motion Pictures, University of North Carolina, Chapel Hill, NC 27514.

Communication Yearbook 11, pp. 177-182

obsolescence of its ostensible object of analysis. "Television," as we have known it since World War II, in a decade may only be a childhood memory to our students—their narrative desires satisfied by interactive computer programs; their "prime time" being whenever they decide to pick up a laser disk at the local video boutique. With Deming, I view television criticism as an academic discipline struggling to emerge, but I see the forces that have forestalled that emergence a bit differently than she does. In what follows, I would like to reframe the "problem" of television criticism slightly and suggest that the television-centered revolution Deming calls for is considerably more advanced than her essay might suggest. Ironically, however, I would also argue that the forces marshaled against it are more formidable than she suspects.

As Deming sees it, the growth of television criticism has been stunted by the devaluing of television programming by the elitist literary establishment. As I have argued elsewhere with regard to the radio soap opera, "aesthetic analysis of broadcasting" was regarded by many as a contradiction in terms long before the advent of commercial television (Allen, 1985). It was only during the 1950s, and with specific reference to the anthology drama, that what we might see as a nascent television criticism began to develop in the United States. These writerly, autonomous, dramatic works most closely resembled texts from accepted aesthetic canons: They could be read as authored, unified, "serious," and often socially relevant works of art. Not surprisingly, when television production migrated to the West Coast, adopted the production mode of the Hollywood B-movie, and dropped the self-contained drama in favor of the series format, the perceived Golden Age of television, and television criticism, turned quickly to brass.

While literary types were either excoriating television or ignoring it altogether, Deming argues, social scientists were busy establishing academic hegemony over it. Television was to be investigated as a social problem: a generator of deleterious effects or a distorted reflection of social reality. So long as television was to be held to some naive standard of realism, there was little to do but bemoan its shortcomings.

But wait a second. There's no *necessary* incompatibility between studying television as a social phenomenon (even a social "problem") and the development of television criticism. Social science does not have to be "scientistic." It was not so much the hegemonic influence of social science per se that stifled the development of American television criticism as it was the empiricism of American media research. There is little room for "criticism" within a philosophical paradigm that regards knowledge only as statistical regularity, theory as empirical generalization, the researcher as an "objective" recorder of facts, and research as the application to social phenomena of investigatory procedures adapted from the laboratory.

It is no coincidence that nearly all of the television scholars whose critical work Deming cites with varying degrees of approval were trained outside of American mass communication research: Fiske, Hartley, Modleski, Ang, Newcomb, Ellis, Thorburn, Williams, Brunsdon, Flitterman. There are a number of others she might have cited as well, many of whom come to the study of television from cinema studies, all of whom—ironically, perhaps—are moving television criticism toward the television centeredness she so desires: Nick Browne (1984), Edward Buscombe (1976), Jeremy Butler (1986), John Caughie (1984), Robert Deming (1985), Phillip Drummond (1976), Jane Feuer (1984), Michele Hilmes (1985), Beverle Houston (1984), E. Ann Kaplan (1986), Marsha Kinder (1984), Patricia Mellencamp (1985), David Morley (1980, 1986), Margaret Morse (1985), Patrice Petro (1986), Laurie Schulze (1986), Cathy Schwichtenberg (1984), Ellen Seiter (1982), John Tulloch (1976), Mimi White (1986), and Patricia Zimmerman (1985)—among others. Furthermore, each meeting of the Society for Cinema Studies brings to light a new group of graduate students whose critical analyses of television are frequently among the best papers presented. If these names are not familiar to readers of *Journal of Broadcasting*, it is because their television criticism appears much more frequently in cinema studies journals *(Cinema Journal, Journal of Film and Video, Quarterly Review of Film Studies, Wide Angle,* and *Screen)* than in those that address mass communication research (with the exception of *Critical Studies in Mass Communication*—although the "critical" in *CSMC* is used in a different sense from that of Deming or myself.

Why has cinema studies over the past 7 years proven to be more fertile ground for "television-centered" criticism than mass communication research? In large measure, because it has either avoided outright or outgrown the two principal problems Deming associates with television criticism's retardation. Although there are still pockets of high-art film criticism, in general, the field left behind the assumptions of elitist literary evaluation 15 years ago. "*Cherche l'auteur*" hasn't been heard in serious film theory and criticism for ages. The idea that textual complexity can be found in the absence of individual artistic genius has been a hallmark of film genre studies for a decade. And the notion that popular, commercial texts—produced in assembly-line fashion, designed to earn the biggest box-office possible—could still be worthy of critical scrutiny was secured when Truffaut and Chabrol's panegyrics to the films of Robert Aldrich and John Ford found their way to America in the early 1960s.

Except for a brief flirtation with "hard" social science in the 1930s (e.g., the Payne Fund Studies), film has escaped the domination of empiricism. This freedom is due in part to film's alliances with "the arts," but more to the fact that by the time cinema studies emerged as an academic discipline in the 1960s in the United States, television had already usurped film's position as the preeminent form of popular entertainment.

Furthermore, graduate programs in film studies have increasingly realized that there are some serious liabilities in identifying a curriculum exclusively with a nineteenth-century, silver-based, preelectronic technology—particularly when that technology's products are seen more widely on 19-inch screens than 30-foot ones.

Finally, the more film scholars turned their attention to television, the more they recognized both the opportunities for immediate application of methods developed for film criticism and the challenges television presents to film criticism. Whereas American mass communication research has little if any use for theory (except as sets of empirical generalizations), film study revels in (and some would say has been obsessed by) theoretical issues, both homegrown and imported from other disciplines.

To the mass communication graduate student, feminist theory and scholarship might well appear to be an unrelated realm of inquiry and advocacy—not without interest and relevance to some students, but hardly at the center of their curricula. To the film graduate student, issues of gender representation and address are at the very heart of their enterprise.

To suggest to film-trained scholars interested in television that feminist scholarship might have some relevance to their work is a bit like suggesting to geologists that rocks might have some relevance to their work. In fact, one of the key motivating factors for some of the film scholars who are now writing about television is the opportunity to explore how television addresses and "genders" its spectators as well as how it represents notions of masculinity and femininity. What these scholars are finding is that although contemporary film theory is useful in gaining a purchase on television's modes of subject construction and address, some of its basic premises are also thrown open to question by the difference of television (see chapters by Flitterman-Lewis, Kaplan, and Fiske in Allen, 1987).

Let me make my point here clear. I certainly do not wish to trivialize the problems Deming sees with the state of television criticism. Critical work on television, particularly that produced within the framework of American mass communication research, is very much in need of a thorough rethinking—a rethinking that could be greatly aided by the insights of feminist scholarship. Nor do I wish to suggest that film studies provides a magical solution to the problems of constructing a "television-centered" and feminist-inflected criticism. The solution is not merely a matter of "applying" film theory to television, but the reinvention of mass communication research. This is Deming's basic argument: that in order to recenter television criticism, scholars in mass communication research need an infusion of ideas from outside their discipline. I am suggesting that Deming and the readers who are persuaded by her analysis would find in film-trained television scholars not just allies in their struggle, but productive coworkers.

When we reframe the situation of contemporary television criticism so that it can be seen not only in relationship to feminist literary theory and mass communication research but also to contemporary film theory, I think we see a lively, vital field of inquiry, drawing methods and inspiration from a wide variety of sources, raising important and sometimes profound questions about television, and, perhaps most encouraging, engaging the energies and intellects of bright young scholars. Surely the scholars I list above are not among those Deming accuses of not being "willing to look as patiently at television as literary critics look at literature." They are willing and able to look closely and perceptively at television because they have been rigorously trained in the analysis of sounds and images and because the theoretical paradigms from which they work encourage the infusion of ideas from other disciplines.

Furthermore, Deming suggests that television critics "have not been able or willing to spend much effort imagining how concepts of empirical research might be adapted to the critical project." I'm not quite sure which scholars she is referring to here, but it is undeniable that in the 1970s and early 1980s the dominant brand of film theory (usually called *Screen* theory, because of its promulgation in that British journal) did not encourage critics to stray very far away from "the text." However, the considerable influence upon film studies of British cultural studies, reception theory, subcultural theory, and the work of Mikhail Bakhtin and Antonio Gramsci (as well as a loosening of the hold of *Screen* theory over film studies) has helped to create a climate much more conducive to the integration of textual and audience analysis. With regard to television, one thinks immediately of the work of David Morley, Charlotte Brunsdon, Dorothy Hobson, and John Tulloch and Albert Moran (Brunsdon & Morley, 1978; Hobson, 1982; Morley, 1980, 1986; Tulloch & Moran, 1986).

The relationship of empirical work to criticism is of enormous interest to some of the television critics I list above, in large measure because it raises so many central questions: Is there a "text"—independent of its reception by viewers—about which the critic can really speak? What are the influences and constraints upon reception? How can we account for variations among decodings of television programs? What is the relationship of other forms of discourse (advertising, gossip, etc.) to the decoding act? What epistemological status should be accorded the articulated responses of viewers? If by "empirical research" Deming means research into the reception of television texts by audience members, then I would say that a number of television critics are keenly interested in its relationship to critical practice. If by "empirical research" she means *empiricist* audience or content analysis, then she is quite right to point out that critics have not concerned themselves with its relationship to criticism—and for good reason.

Which brings me to a final observation, and one much less optimistic than the above description of contemporary television criticism might suggest. The degree to which American mass communication research continues to be dominated by an empiricist paradigm of investigation and knowledge production (research must be objective, quantitative, and modeled after laboratory science; knowledge is to be equated with statistical regularity and predictability) is the degree to which television criticism will continue to be marginalized in mass communication studies. Notwithstanding the assurance of some of my colleagues that empiricism is already dead, I cannot see scholars who have been trained to regard their way of doing things as the only path to truth suddenly embracing a paradigm that undermines this very premise. So long as our curricula distinguish between "research methods" and "criticism," so long as job announcements for scholars in mass communication research equate research skills with quantification, television criticism can expect no more than a grudging tolerance from the mass communication studies community, and scholars trained in other disciplines will continue gleefully and productively to plow the critical field broadcasting scholars have left fallow for a half century.

REFERENCES

Allen, R. C. (1985). *Speaking of soap operas.* Chapel Hill: University of North Carolina Press.

Allen, R. C. (Ed.). (1987). *Channels of discourse: Television and contemporary criticism.* Chapel Hill: University of North Carolina Press.

Browne, N. (1984). The political economy of the television (super) text. *Quarterly Review of Film Studies, 9,* 174-182.

Brunsdon, C. & Morley, D. (1978). *Everyday television: "Nationwide."* London: British Film Institute.

Buscombe, E. (1976). *"The Sweeny"*—Better than nothing? *Screen Education, 20,* 66-69.

Butler, J. (1986). Notes on the soap opera apparatus: Televisual style and "As the World Turns." *Cinema Journal, 25,* 53-70.

Caughie, J. (1984). Television criticism.*Screen, 25,* 109-121.

Deming, R. (1985). Discourse/talk/television. *Screen, 26,* 88-92.

Drummond, P. (1976). Structural and narrative constraints and strategies in "The Sweeny." *Screen Education, 20,* 15-35.

Feuer, J. (1984). Melodrama, serial form and television today. *Screen 25,* 4-16.

Hilmes, M. (1985). The television apparatus: Direct address. *Journal of Film and Video, 37,* 27-36.

Hobson, D. (1982). *Crossroads: The drama of a soap opera.* London: Methuen.

Houston, B. (1984). Viewing television: The metapsychology of endless consumption. *Quarterly Review of Film Studies, 9,* 183-195.

Kaplan, E. A. (1986). History, spectatorship, and gender address in music television. *Journal of Communication Inquiry, 10,* 3-14.

Kinder, M. (1984). Music video and the spectator: Television, ideology, and dream. *Film Quarterly, 38,* 3-15.

Mellencamp, P. (1985). Situation and simulation: An introduction to "I Love Lucy." *Screen, 26,* 30-40.

Morley, D. (1980). *The "Nationwide" audience: Structure and decoding.* London: British Film Institute.

Morley, D. (1986). *Family television: Cultural power and domestic leisure.* London: Comedia.

Morse, M. (1985). Talk, talk, talk—The space of discourse in television. *Screen, 26,* 2-15.

Petro, P. (1986). Mass culture and the feminine: The place of television in film studies. *Cinema Journal, 25,* 5-21.

Schulze, L. (1986). "Getting Physical": Text/context/reading and the made-for/TV movie. *Cinema Journal, 25,* 35-50.

Schwichtenberg, C. (1984). "The Love Boat": The packaging and selling of love, heterosexual romance, and family. *Media, Culture and Society, 6,* 301-311.

Seiter, E. (1982). Promise and contradiction: The daytime television serials. *Screen, 23,* 150-163.

Tulloch, J. (1976). Gradgrind's heirs: The quiz and the presentation of knowledge by British television. *Screen Education, 19,* 3-13.

Tulloch, J., & Moran, A. (1986). *"A Country Practice": Quality soap.* Paddington, Australia: Currency.

White, M. (1986). Crossing wavelengths: The diegetic and referential imaginary of American commercial television. *Cinema Journal, 25,* 51-64.

Zimmerman, P. (1985). Good girls, bad women: The role of older women on "Dynasty." *Journal of Film and Video, 37,* 89-92.

Recentering a Television-Centered Television Criticism: A Political-Economic Response

EILEEN R. MEEHAN
University of Iowa, Iowa City

AT a time when communication behaviorists, ethnographers, political economists, and media critics are finally speaking to each other with some civility ("paradigm dialogue"), Deming's call for a television-centered television criticism could not be more welcome. Besides sketching how such a synthesis of approaches could illuminate the complex phenomenon of television, the essay also inflects that synthesis with a distinctly feminist perspective. Surely the strengths of the essay lay in its multifaceted and multilayered approach to the problem of television in general and to television criticism in particular. Further, in arguing for this new agenda, Deming adroitly avoids two errors common in media criticism: She treats criticism neither as intellectual gymnastics whereby the clever critic elucidates the text's "real" meaning nor as imaginative projections whereby the critic deduces the response that marginalized readers might construct from the text. Thus Deming constructs a role for the critic that avoids the twin traps of critical elitism and elistist polysemy, traps into which most film and television critics have fallen. Instead, Deming argues that the careful, sensitive, and systematic study of both television series and their audiences is necessary in a television-centered television criticism. But more important, she demonstrates that such an approach is possible by drawing from audience research and textual analysis in order to contextualize her own original research on television melodrama. The result is a powerful case for a television criticism that "mediates between textuality and social realities" (p. 171).

Correspondence and requests for reprints: Eileen R. Meehan, Department of Communication Studies, University of Iowa, Iowa City, IA 52242.

Communication Yearbook 11, pp. 183-193

Having pointed out these exemplary features of the essay, I now turn to my institutional function as commentator and critic. While embracing Deming's suggestion that textuality and social realities must play a major role in a television-centered television criticism, I find a more powerful approach to television implicit in the essay. Where Deming suggests that the study of the economic structure of television is a necessary *further* step for an adequate television criticism (p. 173), I suggest that it is *the* necessary *first* step for a television-centered television criticism. While I agree that good criticism mediates between the televisual text and social realities, I would add that good criticism should be firmly grounded in an understanding of the industrial structure of television. Obviously, this industrial structure shapes, constrains, and informs the production of television texts; after all, television programs are produced, distributed, and continued as a result of decisions by corporations from the industries of broadcasting, advertising, product manufacturing, and program rating.

But it is also important to note that social realities are constrained by the larger economic structure based on private, corporate ownership. Whether called "capitalism" or "free enterprise," the current economic structure systematically divides people into classes, genders, races, and so on, and uses these divisions to limit access to resources and opportunities. These limitations generate a social environment within which collectivities of people build shared social realities based on their lived experience of coping, circumventing, and creating in response to their social environment. In television criticism, then, the problem becomes how to relate the manufactured text and the conditions of its production to such differentiated social realities. This relationship should illuminate, first, why some forms and ideas are selected for manufacture and, second, how such manufactures are appropriated by different subcultures within an economically conditioned social reality. If criticism is to mediate successfully between manufactured texts and social realities, then it must be grounded not only in textual analysis and subcultural research, but ultimately in economics.

Is this asking too much of a television critic? The practicality and power of such a grounded approach is suggested in Deming's treatment of two melodramatic forms of television programming. Her knowledge of production constraints and socially constructed gender differences inform her criticism of soap operas and detective programs, allowing her to retrieve oppositional moments from particular texts in an analytically rigorous manner. This rigor is not a matter of postulating an idealized oppositional reader and then "discovering" what that reader might see in the text. Rather, Deming draws on a wealth of feminist work on how women deal with a genderist social environment, supplemented by feminist criticism of media and research on women's readings of genderist texts, especially romances and melodramas. As a critic, Deming grounds herself in an empirically documented subculture of femaleness in order to construct readings of selected examples of televisual melodramas in terms of subcultural rules of femaleness as well as accepted practices in television criticism. However, because Deming implicitly recognizes the importance of industrial constraints on television production, she avoids the all-too-ubiquitous reflection hypothesis, which would treat the texts manufactured *for* women as reflections *of* women made available in the cool, dispassionate, and objective mirror of television.

As Deming repeatedly notes, the process of constructing the televisual text is highly selective and highly constrained due to economic imperatives. Such corporations as advertising agencies, manufacturers of consumer goods, networks, affiliated stations, independent production companies, Hollywood studios, ratings firms, and program syndicators are either directly or indirectly involved in the selection of generic forms as well as the selection of ideas, themes, plots, representations, visions, and styles through which a program achieves its particularity. These types of corporations configure to form a series of distinct markets whose interrelationships produce the television industry. For television programs, the most important are the markets comprising, first, networks, advertisers, and the ratings firm currently positioned as the monopoly producer of national audience measurements; then, the market comprising networks, independent production companies, and studios.

These two markets interconnect to form the economic context for the construction, distribution, and continuation of most television programming. In the first market, the institutional ground rules for national television are negotiated. Advertisers demand access to an audience of consumers; networks promise to provide such an audience; verification of the networks' productivity is provided by the ratings firm.

Since the late 1950s the second market has been characterized by the networks' oligopolistic control over distribution and each network's internal control over its scheduling of programs. This control has allowed them to dictate the economic terms under which they will accept programming as well as the generic form and specific content of that programming. By considering first the immediate constraints on production and then the larger framework in which those constraints are articulated, the importance of the economic as the primary determinant of the televisual text will become clear.

IMMEDIATE CONSTRAINTS: NETWORKS AND PRODUCERS

In the late 1940s, RCA and CBS innovated two different televisual technologies, but both companies defined television as a commercial, broadcast medium that would ultimately replace radio as *the* broadcast distribution system for national programming and advertising. The new medium, however, did not appeal immediately to advertisers. Programming for television was more expensive than radio. Also, in the late 1940s and 1950s television's ability to deliver the commodity audience was not yet demonstrated. While some sponsors agreed to underwrite simultaneous television and radio broadcasts of the same show, others held back. (See Barnouw, 1966,

1968, 1970, 1975, 1978; Bergreen, 1980; Danielian, 1939; Ewen, 1976; Mosco, 1979; Williams, 1975.)

This left television sponsorship relatively undefined. Some companies followed the old model for sponsorship, buying time from the networks and filling that time with inexpensive productions like game shows in the evening or soap operas during the day. In an attempt to get high ratings, many game shows were scripted as melodramas, rather than contests of skill. By 1959 such programming was the target of a congressional investigation. Revelations that the games had been rigged by the advertisers or their agencies were treated by the press and the government as a public outrage. While advertisers were considered sufficiently moral to continue running commercials on television, serious questions were raised as to their ability to provide programming in the public interest. Stepping into this breach, networks promised to assume the burden of programming and scheduling television, thus saving the public interest.

From an economic perspective, the networks' reaction to the quiz scandals allowed the networks to reorganize the system of sponsorship. Under the old system, advertisers had once purchased a time slot as their own and commissioned programs, not only to attract the commodity audience but also to build a particular image of the manufacturer and its product. While some advertisers drew on popular culture, a few others attempted to link their names with high culture, but all ignored the networks' need to build a cohesive, integrated schedule that would maximize the particular network's ability to control ratings for the entire night. Under the new system of sponsorship, networks sought to secure sufficient control over their schedules to achieve that end, without alienating the advertisers.

With the new "magazine" system, advertisers relinquished their direct control of content as well as the cost of producing that content. In return, they could more selectively purchase "spots" throughout the schedule that would secure them access to their targeted portions of the commodity audience. As networks took control of their schedules, they worked to build a seamless progression of programs that would attract and keep at least a third of the commodity audience for the night. The trade-off in efficiency and costing proved attractive for advertisers as well as for the networks.

It also refocused the selection of programming. A program was no longer a distinctive vehicle associated with a particular advertiser, but rather a component in an undifferentiated lineup of programs and ads that merged together to occupy the prime-time slot. Programs that "stuck out," such as serious drama or classical music, disrupted the flow and hence were not as attractive as the intermeshing of familiar forms, faces, and fantasies.

With network control over programming and distribution assured, the market for television programs assumed its basic shape in the 1960s. The networks (ABC, CBS, and NBC) oligopolized distribution to the point that they indirectly controlled and directly commissioned programming from selected producers. When antitrust considerations in 1972 forced the networks to divest themselves of their internal divisions dedicated to production, management ties between the parent companies and their spin-off firms ensured the prominance of these "independents" as program producers. Supplementing these producers were the Hollywood studios whose physical plant and personnel became television factories much as they had once been movie factories. Finally, individual producers formed independent companies; the founders of these firms and most of their employees were usually drawn from the networks or the studios. With deregulation, networks have increasingly entered into coproduction with companies that are considerably less powerful than the networks, given the continued domination of the networks over distribution. In sum, the population of this second market is well interconnected and quite limited.

That smallness is somewhat surprising given the increasing accessibility of production training, the availability of professionally creative people, the availability of studio space from the motion picture companies, and decreasing costs of the necessary technology. If the program is the basic unit of production, then the market should be overflowing with quality product at low prices, especially as training becomes more accessible and costs of technologies go down. However, such competition generates waste and unpredictability for both producers and networks. Such competition requires that producers have programs in hand, ready for competitive viewing. Since only a narrow selection of all possible programs can be purchased, most programs would be unsalable—thus wasting the money, labor, and time invested in them. Similarly, such competitive viewing would make every program selection a unique decision, mitigating against rationalization and routinization of programming.

However, the individual program does not serve as the basis for transactions between networks and producers; rather, the generic program serves as the linchpin in these relationships. A network selects a company based on that company's successes within a specific genre and then commissions the company to produce a program from that genre, often specifying thematic or stylistic elements. This routinizes the selection of producers, generic programs, and content as well as signature items to be featured in the program. Indeed, the networks structure the market as an oligopoly limited to no more than seven producers (spin-offs, independents, studios) with which they contract for programs. Often, the more independent companies must work with studios in order to secure a contract. Here, connections with ex-employers (especially the contracting network or coproducing studio) facilitate the initiation of new relations while an old relationship relies on the company's "track record" in television generally and in the most recent particular genre. The basic assumption is that companies that can successfully produce one detective program should be able to produce a second successful example of that genre. (See Brown, 1971; Cantor, 1971, 1980; Ettema, 1982; Feuer, 1984; Gitlin, 1985; Guback & Dombkowski, 1976; Pekurny, 1982; Smith, 1985; Turow, 1982.)

Producers use this practice to their own advantage. Each company within the charmed circle specializes in one or two genres. This limits competition between members of the circle to rivalries within the narrow confines of specialized genres. Rivalry within genres encourages the development of signature items that crop up across a company's programs and serve to distinguish one firm's product from its rival's product. Of course, should a company's primary genre or its signature earn unacceptable ratings or create political controversy, the firm may be excluded from the market by network fiat. This risk encourages companies to develop track records in at least one other generic form and to cultivate new twists in their approach to their primary and secondary genres. In this way, networks and producers utilize genre as a manufacturing category to routinize and rationalize their transactions. Such rationalization and routinization fosters reliance on the familiar plots, themes, representations, formulae, and so forth. However, generic manufacture also fosters limited creativity within genre as companies differentiate their products through an industrial autuerism that depends on signature items, twists, and the like. For the networks, such small differences in tandem with slight differences in the ratings can make or break a program, can trigger or end a programming trend.

Generic manufacture and industrial auteurism, then, serve the interests of both networks and producers. However, those interests are not always so closely intertwined. In the process of commissioning programs, the networks' control over distribution allows them to dictate the terms of production. Thus production companies absorb the production costs of pilots and episodes. Networks usually specify or retain veto power over the selection of actors and pay the stars' salaries. So, while production companies require at least a five-year run before they can make good their investment via international and domestic syndication, the networks face an increasing cost over the run of a successful program as its stars negotiate for higher salaries. Such costs are not necessarily recouped through higher prices for advertising spots since most series tend to drop out of the 5 top-rated programs and stabilize in the top 20 as the series ages. A program, then, is most attractive for the networks at the point when it is a mixed blessing for the producers—that is, when the network orders more episodes of a new, smash hit with unknown actors paid relatively low salaries. The program becomes more attractive for producers as it nears the possibility of syndication, precisely when network interest begins to wane. This discontinuity of interests between producers and networks becomes an important factor in renewals and syndication and in the commissioning of new programs. The decision to end a successful program may include arrangements between the network and producer that assure the producing company of a "most favored nation" status, thereby further institutionalizing oligopoly and generic manufacture.

THE LARGER FRAMEWORK: ADVERTISERS, NETWORKS, RATINGS

Networks act as corporate gatekeepers whose economically based preferences for some genres, ideas, and so on set the producers' agenda. However, network preferences are themselves shaped by larger economic relationships that define television as a national, commercial medium dedicated to the advertising of relatively ephemeral consumer goods. Two important constraints shape those network preferences: Content and genre must be acceptable to advertisers; the programs resulting from producers' manipulation of genre and content must attract large numbers of consumers as measured by the major ratings firm. These constraints arise from the triangle of relations between networks as sellers of the commodity audience, advertisers as purchasers of that audience, and the rating firm as the reporter of each network's ability to produce the commodity audience. As situations change, this three-sided relationship is negotiated and renegotiated by the relevant firms. (See Banks, 1981; Beville, 1985; Eliot, 1983; Hurwitz, 1983, 1984; Livant, 1979; Meehan, 1983, 1984, 1986; Murdock, 1978; Rubens, 1984; Schiller, 1977; Smythe, 1977.)

While the selection of producing firms is largely a matter of network fiat, the networks' decisions to commission programs are constrained by advertisers' demand that programs be appropriate vehicles for advertising. In practice, this means that programs should neither actively offend nor actively engage the vast majority of consumers across the nation. Thus advertiser demand encourages the networks to rely on the "tried and true"—on familiar genres proven successful in other mass media, filled with familiar characters, themes, plots, and assumptions. While innovation comes from the industrial auteurism of production companies, the success of any particular innovation guarantees advertiser pressure on networks to commission imitations of that successful innovation. The demand for such copies results in a steady stream of imitations within the dominant genre until ratings for "copy cat" programs either stabilize or decline in the face of a new, generic innovation. The introduction of such an innovation sets off another cycle of imitation until saturation is once more reached. Taken together, advertisers' and networks' demand for familiarity and for imitation facilitate the industrialization of program creation through the standardization of component parts and the routinization of their assembly.

Another economic source of pressure on programming is again a function of demand, here the demand for ratings. Both advertisers and broadcasters are interested in obtaining a set of measures estimating audience size and composition for programs to serve as a "floor" on which the buying and selling of audiences can routinely proceed. Such unified demand serves as the basic constraint on ratings production; other measurements of the audience for national programming are simply not required by national advertisers and national networks for their primary transaction. However, not all members of the general public are equally valuable in these transactions. The advertisers of goods for mass consumption have little interest in either the elite 1% of the population or the impoverished 10%-20% of the population. Since networks attempt to attract the audiences that advertisers prefer, networks also have little interest in the extremes of wealth and poverty. To serve this unified demand for an audience of consumers, ratings firms have historically skewed their sampling procedures to select established households from the vast army of consumers rather than the even larger universe of the general population. For example, during the Great Depression when telephone service was a mark of disposable income, the first raters used urban households with telephones listings as the basis of their sample. While this may seem poor science, it was a reasonable business practice that responded to demand.

However, demand is not always so unified, especially when the information produced is used to set prices that advertisers must pay, and networks may demand, for access to the commodity audience. With advertisers and networks committed to working from *a* set of numbers, each faction can lobby for numbers that subtly overestimate or underestimate the audience, thereby indirectly affecting price. Depending on which faction has borne the burden of programming costs, ratings methods have favored advertisers or networks. In dealing with continuities in demand for a set of numbers describing a subset of the population and discontinuities in demand over accuracy of estimates, ratings firms have devised various strategies in their attempts to be accepted by networks and advertisers as *the* producer of national ratings.

This exercise of economic creativity by a ratings firm shapes the definition of the commodity audience and thereby indirectly influences programming. As the ratings' sample becomes the commodity audience, the networks' task is not to respond to the public or even to the mass of consumers, but rather to respond to patterns of preference in the commodity audience/sample. This need is particularly true when the basis of ratings changed from periodic surveys of a telephone sample whose respondents were constantly changing (early monopoly firms: Cooperative Analysis of Broadcasting, 1929-1934, and C. E. Hooper Company, 1934-1946) to the continuous metered measurement of set tuning by a fixed panel of respondents (A. C. Nielsen company, innovated 1944, effective monopoly achieved 1949). When the A. C. Nielsen Company's 1200 metered households became the commodity audience, the networks were presented with a stable sample over which they could vie while advertisers were presented with the opportunity of continuous measurements of a known group of consumers/auditors.

The effects of the fixed sample on programming are indeed significant. When the fixed sample is held constant, networks have longitudinal data on the generic preferences of the sample, allowing some rational basis for the selection of genres. This mitigates for periods of relative stability in television's generic offerings, with innovation limited to signatures of the production oligopoly. When the fixed sample is periodically retaken in response to advertisers' shifting concerns about the consumer subset of the population, programming becomes more problematic. Networks reintroduce genres fallen from favor and become more receptive to new twists and signatures that might appeal to the description of the new sample. As these relationships between networks, raters, and advertisers shift, the parameters of this larger framework change. And changes in that framework create new pressures and new demands for the more immediate constraints on programming—the relationships between networks and producers.

CONCLUSION

The generic form, auteurist signatures, and general content of the televisual text are determined by the economic relations between and among advertisers as well as among networks, production companies, and ratings firms. The primary constraints on televisual texts arise from the fact that such texts are designed as vehicles for advertising and such vehicles are, indeed, mass manufactured for mass distribution and consumption. The manufacture of such vehicles relies on the most commonly decipherable forms, ideas, claims, and representations in order to make these cultural artifacts accessible to the majority of consumers among the 242 million comprising the U.S. population as well as to worldwide millions of consumers who can be reached via commercial syndication. Thus, despite the varied contents, visions, ideas, forms, and so on available from the cultural fund created by human societies across history, the elements preferred by networks and producers tend to support the dominant social order of both the United States and global capitalism—a social order that is both patriarchical and capitalist.

A television-centered television criticism must be grounded in the study of the fundamental element governing television as a technology, a cultural form, and a site of opposition—the economics of television. The relationships between production companies and their employees, production companies and networks, and networks and advertisers and ratings producers constitute a series of markets, layered one upon the other, set the constraints within which the televisual text is assembled, produced, and distributed. When articulated directly, this approach may seem quite a departure from Deming's. However, this approach serves as the base of many of Deming's arguments and as such lies under the surface of the essay. Television's stories—unlike those told by bards or shamens or grandparents—are composed by employees, disseminated by media conglomerates, and designed to attract the group of consumers currently measured by the dominant ratings firm so that advertisers and networks may evaluate the performance of programs in producing the commodity audience.

The issue here is not whether television's stories are less authentic or less narrative than other stories. Rather, the issue is precisely that television's stories are complicated by their duality as show business, as both cultural artifact and economic commodity. The important difference is the domination of the economic—no business, no show—and the effects of that dominance on the manufacture of texts, on the relative autonomy granted the producing company by the distributing conglomerate, and on the operating definition of the audience. Where Deming has rightly celebrated the ambiguities used by auditors/actors to give voice to the oppressed as well as the creativity of those who configure generic and symbolic elements to produce *a* program, I have done my best to illuminate the transindustrial structures that precede and allow such ambiguities, creativites, configurations. Ultimately, of course, both positions must be synthesized for a truly television-centered approach to television scholarship.

REFERENCES

Banks, M. (1981). *A history of broadcast audience research in the United States, 1920-1980 with an emphasis on the rating services.* Unpublished doctoral dissertation, University of Tennessee.

Barnouw, E. (1966). *A tower in Babel.* New York: Oxford University Press.

Barnouw, E. (1968). *The golden web.* New York: Oxford University Press.

Barnouw, E. (1970). *The image empire.* New York: Oxford University Press.

Barnouw, E. (1975). *Tube of plenty.* New York: Oxford University Press.

Barnouw, E. (1978). *The sponsor.* New York: Oxford University Press.

Bergreen, L. (1980). *Look now, pay later.* Garden City, NY: Doubleday.

Beville, H. M., Jr. (1985). *Audience ratings.* Hillsdale, NJ: Lawrence Erlbaum.

Brown, L. (1971). *Televi$ion.* New York: Harcourt Brace Jovanovich.

Cantor, M. G. (1971). *The Hollywood TV producer.* New York: Basic Books.

Cantor, M. G. (1980). *Prime-time television.* Newbury Park, CA: Sage.

Danielian, N. R. (1939). *AT&T.* New York: Vanguard.

Eliot, M. (1983). *Televisions.* New York: St. Martin's.

Ettema, J. S. (1982). The organizational context of creativity: A case study from public television. In J. S. Ettema & D. C. Whitney (Eds.), *Individuals in mass media organizations: Creativity and constraint.* Newbury Park, CA: Sage.

Ewen, S. (1976). *Captains of consciousness.* New York: McGraw-Hill.

Feuer, J. (1984). MTM enterprises: An overview. In J. Feuer, P. Kerr, & T. Vahimagi (Eds.), *MTM quality television.* London: BFI.

Gitlin, T. (1985). *Inside prime-time.* New York: Pantheon.

Guback, T., & Dombkowski, D. (1976). Television and Hollywood: Economic relations in the 1970's. *Journal of Broadcasting, 20,* 511-527.

Hurwitz, D. (1983). *Broadcast "ratings": The rise and development of commercial audience research and measurement in American broadcasting.* Unpublished doctoral dissertation, University of Illinois, Urbana.

Hurwitz, D. (1984). Broadcast ratings: The missing dimension. *Critical Studies in Mass Communication, 1,* 205-215.

Livant, B. (1979). The audience commodity: On the blindspot debate. *Canadian Journal of Political & Social Theory, 3,* 91-106.

Meehan, E. R. (1983). *Neither heroes nor villains: Towards a political economy of the ratings industry.* Unpublished doctoral dissertation, University of Illinois, Urbana.

Meehan, E. R. (1984). Ratings and the institutional approach: A third answer to the commodity question. *Critical Studies in Mass Communication, 1,* 216-225.

Meehan, E. R. (1986). Critical theorizing on broadcast history. *Journal of Broadcasting and Electronic Media, 30,* 393-411.

Mosco, V. (1979). *Broadcasting in the United States.* Norwood, NJ: Ablex.

Murdock, G. (1978). Blindspots about Western Marxism: A reply to Dallas Smythe. *Canadian Journal of Political & Social Theory, 2,* 109-119.

Pekurny, R. (1982). Coping with television production. In J. S. Ettema & D. C. Whitney (Eds.), *Individuals in mass media organizations: Creativity and constraint.* Newbury Park, CA: Sage.

Rubens, W. S. (1984). High-tech audience measurement for new-tech audiences. *Critical Studies in Mass Communication, 1,* 195-204.

Schiller, H. (1977). *Mass communications and American empire.* New York: Augustus Kelly.

Smith, J. E. (1985). *Subtexts of resistance in ideological commodities: The case of "Magnum P.I."* Paper presented at the Iowa Symposium and Conference on Television Criticism, Iowa City.

Smythe, D. (1977). Communications: Blindspot of Western Marxism. *Canadian Journal of Political & Social Theory, 1,* 1-27.

Turow, J. (1982). Unconventional programs on commercial television: An organizational perspective. In J. S. Ettema & D. C. Whitney (Eds.), *Individuals in mass media organizations: Creativity and constraint*. Newbury Park, CA: Sage.

Williams, R. (1975). *Television: Technology and cultural form*. New York: Schocken.

5 Toward a Theory of Mediation

DAVID L. ALTHEIDE
ROBERT P. SNOW
Arizona State University

It is argued that a central feature of all communication, and mass communication in particular, is a process of mediation involving organizing and interpretive schema embedded in specific formats. This mediation process may be conceptualized as a general social form that is used to direct and inform social activity and cultural phenomena. Individual action and meaning in everyday life weaves in and out of these organizing and interpretive schema. Building on symbolic interaction theory, so-called media effects are recast as cultural phenomena or content that derive meaning through symbolic references in the formal (format) properties of specific media.

When the Gods wish to punish us, they answer our prayers.

—Oscar Wilde

Only the gods could see then what we see now. In ways that our predecessors could not even imagine, we have the ability to travel on the "media jet," to negate electronically previously taken-for-granted assumptions about the relationships between time and space. But if the gods only knew then what we know now, then the gods must have been crazy! We want to show why.

In the following pages, we present a perspective for theorizing and investigating the cultural impact of mass communication, particularly television. Through the decades of work we have invested in this ambitious topic, it has become apparent to us that studies of the mass media inform a general theory of communication, which in turn suggest additional topics to investigate. Our intent is to expand the conceptual domain of mass communication into other facets of modern life, for example, computer formats and bureaucracy. Expect to be a bit surprised.

It is in the interaction of communication forms as product and producer

Correspondence and requests for reprints: David L. Altheide, School of Justice Studies, Arizona State University, Tempe, AZ 85287.

Communication Yearbook 11, pp. 194-223

that everyday life takes place and social order is accomplished; *how* something is communicated is prior to *what* is communicated (see Peterson, 1976). Identifying and locating the sources, nature, and consequences of communicative routines, styles, and patterns are therefore central to an understanding of social control as well as an explication of the politics of everyday life. A statement about what we term *mediation* is theoretically appropriate. Mediation (some people prefer *mediatization*) refers to the impact of the logic and form of any medium involved in the communication process. The following materials are offered to illustrate how media logic and formats compatible with popular culture mediate, define, and direct social interaction in contemporary urban Western society.

FROM CONTENT TO THE MESSAGE

The sociology of knowledge informs us that the communication process is problematic, and that history, context, and interaction contribute to the social construction of meaningful information (see Berger & Luckmann, 1967). Social science lacks a theory of mediation that would articulate the relationships among (1) an actor; (2) a context; (3) a phenomenon or event; (4) a medium; and (5) an audience. Each of these contributes to an actor's attention to, and understanding of, relevant information, as well as perception of a "message" (see Blumer, 1969). This conceptualization of the communication process creates a "whole" from what has heretofore been regarded as discrete parts (see Streeter, 1984). Thus, regarding political communication, sociologists have commented on the cultural, economic, and political context (see Barrett, Corrigan, Kuhn, & Wolff, 1979); the event under study (Gitlin, 1980); the media organization (Altheide, 1976; Epstein, 1973; Gans, 1979); and the audience (Gerbner, Gross, Morgan, & Signorielli, 1980; Graber, 1984; Gunter & Wober, 1983). And efforts have been made to join two or three of the pieces theoretically, particularly the context, the event, and the audience (see Bennett, 1983; Glasgow Media Group, 1976; Hall, 1980; Lang & Lang, 1981). Missing from much of this creative work, however, is a theoretical statement about the specific medium per se, particularly how media may contribute to the process suggested by the sociology of knowledge.

It is axiomatic for mass communication scholars that information and imagery are organizational and technological products of the mass media (see Williams, 1975, 1982). Increasingly, what we "know" and are concerned about are events, problems, and issues that are delivered to us in daily doses. But this work is not an essay about "agenda setting" (see Shaw & McCombs, 1977). This chapter is about the organization of the communication process in general and mass communication in particular. We will implicitly make a number of claims as we set forth a unique perspective for resolving a paradox of communication and culture.

Prior to modern technology in Western society, interaction occurred through rules that were constantly reestablished or mediated by the parties directly involved. Third-party mediation was largely a matter of formal institutionalized ritual, such as religious ceremony, oral history, and theatre. By the beginning of the twentieth century another dimension of mediation had emerged, one that developed formal properties and competency requirements independent of existing institutional norms. Consequently, in today's urbanized world, people in business, education, religion—and throughout everyday life—must know how to operate media technology and code and decode specialized media formats before interaction can begin. It is the process, logic, and cultural impact of this competence that occupies our attention in the remainder of this essay.

One explicit point we wish to make is that the nature of contemporary mass communication entails active participation with rather distinctive formats that essentially define the time, place, and manner of social interactions. It is the unique form of the mass media that draws our attention to mediation as a general feature of all communication that has not heretofore been clarified. We regard the mass media as major factors in contemporary social life, rather than merely being "dependent" variables affected by class, status, and power. As will become apparent, we find that mass communication formats are an integral part of the ongoing construction of culture. Indeed, culture is not simply mediated through mass media; rather, culture—in both form and content—is embodied in mass media. In what follows, we will briefly set forth the theoretic context, illustrate what is meant by the logic and form of mediation, and show its relevance for the role of formats in communication behavior. This effort will be followed by some discussion and illustrations of mass media formats, particularly with TV news coverage of terrorism. Next, we will address the significance of mediation for understanding the impact of mass media on audience behavior. Finally, we will briefly turn to other forms of mediation, for example, keyboards and computers.

MEDIATION IN SOCIAL LIFE

Our lives are awash in media. But we are seldom aware of the role these media play because they are such a part of day-to-day experience. Indeed, any effort to try to analyze media effects independently of the life world in which the media operate is doomed to failure, or at best, trivial findings. The major electronic media are but the latest in the human legacy and involvement with all kinds of media. Thus while the electronic media are certainly different from other information media such as newspapers, as well as other experiential and environmental media such as architecture, there remain some conceptual similarities.

The major starting point toward a more adequate view of the audience is the assumption that social life is constituted by and through a communication process. In this sense, it is largely irrelevant whether one is focusing on interpersonal communication or mass communication: There is a communication process at work and any serious effort to develop a coherent theory of any kind of communication must be tied to this basic assumption. This view suggests, then, at least two things: (1) communication, social interaction, and social order are inextricably joined; and (2) scientific assumptions, concepts, and theoretical frameworks seeking to lay claim to subareas of communication, for example, "mass media," will be implicitly or explicitly relevant for this more basic issue.

Media Are Visible

A medium is any process, technique or technology that facilitates in social affairs the emergence of something visible, something tangible. The media we use in everyday life make thoughts, intentions, and meanings come to life, and, in doing so, these media take on a reality and importance that is independent of substantive content in the communication process. Consequently, media are more than a neutral conduit of information transmission; they are concrete action agents that come to represent or stand for the location and establishment of various kinds of meanings. Television is entertainment, news, talk, relaxation, stimulation, and so on. Through forms of appearance and action (media strategy), every medium becomes a visible agent of social affairs.

Social Forms and Mass Communication

We begin with the assumption that the mass media are more than their content or programs (including implicit or explicit ideology). Rather, we seek to articulate the mass media qua media because our previous work suggests that McLuhan and Innis were partly correct that new and emergent forms of communication influence culture. Thus, while it is clear to us that ideology and power do find their way into programming and messages, the resulting content per se does not take us very far in understanding the cultural relevance of new forms of communication. The way audience members interact with these forms will be examined below.

Simmel was one of the first to set forth the notion that sociological forms reflect as well as construct social order. In reviewing what is relevant in Simmel's works for understanding mass media, two related points stand out. The first concerns the fundamental importance of social forms; the second rests on Simmel's basic approach to sociology, which is essentially grounded in notions about communication processes. Beginning with social forms, Simmel followed the Kantian thesis and argued that forms operate as a priori conditions in shaping experience and cultural content. But Simmel departed from Kant (and the Durkheimian approach as well) and rejected the assumption that forms (or structures) are fixed or static and relatively unaffected by pragmatic concerns (Levine, 1971). For Simmel, people act through forms and use them to make sense of their empirical world, but they are not, sui generis, structures. Instead, forms are procedural strategies used to guide behavior and to develop particular kinds of cultural content. Examples include grammar, as the form for using language and establishing meaning; logic, as the form for knowing and establishing proof; geometry, as the form for understanding shape and spatial relations; and music, as a form for organizing sounds into aesthetic rhythms and melodic patterns. In each case, the form makes the production of specific kinds of phenomena possible, and yet the form has an autonomy or independence with respect to that content.

Simmel acknowledged the inherent subjectivism in his sociology of culture but argued that despite the pragmatic origin of a social form, it eventually became autonomous and independent through an objectification process. Initially, social forms emerge out of the need to cope with a new and strange phenomenon or a situation rendered chaotic. However, as the situation persists and the form proves adequate to the task, it becomes objectified and closely tied to praxis (Levine, 1971). Therefore, while social forms and cultural content are rooted in a so-called subjective process, people objectify forms for the apparent stability, predictability, and sensibility that forms provide.

As noted above, a medium does not consist of an object or thing that exists independently of the people who select, define, interpret, and, in short, construct it. It is in this sense that media abound and should be regarded as synonymous with those aspects of a culture involved in the derivation, interpretation, and communication of meaning. This point has been well developed in some of our previous work and will not be repeated here except simply to note that this chapter takes in a lot of territory, for example, buildings, calendars, modes of transportation, dance, fashion, body shape and styles, and, of course, the media explicitly involved with communication (see Altheide & Snow, 1979).

Any medium on which we depend for imagery and information can be treated and analyzed as a social form that has been constructed and organized to achieve a variety of noncommunication messages and purposes that have a social and historical origin and context. The electronic media simply made it possible to take information-for-communication out of its immediate context and transfer it to another place and time. But the biggest difference was largely in the technology, which permitted a small number of people to communicate with a large number of people; the difference was not in the act of communication.

FORMAT

The way media appear, or their essential form, provides a kind of intelligence and interpretation to specific points of information, or content, that they present. We refer to the nature of this appearance as format, or the rules and logic that transform and mold information (content) into the recognizable shape and form of the specific medium. Moreover, all media have a format and can be distinguished by it (see Altheide & Snow, 1979).

Drawing from a considerable body of scholarly discussion, formats are formulas (Chesebro, 1982; Gitlin, 1983; Newcomb, 1974; Smith, 1983) that serve as strategies for presenting categorical subject matter to an audience. For example, broad categories such as international politics, pioneering the West, or the eternal romance triangle are presented through specific formats, such as event-centered news, Hollywood film, or television soap operas. Consequently, depicting a historical event will vary with the type of format or genre (Broadway musical, TV sitcom, Hollywood western) that is used to present and inform that event.

Extending the logic of format as formula or strategy, the term may also be used as an orientation framework or methodology for understanding various cultural phenomena. The question, "When is a particular phenomenon considered to be sports, news, entertainment, politics, or art?" may be answered in terms of format criteria. While news may be what the news media say is news, it could also be argued that almost any event or item can appear as legitimate news when it is presented in a news format. The same could hold true for sports, politics, art, and so on. In sports, for example, newspaper columnists have charged that college and professional sports are becoming an entertainment business. What leads critics to this conclusion is the failure of athletes, owners, and the media to follow the traditional format of team-spirited, fan-oriented competition. Instead, athletes negotiate enormous and complex salary deals through sharp business agents, owners dress up the stadium with entertainment devices, and the media add a circuslike hype and hoopla.

On the other hand, television's preeminence has forced activities that appear on television to accept television's format rules (see Altheide & Snow, 1979). After demonstrating how mediated sports can accommodate narrative myth, individual intimacy, commodification, and rigid time segmentation, Duncan and Brummett (1986) conclude:

> To the extent that the public shares a media logic which influences the makeup of mediated content, then it understands sports in some of the same ways that it understands politics, the news, situation comedies, and lifestyles of the rich and famous. In short, because spectator sports are *mediated* through an institution which inserts its logic into other aspects of experience which it mediates, spectator sports should always be studied in connection with their media and with the other institutions in which they are linked by the media. (p. 16)

For example, when professional football moved to prime time, rule changes occurred that promoted an increased entertainment value—commercial value—for pro football as a televison commodity. Games became higher scoring, more dramatic, less violent, and had greater stadium and crowd theatrics than in the period prior to television broadcasts. Similar changes in basketball and baseball have led to a blurring between the traditional sports contest framework of team competition and the entertainment framework of highly stylized, individualized "big play" action. During the late 1970s, the networks—and ABC in particular—pushed the entertainment-styled sports contest to the limit with slam-dunk basketball and fungo bat home-run contests, bogus competitions among media personalities in tennis, skiing, and schoolyard type activities, as well as *Wide World of Sports* coverage of tobacco spitting, bathtub and bar stool racing, and bubblegum blowing.

A more serious example of infusing a traditional media format with television entertainment is the television "docudrama." Television networks discovered some years ago that the traditional 16mm-educational classroom film was not acceptable to prime-time audiences. However, ratings increased when history was dressed in a high-entertainment format that emphasized backstage life and personal intrigue and confrontation on the order of *Dallas* and *Dynasty*. Similar observations and criticism have been made by newscasters and television critics about the increased entertainment emphasis in network and local news broadcasts.

A final observation on the significance of media formats and social forms concerns Simmel's point that social action can be evaluated as "good" or "bad" form (Wolff, 1950). Everyone is familiar with the notions of good and bad art, good and bad competition, and even good and bad small talk. In turn, media formats have become standardized and accepted to the degree that media professionals commonly refer to good or bad film, television, journalism, and so on. Consistent with Simmel's argument, the criteria used in such evaluations rarely have much to do with content. Instead, evaluations are often based on format criteria, such as edits, camera shots, lighting and sound quality, and other technical matters. In analyzing the judging of television news awards, Altheide (1978) concluded that the primary evaluation criteria consisted of technical or format-oriented matters rather than news content. In that situation, good news meant good television.

Linguistic Form in Media

At the risk of being all too brief, the following illustrations attempt to describe and assess the features and importance of mass communication as specialized languages. A rich and growing body of literature is advancing the thesis that "media effects" must be determined in part through linguistic analysis, such as semiotics and iconography (see Berger, 1981; Fishwick & Browne, 1978; Fiske & Hartley, 1978). Although media linguistics ranges from a psychoanalytic approach to straight grammatological diagrams, its general value lies in the Sapir/Whorf hypothesis (Sapir, 1949; Whorf, 1956) that grammar provides a logic framework for constructing reality.

The linguistic character of mass communication may be observed in its most basic sense by applying the naive approach of identifying the grammar (syntax, inflection, and specialized vocabulary) of a particular media presentation, such as a television program, novel, or radio broadcast (see Snow, 1983). Building on observations of grammatical form rather than content analysis, it is possible to develop a description of the grammatical characteristics unique to each medium and unique to particular formats within a medium. To date, Hollywood and journalistic film have been subjected to the most pronounced grammatical description, and, no doubt, the most famous and still one of the most dramatic examples of film grammar is the chase scene as developed by silent filmmaker D. W. Griffith (circa 1915). Griffith discovered that the illusion of a chase could be constructed on film by switching back and forth between pursuer and pursued in a sequence of edited shots that varied in duration and in distance between the audience viewer and the film subject. As viewers became familiar with this syntax, they were able to anticipate the next visual image in the sequence. Eventually, the film audience became familiar with the syntax of fear in horror genre, gunfights in Westerns, and seduction in love stories.

Similarly, network television news employs a now familiar syntax of introducing stories with the anchorperson followed by a reporter on the scene. This technique is significant in establishing the "news" credibility of the anchorperson in the mind of the viewer. To illustrate further, an on-the-scene report is organized as a series of visual shots superimposed over the reporter's narration. Although the typical viewer's conception is that narration supports the visual images, it is usually a case of wrapping the narrative in whatever appropriate visual scenes are available. The result is that viewers of television news develop their notions about news primarily on the basis of an organization of visual images rather than the more informative oral reports (Altheide, 1985a). It may be concluded that television news consists of seeing an anchorperson talking while seated at a table, followed by a series of pictures that apparently are taken at the scene of the story, and summarized or concluded by a reporter or anchorperson.

Format is that explicit and implicit understanding which joins an activity and/or actor via a medium to an audience. However, since formats comprise "pre-givens" or basics for interaction and communication, they tend to be taken for granted, and thereby excluded from scholarly assessment of the content and process of communication. Furthermore, the perspective contained in these formats is relevant for understanding communication content as well as process (see Altheide, 1976; Epstein, 1973; Gans, 1979; Tuchman, 1978).

The power of the mass media goes beyond mere information transmission; it consists of shaping information along explicit temporal and spatial lines. More is involved than simply a "narrative form"; rather, the narrative is molded by a format logic. For example, TV news "tells time" with visuals, particularly videotape. This method means that all other things being equal, the report with the most relevant visuals available will get the most air time (see Altheide, 1985a; Schneider, 1985). On U.S. TV networks, without such visuals there is little likelihood that an event will receive more than a few seconds if selected at all. Format considerations for events featured on U.S. network TV include the following:

- accessibility—how readily can newsworkers obtain information about an event
- visual quality—the extent and clarity of film, tape, or other visual depictions of the significant action
- drama and action—the graphic, visual, and aural portrayal of movement that can be used to illustrate the event
- audience relevance—the interest an item is perceived by newsworkers to have for a mass audience
- thematic encapsulation—the ease with which an event can be briefly stated and summarized, and joined to a similar event or a series of reports over a period of time or within the same newscast

These format considerations guide both selection and production of news events. For example, a report of an event is more likely to be broadcast if visuals are accessible (and available) and can be used to illustrate the event. If the event is also dramatic and involves action presumed to be familiar to an audience, for example, shooting, running, and so forth, then that event is likely to receive more air time. For a more detailed and comprehensive example, consider the relationship between TV news format requirements and reports about terrorism.

TV NEWS FORMATS AND TERRORISM

In an international study ("TV News and the Production of Reality") of the news coverage in a dozen countries for the week of September 21-27, 1981, we have examined newscasts on the basis of *information units* (IUs; they rarely exceed 10-20 seconds), which are akin to sentences in a report about an *item* (see Altheide, 1985a). The relevance of visuals in TV coverage of terrorism (see Schmid & de Graaf, 1982) can be illustrated by examining the number of IUs in selected reports about terrorism and noting the way visuals were used. Summary reviews of hostages held in Honduras and terrorists in Paris will be followed by an analysis of the way American and British TV covered a terrorist incident in Britain. Together, these materials provide the grist for an analytic scheme, an ideal type, for clarifying how TV news formats influence coverage of terrorism in particular, and international news in general.

Network Coverage of an
Attack on Americans in Honduras

ABC's coverage of an attack in Honduras on American advisors on September 23, 1981, lasted for 20 seconds, consisting of 2 information units.

There was no videotape, only a graphic as a backdrop to the report by Robinson from Chicago.

CBS's coverage of the same attack was quite similar. It lasted 30 seconds—consisting of 3 information units—with the studio anchor, Dan Rather, discussing it over a map of the world. He stated that a Communist group claimed credit. (Note that this statement also served as a transition to the next item, that lasted 2 minutes, 10 seconds, dealing with how the handicapped were treated in the Soviet Union; videotape was used.)

NBC reported the attack in 10 seconds, with one information unit. No visuals were used other than the studio anchor, John Chancellor.

Network Coverage of
Armenian Terrorists in Paris

The network coverage of the Armenian terrorist story in Paris was similar to the Honduras story. On September 24, 1981, all three networks reported that a group of Armenian terrorists stormed the Turkish embassy in Paris. There were different accounts of the number of hostages being held.

ABC gave the report 90 seconds on September 24, the day the event occurred. It was the fifth item in the newscast and was made up of 7 information units. Pierre Salinger was on the scene. Videotape (with the reporter's voice-over) provided the action. ABC had no follow-up report on September 25, although the other networks did (as did at least six countries in our international study—Sweden, Netherlands, Great Britain, Israel, France, Spain).

CBS, on September 24, gave the embassy takeover 80 seconds. It was the ninth item in the news report and consisted of 5 information units. Videotape was used with the reporter on the scene. CBS covered the end of the ordeal on September 25, in 20 seconds. It was the thirteenth item in the news report and consisted of 1 information unit. Some videotape and graphics aided Rather's in-studio summary.

NBC allotted 110 seconds to this report on September 24. It was the fifth item in the newscast and consisted of 7 information units. The reporter did a voice-over of videotape, including talking with officials. NBC gave the release of the hostages 30 seconds on September 25. It was the eighth item, consisting of 2 information units. John Chancellor talked over videotape.

Other Network Coverage of Hostages

Some other hostage reports aired by the networks further suggest the importance of visuals for the amount of coverage. On September 18, 1981, the three networks carried reports about the hijacking of a Polish airliner. ABC and NBC used their respective anchors, Peter Jennings from England and John Chancellor, to talk over some film for 30 seconds. Dan Rather did film voice-over for CBS's 20-second report.

On September 27 another hijacking was reported by the wire services which did not make the American networks. Three Croatian hijackers who had hijacked a Yugoslavian jet bound for Cyprus on the previous night were being returned to Belgrade. The assumption must be that no film was available to the networks of this incident and surrounding events.

These materials demonstrate two points established in prior work (Altheide, 1985a): First, network news time beyond 20 seconds is linked to the visual imagery of videotape; second, the visuals are of dramatic action rather than "talking heads." What we want to emphasize is that the presentation and use of political language and symbols takes place within the media formats.

A detailed case study of the coverage by U.S. and British TV of an IRA bombing on July 20, 1982, in two parks in London further illustrates the role of formats in shaping symbolic messages (see Altheide, 1987). The data will not be presented in the brief section to follow. Instead, we present the analytic framework for clarifying which of four aspects of terrorists' behavior—precipitating social conditions, goals, objectives, or tactics—were more likely to be presented, and if so, in which news formats they would be found—conventional TV news coverage or documentary-type programs (Paletz, Ayanian, & Fozzard, 1982).

Our examples suggest that tactics—and their aftermath—are more susceptible to visual documentation. We will further suggest that the interpretation by Paletz et al. (1982) and others (see Davis & Walton, 1983), that "terrorists . . . are not endowed with legitimacy by television news . . . [and that] terrorists' tactics are stressed in television news" (Paletz et al., 1982, p. 162) is at least partially correct. Format considerations, however, contribute in ways previously unacknowledged to this coverage; what is more compatible with format considerations can lead to certain emphases that have ideological overtones. Moreover, if similar formats and reports can be comparatively examined in the United States and the United Kingdom, we can further clarify the role of the media formats in presenting messages that resonate ideology.

In addition to the logic and grammar (see Altheide & Snow, 1979), TV news formats involve certain elements that have several variates: (1) source(s) of information—officials, actual participants, and so on; (2) specificity of focus and emphasis—"pure description" of some happening, historical context of an event, and so forth; (3) temporal/spatial presentation of information—an individual talking, videotape, or graphics. It is through certain combinations of these elements that make one type of news program—a regular evening newscast—recognizable as different from another—a documentary.

For purposes of this comparative study on TV news coverage of terrorism, it was useful to draw on analytical distinctions for each of the three elements noted above. These analytical tools were used to develop two ideal types of news formats—*event* and *topic*. The former is usually found in regular evening newscasts, while the latter is more typical of documentaries, although numerous exceptions do occur. (The overlap in these formats is apparent, and several British researchers [Schlesinger, Murdock, & Elliott, 1983, p. 36 ff] distinguish between a news bulletin, news magazine, current affairs, and documentary.)

The analytical concepts we have borrowed from previous work are as follows (see Altheide, 1985a; Schlesinger, 1983):

(1) *Open-Closed* refers to the source of information and range of perspectives permitted into the report. Event reports tend to be closed, mainly using official views, while the topic type provides "spaces in which the core assumptions of the official perspective can be interrogated and contexted and in which other perspectives can be presented and examined" (Schlesinger et al., 1983, p. 32).

(2) *Tight-Loose* refers to internal organization of the report itself. If only one definition or slant on a happening is permitted, then the report is tight; if several angles are set forth, and/or permitted to emerge in the course of the report, then the report is loose. Event reports tend to be tight, while topic reports tend to be a bit more loose. The former, more typical of regular news reports, tends to be organized around one central theme or angle, with little ambiguity; loose structuring, more common with certain documentaries, invites comparisons, different points of view, and does not avoid ambiguities or uncertainties.

(3) *Scanning-Object Time.* An additional element must be considered in our attempt to clarify format features of TV news coverage about terrorism. In addition to noting the apparent overlap in tight-loose and open-closed formats, it is also important to add that these formats differ in mode of representation. Schlesinger et al.'s (1983) distinction between "production techniques" for a news bulletin—"film report"—is not as precise as we would prefer (p. 36 ff). Elements of both may be found in a report in a regular evening newscast, as well as in a documentary. What is critical is the role of the imagery in the thematic emphasis of the report. And imagery on television is based on the premise that real life events and objects that exist in at least three dimensions—object time—can be communicated in only two dimensions—scanning time (Altheide, 1985a). Object time is more explicit, and is associated with documentary-type reports: scanning time is more interpretive, relying on the audience's ability to contextualize and fill in what is presented as information in order to make sense of the report and thereby see the connection between an interpretation and visual evidence.

> "Scanning time" is associated with the event type, or conventional TV news reports. On the other hand, it is time transformed through format into space as a visual representation on a TV screen. On the other hand, it is an artistic and technologically mediated interpretation of object time or the context, circumstances, and actual physical layout of the actors, action, and objects contained within the news report. Just as a gifted painter can offer a two-dimensional rendering of a human body, so too can the news producer. In both cases, it is the audience member who is presumed to be able to follow the interpretation, slotting the appropriate slice of time (as visually depicted) within the proper sequence of action. (Altheide, 1985a, p. 107)

Combining the "official" perspective of an incident, along with the thematic emphasis, temporal order, and program type, suggests the scheme presented in Table 1.

The comparative case study of coverage of terrorism showed remarkable consistency. While there was some overlap between program types, regular news reports (event) tended to focus on tactics and the aftermath of an incident, while topic-type interview shows and documentaries (*topic*) provided information about precipitating social conditions, goals, and objectives. This relationship suggests, then, that international events cast in one format provide different public information. While ideology remains important, it is also true that the impact of format cannot be denied.

MEDIATION AND THE AUDIENCE

Our attempt to understand the communication of culture does not, of course, presume that actors are determined and lack choices. Rather, we seek to clarify how the nature, form, and logic of such choices have been altered by media formats.

In part, media power results from an ability of media strategy to transform the temporal and spatial dimensions of an object or event to make it fit with existing (media) formats. In addition, media power exists when audience members treat media depictions as a summary of an event, translate such images back into the event itself, and then act on the event as a reality independent of media influence. In the language of science this reconstruction becomes "media effects." However, unlike most other media effects studies, our approach posits the primacy of form over content.

Form not only precedes content temporally, it provides the spatial arrangement within which content emerges and becomes substantially meaningful. From our standpoint, media power consists of the adoption by audience members of the formal properties of media communication strategy. As content emerges through and becomes defined by the criteria of form, attention may be turned to the kinds of effects discussed in "audience power" studies such as Blumler and Katz (1974). Whereas the "uses and gratifications model" argues that audience perspectives must be taken into account in understanding so-called media effects, we argue that audience perspectives are in part developed on the foundation of various formal (format) properties of media strategy.

The format and shape of a medium communicates a good deal about its purpose, content, and even intent. It is as though each medium is associated with its own code of interpretation that the audience members recognize. Indeed, the members of a culture, or whom Schutz (1967) refers to as "contemporaries," share a historical and cultural awareness of the pre-givens of their respective media, which may seem less clear to their predecessors and successors. For example, archaeologists spend lifetimes trying to unravel

TABLE 1
Ideal-Type News Formats

Event		*Topic*
closed	official perspective	open
tight	thematic emphasis	loose
scanning	temporal order	object
regular newscast	program type	documentary

meanings and contexts of communication that any child who lived at a particular time took for granted. How individuals reflexively use various media must also be understood and integrated within any general theory of mediation in social life.

The point we wish to stress is consistent with a sociology of knowledge perspective, which recognizes that individuals construct meanings about reality and experiences through the formal properties of various institutional and ideological frameworks, such as Christianity, science, and capitalism. Furthermore, we know that over time such frameworks become routinized and reified as "the reality" within the collective consciousness of a society (see Berger & Luckmann, 1967). For example, what is often overlooked in the so-called natural character of paternalism in family organization, or hetero-sexuality in the biology of sexuality, is the fact that both views are taken-for-granted assumptions embedded in Christianity. Similarly, the importance of television format may not be recognized as an actor in the change of format of newspapers and college textbooks. People may miss the fact that it is only through the public's acceptance of television and existing television formats that makes the claim credible that TV political ads are effective, even essential for a winning campaign. Consequently, in claiming that television is important in contemporary political campaigns, it should be recognized that a candidate's physical appearance, mannerisms, and rhetoric are judged within certain formal characteristics of television itself. Certainly, not every television advertisement is effective in eliciting attention and favorable response, but those that follow "good television" principles will have a greater potential appeal than those that fail to meet format criteria.

Placing this approach within a symbolic interaction model suggests that audience members interact with media and vice versa in at least a para-social fashion to develop various meanings based on the symbols employed and interpreted in a specific context (Blumer, 1969; Davis & Baran, 1981; Douglas et al., 1982). In short, symbolic interaction theoretically encapsulates the entire communication process from message formulation to interpretation and action. Indeed, numerous studies on the social construction of messages have been informed by a symbolic interaction perspective (see Adams & Schreibman, 1978), although this debt is not always acknowledged, perhaps because it is assumed to be the case (see McQuail, 1983).

Our point, then, is that media are associated with—indeed, constituted by—a set of grammatical rules for using certain symbols and have developed general perspectives for interpreting various objects and events. In turn, audience members selectively adopt this overall logic and symbol system for making sense of media experience. Individuals become viewers by adjusting to and accepting the rules and logic of the format, which joins the medium with the content, and with their viewing situation. The ease with which this adjustment has occurred and the taken-for-granted character of this inter-action and experience enables media workers and audience members alike selectively to (1) utilize the media as a source of legitimate information on subjects of relevance; (2) accept basic assumptions about how information is "learned"; (3) look to media as a trusted mediation agent in troublesome and potentially chaotic situations; and (4) develop vicarious overt interaction networks for the sake of routine in everyday life.

To carry the last point a bit further, it is suggested that to the extent that mass media formats influence the social organization of other rounds of human activity and participation, these media function in ways similar to a total institution. In other words, some mass media formats have had an impact on other realms of social life, including the temporal and spatial dimensions surrounding the organization and meaning of everyday affairs. In particular, TV organizations and personnel manifest the motives, intent, and logic to guide the time, place, and manner of collective (audience) social actions. First, media producers are interested in attracting an audience, whether broad or narrow (Altheide & Johnson, 1980; McQuail, 1969; Wright, 1965). Second, the motivation of most media messengers goes beyond conveying the message; rather, it is a message with another purpose—enlightenment, manipulations, commercialism, and so on (Comstock, 1980; DeFleur & Ball-Rokeach, 1975). Third, the messages are infused with this purpose, so we always get an explicit and implicit message (Barrett et al., 1979; Gitlin, 1980, 1983). Fourth, media messages are often targeted for particular audiences at a particular place and time (Altheide & Snow, 1979; Epstein, 1973; Schudson, 1978). Fifth, mass media receivers and messages are ubiquitous and essentially without temporal and spatial limitations in the Western world (Snow, 1983). Sixth, all phases of the media production and programming are tightly scheduled, hierarchically organized, and rationally dispersed (Fishman, 1980; Tuchman, 1978; Tunstall, 1977), although video cassette recorders permit viewers to have some control over scheduling (see Levy & Fink, 1984). In this regard, some features of freedom and flexibility may be joined with media technology.

Just as prison wardens communicate control to social actors as inmates, media managers transform actors into target audiences. The audience member's selections are informed by master assumptions and planning by the message producers and disseminators (Seymour-Ure, 1974; Shaw & McCombs, 1977). Over time, the routines and activities of everyday life essentially integrate the prevailing media logic and formats into the audiences' discourse and patterns (Altheide, 1985a; Hall, 1979, 1980; Davis & Baran, 1981; Nimmo & Combs, 1983). Each of the above abound in any mass-mediated social order with varying intensity, duration, and topical emphasis (Tunstall, 1977).

Scheduling and viewing norms, which most explicitly illustrate the communication of control via TV formats, have been identified with regard to purposive content, purposive use, and patterned use (Lull, 1986). The specific programming content may vary, but the media logic of involvement and control persists. Even all-encompassing institutions such as prisons incorporate mass media programs and schedules into their routines! Individual viewing situations are duplicated by the millions to produce macrosocial patterns and effects that have been largely neglected by most mass communication research (see Altheide & Snow, 1979). When viewed from this perspective, no single institution is so pervasive in shaping the viewer's definition of a situation and the meaning of a message (see Snow, 1983). Lull (1986) confirms that

> abundant empirical evidence indicates that the convenient visual medium is woven purposefully into the intricate tapestry of audience members' complicated lives. Uses of television, and the construction of communication in general, is patterned at the microsocial and macrosocial levels of analysis. (p. 610)

The upshot is that messages are not so much received as they are situationally interpreted and constructed for the purpose at hand. And the interaction with the specific medium is also informed by an individual's definition of the time, place, and manner of communication in a situation.

Electronic Time and Space

The organization of communication informs the temporal and spatial order of experience and social interaction (see Altheide, 1985a; Meyrowitz, 1985). As communication formats have changed, so too have previously taken-for-granted assumptions about the time, place, and manner of activities, including the relevance of formats for audiences. This influence is partly a feature of specific program content, but it is also due to the way in which time, place, and manner of media activities routinely occur. When the logic becomes integral to everyday life so that aspects of format are accepted and incorporated into the time, place, and manner of a range of activities, then the media are socially relevant as a social form in their own right, regardless of specific programming content. An examination of the mass media's role in temporal scheduling of daily routines will be followed by a brief look at the impact of communication formats on the interaction process.

The Temporal Order of Everyday Life

What is important about mass communication formats is their institutional pervasiveness. One way to approach the relevance of media for temporal features of the interaction order is to follow Zerubavel's (1981) keen analysis of the nature and relevance of time for social order. For Zerubavel (1981), social organization is tied to temporal symmetry, or synchronizing the activity of many individuals. Four temporal dimensions underlie temporal symmetry: sequential structure, duration, temporal location, and rate of recurrence.

Sequential Structure

The basic idea here is simply that things go in stages as part of a process and cannot be easily altered in social life. However, media logic can significantly amend what may at one time have been constitutive rules. As social actors become accustomed to joining analytically discrete elements or events into a whole, what may have been arbitrary at one time is now seen—and acted upon—as inevitable and necessary (see Berger & Luckmann, 1967).

The mass media bring unique format characteristics to social situations. Keeping in mind that there are numerous exceptions, we can nevertheless state that media logic negates some rigid sequences. The media are widely available and are operable by all age groups. This accessibility suggests that status distinctions between children, adolescents, and adults are mixed when it comes to using media. (More specific qualitative criteria—"ideal norms"— may be imposed to maintain "media age groups," for example, only adults can view X-rated movies; no late night viewing for children.) In this sense, the availability of various media in our culture is becoming a kind of cultural invariant: Group boundaries—whether based on achieved or ascribed criteria—are permeated by media. Meyrowitz (1985) has made a similar point:

> Electronic media . . . bypass the isolating characteristics of place, and they there-
> by blur the differences between people in different socialization processes. . . .
> Young children once depended almost entirely on their parents and teachers as
> channels to information about the world, but today's children sometimes help
> adults keep in touch with outside events. (p. 157)

One can "know" versions of different ages and experiences at will and can identify with the character and dramaturgy of "being a certain age" in a certain place at a given time. For example, a 12-year-old child can have a media experience of what it is like to be 16 or 60 in the 1940s or the 1990s. The upshot is that media break the sequence of life as it may be viewed by "older" people, who in turn seek to control media in order to control experience of the "noneligible" actors.

Duration and Pervasiveness

How long an event is expected to last is tied to a more general question about the nature and uses of scheduling in everyday life. Activities are engulfed by pervasive time frames. TV and electronic media schedules lead us to schedule parts of the day. Evening prime-time TV viewing occurs between 7 and 8 p.m. and 10 and 11 p.m. This segment of time has not only provided people with evening activities at home, but has also led them to plan activities around the viewing schedule.

Media time is pervasive because other activities incorporate media scheduling and imagery into their own concerns. Children spend considerable time watching TV and learn a great deal from it, for example, facts and impressions about events, styles, images, and, of course, consumer choices and behaviors. But, as they interactively view TV with peers, children also learn how to watch TV, what to laugh at, how to make comments sanctioned by their peers, and what to focus on for purposes of later conversations. For example, laugh tracks on TV provide a sense of timing for individual audience members, while commercials come to be recognized as time-outs, where certain behavior and inattention is permissible. Because children experience TV as part of their everyday routine and surroundings—and not something extraordinary that did not used to be available—TV per se is part of the family, so to speak; it is a feature of routine involvements not dissimilar from hugging one's parents, going to bed, or going to school.

Temporal Location

Media formats are increasingly the standards by which other experiences are recognized, judged, and changed. Temporal and spatial parameters are central to formats. Some of the inventions we have used to locate time physically include the clock and the calendar. The former was a mechanical analogue that mainly told us about time-just-passed, time-left, but little about time-now. Early media had a lot in common with time in that they were essentially "owned" and defined and regulated by the same powerful groups. For example, our current calendar, which is marked off in mechanical hours-days, was a religious construction mildly informed by profane insights that helped translate these sacred categories into a model a bit more compatible with our solar system.

Recurrence

The sources and features of legitimacy that provided the formats for daily life have shifted in modern urban society from institutions such as the church to the mass media. Increasingly, people check and compare their perceptions and understandings with the electronic media (see Blumler & Katz, 1974). Specific days have also been creatively and ritualistically set aside for media experiences pervading the entire culture. The Superbowl football game now is played on Super Sunday; Thanksgiving and New Year's Days are parade and football bowl-game days. Similar media rituals for a celebration of American society are the Academy Awards show and the Miss America Pageant. Even nonmedia rituals such as Halloween, July Fourth, Christmas, Easter, and Mardi Gras have become occasions fraught with media definitions.

The impact may be most visible when one season associated with some events undergoes a practical rearrangement for media purposes. A recent example is the rise and fall of the United States Football League (USFL), which played during the late spring and summer, rather than the traditional football seasons of fall and winter. The critical question for the founders of the

USFL was whether or not there was a large enough audience "out there" who would be willing to watch football any time of the year, and that the revenues from a TV contract could essentially carry the new league, regardless of how many people actually paid to attend the football games. When TV contracts stopped, so did the league. Indeed, a subsequent court case claimed that the National Football League had conspired to destroy the USFL by working to deny it adequate TV coverage.

Time is also marked off by media formats through the definition and use of certain media forms and channels. Thus an individual can be somewhat identified by the media he or she uses and by the specific selections made from each. Specifically, there is a sound and location on the "dial" for finding liberal or conservative music, politics, racial/ethnic music and talk, and general identity. Who you are is easily shown through media formats that identify you as the kind of person who "does this kind of music, TV, etc." (see Larson & Kubey, 1983; Snow, 1983).

Zerubavel's (1981) insights about the social foundations of time provide an opportunity for students of communication conceptually to join time keeping with event making. We have suggested that institutional dominance is partially a feature of communicative dominance, which in turn is manifested in establishing and maintaining a temporal order.

The logic and use of communication formats shape and limit content within their own parameters; formats of communication contain, limit, and essentially define the rules and procedures for dealing with content (messages). Giddens (1984) has referred to the process through which rules reflect the order they produce as *structuration*.

> According to the notion of duality of structure, the structural properties of social systems are both medium and outcome of the practices they recursively organize. Structure is not 'external' to individuals . . . [and] is not to be equated with constraint but is always both constraining and enabling. . . . The reification of social relations, or the discursive "naturalization" of the historically contingent circumstances and products of human action, is one of the main dimensions of ideology in social life. (p. 25)

In this sense, formats are meta-communication statements or rules for the recognition, retention, organization, and presentation of information and experience. Their power resides in employing a logic that joins the manner of specific acts to a temporal and spatial order. Our analyses indicate that the mass media increasingly play this role and, perhaps more important, contribute to the nature of social interaction in everyday life.

Formats and Social Interaction

Perhaps no area of communication research is more emphasized than interaction effects. Most studies about media effects are actually oriented to various forms of social interaction, for example, violent behavior, voting behavior, buying behavior, and so forth. Indeed, with few exceptions, the "effects of the mass media on behavior" refers to the nature, origin, and consequences for social interaction. Moreover, many of the topics for media research, such as "media violence," have been largely defined, initiated, and sustained through mass media attention rather than a comprehensive theory of communication and mediation in social life. The cultural analysis of media effects, particularly mediation, turns our attention to the routine and mundane features of everyday life that constitute social order. These may include things we take for granted as well as things we do not attend to. As Davis and Baran (1981) state:

> Equally important, none of the existing effects perspectives discuss how we use mass communication to help us avoid doing certain things. But mass communication can help us avoid reflecting upon ourselves, other people, or our social environment. . . . The media's most significant effects, then, are not necessarily the most observable or dramatic. They may be those that alter our lives in subtle but meaningful ways. (p. 9)

Scheduling and viewing norms have been identified that suggest that prevailing media logic and formats are integrated into audience members' discourse and interaction patterns (see Altheide, 1985a; Davis & Baran, 1981; Hall, 1979, 1980; Nimmo & Combs, 1983). For example, Davis and Baran (1981) illustrate the ways in which the mass media engage in subtle but important forms of social control, including providing framing cues to each other, disrupting social conversations, and disrupting how we tell stories and enact drama in everyday discourse. While such forms of control are most salient to "self systems" and the interaction process, the routinized use of mass mediated genres can frame how we interpret problems and issues. More recently, Lull (1986) offers three kinds of rules implicit in TV formats, which join individual viewing situation in "microsocial" contexts to "macrosocial" patterns.

First, there are *habitual rules* regulating behavior which emerge from and are sanctioned by more powerful family members. For example, older siblings control programming selections at certain days and times (Saturday mornings). Other children's choices are informed by these scheduling practices, leading them to capture other periods as their own. Lull (1986) affirms that

> macrosocial habits take the form of national patterns of exposure to television. . . . Commercial television presents a fairly inflexible agenda wherein particular times of the day are associated with types of television programs. Furthermore, the presentational format of network television—the rhythm of program segment/commercial/program segment/commercial, etc.—is a prescribed habitual mode of commercial programming. The formula is so ingrained in the medium and its audience that even noncommercial television systems and stations have had to adopt similar breaks in their programming. . . . Broad

patterns of social behavior are simulated in the process as audience members typically adjust their routines to fit television schedules. (pp. 603-604)

Second, *parametric rules* refer to a range of behaviors and options selected to accompany viewing times, for example, what may be watched and for how long, but each of these may require some supervision and decision by adults. Broader social issues are reflected in the options viewers have and exercise. First, viewers cannot alter the TV messages; they can only turn them off. Second, age groups tend to have strikingly common tastes for programs, particularly when the viewers see program advertising as part of the regular commercial breaks. Third, there are few choices for comparative information on products, imagery, or ideologies.

Third, *practical rules* are "methodical interactions that people create in order to accomplish interpersonal goals" for influencing desired social relations and outcomes; creating interpersonal distances; a source of status and control in its own right through the application of information from TV to one's own family; and perhaps most basic, TV programming can be used to represent competence, membership, and affiliation (Lull, 1986, p. 606).

When millions of people engage in similar activities via media formats, a macrosocial effect can be identified, particularly in cultivating values and giving them a visual identification. As stated by Lull (1986):

> These cultural lessons are assimilated to some degree by audience members throughout the country who then incorporate elements of the sponsored imagery into their everyday interpersonal relations. In this way, patterns develop across the country that are often first suggested and later reinforced by television. These lessons advocate special ways of thinking. Consumerism may be the most pervasive case in point because the creation of a climate for consumption is fundamental to commercial broadcasting. . . . The first step on macrosocial, tactical communication is the effective transmission of values through television programming. The second step is the employment of these suggestions by viewers as they construct their daily lives. (p. 607)

The upshot of these examples is that a frame for discourse and social interaction is apparent in mass media formats. When the temporal and spatial organizing features of media messages and imagery become incorporated into extra-media contexts, then a theoretically informed "media analysis" merges into cultural analysis. For this reason we examine other instances of mediation.

OTHER FORMS OF MEDIATION

Obviously, calling for an understanding of mediation in social life requires looking beyond conventional communication forms such as the mass media.

If mediation and formats do affect cultural affairs, then we should be able to see manifestations in other realms of social life. Computers in particular, and keyboard communication in general, pervade the worlds of work and play in technological societies, but they have seldom been treated as significant formats in their own right.

While major steps have already been taken to integrate mass communication within a general theory of communication (see Altheide, 1985a; Meyrowitz, 1985), the role of computer formats in social life, and particularly bureaucratic structures, remains to be explicated (see Danziger, Dutton, Kling, & Kraemer, 1982; Tomeski & Lazarus, 1975; Wessel, 1974). The task, then, is to illustrate and demonstrate how computer formats express temporal and spatial dimensions in particular, and contribute to the communication process in general.

Computer Formats

While formats are vital for all forms of communication, only recently have computer communication formats come to dominate and essentially differentiate large segments of everyday life (see Altheide, 1985c; Altheide & Snow, 1979; Giddens, 1984; McLuhan, 1960, 1962). Both main frame and micro (personal) computers illustrate unique communication processes. It is not just the computers per se that are important, but rather the effects on the logic-in-use by bureaucratic personnel who increasingly modify definitions of situations to comply with features of computer formats.

The operation of the "computer system" still depends on a "manual system" of a different kind. Supplementing stacks of paper and handwritten notes from files, computer formats necessitate using keyboards to interact with the machine. The rules and logic of such interaction, along with the temporal and spatial parameters of this interface, have added yet another specialization to the bureaucracy. A keyboard may be defined as any device in which parts are purposefully manipulated in a social situation according to a logical scheme, in order to create, interpret, send, or receive symbolically meaningful information. Already institutionalized throughout social life in the guise of musical keyboards, telephone dialing equipment, electronic tuning equipment, microwave ovens, videogames, and a host of children's toys, the fingertip control of keyboards is the hallmark of computer interaction (see Altheide, 1985c).

Any technology carries with it assumptions, logic, and a cosmology (see Berger & Luckmann, 1967). The original purpose of an invention is quickly forgotten as the innovation is simultaneously incorporated into the process of stability and change, and thereby contributes to its character. For example, one forerunner of computers was the mechanical sorting of punched "Hollerith" cards to provide faster census information (see Austrian, 1982). This process was originally intended merely to process information rather than define and shape the nature of the information collected. Subsequently, this expanded technology has spawned an orientation to research that equates the use of computer techniques with knowledge and science. Technicians are now trained to produce and seek out information in a form that can be transformed into a "machine readable" form (see Mills, 1959; Sorokin, 1956). Similarly, the computer form is increasingly deemed to be essential to bureaucratic work and, indeed, our "contemporary" world:

> The belief in the indispensability of the computer is not entirely mistaken. The computer becomes an indispensable component of any structure once it is so thoroughly integrated with the structure, so enmeshed in various vital sub-structures, that it can no longer be factored out without fatally impairing the whole structure. That is virtually a tautology. The utility of this tautology is that it can reawaken us to the possibility that some human actions, e.g., introduction of computers into some complex human activities, may constitute an irreversible commitment. (Weizenbaum, 1976, p. 28)

Computers exemplify "pure work," or the unreflexive pursuit of tasks. However, since all human work—even in a bureaucracy—is reflexive, contextualized, and therefore somewhat ambiguous, major translations are necessary to bring people back in, particularly when the original purpose is forgotten. The entrapment of content by form via computer logic has been suggested by Weizenbaum's (1976) analysis of a researcher who confronts a problem:

> When this limitation seems to him to be entirely computational, and when a computer is offered to help remove it, he may well launch a program of intensive, time-consuming "research" aimed simply at "computerizing" his technique. Such programs usually generate subproblems of a strictly computational nature that tend, by virtue of their very magnitude, to increasingly dominate the task and, unless great care is taken to avoid it, to eventually become the center of attention. . . . The collection of subproblems together with the lore, jargon, and subtechniques which crystallized around them, becomes reified. (p. 36)

The management of our complex tax system (Samuelson, 1986) and a less than efficient welfare antisystem have been partially buttressed by computer systems and data bases. The way computer formats were employed to mediate and salvage a welfare system, which implicitly conforms to an ideology of social control, has been suggested by Weizenbaum (1976):

> The very erection of an enormously large and complex computer based welfare administration apparatus, however, created an interest in its maintenance and therefore in the perpetuation of the welfare system itself. And such interests soon become substantive barriers to innovation even if good reasons to innovate later accumulate. . . . The computer, then, was used to conserve America's social and political institutions. It buttressed them and immunized them, at least tempo-rarily, against enormous pressures for change. (p. 31)

This way of working and interacting with substantive problems simultaneously influences criteria for "good work" and changes the organizational product. Worker competence and the legitimacy and processing of "official information" are but a few of the effects computer formats and mediation have had on social life. One result has been an acceleration toward the reduction of information, which amounts to bureaucratic propaganda (see Altheide & Johnson, 1980; Douglas, 1971). The latest form this has taken is the data base.

One consequence of data base use is that our lives are affected by predictors based on information that may lack validity when applied to individuals, yet is utilized because it is available. An illustration is the way insurance companies use data bases to the detriment of many individuals, a process Wessel (1974) has referred to as "data-in-gross":

> Few people seem to realize how enormously we are already affected by data-in-gross. Our fire insurance and automobile premiums are fixed by unrelated experience in the areas in which we reside, in large part even to the exclusion of individual experience.... Unlike transactional data where individual rights have long been the subject of some common law concerns, there is almost no legal precedent to help us handle data-in-gross.... The problem is that the computer makes so much more of this possible, that data-in-gross can ultimately become as much of a concern as individual data. (pp. 38-39)

Despite the fact that statisticians have long been aware of the "ecological fallacy" of attributing aggregate characteristics to individual cases, the insurance companies use this information because it is organizationally useful for legitimating rates.

Computer formats operate well within bureaucratic settings because of common assumptions about rational organization and that clear distinctions exist between means and goals. From one perspective, bureaucracy "looks" like computerization, keyboard products and images, and efficiency. But from the interactionist interest in the definition of the situation, it is clear that process and product have not only come together, but are now Janus-like. The time, place, and manner of an expanding array of bureaucratic activity involve and reflect computer formats. The implications for social control have been suggested by Couch (1984):

> The inventors of new communication systems, record keeping procedures, and production methods are offering the possibility of all human transactions taking the form of mediated contact.... More and more, coordinated action is action that is subordinated to machines. All are becoming machine like. Rationality is equated with subordination of human activity to machines. (p. 369)

The social definition of computer technology has transcended being a tool; it is a communicative frame for transforming topics into resources massaged by a format that symbolically reifies itself through its use, while denying human agency.

CONCLUSION

The reflexive character of the communication process is of central importance for the sociology of everyday life. While scholars have long recognized that symbolic communication joined retrospective and prospective meanings of a situation, the role of mediation itself has not been previously delineated. It has been suggested that an analysis of television and other media formats provides some insight into the way experience and information is organized in terms of an actor, a context, a phenomenon or event, a medium, and an audience.

Identifying communication formats in social life and assessing their effects is no trivial pursuit. How we communicate precedes and limits what we communicate. When a medium used in daily affairs operates on the basis of a distinctive logic, then communication is subject to format, which in turn informs its content and situated use. The impact is even greater when, as in the case of computers, they are symbolically legitimated. Recognizing this format and charting its implications and effects is an act of freedom.

Format is also offered as a theoretical construct for clarifying the meaningful way in which experience is symbolically mediated. More than a vessel, mediation is itself organized and interpreted by actors in a situation. Moreover, as the logic of a medium—for example, television—pervades a social order, more than content is affected; the temporal and spatial dimensions of social order and everyday routines can themselves be altered and routinized. Such a meta-communication perspective is implied in a reflexive definition of the situation.

Any theory of social organization must implicitly or explicitly make claims about a communication process joining actors to a definition of the situation. For example, Durkheim (1965) argued that the collective consciousness flowed from, and was sustained by, meaningful religious rituals that were spatially and temporally organized, recognized, and interpreted. Religion was the dominant institution. Social life was "religious"; at every turn the sacred was meaningfully communicated and affirmed.

With the division of labor and the rise of a rationalistic contract society, social life has become increasingly differentiated, and the logic of bureaucratic form has become central in social control. Indeed, Weinstein (1985) suggests that a new form of collective consciousness, albeit fragmented, is realized through mass media images and forms produced for the celebration of instrumental values and interests. From this perspective, the mass media in general, and television in particular, provide the means for cultural expression of social structure.

The important feature of a social form is the way in which it is used as a structural device. As alluded to earlier, this structuration occurs in two principal ways: (1) as a strategy for social action, which includes interaction in an elementary fashion as well as more complex institutional patterns; and (2) as an interpretive schema. As a strategy for social action, Simmel saw social forms operating in four categories or levels: elementary interaction, institutional patterns, autonomous play forms, and society as a generic abstraction. Applying this categorization to mass communication, it is argued that mass communication is accepted as a basic form of interaction in modern urban society, that mass media operate as a distinct institutional strategy, that mass communication may operate as an autonomous play form of communication, and, to some people, mass media may come to represent society in a generic sense. When operating as an interpretive schema, mass media operate as perspectives that inform conceptions of reality. As such, media become a means of informing the process of creating culture.

The mass media are changing our lives because they can bring an image of one moment into another. This is particularly crucial when electronic media rapidly link one place (space) with another; we, in our living rooms, see people in their living rooms, on battlefields, on the moon, at work. These images make little sense unless we can locate them within our own stock of knowledge and taken-for-granted routines (see Schutz, 1967). And, since a key feature of our ability to interpret events is our own position in time and place, we will incorporate this event—occurring in its own time, place, and manner—within our perspective. Thus the event we are experiencing is essentially interpreted as not fundamentally different after all, but simply a different version of an already familiar order.

Now, a strange event can become meaningful when it is made available to us through a familiar medium. This sense making can be accomplished in several ways: First, we can be physically located in a place, therefore encountering the event in a manner that is taken for granted. For example, we may be sitting in a familiar chair in our own homes when we encounter the strange event. Second, we can acquire information about an event in a variety of ways, but in the case of news events, most of this information comes from newspapers, radio, or TV. Not only is the language in which the information is delivered important, but so too is the explicit medium. As we have become familiar with various types of media, we take them for granted and are unaware that the information is mediated by them; it appears as though we are getting a straight dose of the event, particularly in the case of television, in which pictures are used on "the scene." Third, the specific message about the event can be cast in terms already familiar to us, for example, conflict, dishonesty, or corruption. Fourth, the way the information is formatted can seem quite familiar and therefore not noticed, although such formats can significantly affect how a report will be presented. For example, viewers of TV have developed what may be termed *media consciousness*, a perspective for allowing the format in use to stand for the event itself (Snow, 1983). This substitution can include scheduling, pace, tempo, and organization. Thus as viewers routinely receive "world and national news" on telecasts within a 5-minute block, they may also expect it, and therefore may not find it strange or presumptuous that the entire world's significant events of the day can be so quickly encapsulated. In short, what has developed over time is a perspective of information that has been provided by the media format itself; media may be viewed from the standpoint of media, and that is why the world seems normal (see Schneider, 1985). As a central feature of the logic-in-use in everyday life, these media formats need not be wholly constitutive to have sociological significance; theoretically, it is enough that they help construct the time, place, and manner of experience in social affairs. Clearly, the gods would be envious.

REFERENCES

Adams, W. C., & Schreibman, F. (Eds.). (1978). *Television network news: Issues in content research.* Washington, DC: George Washington University.
Altheide, D. L. (1976). *Creating reality: How TV news distorts events.* Newbury Park, CA: Sage.
Altheide, D. L. (1978). RTNDA news award judging and media culture. *Journalism Quarterly, 55,* 164-167.
Altheide, D. L. (1985a). *Media power.* Newbury Park, CA: Sage.
Altheide, D. L. (1985b). Symbolic interaction and "uses and gratification": Towards a theoretical integration. *Communications: The European Journal of Communication, 3,* 73-82.
Altheide, D. L. (1985c). Keyboarding as a social form. *Computers and the Social Sciences, 1,* 97-106.
Altheide, D. L. (1987). Format and symbols in TV coverage of terrorism in the United States and Great Britain. *International Studies Quarterly, 31,* 161-170.
Altheide, D. L., & Johnson, J. M. (1980). *Bureaucratic propaganda.* Boston: Allyn & Bacon.
Altheide, D. L., & Snow, R. P. (1979). *Media logic.* Newbury Park, CA: Sage.
Austrian, G. D. (1982). *Herman Hollerith: Forgotten giant of information processing.* New York: Columbia University Press.
Barrett, M., Corrigan, P., Kuhn, A., & Wolff, U. (Eds.). (1979). *Ideology and cultural production.* New York: St. Martin's.
Bennett, W. L. (1983). *News: The politics of illusion.* New York: Longman.
Berger, A. A. (1981). Semiotics and TV. In R. P. Adler (Ed.), *Understanding television* (pp. 91-114). New York: Praeger.
Berger, P., & Luckmann, T. (1967). *The social construction of reality.* Garden City, NY: Anchor.
Blumer, H. (1969). *Symbolic interactionism: Perspective and method.* Englewood Cliffs, NJ: Prentice-Hall.
Blumler, J., & Katz, E. (Eds.). (1974). *The uses of mass communications: Current perspectives on gratifications research.* Newbury Park, CA: Sage.
Chesebro, J. W. (1982). Communication, values, and popular television series—A seven year assessment. In G. Gumpert & R. Cathcart (Eds.), *Inter/media: Interpersonal communication in a media world* (pp. 468-519). New York: Oxford University Press.
Couch, C. J. (1984). *Constructing civilizations.* Greenwich, CT: JAI Press.
Comstock, G. (1980). *Television in America.* Newbury Park, CA: Sage.
Danziger, J. N., Dutton, W. H., Kling, R., & Kraemer, K. L. (1982). *Computers and politics: High technology and American local governments.* New York: Columbia University Press.
Davis, D. E., & Baran, S. J. (1981). *Mass communication and everyday life.* Belmont, CA: Wadsworth.
Davis, H., & Walton, P. (Eds.). (1983). *Language, image, media.* Oxford, England: Basil Blackwell.
DeFleur, M., & Ball-Rokeach, S. (1975). *Theories of mass communication.* New York: David McKay.

Douglas, J. D. (1971). *American social order.* New York: Free Press.

Douglas, J. D., Adler, P., Adler, P., Fontana, A., Freeman, C. R., & Kotarba, J. (1982). *An introduction to the sociologies of everyday life.* Boston, MA: Allyn & Bacon.

Duncan, M. C., & Brummett, B. (1987). The mediation of spectator sport. *Research Quarterly for Exercise and Sport, 58,* 168-177.

Durkheim, E. (1965). *The division of labor in society* (G. Simpson, Trans.). New York: Free Press.

Epstein, E. J. (1973). *News from nowhere.* New York: Random House.

Fishman, M. (1980). *Manufacturing the news.* Austin: University of Texas Press.

Fishwick, M., & Browne, R. B. (Eds.). (1978). *Icons of America.* Bowling Green, OH: Bowling Green Press.

Fiske, J., & Hartley, J. (1978). *Reading television.* London: Methuen.

Gans, H. J. (1979). *Deciding what's news.* New York: Free Press.

Gerbner, G., Gross, L., Morgan, M., & Signorielli, N. (1980). The "mainstreaming" of America: Violence profile no. 11. *Journal of Communication, 30*(3): 10-29.

Giddens, A. (1984). *The constitution of society: Outline of the theory of structuration.* Berkeley: University of California Press.

Gitlin, T. (1980). *The whole world is watching.* Berkeley: University of California Press.

Gitlin, T. (1983). *Inside prime time.* New York: Pantheon.

Glasgow Media Group. (1976). *Bad news.* London: Routledge & Kegan Paul.

Goffman, E. (1961). *Asylums: Essays on the social situation of mental patients and other inmates.* Garden City, NY: Doubleday.

Goffman, E. (1974). *Frame analysis.* New York: Harper & Row.

Graber, D. A. (1984). *Processing the news: How people tame the information tide.* New York: Longman.

Greenfield, P. M. (1984). *Mind and media: The effects of television, video games, and computers.* Cambridge, MA: Harvard University Press.

Gronbeck, B. E. (1981). McLuhan as rhetorical theorist. *Journal of Communication, 31*(3), 117-128.

Gumpert, G., & Cathcart, R. (1979). *Intermedia: Interpersonal communication in a media world.* New York: Oxford University Press.

Gunter, B., & Wober, M. (1983). Television viewing and public perceptions of hazards to life. *Journal of Environmental Psychology, 3,* 325-335.

Hall, S. (1979). Culture, the media and ideological effect. In J. Curran, M. Gurevitch, & J. Woolacott (Eds.), *Mass communication and society* (pp. 315-345). Newbury Park, CA: Sage.

Hall, S. (1980). Cultural studies and the centre: Some problematics and problems. In S. Hall, D. Hobson, A. Lowe, & P. Willis (Eds.), *Culture, media, language: Working papers in cultural studies, 1971-79* (pp. 15-47). London: Hutchinson.

Lang, G. E., & Lang, K. (1981). Mass communication and public opinion: Strategies for research. In M. Rosenberg & R. H. Turner (Eds.), *Social psychology: Sociological perspectives* (pp. 653-681). New York: Basic Books.

Larson, R., & Kubey, R. (1983). Television and music: Contrasting media in adolescent life. *Youth and Society, 15,* 13-31.

Levine, D. N. (1971). *Georg Simmel on individuality and social forms.* Chicago: University of Chicago Press.

Levy, M. R. (1979). Watching TV news as parasocial interaction. *Journal of Broadcasting, 23,* 69-80.

Levy, M. R., & Fink, E. L. (1984). Home video recorders and the transcience of television broadcasts. *Journalism Quarterly, 34,* 56-71.

Lull, J. (1982). The social uses of television. In D. C. Whitney et al. (Eds.), *Mass communication review yearbook* (Vol. 3, pp. 397-409). Newbury Park, CA: Sage.

Lull, J. (1986). Ideology, television and interpersonal communications. In G. Gumpert & R. Cathcart (Eds.), *Inter-Media: Interpersonal communication in media world* (pp. 597-610). New York: Oxford University Press.

McLuhan, M. (1960). *Explorations in communication.* Boston: Beacon.

McLuhan, M. (1962). *The Gutenberg Galaxy: The making of typographic man.* Toronto: University of Toronto Press.

McLuhan, M. (1964). *Understanding media: The extensions of man.* New York: McGraw-Hill.

McQuail, D. (1969). *Towards a sociology of mass communications.* London: Collier-Macmillan.

McQuail, D. (1983). *Mass communication theory.* Newbury Park, CA: Sage.

Meyrowitz, J. (1985). *No sense of place: The impact of electronic media on social behavior.* New York: Plenum.

Mills, C. W. (1959). *The sociological imagination.* New York: Oxford University Press.

Newcomb, H. (1974). *TV, the most popular art.* Garden City, NY: Doubleday/Anchor.

Nimmo, D., & Combs, J. E. (1983). *Mediated political realities.* New York: Longman.

Paletz, D., Ayanian, J. Z., & Fozzard, P. A. (1982). Terrorism on television news: The IRA, the FALN, and the Red Brigade. In W. Adams (Ed.), *Television coverage of international affairs* (pp. 143-165). Norwood, NJ: Ablex.

Peterson, R. A. (Ed.). (1976). *The production of culture.* Newbury Park, CA: Sage.

Samuelson, R. J. (1986, April 21). The true tax burden. *Newsweek,* p. 68.

Sapir, E. (1949). Time perspective in aboriginal American culture: A study in method. In D. G. Mandlebaum (Ed.), *Selected writings in language, culture, and personality.* Berkeley: University of California Press.

Schlesinger, P. (1978). *Putting "Reality" Together.* London: Constable.

Schlesinger, P., Murdock, P. G., & Elliott, P. (1983). *Televising "terrorism": Political violence in popular culture.* London: Comedia Publishing Group.

Schmid, A. P., & de Graaf, J. (1982). *Violence as communication: Insurgent terrorism and the Western news media.* Newbury Park, CA: Sage.

Schneider, F. (1985). *The substance and structure of network television news: An analysis of content features, format features, and formal features.* Unpublished doctoral dissertation, Syracuse University.

Schudson, M. (1978). *Discovering the news: A social history of American newspapers.* New York: Basic Books.

Schudson, M. (1984). *Advertising, the uneasy persuasion: Its dubious impact on American society.* New York: Basic Books.

Schutz, A. (1967). *The phenomenology of the social world.* Evanston, IL: Northwestern University Press.

Seymour-Ure, C. (1974). *The political impact of mass media.* Newbury Park, CA: Sage.

Shaw, D. L., & McCombs, M. E. (1977). *The emergence of American political issues: The agenda-setting function of the press.* St. Paul, MN: West.

Smith, V. J. (1983). *Programming for radio and television.* Washington, DC: University Press of America.

Snow, R. P. (1983). *Creating media culture.* Newbury Park, CA: Sage.

Sorokin, P. A. (1956). *Fads and foibles in modern sociology.* Chicago: Regnery.

Streeter, T. (1984). An alternative approach to television research: Developments in British cultural studies in Birmingham. In W. D. Rowland, Jr., & B. Watkins (Eds.), *Interpreting television: Current research perspectives* (pp. 74-97). Newbury Park, CA: Sage.

Tomeski, E. A., & Lazarus, H. (1975). *People-oriented computer systems: The computer in crisis.* New York: Van Nostrand Reinhold.

Tuchman, G. (1978). *Making news.* New York: Free Press.

Tunstall, J. (1977). *The media are American.* New York: Columbia University Press.

Weinstein, D. (1985, Winter). Television as religion: The reemergence of the conscience-collective. *Listening, 20,* 6-16.

Weizenbaum, J. (1976). *Computer power and human reason: From judgment to calculation.* San Francisco: W. H. Freeman.

Wessel, M. R. (1974). *Freedom's edge: The computer threat to society.* Reading, MA: Addison-Wesley.

Whorf, B. (1956). *Language, thought, and reality* (J. B. Carrol, Ed.). Cambridge, MA: M.I.T. Press.

Williams, R. (1975). *Television, technology and cultural form.* New York: Shocken.

Williams, R. (1982). *The sociology of culture.* New York: Shocken.

Wolff, K. H. (1950). *The sociology of Georg Simmel.* New York: Free Press.

Wright, C. R. (1965). *Mass communication: A sociological perspective.* New York: Random House.

Zerubavel, E. (1981). *Hidden rhythms.* Chicago: University of Chicago Press.

On Mediated Communication Theory: The Rise of Format

TIMOTHY P. MEYER
University of Wisconsin—Green Bay

T HE notion of format as a key concept in understanding mediated communication has been overlooked either entirely or has been given only scant attention. It may be that formats are such obvious givens in the consideration of mediated communication that it seems hardly necessary to consider their implications. As the essay by Altheide and Snow and, I hope, this one make clear, the consequences of media formats are indeed far-reaching and significant. It is the purpose of this review to elaborate upon the authors' treatment of format; this elaboration is intended to enhance the significance of media formats and their consequences and to enhance our grasp of the process of mediated communication and its impact on individuals.

In commenting upon the importance of format in mediated communication, Altheide and Snow stress: "since formats comprise 'pre-givens' or basics for interaction in communication, they tend to be taken for granted, and thereby excluded from scholarly assessment of the content and process of communication" (p. 201). They go on to observe that media formats shape events in the creation of content by manipulating the dimensions of space and time to suit a variety of purposes. Some of these purposes are dictated by the time or space constraints, others reflect the nature of the media institution producing the content and the underlying values and goals of these institutions, while still others would include the particular goals of those directly responsible for creating the content (e.g., reporters or editors). Thus, format considerations help to determine which events are selected for presentation and how they will be "packaged."

Correspondence and requests for reprints: Timothy P. Meyer, Department of Communication and the Arts, University of Wisconsin, Green Bay, WI 54301.

Communication Yearbook 11, pp. 224-229

While Altheide and Snow focus on the coverage of events in television news contexts, their observations can and should be extended to the arena of media presentations of so-called entertainment content as well. Moreover, even what they have presented regarding television news would profit from further elaboration. They provided a good starting point in their thinking on the value of examining format as a crucial determinant of mediated communication and its effects on individuals and audiences. A great deal more, however, needs to be said.

Regarding the presentation and creation of content in television news, the authors list format features that shape the news events that are selected and produced. These features include accessibility, visual quality, drama and action, audience relevance, and thematic encapsulation. Of course, only thematic encapsulation would seem to require a definition; the authors tell us the TV journalists look for the ease with which an event can be briefly presented and linked to a similar event or a series of reports in a particular newscast or over a period of time.

An obvious oversight in this list of features is the singular notion of encapsulation of an event. Here it should be noted that all events selected for coverage in news media from the many potential events must be able to fit the strict time constraints dictated by the commercial nature of the media. This requirement also means, however, that events must be transformed into stories and shot and edited a certain way. What is created in television lingo is the "package." A package is usually 90 seconds or less in length, only rarely longer than 90 seconds. Even a news story that is featured or "stripped" across two or more consecutive newscasts will be subjected to minute-and-a-half chunks. These packages also feature a reporter who has been assigned to the event and shoots tape stock of the event in film style, that is, out of sequence. Having viewed the photographer's footage, the reporter selects how much of what stock and in what order for the creation of a package. The voice-over is then added to complete the package, which is now available complete with a fixed time for use on the upcoming newscast(s). The upshot of this notion is indeed highly consequential in that the events selected must accommodate themselves to the virtually nonnegotiable demands of the package. Only the news that fits gets reported. Of course, what does not fit is either discarded or never considered in the first place. Many people who are interviewed for TV news for the first time are invariably surprised to see how little of the entire interview that was recorded actually makes it into the story.

The constraints of this packaging process also mean that another feature of mediated news content emerges due to format considerations. Complexity is avoided either entirely or is cast in overly simplistic terms. Here, the needs of the audience are supposedly taken into account in that people will not be able to make sense out of a very complicated situation. Given the uncompromising time constraints and the limited abilities of reporters who must cover a wide range of often disparate events, it is no wonder that complex issues are either ignored or dealt with only in the most superficial ways. And since much that is complex does not also lend itself easily to being visualized or capable of dramatic action, TV news remains relegated to presenting whatever it does best—but that is certainly not complex issues. Thus an entire repertoire of events worthy of coverage and perhaps even essential to the audience's attention is largely neglected.

Additional observations are also in order regarding the articulation of the feature termed *drama and action* by Altheide and Snow. The kinds of drama that are incorporated into TV news include those that mostly mirror the stories presented in TV entertainment programs, or perhaps the term *non-news programs* is better. While fictionalized content in television generally presents the kinds of dramatic plots that involve human against nature or human against humanity (to the usual exclusion of person against self, person against a supreme being, etc.), events that are transformed into news stories usually come out looking and sounding very similar. Such blurring of fantasy and reality content has the effect of giving the viewer some comfort and ease of identification; a familiar framework that is immediately recognizable and is predictable is used for structuring TV news stories. Bad weather becomes packaged in a classic human-nature confrontation as people in the station's coverage area are shown coping with a colossal snowstorm, flooding due to heavy rains, drought from hot sun and no rain and its effects on farmers' crops, and so on. Action items at the local city council are covered from the angle of conflict between or among advocates and opponents of a particular piece of legislation. Again, such "storylines" are both familar to viewers and are comfortably predictable. Events, when fit to TV's format requirements, must either be usable for TV's definition of what constitutes news or it will be molded or "fabricated" to fit the pattern that must be followed. This claim is not to imply that such fabrications involve deceiving viewers in the sense that an event is made up out of thin or polluted air; only that most events that occur in real life do not usually lend themselves in their entirety to TV's sense of what makes an event a story. They must therefore be created by the reporter.

Another major area suggested by Altheide and Snow is the idea of media using formats that carry with them a series of conventions that must be considered a vital part of the overall process of mediated communication that makes it unique from all other forms of communication. It is this concept of format conventions that brings to mind Epstein's work on journalism (both print and electronic) conventions.

Epstein (1973) has noted that the news media's reliance on the traditional canons of journalism in both reporting and writing/broadcast techniques brings with it rigorous format constraints on what gets reported and how. Techniques such as the five-Ws lead, the inverted pyramid, the reliance on those news sources that have always been newsworthy, and so forth all help to determine the content. The consequences, according to Epstein, are profound. Such techniques are more than just procedure for dealing with news in a systematic and orderly fashion. They effectively determine what can be written/packaged in the first place:

In this sense the techniques of journalism define what is considered to be real: what can be written about and how it can be understood. From the standpoint of the audience the techniques of journalism determine what the audience can think—the range of what is taken to be real on a given day. If something happens that cannot be packaged by the industrial formula, then, in a fundamental sense, it has not happened, it cannot be brought to the attention of the audience. If something happens that is only rendered in distorted fashion by the canons of journalism, then it is rendered in such a distorted fashion, often without correction. (p. 81)

Epstein also emphasizes that what is left out as a result of format considerations may be more important than what is included, mainly information on historical background and continuity, motives and agendas of those who shape or determine major events, and the impact of technology, demographic and physiological change, and other impersonal forces that play such major roles in defining society as individuals come to know and experience it. He concludes, "What we lamely call the conventions of journalism were developed for another time and place. They were designed to report an orderly world of politics and international alignments, class structure, and culture" (p. 81). But the world of the late twentieth century is characterized by a changing, evolving structure; cultural meanings are not at all set, but often are in a state of flux, or a catalogue of meanings exists for a variety of different cultural groupings simultaneously, reflecting a diversity that is difficult to comprehend. By using outdated conventions, however, our society is put in the unfortunate position of having to filter events through "conventional glasses which reduce them to type, which exorcise the realities of the world through conventional stylistics and conventional names" (p. 82).

Altheide and Snow spend much of their essay dealing with the media, principally television, as they operate in news contexts. While these analyses are both enlightening and useful, the implications of format consequences seem to be equally if not even more profound for fictional content. As I indicated earlier, the efforts of news media to shape events into stories that mirror the fictional representations of the media seem unusually dedicated to constructing as accurate a reflection as possible, at least regarding the conventions of fictional narratives. There seems, however, to be more going on in the process of packaging content according to stringent format constraints than simply this "mirroring effect."

Altheide and Snow write that formats are more than merely formulas or strategies. Format as term can also be used "as an orientation framework or methodology for understanding cultural phenomena" (p. 199). In this sense, then, format as the focus in its role a determiner of impact on individuals who interface with media takes on even more significance. Commonly accepted formats are used by audiences to grasp events that occur around them, becoming tools of vicarious experience for viewers and readers. Moreover, individuals then must integrate the mediated content—the meaning of which is greatly influenced and determined by the format in which it is presented—into existing meaning frameworks. It is this interpretation process that would ultimately shape the course of human actions and interactions.

It is clear that individuals are exposed to far more fictional content than nonfictional content. This claim is certainly true when it comes to television viewing patterns. Most Americans watch relatively little news/nonfictional programming in comparison to fictional content. And, given the close resemblance between the formats used for nonfiction and fiction content alike, the impact of fictional content, complete with its format constraints, would seem to be of considerable consequence.

One of the consequences of format-induced effects for viewers is the apparent confusion between fact and fiction. The authors insightfully describe the dilemmas posed by the creation and presentation of docudramas, part fiction and part fact (where the alleged facts begin and end is evidently left up to viewers, most of whom probably couldn't care less). But much of the fictional content has the look of nonfiction. While most viewers do not presumably lose track of the fictional nature of this content, the consequences of exposure to and interpretation of the narrative formulas still manifest themselves. For example, television narratives nearly always follow the formula that demands the resolution to problems or conflicts that are generated by the narratives. That problems, regardless of how seemingly insurmountable, are invariably solved is a curious distortion of reality in and of itself. What it suggests to viewers, over and over, is that problems and conflicts have solutions. This suggestion may prompt viewers to expect solutions a la the world of television, an expectation that may be inappropriate for either specific individuals or circumstances. Such expectations may also transcend to political arenas in which politicians seeking elective office feel the need to promise solutions to complex problems and for those running against incumbents to criticize those in office for not "solving" problems. The campaign will usually degenerate to the incumbent claiming that progress has been made or that solutions have been found, while the opponent promises to do a better job and solve the problems beyond the grasp of the incumbent and his or her administration.

Another consequence of exposure to media solutions to various problems stems from the extreme superficiality of the situations that television presents. The nature of the medium—indeed, the format and formula considerations that dictate form and content—allows only certain aspects of situations to be presented. Such superficiality can give the impression to viewers that most things are not at all complicated and are amenable to immediate, effective solutions.

The greatest impact of media formats on viewers may thus results from the creation and presentation of fictional content, content that is treated by viewers as having a direct correspondence to their own reality constructions. Viewers are then reinforced for such interpretations when content is blurred (docudramas) or when nonfiction mirrors fictional formulas as is the case with television news. It may matter little what the verifiable "facts" are in a given situation. Only what appears to be a plausible account will suffice.

Altheide and Snow have presented some provocative and valuable insights into mediated communication. Most important, they have drawn our much-needed attention to media formats. The need to examine the implications of formats seems substantial. Altheide and Snow have gone a long way in urging a continued, rigorous investigation of media formats. It seems that format may hold one of the essential keys to our continued quest for a comprehensible theory of mediated communication.

REFERENCE

Epstein, E. J. (1973). *News from nowhere*. New York: Random House.

Linguistic Character and a Theory of Mediation

GARY GUMPERT

Queens College

A DOPT, for the moment, a totally hypothetical stance. A new, unspoiled civilization has just been discovered, one unspoiled by the seductive guile of media intrusion, yet, through some mysterious, perhaps divine intervention, totally literate. Accept, with all of its improbability, your calisthenic assignment and responsibility of phasing all of our twentieth-century virtuoso media paraphernalia into a society that has practiced media abstinence from the beginning of time. It is assumed that you—being endowed with beneficent wisdom, a pool of sagacity, and extraordinary media logic—will make decisions grounded upon theoretical bases and not upon intuition or ignorance.

Apparently, there is no great mystery about the nature of human communications—those moments when interaction flows unimpeded without the interference and influence of intervening forms of communication. But there was a time when the pundit and sages of old did not understand, could not account for, the impact of mediating forces upon the communication process. But that was in the past, and now, after years of meditation and study, you are prepared for this moment—the chance to articulate a media reality founded on a "Theory of Mediation." Now is the time to return to your mentors of yesteryear, to the data banks of media research, to a lexicon of effects, and choreograph a mediated paradise. But to whom do you turn? What do the scholars have to offer? Do we turn to McLuhan (1964), Ong (1967), Innis (1964), McQuail (1983), Wright (1965), or Altheide and Snow (1987)? Who shall be our Tiresias in this journey in search of a theory?

In the sober reality of 1987 it becomes clear that, while we have made stupendous technological strides in all areas of communication, we know little in regard to development, planning, and the effects of mediation upon human

Correspondence and requests for reprints: Gary Gumpert, Department of Communication, Queens College, Flushing, NY 11367.

Communication Yearbook 11, pp. 230-236

interaction. We have progressed in terms of the scientific study of communication and its variables, and although one can point to particular effects and influences, there is still no comprehensive perceptual matrix facilitating the orchestration of communication in our contemporary world. It is curious that the notion of *mediated communication* remains somewhat of an intellectual aberration—not yet in the mainstream of communication scholarship.

There are a number of reasons for this state of intellectual conservatism. One cause is a dilemma into which scholars are lured as they are encouraged to define and delimit their own academic turf and identity. Interpersonal, nonverbal, small group communication, and mass communication, for example, become self-protective cocoons instead of heuristically oriented points of departure. Another reason is the historical antecedents from which our present academic departments and schools of criticism have emerged. Thus departments of communication that developed from a speech and rhetoric tradition have essentially ignored the omnipresent relationship of media and communication. On the other hand, those departments that grew out of a journalistic or broadcasting past chose to embrace a professional orientation in which communication theory seldom was recognized. A third factor that has retarded the mediated communication perspective is the economic and social institutions from which media technology materialized, which in turn governed their development. Therefore, ideology and form become superimposed on media and become its primary characteristics rather than its governing factors.

The above intervening factors detract from a focus that attempts to examine the media of communication with the assumption that they are *more* than merely neutral channels that transmit and transport information from one place or time to another. Altheide and Snow's theory of mediation asserts that

> a medium does not consist of an object or thing that exists independently of the people who select, define, interpret, and, in short, construct it. It is in this sense that media abound and should be regarded as synonymous with those aspects of a culture involved in the derivation, interpretation, and communication of meaning. (p. 198)

The premise of media nexus, which states that the creation, perception, and influence of content is always connected with mediating variables, must guide any theory of mediation. Subsumed within that premise is the tenet that human beings live in a symbolic, interdependent relationship with mediated forms.

With these ideas in the background, I now turn to "Toward a Theory of Mediation" by Altheide and Snow. Their premise is stated quite simply in the development of their argument.

> Mediation refers to the impact of the logic and form of any medium involved in the communication process. The following materials are offered to illustrate

how media logic and formats compatible with popular culture mediate, define, and direct social interaction. (p. 195)

A need does exist for the development of "a theory or theories of mediation" and certainly both authors have done much in that direction in their past contributions. While I approached "Toward a Theory of Mediation" with intellectual hope, I left it less than satisfied because of its unfulfilled promise. The source of my frustration is found in the manuscript's several weaknesses: the singular vision of mass communication; the ambiguity of the "format concept"; and the lack of continuity and support in the development of the supporting arguments.

Altheide and Snow observe that "social science lacks a theory of mediation that would articulate the relationships among (1) an actor; (2) a context; (3) a phenomenon or event; (4) a medium; and (5) an audience" (p. 195), and there-fore seek to develop a *general* theory of mediation. However, those theoretical observations that materialize are most directly linked to *mass communication* as a particular manifestation of mediation. Altheide and Snow embrace a position that transcends a mono-medium theory and yet their focus in "Toward a Theory of Mediation" is primarily the mass medium of television. In Cathcart and Gumpert (1983), we stated a position that seeks to clarify the relationship of *medium* and *mass medium*:

> *All media are not mass media.* Any so called mass medium can be used for point to point transmission. . . . Mass communication refers to a specific utilization of medium; a circumstance of communication in which a medium replicates, duplicates, and disseminates identical content to a geographically wide spread population. Therefore, the term "media" does not characterize a distinct type of communication because it does not account for or suggest its use. In the typology of human communication, "media" should not be relegated solely to the category "mass communication." (p. 168)

This distinction is not to deny the extraordinary impact of the mass media, particularly television, upon the cultural persona of most industrialized nations. I would merely argue that any theory of mediation must encompass all media, both electronic and nonelectronic, and imply the intricate interrelationship of media with each other. The concept of "mass communication" emphasizes the institutionalization or the organizational patterns of a medium and only features one property of the particular medium's intrinsic character—that is, the simultaneous transcendence of time and space.

One of the important features of the Altheide and Snow thesis is their conception of "form" in the articulation of a theory of mediation. They intend to "illustrate what is meant by the logic and form of mediation" (p. 196), but some degree of confusion results in the process.

> The way media appear, or *their essential form*, provides a kind of intelligence and interpretation to specific points of information, or content, that they present.

> We refer to the nature of this appearance *as format, or the rules and logic that transform and mold information (content) into recognizable shape and form of the specific medium.* Moreover, all media have a format and can be distinguished by it. (pp. 198-199; emphasis added)

On the one hand, format refers to "rules and logic," while on the other hand, format is defined as "formulas that serve as strategies for presenting categorical subject matter to an audience (p. 9). The distinction is not clear. This orientation to form suggests genre as the basic unit of analysis—one that is indigenous to a specific medium. But the formats with which Altheide and Snow are concerned appear to be imposed by extraneous forces. The authors' response to "when is a particular phenomenon considered to be sports, news, entertainment, politics, or art?" is that the question can be "answered in terms of format criteria" (p. 199). As an example, the field of sports is used to illustrate their point by showing that television has forced its own format rules, governed by the economics of entertainment, upon those athletic events that appear on television.

> For example, when professional football moved to prime time, rule changes occurred that promoted an increased entertainment value—commercial value—for pro football as a television commodity. Games became higher scoring, more dramatic, less violent, and had greater stadium and crowd theatrics than in the period prior to television broadcasts. (pp. 199-200)

Further proof of impact of format is provided in the development of the "docudrama" genre as the result of the commercializing of the more traditional 16-mm educational classroom film. "Ratings increased when history was dressed in a high-entertainment format that emphasized backstage life and personal intrigue and confrontation on the order of *Dallas* and *Dynasty*" (p. 200).

I would agree that media economics impose fundamental criteria and thereby alter genre, but I would disagree that such criteria are intrinsic to media. They are imposed by a social system that is structured and guided by economic principles. Altheide and Snow get much closer to the intrinsic elements of mediation when they discuss linguistic form in media, although even here I have an argument with their approach. It is my contention that a *theory of mediation* must begin with *the language of the system.* Therefore, the Altheide and Snow emphasis on linguistic form provides the basis from which formats develop. They write:

> The linguistic character of mass communication may be observed in its most basic sense by applying the naive approach of identifying the grammar (syntax, inflection, and specialized vocabulary) of a particular media presentation. . . . Building on observations of grammatical form rather than content analysis, it is possible to develop a description of the grammatical characteristics unique to each medium and unique to particular formats within a medium. (pp. 200-201)

There is no doubt that the concept of format is linked and influenced by the formal features that constitute a medium and that are the result of the very technology creating it. We have tried to establish this position previously (Gumpert & Cathcart, 1985):

> Every medium, not just television, is structured and characterized by technical elements which define it. That is to say, a medium of communication is a technical manifestation, a result of technological connection and combination. All conventions in turn evolve through application to a new medium of those grammatical rules and norms which have been used to determine meaning in already existing media. (p. 26)

The linguistic character being described emerges from a medium, but *not* necessarily *a mass medium*. The concept of "mass" is superimposed upon medium by a nonindigenous structure. While Altheide and Snow may be quite correct in asserting the importance of "formats" as influential in transforming and altering the cultural response of an audience to a medium, I contend that the intrinsic linguistic character, or the grammar of the medium, is an analytical concept that is a precursor to format. The implication in this basic philosophical disagreement is that it is necessary to distinguish between those "media effects" attributed to properties of a medium and those that more accurately are traits of the institution imposed upon the medium.

Altheide and Snow have set up a difficult and important task for themselves. The need exists for the establishment of a theory that super-imposes the potent and ubiquitous variable of mediation upon the communication process. Media is not a communication subarea, but a constant—whether the immediate focus of analysis is mediated or not is irrelevant. A theory must provide a series of propositions explaining the operation of a class of phenomenon. The requirement for the development of a theory is to establish a series of supprting interrelating assertions to support the model inherent in the theory. One hopes that from the theory will emerge operational definitions that are "experimental" or "testable." "Toward a Theory of Mediation" presents somewhat of a problem because the supporting arguments are disparate, are not agents of the theory, and are not developed as well as they should be.

The discussion of the television news coverage of terrorism as an illustration of mass media formats is interesting, but it is not developed enough to stand as a supporting assertion of the theory. The presentation of tools for the purpose of analyzing news formats is extremely valuable, but seems to constitute a separate study the purpose of which is to demonstrate the connection of political ideology and the news format. I would agree that "the format and shape of a medium communicates a good deal about its purpose, content, and even intent. It is as though each medium is associated with its own code of interpretation that the audience members recognize" (p. 206). This relationship is an extraordinarily fertile area of media theory that would support a theory of mediation, but the discussion of television news coverage of international terrorism does not support the basic premise of the theory. It does demonstrate the power and complexity of the newscast format and the authors provide an excellent analytical tool.

From the specificity of the newscast, Altheide and Snow shift their attention to the more general subject of media impact, particularly the effects of the mass media upon audience behavior. Their observation is critical—that the major influence of electronic media on viewers is that the "individuals become viewers by adjusting to and accepting the rules and logic of the format, which joins the medium with the content, and with their viewing situation" (p. 208). The discussion that follows devoted to the interconnection of "mass media" apperception and the "temporal scheduling of daily routines" and the impact of formats upon the interaction process is well presented. However, habitual, parametric, and tactical rules are descriptions of conduct influencing the relationship of audience to television viewing. Certainly, television formats become influential in the determination of viewers' rituals and social strategies, but this particular aspect requires further development and a stronger link to "a theory of mediation."

The impact of computers is simply not understood by most media critics and so the last section of "Toward a Theory of Mediation," devoted to computers and mediation, is extremely important. While it further crystallizes my admiration for the work of Altheide and Snow, it also illustrates my ambivalence with their approach. It is the same problem noted earlier—the ambiguity found in the use of "format" and "form." I maintain that formats grow out of form and institutionalization, while Altheide and Snow proclaim the primacy of "format." This disagreement may be quite fundamental since the "logic" of theory building takes us down divergent paths because of this semantic distinction. We arrive at similar conclusions, but differ in the approach that links ideology to the medium. Is the "fallacy of data base validity" inherent in the medium of the computer or does it represent an attitude resulting from the collision of media generations? Is it possible for computer formats to operate in a "nonbureaucratic setting?" What needs to be demonstrated by Altheide and Snow is the specific nature of computer form and logic.

"Toward a Theory of Mediation" is an important step in the right direction because it represents a theoretical approach fusing intellectual approaches rather than splitting them into neat academic cubicles. All critics project their own perceptions of the world in their analysis. In that sense, I am no different, although I am very much in sympathy with my colleagues' quest for a coherent theory of mediation.

REFERENCES

Altheide, D., & Snow, R. P. (1979). *Media logic.* Newbury Park, CA: Sage.
Cathcart, R. P., & Gumpert, G. (1983). Mediated interpersonal communication: Toward a new typology. *Quarterly Journal of Speech, 69,* 267-277.

Gumpert, G., & Cathcart, R. P. (1985). Media grammars, generations, and media gaps. *Critical Studies in Mass Communication, 2*, 23-35.

Innis, H. A. (1964). *The bias of communication.* Toronto: University of Toronto Press.

McLuhan, M. (1964). *Understanding media: The extensions of man.* New York: McGraw-Hill.

McQuail, D. (1983). *Mass communication theory.* Newbury Park, CA: Sage.

Ong, W. J. (1967). *The presence of the word: Some prolegomena for cultural and religious history.* Minneapolis: University of Minnesota Press.

Wright, C. R. (1965). *Mass communication: A sociological perspective.* New York: Random House.

SECTION 3

HEALTH CARE: COMMUNICATION POLICIES AND PRACTICES

6 The Pervasive Role of Information in Health and Health Care: Implications for Health Communication Policy

GARY L. KREPS
Northern Illinois University

Beginning with the communication processes by which we assess our own state of sickness and health, this article moves to consider the interpersonal and mass communication components of health and health care for consumers, providers, and administrators. The article concludes with an analysis of effective policy for health-care communication.

THE COMMUNICATION OF HEALTH INFORMATION

The communication of relevant information is a central element of health care. Key information about health and illness, health information, is used to direct individual and conjoint behaviors toward the accomplishment of health evaluation and maintenance. The need for accurate and timely health information is not limited to health-care professionals, but is a crucial input for all individuals involved in the health-care system. For example, health-care consumers, providers, and administrators depend on health information to accomplish many of their goals. Consumers depend on relevant health information to monitor their own health, to seek evaluations of health status from experts, and to identify strategies for maintaining optimal levels of health. Health-care providers need information to keep abreast of key advances in health-care knowledge, to interpret clients' complaints in diagnosing health problems, to monitor changes in clients' health conditions, as well as to direct provision of health-care services. Similarly, administrators

Correspondence and requests for reprints: Gary L. Kreps, Department of Communication Studies, Northern Illinois University, De Kalb, IL 60115.

Communication Yearbook 11, pp. 238-276

of health-care organizations need information about the quality and kind of services clientele have sought and will seek in the future to ensure selection of appropriate staff, equipment, and supplies for their organizations. Furthermore, in addition to seeking timely and relevant health information, consumers, providers, and administrators need to supply each other with pertinent health information to facilitate accomplishment of cooperative health-care activities.

Human communication is used as a primary tool to seek, process, and share health information. Yet, the role of communication in health care is so "pervasive, ubiquitous, and equivocal" that key communication activities are often taken for granted, and complexities and subtleties of health communication are often unnoticed, incompletely analyzed, and poorly utilized (Fisher, 1978, p. 91). Health communication is pervasive because human communication is the critical process that enables participants in health-care delivery systems to seek and send timely and relevant information that is crucial to evaluating health complaints, determining appropriate health-promoting and preserving activities, and eliciting cooperation. Health communication is ubiquitous because communication processes must be continuously employed by participants in health-care delivery systems to seek, interpret, and share vast amounts of information relevant to the preservation of human health. Health communication is equivocal due to the complex and idiosyncratic nature of human communication processes, as well as due to the intangible, multifaceted nature of health risks that are often complex and difficult to fully diagnose. This chapter will provide a selective review of research and theory to explain the pervasive, ubiquitous, and equivocal roles of communication and information processes in human health and health care at five primary interrelated hierarchical levels of interaction (the intrapersonal, interpersonal, group, organizational, and societal settings). Key issues concerning communication and health will be identified at each of the five hierarchical levels, and relevant health communication knowledge will be applied to the advancement of public health policy to facilitate effective use of health information in society.

INTRAPERSONAL ASPECTS OF HEALTH AND HEALTH CARE

Intrapersonal interaction is the most basic level of human communication; it is at the intrapersonal level of communication that information is processed, individual health-care decisions are made, and meanings for health, illness, and health-care treatment are created. At its most basic level, intrapersonal communication is used as a self-regulatory biological tool: "It appears to function as one of the central biological processes" (Smith, 1971, p. 11). Human beings continuously relay internal physiological messages through their nervous systems to actuate bodily processes and to coordinate biological activities (Nason, 1968). Without such self-regulatory physiological intra-personal communication via the nervous system, human beings would not be able to monitor and coordinate basic physical activities, nor would they be able to maintain personal health.

Creating Meanings

Encoding and decoding messages are intrapersonal communication pro-cesses where health information is interpreted and health messages are created. Human beings select relevant data from a wide range of message sources both internal and external to themselves, interpreting these data to make sense of and respond to their worlds (Barnlund, 1962, 1970; Hunt, 1982). Intrapersonal communication is the inner dimension of human communication, where the process of selecting relevant data, assigning information values to these data, and creating message strategies is accom-plished (Barker & Wiseman, 1966; Goldman, 1979).

Symbolic interpretations about health status are created intrapersonally. "Human illness is not only a physical condition but a symbolic one as well" (Barnlund, 1976, p. 718). Health and illness are perceptual judgments made about the relative quality of physical and psychological condition. When individuals believe themselves to be ill, they create personal meanings in response to health information they receive. Similarly, when individuals believe themselves to be in a state of health, they are also using health information to interpret their condition. The judgments consumers make about their health do not always match providers' evaluations. A man with a serious heart condition, for example, can deny his condition, ignore the advice of health-care providers, and act as though he were in perfect health. This person has chosen not to recognize his heart condition or allow it to constrain his activities and perception of self. Another person may react to his or her physical condition completely differently, by feeling totally incapacitated when experiencing a mild headache.

The meanings assigned to health and illness strongly influence the health-care choices and decisions individuals make, as well as the levels of confidence and commitment they have for health-care treatment. For example, a man whose interpretation of his health condition is that he is a "cancer victim," with all of the negative symbolism that identification encompasses, may hold little hope for effective treatment and recovery (Blumberg, Flaherty, & Lewis, 1982; Northouse, 1986). The man may even refuse treatment because he believes such health care to be futile in reversing the illness. This reaction may be contrary to current medical information that indicates the viability of specialized treatment for this particular illness, but the man's reactions are consistent with his symbolic evaluation of the health condition. In this example, the man's symbolic evaluation of illness is influencing his subsequent perception and interpretation of relevant health-care information and strategies. As Watzlawick, Beavin, and Jackson (1967) have suggested, the ways people see themselves will influence the ways they "punctuate" reality. The symbolic aspects of health and illness strongly influence the ways individuals select, process, and react to health information.

Decision Making

Health beliefs strongly influence the health-related behaviors that people choose to perform (Becker, 1974a, 1974b; Becker, Maimon, Kirscht, Haefner, & Drachman, 1977; Gochman, 1972a, 1972b). The beliefs, values, and attitudes people hold about health and health care color the way these individuals interpret and present health complaints, as well as the way they choose to utilize health information (Mechanic, 1972a; Seibold & Roper, 1979; Simonton & Matthews-Simonton, 1975). A member of a religious sect whose culturally induced health beliefs condemn medical technology as evil will react very differently to hospitalization in a modern health-care center from an individual whose health beliefs glorify the development and use of the latest technologies in health-care treatment. Health-care beliefs inform individuals of the legitimacy of different health-care actions and influence their reactions to health information.

The meanings people assign to their states of health not only influence the perceptions, choices, and decisions they make about health-care opportunities, but also influence the actual physical responses they exhibit in response to health-care treatment. For example, Frank (1973, 1975), has indicated that the success of a health-care treatment is often directly related to the amount of faith consumers exhibit for the effectiveness of that treatment. A long tradition of scientific research on the placebo effect has demonstrated that personal belief in the efficacy of inert pharmacological agents generally result in significant physiological influence of these drugs (Beecher, 1955; Bok, 1974; Byerly, 1976; Shapiro, 1964; Whitehorn, 1958; Wolf, 1950). Other research has demonstrated that humans have the ability to influence their physiology consciously, controlling stress and pain through meditation, imagery, biofeedback methods, and hypnosis (Ewin, 1978; Mines, 1974; Wallace & Benson, 1972). Furthermore, psychosomatic aspects of illness are examples of intrapersonal self-fulfilling prophesies where interpretations of health can directly influence physiology (Alexander, 1950; Herrick, 1976; Hopkins & Wolff, 1965). The ways human beings internally process health information directly influences their physical conditions.

The intrapersonal level of human communication has a major influence on human health and health care. It is at the intrapersonal level that information is processed, individual health-care decisions are made, and meanings for health, illness, and treatment are created. The ability to communicate effectively intrapersonally enables human beings to interpret health information reliably and direct health-care activities.

INTERPERSONAL ASPECTS OF
HEALTH AND HEALTH CARE

Interpersonal communication adds an important dimension to health communication—the opportunity to develop interpersonal relationships, where relational partners exchange messages to facilitate interpersonal coordination and cooperation. Interpersonal relationships have the potential for providing relational partners with many health-related benefits. For example, relational partners often provide each other with information to evaluate health status and direct health care (Feldman, 1976; Kreps, Ruben, Baker, & Rosenthal, 1987; Ruben & Bowman, 1986). Relational partners can also offer one another emotional support to help each cope with health threats (Albrecht & Adelman, 1984; Office of Cancer Communications, 1985; Sullivan & Reardon, 1986). There is even evidence that the absence of meaningful relationships can have negative medical consequences on individuals, at times leading to death (Lynch, 1977).

HEALTH-CARE RELATIONSHIPS

Health-care relationships are primary channels for acquiring and seeking health information, and as such are crucial delivery vehicles for a wide range of health-care services (Kreps & Thornton, 1984). The communication relationships established by health-care providers and consumers have a major influence on the behaviors they engage in during health-care practice (Smith, 1976). An unspoken "implicit contract" is developed between relational partners, such as in health-care provider/consumer relationships, directing interactants to behave in accordance with the behavioral boundaries of each other's role expectations (Kreps, 1986a; Rossiter & Pearce, 1975). Health-care relationships develop when individuals establish an implicit contract providing for often unspoken but mutually recognized and agreed upon expectations for one another's behavior, outlining the health-care roles they will engage in with one another. The messages they exchange indicate the kinds of roles they expect each other to perform and encourage health-care providers and consumers to act in accordance with mutual expectations. Effective health-care relationships have clearly understood and agreed upon implicit contracts, where relational partners work at continually updating their awareness of mutual expectations by giving and seeking interpersonal feedback, enabling them to continue to act appropriately toward each other as their relationship grows (Kreps, 1986d). The effectiveness of health-care relationships have major influences on the success of health care, influencing both the outcomes and satisfaction people derive from such situations (Korsch & Negrete, 1972; Lane, 1983; Street & Wiemann, 1987).

Interpersonal communication provides interactants with information about the kinds of roles expected of them by relational others, and the actual performance of these interpersonal roles directs the ways interactants interpret each other's messages (Wilmot, 1980). Roles perform a key information processing function in health-care relationships by directing health-care providers' and consumers' interpretations of interpersonal messages as well as directing their responses to messages. When a consumer asks a doctor to help with a health problem, the consumer is not only communicating on a content information level about his or her health condition, but is also providing relationship information that defines the doctor's "helper" role and his or her own "helpee" role (Bateson, 1958; Watzlawick, Beavin, & Jackson, 1967). Once helper/helpee relational roles are established, all future interpersonal message exchanges are interpreted in light of the interactants' relational positions (Bateson, 1958).

Content and Relationship Information

The messages health-care providers and consumers send each other provide them with both "content"-oriented information about health care and "relationship"-oriented information about the feelings each has about the other and the health-care situation (Watzlawick et al., 1967). Relationship aspects of messages demonstrate interactants' relative levels of sensitivity or insensitivity toward their relational partners. Unfortunately, insensitive interpersonal message exchanges are a common occurrence in health care (Gazda, Walters, & Childers, 1975; Kane & Deuschle, 1967; Korsch & Negrete, 1972; Lane, 1981). Insensitive interactants either fail to recognize the relationship information implications of their statements, and become preoccupied with the content-related aspects of their message exchanges, or do not care to send sensitive relational messages. Health-care providers may often be too involved with the mechanics of accomplishing their health-care tasks to communicate in a genuinely caring manner to their clients (Pettegrew et al., 1980). Similarly, consumers may be too wrapped up in their own health problems to be aware of the perspective of and communicate sensitively to health-care providers (Kreps & Thornton, 1984).

At times seemingly sensitive interpersonal message strategies may also limit the effectiveness of health communication by diminishing the potential of the individual to withstand and combat health threats. Relational messages have potentially powerful influences on the roles individuals adopt in health-care situations, and messages that inform persons that they are ill often influence these people to adopt behavior patterns known as the "sick role" (Becker, 1974b; Carne, 1975; Kasl & Cobb, 1966; Twaddle, 1972). For example, interpersonal messages such as "stay in bed and get plenty of rest"; "poor baby, be sure to take your medications"; or "don't exert yourself" clearly identify the limited social expectations others have for the person's role performance, and reinforce adoption of a socially limited sick role (Colm, 1953). Parsons (1951, 1958) suggests the sick role limits the social influence of individuals by defining them as socially deviant.

They are deviant because they are restricted from performing their normal social roles and must be encouraged to seek help to "return to a state of normalcy or health" (Crane, 1975, p. 131). Sick-role interpersonal messages may result in an interpersonal self-fulfilling prophesy encouraging message recipients to engage in sick-role behaviors. For example, "once an individual is classified as mentally ill others will often respond to that definition by reinforcing sick behavior" (Wilmot, 1979, p. 118). Interpersonal messages that tell people they are seen as being mentally ill provide those persons with reinforcing information about others' expectations for their behavior, encouraging them to act in mentally unstable ways (Gergen, 1968). Therefore, to promote health it is important for interpersonal communicators to encourage others to view themselves as powerful, able to withstand and combat health risks.

Health-care provider/consumer relationships are not only influenced by the relational information in the message each sends, but are also affected by content information in interpersonal messages that provide health-care interactants with information about the nature of health problems and strategies for treatment (Roter, 1983). Both providers and consumers need accurate and timely health information. Providers depend upon reliable information from consumers to diagnose patients' health problems adequately and design effective treatment regimens, while consumers need clear information from practitioners about diagnoses and treatments to make informed health-care choices (McIntosh, 1974).

Research has shown that health-care providers, especially physicians, have the potential to promote public health and health-risk prevention strongly by providing their clients with relevant health information through interpersonal counseling and health education (Center for Health Education, 1984a, 1984b; Maibach & Kreps, 1986; Pierce et al., 1984; Relman, 1982). For example, a recent national survey identified primary care physicians as the most preferred source of health information in America with 84% of the 1250 persons surveyed identifying an interpersonal discussion with their personal physicians as the most useful source of health information (Kreps et al., in press). Yet a large body of research suggests that many physicians' communication practices often fail to supply their clients with satisfactory levels of health information (Hess, Liepman, & Ruane, 1983; Kreps et al., in press; Maibach & Kreps, 1986; Newell & Webber, 1983; Relman, 1982; Ruben, 1986; Ruben & Bowman, 1986). The Center for Health Education (1984a) has concluded that inadequate interpersonal communication skills, lack of prevention-oriented training, concerns about patient compliance, perceived lack of support services, and administrative constraints are among the key factors that inhibit the success of physicians' health education efforts.

Health-care provider and consumer efforts to share relevant information are often deterred by miscommunications, the misinterpretation of information communicated interpersonally (Kreps & Thornton, 1984). Miscommunication occurs in many interpersonal communication situations, often because of the idiosyncratic ways individuals process information and create meanings, but there are several reasons information misinterpretations happen as frequently as they do in health-care interactions. The complexity of health-care problems, diagnoses, and treatments makes it difficult to create and interpret health-care messages without ambiguities and information loss, which leads to miscommunications; the overuse of medical jargon by health-care providers often confuses consumers of health care, leading consumers to misinterpret messages (Barnlund, 1976; Woods, 1975); the urgency and emotionality of many health-care situations often results in hastily created and interpreted messages by both providers and consumers, leading to miscommunications (Altman, 1972; Sethee, 1967); and the differences in education and experience between providers and consumers often leads to semantic distance in their interpretations of interpersonal messages (Barnlund, 1976). Miscommunications often cause serious difficulties in health care because they misdirect intricate interdependent health-preserving behaviors. Miscommunications lead consumers to interpret incorrectly the health-care instructions explained to them by providers, making it virtually impossible to comply with health-care regimens. Providers, on their side, can misinterpret messages patients give them, resulting in incorrect diagnoses and inappropriate treatments. Health-care providers and consumers must communicate clearly and seek feedback to avoid miscommunications (Cline, 1983; Kreps & Thornton, 1984).

The moral and legal principle of informed consent—which charges providers with the responsibility for clearly explaining health-care treatment options and implications to clients so these consumers can make knowledgeable choices about the health-care services they wish to receive—illustrate the importance of providing content-rich health information interpersonally (Alfidi, 1971; Horty, 1971; Ingelfinger, 1972; President's Commission for the Study of Ethical Problems in Medicine and Biomedical and Behavioral Research, 1982a, 1982b, 1982c). Yet research has indicated that many health-care providers are not personally motivated or well trained to provide their clients with full and clear health information (Brauer, 1965; Maibach & Kreps, 1986; Waitzkin & Stoekle, 1976).

Since the health-care provider has access to diagnostic and health-care regimen information that is often not available to consumers, and is of vital importance to them, the provider can wield a great deal of power over consumers by giving, withholding, or altering relevant health information (Meyer, 1969; Pettigrew, 1972). The provider/consumer relationship can be viewed as a micropolitical situation, where "information control is used, at least in part, to maintain patterns of dominance and subordination" by health-care practitioners over their clients (Waitzkin & Stoekle, 1976, p. 265). Health-care providers may withhold relevant information as an act of paternalistic control over the health-care situation or to establish power within the provider/patient relationship as a form of information politics (Hunt & Rhodes, 1983; Johnson, 1972; Quint, 1965; Waitzkin & Stoekle,

1972). Paternalistic control of pertinent health information can dehumanize health-care consumers because it infers that they are not capable of making choices for themselves about their health-care treatment. The withholding of relevant information allows health-care providers to maintain a one-up power position in the health-care relationship which can intimidate and confuse consumers and limit the effectiveness of health communication (Ley, Bradshaw, Eaves, & Walker, 1973).

Communication and Compliance

Compliance is a commonly examined issue in health-care research that has rarely been studied from a relational communication perspective (Arntson, 1985; Lane, 1983). The primary areas of compliance research have focused on patient compliance with health-care appointments (Alpert, 1964; Hertz & Stamps, 1977), regimens (Caron, 1968; Davis & Eichorn, 1963; Lane, 1982), and use of prescribed drugs (Blackwell, 1973; Hulka, Cassel, & Kupper, 1976; Hulka, Kupper, & Cassell, 1975). Although most of the compliance literature focuses on the characteristics of patients that lead to poor compliance, an interactive perspective on the compliance issue explores the level of cooperation elicited in the provider/consumer relationship (Kreps, 1986d; Kreps & Thornton, 1984; Lane, 1982, 1983). From a relational perspective, the responsibility for health-care cooperation is shared jointly by consumer and provider and compliance is encouraged by the specific interpersonal influence strategies used by communicators (Arntson, 1985; Speedling & Rose, 1985). Evidence suggests that the quality of interaction between health-care providers and consumers strongly influences the level of cooperation engendered between these health communicators (Lane, 1982; Stone, 1979).

Therepeutic Communication

A key health-care function of interpersonal relationships is the provision of mutual social support between relational partners (Albrecht & Adelman, 1984; Froland, Brodsky, Olson, & Stewart, 1979; Gottlieb, 1981; Query, 1985). Interpersonal communication has great potential for providing therapeutic benefits for relational partners through the provision of relevant and supportive content and relationship information. Interpersonal relationships "are regarded as therapeutic when they provoke personal insight or reorientation, and when they enable persons to participate in more satisfying ways in future social encounters" (Barnlund, 1968, p. 614). Providers can communicate therapeutically to their clients by providing them with relevant health information enabling patients to gain insights into the nature of their health problems and acquire information about how they can improve their health status, as well as by encouraging patients to become personally involved in directing their health care. The provision of therapeutic communication is not just limited to trained health-care professionals, nor is it offered only during health-care practice; anyone has the potential to communicate therapeutically (Kreps, 1981). For example, hairdressers and bartenders often provide their clients with therapeutic counsel (Cowen et al., 1979; Cowen, McKim, & Weissberg, 1981; Wiesenfeld & Weiss, 1979). All interpersonal relationships are potentially therapeutic to the extent that interactants provide one another with informative feedback leading to enlightenment and redirection (Burke, Weir, & Duncan, 1976).

The Health-Care Interview

The health-care interview is an important interpersonal communication setting for the exchange of content and relationship information between providers and consumers (Benjamin, 1981; Cline, 1983; Roter & Hall, 1986). An important communication function of the interview is to initiate the development of effective health-care relationships and the development of provider and consumer health communication rules. The relational messages interview participants send one another establish the guidelines for an implicit contract between health-care provider and consumer. In effective interviews, care is taken by practitioners to put patients at ease so they feel comfortable about sharing personal health information and are receptive to health information provided to them. Interview participants also depend upon their interpersonal messages to elicit full and clear content information to inform diagnoses, explore treatment options, and make informed health-care decisions.

Traditionally, health-care providers are charged with the responsibility of maintaining control of the interview by keeping it focused, establishing rapport with the patient by communicating in a sensitive and caring manner, and bringing closure to the interview by responding to patient questions and clearly explaining future health-care activities the patient should engage in (Foley & Sharf, 1981). Yet health-care consumers, despite their personal stake in the health-care situation, are not routinely given, nor do they often take, opportunities to control health-care interviews by directing questions to their providers and voicing their concerns and suggestions about health-care treatments (Greenfield, Kaplan, & Ware, 1985). If interview participants can coordinate the exchange of content and relationship information, the health-care interview can provide them with a structured setting for gathering relevant health information and establishing effective provider/consumer relationships (Carroll & Monroe, 1980; Cassata, 1983).

Interpersonal communication is a very important level of human inter-action and health communication. It is a primary method of exchange between patient and provider, providing a personal means of acquiring relevant health-related information and opportunities to develop provider/consumer relationships by establishing implicit contracts for coordinating interdependent health-care activities. A clear understanding of the dynamics of interpersonal communication and the ability to competently communicate interpersonally are crucial aspects of effective health communication and health-care practice.

GROUP ASPECTS OF HEALTH AND HEALTH CARE

Groups are a primary unit of social organization in health care, where group members are coordinated in a network of interdependent interpersonal relationships working toward the accomplishment of collective goals (Bion, 1952; Mabry & Barnes, 1980). Specialized groups are used in health care to help process information through the coordinated communication efforts of group members (Thornton, 1978). Groups, like interpersonal relationships, are particularly well suited for providing members with social support through the expression of inclusion, acceptance, and validation, as well as by providing members with therapeutic insights into their personal problems (Albrecht & Adelman, 1984; Cobb, 1976; Query, 1985). Groups are often used for working through complex health-care problems that demand a great deal of specialized knowledge and responsibility (Kreps & Thornton, 1984; Schaefer, 1974; Scheff, 1963; Schwartz, 1975). Group members can help one another process the information equivocally inherent in complex health-care issues (Weick, 1969), sharing personal expertise in evaluating the merits of alternative solutions, and sharing practical, moral, and legal responsibility for health-care decisions that often have far-ranging implications (Wise, 1974).

Communication in Health-Care Teams

The ever increasing specialization of information (and technologies) in health-care delivery has resulted in the development of a wide range of interdependent specialized health-care provider roles and functions. The interdependent functioning of specialists in the delivery of health-care services depends on the ability of these individuals to elicit cooperation and coordination. Health-care specialists must collaborate on strategies, share relevant health information, and coordinate professional activities to provide effective health-care services (Given & Simmons, 1977; Nagi, 1975). "A team is a group with a purpose, the accomplishment of which requires inter-dependent and collaborative efforts of its members" (Thornton, 1978, p. 539). The activities of health-care team members revolve around the specific needs of health-care consumers, who should be recognized as key members of such teams, and human communication is the means by which health-care team members (including consumers) share information and elicit cooperation in health-care delivery (Baldwin et al., 1980; Kreps & Thornton, 1984; Wise, 1972).

Members of health-care teams often conflict with one another, especially when the communication structure of the team is hierarchical as opposed to egalitarian (Thornton, 1978). It is difficult to facilitate open sharing of information if any one team member attempts to dominate decision making. Physicians often take charge of health-care teams, based upon the "legitimate" power they possess due to the social status of their profession (French & Raven, 1968; Friedson, 1970; Yanda, 1977). Yet in most health-care situations, physicians do not possess all the specialized knowledge needed to provide the highest-quality health care. For example, physicians can often benefit from the pharmacological information that pharmacists have, the nutritional information dieticians possess, or the personal history information the consumers of health care possess (Brodie, Kroben, & Wertheimenr, 1973; Hussar, 1976). Information sharing in hierarchically structured health-care teams is influenced by the relative status of the different health-care specialty areas represented, and the articulation of roles in these teams develops primarily as a result of accommodation of lower-status team members to those members of higher status (Nagi, 1975). The effectiveness of health-care teams is dependent to a large extent on the abilities of the team members to overcome interprofessional status barriers to communication (Kreps & Thornton, 1984).

Support Networks

Small groups have served an important health-care function in recent years as a setting for social support and therapy for health-care consumers (Wagner, 1966; Droge, Arnston, & Norton, 1981; Froland, 1981). The family is a primary group that has a great potential for providing social support and therapy to its members (Kitson, Moir, & Mason, 1982; Litman, 1966). Peer support and counseling groups provide important health communication functions for a wide range of different health-care consumers, helping individuals cope with such diverse issues as unemployment (Gore, 1978), bereavement (Cluck & Cline, 1985), divorce (Chiraboga, Coho, Stein, & Roberts, 1979), epilepsy (Droge et al., 1981), cancer (Morrow, Hoagland, & Carnrike, 1981; Peters-Golden, 1982; Wortman & Dunkel-Schetter, 1979), old age (Campbell & Chenoweth, 1981; Gronning, 1982; Kreps, 1986c; Nussbaum, 1983; Query, 1985), and mental illness (Froland et al., 1979; Horowitz, 1977; Pattison & Pattison, 1981). Peer support groups routinely provide their members with information about relevant health-care methods and services, problem-solving interaction, referral services, friendly visits, and assistance in making choices about health-care options available to them. These groups help members feel good about themselves and assert control of their own health care. For example, Droge et al. (1981) describes how self-help groups for epileptic patients provide these individuals with social support, helping them to express their feelings, seek reassurance from each other, and provide each other with information for problem solving.

Group psychotherapy sessions are therapeutic health communication situations where members offer information to and receive feedback from each other (Posser, 1966; Rose, 1977). Therapy groups have proven to be successful at helping individuals cope with their problems because they provide group members with intersubjective validation and feedback through group interaction (Haley, 1977). Group therapy can help individuals learn how to cope with reality by enabling members to experience controlled therapeutic contact with people possessing different communication styles and perspectives (Berger, 1958; Talland & Clark, 1954).

Group interaction is an extremely important level of health communication because groups provide consumers and providers with important health communication networks for processing and sharing relevant health information and social support. In health-care teams, interdependent health-care providers share their expertise and experiences to coordinate their health-care delivery activities. Providers and consumers work together in groups to share their often disparate perspectives in making difficult health-care decisions. Consumers also can provide one another with peer support and the benefit of their insight and feedback in therapeutic group communication situations.

ORGANIZATIONAL ASPECTS
OF HEALTH AND HEALTH CARE

Organizations have developed as primary sites for health-care delivery in the modern world (Starr, 1982). Hospitals, medical centers, nursing homes, convalescent centers, health maintenance organizations, and clinics are settings where health-care professionals provide numerous health-care services to the public. As knowledge about health and health care has progressed, the provision of health-care services has grown increasingly complex (Mechanic, 1972b; Mendelsohn, 1979). The need to coordinate the activities of many different specialists and technologies in health care has increased the need to develop bureaucratic health-care delivery systems (Perrow, 1965). With the growing sophistication of health-care practice, the delivery systems for health care have become larger, more structured, and more technologically sophisticated than ever in the past (Georgopoulos, 1974, 1975). Communication is a crucial tool for coordinating people and technologies in complex health-care organizations (Costello & Pettegrew, 1979; Kreps, 1986a).

Organizations as Information Processors

Organizations provide social structures for facilitating human adaptation through processing of information (Kreps, 1986a; Weick, 1969). Organizational affiliations help people adapt to environmental constraints and cope with complex problems they encounter. Health-care organizations provide consumers with information-processing resources to help them solve their health problems. Coping with threats to individual health is an information-processing problem for most people since serious health problems are often too equivocal for individuals to fully interpret, understand, and adequately respond to by themselves (Kreps & Thornton, 1984; Zola, 1963). Consumers need specialized information to direct their health-preserving activities. With the help of knowledgeable others, consumers can cope with complex health threats. The more equivocal health problems are, the more equivocal health-care processes for interpreting and effectively responding to these problems must be (the principle of requisite variety), and the more likely consumers are to need the information processing resources of health-care organizations (Weick, 1969; Kreps & Thornton, 1984). Routine health-care ailments, such as headaches or common colds, pose less complex information-processing problems, necessitating less information-processing power than an acute, highly equivocal health-care problem like a brain tumor. Equivocal problems demand the information-processing resources of a health-care organization; tests have to be conducted, specialists must be consulted, and complex treatments and operations may have to be performed. Only health-care organizations, with well-trained personnel and specialized equipment, can help clients with highly equivocal health-care problems.

Internal and External Organizational Communication

Information flow in health-care organizations must be directed and coordinated internally and externally for organizations to function effectively (Kreps, 1986a). Health-care organizations are complex social systems composed of networks of interdependent groups of health-care providers and support staff whose activities must be coordinated (Perrow, 1965). Health-care administrators direct internal organizational information flow between different departments and divisions to coordinate internal health preserving and administrative activities of the system (Pfeffer & Salancik, 1977). Administrators must also be able to see beyond the boundaries of their organization to proactively direct their organizations' interaction with its relevant environment (Kreps, 1986b). For example, fund raising, lobbying, personnel recruitment, and media relations are all potentially important functions within external information systems in health-care organizations (Kreps, 1986a; Pfeffer, 1973).

Organizations, like human beings, must be able to adapt to survive. Health-care organizations constantly need feedback about their performance from internal and external information sources to identify performance gaps and initiate constructive change. An important source of feedback for an organization is its members—especially those who work with consumers (cosmopolites) since they can provide the organization with information about both the internal environment, of which they are a part, and the external environment, with which they have daily contact. Nurses, for example, are important information sources within health-care organizations since they are involved with many of the internal activities of the organization and have daily contact with incoming and outgoing patients as well as other members of the hospital's relevant environment (Kreps, 1986b). These communication contacts provide nurses with valuable information (organizational intelligence) about how to get things done in their organization (Kreps, 1986a). Yet leaders of health-care organizations often fail to recognize and fully utilize the information resources nurses possess (Kreps, 1986b). This administrative neglect can lead to frustration among nurses and subsequent high rates of turnover (Filoromo & Ziff, 1980; Mobley, 1977, 1982; Wandelt, Pierce, & Widdowson, 1981; Wolf, 1981).

Interprofessional relationships between the many different providers in health-care organizations must be managed. Ineffective interprofessional relationships established between health-care providers is a major problem in health-care delivery systems (Boyer, Lee, & Kirschner, 1977; Frank, 1961; Hill, 1978; Kindig, 1975). Power and status discrepancies between practitioners can lead to professional domination and conflict between health-care providers (Friedson, 1970). Differences in education, orientation to health care, and evaluations of the value of other health-care disciplines can make interprofessional relations uneasy. Health-care professionals are often ethnocentric about the legitimacy of their profession in comparison to other groups of health-care professionals, leading to conflict over domain consensus and authority due to the overlapping responsibilities and interdependent activities that health-care providers often share (Kreps & Thornton, 1984; Starr, 1982).

Providers often experience problems of role conflict and role strain in health-care organizations, increasing their levels of job-related stress and burnout (House, 1970; Pettegrew et al., 1980; Ray, 1983). A common cause of role conflict problems are the mutually contradictory directives health-care providers receive from multiple sources of authority in health-care organizations (House, 1970). Nurses often receive several demands on their time for different health-care activities from equally legitimate sources such as staff physicians, head nurses, patients, patients' private physicians, as well as from hospital administrators. Because health-care organizations have many sources of authority, such double-bind situations often cause role conflict, role strain, job-related stress, burnout, and information-processing problems for health-care providers, limiting the effectiveness of organizational communication (House, 1970; Woodlock, 1983).

Health-Care Delivery Organizations and Consumers

The complexity of health-care organization processes often leads these organizations to become extremely bureaucratic, with many rules to direct activities (Costello & Pettegrew, 1979; Perrow, 1965; Starr, 1982). Such regulations provide health-care personnel with content information that helps them to direct their activities and helps to maintain order within the organization. On a relationship level, however, the proliferation of rules and regulations in health-care organizations can be stifling and dehumanizing. For many individuals, hospitalization is tantamount to incarceration (Kreps, 1986c; Mendelsohn, 1979). The many rules that govern patient behavior limit the social potential of the individual and tend to reinforce the sick role, and the roles governing hospital personnel may stifle and frustrate them.

Institutionalization often has a dehumanizing influence on patients, especially long-term care patients, such as elderly residents of nursing homes (Kreps, 1986c; Mendelson, 1974). Entry into health-care systems, such as hospitals or nursing homes, severely constrain elders' freedom of choice. As a patient, the elder is generally "assigned" a patient number, a patient chart, a bed, a room, and a medical regimen, and sometimes is even given institutionally approved garments to wear. Patients must adapt to the health-care system's schedule of events, rather than choosing their own activities, including many hygienic schedule choices they are used to choosing for themselves (such as when to eat, when to sleep, and when to use the toilet). Daily events are often scheduled for the elder, with little or no heed for the individual's wishes. Elderly patients are often given little choice about what foods they want to eat; dieticians make those choices for them. Hospital personnel take the elder for lab tests, therapy sessions, and even surgical operations according to a schedule prepared for the patient, often with little or no collaboration with the elder. The elder is regularly told when to sit up, when to lie down, when to stand up, regardless of their own wishes. Evidence indicates the institutionalization of health-care delivery in many organizations can limit the effectiveness of health-care treatment by alienating and dehumanizing health-care recipients (U.S. Senate Special Committee on Aging, Subcommittee on Long Term Care, 1974; 1975).

Communication Technologies in Health-Care Organizations

Modern health-care organizations commonly utilize a broad range of specialized communication technologies to help handle their complex health information needs (Brenner & Logan, 1980; Day, 1975; Park & Bashshur, 1975). Many health-care organizations regularly use in-house computer and audiovisual information technologies for patient education, information exchange for personnel between shifts, medical procedure documentation, and in-service training (Cassata, Harris, Bland, & Ronning, 1976; Cassata, Conroe, & Clements, 1977; Cassata & Clements, 1978; Elmore, 1981; Portis & Hunter, 1975; Stoeckle, Lazare, Weingarten, & McGuire, 1971; Wagner, 1967). The computer has emerged as one of the most powerful communication technologies for storing, processing, and retrieving health information in organizations (Davis, 1973; Makris, 1983; Sterling, Pollack & Spencer, 1973). Computers are used to store and process medical records, information about health-care treatment, referral, and research, as well as to analyze laboratory tests, interpret diagnostic data, track physiological monitoring systems, and conduct tomographic scans and noninvasive imaging procedures in nuclear medicine (Anderson & Jay, 1985; Hawkins, Day, Gustafson, Chewning, & Bosworth, 1982; Hinchcliff-Pelias, 1983; Kreps, Hubbard, & DeVita, in press; Makris, 1983; Park & Bashshur, 1975; Slack, Hicks, Reed, & VanCura, 1966; Slack et al., 1974; Zimmerman, 1978).

Makris (1983) describes two different ways computers are used to handle many of the information-processing needs (informatics) of health-care organizations, "medical informatics" and "health informatics" (p. 206). Medical informatics are used to improve health-care delivery by increasing the sophistication of medical instruments, assisting research into epidemiology, and enhancing decision making in clinical medicine (Baker, 1974; Makris, 1983, p. 206; Friedman et al., 1977). Health informatics are used to increase the efficiency of health organizations by managing health information processes. Health informatics "assist the management of: the administrative functions of a hospital (accounting, billing, inventory, payroll), patient care functions (admitting, appointment scheduling, dietary, laboratory, nurse scheduling, pharmacy), and general management control functions (budgeting, productivity analysis, utilization review)" (Makris, 1983, p. 206).

Computerization of medical records serves both clinical and administrative information functions in health-care organizations by giving providers easy access to information for diagnosis and treatment and giving administrators records of health-care services and resources (Zimmerman, 1978). (The availability of computerized patient information also implies that health-care organizations must be careful to protect the individual's information privacy.) Computerized appointment scheduling and shift scheduling has helped to solve many time-management problems in health-care organizations (Covvey & McAlister, 1980; Nelson, 1981). Patient history taking by computer has been used effectively to gather sensitive information anonymously, provide consumers with an interactive means of seeking health information, as well as store and process patient health information (Cohen, 1981; Haessler, Holland, & Elshtain, 1974; Slack et al., 1966, 1974).

Along with the many useful applications and benefits of computerized hospital information systems, several communication problems have also arisen. Some of the problems associated with the computerization of health-care organizations include too much and too little access to health information (Brenner & Logan, 1980; Covell, Uman, & Manning, 1985; Friedman, 1977; Kaplan, 1985; Kreps & Naughton, 1986; Morrell, Podlone, & Cohen, 1977). The storing of private medical records on computer files often allows people of questionable integrity, who have no legitimate right to private medical information, access to these data. For example, in 1986 information was leaked to the mass media from the medical records computer files of the Clinical Center of the National Institutes of Health (NIH) concerning the health-care treatment being offered to Roy Cohn, a famous New York lawyer who was under investigation. Mr. Cohn had repeatedly told media representatives that he was being treated for a liver ailment. Subsequent newspaper reports about his medical records from the NIH indicated he was being treated for AIDS, contradicting Mr. Cohn's previous statements and potentially causing him unnecessary distress. Other unwarranted uses of health information have occurred when suppliers of health-care products and services have accessed computerized medical files to establish mailing lists for identifying potential customers to market their wares to. Problems concerning limited access to health information also occur when those who need the information have difficulty getting it or understanding it, such as when the coding of information on computer files makes the data difficult to interpret or when data are omitted from the files. Additional problems of limited access include lack of receptiveness of health-care staff to computer information systems and limited abilities to utilize computer technologies.

As health knowledge has increased, health-care services have become more complex, and the need for organizations to help handle the management of health information has become more pronounced, making organizations important sites for health-care delivery. Effective communication of relevant information, often with the use of health-care systems, enables organizational adaptation to ever changing health-care issues. Adaptation of health-care organizations to emergent health information constraints enables viable health-care service delivery in the modern world. Optimally, health-care organizations provide the structure, personnel, and technology for coping with complex health-care situations, and helping to process health information, although limitations in the effectiveness of health-care organizations can often exacerbate health problems (Davis, 1973; Kreps & Thornton, 1984; Mendelsohn, 1979).

SOCIETAL ASPECTS OF HEALTH AND HEALTH CARE

For the health-care system to work effectively, there must be active sharing of relevant information to facilitate coordination of activities between key members of societal interorganizational fields (Aiken & Hage, 1968; Georgopoulos, 1975; Levine, White, & Paul, 1963; Turk, 1973; Warren, 1967). For example, if hospital organizations are to accomplish their health-care goals, they must be able to elicit cooperation from a wide range of different organizations that provide them with specialized services and products such as equipment sales and service organizations, health care personnel unions, pharmaceutical companies, laundry services, insurance companies, food services companies, private ambulance services, and government agencies. Because rules and regulations have a major influence on health-care organizations, it is important for such organizations to gather information from government sources and attempt to influence relevant governmental legislation (Conant, 1968; Lewis, 1955). Lobbying activities and selection of members of hospital boards of directors that represent government agencies and other members of hospitals' interorganizational fields are common strategies used to accomplish societal information exchange and influence (Kreps, 1986a; Pfeffer, 1973; Turk, 1973). Health-care organizations use societal communication contacts to share information with government agencies and to influence these agencies.

Mediated Communication and Health Information

Modern societies have become increasingly dependent upon media to disseminate health information, enabling the sharing of relevant health information among many different people, groups, and organizations within modern societies (Wright, 1975). Media provide forums for information that help societal members recognize and evaluate environmental opportunities and constraints, coordinate their resources and activities in response to their environment, learn about culturally relevant phenomena, and pass on (timebind) knowledge and cultural information to future societies as a form of social inheritance (Lasswell, 1948; Schramm, 1954). Mediated communication is often used in public health education campaigns by channeling health information to consumers about health-promoting behaviors (Atkin, 1979, 1981; Flay & Cook, 1981). For example, mediated communication has been used, with differing levels of success, to provide consumers with information about the uses and abuses of drugs (Atkyns, McEwen, & Hanneman, 1975; Feingold & Knapp, 1977; Fejer, Smart, & Whitehead, 1971; Goldstein, 1965; Hanneman, 1973), the importance of good nutrition (Kaufman, 1980), how to avoid heart disease (Macoby & Farquhar, 1975; Solomon, 1984), preventing drunk driving (Atkin, Garramore, & Anderson, 1986), the importance of giving up smoking (O'Keefe, 1971; Puska et al., 1979), and reasons and methods for effective contraception (Udry, 1972).

Print media, such as newspapers, books, magazines, journals, and pamphlets, have great utility as health communication tools to educate consumers about health risks, health maintenance, and health-care services (Kreps & Thornton, 1984). In a survey of the comparative use of newspapers, radio, magazines, and television as sources of health information, Wright (1975) found that newspapers and magazines are used most often by respondents, and printed media were identified as the most useful source of health information. Bishop (1974) found that the more anxious consumers are about a specific health problem, the more likely they are to seek and utilize printed health information. Pamphlets and booklets are examples of technologically simple, but important, print media used by many health-care systems to provide their relevant publics with health information (Feldman, 1966). These print media are often used to help consumers recognize and understand symptoms of health problems, adopt appropriate strategies for resisting and coping with health risks, and identify where and how they can obtain health-care services.

Health Information and the Health-Care Professions

Print media, specifically biomedical journals and textbooks, are an important and preferred source of health information for health-care providers, helping them learn about the latest techniques for diagnosing and treating health problems (Covell, Uman, & Manning, 1985; Currie, 1976). Yet advances in health-care knowledge are expanding at such a rapid rate that it is increasingly difficult for those providers who depend upon state-of-the-art health information to keep up to date (Bernier & Yerkey, 1979; Harlem, 1977; Haynes et al., 1986; Kreps, Hubbard, & DeVita, in press). Bernier and Yerkey (1979) estimated that approximately 2 million articles are published in the biomedical literature annually; the publication rate was increasing geometrically, making it virtually impossible for health-care providers to keep abreast of the relevant literature on health-care advances. In fact, evidence suggests that the longer it has been since physicians have graduated from medical school, the more outdated their health-care knowledge and practices become (Haynes et al., 1986).

Computerized information systems, like Physician Data Query and Internist/Cadeceus, are relatively new media that can help providers and consumers by enabling them to identify relevant health-care literature and quickly access the latest health-care information (Haynes et al., 1985; Kreps et al., in press; Kreps, Maibach, Naughton, Day, & Annett, 1986; Miller, Pople, & Myers, 1982). These information systems help bridge the information gap that often exists between the clinical research community that generates state-of-the-art advances in health care-treatment and the specialized practice community, the general practice community, and health-care consumers who need to utilize such health information (Kreps & Naughton, 1986).

Computerized information and decision-making systems have great potential for helping health-care providers and consumers identify and apply relevant health information to their health-care activities. Yet there is serious concern that computer applications in health care have not been well diffused into the health-care system, nor have they been utilized to their fullest potential. This failure is due to many providers' and consumers' reticence to adopt and utilize communication technologies as well as to many complexities that are part of current computer systems that hinder their effective implementation and frustrate computer users in health-care settings (Kaplan, 1985; Kreps et al., 1986).

Mediated Public Health Information

In recent years, the telephone has been increasingly utilized as an interactive health information dissemination medium, with telephone mediated hot lines and referral services developing as important channels providing support, information, and referral for callers who suffer from assorted health risks such as AIDS, poisoning, domestic violence, alcoholism, drug addiction, and cancer. Local and national telephone hot lines provide millions of callers with crisis counseling helping lonely, depressed, and suicidal callers to work through their emotional problems (Fish, 1986). The National Cancer Institute has developed a cancer information hot line, the Cancer Information Service, that can be reached by anyone in the United States via a toll-free telephone number for up-to-date information regarding cancer treatment, referral, and clinical research (Stein, 1985). The Cancer

Information Service hot line has been used successfully in concert with other communication media as well as with print, radio, and television advertisements, commercials, and public service announcements to promote the hot line to the public (Hammond, 1986; Kreps & Naughton, 1986; Stein, 1985).

Radio and television have become increasingly health oriented in recent years, with increased programming of health education shows (Kreps & Thornton, 1984; Wright, 1975). News programs often include special "health segments" and may even employ "health reporters." Nationally televised news magazine shows, such as *60 Minutes*, *20/20*, and *Hour-Magazine*, generally offer special segments devoted to health issues such as nutrition, heart disease, exercise, and new health-care treatments. Discussion-oriented television shows, such as *Donahue*, often invite nationally recognized health experts or individuals with life-threatening health problems to interact with a studio audience about health topics. Exercise shows provide their audience with health-promoting ideas and activities. Radio talk-shows often discuss health issues and provide listeners with health-care tips. To the extent that the health information presented is correct, trends in health programming have helped make television and radio important channels for health promotion.

Unfortunately, information presented through mass media do not always promote public health. For example, advertisements for cigarettes and alcoholic beverages have downplayed these products' health risks, aligned their consumption with virility, sophistication, and athletic prowess, and, most dangerously, are often directed toward high-risk segments of the population, such as youths who may develop hard-to-break negative health habits early in their lives (Jacobson & Amos, 1985; Trauth & Huffman, 1986). Furthermore, dramatic programs on television and popular films often present distorted images of the health-care system, either representing the health-care professional as omnipotent or representing the health-care system as totally inept (Kreps & Thornton, 1984; McLaughlin, 1975). These exaggerated media portrayals of the health-care system can lend support to societal stereotypes about the roles of health-care providers and consumers and may promote many unrealistic expectations (Blackwell, 1967; Gochman, 1969; Mechanic, 1972b; Myerhoff & Larson, 1965; Nelson, 1973; Tagliacozzo & Mauksch, 1972). Media advertisements that glorify the use of products associated with serious health risks and stereotypical media portrayals of health-care situations can reinforce unrealistic expectations for health and health-care practice, and help to socialize unproductive public health beliefs (Kasl & Cobb, 1966).

Cultural Influences on Health Communication

Stigma, or the loss of social identity and status, is a primary problem facing many people seeking health care (Goffman, 1963; Thompson & Seibold, 1978). Stigma is a social situation that occurs when a person's public image is "reduced in our minds from a whole and usual person to a tainted, discounted one" (Goffman, 1963, p. 3). Due to the perceived deviance associated with the sick role, those seeking health care often suffer from stigma (LaFargue, 1972; Lennane & Lennane, 1973). Media portrayals of health-care consumers can reinforce the powerless stereotype embodied by the sick role (Cassata, Skill, & Boadu, 1979; McLaughlin, 1975). Cultural stereotypes often lead to stigma and prejudicial treatment of many groups of health-care consumers, such as AIDS sufferers (Hughey, Norton, Edgar, & Adamson, 1986), the aged (Kreps, 1986c), the poor (Kosa & Zola, 1975), blacks (White, 1974), Hispanic Americans (Hoppe & Heller, 1975; Martiney, 1978; Quesada & Heller, 1977), women (Chesler, 1972; Corea, 1977; Mendelsohn, 1981), the mentally retarded (Baran, 1977), and the disabled (Braithwaite, 1985; Dahnke, 1982; Emry & Wiseman, 1985; Thompson, 1981).

Societally based cultural perspectives on the health-care system have a dramatic influence on health and health care (Kleinman, 1980). For example, Mendelsohn (1981) suggests a modern American cultural orientation to health care that views health care as though it were a religion. The "religion of health care" is steeped in mysticism, too dark and mysterious for the average "parishioner" (patient) to understand. Consumers must have faith in the wisdom of the high priests and priestesses of health care (providers) to interpret the gospel of health care and direct health-preserving activities (Frank, 1975; Mendelsohn, 1981). Religion as a metaphor for health care reinforces the passive, almost obsequious, role many health-care consumers adopt (Kreps & Thornton, 1984). Societal members' dependence on the mysticism and ritual of health care in controlling illness and providing health care promotes unrealistic consumer expectations for health-care outcomes, places the provider in a one-up power position in the patient/provider relationship, and discourages consumers from taking active roles in their own treatment (Becker, 1974a, 1974b; Blackwell, 1967; Colm, 1953; Crane, 1975; Gochman, 1969; Mechanic, 1972b; Myerhoff & Larson, 1965; Roth, 1957).

Ethical Constraints on Health Communication

Ethical standards for health communication are developed to govern the moral acceptability of health-related behaviors of societal members (Barry, 1982; President's Commission for the Study of Ethical Problems in Medicine and Biomedical and Behavioral Research, 1982a, 1982b, 1982c, 1982d). Ethical standards for health behaviors are established through information generated by interaction within a given community and as such are largely culturally bound (Kreps & Thornton, 1984). Health behaviors, then, are ethical to the extent they are appropriate to the cultural orientations of health communicators. Moral dilemmas develop when there are contradictory cultural values guiding health behaviors (Campbell, 1975). Representatives of different cultures often have very different orientations of what is ethical health behavior. Even within a single cultural perspective, health-care issues such as euthanasia can pose moral dilemmas for individuals. In the case of euthanasia, the mutually opposing cultural values of preserving human life, limiting human suffering, and respecting an individual's personal health decisions conflict to cause moral dilemmas. Ethical issues are complex and are not easily resolved, but communication among members of a community of peers and professionals can be used to help individuals gather and examine intersubjective information about health-care issues and make ethical health-care decisions (Kreps & Thornton, 1984).

The societal level of communication performs several very important information functions in health and health care. It is at the societal level of communication that the coordination of health information and health-care services between interdependent groups and organizations is accomplished. Mass media have powerful influences on public health and health care due to their use as key societal channels for health information. Culturally bound interpretations of health information strongly influence social constraints on the health-care activities of providers and consumers.

IMPLICATIONS FOR
HEALTH COMMUNICATION POLICY

The pervasive uses of health information at each of the micro and macro levels of human interaction, examined in this essay, illustrate the important functions of human communication in health and health care. Yet, acknowledgment of the important relationships between communication, information, health, and health care opens a Pandora's box of complex questions about how best to utilize communication and information in promoting human health. These questions are especially difficult to answer since current knowledge about the effective use of communication in health care is incomplete and fragmented (Arntson, 1985; Thompson, 1984). In the remainder of this chapter, several directions for the development of health communication policies will be suggested for government agencies, health-care delivery organizations, educational institutions, professional societies, and accrediting bodies.

Governmental Health Communication Policy

Federal and local government can begin to help promote effective health communication through development and implementation of legislation as well as through careful implementation of existing laws regulating health care and health promotion. Laws can be designed to help protect health-care consumers' and providers' rights to receive relevant and accurate health information through the mass media and in health-care organizations, as well as protect their rights to privacy of personal health information although laws have limited influence on the communication behaviors individuals engage in. For example, although failure by health-care providers to secure informed consent from their clients is viewed in most states of this country as illegal—a form of medical malpractice subject to negligence law—patients are routinely treated in health-care systems without receiving full disclosure about treatment procedures and risks, nor are they given clear opportunities to refuse treatment (President's Commission for the Study of Ethical Problems in Medicine and Biomedical and Behavioral Research, 1982a). Many consumers are not aware that they have the right to informed consent, and in a national survey more than 75% of the physicians interviewed did not know what the legal requirements for informed consent were in their home states (President's Commission for the Study of Ethical Problems in Medicine and Biomedical and Behavioral Research, 1982a, 1982b). Efforts must be taken to disseminate information about the legal requirements for informed consent to health-care providers and consumers and to implement steps to encourage providers to live up to the law.

Government agencies dealing with public health and research, such as the Federal Drug Administration (FDA), the National Institutes of Health (NIH), the Centers for Disease Control (CDC), as well as state and local agencies concerning public health, can make the provision of relevant health information to health-care providers and consumers a primary institutional goal by designating substantial funding and efforts to health information dissemination (Green, 1978). For example, the National Cancer Institute (NCI) of the National Institutes of Health has established exemplar health communication programs for disseminating health information. NCI operates the Cancer Information Service for disseminating cancer information to the public via telephone and the mails; the Office of Cancer Communications, which initiates communications with government, scientific, and medical groups, as well as with the press and the public, to increase understanding of cancer prevention, control, and cure via television and radio, pamphlets, booklets, and through direct contact with the public and relevant organizations; and the International Cancer Information Center, which collects and disseminates relevant scientific information about cancer research through journals and computer information system databases. The NCI's substantial investment in health communication programs illustrate their recognition of the primary role of health information in public health and health care. Other government agencies can also develop appropriate communication programs for disseminating health information to their relevant publics.

Organizational Health Communication Policy

Health-care delivery organizations can help promote effective health communication through development of policies and in-house training guidelines for helping their personnel to recognize the communicative demands of their jobs and develop optimal communication skills (Ruben & Bowman, 1986). Orientation programs for employees and consumers can emphasize the importance of trust and cooperation in health care and stress the organization's support for good communication. Ombudsmen can be made available to ameliorate conflicts, helping providers and consumers identify answers to their questions and solve problems they are facing. Systems for gathering feedback from consumers and employees about organizational performance should be made available, and such feedback should be utilized in directing organizational development, problem solving, and innovation (Kreps, 1986b; Ruben & Bowman, 1986). Health-care organizations can utilize communication technologies such as slide-shows, videotape programs, closed circuit television systems, and computer systems to help educate providers and consumers, as well as to help collect, process, and deliver relevant operational and health information (Elmore, 1981). Health-care organizations can also share their health information resources with the public by implementing health education programs and health fairs to promote public health and goodwill and to gather information fro these audiences about their specific health-care concerns, needs, and problems.

Self-help organizations can be established in communities to provide consumers with important health information (Kreps, 1986c). For example, community wellness centers and senior centers in some neighborhoods currently provide health promotion and health maintenance services to local residents. These centers often offer classes to community members on weight control, retirement planning, physical fitness, stress management, and nutritional awareness and provide community residents with health-care referrals when needed. Local residents can easily partake in the health-promoting activities of nearby centers without many of the formalities of seeking help at more bureaucratic and intimidating health-care organizations.

Educational Health Communication Policy

Educational institutions can develop curricula to help future health-care providers—as well as health-care consumers—develop both appreciation for the importance of effective communication in health care and enhanced abilities to communicate competently in health-care situations (Barnlund, 1976; Cassata, 1980). Providers and consumers need support in developing knowledge and skills of competent human communication for use in seeking, interpreting, and providing relevant health information (Association of American Medical Colleges, 1984, 1985; Kreps & Query, 1986). Health communication education can be implemented several ways at different educational levels. For example, in elementary schools, lessons for school children about how to talk about health problems at home and in health-care systems and to utilize communication to help others can be integrated into basic health courses; in schools of nursing, pharmacy, dentistry, allied health, social work, and medicine, health communication courses or course sections can supplement existing courses for health-care providers; continuing education programs for health-care providers can offer programs concerning health communication issues and competencies; undergraduate and graduate college communication programs can also add health communication courses to their curricula. Optimally, college health communication courses can be presented to interprofessional groups of students representing different health-care professions, as well as consumers, to promote the development of interprofessional understanding that can translate into cooperation and teamwork in the delivery of health care (Hill, 1978; Kreps, 1985).

Professional Society and Accrediting
Agency Health Communication Policy

Educational institutions and professional societies (such as the American Medical Association and the International Communication Association) can help stimulate and support health communication research, such as research designed to identify specific communication competencies needed by health-care providers and consumers to promote effective health care. Communication competence is not merely the development of specific, isolated communication skills, but the development of appropriate contextually based communication motivation, knowledge, and competence (Spitzberg, 1981, 1983; Spitzberg & Cupach, 1984; Wiemann, 1977). Research by Morse and Piland (1981) has identified five "essential" communication skills for health-care providers: (1) listening, (2) exchanging routine information, (3) managing conflict, (4) communicating in small groups, and (5) instructing. Future research can help ascertain the most effective communication strategies providers and consumers can use in health-care situations, identify information needs of health consumers and providers, evaluate current health information sources, and constitute strategies for helping providers and consumers best utilize health information (Kreps & Query, 1986).

Institutions offering health provider educational programs, professional societies for health-care providers, and accrediting bodies for both health-care organizations and educational programs have the opportunity to establish standards and criteria for effective provider health communication and for educational programs that help health-care providers develop effective communication skills. These organizations can develop criteria for accrediting health-care personnel, educational programs, and organizations by assessing the quality of health communication in health-care practice. Such assessment and accreditation activities can spur the introduction and dissemination of health communication education and facilitate improvements in health communication practices. For example, a report of a recent national review of medical and premedical education programs conducted by the Association of American Medical Colleges indicated that many medical faculties were lagging behind in the development, teaching, and evaluation of physician communication skills and recommended that medical "faculties should teach effective communication with patients (including the medical interview) and must evaluate students' communication with patients with much more care than they do at present" (Association of American Medical Colleges, 1985, p. 126).

Interorganizational Collaboration

Collaboration among governmental, educational, health-care delivery, professional, and industrial organizations can help improve development and dissemination of health information. For example, a recent consensus conference was conducted at the National Institutes of Health to establish current knowledge and directions for health promotion concerning blood cholesterol level and heart disease: Conference participants included expert personnel from federal agencies, medical schools, health-care delivery systems, professional societies, and public interest groups, who examined current biomedical evidence and answered questions concerning the relationship between blood cholesterol levels and heart disease, identification of the levels of blood cholesterol at which health-care interventions should be introduced, whether attempts should be made to reduce blood cholesterol levels of the general population, and what research directions should be pursued on the relationship between blood cholesterol and coronary heart disease (National Institute of Health, 1986). The findings of this conference were widely disseminated to health-care providers throughout the world and are currently being used by health-care providers as standards for practice concerning cholesterol and heart disease. Similar collaborative efforts can be used to identify state-of-the-art knowledge about additional health-care issues and establish clear standards for practice.

Health communication practice can be enhanced by translating communication knowledge into public health communication strategies, practices, and policies. The preliminary policy suggestions provided here identify just a few of the many areas for improving health communication in the modern world. Additional health communication research and policy should address, among other issues, how to facilitate the public's identification and utilization of health information sources, technologies, and programs to promote public health through effective applications of relevant health information. By identifying and promoting effective use of health communication and health information, health care can be improved and public health can be enhanced.

REFERENCES

Aiken, M., & Hage, J. (1968). Organizational interdependence and intraorganizational structure. *American Sociological Review, 33*, 912-930.

Albrecht, T., & Adelman, M. (1984). Social support and life stress: New directions for communication research. *Human Communication Research, 11*, 3-32.

Alexander, F. (1950). *Psychosomatic medicine.* New York: W. W. Norton.

Alfidi, R. (1971). Informed consent: A study of patient reaction. *Journal of the American Medical Association, 216*, 1325-1329.

Alpert, J. (1964). Broken appointments. *Pediatrics, 34*, 124-132.

Anderson, J., & Jay, S. (1985). Computers and clinical judgment: The role of physician networks. *Social Science and Medicine, 20*, 969-979.

Arntson, P. (1985). Future research in health communication. *Journal of Applied Communication Research, 13*, 118-130.

Association of American Medical Colleges. (1984). *Physicians for the twenty-first century.* Washington, DC: Author.

Association of American Medical Colleges. (1985). Report of the working group on fundamental skills. *Journal of Medical Education, 59*, 125-134.

Atkin, C. (1979). Research evidence on mass mediated health communication campaigns. In D. Nimmo (Ed.), *Communication yearbook 3* (pp. 655-668). New Brunswick, NJ: Transaction.

Atkin, C. (1981). Mass media information campaign effectiveness. In R. Rice & W. Paisley (Eds.), *Public communication campaigns* (pp. 265-280). Newbury Park, CA: Sage.

Atkin, C., Garramore, G., & Anderson, R. (1986, May). *Formative evaluation research in health campaign planning: The case of drunk driving prevention.* Paper presented at the annual meeting of the International Communication Association, Chicago.

Atkyns, R., Gordon, T., & Couch, W. (1986, May). *Adolescent health promotion audience segmentation: Source influence, preference, and information acquisition.* Paper presented at the annual meeting of the International Communication Association, Chicago.

Atkyns, R., McEwen, W., & Hanneman, G. (1975). Sources of drug information among adults. *Journal of Drug Education, 5*, 161-169.

Atman, N. (1972). Understanding your patient's emotional response. *Journal of Practical Nursing, 22*, 22-25.

Baker, S. (1979). The diffusion of high technology medical innovation: The computed tomography scanner example. *Social Science and Medicine, 13*, 155-162.

Baldwin, D., et al. (1980). *Interdisciplinary health care teams in teaching and practice.* Reno: University of Nevada/New Health Perspectives, Inc.

Baran, S. (1977). TV programming and attitudes toward mental retardation. *Journalism Quarterly, 54*, 140-142.

Barker, L., & Wiseman, G. (1966). A model of intrapersonal communication. *Journal of Communication, 16*, 172-179.

Barnlund, D. (1962). Toward a meaning-centered philosophy of communication. *Journal of Communication, 12*, 197-211.

Barnlund, D. (1968). Therapeutic communication. In D. Barnlund (Ed.), *Interpersonal communication* (pp. 613-645). Boston: Houghton Mifflin.

Barnlund, D. (1970). A transactional model of communication. In *Foundations of communication theory* (pp. 83-102). New York: Harper & Row.

Barnlund, D. (1976). The mystification of meaning: Doctor-patient encounters. *Journal of Medical Education, 51*, 716-725.

Bateson, G. (1958). *Naven* (2nd ed.). Palo Alto, CA: Stanford University Press.

Becker, M. (1974a). The health belief model and personal health behavior: Introduction. *Health Education Monographs, 2*, 326-327.

Becker, M. (1974b). The health belief model and sick role behavior. *Health Education Monographs, 2*, 409-419.

Becker, M., Maimon, L., Kirscht, J., Haefner, D., & Drachman, R. (1977). The health belief model and prediction of dietary compliance: A field experiment. *Journal of Health and Social Behavior, 18*, 348-366.

Beecher, H. (1955). The powerful placebo. *Journal of the American Medical Association, 159*, 1602-1606.

Benjamin, A. (1981). *The helping interview* (3rd ed.). Boston: Houghton Mifflin.

Berger, M. (1958). Nonverbal communications in group psychotherapy. *International Journal of Group Psychotherapy, 8*, 161-178.

Bernier, C., & Yerkey, A. (1979). *Cogent communication: Overcoming information overload.* Westport, CT: Greenwood.

Bion, W. (1952). Group dynamics: A re-view. *International Journal of Psycho-Analysis, 33*, 235-247.

Bishop, R. (1974). Anxiety and readership of health information. *Journalism Quarterly, 51*, 40-46.

Blackwell, B. (1967). Upper middle class adult expectations about entering the sick role for physical and psychiatric dysfunctions. *Journal of Health and Social Behavior, 8*, 83-95.

Blackwell, B. (1973). Patient compliance. *New England Journal of Medicine, 289*, 249-252.

Blumberg, B., Flaherty, M., & Lewis, J. (Eds.). (1982). *Coping with cancer*. (NIH Publication 82-2080). Bethesda, MD: National Cancer Institute.

Bok, S. (1974). The ethics of giving placebos. *Scientific American, 231*, 17-23.

Boyer, L., Lee, D., & Kirschner, C. (1977). A student-run course in interprofessional relations. *Journal of Medical Education, 52*, 183-189.

Braithwaite, D. (1985, November). *Impression management and redefinition of self by persons with disabilities*. Paper presented at the annual meeting of the Speech Communication Association, Denver.

Brauer, P. (1965). Should the patient be told the truth? In J. Skipper & R. Leonard (Eds.), *Social interaction and patient care* (pp. 23-46). Philadelphia: Lippincott.

Brenner, D., & Logan, R. (1980). Some considerations in the diffusion of medical technologies: Medical information systems. In D. Nimmo (Ed.), *Communication yearbook 4* (pp. 609-623). New Brunswick, NJ: Transaction.

Brodie, D., Kroben, J., & Wertheimenr, A. (1973). Expanded roles for the pharmacist. *American Journal of Pharmaceutical Education, 37*, 591.

Burke, R., Weir, T., & Duncan, G. (1976). Informal helping relationships in work organizations. *Academy of Management Journal, 19*, 370-377.

Byerly, H. (1976). Explaining and exploiting the placebo effect. *Perspectives in Biology and Medicine, 19*, 423-436.

Campbell, R., & Chenoweth, B. (1981). *Peer support for older adults*. Ann Arbor: University of Michigan Press.

Caron, H. (1968). Patients' cooperation with a medical regimen. *Journal of the American Medical Association, 203*, 922-926.

Carroll, J., & Monroe, J. (1980). Teaching clinical interviewing in the health professions: A review of empirical research. *Evaluation and the Health Professions, 3*, 21-45.

Cassata, D. (1980). Health communication theory and research: A definitional overview. In D. Nimmo (Ed.), *Communication yearbook 4* (pp. 583-589). New Brunswick, NJ: Transaction.

Cassata, D. (1983). Physician interviewing and counseling training. *International Journal of Advanced Counseling, 5*, 297-305.

Cassata, D., Conroe, R., & Clements, P. (1977). A program for enhancing medical interviewing using videotape feedback in the family practice residency. *Journal of Family Practice, 4*, 673-677.

Cassata, D., Harris, I., Bland, C., & Ronning, G. (1976). A systematic approach to curriculum design in a medical school interview course. *Journal of Medical Education, 51*, 939-941.

Cassata, D., & Clements, P. (1978). Teaching communication skills through videotape feedback: A rural health program. *Biosciences Communications, 4*, 39-50.

Cassata, M., Skill, T., & Boadu, S. (1979). In sickness and in health. *Journal of Communication, 29*, 73-80.

Center for Health Education. (1984a). *Physician involvement in cancer risk reduction education*. Baltimore: Author.

Center for Health Education. (1984b). *Needs assessment: Physician's role in cancer risk reduction*. Baltimore: Author.

Chesler, P. (1972). *Women and madness*. New York: Avon.

Chiraboga, D., Coho, A., Stein, J., & Roberts, J. (1979). Divorce, stress, and social supports: A study in help seeking behavior. *Journal of Divorce, 3*, 121-135.

Cline, R. (1983). Interpersonal communication skills for enhancing physician-patient relationships. *Maryland State Medical Journal, 32*, 272-278.

Cluck, G., & Cline, R. (1985, May). *The circle of others: Self help groups for the bereaved*. Paper presented at the annual meeting of the Eastern Communication Association, Providence, RI.

Cobb, S. (1976). Social support as a moderator of life stress. *Psychosomatic Medicine, 38,* 300-314.

Cohen, S. (1981). Experience with a computerized medical history system in private practice. *Proceedings of 5th Annual Symposium on Computer Applications in Medical Care* (pp. 121-123). Silver Springs, MD: IEEE.

Colm, H. (1953). Healing as participation: Comments based on Paul Tillich's existential philosophy. *Psychiatry, 16,* 99-111.

Conant, R. (1968). *The politics of community health.* Washington, DC: Public Affairs Press.

Corea, G. (1977). *The hidden malpractice: How American medicine treats women as patients and professionals.* New York: William Morrow.

Costello, D., & Pettegrew, L. (1979). Health communication theory and research: An overview of health organizations. In D. Nimmo (Ed.), *Communication yearbook 3* (pp. 607-623). New Brunswick, NJ: Transaction.

Covell, D., Uman, G., & Manning, P. (1985). Information needs in office practice: Are they being met? *Annals of Internal Medicine, 103,* 596-599.

Covvey, D., & McAlister, N. (1980). *Computers in the practice of medicine.* Menlo Park, CA: Addison-Wesley.

Cowen, E., Gestin, E., Boike, M., Norton, P., Wilson, A., & DeStefano, M. (1979). Hairdressers as caregivers I: A descriptive profile of interpersonal help-giving involvements. *American Journal of Community Psychology, 7,* 633-648.

Cowen, E., McKim, B., & Weissberg, R. (1981). Bartenders as informal interpersonal help agents. *American Journal of Community Psychology, 9,* 715-729.

Crane, D. (1975). The social potential of the patient: An alternative to the sick role. *Journal of Communication, 25,* 131-139.

Currie, B. (1976). Continuing education from medical periodicals. *Journal of Medical Education, 51,* 240-244.

Davis, L. (1973). A system approach to medical information. *Methods of Information in Medicine, 12,* 1-6.

Dahnke, G. (1982). Communication between handicapped and nonhandicapped persons: Toward a deductive theory. In M. Burgoon (Ed.), *Communication yearbook 6* (pp. 92-135). Newbury Park, CA: Sage.

Davis, M., & Eichorn, R. (1963). Compliance with medical regimens: A panel study. *Journal of Health and Human Behavior, 4,* 240-249.

Day, S. (1975). *Communication of scientific information.* New York: Karger.

Department of Health and Human Services. (1980). *Promoting health/preventing disease: Objectives for the nation* (DHEW Publication No. 79-55071 A). Washington, DC: Author.

Droge, D., Arnston, P., & Norton, R. (1981, May). *The social support function in epilepsy self help groups.* Paper presented at the annual meeting of the International Communication Association, Dallas.

Elmore, G. (1981, October). *Integrating video technology and organizational communication.* Paper presented at the annual meeting of the Indiana Speech Association, Indianapolis.

Emry, R., & Wiseman, R. (1985, November). *An intercultural understanding of ablebodied and disabled persons' communication.* Paper presented at the annual meeting of the Speech Communication Association, Denver.

Ewin, D. (1978). Relieving suffering and pain with hypnosis. *Geriatrics, 33,* 87-89.

Feingold, P., & Knapp, M. (1977). Anti-drug abuse commercials. *Journal of Communication, 27,* 20-28.

Fejer, D., Smart, R., & Whitehead, P. (1971). Sources of information about drugs among high school students. *Public Opinion Quarterly, 35,* 235-241.

Feldman, J. (1976). *The dissemination of health information.* Chicago: Aldine.

Filoromo, T., & Ziff, D. (1980). *Nurse recruitment: Strategies for success.* Rockville, MD: Aspen.

Fish, S. (1986, November). *The crisis "hotline" as mediated therapeutic communication.* Paper presented at the annual meeting of the Speech Communication Association, Chicago.

Fisher, B. (1978). *Perspectives on human communication.* New York: Macmillan.

Flay, B., & Cook, T. (1981). Evaluation of mass media prevention campaigns. In R. Rice & W. Paisley (Eds.), *Public communication campaigns* (pp. 239-264). Newbury Park, CA: Sage.

Foley, R., & Sharf, B. (1981). The five interviewing techniques most frequently overlooked by primary care physicians. *Behavioral Medicine, 11*, 26-31.

Frank, J. (1973). *Persuasion and healing* (rev. ed.). Baltimore: Johns Hopkins University Press.

Frank, J. (1975). The faith that heals. *Johns Hopkins Medical Journal, 137*, 127-131.

Frank, L. (1961). Interprofessional communication. *American Journal of Public Health, 51*, 1798-1804.

Freidson, E. (1970). *Professional dominance: The social structure of medical care*. Chicago: Aldine.

French, J., & Raven, B. (1968). The basis of social power. In D. Cartwright & A. Zander (Eds.), *Group dynamics: Research and theory* (3rd. ed., pp. 259-269). New York: Harper & Row.

Friedman, R. (1977). Computers in clinical medicine: A critical review. *Computers and Biomedical Research, 10*, 199-204.

Froland, C., Brodsky, G., Olson, M., & Stewart, L. (1979). Social support and social adjustment. Implications for mental health professionals. *Community Mental Health Journal, 15*, 82-93.

Froland, C. (1981). *Helping networks and human services*. Newbury Park, CA: Sage.

Gazda, G., Walters, R., & Childers, W. (1975). *Human relations development: A manual for health sciences*. Boston: Allyn & Bacon.

Georgopoulos, B. (Ed.). (1974). *Organization research on health institutions*. Ann Arbor, MI: Institute for Social Research.

Georgopoulos, B. (1975). *Hospital organization research: Review and source book*. Philadelphia: W. B. Saunders.

Gergen, K. (1968). Personal consistency and the presentation of self. In C. Gordon & K. Gergen (Eds.), *The self in social interaction* (Vol. 1, pp. 299-308). New York: John Wiley.

Given, B., & Simmons, S. (1977). The interdisciplinary health care team. *Nursing Forum, 16*, 164-184.

Gochman, D. (1969). Measuring health-relevant expectancies. *Psychological Reports, 24*, 880-886.

Gochman, D. (1972a). The development of health beliefs. *Psychological Reports, 31*, 259-266.

Gochman, D. (1972b). The organizing role of motivation in health beliefs and intentions. *Journal of Health and Social Behavior, 13*, 285-293.

Goffman, E. (1963). *Stigma: Notes on the management of spoiled identity*. Englewood Cliffs, NJ: Prentice-Hall.

Goldman, A. (1979). *Unveiling the self: Frontiers in human communication*. Dubuque, IA: Kendall/Hunt.

Goldstein, H. (1965). Guidelines for drug education through electronic media. *Journal of Drug Education, 14*, 157-171.

Gottlieb, B. (1981). *Social networks and social support*. Newbury Park, CA: Sage.

Green, L. (1978). Determining the impact and effectiveness of health education as it relates to federal policy. *Health Education Monographs, 6* (Suppl. 1), 29-66.

Greenfield, S., Kaplan, S., & Ware, J. (1985). Expanding patient involvement in care: Effects on patient outcomes. *Annals of Internal Medicine, 102*, 520-528.

Gronning, N. (1982, November). *Peer counselor training in gerontology*. Paper presented at the annual meeting of the Speech Communication Association, Louisville, KY.

Haessler, H., Holland, T., & Elshtain, E. (1974). Evolution of an automated database history. *Archives of Internal Medicine, 134*, 586-591.

Haley, J. (1977). *Problem solving therapy*. San Francisco: Jossey-Bass.

Hammond, S. (1986, May). *Health advertising: The credibility of organizational sources*. Paper presented at the annual meeting of the International Communication Association, Chicago.

Hanneman, G. (1973). Communicating drug-abuse information among college students. *Public Opinion Quarterly, 37*, 171-191.

Harlem, O. (1977). *Communication in medicine*. Paris: S. Karger.

Hawkins, R., Day, T., Gustafson, D., Chewning, B., & Bosworth, K. (1982, May). *Using computer programs to provide health information to adolescents: BARNY.* Paper presented at the annual meeting of the International Communication Association, Boston.

Haynes, R., McKibbon, K., Fitzgerald, D., Guyatt, G., Walker, C., & Sackett, D. (1986). How to keep up with the medical literature: 1. Why try to keep up and how to get started. *Annals of Internal Medicine, 105,* 149-153.

Haynes, R., McKibbon, K., Walker, C., Mousseau, J., Baker, L., Fitzgerald, D., Guyatt, G., & Norman, G. (1985). Computer searching of the medical literature: An evaluation of MEDLINE searching systems. *Annals of Internal Medicine, 103,* 812-816.

Herrick, J. (1976). Placebos, psychosomatic and psychogenic illnesses and psychotherapy: Their theorized cross-cultural development. *Psychological Record, 26,* 327-342.

Hertz, P., & Stamps, P. (1977). Appointment-keeping behavior re-evaluated. *American Journal of Public Health, 67,* 1033-1036.

Hess, J., Liepman, M., & Ruane, T. (1983). *Family practice and preventive medicine: Health promotion in primary care.* New York: Human Sciences.

Hill, S. K. (1978). Health communication: Focus on interprofessional communication. *Communication Administration Bulletin, 25,* 31-36.

Hinchcliff-Pelias, M. (1983, November). *The use of computer aided instruction for systematic desensitization in the treatment of communication apprehension.* Paper presented at the annual meeting of the Speech Communication Association, Washington, DC.

Hopkins, P., & Wolff, H. (1965). *Principles and psychosomatic disorders.* Oxford: Pergamon.

Hoppe, S., & Heller, P. (1975). Alienation, familism, and the utilization of health services by Mexican-Americans. *Journal of Health and Social Behavior, 16,* 304-314.

Horowitz, A. (1977). Social networks and pathways to psychiatric treatment. *Social Forces, 56,* 86-105.

Horty, J. (1971). Informed consent: New rule puts burden of proof on patient. *Modern Hospital, 116*(2), 54-55.

House, R. (1970). Role conflict and multiple authority in organizations. *California Management Review, 12,* 53-60.

Hughey, J., Norton, R., Edgar, T., & Adamson, B. (1986, November). *An explanatory analysis of the media coverage of AIDS and men at risk.* Paper presented at the annual meeting of the Speech Communication Association, Chicago.

Hulka, B., Cassel, J., & Kupper, L. (1976). Communication compliance, and concordance between physicians and patients with prescribed medications. *American Journal of Public Health, 66,* 847-853.

Hulka, B., Kupper, L., & Cassel, J. (1975). Medication use and misuse: Physician-patient discrepancies. *Journal of Chronic Diseases, 28,* 7-21.

Hunt, G., & Rhodes, L. (1983). Patient education: The importance of a reciprocal relationship. *Maryland State Medical Journal, 32,* 299-302.

Hunt, M. (1982). *The universe within.* New York: Simon & Schuster.

Hussar, D. (1976). Pharmacy practice: The importance of effective communications. *American Journal of Pharmacy, 148,* 136-147.

Ingelfinger, F. (1972). Informed (but uneducated) consent. *New England Journal of Medicine, 287,* 465-466.

Jacobson, B., & Amos, A. (1985). *When smoke gets in your eyes: Cigarette advertising policy and coverage of smoking and health in women's magazines.* London: British Medical Association/Health Education Council.

Johnson, T. (1972). *Professions and power.* London: Macmillan.

Kane, R., & Deuschle, K. (1967). Problems in doctor-patient communication. *Medical Care, 5,* 260-271.

Kaplan, B. (1985). Barriers to medical computing: History, diagnosis, and therapy for the medical computing lag. In G. Cohen (Ed.), *Proceedings of the Ninth Annual Symposium on*

Computer Applications in Medical Care (pp. 400-404). Silver Spring, MD: IEEE/Computer Society Press.

Kasl, S., & Cobb, S. (1966). Health behavior, illness behavior and sick role behavior. *Archives of Environmental Health, 12*, 246-266, 531-541.

Kaufman, L. (1980). Prime-time nutrition. *Journal of Communication, 30*, 37-46.

Kindig, D. (1975). Interdisciplinary education for primary health care team delivery. *Journal of Medical Education, 50*, 97-110.

Kitson, G., Moir, R., & Mason, P. (1982). Family social support in crises: The special case of divorce. *American Journal of Orthopsychiatry, 52*, 161-165.

Kleinman, A. (1980). *Patients and healers in the context of culture.* Berkeley: University of California Press.

Knapp, M. (1978). *Social intercourse.* Boston: Allyn & Bacon.

Korsch, B., & Negrete, V. (1972). Doctor-patient communication. *Scientific American, 227*, 66-74.

Kosa, J., & Zola, I., (Eds.). (1975). *Poverty and health: A sociological analysis.* Cambridge, MA: Harvard University Press.

Kreps, G. (1981, October). *Therapeutic communication in the interview process.* Paper presented at the annual meeting of the Indiana Speech Association, Indianapolis.

Kreps, G. (1984). Communication and gerontology: Health communication training for providers of health services to the elderly. In G. Kreps & B. Thornton, *Health communication* (pp. 210-217). New York: Longman.

Kreps, G. (1985, May). *The development and presentation of an interdisciplinary survey course in health communication.* Paper presented at the annual meeting of the Eastern Communication Association, Providence, RI.

Kreps, G. (1986a). *Organizational communication: Theory and practice.* New York: Longman.

Kreps, G. (1986b). Description and evaluation of a nurse retention organizational development research program. In H. Gueutal & M. Kavanagh (Eds.), *Fifty years of excellence in management research and practice: Proceedings of the Twenty-Third Annual Meeting of the Eastern Academy of Management* (pp. 18-22).

Kreps, G. (1986c). Health communication and the elderly. *World Communication, 15*, 55-70.

Kreps, G. (1986d, February). *A relational analysis of the role of information in health and health care.* Paper presented at the Communicating with Patients Conference, University of South Florida, Tampa.

Kreps, G., Hubbard, S., & DeVita, V. (in press). Overview of the Physician Data Query on-line cancer information system's role in health information dissemination. *Information and Behavior.*

Kreps, G., Maibach, E., Naughton, M., Day, S., & Annett, D. (1986). PDQ usage trends: Implications for evaluation. In A. Levy & B. Williams (Eds.), *Proceedings of the American Association for Medical Systems and Information Congress* (pp. 71-75).

Kreps, G., & Naughton, M. D. (1986). The role of PDQ in disseminating cancer information. In R. Salamon, B. Blum, & M. Jorgensen (Eds.), *MEDINFO 86* (pp. 400-404). Amsterdam: Elsevier.

Kreps, G., & Query, J. (1986, November). *Assessment and testing in the health professions.* Paper presented at the annual meeting of the Speech Communication Association, Chicago.

Kreps, G., Ruben, B., Baker, M., & Rosenthal, S. (1987). A national survey of public knowledge about digestive health and disease: Implications for health education. *Public Health Reports, 102*, 270-277.

Kreps, G., & Thornton, B. (1984). *Health communication.* New York: Longman.

LaFargue, J. (1972). Role of prejudice in rejection of health care. *Nursing Research, 21*, 53-58.

Lane, S. (1981, November). *Interpersonal situation: Empathic communication between medical personnel and patients.* Paper presented at the annual meeting of the Speech Communication Association, Anaheim, CA.

Lane, S. (1982). Communication and patient compliance. In L. Pettegrew (Ed.), *Straight talk: Explorations in provider patient interaction* (pp. 59-69). Louisville, KY: Humana.

Lane, S. (1983). Compliance, satisfaction, and physician-patient communication. In R. Bostrom (Ed.), *Communication yearbook 7* (pp. 772-799). Newbury Park, CA: Sage.

Lennane, K., & Lennane, R. (1973). Alleged psychogenic disorders in women: A possible manifestation of sexual prejudice. *New England Journal of Medicine, 288,* 288-292.

Levine, S., White, P., & Paul, B. (1963). Community interorganizational problems in providing medical care and social services. *American Journal of Public Health, 53,* 1183-1195.

Lewis, O. (1955). Medicine and politics in a Mexican village. In B. Paul (Ed.), *Health, culture, and community* (pp. 403-434). New York: Russell Sage Foundation.

Ley, P., Bradshaw, P., Eaves, D., & Walker, C. (1973). A method of increasing patients' recall of information presented by doctors. *Psychological Medicine, 3,* 217-220.

Litman, T. (1966). The family and physical rehabilitation. *Journal of Chronic Diseases, 19,* 211-217.

Lynch, J. (1977). *The broken heart: The medical consequences of loneliness.* New York: Basic Books.

Mabry, E., & Barnes, R. (1980). *The dynamics of small group communication.* Englewood Cliffs, NJ: Prentice-Hall.

Maccoby, N., & Farquhar, J. (1975). Communication for health: Unselling heart disease. *Journal of Communication, 25,* 114-126.

Maibach, E., & Kreps, G. (1986, October). *Communicating with patients: Primary care physicians' perspectives on cancer prevention, screening, and education.* Paper presented at the International Conference on Doctor-Patient Communication, University of Western Ontario, London, Ontario, Canada.

Makris, P. (1983). Informatics in health-care delivery systems. *Information Age, 5,* 205-210.

Martiney, R. (1978). *Hispanic culture and health care: Fact, fiction and folklore.* St. Louis: C. V. Mosby.

McIntosh, J. (1974). Process of communication, information seeking control associated with cancer: A selected review of the literature. *Social Science and Medicine, 8,* 167-187.

Mechanic, D. (1972a). Social psychological factors affecting the presentation of bodily complaints. *New England Journal of Medicine, 286,* 1132-1139.

Mechanic, D. (1972b). *Public expectations and health care: Essays on the changing organization of health services.* New York: John Wiley.

Mendelsohn, R. (1979). *Confessions of a medical heretic.* Chicago: Contemporary Books.

Mendelsohn, R. (1981). *Male practice: How doctors manipulate women.* Chicago: Contemporary Books.

Mendelson, M. (1974). *Tender loving greed.* New York: Knopps.

Meyer, B. (1969). Truth and the physician. *Bulletin of the New York Academy of Medicine, 45,* 59-71.

Meyerhoff, B. (1978). *Number our days.* New York: Simon & Schuster.

Miller, R., Pople, M., & Myers, J. (1982). INTERNIST-1, an experimental computer-based diagnostic consultant for general internal medicine. *New England Journal of Medicine, 307,* 468-475.

Mines, S. (1974). *The conquest of pain.* New York: Grosset & Dunlap.

Mobley, W. (1977). Intermediate linkages in the relationship between job satisfaction and employee turnover. *Journal of Applied Psychology, 62,* 237-240.

Mobley, W. (1982). Some unanswered questions in turnover and withdrawal research. *Academy of Management Review, 7,* 111-116.

Morrell, J., Podlone, M., & Cohen, S. (1977). Receptivity of physicians in a teaching hospital to a computerized drug interaction monitoring and reporting system. *Medical Care, 15,* 66-78.

Morrow, G., Hoagland, A., & Carnrike, C. (1981). Social support and parental adjustment to pediatric cancer. *Journal of Consulting and Clinical Psychology, 49,* 763-765.

Morse, B., & Piland, R. (1981). An assessment of communication competencies needed by intermediate-level health care providers: A study of nurse-patient, nurse-doctor, nurse-nurse communication relationships. *Journal of Applied Communication Research, 9,* 30-41.

Myerhoff, B., & Larson, W. (1965). The doctor as cultural hero: The routinization of charisma. *Human Organization, 24,* 188-191.

Nagi, S. (1975). Teamwork in health care in the United States: A sociological perspective. *Milbank Quarterly.*

Nason, A. (1968). *Essentials of modern biology.* New York: John Wiley.

National Cancer Institute. (1986). *Scientific information services of the National Cancer Institute* (NIH Publication No. 86-2683). Bethesda, MD: Author.

National Institutes of Health. (1986). *Lowering blood and cholesterol level to prevent heart disease* (Vol. 5, No. 7). Bethesda, MD: Author.

Nelson, B. (1973). Study indicates which patients nurses don't like: The unpleasant, the long term, the mentally ill, the hypochondriacs, and the dying. *Modern Hospital, 119,* 70-72.

Nelson, R. (1986, July/August). What is the payoff in computerized appointment scheduling. *Medical Group Management,* pp. 18-21.

Newell, G., & Webber, C. (1983). The primary care physician in cancer prevention. *Family and Community Health, 5,* 77-84.

Northouse, P. (1986, February). *Communication and cancer: Issues confronting patients, health professionals and family members.* Paper presented at the Communicating with Patients Conference, University of South Florida.

Nussbaum, J. (1983). Relational closeness of elderly interaction: Implications for life satisfaction. *Western Journal of Speech Communication, 47,* 229-243.

Office of Cancer Communications. (1985). *Taking time: Support for people with cancer and the people who care about them* (NIH Publication No. 85-2059). Bethesda, MD: Author.

O'Keefe, M. (1971). The anti-smoking commercials: A study of television's impact on behavior. *Public Opinion Quarterly, 35,* 242-248.

Park, B., & Bashshur, R. (1965). Some implications of telemedicine. *Journal of Communication, 25,* 161-166.

Parsons, T. (1951). *The social system.* New York: Free Press.

Parsons, T. (1958). Definitions of health and illness in light of American values and social structure. In E. Jaco (Ed.), *Patients, physicians, and illness.* New York: Free Press.

Pattison, E., & Pattison, M. (1981). Analysis of a schizophrenic psychosocial network. *Schizophrenia Bulletin, 7,* 135-143.

Paul, B. (1955). *Health, culture, and community.* New York: Russell Sage Foundation.

Perrow, C. (1965). Hospitals, technology, structure and goals. In J. March (Ed.), *Handbook of organizations.* Chicago: Rand McNally.

Peters-Golden, H. (1982). Breast-cancer: Varied perceptions of social support in the illness experience. *Social Science and Medicine, 16,* 483-491.

Pettegrew, L., Thomas, R., Costello, D., Wolf, G., Lennox, L., & Thomas, S. (1980). Job-related stress in a health care organization: Management/communication issues. In D. Nimmo (Ed.), *Communication yearbook 4,* (pp. 626-652). New Brunswick, NJ: Transaction.

Pettigrew, A. (1972). Information as a power resource. *Sociology, 6,* 187-204.

Pfeffer, J. (1973). Size, composition and function of hospital boards of directors: A study of organization-environment linkage. *Administrative Science Quarterly, 18,* 449-461.

Pfeffer, J., & Salancik, G. (1977). Organizational context and the characteristics and tenure of hospital administrators. *Academy of Management Journal, 20,* 74-88.

Pierce, J., Watson, D., Knights, S., Glidden, T., Williams, S., & Watson, R. (1984). A controlled trial of health education in the physician's office. *Preventive Medicine, 13,* 185-194.

Portis, B., & Hunter, A. (1975). In-service training by mass media. *Journal of Communication, 25,* 167-170.

Poser, E. (1966). The effect of therapists' training on group therapeutic outcome. *Journal of Consulting Psychology, 30,* 283-289.

Pratt, L., Seligmann, A., & Reader, G. (1957). Physicians' view on the level of medical information among patients. *American Journal of Public Health, 47,* 1277-1283.

President's Commission for the Study of Ethical Problems in Medicine and Biomedical and Behavioral Research. (1982a). *Making health care decisions: The ethical and legal implications of informed consent in the patient-practitioner relationship* (Vol. 1). Washington, DC: Government Printing Office.

President's Commission for the Study of Ethical Problems in Medicine and Biomedical and Behavioral Research. (1982b). *Making health care decisions: The ethical and legal implications of informed consent in the patient-practitioner relationship* (Vol. 2). Washington, DC: Government Printing Office.

President's Commission for the Study of Ethical Problems in Medicine and Biomedical and Behavioral Research. (1982c). *Making health care decisions: The ethical and legal implications of informed consent in the patient-practitioner relationship* (Vol. 3). Washington, DC: Government Printing Office.

President's Commission for the Study of Ethical Problems in Medicine and Biomedical and Behavioral Research. (1982d). *Splicing life: The social and ethical issues of genetic engineering with human beings.* Washington, DC: Government Printing Office.

Puska, P., Koskela, K., McAlister, A., Pallonen, V., Vartlanian, E., & Homan, K. (1979). A comprehensive television smoking cessation programme in Finland. *International Journal of Health Education, 22*, 1-29.

Query, J. (1985, October). *Small group processes and support groups: An impetus.* Paper presented at the annual meeting of the Speech Communication Association of Ohio, Columbus.

Quesada, G., & Heller, R. (1977). Sociocultural barriers to medical care among Mexican-Americans in Texas. *Medical Care, 15*, 93-101.

Quint, J. (1965). Institution practices of information control. *Psychiatry, 28*, 119-128.

Ray, E. B. (1983). Job burnout from a communication perspective. In R. Bostrom (Ed.), *Communication yearbook 7* (pp. 738-755). Newbury Park, CA: Sage.

Relman, A. (1982). Encouraging the practice of preventive medicine in health promotion. *Public Health Reports, 97*, 216-219.

Rose, S. (1977). *Group therapy: A behavioral approach.* Englewood Cliffs, NJ: Prentice-Hall.

Rossiter, C., & Pearce, W. (1975). *Communicating personally: A theory of interpersonal communication and human relationships.* Indianapolis: Bobbs-Merrill.

Roter, D. (1983). Physician/patient communication: Transmission of information and patient effects. *Maryland State Medical Journal, 32*, 260-265.

Roter, D., & Hall, J. (1986, October). *Meta analysis of correlates of provider behavior: A contribution to a theory of effective provider behavior.* Paper presented at the International Conference on Doctor-Patient Communication, University of Western Ontario, London, Ontario.

Roth, J. (1957). Ritual and magic in the control of contagion. *American Sociological Review, 23*, 311-312.

Ruben, B. (1986). Public perceptions of digestive health and disease. *Practical Gastroenterology, 10*(2), 35-42.

Ruben, B., & Bowman, J. (1986). Patient satisfaction (part 1): Critical issues in the theory and design of patient relations training. *Journal of Healthcare Education and Training, 1*, 1-5.

Schaefer, J. (1974). The interrelatedness of decision making and the nursing process. *American Journal of Nursing, 74*, 1852-1855.

Scheff, T. (1963). Decision rules, types of error and their consequences in medical diagnosis. *Behavioral Science, 8*, 97-107.

Schramm, W. (1954). How communication works. In W. Schramm (Ed.), *The process and effects of mass communication*, Urbana, IL: University of Illinois Press.

Schwartz, W. (1975). Decision analysis: A look at the chief complaints. *New England Journal of Medicine, 300*, 556-559.

Seagull, A. (1976). Sociocultural variation in sick role behavioral expectations. *Social Science and Medicine, 10*, 47-51.

Seibold, D., & Roper, R. (1979). Psychosocial determinants of health care intentions: Test of the Triandis and Fishbein models. In D. Nimmo (Ed.), *Communication yearbook 3* (pp. 626-643). New Brunswick, NJ: Transaction.

Seligman, A., McGrath, N., & Pratt, L. (1957). Level of medical information among clinic patients. *Journal of Chronic Disorders, 6*, 497-509.

Sethee, U. (1967). Verbal responses of nurses to patients in emotion-laden situations in public health nursing. *Nursing Research, 16*, 365-368.

Shapiro, A. (1964). Factors contributing to the placebo effect: Their implications for psychotherapy. *American Journal of Psychotherapy, 18*, 73-88.

Siegal, E. (1982). Transfer of information to health practitioners. In B. Dervin & M. Voight (Eds.), *Progress in communication sciences* (Vol. 3, pp. 311-334). Norwood, NJ: Ablex.

Simonton, O., & Matthews-Simonton, S. (1975). Belief systems and management of the emotional aspects of malignancy. *Journal of Transpersonal Psychology, 7*, 29-47.

Slack, W., Hicks, W., Reed, C., & VanCura, L. (1966). A computer-based medical history. *New England Journal of Medicine, 274*, 194-198.

Slack, W., Porter, D., Witschi, J., Sullivan, M., Buxbaum, R., & Stare, F. (1974). Dietary interviewing by computer. *Journal of the American Diabetics Association, 69*, 514-517.

Smith, D. (1971). From id to information: A biological view of communication. *Today's Speech, 19*, 11-15.

Smith, R. (1976). *Doctors and patients.* Boise, ID: Syms-York.

Solomon, D. (1984). Social marketing and community health promotion: The Stanford heart disease prevention project. In L. Fredericksen, L. Salomon, & K. Brehony (Eds.), *Marketing health behavior: Principles, techniques, and applications* (pp. 115-135). New York: Plenum.

Speedling, E., & Rose, D. (1985). Building an effective doctor-patient relationship: From patient satisfaction to patient participation. *Social Science and Medicine, 21*, 115-120.

Spitzberg, B. (1981, November). *Competence in communicating: A taxonomy, review, critique, and predictive model.* Paper presented at the annual meeting of the Speech Communication Association, Anaheim, CA.

Spitzberg, B. (1983). Communication competence as knowledge, skill, and impression. *Communication Education, 32*, 323-329.

Spitzberg, B., & Cupach, W. (1984). *Interpersonal communication competence.* Newbury Park, CA: Sage.

Starr, P. (1982). *The social transformation of American medicine.* New York: Basic Books.

Sterling, T., Pollack, S., & Spencer, W. (1973). The use of an information system to "humanize" procedures in a rehabilitation hospital. *International Journal of Bio-Medical Computing, 5*, 51-57.

Stoeckle, J., Lazare, A., Weingarten, C., & McGuire, M. (1971). Learning medicine by videotaped recordings. *Journal of Medical Education, 46*, 518-524.

Stone, G. (1979). Patient compliance and the role of the expert. *Journal of Social Issues, 35*, 34-59.

Street, R., & Wiemann, J. (1987). Patients' satisfaction with physicians' interpersonal involvement, expressiveness, and dominance. In M. McLaughlin (Ed.), *Communication yearbook 10.* Newbury Park, CA: Sage.

Sullivan, C., & Reardon, K. (1986). Social support satisfaction and health locus of control: Discriminators of breast cancer patients' styles of coping. In M. McLaughlin (Ed.), *Communication yearbook 9* (pp. 707-722). Newbury Park, CA: Sage.

Tagliacozzo, D., & Mauksch, H. (1972). The patient's view of the patient's role. In E. Gartley Jaco (Ed.), *Patients, physicians and illness* (2nd ed.). New York: Free Press.

Talland, G., & Clark, D. (1954). Evaluation of topics in therapy group discussion. *Journal of Clinical Psychology, 10*, 131-137.

Thompson, T. (1981). The development of communication skills in physically handicapped children. *Human Communication Research, 7*, 312-324.

Thompson, T. (1984). The invisible helping hand: The role of communication in health and social service professions. *Communication Quarterly, 32*, 148-163.

Thompson, T., & Seibold, D. (1978). Stigma management in "normal" stigmatized interactions: Test of the disclosure hypothesis and a model of stigma acceptance. *Human Communication Research, 4*, 231-242.

Thornton, B. (1978). Health care teams and multimethodological research. In B. Ruben (Ed.), *Communication yearbook 2* (pp. 538-553). New Brunswick, NJ: Transaction.

Trauth, D., & Huffman, J. (1986, May). *Regulation of alcoholic beverage advertising: Its present status and future directions.* Paper presented at the annual meeting of the International Communication Association, Chicago.

Turk, H. (1973). Comparative urban structure from an interorganizational perspective. *Administrative Science Quarterly, 18,* 37-55.

Twaddle, A. (1972). The concepts of the sick role and illness behavior. *Advances in Psychosomatic Medicine, 18,* 162-179.

Udry, J. (1972). Can mass media advertising increase contraceptive use? *Family Planning Perspectives, 4,* 37-44.

U.S. Senate Special Committee on Aging, Subcommittee on Long Term Care. (1974). *Nursing home care in the United States, failure in public policy: Introductory report.* Washington, DC: Government Printing Office.

U.S. Senate Special Committee on Aging, Subcommittee on Long Term Care. (1975). *Nursing home care in the United States, failure in public policy: Introductory report and nine supporting papers.* Washington, DC: Government Printing Office.

Wagner, H. (1967). Videotape in the teaching of medical history taking. *Journal of Medical Education, 42,* 1055-1058.

Wagner, M. (1966). Reinforcement of the verbal productivity in group therapy. *Psychological Reports, 19,* 1217-1218.

Waitzkin, H., & Stoekle, J. (1972). The communication of information about illness. *Advances in Psychosomatic Medicine, 8,* 180-215.

Wallace, R., & Benson, H. (1972). The physiology of meditation. *Scientific American, 226,* 84-90.

Wandelt, M., Pierce, P., & Widdowson, R. (1981). Why nurses leave nursing and what can be done about it. *American Journal of Nursing, 81,* 72-77.

Warren, R. (1967). The interorganizational field as a focus of investigation. *Administrative Science Quarterly, 12,* 396-419.

Watzlawick, P., Beavin, J., & Jackson, D. (1967). *Pragmatics of human communication.* New York: W. W. Norton.

Weick, K. (1969). *The social psychology of organizing.* Reading, MA: Addison-Wesley.

Weiner, M., Brok, A., & Snadowsky, A. (1978). *Working with the aged.* Englewood Cliffs, NJ: Prentice-Hall.

White, E. (1974). Health and the black person: An annotated bibliography. *American Journal of Nursing, 74,* 1839-1841.

Whitehorn, J. (1958). Psychiatric implications of the placebo effect. *American Journal of Psychiatry, 114,* 662-664.

Wiemann, J. (1977). Explication and test of a model of communicative competence. *Human Communication Research, 3,* 195-213.

Wiesenfeld, A., & Weiss, H. (1979). Hairdressers and helping: Influencing the behavior of informal caregivers. *Professional Psychology, 10,* 786-792.

Wilmot, W. (1980). *Dyadic communication* (2nd ed.). Reading, MA: Addison-Wesley.

Wise, H. (1972). The primary care health team. *Archives of Internal Medicine, 130,* 438-444.

Wise, H. (1974). *Making health teams work.* Cambridge, MA: Ballinger.

Wolf, G. (1981, April). Nursing turnover: Some causes and solutions. *Nursing Outlook,* pp. 233-236.

Wolf, S. (1950). Effects of suggestion and conditioning on the action of chemical agents in human subjects: The pharmacology of placebos. *Journal of Clinical Investigation, 29,* 100-109.

Woods, D. (1975). Talking to people is a doctor game that doctors don't play. *Canadian Medical Association Journal, 113,* 1105-1106.

Woodlock, B. (1983). Levels of exchange and organizational communication. In R. Bostrom (Ed.), *Communication yearbook 7* (pp. 756-771). Newbury Park, CA: Sage.

Wortman, C., & Dunkel-Schetter, C. (1979). Interpersonal relationships and cancer. *Journal of Social Issues, 35,* 132-155.

Wright, W. (1975). Mass media as sources of medical information. *Journal of Communication,* *25,* 171-173.

Yanda, R. (1977). *Doctors as managers of health care teams.* New York: AMACOM.

Zimmerman, J. (1978). Physician utilization of medical records: Preliminary determinations. *Medical Informatics, 3*(1), 27-35.

Zola, I. (1963). Problems of communication, diagnosis, and patient care: The interplay of patient, physician and clinic organization. *Journal of Medical Education, 38,* 829-838.

7 The Role of Persuasion in Health Promotion and Disease Prevention: Review and Commentary

KATHLEEN KELLEY REARDON
University of Southern California

Centering on persuasion theory and research as it informs efforts in disease prevention and cure, Reardon examines strategies for motivating change in health-related behaviors, heightening probabilities of recovery from illness through social support and treatment compliance, and coping with serious and terminal illnesses. She then turns to an examination of Kreps's policy arguments closing with an agenda for health-care persuasion research.

C OMMUNICATION rcsearchers have only recently recognized the important role they might play in discovering how people are motivated to adopt healthful lifestyles. Communication, particularly via mass media, has been considered a weak vehicle for influencing people to adopt healthful behaviors (Solomon & Maccoby, 1984). Recent work indicates that communication is a key factor in both disease prevention and cure. Research on diffusion of health information, doctor-patient relationships, compliance with therapy, smoking cessation, alcohol, drug abuse, diet, stress, and cancer include communication as a major component in efforts to reduce disease onset rates and to increase recovery rates. It has become clear that illness is not only a personal experience, but a social experience as well. What doctors, nurses, family members, friends, acquaintances and media sources say, write, and do concerning a particular illness can influence patients' perceptions of cure, compliance with treatment, and efforts to survive.

Building on Kreps's comprehensive overview of the role of information in health care, this chapter will examine the role of persuasion in both disease prevention and cure. In the second section, I will respond to Kreps's review

Correspondence and requests for reprints: Kathleen Kelley Reardon, Business School, Bridge Hall 401G, University of Southern California, Los Angeles, CA 90089-1421.

Communication Yearbook 11, pp. 277-297

and the suggestions he made for future research and conclude with a brief research agenda.

DISEASE PREVENTION

Among the many lessons learned throughout the history of medicine is that prevention of disease usually is more effective and cost-effective than modes of treatment and cure. This lesson was emphasized in the 1984 surgeon general's report. It called for greater responsibility by individuals, communities, and societies in preventing diseases. This report indicated that behavior and lifestyle are implicated in onset of and mortality from life-threatening diseases. As a host of illnesses continue to defy medical science, improvements in health will require changes in health-related behaviors such as diet, exercise, and stress. And as the burden of health maintenance shifts from health practitioners to individuals and societies, research is needed to understand how people might be persuaded to take greater responsibility for prevention of illness and for their own cure once illness has occurred (Green, 1984).

Much existing disease prevention and health promotion research indicates that people do not easily change health-related behaviors. Those of us who have studied persuasion are not likely to find this resistance surprising. For decades, social scientists have been trying to determine what motivates people to change their behaviors. Adopting conditioning model explanations, we might propose that reinforcement for health-enhancing behavior and punishment or withholding positive reinforcers are promising approaches. Following Bandura's (1977) modeling approach, observations of the health-enhancing behaviors of others might offer some promise. Consistency theories, on the other hand, would suggest that people engaging in health-threatening behavior should be confronted with the contradiction between their desire to live a long and happy life and their current behavior. Finally, from theories that focus on the reasoning capacities of human beings (Ball-Rokeach, Rokeach, & Grube, 1984; Reardon, 1981, 1986) we might conclude that health-enhancing behaviors are elicited by guiding the persuadees through reasoned consideration of their current problematic behavior.

While there is much to be gained from persuasion theory and research, changing health-related behaviors does not appear to be a one-approach proposition. What works with one age group or type of illness does not necessarily work with another. We need only take a look at disease prevention research to see that there are no simple answers to the question, What are the best strategies for motivating people to adopt healthful lifestyles? Research on smoking, alcoholism, adolescent drug abuse, and AIDS indicates that we have much to learn about effective means of persuading people to adopt healthful behaviors.

Smoking

Cigarette smoking is the single most important environmental factor contributing to early death in the United States. Between 1964 and 1983 over 30 million smokers have quit smoking, but this cessation has primarily been accomplished among "lighter" smokers, leaving a heavier smoking group behind (Shopeland & Brown, 1985). Persuading heavy smokers to quit constitutes a significant societal health-promotion challenge. A number of antismoking education programs have been developed and implemented over the years by schools and voluntary health agencies. Most of these programs have been based on the premise that teaching children why cigarette smoking is bad for them will encourage them to resist smoking. It appears that such programs have succeeded in changing children's knowledge, but few have consistently reduced the onset of smoking behavior (Green, 1979; Thompson, 1978). During the 1980s, researchers have attempted to discover the psycho-social processes involved in becoming a cigarette smoker. In a review of these programs, Flay (1986) reports that the most rigorous studies to date indicate that the social influences approach to smoking prevention (i.e., teaching children about the social norms regarding smoking, about the social influences to smoke, and providing them with resistance skills) can be effective some of the time. More research is needed to determine when and for whom it is effective.

For adult smokers other techniques are common. Aversion strategies are based on the learning model principal that smokers have learned to associate certain situations with smoking. By pairing the urge to smoke with electric shock, rapid smoking, excessive smoking, or aversive images, smokers are expected to experience an aversion to smoking.

Self-control strategies encourage smokers to rearrange the circumstances in which smoking usually occurs or to arrange "no smoking contracts" with other persons. They also include behavioral programming in which the smokers administer their own rewards and punishments, or cognitive control in which smokers use self-instruction to control smoking behavior (Benfari, Ockene, & McIntyre, 1982).

Other strategies such as the combining of aversion and self-control or the use of nicotine substitutes have also been used. The research to date indicates that almost any intervention can be effective in eliminating smoking behavior. The major problem appears to be the rapid decrease of treatment effects. We simply do not know enough about creating interventions that overcome the power of addictions.

Research by Schwartz and Inbar-Saban (1987) suggests that changing values may be one way to accomplish long-term effects. Using Rokeach's self-confrontation approach with obese adults, Schwartz and Inbar-Saban were able to obtain adherence to diets for 14 months. They achieved this result by confronting participants with value differences between people who diet effectively and those who do not. Specifically, they found that effective dieters score high on wisdom and low on happiness as guiding principles in their lives when compared to those who fail at diets. Respondents were confronted with this information and given the opportunity to compare their own positions on these values with those of successful and unsuccessful dieters. These respondents surpassed a discussion group and control group in the average amount of weight lost. This weight loss persisted until the end of the study at 14 months. Two months into the study, the value self-confrontation procedure was administered to both the discussion and control groups as a second test of the effects of this treatment. The effects of value self-confrontation were significant for the control group but not for the discussion group. The researchers concluded that the value self-confrontation procedure was a "robust method which can be adapted to different settings and behaviors." The fact that weight loss due to value self-confrontation persisted over a year suggests that adapting strategies to suit the values of subjects may prove more promising than methods that ignore variations in subjects' value orientations.

Alcoholism

Alcohol abuse is another serious health threat affecting American youths, adults, and their families. Not only has alcohol abuse been linked with cirrhosis of the liver, heart dysfunction and a variety of physical problems, but excessive consumption of alcohol increases the likelihood of injury or death from automobile accidents, homicide, and suicide (Berg, 1976). Recent research in prevention of alcoholism indicates that educational programs are moderately successful in increasing knowledge about alcohol but less successful in producing attitude change and behavioral change (Engstrom, 1984).

While there is consensus concerning the need to combat alcoholism, there appears to be little consensus concerning the most effective means. Some researchers see alcoholism as the result of a host of normative beliefs about its use. They propose that the social and cultural factors influencing alcohol use must be identified and changed to reduce excessive alcohol consumption (see Blane, 1976). Other researchers operate on the premise that such factors as availability of alcohol, laws controlling its use, and the extent to which environments and people (e.g., bartenders and friends) encourage excessive consumption should be the target of persuasion efforts (see Moore & Gerstein, 1981). A third group of researchers propose that alcoholism is a treatable disease and that efforts should be devoted to identifying high-risk groups and focusing prevention efforts on them (see Mello, 1976).

Each of these models has advantages and disadvantages (see Tuchfeld and Marcus, 1984). It is also quite possible to adopt more than one as they do not stand in opposition to each other but rather propose somewhat different targets of attention. More research is needed to compare the effects of strategies for prevention of alcoholism. For example, does legal regulation of alcohol consumption decrease alcoholism? Are there strategies that involve the potential or current alcoholic and his or her family that might lead to greater reduction and cessation of alcohol consumption? Are there age, socioeconomic, gender, regional, and other factors implicated in the selection of effective strategies for reducing alcohol consumption? What effects to advertising and mass media programming have on perception of alcohol use and actual consumption? These are some of the questions that might be answered by communication research.

Drug Abuse

Adolescent drug abuse is another important area for prevention research. During the last decade, there has been an increase in research on training adolescents to resist pressure to use drugs. Interpersonal skills for resisting drug use are being adopted in schools across the United States. Researchers are finding a relationship between social competence and prevention of drug use. It appears that social competence acts to lessen the impact of social pressure to use drugs (Botvin, Eng, & Williams, 1980; Hurd, Johnson, Luepker, Pechacek, & Jacobs, 1980; Pentz, 1985; Perry, Killen, Telch, Slinkard, & Danaher, 1980; Schinke & Gilchrist, 1983). Other researchers are attempting to discover the type of noncompliance strategies adolescents can be expected to use in actual interactions with peers (Reardon, Sussman, & Flay, 1987). We are learning that it is not enough to want adolescents to "Just say no" to drugs. It is important to know what they feel comfortable saying to friends and acquaintances in dyads and in groups. For example, Reardon et al. (1987) found that high-risk adolescents (those who expect to smoke sometime in their lifetime and those who have smoked a cigarette) are less likely to use highly rejecting strategies when refusing the offer of a cigarette. They also found that when adolescents are in a group, they are less likely to use highly rejecting strategies than when they are with one person.

Recent research on the influence of stress on cigarette and alcohol use indicates that personal relationships can play a role in reducing onset rates. Wills (1986) found that young adolescents who received emotional support from their parents were less likely to use cigarettes and alcohol. He also found, however, that peer support was positively related to cigarette and alcohol use. It appears that social support is not necessarily an inhibitor of drug abuse. The nature and source of support may be crucial factors.

Persuading adolescents to resist drugs is a complex activity. The child's level of stress, parental support, peer support, and the context of invitations to use drugs are only a few of the many factors that play a role in the onset and maintenance of drug use and abuse. Persuasion research in this area cannot afford to ignore these factors. We cannot expect effectively to reduce drug use among adolescents merely by teaching them noncompliance strategies that they may find difficult or impossible to employ. Research in this area must become increasingly sensitive to the psychological and social factors that impinge on adolescents' decisions about drugs.

AIDS

A fourth major health concern for the United States and the world in general is the spread of AIDS through intravenous drug use and unsafe sexual practices. Prevention is the primary means of reducing the threat since there is no cure for AIDS. By 1991, it is estimated that over 270,000 people will have contracted AIDS and 179,000 will have died. The only way to reduce these numbers is through educating people about high-risk behaviors and persuading them to engage in safe practices.

One of the major obstacles in the path of persuading heterosexuals and homosexuals to take precautions against AIDS is that the onset of AIDS may be delayed for three to seven years or more following exposure to the HTLV-III virus (Department of Health and Human Services, 1985). Since the immediate consequences of sexual activity are reinforcing and the potential negative consequences of high risk activities are uncertain, knowledge of AIDS and even fear of it may fail to motivate people to change their behaviors (Kelly & St. Lawrence, 1986).

Research suggests that the mass media have contributed to decreases in high-risk behavior among homosexual men. In San Francisco, the proportion of homosexual and bisexual males who reported that they were monogamous, celibate, or practiced "unsafe" sex only with their steady partner increased from 69% in 1984 to 81% in 1985 (Puckett & Bart, 1985). According to two Gallup polls conducted for the New York City Department of Health, 95% of the U.S. population has heard of AIDS; 80% realize that most AIDS patients are homosexuals and 84% know that intravenous drug users who share needles are at high risk for AIDS (Clarke & Sencer, 1985).

Despite the high level of awareness about the existence of AIDS, many people at risk engage in denial. Recent research suggests that the fight against AIDS may require joint interpersonal and mass communication campaigns in which opinion leaders and other trusted sources assist those at risk to realize that AIDS can happen to them (Reardon & Richardson, 1986). Interpersonal communication may be especially useful in discouraging those at risk for AIDS from finding ways to reduce the dissonance elicited when they engage in high-risk behaviors and in encouraging them to believe that AIDS can happen to them.

Communication and persuasion are the two primary means of deterring the spread of AIDS. Locating effective strategies for persuading people to engage in safe sexual practices and to avoid the sharing of intravenous needles is a communication issue that remains unresolved. AIDS is a disease surrounded by emotional turmoil and horror. Its association with sexuality makes it difficult to get people to listen to recommendations, let alone adopt them.

Research is needed to identify both interpersonal and mass media strategies for motivating people at risk for AIDS to use greater caution.

Diet

A fifth major health problem that may be alleviated by effective communication and persuasion efforts is diet. There is still considerable controversy regarding the role specific types of food play in promoting and threatening health. It is clear, however, that diet is implicated in a number of chronic diseases. The great majority of Americans, for example, suffer from overconsumption of food. Obesity affects about 20% of the population. Although diseases like cancer, heart disease, and hypertension have multiple causes, each of them is practically nonexistent in some populations with dietary habits that differ from our own (Hegsted, 1984). The high-fat diet of Americans has been implicated in heart disease, some cancers, and hypertension. Intake of dietary fiber appears to influence occurrence of cancer of the lower bowel as well as constipation and diverticulosis. Although, at this time, it is difficult to establish exact, quantitative desirable levels of certain types of foods, the evidence clearly indicates that diets high in saturated fat and cholesterol and low in fruits, vegetables, and whole grains are likely to promote one or more serious illnesses (Harper, 1984).

Persuading people to alter their diets is no easy matter. There appear to be biological, cultural, and perhaps genetic predispositions to food types and amounts. Moreover, consumers are confused by conflicting statements about nutrition. Further, those who do feel confident about the types of food conducive to health may be unable to purchase those foods since many foods are overprocessed or contain hidden amounts of salt, sugar, and preservatives. Encouraging people to eat well when they are surrounded by so many opportunities to do otherwise is another health communication challenge.

HEALTH PROMOTION AFTER
THE ONSET OF SERIOUS ILLNESS

There is little doubt that persuasion theory and research can be useful in the development of educational models of disease prevention. Research also indicates that persuasion styles and strategies play a vital role in increasing the chances of recovery for those people who have contracted serious illnesses. The second section of this chapter will focus on what has been learned about the role of persuasion in the treatment of serious illnesses such as cancer and AIDS. We will examine the role that persuasion plays in three aspects of the coping process: (2) attributing causality, (2) social support, and (3) compliance.

Attributing Causality

Attribution theory maintains that when one encounters a sudden threat or change in one's environment, the individual will initiate a causal search for the reasons behind that threat or change (Harvey & Weary, 1981; Pyszczynski & Greenberg, 1981; Wong & Weiner, 1981). The purposes of such searches are to understand, predict, and control threat (Kelley, 1967). Research suggests that cancer patients and other seriously ill people form theories about the origins of their illness (Taylor & Levin, 1976). Some research suggests that the need to answer the question, "Why me?" is so great that seriously ill patients create illusions, or ways of looking at the facts, that allow them to derive satisfactory answers (Taylor, 1983). By creating acceptable and alterable causes (e.g., poor diet, high stress, deficient amounts of exercise), patients gain a sense of mastery over the otherwise unknown.

The preponderance of work in this area has been conducted by psychologists. Their approach is to understand the cognitive and emotional processes that lead to causal attributions about the onset of illness. The fact is, however, that attributions of this sort do not occur in a vacuum. The attributional process is typically relational. Stigmatizing conditions such as breast cancer and AIDS present social problems for both the victim and those with whom they interact. In their book, *Stigma*, Jones et al. (1984) conclude that what they call "marked" people may arouse in others a prescient sense of danger. The source of this threat may not be physical but symbolic. "The carriers of stigmatizing marks symbolize something perceived as threatening to our individual and collective sense of well-being" (p. 82). Just as cancer patients or AIDS patients may create rationales to understand why this dread disease afflicted them, their friends, relatives, and acquaintances may also create rationales to assure them that the same will not happen to them. Ernest Becker (1973) describes humans as animals with no defense against full perception of the external world, animals "completely open to experience" (p. 50). Unlike our perception of most animals, we live in the past and the future. Our certain knowledge of impending death is nothing short of "appalling" (p. 51). To avoid dealing directly with death, we may avoid dealing with people who are seriously ill.

It seems only natural, then, that we should protect ourselves from those who force us to consider our own vulnerability. This resistance does not mean that no individuals exist who can rise above fear to be of assistance to seriously ill people. Hospices and volunteer programs reject that hypothesis. Yet even these people have the need to order their world. They must find reasons for their invulnerability to the affliction of others. In doing so, they may directly or indirectly influence the attributional process of the patient. Even coping "too well" may be disparaged by others. Jones et al. (1984) argue that some people show irrational irritation for those marked individuals who appear insufficiently daunted by their conditions and who seem to violate the expected order by coping with or even overcoming them.

The self is a social product. As such, any experience of illness that disrupts the self cannot be other than social as well. Most people have a poor idea of what adequate coping with cancer is and hence turn to others to learn what it means to cope well. We now know that cancer patients tend to compare downward. That is, in contrast with Festinger's Social Comparison Theory (1954), many cancer patients do not compare themselves with those better off than they, nor do they aspire to be like those people. Instead, they see themselves as better off than other cancer patients. For example, a married breast cancer patient might focus on her advantage over less fortunate single patients. If she has had a lumpectomy (removal of only the tumor and surrounding tissue), she might compare herself with someone who has had a mastectomy. Apparently, it is always possible to be better off than someone else (see Taylor, 1983; Taylor, Dakoff, & Reardon, 1987).

A fascinating aspect of human beings is their tendency to seek understanding and mastery of misfortune. For people with serious illnesses such as cancer and AIDS, this process can influence recovery and/or quality of life during the years or months of survival. With the exception of some social support research, communication scholars have not yet found their way into this interesting area of study. If we think of illness as a social as well as personal experience, the role of communication becomes obvious. We need more research into the types of communication that facilitate a sense of well-being. For example, Burleson's (1984) studies of comforting strategies might be productively applied in health settings. What types of comforting strategies facilitate the development of health-promoting attitudes and behaviors? More research is needed that focuses on the effects of mass media messages on patients' perceptions of the likelihood of their recovery and self-worth. In our tendency to see illness as a personal experience, we may be overlooking an important avenue of communication research. What types of strategies used by cancer patients and AIDS patients encourage others to feel less threatened and more supportive? How do seriously ill people use and interpret mass media messages about their disease? What type of social environment is needed to maintain rationales that facilitate recovery and quality of life? How do interpersonal and mass media dependency influence the course of illness? These are some of the questions that health communication research might answer.

Social Support

The term *social support* is typically used to refer to the ways in which interpersonal relationships protect people from the deleterious effects of stress and illness. Research on the impact of social support on health outcomes generally indicates a beneficial effect (Berkman & Symo, 1979; Blazer, 1982; Broadhead, Kaplan, & James et al., 1983; Dunkel-Schetter & Wortman, 1982; Funch & Marshall, 1983).

Social support has not been studied from a persuasion perspective. However, research clearly indicates that it can encourage or discourage patients from obtaining and maintaining appropriate treatment and can influence the extent of effort they commit to survival. Among cancer and AIDS patients, emotional support may be very important. A positive relationship between emotional support from family members and degree of physical and/or psychological adjustment to cancer has been found (Bloom, 1982; Carey, 1974; Weidman-Gibbs & Achterberg-Lawlis, 1978). Longitudinal studies have indicated that social support at time of diagnosis is associated with less emotional distress and longer life (Weisman & Worden, 1975).

Among cancer or AIDS patients, social support is very important. However, recent research has raised two important questions: (1) What type of social support is needed, and (2) is social support always positive? The answers to these questions depend to a large extent on the nature of the illness and often on timing. In terms of cancer and AIDS patients, providing information may be a useful form of support immediately after initial diagnosis. Wortman (1984) explains, "Since the major adaptive task required of the patient at diagnosis is to appraise symptoms and initiate treatment, the provision of information may be more stress-reducing than other types of support" (p. 2343). Of course, the question remains, how much information is too much or too little?

The likelihood of social support having positive effects on patient recovery may also depend on whether support is reciprocated. DiMatteo and Hays (1981) argue that the support a patient receives may depend in part on the support family and friends receive themselves. If the patient does not provide some emotional return to those supporting him or her, support may cease or be less than optimal. DiMatteo and Hays also point out that social support can be detrimental to treatment if the treatment goes against supporters' values and beliefs. They may subvert the treatment regimen or cause it to be ignored.

The effectiveness of social support also appears to depend on who is doing the supporting. Support from the wrong person can cause anxiety for the patient (Heller, 1979; Wortman, 1984). Wortman (1984) explains that the comment, "I know how you feel," might be perceived as very supportive if made by a fellow cancer patient, but might be infuriating if made by a healthy friend or acquaintance.

Overall, the literature pertaining to social support and cancer raises a number of important issues but leaves many others unresolved. Health communication researchers might focus efforts on understanding the types of social support that encourage patients to adopt health-enhancing coping styles. What strategies are useful with seriously ill patients, and are certain strategies more effective at certain times in the course of treatment and recovery? How might cancer and AIDS patients be trained to elicit social support from others and to reciprocate it? And whose support is vital and whose support might even be counterproductive to recovery?

Compliance

Another area in which persuasion plays a crucial role in recovery from serious illness is compliance with treatment regimens. One of the most vexing problems facing the physician is the treatment dropout rate of both inpatients and outpatients. The treatment of many chronic diseases is hampered by patients failing to persevere in treatment—a situation exacerbated by increasing treatment options and expenses (Baekeland & Lundwall, 1975). It is therefore important to identify factors that contribute to dropout rates and to identify strategies that health professionals and patients' friends and families may use to increase compliance.

Research on medication compliance among children has elicited a set of factors. Among these factors are duration of medication, familiarity with the physician, side effects, accuracy of pharmacist instructions, provider-parent interaction, family and demographic factors, psychological factors, and social factors. Improved compliance when treating children appears to result from intervention strategies that are informational (i.e., involving the transfer of information about the disease and its treatment from clinicians to parents) and behavioral (i.e., focusing on the specific behavior involved in compliance) (Dickey, Mattar, & Chudzik, 1975; Thibaudeau & Reidy, 1977). Providing information without assistance in changing behavior is not likely to achieve the desired results of medication compliance (Shope, 1981).

Potter and Roberts (1984) identified another factor implicated in children's compliance—their perception of the illness. They propose that helping children to understand illness could improve treatment regimen compliance and lessen anxiety. Unfortunately, many pediatricians take the more traditional approach of dealing primarily with the parents (Bibace & Walsh, 1980). Few researchers have focused their attention on strategies and guidelines for explaining illness to children of different ages. This is an area where communication research is needed.

Among the elderly, compliance with drug regimens is a significant problem. Recent research indicates that the elderly often do not understand the purpose of their drug therapy (Smith & Andrews, 1983). They also tend to make serious medication errors, with omission (forgetting, misunderstanding of regimen, being too sick, or lacking money to buy medication) being the most frequent problem (Schwartz, Wang, Zeitz, & Goss, 1962). And, surprisingly, much noncompliance is intentional with patients believing that the drug is unnecessary (Cooper, Love, & Raffoul, 1982).

The fact that the elderly use more medications than other groups increases the likelihood of misuse or neglect. But there appears to be more to the issue of elderly medical noncompliance than might be accounted for by numbers of medications alone. Memory problems, failing eyesight, heightened arousal of the autonomic nervous system, slowed responses, and auditory problems are implicated (Richardson, 1986). It is clear that educational programs must be specifically designed for the elderly. This approach is referred to as "behavioral tailoring" (Boczowski & Zeichner, 1985). What is less clear is that there may be times when, in our efforts to achieve compliance, we may overlook the simple fact that not everyone wants to live longer if it means a significant diminishment in their quality of life.

Communication researchers have much to offer the study of medical compliance. Research indicates that increasing compliance requires "behavior tailoring" of programs to the needs, concerns, limitations, and personalities of patients. Little research exists identifying strategies that work best with children, adolescents, the elderly, and the seriously ill. This area of health study is clearly relational in nature and clearly an area in need of communication research.

ALTERNATIVE AND EXPANDED VIEWS ON THREE ISSUES RAISED BY KREPS

Persuading people to change their health-related behaviors is a complex activity. Kreps argues that this complexity is often overlooked and incompletely analyzed. In this section, I will address three areas where inattention to complexity has limited the vision of health researchers. The first section addresses some misconceptions about what it means to cope with serious illness. The second section challenges the notion that taking responsibility for one's own health always facilitates recovery. The third section provides some guidelines for using new technologies to encourage people to adopt healthful lifestyles.

Coping with Serious Illness

A considerable amount of research has been devoted to identifying optimal styles of coping with serious illness. The results have been less than satisfying. To date, not only is there extensive controversy over how to measure coping styles, but researchers are beginning to wonder whether they have been asking the right questions. We are beginning to realize that there may not be a best overall strategy for coping with serious illness, that people don't cope in a single fashion throughout the course of an illness. Recent research also suggests coping styles that facilitate recovery from one illness may be dysfunctional to recovery from another illness. There is also mounting evidence that coping is as much an interpersonal process as an intrapersonal process. It may be that the success of a particular coping style is largely dependent on the support the patient receives from significant others for using that style.

This finding does not necessarily mean that long-term denial facilitates recovery. Some researchers emphasize that denial can lead to serious delay in seeking help (Greene, Moss, & Goldstein, 1974; Simon, Feinleib, & Thompson, 1972). But as Simonton and Shook (1984) suggest, temporary diversions into less than admirable forms of coping may well be natural. There may be pivot points in the cancer recovery process, for example, each marking increased progress and each characterized by a variety of coping activities. We also know that good copers (those who resolve problems and have little distress) use a wider variety of coping styles than do poor copers (Weisman, 1976; Weisman & Worden, 1975; Weisman, Worden, & Sobel, 1980).

From this research, we may conclude that encouraging patients to adopt culturally or personally favored coping styles can be dysfunctional to recovery. It is easy for people who are not ill themselves to confuse and frustrate patients with ill-founded expectations about "good coping." Such expectations may be difficult, if not impossible, to achieve in the early phases of serious illness. Coping is a process of reasoning about emotion (Reardon & Buck, 1984). When emotional reactions are strong, certain types of reasoning may be impossible. When people first learn that they have cancer or AIDS, for example, they may need to deny or react passively for a time. They may find it necessary to cope, at least temporarily, in ways not admired by significant others.

To understand when and for whom particular coping styles are functional to recovery, we must begin to identify stages of the recovery process for a variety of illnesses. We must also direct our attention to what Kreps describes as the symbolic interpretations of patients. Patients' perspectives on their illnesses are equally important to actual physical status in terms of understanding and appreciating their coping styles. Until this understanding is accomplished, gaining compliance from patients will be difficult. We cannot expect to persuade deniers to take medication or undergo debilitating treatments. If, however, we can place denial into a time frame, accept that it may be functional to recovery at certain points, and find ways to move patients into different coping styles when denial ceases to facilitate recovery, then the chances of gaining compliance may be improved.

Another blind spot in coping research is evidenced by the minimal amount of attention given to the social and cultural contexts of coping. Researchers are beginning to recognize that coping is not solely an intrapersonal process. People do not cope in isolation. Friends, relatives, acquaintances, and strangers can influence patients' symbolic interpretations of their illnesses as well as the behavioral coping styles they select. For example, Hackett and Weisman (1969) argue that to the extent that significant others honestly endorse the optimism they offer patients, the effectiveness of the patient's denial is not undermined. However, to the extent that others cannot genuinely reciprocate optimism, the patient may see through the facade of hopefulness and begin to experience doubt and fear.

Another way that signficant others can influence the coping success of patients involves the extent to which what they expect of the patient is something that the patient can comfortably deliver. Wortman and Dunkel-Schetter (1979) argue that seriously ill patients are often victims of their own families and circle of friends. When it is difficult for others to cope with the idea of cancer, for example, they may isolate or reject the patient. Even when this rejection does not occur, family members and friends may discourage cancer patients from discussing the illness, the possibility of recurrence, or other issues that the patient may need to discuss (Lichtman, 1982; Taylor, 1983).

Mass media sometimes exacerbate this problem. Taylor and Levin (1976) have argued that in the absence of other cancer patients with whom to compare reactions, patients and their families may rely on the media. However, media coverage of cancer is often biased—focusing on "super-copers" who appear to have easily picked up their lives where they left off before cancer surgery and treatment. According to Taylor and Levin, an unfortunate consequence of this media bias is that cancer patients exposed to supercoper models and experiencing bouts of depression, fear and self-doubt may feel inadequate.

Coping styles facilitate recovery to the extent that they (a) allow the patient some alleviation from stress or channel stress in some productive manner, (b) do not inhibit necessary treatment, and (c) are encouraged, or at least appreciated, by significant others. It will be difficult for persuasion research to make headway in terms of finding ways to encourage patients to adopt optimal coping styles until researchers cease to study them as if styles are inherently good or bad and are adopted by patients in isolation of the opinions of others.

The Issue of Patient Responsibility

A second issue raised by Kreps that may profitably be viewed from a somewhat different vantage point is the belief that patients should be encouraged to take responsibility for their own recovery. Kreps argues that to promote health, "It is important for interpersonal communicators to encourage others to view themselves as powerful, able to withstand and combat health risks."

Considerable research supports Kreps's assertion, but there is another side to the issue of patient responsibility that is often overlooked as we strive to convince patients to feel a sense of power over their recovery. That is, responsibility can be taken too far. When this happens, patients make dangerous decisions.

Each year the public spends approximately $4 billion on unproven cancer cures. These people are usually educated, middle to upper class, and often curable. In place of traditional treatments, many of them choose metabolic therapy, diet treatments, megavitamins, mental imagery to reduce the size of tumors, faith healing, or some other unorthodox treatment method.

Cassileth and Brown (1986) report that these people are equally or better informed than patients who do not use the "unproven methods." This, they argue, can be explained in part by the fact that several features of these unproven methods require time, financial resources, and an educated, questioning approach to illness. These people are usually quite knowledgeable about conventional treatments, have obtained second and third opinions, and have read relevant orthodox medical publications.

When it comes to cancer, well-educated, information-seeking patients and their families often know people who died of the disease. They are unimpressed with 50% cure rates for many cancers and often feel that unconventional treatments offer the same opportunity for cure with the added benefit of being "natural and nontoxic" (Cassileth & Brown, 1986). As a result, people die who might have been saved.

The mass media are replete with information about taking care of yourself. We are again in an era of home remedies and self-diagnosis kits. While there are obvious advantages to encouraging members of a society to take responsibility for their own health (e.g., to ask questions of their doctors and to get second opinions) and while some methods like meditation and hypnosis have been useful as complementary therapies to traditional treatments, most people are unaware of just how much responsibility is too much.

This discussion is not meant to imply that encouraging patients to take an active role in their recovery is somehow wrong or that established medical science is always right. It merely suggests that when we encourage people to take such a role, they should be apprised of the extent of available misinformation and quackery that even well-meaning people might suggest. In terms of persuasion research, it may mean developing strategies to encourage people to adopt healthful lifestyles and to take an active role in assuring their own health while also inoculating them against the likelihood that they will be encouraged to adopt methods of so-called health promotion, disease prevention, and cure that may reduce their chances of a long healthful life.

The Role of Technology in the
Dissemination of Health-Care Information

It is tempting to become enamored with communication technologies. They seem to hold such promise. The truth is, however, that we know very little about how technologies of any sort affect social relations, community, and lifestyles. Fischer (1985) argues that there is "an empirical vacuum of startling proportions on the social consequences of technology."

Many discussions of technology assume homogeneous effects—that all the consequences of a specific technology operate in parallel or that all people are affected in the same ways whether rich or poor, urban or rural, male or female (Fischer, 1985). Yet there is no evidence that the effects of similar or even the same technologies have consistent effects, nor that all people react similarly to them.

Existing research suggests that common generalizations about media as content sources may be misleading (Dervin, 1981; Williams, Dordick, & Horstmann, 1977). Ball-Rokeach and Cantor (1986) argue that the media audience is not to be understood as passive consumers, but as active individuals who consume media products in the context of their personal and social goals. This is not a novel perspective on the effects of mass media, but one that bears repeating. People vary in their dependency on mass media for health information. *Media system dependency* is the term used to describe the extent to which attainment of personal and social goals is contingent on the use of mass media (Ball-Rokeach et al., 1984). To the extent that people find mass media useful in meeting health-related goals, we may expect mass media health messages to influence their attitudes and behaviors. To the extent that people depend on nonmedia sources such as family and friends for health information, the effects of media are likely to be reduced.

A number of health-related research projects have combined mass and interpersonal communication (see Flay, 1981). Research indicates that the social context in which communication technologies are used to disseminate health information can influence the extent of increased awareness and behavioral change (Flay, 1981; Rogers, 1986). Interpersonal networks often play a crucial role in the diffusion of health-related information. While it appears that mass media can effectively increase awareness and change knowledge about health issues, they are less effective in changing behaviors and encouraging maintenance of any new behaviors. The blending of mass media and interpersonal communication promises a higher likelihood of effectiveness (Flay, 1981).

There is, however, a tendency to add interpersonal components to health campaigns with little regard for the nature of those components. Just getting people to talk about media messages may not be enough to ensure lasting effects. Effective, satisfying interpersonal communication is more than just talking. Who is talking with whom, about what, using what styles and strategies and at what levels of competence are only a few of the questions that should be asked before interpersonal communication is integrated into health campaigns.

Unfortunately, the historical separation between interpersonal and mass media scholars has inhibited combining the best perspectives from each. A chasm exists between interpersonal and mass media scholars born of departmental separation and struggles for clear identities and credibility in the social scientific community. This "false dichotomy" in our field hinders theory and research on the diffusion of health information (Delia, 1987; Reardon & Rogers, 1986).

It is not sufficient for communication researchers merely to add an underdeveloped interpersonal component to media campaigns. This kind of token attention to interpersonal communication can only lead to erroneous conclusions. To be effective, health campaigns should draw upon the best available resources. We must explore how various types of interpersonal communication facilitate changes in health-related attitudes and behaviors. We need to look at how new communication technologies can be allied with other resources rather than expecting them always to play the key role in all our diffusion efforts. Breslow (1982) argues that campaigns, such as those against smoking, need comprehensive strategies that mobilize all available resources most effectively. This effort means stepping beyond common assumptions about the power of technology. It means greater use of ethnography, field surveys, and quasi-experimental methods. It means getting to know how and why people use media and other new technologies to acquire health information. And it means identifying obstacles in the path of dissemination and developing strategies to meet the needs of quite different segments of the population.

A PERSUASION RESEARCH AGENDA

Obviously, changing health-related behaviors is not a one-approach proposition. There appear to be no simple answers. We have learned that illness is a social as well as personal process. Few people cope with illness in isolation. Few make major changes in their health-related behaviors and maintain those changes without encouragement from significant others.

Once we begin to view illness, in part, as a social experience, the course of research is altered. As we have discussed, it may be unproductive and even destructive to persuade patients to adopt coping styles that are discouraged in their families. We cannot effectively teach adolescents to resist smoking and drugs if we do not understand the social contexts in which they live. Efforts to employ new communication technologies to disseminate health information and to alter current health-threatening behaviors may be wasted if we do not understand the social and cultural contexts of their usage and how these technologies might help people meet their health goals.

There is much groundwork to be done. As I mentioned, this work will often require putting aside assumptions about target audiences or individuals in order to conduct exploratory research. A preference for quantitative research methodology may blind many of us to the important role that field surveys, ethnography, and other methods might contribute to our understanding of the people we are trying to persuade and how they might utilize the methods we have developed to meet their personal and social goals. Whether stated or implied, one of the primary messages to be derived from Kreps's chapter and this one is that there are no simple answers. Communication and persuasion are processes. We cannot expect to inform people and change their health behaviors without an understanding and appreciation of their values and needs.

REFERENCES

Baekeland, F., & Lundwall, L. (1975). Dropping out of treatment: A critical review. *Psychological Bulletin, 82,* 738-783.

Ball-Rokeach, S. J. (1986). Changing and stabilizing political behavior and beliefs. In S. J. Ball-Rokeach & M. G. Cantor (Eds.), *Media, audience, and social structure* (pp. 280-290). Newbury Park, CA: Sage.

Ball-Rokeach, S. J., & Cantor, M. G. (1986). The media and social fabric. In S. Ball-Rokeach & M. Cantor (Eds.), *Media, audience, and social change* (pp. 10-20). Newbury Park, CA: Sage.

Ball-Rokeach, S. J., Rokeach, M., & Grube, J. W. (1984). *The great American values test.* New York: Academic Press.

Bandura, A. (1977). *Social learning theory.* Englewood Cliffs, NJ: Prentice-Hall.

Becker, E. (1973). *The denial of death.* New York: Free Press.

Benfari, R. C., Okene, J. K., & McIntyre, K. M. (1982). Control of cigarette smoking from a psychological perspective. *Annual Review of Public Health, 3*, 101-128.

Berg, R. L. (1976). The high cost of self-deception. *Preventive Medicine, 5*, 483-495.

Berkman, L. F., & Syme, S. L. (1979). Social networks, host resistance, and mortality: A nine-year follow-up study of Alameda County residents. *American Journal of Epidemiology, 109*, 186-204.

Bibace, R., & Walsh, N. E. (1980). Development of children's concepts of illness. *Pediatrics, 66*, 912-917.

Blane, H. T. (1976). Issues in preventing alcohol problems. *Preventive Medicine, 5*, 176-186.

Blazer, D. G. (1982). Social support and mortality in an elderly community population. *American Journal of Epidemiology, 115*, 684-694.

Bloom, J. R. (1982). Social support, accommodation to stress and adjustment to breast cancer. *Social Science Medicine, 16*, 1329-1338.

Boczkowski, J. A., & Zeichner, A. (1985). Medication compliance and the elderly. *Clinical Gerontologist, 4*, 3-15.

Botvin, G., Eng, A., & Williams, C. (1980). Preventing the onset of cigarette smoking through life skills training. *Preventive Medicine, 9*, 135-143.

Breslow, L. (1982). Control of cigarette smoking from a public policy perspective. *Annual Review of Public Health, 3*, 129-151.

Broadhead, W. E., Kaplan, B. H., & Jones, S. A., et al. (1983). The epidemiologic evidence for a relationship between social support and health. *American Journal of Epidemiology, 117*, 521-537.

Burleson, B. (1984). Age, social-cognitive development and the use of comforting strategies. *Communication Monographs, 51*, 140-153.

Carey, R. (1974). Emotional adjustment in terminal patients: A quantitative approach. *Journal of Counseling Psychology, 21*, 433-439.

Cassem, N. H., & Hackett, T. P. (1971). Psychiatric consultation in a coronary care unit. *Annals of Internal Medicine, 75*, 9-14.

Cassileth, B. R., & Brown, H. (1986). *Unorthodox cancer medicine.* Unpublished manuscript. University of Pennsylvania Cancer Center.

Clarke, P. D., & Sencer, J. (1985, August 23). Results of a Gallop Poll on Acquired Immunodeficiency Syndrome: New York City, United States. *Morbidity and Mortality Weekly*, pp. 513-514.

Cooper, J. K., Love, D. W., & Raffoul, P. R. (1982). Intentional prescription nonadherence (noncompliance) by the elderly. *American Geriatrics Society, 30*, 329-333.

Delia, J. G. (1987). Twentieth-century communication research: An historical perspective. In C. R. Berger & S. H. Chaffee (Eds.), *Handbook of communication science.* Newbury Park, CA: Sage.

Dickey, F., Mattar, M., & Chudzik, H. (1975). Pharmacist counseling increases drug regimen compliance. *Hospitals, 49*, 85-86, 88.

DiMatteo, M. R., & Hays, R. (1981). Social support and serious illness. In B. H. Gottlieb (Ed.), *Social networks and social support* (pp. 117-148). Newbury Park, CA: Sage.

Dunkel-Schetter, C., & Wortman, C. (1982). The interpersonal dynamics of cancer: Problems in social relationships and their impact on the patient. In H. Griedman & M. DiMatteo (Eds.), *Interpersonal issues in health care.* New York: Academic Press.

Engstrom, D. (1984). A psychological perspective of prevention in alcoholism. In J. Matarazzo, S. Weiss, J. Herd, N. Miller, & S. Weiss (Eds.), *Behavioral health* (pp. 1047-1058). New York: John Wiley.

Festinger, L. A. (1954). A theory of social comparison processes. *Human Relations, 7,* 117-140.

Fischer, C. S. (1985). Studying technology and social life. In M. Castells (Ed.), *High technology, space, and society* (pp. 284-300). Newbury Park, CA: Sage.

Flay, B. R. (1981). On improving the chances of mass media health promotion programs causing meaningful changes in behavior. In M. Meyer (Ed.), *Health education by television* (pp. 56-91). Munich, Germany: Saur.

Flay, B. R. (1986). Psychosocial approaches to smoking prevention: A review of findings. *Health Psychology.*

Funch, D. P., & Marshall, J. (1983). The role of stress, social support, and age in survival from breast cancer. *Journal of Psychosomatic Research, 27,* 77-83.

Green, D. E. (1979). Youth education. *Smoking and Health: A Report of the Surgeon General.* Washington, DC: Department of Health, Education, and Welfare.

Green, L. W. (1984). Health education models. In J. Matarazzo, S. Weiss, J. Herd, N. Miller, & S. Weiss (Eds.), *Behavioral health* (pp. 181-198). New York: John Wiley.

Greene, W. A., Moss, A. J., & Goldstein, S. (1974). Delay, denial, and death in coronary heart disease. In R. S. Eliot (Ed.), *Stress and the heart.* Mount Kisco, NY: Futura.

Gusfield, J. (1976). The prevention of drinking problems. In W. Filstead, J. Rossi, & M. Keller (Eds.), *Alcohol and alcohol problems: New thinking and new directions.* Cambridge, MA: Ballinger.

Hackett, T. P., & Weisman, A. D. (1969). Reactions to the imminence of death. In G. Grosser, H. Wechsler, & M. Greenblat (Eds.), *The threat of impending disaster* (pp. 300-311). Cambridge: MIT Press.

Harper, A. E. (1984). A healthful diet and its implications for disease prevention. In J. Matarazzo, S. Weiss, J. Herd, N. Miller, & S. Weiss (Eds.), *Behavioral health* (pp. 575-589). New York: John Wiley.

Harvey, J. H., & Weary, G. W. (1981). *Perspectives on attributional processes.* Dubuque, IA: W. C. Brown.

Hegsted, D. M. (1984). What is a healthful diet? In J. Matarazzo, S. Weiss, J. Herd, N. Miller, & S. Weiss (Eds.), *Behavioral health* (pp. 552-574). New York: John Wiley.

Heller, K. (1979). The effects of social support: Prevention and treatment implications. In A. Goldstein & F. Kanfer (Eds.), *Maximizing treatment gains: Enhancement in psychotherapy.* New York: Academic Press.

Hurd, P. D., Johnson, C. A., Leupker, R. V., Pechacek, T. F., & Jacobs, D. R. (1980). Prevention of cigarette smoking in seventh grade students. *Journal of Behavioral Medicine, 3,* 15-28.

Jones, E. E., Farina, A., Hastorf, A. H., Markus, H., Miller, D. T., & Scott, R. A. (1984). *Social stigma.* San Francisco: W. H. Freeman.

Kelley, H. H. (1967). Attribution theory in social psychology. In D. Levine (Ed.), *Nebraska Symposium on Motivation* (Vol. 15, pp. 192-238). Lincoln: University of Nebraska Press.

Kelly, J. A., & St. Lawrence, J. S. (1986). Behavioral intervention and AIDS. *Behavior Therapist, 9,* 121-125.

Lichtman, R. R. (1982). *Close relationships after breast cancer.* Unpublished doctoral dissertation, University of California.

Mello, N. K. (1976). Some issues in research on the biology of alcoholism. In W. J. Filstead, J. J. Rossi, & M. Keller (Eds.), *Alcohol and alcohol problems: New thinking and new directions.* Cambridge, MA: Ballinger.

Moore, M. H., & Gerstein, D. R. (Eds.). (1981). *Alcohol and public policy: Beyond the shadow of Prohibition.* Washington, DC: National Academy Press.

Penz, M. A. (1985). Social competence and self-efficacy as determinants of substance use in adolescence. In *Coping and substance use* (pp. 117-142). New York: Academic Press.

Perry, C., Killen, J., Telch, M., Slinkard, L., & Danaher, B. (1980). Modifying smoking behavior of teenagers: A school-based intervention. *American Journal of Public Health, 70,* 722-725.

Potter, P. C., & Roberts, M. C. (1984). Children's perceptions of chronic illness: The roles of disease symptoms, cognitive development, and information. *Journal of Pediatric Psychology, 9*, 13-24.

Puckett, S. B., & Bart, M. (1985, November 8). Self-reported behavioral changes among homosexual and bisexual men—San Francisco. *Morbidity and Mortality Weekly Report*, pp. 2537-2538.

Pyszcynski, T. A., & Greenberg, J. (1981). The role of disconfirmed expectancies in the instigation of attributional processing. *Journal of Personality and Social Psychology, 40*, 31-38.

Reardon, K. K. (1981). *Persuasion: Theory and context*. Newbury Park, CA: Sage.

Reardon, K. K. (1986). *Interpersonal communication: Where minds meet*. Belmont, CA: Wadsworth.

Reardon, K. K., & Buck, R. (1984, May). *Emotion, reason, and communication in coping with cancer*. Paper presented at the annual meeting of the International Communication Association, San Francisco.

Reardon, K. K., & Richardson, J. L. (in press). The important role of mass media in the diffusion of accurate information about AIDS. *Journal of Homosexuality*.

Reardon, K. K., & Rogers, E. M. (1986). *Interpersonal and mass media communication: A false dichotomy*. Paper presented at the annual meeting of the Speech Communication Association, Chicago.

Reardon, K. K., Sussman, S., & Flay, B. R. (1987). *Can adolescents just say "no" to smoking?* Unpublished manuscript, University of Southern California.

Richardson, J. L. (1986). Perspectives on compliance with drug regimens among the elderly. *Journal of Compliance in Health Care, 1*, 29-41.

Rogers, E. M. (1986). *Communication technology: The new media society*. Newbury Park, CA: Sage.

Rokeach, M. (1973). *The nature of human values*. New York: Free Press.

Schinke, S. P., & Gilchrist, L. E. (1983). Primary prevention of tobacco smoking. *Journal of School Health, 53*, 416-419.

Schwartz, D., Wang, M., Zeitz, L., & Goss, M. E. (1962). Medication errors made by elderly chronically ill patients. *American Journal of Public Health, 52*, 2018-2029.

Schwartz, S. H., & Inbar-Saban, N. (1987). *Value self-confrontation as a method to aid in weight loss*. Unpublished manuscript, Hebrew University of Jerusalem.

Shope, J. T. (1981). Medication compliance. *Pediatric Clinics of North America, 28*, 5-21.

Shopeland, D. R., & Brown, C. (1985). Current trends in smoking control. *Annals of Behavioral Medicine, 7*, 5-8.

Simon, A. B., Feinleib, M., & Thompson, H. K. (1972). Components of delay in the prehospital phase of acute myocardial infarction. *American Journal of Cardiology, 30*, 476-482.

Simpkins, P., & Andrews, J. (1983). Drug compliance—not so bad, knowledge—not so good: The elderly after hospital discharge. *Age and Aging, 12*, 336-342.

Solomon, D. S., & Maccoby, N. (1984). Communication as a model for health enhancement. In J. Matarazzo, S. Weiss, J. Herd, N. Miller, & S. Weiss (Eds.), *Behavioral health* (pp. 209-211). New York: John Wiley.

Taylor, S. E. (1983, November). Adjustment to threatening events: A theory of cognitive adaption. *American Psychologist*, pp. 1161-1173.

Taylor, S. E., Dakoff, G., & Reardon, K. K. (1987). *Cancer patients' responses to stories about cancer*. Unpublished manuscript, University of California, Los Angeles.

Taylor, S. E., & Levin, S. (1976). *The psychological impact of breast cancer: A review of theory and research*. San Francisco: West Coast Cancer Foundation.

Taylor, S. E., Lichtman, R. R., & Wood, J. V. (1984). Attributions, beliefs about control, and adjustment to breast cancer. *Journal of Personality and Social Psychology, 46*, 489-502.

Thibaudeau, M., & Reidy, M. (1977). Nursing makes a difference: A comparative study of the health behavior of mothers in three primary care agencies. *International Journal of Nursing Studies, 14*, 97-107.

Thompson, E. L. (1978). Smoking education programs, 1960-1976. *American Journal of Public Health, 68,* 250-257.

Tuchfeld, B. S., & Marcus, S. H. (1984). Social models of prevention in alcoholism. In J. Matarazzo, S. Weiss, J. Herd, N. Miller, & S. Weiss (Eds.), *Behavioral health* (pp. 1041-1046). New York: John Wiley.

Weidman-Gibbs, H., & Achterberg-Lawlis, J. (1978). Spiritual values and death anxiety: Implications for counseling with terminal cancer patients. *Journal of Counseling Psychology, 25,* 563-569.

Weisman, A. D. (1976). Early diagnosis of vulnerability in cancer patients. *American Journal of the Medical Sciences, 271,* 187-196.

Weisman, A. D., & Worden, J. W. (1975). Psychological analysis of cancer deaths. Omega, 6, 61-75.

Weisman, A. D., Worden, J. W., & Sobel, H. J. (1980). *Psychosocial screening and intervention with cancer patients.* Cambridge, MA: Harvard University Press.

Williams, F., Dordick, H. S., & Horstmann, F. (1977). Where citizens go for information. *Journal of Communication, 27,* 95-99.

Wills, T. A. (1986). Stress and coping in early adolescence: Relationships to substance use in urban school samples. *Health Psychology, 5,* 503-529.

Wong, P.T.P., & Weiner, B. (1981). When people ask "why" questions, and the heuristics of attributional research. *Journal of Personality and Social Psychology, 40,* 650-663.

Wortman, C. B. (1984). Social support and the cancer patient: Conceptual and methodological issues. *Cancer, 53,* 2339-2359.

Wortman, C. B., & Dunkel-Schetter, C. (1979). Interpersonal relationships and cancer: A theoretical analysis. *Journal of Social Issues, 35,* 120-155.

Theoretical Plurality in
Health Communication

LOYD S. PETTEGREW
University of South Florida

PROFESSORS Kreps and Reardon have presented a number of important issues in their respective essays on health communication. I have been asked to respond to their ideas and hope to accomplish three tasks: (1) to review briefly the health-care context particularly as it exists in the United States; (2) to shed some critical light on Kreps's and Reardon's chapters; and (3) to offer an alternative to the information and persuasion perspectives.

Since health communication is a context involving all levels of human interaction, I must comment at least briefly on this context. Ethnographers like Bateson and Goffman have disabused us of the notion that there is such a thing as "generic" human communication. We are therefore obliged to make some sense out of the particular contexts in which communication takes place.

My main role is to examine critically some of the key positions each author has taken. Although their information and persuasion perspectives are not antagonistic, they are distinct enough to deserve separate treatment. I selectively comment on issues I find important to the health communication area.

Finally, I conclude my remarks by introducing an additional communication point of view—the narrative perspective. There is good reason to believe that health communication research and practice can be both informed and enriched by communication-centered approaches like narrative theory. I use the various levels of communication analyzed by Kreps to illustrate briefly how the narrative perspective might be usefully applied to communication in the health-care context. I confess to doing little more than scratching the surface of this engaging point of view since more worthy presentations are prominent in the communication literature. I distinguish

Correspondence and requests for reprints: Loyd S. Pettegrew, Department of Communication, University of South Florida, Tampa, FL 33620-5550.

Communication Yearbook 11, pp. 298-308

two types of narrative perspectives. The first uses narrative as the basic unit of communication analysis. The latter use of narrative theory coincides with the formulations advanced by Walter Fisher and others. The former use is more loosely interpretive, while the latter is more parochial.

THE HEALTH-CARE CONTEXT

The social context in which health care is sought and delivered in the United States differs from every other country. Health care is culturally bound. White Anglo physicians from the United Kingdom visit the United States and are dismayed at how some Americans receive markedly different health care than others depending on socioeconomic status. Their American counterparts visiting England are shocked to find that kidney dialysis is not offered to everyone who needs it but is rationed on a priority basis. Health care in Third World countries is exponentially even more idiosyncratic.

To complicate the issue surrounding health communication, we must also recognize significant subcontexts. During my tenure at an academic medical center, I was continuously struck by how the dissemination of modern medical information was hoist by the petard of contextuality.

Stories abound about how the white, first-year medical resident would admonish the obese, diabetic black woman from the projects to follow her 1500-calorie diet and avoid starchy foods in favor of meat exchanges. Every month the woman would return with a worsening diabetic condition and the medical resident would scold and implore the patient, failing to see that the woman's culture did not allow for the recommended diet. From the medical resident's perspective, if the woman didn't care enough about her health or was too stupid to understand, the surgery folks would be seeing her eventually to cut off a gangrenous leg. Health information was being sent reliably from the health-care sender through the channel of speech to the receiver. It was the latest health information presented "by the book." Unfortunately, the book contained the message but did not consider the audience or her subculture.

However true it may be that people in our field know more about the human communication enterprise than most health-care practitioners, we have all but ignored the communication context. Our literature is saturated with studies of human communication that, borrowing a theme from Meyrowitz (1985), fail to question place. We have yet to develop a grammar of social context in spite of the fact that human relationships develop and communication takes place within such a frame.

It would seem patent that understanding health communication cannot advance without giving concerted attention to the context in which health care is practiced here and in other countries. Without this foundation, our speculations about health communication risk being as helpful as the admonitions of the white medical resident to her diabetic patient. While this is cause for concern, hope for the future need not be abandoned as long as we recognize the contextual necessities of health communication, both the caregiving context itself and the cultural subcontexts within which health-care delivery is practiced.

In the chapters by Kreps and Reardon, we find a melding of health, health care, and the contextual fabric within which all of this takes place. I would favor a more restricted definition of the health-care context that focuses primarily on formal health-care delivery. In so doing, I recognize that a significant portion of health care in this country is delivered informally. The multibillion dollar over-the-counter prescription market attests to the scope of self-medication and the informal health-care context. Still, when informal delivery systems fail, Americans wind up at doctors' offices, clinics, and hospitals. This type of health-care delivery is categorically different than fad diets, fitness centers, health food stores, and tanning spas. While all of these are generally tied to the pursuance of a more healthy lifestyle, they do not deliver health care. While the communication in such places may be interesting to us, we should set some contextual parameters for our field of study.

A CRITIQUE OF COMMUNICATION
AS INFORMATION OR PERSUASION

At first blush, the essays offered by Professors Kreps and Reardon offer some *déjà vu* to the historical development of our field. They hint at two competing perspectives. Should communication in the health-care context be viewed as information or persuasion? The titanic Madison Avenue product wars are not lost on this issue. Such arguments conjure up two well-known commercial lines: "Is Certs a candy mint or a breath mint?" and "Is Miller Lite good because it tastes great or is less filling?" Usually, the best answer may not rest with resolving the dichotomy.

The fact that the information/persuasion issue is still considered useful controversy in the area of health communication reveals something about its newness. Communication study in the health-care context is little more than 15 years old. More important, communication in the health-care context has been dominated by views from other disciplines such as medicine, social psychology, sociology, and the like.

Imparting a more communication-centered perspective on health-care practitioners is a tedious endeavor. Typically, the health communication researcher, as a relative neophyte to the health-care context, faces both a credibility problem and the orientation of medicine to be concerned primarily with facts and information instead of affect and persuasion. I have argued elsewhere that other disciplines still dominated the way communication has been viewed in the health-care context (Pettegrew & Logan, 1987). The preparadigmatic state of the communication field encourages the information/persuasion controversy. For many health-care practitioners, such arguments are new and engaging.

The ground around health communication has shifted significantly during its development. As Kreps and Reardon point out, change in the health-care arena has been pervasive. In contrast to 15 years ago, patients are now encouraged to participate in their health care; successful health care has become a marketable commodity; health insurers and in fact all facets of health care have become more cost conscious; health promotion and preventive medicine have taken their rightful place beside pathogenic medicine.

I see more problems in the assumptions each author makes about the health-care context than in the information/persuasion perspectives each emphasizes. Kreps would have us believe that communication and health are virtually isomorphic and that communication therefore is the direct link to health across the board. He takes this implicit argument one step further by suggesting the formulation of a "health communication policy" or standard that should be instituted to guarantee more effective health-care practice. The communication responsibility from Kreps's point of view rests squarely on the shoulders of the health-care provider.

Reardon is more cautious. She believes we need to go beyond the role of health communicator as disseminator of health information and deal with strategic communication. She poses a very important and controversial question: "What are the best strategies for motivating people to adopt healthful lifestyles?" (p. 278). Reardon believes that persuasion theory can be applied usefully to health communication at all levels of interaction. Her well-constructed applications belie the rich treatment afforded persuasion from the communication tradition. While I do not doubt that social psychology has much to offer those interested in viewing health communication from a persuasion perspective, there is much that can also be applied from our rhetorical traditions. Reardon also neglects to consider the role communication plays in determining what is healthful. Each of these essays is considered in separate critiques.

THE PROBLEMATIC ROLE OF
INFORMATION IN HEALTH CARE

While I find Kreps's paper confirming of my academic tradition, I believe two implications of his arguments are problematic and deserve resolution. First, Kreps often uses information and communication interchangeably. This gives rise to conceptual fuzziness at a time when health communication needs greater precision and credibility. Second, although the association between communication and health has yet to be tested rigorously, Kreps prescribes more and better communication. If we are as yet unsure of the question, how credible can communication answers be?

Information/Communication as Interchangeable

Kreps compounds the equivocal role he identifies for communication in the health-care context by referring to communication and information interchangeably. If there is one thing our field has reached agreement on, it is that information with affect or relational components is no longer simply information. We must strive to understand that there may in fact be very little pure information in the health-care context. Just as there is no such thing as a theory-free language, health facts may seldom if ever exist independent of affective or relational baggage. Perhaps the term *health information* is as hollow as message content during the Shannon and Weaver days. They exist by themselves only in a theoretical world and not a world of contextual practice. Arntson and Droge (1983) have argued eloquently that even research *about* communication in the health-care context has manifest sociopolitical consequences. Perhaps health communication scholars can perform a needed last rites on the concept of health information, disabusing those in the health-care context from viewing communication as simply or primarily informational.

The Missing Link Between
Health and Communication

It would help the legitimacy of our work if we could provide strong empirical evidence about the link between health and communication. What evidence Kreps has accumulated for this bold claim is in most cases either anecdotal or the logic of common sense. From our own corner of the academic world such appeals seem intuitive, but are they legitimate?

Karl Weick (1983) once admonished scholars of communication in the organizational context to produce a "Hawthorne Study" of the field if they hoped to gain legitimacy. I would echo Weick's suggestion for health communication. Kreps would have us believe that health and communication are inextricably bound (p. 238). He provides a series of claims about the role of communication in the health-care context. These claims should be viewed more as working hypotheses to be tested than as ultimate truths. While they may have support in the general communication literature, we must remember the idiosyncratic nature of the health-care context. What obtains for a general social context may simply not apply at all in health care.

Let us turn a critical eye to some of these claims for a moment. Are satisfied or informed patients necessarily healthier (p. 242)? Are insensitive relational messages less effective in the health-care context (p. 243)? By whose standards should sensitivity be judged? Is encouraging others to view themselves as powerful or able to withstand and combat health risks either appropriate or effective (p. 244)? Do "effective health-care relationships have clearly understood and agreed upon implicit contracts . . . enabling them to continue to act appropriately toward each other as their relationship grows" (p. 242)?

The fact is that no matter how "right" or logical these claims appear, there is no strong evidence to back them up. For example, relationships in the health-care context have undergone dramatic change during the past decade. HMOs, team nursing, and team medicine have all done away with continuous, personal health-care relationships. In spite of the negative things the popular press has to say about HMO care, more Americans are joining HMOs and being cared for appreciably well.

The evidential dilemma of Kreps's thesis rests with three problems in health communication research. First, we are unclear about what constitutes an effective health-care relationship or effective health care. There is no accepted criterion validity for health or effective health-care relationships. Second, we simply do not understand the association between communication and health at the interpersonal level let alone the other four levels Kreps describes in his chapter. We have been content to focus on smaller research issues rather than test our own legitimacy (Bochner & Eisenberg, 1984). Third, as a result, we cannot prescribe appropriately a stronger or better dose of communication to solve human health problems because the efficacy of such medicine has not been fully tested.

The Utopian Syndrome

Kreps takes the ultimate step in arguing that communication and health are linked. He urges that a national policy or standard for health information be established. His goal is to establish greater communication competency among health-care providers. He believes that we can and should institutionalize "standards and criteria for effective provider health communication" (p. 263).

I find several problems with this suggested course of action. If the field of communication cannot agree on what constitutes effective communication as evidenced by competing constructs like rhetorical sensitivity and communication competence, how can "standards" of communication be set for the health-care context? Regulation demands greater certainty than presently exists about effective or appropriate communication behavior.

Providing simple or patent solutions to complex problems promises to create worse problems than existed before the solution. We risk getting trapped by what Watzlawick, Weakland, and Fisch (1974) have termed the "Utopian Syndrome." The communication needs of a pathologist are markedly different from someone in family medicine. Are we to hold students in each specialty accountable for the same level of communication skill? What happens when we generate new evidence that calls into question some of our assumptions about the link between communication skills and outcomes in the health-care context? Policy is not that easily changed. Who will enforce this policy when licensed health-care practitioners fail in their communication obligations? Finally, why is the onus for effective communication primarily the responsibility of the health-care practitioner when such a notion stands in the face of the concept of communication relationship?

COMMUNICATION-CENTERED PERSUASION

Reardon has written definitively on the subject of persuasion in a general social context (Reardon, 1981). There is no reason to challenge her expertise on the subject. I do feel, however, that the tradition of social psychology is emphasized to the neglect of rhetorical theory. I have argued elsewhere (Smith & Pettegrew, 1986) that the doctor-patient relationship lends itself to the study of persuasion, particularly rhetorical notions of persuasion. Reardon's orientation toward persuading people to change their habits and behaviors to more healthful trends can be informed by rhetorical concepts.

For example, the issue of medical noncompliance can be informed by the rhetorical notion of identification. Many medical regimens have not been developed with the elderly in mind. While Reardon cites some success with the "behavioral tailoring" of educational programs, the communication tradition may have equally effective and more humane approaches to such problems. Young physicians and other health-care practitioners make youthful assumptions about patient needs and world views. Treatment regimens developed specifically to identify with elderly patients might offer rhetorical solutions to problems of medical noncompliance.

Some failures in medical treatment might be viewed usefully as the inability to determine and/or reconcile the exigencies of partners in health-care relationships. We can learn from the "high touch" health professions like chiropractic and osteopathy. Many patients come to providers for reassurance and the laying on of hands. Modern medicine comes ready to prescribe medication and perform diagnostic tests. When such differences in exigency collide, it is not surprising that problems arise.

The assumption that the problems in health care reside either with poor health communicators or impaired patients, be they elderly or simply noncompliant, favors a linear model of communication rather than a relational model mediated by context and situation. In fact, health communication at a variety of levels might be seen as rhetorical situations, some of which are more interactive than others. The issue of responsibility in health maintenance, particularly given the increasing role of the mass media, lends itself to rhetorical ideas.

Mass-mediated programming on health issues must be seen as more than the dissemination of health information. The fact that the mass media are even involved in health communication changes the context itself (Meyrowitz, 1985). Researchers involved with AIDS have been frustrated at the refusal of the mass media to assist in the promotion of safe sexual practices. Such issues can be addressed provocatively and effectively through rhetorical theories.

I agree with Reardon that a "preference for quantitative research methodology may blind many of us to the important role that . . . other methods might contribute to our understanding of the people we are trying to persuade" (p. 293). I would suggest that the resolution to this dilemma lies not in methodological diversity but in theoretical plurality. Relying primarily on social psychological theories will only ever make us junior social psychologists. Our future lies in integrating our rhetorical traditions or proving their limitations in the health-care context.

NARRATIVE THEORY AS AN ALTERNATIVE

Social necessity is often the mother of invention. Feyerabend (1975) argues that science itself is founded on advances born out of necessity or serendipity rather than adherence to disciplinary rigor. We have a debt to pay to Dwight Conquergood (1986), who was the first scholar in our field to explore the uses of narrative theory in the health-care context. Smith (1987) has since applied narrative theory to the subject of ethics and human values in medicine. I hope to extend this line of inquiry to health communication in general. My enthusiasm is founded on the belief that narrative theory compliments information and persuasion theory, particularly in the health-care context.

Narrative Theory

Narrative theory is an interpretive theory. It was formulated by Walter Fisher (1984a, 1984b) and applied to the issue of public discourse. Narrative theory is founded on the concept *homo narrans*. Human beings are most fundamentally storytelling creatures. It is through the active use of stories that humans come to be socialized into a particular culture and it is through stories that the social process is continued.

In narrative theory, stories become the primary unit of human communication analysis. The concept of information is subordinated to the culturally bound story. Information and narrative share a relationship analogous to task and role in social theory. The latter concept is the social gestalt of many instances of the former.

Not all narratives are, of course, equal. Some are more compelling than others; their social affect is consequently greater. Fisher (1984a) outlines the concepts of narrative rationality and narrative fidelity by which all stories can be assessed. These are, however, not absolute. "Human communication in all of its forms is inbued with 'mythos'—ideas that cannot be verified or proven in any absolute way . . . liberation of the human spirit would seem to call for an acceptance of these facts" (p. 86).

NARRATIVES IN THE HEALTH-CARE CONTEXT

The proof of the narrative pudding is a long way away. In this section I briefly describe how narrative theory might be applied usefully to various levels within the health-care context. This is meant to challenge the reader to consider narrative theory but is far from a definitive application of the subject.

Intrapersonal Level

Kreps suggests that health and illness are symbols that reside intrapersonally (p. 239). I believe such symbols may possess more coherence and form than the laundry list of isolated symbols suggested. Health and illness may actually represent internal dramas with attendant plots, actors, settings, and the like. It might very well be that part of regaining health involves replacing illness narratives with healthful ones. Symbolic denial of one's health status may legitimately be a rejection of unconvincing or untenable narratives about one's role in life. The notion of AIDS as sexual/biological victimization may simply not ring true to someone who does not see himself or herself as a victim. It may therefore be easier to deny the disease than to accept a narrative that is demeaning or at odds with one's self-concept.

Interpersonal Level

Reardon believes that we "cannot effectively teach adolescents to resist smoking and drugs if we do not understand the social contexts in which they live"(p. 293). She believes that all the communication technology in the world may be wasted if their use fails to integrate the person in his or her social milieu. I suggest that narrative theory may be an effective vehicle for understanding and changing health behaviors.

Health-care practitioners might pay greater attention to the patient's story about why she or he is there. Using Reardon's example, the health professional may learn that the nagging cough is simply a by-product of the feeling of independence and power a teenager gets from smoking cigarettes. Curing chronic bronchitis in a teenaged patient may involve replacing one symbol of power for another and providing the patient with a new, more healthful narrative. Guilt and logic continue to fail miserably in this enterprise.

Organizational Level

Kreps (p. 249) believes that individuals may need assistance from others in coping with health threats. They may in fact need the information-processing resources of health-care organizations. Yet sometimes this provision is precisely the wrong road to effective coping or renewed health. Take the plight of the AIDS patient or the Vietnam veteran as cases in point. From the stories of both groups, one learns that the organizations offering help are precisely the groups that cannot be trusted. These groups' narratives of untrustworthy, if not sinister, organizations like the Veterans Administration or the Centers for Disease Control militate against help seeking.

In such cases, alternative organizations, such as vet centers and AIDS Buddies, must be offered to replace incredible characters in the patients' narratives. Narrative theory suggests that the road to improved health may not rest with disseminating information about the availability of help. Rather, renewed health may depend on a new and more elaborate story of trust and hope. It is not likely that Vietnam veterans, AIDS patients, or any others will take advantage of health care in institutions they do not believe in.

Mass Media and Societal Level

Clearly, there is no dearth of health information available to the American public. Billions of dollars are spent annually by local, state, and federal governments to promote health. But, my guess is that health promotion at the mass media/societal level fails to create a strong identification with the various audiences it seeks to reach. Narrative theory suggests that information reaches these people but fails to create an affective response. The answer may lie in the fact that people make sense out of their world via stories and not isolated or contextually sterile bits of information.

To change the habits of cigarette smokers, substance abusers, and others who routinely engage in unhealthy behaviors, we must identify with them rather than merely inform them. We must understand their world and the stories that give their world meaning. I believe that narrative theory can play a key role in this process. We should take the opportunity to explore the systematic integration of health into the human story of life.

REFERENCES

Arntson, P., & Droge, D. (1983). *The socio-political consequences of health communication research.* Paper presented to the Health Communication Division of the International Communication Association Convention, Dallas.

Bochner, A. P., & Eisenberg, E. M. (1984). Legitimizing speech communication: An examination of coherence and cohesion in the development of the discipline. In T. W. Benson (Ed.), *Speech communication in the twentieth century.* Carbondale: Southern Illinois University Press.

Conquergood, D. (1985). *Emissaries of pity, science, and progress: The epistemological and ethical issues in the intercultural encounter between Western medicine and tribal folk beliefs.* Paper presented to the Health Communication Division of the International Communication Association Convention, Chicago.

Feyerabend, P. (1975). *Against method.* London: N.L.B.

Fisher, W. R. (1984a). Narration as a human communication paradigm: The case of public moral argument. *Communication Monographs, 51,* 1-22.

Fisher, W. R. (1984b). The narrative paradigm: In the beginning. *Journal of Communication, 35,* 74-89.

Meyrowitz, J. (1985). *No sense of place: The impact of electronic media on social behavior.* New York: Oxford University Press.

Pettegrew, L. S., & Logan, R. (1987). Communication in the health care context. In C. Berger & S. Chaffee (Eds.), *Handbook of communication science.* Newbury Park, CA: Sage.

Reardon, K. K. (1981). *Persuasion: Theory and context.* Newbury Park, CA: Sage.

Smith, D. H. (1987). *The use of narrative theory in understanding bioethical issues in medicine.* Paper presented at the Second Annual South Florida Conference on Doctor-Patient Communication, St. Petersburg.

Smith, D. H., & Pettegrew, L. S. (1986). Mutual persuasion as a model for doctor-patient communication. *Theoretical Medicine, 7,* 127-139.

Watzlawick, P., Weakland, J., & Fisch, R. (1984). *Change*. New York: W. W. Norton.
Weick, K. (1983). Organizational communication: Toward a research agenda. In L. Putnam & M. Pacanowsky (Eds.), *Communication and organizations: An interpretive approach*. Newbury Park, CA: Sage.

SECTION 4

ORGANIZATIONS: MEDIA AND EMPOWERMENT

8 Meaning and Action in the Organizational Setting: An Interpretive Approach

JOSEPH J. PILOTTA
TIMOTHY WIDMAN
SUSAN A. JASKO
Ohio State University

Building on a review of the traditions that led to the cultural perspective and treating organizations as frameworks, this article uses Luhmann's neofunctional model as the conceptual device to illuminate cultural theory. Organizational cultures are seen as systems of signification and as communication media by which the premises of action are developed, maintained, and transmitted.

EMPLOYING the concept of culture in the study of organizations raises a number of important questions. For instance, in what ways do organizations resemble cultural systems communicating meaning across time? Is there a unit of analysis in the organizational setting that corresponds, even if only roughly, to the usages of culture by social and symbolic anthropology? How do the cultural texts, reputed to underpin organizational discourse, get created? Are research practices constructed around the concept of organizational culture necessarily forced to take the form of ethnographies? Are these methods capable of producing insights into underlying communication processes? Can interpretive methods focused upon the cultural aspects of organizational life be employed to examine the practical factors with which organizational members must continually cope?

Organizational culture has provided an opportunity for advocates of interpretive approaches to gain a foothold in the organizational arena. Theory development with respect to the concept of organizational culture is certainly a desideratum. In too many cases, however, interpretive methodologies appear more intent upon exorcising the ghosts of positivism and functionalism than upon articulating principled methodologically and theoretically accountable tools of their own. Therefore, even while accepting the legitimacy

Correspondence and requests for reprints: Joseph J. Pilotta, Department of Communication, Ohio State University, Columbus, OH 43210.

Communication Yearbook 11, pp. 310-334

of the "cultural perspective," it is also acknowledged that adequate theoretical explication of this perspective remains unavailable. Given its underdevelopment as a theoretical framework, reasoned assessment of the research outcomes emanating from the cultural perspective must await clarification of some of the core concepts attached to this perspective.

For present purposes, the explanations offered here presume the three following points. First, we distinguish between the social-psychological perspective and the communication perspective to delineate a "cultural" domain within organizational theory and research. Where this differentiation of fundamental viewpoints is either absent entirely or incompletely worked through, "organizational culture" will yield products like atheoretical ethnographies, reformulations of traditional "climate" variables, and storytelling. Second, we believe that organizations are by nature practical domains or "action frameworks." Consequently, the cultures of organizations are first of all functional configurations and performances, and only secondarily rhetorical or even mythopoetic phenomena. Third, organizational culture serves the maintenance and development of organizations by providing important ordering mechanisms that further the organization's domination of complex information environments.

The point of view elaborated in this chapter draws liberally upon contemporary European phenomenology within the Husserlian tradition. It employs especially Niklas Luhmann's neofunctional system's model, which contains a particularly elegant extension of phenomenological principles in application to the analysis of social action systems. The chapter highlights generalized communication processes at work in organizational life that furnish the raw material molded by particular organizations in creating their particular cultural forms. Because this cultural process is a communication process before it is a social-psychological process, the discussion begins by distinguishing between questions more appropriate to social psychology than to communication, and by briefly characterizing organizational research traditions in light of this distinction. Next, the discussion offers a specific intepretation of the "cultural perspective" that treats it as a functional construct bound by the practical requirements of achieving tasks, producing products, and effecting organizational aims in its environment. Finally, the chapter surveys some particular ways that cultural meanings "work."

THE PROBLEMATIC OF
ORGANIZATIONAL COMMUNICATION

For conceptual as well as practical reasons, the field of human communication needs to develop a more clearly communication-based perspective of formal organizations and organizational behavior. To this end, it is necessary to begin by distinguishing such a perspective from a standpoint of organizational research based upon social psychology. Organizational communication research has looked at issues related to, but apart from, that of communication at the level of the organization. It has examined interpersonal communication among individual members of organizations, and sought to measure that interaction through employee self-reports and an assortment of observational protocols, or in terms of productivity and efficiency. Only rarely has the literature suggested that organizational communication might involve a level of communication that differs significantly from interpersonal or group interaction. The absence of a clear distinction between social psychological and communication perspectives has resulted in this heavy dependence upon interpersonal and small group designs by communication research and theory treating organizations and organizational behavior.

For social psychology, the primary object of analysis consists of intra-individual psychological processes; these processes are by definition hidden to the researcher. Consequently, the social psychological researcher turns to communication behaviors and employs them as *indicators* for the purpose of accessing psychological events. But regardless of how much effort is devoted to interpreting communication behaviors, it is ultimately the underlying psychological processes that the social psychologist is interested in. Psychological observations and theories about them establish the baseline for any explanation about actual behaviors and fix the guidelines for any possible interventions. In other words, from the standpoint of social psychology, communication behaviors and events are *secondary* operationally and *derivative* causally. Human psychological behavior forms the major object of concern for social psychological investigation.

Even among current writers and organizational researchers, there is a persistent and sometimes overwhelming tendency to fall back upon speculation and description of these inner and hidden psychological properties and occurrences when examining communication in the organization. Often, where these are not descriptions of communicator traits or context stimuli, the resulting analyses are remarkably similar to literary analysis. For present purposes, it is important to acknowledge that although the social-psychological aspects of human communication are fascinating and undeniably contribute to our self-understanding as communicators, such accounts of communication behavior do not augment our knowledge about how meaning is shared and structured among individuals; instead they describe how individuals *experience* the transference of that meaning. Little or nothing is disclosed about the transference process itself or about its social construction. Examination of the communication process needs to emphasize the extra-psychological, the extraindividual aspects of meaning transmission. An emphasis upon process characteristics views communication behaviors and events as operationally primary and causally effective. In other words, communication processes take precedence over individuals, whether singly, in dyads, or in groups.

In the first chapter of *Organizations and Communication: An Interpretive Approach,* Karl Weick (1979) assumes the considerable task of presenting possibilities for the development of a new research agenda for researchers examining organizational phenonena. He begins by reminding the reader about Berstein's description of the field of organization communication as "a discipline in search of a domain" (Putnam & Pacanowsky, 1983, p. 2). For any communication researcher seeking to address some aspect of organizational research, this reminder is still the place to begin (Etzioni, 1971; Goodall, 1984; Perrow, 1979; Peters & Waterman, 1982; Warren, 1984).

What is the province of organizational communication? It is the question that arises from the lines of research reports, journal articles, and conference papers, amidst which one quickly becomes lost in a sea of variables, of aspects of behavior frequently encountered in the organizational setting. Such studies offer examinations of cohesiveness, conflict, competition, task orientation, leadership emergence, fantasy themes, and the relationship between groups within the larger organizational structure. These all represent applications and elaborations of social-psychological models.

The examination of group behavior focuses inevitably upon the behavior of the individuals composing that group, more specifically upon how individual behaviors are affected by group dynamics. It presupposes a circular model, the outgrowth and extension of the interpersonal model, that is, of the dyad. To the degree that that model is based upon a mechanistic model including feedback loops, channel noise, and an (assumed) separation between the message and the medium/channel, it thereby focuses the research questions upon isolated communicators in highly contextualized circumstances. The communication variables in this setting are characteristics of idiosyncratic communication performances. In short, the focus is upon the trees and not the forest.

From the positivistic tradition, in an attempt to import and impart scientific objectivity and rigor in the examination of human social phenomena, quantitative methods and assumptions were applied to studies of individuals, groups, and organizations/institutions. One immediately thinks of the famous Hawthorne studies, which ironically produced the conclusion—the "Hawthorne Effect"—demonstrating that effects are not so simply anticipated when the research object is human behavior (in that case, productivity). Structural and mathematical models continue in the literature surrounding research about organizations, and often form an important part of the curriculum of MBA programs.

An interest in structure as the defining characteristic of organizations has yielded an emphasis upon hierarchy, authority, power, and control, with the complementary view of employees as unmotivated, uncommitted, untrustworthy, and unreliable. Organizational goals have been seen as dictates handed down from above via commands; thus goals are achieved through punishment and reward. It is characteristic of this research that all organizations are looked upon as essentially alike along all important dimensions (i.e., no differentiation is made as to product or to goals) and as essentially self-contained.

The human relations school of thought developed as if in reaction to this viewpoint, emphasizing worker attitudes, self-actualization, loyalty, and an assortment of lateral structures like participation in decision-making practices. The focus of attention was on leadership, communication, participation, and conflict. Individual self-expression and self-actualization and, in turn, group interaction (often in terms of leadership emergence) became the central concerns. It was assumed that because organizations are composed of individuals, understanding individuals and individuals as members of small groups will inform us about organizational behavior, and provide the basis for useful explanatory models.

Despite the differences among these viewpoints they all nonetheless share the assumption that individuals and collections of individuals constitute the ultimate building blocks of complex organizations. But, as Charles Perrow (1979) notes in his critical essay *Complex Organizations*: "One cannot explain organizations by explaining the attitudes and behaviors of individuals or even small groups within them. We learn a great deal about psychology and social psychology but little about organizations per se in this fashion" (p. 149). Taking Perrow's admonition to heart, this discussion relinquishes "individuals" as the basic unit of analysis for the study of organizations, and consequently takes issue with the use of "interaction between individuals" as the basis for the analysis of organizational *communication*. The complexities of organizing imply a form of communication much more efficient and compressed than can be understood employing models ultimately derived from face-to-face interaction.

The work of March and Simon (1958) seems at least to be hinting at a domain beyond the social psychological approaches when they observe, for example, that instead of the organization controlling the decision-making process, it controls the *premises* of decision making. March and Simon distinguish the *premises* of decision making from an individual's decision-making capacity/ability. In this way, such premises can be said to supersede individuals in given positions by establishing specific role expectations, irrespective of the individuals involved.

Extending the ideas of March and Simon, Perrow (1979, pp. 146-153) directs our attention to the notion of control within the organization. Perrow dismisses the command model and its rules-based extensions as both too simplistic as well as unreflective of accounts of actual organizational life. Perrow points out that perhaps as little as 20% of all activity in an organization can be accounted for by such obtrusive control means. He continues by applauding the insights offered by March and Simon with respect to their description of unobtrusive control mechanisms. These later mechanisms are to be distinguished from the more common control mechanisms typically employed by social scientists to explain daily organizational life: mechanisms like training, habit, socialization, standards, and peer pressure. Instead, March and Simon suggest that there is a more subtle means of control effected by decisional premises through such forms as the standardization of raw materials, the development of an organizational vocabulary, and the absorption of environmental uncertainty. It is not that socialization and professional training are examples of these premises, it is rather that these premises *ground* and *predetermine* the character of socialization and professional training. In discussing this aspect of March and Simon's work, Perrow alludes to an entire level of organizational analysis as yet incompletely examined by researchers and scholars in the field of communication.

There is significant dissatisfaction with the current state of organizational research among some theoreticians, which has been reflected directly and indirectly in the work of Karl Weick (1979). Weick takes explicit note as well of the common managerial complaint about the inapplicability of research results and conclusions to actual organizational settings. Organizational research is out of touch with important parameters determining organizational reality. Like March and Simon, Weick attempts to change current and longstanding views of organizations by applying new metaphors and by suggesting radical views of organizing as human behavior. He questions the applicability of the rational model to human individual or collective behavior. Weick also challenges traditional views about the relationship between goals or plans and action. Both rationalization and explanation, according to Weick, are accomplished after the fact of any action. Nevertheless, orders of discourse are built into those rationalizations that convincingly reflect preestablished organizational aims. In other words, first we act; second, we construct an explanation; and third, we ignore or forget that the action preceded the explanation. The mesh between the action and the supervening rationalization is achieved at the organizational level, as distinguished from the interindividual level, in such a way that rationalization functions as a simple extension of the action already undertaken.

Drawing upon March and Simon, we can suggest that this is possible, as well as not counterproductive for the organization by virtue of the shared base of premises that unobtrusively, yet efficiently and consistently, guide action selection. If this is assumed to be true, then at least two questions are raised for the organizational researcher: How are the premises created? How do these premises come to be shared? For present purposes, a third question is also relevant: Is this directly related to communication in organizations?

This chapter argues that such premises are to be found in a symbolically generalized form; that is, they are embedded in *communication codes*, which operate at the level of organizational functioning (Luhmann, 1979, 1982). As such, the analysis of these codes and of their operation offer appropriate objects for researchers interested in communication in organizations.

Recently the topic of communication in organizations has begun to be addressed from a cultural perspective. Responding to a sense of frustration on the part of the organizations themselves and perceiving stagnation of research propositions, a growing number of researchers have called attention to the metaphor of "culture" as a tool for understanding certain facets of organizations (Putnam & Pacanowsky, 1983). Utilizing interpretive methods, this effort to apply the metaphor of culture to organizations by and large suggests an attempt to encompass theoretically some evident complexities that are as yet unaccounted for by organizational communications research. These analyses, however, remain for the most part at the level of interpersonal or group interaction; they provide richer descriptive detail, but they do not furnish equivalently robust theory.

Organizational culture in many respects represents a reformulation of variables previously grouped under the heading "climate" by traditional organizational literature. Organizational culture has achieved a growing prominence in the literature and vocabulary of communication partly in response to several very popular and successful books addressing the issue of success and failure among corporations in America. Perhaps the most well-known of these volumes is Peters and Waterman (1982), *In Search of Excellence*, which presents eight governing principles for corporate success (see also Deal & Kennedy, 1982). Each of these principles is related to or embodies some aspect of organizational culture; that is, the principles identify and describe unwritten, lived rules of daily activity characterizing "successful" corporations (as defined by the authors). But, in fact, the book's net effect amounts to anecdotal description of the paradoxes resident in organizations. Although enjoyable, the book's practical implications are unclear, and its heuristic value not established. Nonetheless, by pointing out those resident paradoxes, the book holds a clue for scholars concerned with identifying communication processes operating at the level of the organization; for the effectiveness of these paradoxes in creating successful organizations points to an ambiguity that can be resolved only at some other level of communication analysis.

At the organizational level, communicating a selected, preferred meaning involves a task of managing such tremendous contingencies that even language is overburdened. Yet this task is essential to the process of routinizing face-to-face interaction, making possible the stabilization and development of organizations. Communication within an organization must occur *not only* at the interpersonal level.

Perhaps, as some have suggested, communication of this sort in organizations occurs at the level of culture. While this is an intriguing proposition, actual applications of the cultural metaphor to organizations by communications researchers have often neglected the very object of their research interest—namely, communication. In these cases, communication comes to mean only that collection of activities (labeled as rites and ceremonies) which the researcher has identified as symbolic in nature. Left at this level, it is easy to understand the conclusion posited by some of this research: Organizations can be comprehended only individually. While such accounts may inform us about our own culture or subcultures thereof, they do little to further our understanding of the processes taking place in organizations, which make the generation and continuity of cultural forms either necessary or possible.

Niklas Luhmann (1970, 1975, 1979, 1982) provides one possible answer to what that underlying process is and how it operates. For Luhmann, it is communication of a particular sort that makes possible all forms of social complexity. He postulates communication media codes, which are specialized, symbolically generalized codes that reduce complexity by simultaneously transmitting both a selected alternative from among multiple action possibilities and the motivation for the acceptance of that selection. Luhmann suggests, then, that communication lays at the heart of the possibility of all social complexity, including organizations.

THE CONCEPT OF CULTURE
AND ORGANIZATIONAL PROCESSES

The first task faced by the researcher who wishes to employ a cultural standpoint for the analysis of formal organizations involves deciding upon a unit of analysis for the organizational setting that corresponds, at least roughly, to already established concepts of culture. Of course, it is unlikely that "organizational culture" correlates to anything more real, though probably no less so, than does any other research dimension upon organizational life. Nonetheless, metaphors like text, fabric, system, and the like ought not to yield unneeded hypostatizations that tempt the analyst to attribute efficient causality to them. The organizational interpretive matrix, comprising such elements as symbols, legends, customs, rites of passage, and so forth, does not imply the existence within any given organization or organizational subunit of a cultural unit of analysis. In the realistic sense of a fixed, deterministic constellation, there is no set of inherited practices and attitudes that "defines those" who "belong to it" by constituting a "mighty system of circular causality" (Bidney, 1954). In other words, the empirically disclosed redundancy of perceptual patterns (mind-sets) and symbol-laden practices (customs) can mislead the researcher into supposing the existence of a self-contained communication circuitry that artificially generates social cohesion by regulating and, to some important degree, regimenting the behaviors and beliefs of organizational actors.

Keeping these caveats in mind, organizational culture can be defined as follows: *Organizational culture consists primarily of an open-ended context framed by significant symbols and modes of legitimated social action that enables selective responses to changes in the communication environment.* This definition of organizational culture does not presuppose a particular a priori distinction between intraorganizational and extraorganizational communication relationships or one between formal and informal interpersonal relationships within organizations. Such distinctions are instead regarded as changeable empirical delimitations forming important components of the frameworks that are constructed differently from organization to organization and from environment to environment.

The principal conceptual and research orientations suggested by this definition of organizational culture can be summarized as follows:

(1) Attention must be paid to the rich diversity among organizations instead of swallowing them up as a whole into an image of formal organization that deprives actual organizations of their intrinsic content. From the cultural perspective, what is interesting is not so much the structural composition of formal organizations as the largely ad hoc generation of meaning-networks that binds each of them idiosyncratically. Conversely, what is held in common by different organizations are the communication process characteristics that furnish the mechanisms for the stabilization of viable cultural forms.

(2) Bureaucratization should be regarded as a set of *social* relationships composed of meaningful behaviors and not only as the formalization of an isolated communication system. This requires a historical and structurational perspective upon organizational bureaucratization that treats it as a purposive human enterprise. This perspective views organizational goals/ends as internal parameters within the interpretive context delineated by the organization and suggests the variability and indetermination of environmental ends by defining them as historically situated dependent variables construed by the interpretive process.

(3) The relational communication functions performed by an organization with respect to external (so-called peripheral) social forms as well as with respect to the various intraorganizational subgroupings (subsystems) indicates the importance of the services performed by both symbolic differentiation and of the legitimation of interest for the comprehension of organizational behavior from any particular vantage point, either inside or outside the organization. Stated in simpler terminology, organizational cultures are not seamless fabrics; any standpoint upon them or within them is inherently local and partial.

(4) Given the symbolic and functional character of organizational sociality, no reliable prediction of the organization's future can be ventured based solely upon knowledge about the organization's historical conditions, which are extensions of established communication structures and events. The temporal structure of organizational culture is not linear, instead it is spiral-like. The viability and effectiveness of the particular interpretive context endures only by virtue of its continuous reinterpretation and use by the organizational actors. Organizational tradition guides without governing, otherwise the least circumstantial novelty in the communication environment could in principle render the tradition ineffectual, and so vulnerable to irrelevance.

Effective employment of the concept of culture in the setting of organizations requires that we pay attention to the communicative interlocking of sense and situation in a manner that stresses cultural process as well as cultural product, and accordingly looks upon organizational culture as a field encompassing complex variations within present communication events, and not simply as an amalgam of routine traditions made up of typified communication outcomes. To this end, we propose that organizations be viewed as action systems integrated through the symbolic reproduction of generalized communication media. In so doing, the focus is upon function, communication, and relationship, rather than upon structure, position, or person.

A cultural scheme provides a setting for self, other, and world interpretation and coorientation incorporated into an elaborate system of practices and codes. Inborn predisposition and social invention, purposive ideality and mindless reality, the natural and the fabricated—each of these facets of the human landscape are linked, arrayed, selected, and integrated by a "third common term," by meaning.

Cultures can be viewed as space/time sense-making systems. Regarded in this manner, a culture consists principally of a system of codes interlocked in a semiotic ecology of interdependent communication structures and processes. When they are looked upon as simple classes of objects, human beings, natural phenomena, and technological implements coexist by fact of mere juxtaposition in space and time. But when they are regarded as elements articulated within elaborate communication systems, they take on the form of lived patterns of meaning, of distinctively cultural unities.

Signification systems express complicated combinations of sense and nonsense discriminations, of "what counts" selections, with respect to an information environment. These signification systems have gradually been fashioned over time into taken-for-granted (often seemingly autonomic) conventional grammars of contingently serviceable lived meanings. As the consequence, the "what" and "how" something is or becomes meaningful within a cultural setting depends largely upon a temporally evolved semiotic ecosystem, whose many dimensions and points of intersection include unexplored vectors of meaning orientation upon cultural self-selection.

The complicated interdependence of the many apparently distinct elements framed by the communication structures describing the semiotic ecosystem has regularly been confirmed by the complex impacts exercised by sudden internal disruptions or exogenous influences. The seemingly adventitious collateral impacts brought about by some alteration in the cultural milieu can generate entire series of unanticipated interactions and problems. The introduction of literacy or of iron weapons are well-known examples from cultural anthropology. But more to the point, much the same can be said about the advent of state capitalism at the beginning of the century or, more recently, the introduction of new technologies into the workplace or manufacturing facility, and the importing of Japanese management techniques by American firms. Novelties like these can tremendously strain the local societal capacity for ordering meanings and managing decision practices—hence, discussions about the trade-offs between adaptation versus evolutionary (change) potential.

A cultural world is never given as a totality that can become in principle an "object" of experience or investigation; but it always contains a "more" that is enacted long before it can be represented by thought. It is precisely the apparently inexhaustible human capacity to create, modify, and transform meaning relationships that underlies the complex differential sign-system articulations of their information environments and that consequently makes possible distinct cultural systems. This marvelous experiential plasticity permits the human organism to adapt situationally without thereby becoming "adapted." Cultural "continuity" is constructed upon this basic, experientially rooted sign-system flexibility. By their very nature, cultural configurations describe open-ended contexts for structured variations and innovation.

The integration or, perhaps better, the cross-fertilization of concepts of communication and concepts of culture by way of these semiotic metaphors centers upon the topics of the generation, reproduction, and transformation of bounded domains of signification complexes (actually, "intersignifica-tions"). While keeping in mind that cultures are not languages, and that linguistic analogies can lead to serious misunderstandings, still a comparison of language and culture is useful at this point. Cultures, like languages, display the capacity for complex intercombinations that construe—that is to say, retain, select, and invent—relationships between individuals, between human and natural domains, and between individuals and them-selves. They integrate complex idiolects of human experience including, to use traditional faculty psychology, cognitive, emotive, and conative features. In saying this much, however, we are already speaking from the semiological, rather than the linguistic level. At the linguistic level, strictly speaking, we encounter complicated signaling systems composed of units, combination rules, and applications; it is at the semiological level that signaling systems, and language is only one such system, serve as vehicles of signification (Lyons, 1979). In other words, using Pierce, there is no sign without signification and interpretation; signs in the semiotic sense occur only as part of the intersection of exchange, interpretation, and effect (Bailey, Steiner, & Matejka, 1980).

Thus at the level of semiotic ecosystem there exists no such thing as a "simple" culture. The forces, tensions, and competitions between avenues for meaning become concretely experienced by individual human subjects in terms of sense-making discriminations available within the cultural milieu. It is, finally, the essential contingency of the cultural communication system's reactiveness to its environment that establishes selective orientations, vectors of signification, guiding the culture's flexible management of novel physical, social, political, credal, and technological factors. Cultures change only in becoming changed; human beings are simultaneously the creatures and the creators of cultures.

Some attempts to apply the cultural perspective in the organizational setting have not successfully avoided the natural tendency to reify their unit of analysis. For example, it might be heuristically beneficial to treat organi-zations as if they were texts that require patient and skillful interrogation on the part of the analyst in order to reveal the indices of institutionalized signification embedded within them—a kind of organizational hermeneutic

(Deetz, 1982). But at the same time it is equally important that we examine the communication contingencies animating the collective authorship of these texts. How do individuals allow themselves to be convinced? How far do these texts genuinely reflect organizational life? Moreover, culture does not consist only of the transmission of complex behaviors through symbolic acquisitions, as it did for anthropologists like E. B. Tylor (1889) or Lowie (1937); it also represents a medium for concerted historical invention and individual virtuosity (Landmann, 1974). Acknowledging that the "natives" conceptualize their sociality, however naively, should also produce insight into how and to what ends they do so. The analysis of the elements composing the organizational text must be complemented by the analysis of their function.

Cultural inventions generally, and most particularly those produced by organizations, are inseparably bound up with the domain of practical necessity. Organizational culture contributes instrumental and adaptive responses to naturally occurring features of the work environment. As the result, the artifacts contained in an organization's culture, whether material or symbolic, are practical devices long before they become objects for the researcher's specialized cognitive endeavors. Context and message, structure and function, provide useful analytic distinctions; but the synchrony of codified symbol and action routine has greater significance than the diachrony of the living cultural processing of organizational interaction only from the standpoint of the nonparticipating observer. From the standpoint of the organization and its members, the relationship is exactly the *reverse*: the communication apparatus provided by significant symbols and structured interactions forms a virtual organizational memory that not only contains the organization's past but, more important, also sustains a constantly renewed and adaptable living present. Seen in this light, organizational culture furnishes organizational actors with the communication context that enables the informed case-by-case specification of the instrumental "how" of workability and the epistemic "why" of institutional rationality.

No less important than the definitional and methodological problems of how best to go about conceptualizing the cultural unit of analysis are the empirical as well as phenomenological problems of acquiring insight into (1) how the organizational texts themselves establish reliable interpretations for ongoing organizational actions and their agents, and (2) how through their daily application such texts are subjected to an ongoing process of reinterpretation that guides and is guided by the everyday intercourse of organizational members within their work environments.

But much as the unwarranted reification of social systems can be avoided by underscoring their indetermination and equifinality in responding to and manipulating their environments, a similar reification of organizational communication patterns might also be avoided if we stress the selective variability and multivocality of symbol use with respect to any organization's communicative transactions (Luhmann, 1982; Weick, 1979). In other words, principles of selection and generalization, which can be said to hold with respect to the external boundaries of organizational activity, also apply to its internal differentiations and contours (Luhmann, 1982).

Many concepts of formal organization involve notions of social hierarchy, laterality, collectivity, membership, and shared meanings. But, while justifiably acknowledging these factors, researchers often neglect the most salient characteristic of any formal organization: that it is assembled for the purpose of some particular activity, to accomplish some end through some process, to get something done. It is for this reason that organizations have goals, charters, objectives, and bottom lines. Organizations engage in task activities yielding more or less tangible products; such products may include decisions and technical services. Organizations, then, are "doing" or action environments.

According to Niklas Luhmann (1970, 1982), we can view formal organizations as articulated action systems formed within a larger and more highly complex environment. For any number of reasons, including the limitations of human beings for coping with ever present and increasing complexity in a direct (sensory) way, as well as the temporal and contextual limitations of face-to-face interactions, it is convenient and possible to regard the formation of systems as a response to the "problem" of environmental complexity (Luhmann, 1979). Social action systems, then, take shape in order to achieve the reduction of complexity; that is, they simplify life, make it controllable, manageable, comprehensible (Luhmann, 1982). In other words, social systems represent "islands of lower complexity . . . within fields of higher complexity." They encode "what counts" selections. Social systems become constituted and operate through the communication of meanings (1982).

This abbreviated description of Luhmann's functional systems viewpoint allows us to fill in between the broad brushstrokes of the image conjured by Weick's (1979) evocative statement that "Organizations enact, adapt to, and survive amidst an environment of puns" (p. 171). What Weick poetically terms "puns," Luhmann conceives as complexities that surround and arise within modern organizations. In turn, echoing Luhmann's analogy about organizations as "islands of lower complexity," Weick describes the function of organizing in the following way:

> Organizing serves to narrow the range of possibilities, to reduce the number of "might" occurs. The activities of organizing are directed toward the establishment of a workable level of certainty. An organization attempts to transform equivocal information into a degree of unequivocality with which it can work and to which it is accustomed. (p. 6)

"Possibilities" and "might occurs" are the contingencies that concern Luhmann. It is the role and function of communication media to further the system/organization's efforts at "narrowing the range" and "reduce[ing] the number" of alternative actions. It is in this way and by exactly this means that an organization is able to "transform equivocal information into a degree of unequivocality."

Pattern-engendering differentiation vis-à-vis the environment occurs through the reduction of the environment's inherent complexity. Action systems do not reproduce their environments. Although rooted firmly in their surroundings, they correspond to their environments neither structurally nor causally, any more than cultures are reducible to geography, climate, or race. Instead, action systems selectively process and reconstitute their environments through selective generalization (Luhmann, 1975).

Selective generalization has immediate theoretical application for the cultural standpoint on the study of modern organizational behavior. Experimental exercises with small groups and organizations that have introduced changes into the work environment, whether physical, social, or organizational, for the purpose of influencing productivity have been sufficiently ambiguous in their outcomes so as to suggest that social interactions are not so rigidly deterministic that specific manipulations lead predictably to dependent variations (Perrow, 1979; Luhmann, 1982). Luhmann (1982), for one, offers an alternative conceptualization of these interaction processes. "Typically a system has several alternatives at hand with which it can intercept and neutralize changes in its environment. It is precisely upon this elasticity that its stability rests, as well as its ability to find favorable conditions of existence" (p. 38).

In application to organizational culture, it is important that the concepts of selectivity and generalization not be uncritically transposed from the organic and zoological niveau to the human and social level. These concepts perform their function in fundamentally different senses in the two material regions. Selective generalization serves in the former to close the system upon its environment, while in the latter selective generalization opens the system to the environment. It is for this reason that it makes little if any sense to talk about a natural habitat with reference to human beings.

Selective generalization serves biological maintenance by establishing restrictive "filters" constraining the organism to a limited sector of the environment by making it insensitive to those features of its domain that do not act as "signals" triggering adaptive response mechanisms (compare Kohler's [1925] invariant valences embedded in rigid gestalts, Washburn's [1968] human utilization of space, Luria's [1981] analysis of animal "communication," and von Uexkull and Kriszat's [1934] discussion of "habitat"). For human beings, by contrast, selective generalization serves not to establish a mesh with the environment but rather to *constitute* it.

Selective generalization takes two general forms in cultural life: with regard to the environment "experience" and with regard to the social system "action" (Luhmann, 1982, p. 291). Selective generalization releases human beings from their surroundings by making these surroundings "available and manipulable in a meaningful way." For human beings, there exists a hiatus between inner drive and external world, which allows the human individual, in the phraseology of Plessner, to live "excentrically" by "orienting him/herself by the world" as well as "orienting the world on him/herself." Therefore, culture is enabling in the broad sense: It releases human beings from the dogmatism of their milieu.

The need to effect systemic manipulations of constantly shifting environments suggests that the identity of an organization consists in purposive adaptations achieved through processes of selection. Selections are stored, coordinated, retrieved, and recombined through repeated enactments. The vital function performed by selection in establishing the criteria for organizational integrity implies that organizations can be conceived as self-interpreting configurations of meanings. As has already been proposed the processes steering organizational self-interpretation must involve more than simply deciding between available alternatives; for such decisions already presuppose interpretation, and therefore indicate the ready application of generally accepted premises that are not themselves potential objects of choice. To attend to something past, to study it, to relate it to the present, to anticipate a future that selects a relevant past, to modify, embrace, or endeavor to eliminate what is, was, or will be; in short, the entire temporal organization of information-processing activities invariably interpretively particularizes some generalized premise.

Some of the limitations of the Weberian means/end schemes for understanding organizational decisions are implicit in these remarks. First, structure itself creates as well as manages contingency. Second, ends constitute functional variables that instruct the system in the selection of differentiation maintaining inputs and outputs. Organizations (like cultures) that fail to adapt means/ends prudently tend toward collapse; one needs to think only about the current pressures on the American automobile industry or try to imagine academic institutions stripped of the political technology of research subsidies and endowments. Third, action systems can successfully maintain more than one systems state, and therefore means/ends orientation, in relation to the same environment; this capacity is perhaps the only remaining functional difference between state and corporate capitalism. Fourth, ends are not always adequately instructive. There are always gaps in the interpretive system. Selective generalization does not provide the details of institutional and extrainstitutional arrangements. Were it to do so, the organization would risk becoming overly adapted to a particular material or symbolic situation and be therefore deprived of the very plasticity it requires for its structural integrity. Accordingly, effective management not only requires "knowing the ropes" but also their resourceful manipulation. Meaning constellations emerge and become elaborated within an organization on an ad hoc basis; they are rooted in the *accumulation of generalized selections* (including rationalizations) shaping the communication environment (Luhmann, 1975).

The role of meaning in linking organizational membership independently of individual personalities and attitudinal preferences should not be ignored in any analysis that wishes to understand organizational behavior from the standpoint of an interpretive system. Organizations, understood as systemic units of possible significations, "belong to" no identifiable party or parties affected by implicit or explicit participation in the organization, whether these be stockholders, managers, laborers, product divisions, competency- and task-differentiated departments, social and political interest mediators or regulators, the public, or whatever. Each of these represent legitimate interest roles sharing a "common" symbolic referent. The "meaning" of the organization, and consequently its ontological "what" as well as the legitimated scope of its responsibilities and its power, consists chiefly of the historically evolved communication network connecting the various interacting influence attempts undertaken by all parties sharing the organization as a common point of experiential or action reference.

Conversely, for "its" part, the organization selects and utilizes all relevant communication media within its environment, regardless of whether these are socially legitimated psychological value-codes like self-esteem, industriousness, and honesty or "material" codes like scarcity of employment opportunities or the dependence of local economies upon regular organizational inputs. Such available meaning codes are absorbed and manipulated in order to influence the premises of action for organizational members and nonmembers alike. Such environmental codes contribute significantly to the organization's ability to discover favorable conditions for existence, to neutralize irritants, and shape its environment. In exchange, the system responds selectively to external influences exercised by factors like politically mediated limitations upon market and resource exploitation, expectations about minimal working conditions, unions, community standards, competitors, philanthropic pressures, and the like.

The plasticity of the organizational system hinges upon the selective permeability of its communication horizons. This permeability in turn triggers system responses as a whole, producing differentiation along available discretionary dimensions that enable organizationally purposive adjustment to the end of maintaining maximal manipulatory latitude with respect to its environment. In this light, we might understand, for example, how the Marxist critique of corporate capitalism actually promotes the survival of the corporate system toward accommodating potentially dysfunctional contingencies in its communication environment. Through responding selectively, the capitalist system has been able to detach the issues pertaining to working-class interests from the substantive contradiction of class consciousness. By so reconstituting the corporate posture, Marxism assists the capitalists as a class in rendering Marxist polemics ineffectual among the working class. In short, to borrow upon classical imagery, Procrustes and Proteus describe limited cases of organizational communication system states.

SYMBOL AND ACTION: THE FUNCTION
OF COMMUNICATION MEDIA CODES

In *Illusions*, Richard Bach (1977) writes, "Argue your limitations, and sure enough they're yours" (p. 100). In a similar vein, Weick (1979) has observed that "people in organizations repeatedly impose that which they later claim imposes on them" (p. 153). These observations point out the mutual articulation linking organizational members and the organization, and highlight two aspects of that relationship. First, we are reminded that it is people—organizational members—who first do the imposing. Second, the original act of selection is forgotten, thereby in effect setting the reality of the organization apart from its immediate (and not just original) context of creation. Thus the "rules" of organizational life, the meaningful fabric steering individual actions and orienting collective choices, is constantly recreated by everyone and, therefore, by no one. Moreover, these ground rules informing the selection and the interpretation of organizational activity function the most efficiently when they are both invisible and condensed, therefore obviating the need for deliberate reenactment of some original circumstance. Such rules include, but are not limited to, standard operating procedures that enable the matter-of-fact handling of day-to-day work activities.

The importance of this anonymous influence, of a "communal presence," to the organization's efficiency becomes nowhere more clear than when this "text" becomes an object of conscious attention on the part of the organization's members. When it is raised to public scrutiny it becomes problematic, so that its effectiveness is impaired and can even become lost altogether. To be sure, whatever flexibility is inherent to that which remains unspoken, hence incompletely articulated, is also forsaken because constant examination and the demand for clarification institutes a far more rigid rhetorical structure than is ordinarily encountered in completing daily functions. In such a circumstance, the possibility for individual variation upon a generic interpretive template can become almost nonexistent. Rational perspective is lost because what had served as background becomes foreground, so that only foreground remains. Heretofore self-evident procedures for making sense of action and information become muddled. The organizational environment, previously apparently ordered and balanced, now seems confusing and inordinately complex.

As part of the requirements for functioning effectively, the organization needs to possess mechanisms that communicate meanings that order the options available to the various individuals within the system. As a vehicle for sending clear messages that create the expectation for preferred organizational meanings, namely, guiding choice, the language code is insufficient. By its very nature, language contains both the possibility for affirmation (compliance) and for negation (rejection). The more complex the action system, the greater the need for a functional differentiation between the language code in general and special, symbolically generalized communication media like power, trust, truth, or money. Such media condition and regulate the motivation for accepting offered selections across entire ranges of different contexts. These devices consequently greatly increase the efficiency of the system by instituting collectively taken-for-granted reality constructs.

In part, generalized constructs of this sort account for what researchers have described as the "climate" of a given organization—for example, the intangible quality of AT&T that distinguishes it from IBM, especially in the mind of the organizational member. It accounts for things like company philosophy, for "the way things are done," for both typical behaviors and the deviations that are permitted to coexist. It accounts for the 1001 day-to-day actions that ensure that business is conducted in an unassuming, dependable, and self-perpetuating manner. It is the stuff that "is" the organization; the living matter that, like the cells in the body, renews itself through passing along the patterns containing blueprints for the entity's structure and purposes. It frames a composite of individual units that is nonetheless more than their simple collection, and so enables growth and adaptation. Such constructs serve as the coding scheme for the organization, and as gatekeepers monitoring ever present and changeable external and internal contingencies. A task this immense would soon exhaust the utility of language, thus specialized communication media carry out these functions for the organization.

A communication medium is defined as a mechanism for transferring meanings in addition to or as a supplement to language; it is a code of generalized symbols that guides the transmission of selections. "The theme of factual experience always relates to other possible, but unrealized, experiences. The world gains its unity solely from the boundaries of this 'et cetera' " (Luhmann, 1979, p. 52). Luhmann (1979) also states:

> Through the generalizing capacity of such media, structures of expectation and patterns of motivation are formed which make it possible for selections made by one individual to be relevant to another, in the sense that he/she is aware of them and does not treat them as an open question, but performs his/her own selections as consequences of them. (p. 48)

As such, the code guides the purposive selection from among the innumerable cues empirically present in any particular context: It filters simple context information to permit serviceable "what counts" determinations. Most important, the communication medium can perform this function so efficiently and unobtrusively that the fact that selections are actively being performed never receives a second thought. Seen in this light, communication media clearly have a motivational function; in other words, they "urge the acceptance of (the other's) selections and make that acceptance the object of expectation" (Luhmann, 1979, p. 111). When one member's selection serves simultaneously as a vehicle motivating some other member's choices, a communication medium can be said to have been formulated. A media code is self-reinforcing; it makes the following two assumptions:

(1) Media-guided communication processes bind partners who complete their own selections and know about this from each other.
(2) The transference of selections entails the reproduction of selections in simplified conditions abstracted from their initial contexts (Luhmann, 1979, p. 112).

The command/consensus dichotomy offers a convenient illustration of the kinds of processes involved. First off, commands are exceptions to the rule of procedure. Indeed, command/acceptance can actually become dysfunctional when it restricts the subordinate so severely as to negate the natural plasticity of individual initiative and competence. Second, the most effective command is doubtlessly the unspoken one. Generalized authority—or, if you prefer, the power to command—selects the other's premises of action in such a way that the subordinate anticipates on his or her own accord the appropriate activity (Luhmann, 1975). When they must be employed, spoken commands can tend to personalize superior-subordinate relations to such a degree that the persons become the theme of interaction instead of the means/end particularity of the task situation. Personalization of this sort can in turn introduce a vast array of communication contingencies that the established channels of communication may or may not be equipped to handle.

Cooperative action among different actors and elements within organizations is not as much a matter of consensus as it is a matter of the coordination of particular interests. This coordination is accomplished through the elicitation of commitments from the affected parties. Networks of mutual obligation form important, if often covert, communication systems in their own right. Commitment transforms private concerns into public themes, while permitting continued relatively free play to personal rationalization and interpretive mechanisms.

From the process standpoint, what is happening is that commitments, regardless of how obtained, generate communication structures that are indifferent albeit hardly irrelevant to individual premises (ideas, values, motives, etc.). Formally or informally achieved commitments, whatever their grounds, frame communication relationships that can readily be evaluated by the affected parties in the simplest, most immediate terms—namely, as the *irretrievable allocation of scarce communication resources*. Trust, goodwill, influence, information, command, respect, integrity, self-esteem, and the like are examples of such resources. More than that, an individual's personal evaluation of the relationship readily becomes translated into palpable behavior for organizational actors on the basis of the relative cost/benefit to each party of reneging/honoring/extending the commitment. Thus commitment secures both a basis for cooperation and a framework for evaluation against which various interests can assess their allocations.

The processes of simplification and abstraction highlighted by the nature of relational commitments presuppose symbolically generalized codes. To take the analysis one step further, the illustrations provided by Luhmann's (1979) discussion of power furnishes a clear example of the motivational role of media codes. Power serves as a communication medium by ordering situations containing binary selectivity (yes/no). Power assumes the following:

(1) Uncertainty exists in relation to the power holder's selections. In other words, for whatever reason, the power holder has more than one available option. Moreover, executing this choice produces or removes uncertainty with respect to the power receiver.
(2) Alternatives are available to the power receiver.

Power can be said to be greater if it can exert influence in the face of attractive alternatives, and it increases proportionately as there is an increase in freedom for the power receiver.

Because the function of a communication medium is to transmit reduced complexity, rather than to emphasize actual applications of power, Luhmann's (1979) perspective underscores the structuring of the other's possible selections. In this way, power as a media code regulates contingency by relating to a possible, and not merely an actual, discrepancy between the preferred selections of the power holder and power receiver, and removing that discrepancy. Power secures possible chains of effects independently of the will of the power receiver; not against the receiver's will, but indifferently/independently of that will. Because, from this point of view, power is not a cause but rather a catalyst: It accelerates events, and thereby increases the probability of the ratio of effective connections between the system and the environment. In other words, "power is an opportunity to increase the probability of realizing improbable selection combinations (Luhmann, 1979, pp. 113-114).

To recapitulate, power within an organizational (action) system exhibits the capacity to influence individual choices among available selections simply by translating preferred selections into expectations. In this way, power helps articulate and integrate the organization's "doing" environment without constraining individuals.

By defining power as a communication medium, it becomes possible to avoid concepts of power that regard it as either a possession or as an attribute of individuals. Rather, in order to employ power successfully within any organization, the individual must learn to access the power code. It is true that such theories of power abound in sociological literature, and are imported by a number of disciplines, including communication. One characteristic shared by most, if not all, of these theories is the view that power is somehow communicated, and not something that *communicates*. This is a significant and theoretically useful distinction, for it follows from this distinction that power, as a communication medium—something that "communicates"—is an extension of the organizational system much in the same way that any technology generally represents an articulated extension of its environment.

Luhmann (1979) points out that "in organizations, power creates countervailing power" (p. 179). This is to say that, speaking from a structural viewpoint, the power of subordinates resides in their position *as subordinates*. To deny in some respect the subordinate condition can become, then, a means for management to reorganize purposively the power of subordinates. This final illustration offers a vivid example of code functions.

"Employee involvement" and "worker participation" are phrases that, in retrospect, heralded the arrival of quality circles onto the scene of contemporary corporate management strategies. Although quality circles represented attempts to increase employee input into the decision-making process, and sought to engender greater employee identification with the organization, Weick sees such innovations as direct threats to the survival of an organization. Luhmann (1979) also criticizes these attempts by management to systematize, domesticate, and legislate the power of subordinates by means of "participation."

> Thus "emancipation" becomes management's last trick: denying the difference between superior and subordinate and thus taking away the subordinate's power base. Under the pretense of equalizing power, this simply reorganizes the power which subordinates already possess. (p. 180)

We could say that through the institution of quality circles, management has further elevated its own position with respect to subordinates by asserting control of the definition of the relation between management and subordinates—in this case, as one of peers. Such an assertion on the part of management in effect extends its control over the behaviors of subordinates.

CONCLUSION

It is important to recognize that the word *communication* is among the most often bandied-about pseudotechnical terms; created as a by-product of a genre of popular literature that flourished particularly in the late 1960s and well into the 1970s devoted to self-help that consisted largely of popularized psychological concepts. In many cases, "communication" became a catchall panacea through its regular employment as a social psychological Band-Aid.

The eagerness with which popular writers took up "communication" in a wide variety of contexts is matched perhaps by the efforts of scholars and researchers to dissect and more perfectly understand communication as a uniquely human process. But the perspective of communication scholars differs dramatically from that of popular practitioners, and it is at least in part this dramatic difference that accounts for the complaints from those employed in nonacademic professional organizations that the promises implicit in communication as a *slogan* do not match up with the actual accomplishments of communication as a *science* of human behavior. Each side begins from different assumptions and employs discernibly unique vocabularies, so that even should they arrive at the same conclusion, it is likely that neither party would be able to recognize the scene the other describes.

As obvious and simplistic as this point may appear, it still bears mentioning and requires a moment of elaboration. Far more than agreeing upon definitions and sharing a common set of concerns is needed to bridge this difference. For theory, research, and analysis cannot be restricted to the plane of everyday experience, as though it might somehow be of greater scientific value to limit oneself to the view from the inside, in contradistinction to the researcher's customary "outside" perspective. Instead, the lesson to be drawn here is much more troublesome to put into practice. It is that theory and research need to be informed by the "inside" vantage point while retaining the freedom to seek comprehension of a larger and more intricate picture, that is, an enlightened view from the "outside."

It seems difficult, if not impossible, to imagine an organization that is not based upon an information economy. Organizations are composites of units differentiated according to certain types of information, knowledge, and skills. Under this circumstance, there is a clear relationship between information and mobility, power and control. That it makes conceptual sense to equate information, mobility, and power reflects a significant part of daily life within the organization. But, what is important for our purposes to recognize is that elements such as these are driven by emergent, structurational communication processes.

In *The Social Psychology of Organizing* Carl Weick (1979) writes, "People in organizations repeatedly impose that which they later claim impose on them." In an important sense, this remark epitomizes what he means by the "enacted environment" of organizations (p. 153). For Weick, enactments articulate environments, such that it is more representative to say that in the case of organizations what takes place is the "invention of rather than discovery of the environment" (p. 166). It is at this point where analogies for an organization based on the relationship of an organism to its environment break down. Not only are human beings capable of altering their environments, they also are capable of creating that environment. The creation of an environment, as distinguished from sheerly inhabiting an environment, is precisely the capacity for culture.

These enactments determine the contours and character of an organization, defining at the same time external organizational borders. The cultural "text" is the totality of the guidelines employed for the interpretation of all organizational action; it grounds the "hows" and "whys" giving meaning to the already enacted "what." It is the stuff of imputed motivations in the organizational setting. Luhmann (1979) describes the relationship between social action and motive this way:

> Motives are not necessary for action, but are necessary if actions are to be comprehensively experienced. A social order will thus be much more closely

integrated on the level of the attribution of motives than on the level of action itself. The understanding of motives thus helps retrospectively in recognizing whether an action has occurred at all. (p. 120)

From an external perspective, it may not be immediately obvious why and how organizing, or some dimension thereof, can become problematic. Nor is it likely that the repercussions of such a situation are easily discernible. Organizations, particularly bureaucracies, often appear to be tremendously stable, powerfully well-rooted, and blessed by incredible inertia. Weick suggests a very different sort of an image of organizations, one that anyone with experience in formal organizations would regard as all too familiar: "Organizations enact, adapt to, and survive amidst an environment of puns" (p. 171). To be sure, the larger the organization, the more clearly this image rings true. Elaboration upon this analogy, Weick (1979) contends that organizations must find ways to deal collectively, efficiently, and reliably with equivocal information generated both externally and internally to the organization. There exists, for this reason, tremendous pressure upon the organizational system constantly to interpret and rationalize, so that there develops a great "need for context . . . to reduce the population of puns and the meaning of puns" (p. 183). This leaves open the possibility that given a shift or break in context, previously unequivocal information would likely become equivocal.

Speaking from an analytic perspective, one typically is restricted to the social psychological level; for "failed communications" raise questions such as these: "How is it possible to identify more reliably which of the meanings is intended by the speakers?" "Do individuals hang consistently onto one definition, or alternate definitions as circumstances or personal/professional roles alter?" "If organizations are such highly structured entities, then how is such instability in usage possible?" "Are definitions tied directly to roles/ positions or to the individuals, and why?" "Why is communication a topic at all?"

It is the last of these questions that is perhaps the most convoluted, and for a variety of reasons, the most intriguing: Communication is a social bonding agent, even in the case of disagreement and conflict; participation is presupposed. So how is it that communication can become a point of fracture or be blamed as a source for a variety of organizational ills? It is an amazing feat of human creativity, epitomizing our remarkable capacity as human beings to be able to transform a complicated, ambiguous, changeable information environment into one permitting dependable, even routine, exchanges of an entire spectrum of meanings. It is the wonder that lies at the heart of human communication as a discipline. It is a process presupposing that individuals step beyond their individuality, that is, get beyond immediate and idiosyncratic sensory experience. For human beings, it is the actuality of communication that undergirds the reality of their social nature.

Each individual is shaped by culture as the enabling condition of participating in his or her social milieu. Cultures, like organizations, presuppose the individual in the very instant that they surpass him or her. Still it is the reciprocal articulation that describes cultural life: In anticipating the individual, culture is anticipated by the individual. Preservation and transmission are accomplished only through use and resignification. The mere fact that the cultural text is written by no one does not change the fact that it must be written nonetheless, nor does it make any less valuable the understanding of the means, orientations, and processes through which communication processes effect its authorship. From this standpoint, organizations represent communication systems symbolically interlocking sense and situation, meaning and action.

REFERENCES

Bach, R. (1977). *Illusions: The adventures of a reluctant messiah.* Garden City, NY: Doubleday.

Bailey, E., Steiner, T., & Matejka, E. (Eds.). (1980). *Sign: Semiotics around the world.* Chicago: University of Chicago Press.

Bidney, D. (1954). *Theoretical anthropology.* New York: Columbia University Press.

Deal, T., & Kennedy, A. (1982). *The rites and rituals of corporate life.* Reading, MA: Addison-Wesley.

Deetz, S. (1982). Critical interpretive research in organizational research. *Western Journal of Speech Communication, 46,* 131-149.

Etzioni, A. (Ed.). (1971). *A sociological reader on complex organizations* (2nd ed.). New York: Holt, Rinehart & Winston.

Goodall, H. L. (1984). The status of communication studies in organizational contexts: One rhetorician's lament after a year-long odyssey. *Communication Quarterly, 1,* 133-147.

Kohler, W. (1925). *The mentality of apes.* New York: Harcourt, Brace.

Landmann, M. (1974). *Philosophical anthropology* (D. Parent, Trans.). Philadelphia: Westminster Press. (Original work published 1955)

Lowie, R. (1937). *The history of ethnological theory.* New York: Holt, Rinehart & Winston.

Luhmann, N. (1970). *Soziologische Aufklarung: Aufsatze zur Theorie Soziales Systeme.* Koln: Westdeutscher Verlag.

Luhmann, N. (1975). *Macht.* Stuttgart: Ferdinand Enke.

Luhmann, N. (1979). *Trust and power* (H. Davis, J. Raffan, & K. Roony, Trans.). New York: John Wiley.

Luhmann, N. (1982). *The differentiation of society* (S. Holmes & C. Larmore, Trans.). Cambridge: Cambridge University Press.

Luria, A. (1981). *Language and cognition.* New York: John Wiley.

Lyons, J. (1979). *Semantics* (Vol. 1). Cambridge: Cambridge University Press.

March, J. G., & Simon, H. A. (1958). *Organizations.* New York: John Wiley.

Perrow, C. (1979). *Complex organizations: A critical essay* (2nd ed.). Glenview, IL: Scott, Foresman.

Peters, T., & Waterman, R. (1982). *In search of excellence: Lessons from America's best-run companies.* New York: Warner.

Putnam, L., & Pacanowsky, M. (Eds.). (1983). *Communication and organizations: An interpretive approach.* Newbury Park, CA: Sage.

Tylor, E. B. (1889). *Primitive culture.* New York: Henry Huff.

von Uexkull, J., & Kriszat, G. (1934). *Streifzuge durch die Umwelten der Tieren und Menschen.* Berlin: J. Springer.

Washburn, S. L. (1968). One hundred years of biological anthropology. In J. Brew (Ed.), *One hundred years of anthropology.* Cambridge, MA: Harvard University Press.

Weick, K. (1979). *The social psychology of organizing* (2nd ed.). Reading, MA: Addison-Wesley.

Cultural Studies: Studying Meaning and Action in Organizations

STANLEY DEETZ

Rutgers University

C ULTURAL studies in organizations have been a focus of attention for about 10 years now. Both the conceptual and theoretical work as well as the empirical studies have raised essential questions about the nature of organizational life and how it might be productively studied. Such studies have reconceptualized the nature of communication in organizations and have given far greater significance to communication processes in organizational structure, development, and maintenance.

Certainly for some time such works were quite faddish, based on rather grand claims and advanced by a score of popular writers. Perhaps today this work is more appropriately described as fashionable—part of being appropriately modern in thinking about organizations. The question remains among many, however, as to whether there is really anything new to this work. The answer will come not from debates about whether cultural studies are different from research on climate variables (Falcione & Kaplan, 1984) but from the production of evocative, sense-making concepts and the continued production of systematic, data-based research reports.

I will confess to being somewhat disappointed in the work thus far, particularly on the second account. Most papers have presented a useful overview of new conceptions and research methods, or have provided excellent anecdotes exemplifying practices, or have provided an excellent theoretical overview and insightful anecdotes but without a dependency relationship between them. The recent work by Mumby (1987, 1988), Eisenberg (in press), and Witten (1986) may have overcome this somewhat. But, even in these works, the independence between the massive theoretical

Correspondence and requests for reprints: Stanley Deetz, Department of Communication, Rutgers University, New Brunswick, NJ 08903.

Communication Yearbook 11, pp. 335-345

apparatus and isolated insights into organizational life is still felt on a close reading. To be fair, however, this gap is far less than that felt in most social science research in organizations.

GOALS OF CULTURAL STUDIES

Cultural studies in organizations can be organized around two essential goals, each with unique projected outcomes, types of generalization, and theoretical and methodological limits. The first goal is to generate insight into basic cultural processes, to understand how human beings at this particular historical juncture organize sense and meaning in their lives, and to demonstrate how the organization of work life articulates more basic cultural processes. The second goal is to work toward the continued development and reformation of organizational practices focusing primarily on decision making within a complex changing environment with a number of "stake-holders" with competing interests. While these goals can be largely comple-mentary, they demonstrate a profoundly different interest in organizational studies. The first is preservationist in intent, trying to record and preserve a way a people have "chosen" to live meaningfully. The second is change oriented, trying to identify and enable new choices. I wish to develop each briefly here to articulate the difference such a difference makes and to frame an agenda to which the Pilotta, Widman, and Jasko work might be compared.

Organizations as Cultural Artifacts

Cultural researchers taking the first perspective assume that the task of studying organizations is not substantially different from that of the historian or anthropologist as they enter another time or place to understand, record, and preserve the particular way that people in that time and place organized their lives and meaning (Gudykunst, Stewart, & Ting-Toomey, 1985; Smircich, 1985). In this type of organizational hermeneutics, the strangeness (distantiation) of the researcher is essential to seeing, in the insiders' take-for-granted meanings and social practices, their modes of production and perpetuation. Organizations in these studies are not essentially different in form or often function from other social institutions. The meaning of life and how people manage to live in ways that their basic physical and symbolic needs are fulfilled remains central. In this sense, organizational rituals, myths, stories, and practices share more than a metaphorical relation to preindustrial tribal practices.

From an abstract standpoint, Pilotta et al. are right: These studies rarely engage in theory testing. They are not based on a deductive model. It would be in error, however, to suggest that theory is not central to this work. Internal and external validation and generalization are present. Internal validation usually follows a circular abductive process of relating the part to the whole and the whole to the part. In each turn, an individual part or observation is clarified, and in turn, enriches the more general theoretical principles that further clarify individual parts. Ultimately, this explicit conceptual understanding is sufficiently homologous with tacit "native" understandings that the researcher could "pass" as a member. This understanding makes possible certain "rule of thumb" principles such as whether the researcher can tell and understand a cultural joke.

External validation comes first from demonstrating the relationship between the organizational culture and the larger culture of which it is a part. In the extension of the part/whole relationship, both the organizational culture and the larger culture are further elucidated. Further, validation and insight arise in demonstrating the relation to cross-cultural and cross-time principles of social organization. Such a process moves both toward a universalization and particularization of meaning and action structures. Finally, meaning and action structures can be examined in their historical development, thus identifying historical continuity, mutations, and disjunctures.

The generality of these studies has always been difficult to understand from a more "traditional" social science orientation. When generalization is limited to reconstructed knowledge, these studies might not seem to have much practical extension. The real issue is whether insight gained from "concept-formation" will be given a complementary role with knowledge gained from "concept-application" (see Apel, 1973/1980; Deetz, 1982; Rorty, 1979). The understanding of human organization was greatly advanced in the prescientific day when anthropology and sociology were more like literature and philosophy (see Gergen, 1978). Generative, sensitizing theory, perhaps best seen in a concrete incident, is cumulative and general in ways quite unlike abstract theoretical generalizations.

The insightful description of a single organization does sensitize our "vision" in other organizations and our sense of being in touch with deep human needs. Ironically, such insight may be more in touch with the large number of intuitive decision-making managers (Mitroff, 1983) than are the data-based studies. The power of the good story or good joke is not based on irrationality, but on a kind of rationality perhaps best served by this type of cultural study. Given the methodological problems of sampling and the almost always flawed assumed relation between sample and population in social scientific generalizations in organizations, few knowledge production studies can be generalized beyond the particular organization. Perhaps all organizational studies must be judged on their cultural story-value and the most important thing we can know is how particular stories work as they do.

Organizational Reformation

The second type of goal characterizing cultural studies in organizations is far more applied in nature. Culture is of interest in these studies because by knowing about it we understand better how things like productivity and employee happiness occur and may be influenced. Processes of decision making are of interest since enhancing the fulfillment of human goals through organization is central. These studies differ greatly, however, in the nature of these goals and the conception of processes hindering fulfillment.

The more conservative of these studies (see Martin, Feldman, Hatch, & Sitkin, 1983; Peters & Waterman, 1982; Pondy, 1983; Wilkins, 1983) treat culture as a variable that might potentially be manipulated by managers for better fulfillment of corporate goals. The more radical studies see culture as the historically derived manner in which a cluster of competing interests play themselves out, often to the disadvantage of certain organizational stakeholders (Jehenson, 1984; Morgan, 1986; Mumby, 1988; Riley, 1983). Since an organization is composed of a number of "stakeholders," such as workers, stockholders, suppliers, and consumers, the study of culture is the study of how these interests get articulated and represented in decisions that are made.

I, of course, believe that these more radical studies have much to offer the study of communication in organizations (for development see Deetz, 1985a; Deetz & Kersten, 1983; Deetz & Mumby, 1985). Cultural studies may tell us something about the nature and production of meaning in life and may help managers make "better" decisions, but, most important, they help reveal the forces and means by which certain interests hold sway over others and human need fulfillment is distorted. Four claims form a basis for this notion. While Pilotta et al. would seem to agree with these claims, they consider none of the rather large number of studies that develop them.

(1) *Organizations are social-historical constructions.* As Pilotta et al. made clear, organizations are always human constructions—made and transformed by individuals. Yet clearly they are intrinsically interrelated with larger social, historical, and economic forces of the culture of which they are a part and they are sustained and transformed by processes both internal and external to them. Further, individuals do not in each generation construct them anew. They are made from historical "blueprints" and sustained across time by mechanisms enacted unwittingly by individuals who have only a vague understanding of either the mechanisms or their effects.

(2) *Organizations embody and represent certain human interests.* Different stakeholders have widely different interests in the organization. Each particular organizational structure, communication system, technological innovation, work design, reward structure, and environmental contact influences the representation and fulfillment of different human interests. "Whose" and "what" interests are being served must be a central question in studying all aspects of organizational life (Cameron & Whetten, 1983; Deetz, 1985a; Keeley, 1984).

(3) *Interest representation and organizational decision making often become distorted.* Normative systems, access to communication forums, universalization of sectional interests as everyone's interest, and standard

practices may lead particular interests or particular people's interests to be arbitrarily privileged. In such conditions, the organization's actions may be severed from the communities it serves and individuals' decisions may be unwittingly opposed to their own interests.

(4) *Research is to be primarily in the service of redressing distorted interest representation and enhancing fulfillment of openly selected goals.* The choice of research conceptions, questions, and methods is always value laden. Wider interest representation is morally right and necessary for positive human development (Apel, 1973/1980; Deetz, 1985b; Keeley, 1984). Cultural studies have generally done well in describing how stories, myths, symbols, and norms arise in organizations and function to create and sustain the consensus necessary for working together. They have often failed, however, to consider how these same cultural elements hide contradictions, distort the experience and expression of member interests, and create and sustain false consensus.

LUHMANN-ATING CULTURAL
STUDIES OR A TURN TO THE WEICK?

The contribution of the Pilotta et al. chapter rests principally with whether the translation of existing cultural study conceptions into Luhmann's terms can cast them into a different light and in doing so can both integrate and theoretically ground them. Unfortunately, the justification for the chapter's development is based on a curious and flawed assertion. Quoting the authors:

> Therefore, even while accepting the legitimacy of the "cultural perspective," it is also acknowledged that adequate theoretical explication of this perspective remains unavailable. Given its underdevelopment as a theoretical framework, reasoned assessment of the research outcomes emanating from the cultural perspective must await clarification of some of the core concepts attached to this perspective. (pp. 310-311)

Such an assertion is as inexplicable as the omission of any discussion of most of the major theoretical works in the area.

While there are works lacking in adequate theoretical grounding, most have been explicitly grounded in the works of major theorists such as Giddens (1979, 1982), Clegg (1979, 1981), Berger and Luckmann (1967), Habermas (1975, 1979), Jung (1959), Therborn (1980), and Lukács (1971). Even the ethnographies, which might generally eschew the heavy dependence on theoretical guidance, explicitly ground their work in theorists such as Douglas (1982), Hymes (1967), and Barthes (1957/1972). As a whole, cultural studies in organizations demonstrate considerably more theoretical concern and sophistication than most work in organizations.

Further, a certain political neutrality or even conservativism is accepted with the Pilotta et al. treatment. The authors apparently assume the

possibility of political neutrality in research methods and theoretical conceptions. It is unclear why they would hold such a position in light of the tradition
out of which they work and the presence of compelling works such as those of
Hamnett, Porter, Singh, and Kumar (1984), Gustavsen (1979), and Morgan
(1983). Luhmann's own work justifying the distinction of political concerns of
political institutions from the particular functional configuration of other
institutions is omitted from discussion here (see Luhmann, 1982). While the
authors clearly recognize the inevitable partiality (one-sided and favoring that
side) of any internal or external perspective on an organization, they never
position the research enterprise itself in relation to the organization or the
privilege associated with certain partial perspectives.

The narrow treatment of organizational culture literature and political
naivete is evident in the three central principles given by the authors. Allow me
to discuss them briefly before I turn more directly to the contribution
Luhmann's work might make.

First, the authors claim that they "distinguish between the social-
psychological perspective and the communication perspective to delineate a
'cultural' domain within organizational theory and research" (p. 311). I doubt
that any serious cultural researcher would argue against such a principle; in
fact, most would go well beyond the account given. Pilotta et al. focus on this
issue as an inadequacy of researcher conception. Nowhere in the lengthy
discussion of this principle do they attempt to account for the presence of
"psychologizing" as a cultural feature of organizations or the relation of it to
the frequent acceptance of the social-psychological research perspective in
organizational studies. The individualistic, subject-centered orientation is
useful for managerial interests in organizations for control, for blaming the
individual for structural defects, and for justifying an individual promotion
process. If perception and action in organizations is subjective in character,
only power is left to determine which perceptions and actions will rule. The
communication perspective is not only necessary in an academic sense for
creating a cultural domain for inquiry, but essential for an understanding of
power and domination in the organization at all.

Second, the authors argue that "cultures of organizations are first of all
functional configurations and performances" (p. 311). In one sense, this claim
seems almost obviously true and is certainly in line with most ethnographies
today, particularly those operating within a structural-functionalist paradigm.
As Pilotta et al. say, "Organizational culture contributes instrumental and
adaptive responses to naturally occurring features of the work environment"
(p. 321). Culture is a configuration of recipes and scripts developed and used to
accomplish specific ends. And, as Weick would add, the ends of different
actors need not be the same for them to interact and coordinate in the
production of organizational decisions. But again the analysis does not go far
enough. The organization and organizational constraints are not simply
created by actors for goal accomplishment.

Organizations are historically created structures. They are created in most cases in response to environmental problems and social needs that are past and created then to meet the needs of those in power. Secondary mechanisms frequently protect such structures from critical examination and change. The emphasis Pilotta et al. place on the individual's capacity to select from a "variability and multivocality of symbol use" (p. 321) potentially hides the sedimentation of power relations in available symbols and the limited choices available, a limitation not often experienced by the actor as enmeshed in a culture. The trick is to neither see culture as monolithic and closed nor believe that the possibility of choice is equal to actual choices in organizational contexts.

Culture "qualifies" in the double sense of enabling the actor to have and make functional choices and to be limited and one-sided in choice making. People acquire both their ends and goals as well as the means of accomplishment through acculturation. The presence of ideology denotes the absence of examination of ends or means. The gaps between real human needs and culturally inscribed ones may be great. Cultural choices may be often maladaptive and dysfunctional. The desire for a higher position, greater organizational size, rapid implementation of new technologies, or even control of a large office may be based on cultural scripts adaptive to a past and even ancient practical context, which is reproduced in the institutional memory but is highly dysfunctional in the present context. Given the presence of vested power interests and cultural reproductive mechanisms, adaptive new forms may well result more from accident or even socially described insanity than from human actors purposively selecting from multivocalic cultural codes.

Finally, the authors argue, "Organizational culture serves the maintenance and development of organizations by providing important ordering mechanisms that further the organization's domination of complex information environments" (p. 311). Unless I take the authors wrong, they are here reiterating a point in Luhmann's terms, which was made explicit and clear in Gehlen's (1956) theory of institutions and brought to organizational studies through Berger and Luckmann (1967). Since environmental complexity would overwhelm the individual sense-maker due to the lack of instinctual scripts and the openness of human perception, institutions serve to select and interpret environmental data and order choice-making. In the process, the individual acquires historically inscribed wisdom (rather than genetically inscribed wisdom) and life is made relatively efficient and effortless. Organizational cultures order work life in ways not unlike how other institutions order other aspects of life. Again, I take little issue with the basic idea, but let us play their theme out a step further.

Certainly, it is individuals who make the institutional apparatus as much as it makes them, but all organizational members do not contribute equally in the constitutive processes. In that sense, the ordering mechanisms are far more composed by the will of some and imposed on others, thus fulfilling some interests better than others. As an analogue, if astronomers owned the lens companies, we might well expect far better understanding of the stars than microorganisms. Clearly, organizations do not simply dominate complex information environments; they are built to dominate people also. Organizational information is constituted within hidden power structures and vested interests (Deetz & Mumby, 1985). To suggest that organizations manage information from complex environments without reflecting on the representational privilege particular groups enjoy misses a critical element of organizational life.

Despite inadequacies in the analysis of existing studies and the role of social research, Pilotta et al. provide useful insight into how Luhmann's conceptions can add to current theory in unique and significant ways. A careful look at Luhmann's work by U.S. organizational researchers is long overdue. Important potential contributions can come from the inclusion of concerns made clear in Luhmann's neofunctionalist systems model.

The most important and difficult conception Pilotta et al. introduce is that of "communication media." Such a conception draws attention to the systemic rather than casual connections that exist among organizational phenomena. Such "media" exist as hidden implicative structures that create "logical" dependencies among particular beliefs, perceptions, social practices, and decisions. Such networks, which include but are far more extensive than the language system, provide the relatively stable institutional background for organizational activity and meaning.

Pilotta et al. do an excellent job of developing this concept and providing examples of such systems. Like the work of the structurationists (Giddens, 1979) and rule theorists (Pearce & Cronen, 1980), this work provides insight into the deep structures of organizational life missed by the ethnographers and social psychologists. The process of change and choice is perhaps better described through this account than through the structuration model. Certainly, the impact of the historical material structure of the organization is better treated here than by the rule theorists.

Further, like structuration and rules models, a focus on "communication media" enhances a careful examination of the gap between "intention" and "effect" in organizational communication and decision making. Worker participation programs are certainly not the first organizational innovation where the advocates have had to ask whether the actual outcome is at all consistent with the intended outcome. An in-depth description of how intended outcome A becomes actual outcome B is essential. Luhmann's work holds great promise in this task.

The example analysis of power in organizations is quite instructive and is certainly in line with comparable modern works (see Mumby, 1988). Power is not a personal possession but arises out of a set of discursive relationships. The account given, however, while demonstrating the logic of meaning, does not do justice to the full force of power. Clearly, power in organizations creates "countervailing power." But all power is not equal. As an analogy, in the classroom students always have a power as students, that is, if they refuse to play student the instructor cannot play instructor. However, if there was a power struggle, I have no doubt that I would prefer to be the instructor.

If the ethnographer can provide detailed descriptions of how organizational actors think, feel, and act, Luhmann's work can describe how they come to think, feel, and act as they do through an elaborated description of the systems in which organizational actors confront life. Without a doubt, ethnographies that focus on the actor meanings motivating action need to be supplemented with a functional account of the outcome of such actions. Most cultural studies, however, have not been ethnographies. Most, like the Pilotta et al. piece, suffer more from the lack of concrete empirical descriptions of the structural mechanism by which such systems work than they do by conceptual inadequacy. To name and conceptualize such mechanisms as "communication media" is a useful step toward such descriptions. I look forward to the production of theoretically grounded studies with the descriptive richness of ethnographies.

REFERENCES

Apel, K. O. (1980). *Towards a transformation of philosophy* (G. Adey & D. Frisby, Trans.). London: Routledge & Kegan Paul. (Original work published 1973)

Barthes, R. (1977). *Mythologies* (A. Lauers, Trans.). New York: Hill & Wang. (Original work published 1957)

Berger, P., & Luckmann, T. (1967). *The social construction of reality.* Garden City, NY: Doubleday.

Cameron, K., & Whetten, D. (1983). Organizational effectiveness: One model or several? In K. Cameron & D. Whetten (Eds.), *Organizational effectiveness: A comparison of multiple models* (pp. 1-24). New York: Academic Press.

Clegg, S. (1979). *The theory of power and organization.* Boston: Routledge & Kegan Paul.

Clegg, S. (1981). Organization and control. *Administrative Science Quarterly, 25,* 545-562.

Clegg, S., & Dunkerley, D. (1980). *Organization, class and control.* Boston: Routledge & Kegan Paul.

Deetz, S. (1982). Critical interpretive research in organizational communication. *Western Journal of Speech Communication, 46,* 131-149.

Deetz, S. (1985a). Critical-cultural research: New sensibilities and old realities. *Journal of Management, 11,* 121-136.

Deetz, S. (1985b). Ethical considerations in cultural research in organizations. In P. Frost, L. Moore, M. Louis, C. Lundberg, & J. Martin (Eds.), *Organizational culture* (pp. 251-269). Newbury Park, CA: Sage.

Deetz, S. (1986). Metaphors and the discursive production and reproduction of organization. In L. Thayer (Ed.), *Communication—Organization* (pp. 168-182). Norwood, NJ: Ablex.

Deetz, S., & Kersten, A. (1983). Critical models of interpretive research. In L. Putnam & M. Pacanowsky (Eds.), *Communication and organizations: An interpretive approach* (pp. 147-171). Newbury Park, CA: Sage.

Deetz, S., & Mumby, D. (1985). Metaphor, information, and power. *Information and Behavior, 1,* 369-386.

Douglas, M. (1982). *Natural symbols: Explorations in cosmology.* New York: Pantheon.

Eisenberg, E. (in press). Conflict at Disneyland: A root-metaphor analysis. *Communication Monographs.*

Falcione, R., & Kaplan, E. (1984). Organizational climate, communication, and culture. In R. Bostrom (Ed.), *Communication yearbook 8* (pp. 285-309). Newbury Park, CA: Sage.

Gehlen, A. (1956). *Urmensch and Spatkultur.* Bonn: Athenäum.

Gergen, K. (1978). Toward generative theory. *Journal of Personality and Social Psychology, 36,* 1344-1360.

Giddens, A. (1979). *Central problems in social theory.* Berkeley: University of California Press.

Giddens, A. (1982). *Profiles and critiques in social theory.* London: Macmillan.

Gustavsen, B. (1979). Liberation of work and the role of social research. In T. Burns, L. Karlsson, & V. Rus (Eds.), *Work and power* (pp. 341-356). Newbury Park, CA: Sage.

Gudykunst, W., Stewart, L., & Ting-Toomey (Eds.). (1985). *Communication, culture, and organization processes.* Newbury Park, CA: Sage.

Habermas, J. (1975). *Legitimation crises* (T. McCarthy, Trans.). Boston: Beacon.

Habermas, J. (1979). *Communication and the evolution of society* (T. McCarthy, Trans.). Boston: Beacon.

Hamnett, M., Porter, D., Singh, A., & Kumar, K. (1984). *Ethics, politics, and international social science research: From critique to praxis.* Hawaii: East-West Center and University of Hawaii Press.

Hymes, D. (1967). Models of the interaction of language and social setting. *Journal of Social Issues, 2,* 8-28

Jehenson, R. (1984). Effectiveness, expertise, and excellence as ideological functions: A contribution to a critical phenomenology of the formal organizations. *Human Studies, 7,* 3-21.

Jung, C. G. (1959). *Archetypes and the collective unconscious.* Princeton, NJ: Princeton University Press.

Keeley, M. (1984). Impartiality and participant-interest theories of organizational effectiveness. *Administrative Science Quarterly, 29,* 1-25.

Luhmann, N. (1982). *The differentiation of society* (S. Holmes & C. Larmore, Trans.). New York: Columbia University Press.

Lukács, G. (1971). *History and class consciousness* (R. Livingstone, Trans.). Cambridge: MIT Press.

Martin, J., Feldman, M., Hatch, M., & Sitkin, S. (1983). The uniqueness paradox in organizational stories. *Administrative Science Quarterly, 28,* 438-453.

Martin, J., & Powers, M. (1983). Truth or corporate propaganda: The value of a good war story. In L. Pondy, G. Morgan, P. Frost, & T. Dandridge (Eds.), *Organizational symbolism* (pp. 93-107). Greenwich, CT: JAI.

Mitroff, I. (1983). *Stakeholders of the organizational mind.* San Francisco: Jossey-Bass.

Morgan, G. (1986). *Images of organization.* Newbury Park, CA: Sage.

Morgan, G. (Ed.). (1983). *Beyond method.* Newbury Park, CA: Sage.

Mumby, D. (1987). The political function of narrative in organizations. *Communication Monographs, 54,* 113-127.

Mumby, D. (1988). *Communication and power in organizations: Discourse, ideology, and domination.* Norwood, NJ: Ablex.

Pearce, W. B., & Cronen, X. (1980). *Communication, action and meaning.* New York: Praeger.

Peters, T., & Waterman, R. (1982). *In search of excellence: Lessons from America's best-run companies.* New York: Harper & Row.

Pondy, L. (1983). The role of metaphors and myths in organization and in the facilitation of change. In L. Pondy, P. Frost, G. Morgan, & T. Dandridge (Eds.), *Organizational symbolism* (pp. 157-166). Greenwich, CT: JAI.

Riley, P. (1983). A structurationist account of political culture. *Administrative Science Quarterly, 25,* 414-437.

Rorty, R. (1979). *Philosophy and the mirror of nature.* Princeton, NJ: Princeton University Press.

Smircich, L. (1985). Is the concept of culture a paradigm for understanding organizations and ourselves? In P. Frost, L. Moore, M. Louis, C. Lundberg, & J. Martin (Eds.), *Organizational culture*. Newbury Park, CA: Sage.

Therborn, G. (1980). *The ideology of power and the power of ideology*. London: Verso.

Wilkins, A. (1983). Organizational stories as symbols which control the organization. In L. Pondy, G. Morgan, P. Frost, & T. Dandridge (Eds.), *Organizational symbolism* (pp. 81-92). Greenwich, CT: JAI.

Witten, M. (1986, May). *Storytelling and obedience at the workplace*. Paper presented at the annual meeting of the International Communication Association, Chicago.

The Cultural Perspective:
New Wave, Old Problems

SUE DeWINE
Ohio University

S TUDYING organizations from a cultural perspective has become the latest "new wave" in social science research. In the beginning of the Pilotta, Widman, and Jasko article a number of questions are raised about this approach, but one stands out as particularly important: "Can interpretive methods focused upon the cultural aspects of organizational life be employed to examine the practical factors with which organizational members must continually cope?" (p. 310). Interpretive methods often appear to provide more insights for the researchers than for the practitioners. An additional question that might be asked is, "Are we writing for ourselves because we are intrigued with our own thoughts or are we writing for the benefit of those working in the cultures we are attempting to study?" Unfortunately, Pilotta et al. appear to fall prey to the very criticism they have of other research efforts: "Interpretive methodologies appear more intent upon exorcising the ghosts of positivism and functionalism than upon articulating principled methodologically and theoretically accountable tools of their own" (p. 310).

One might also add that, in addition to a lack of clearly articulated methods for interpretive research, there is very little attempt to demonstrate how the few tools that are available might be applied. The Pilotta et al. article is another in a long line of writings suggesting that interpretive research is an appropriate approach for organizational communication researchers but provides no example of research efforts carried out within this framework.

This commentary, first, identifies pragmatic problems I have uncovered in conducting interpretive and cultural research and assesses the criticisms leveled

AUTHOR'S NOTE: I wish to thank the following individuals for their comments on an earlier draft of this article: Tom Daniels, Anita James, and Chad Compton.

Correspondence and requests for reprints: Sue DeWine, School of Interpersonal Communication, Ohio University, Athens, OH 45701.

Communication Yearbook 11, pp. 346-355

against traditional empirical research formats. Some of these criticisms are justified and others are evangelistic persuasive techniques. Next, "commandments" of the Pilotta et al. article for doing culture research are critiqued. Finally, the article develops criteria for selecting appropriate research methods and avoiding one of Dickens's (1983) laws of experimental research: "The best test of a true experimentalist is his [sic] ability to present as foresight what he has learned from hindsight" (p. 73), or for an interpretive researcher, presenting as foresight what he or she should have inductively derived only from the data set.

IN WITH THE NEW

Interpretive theorizing appears to be far more attractive than interpretive methods. When one attempts to use an interpretive approach, many pragmatic issues arise. In an attempt to provide some examples of interpretive research projects, five studies are examined below. While the results frequently provided "rich" insights, potential drawbacks to applying the interpretive approach are identified.

In the first study, stories were collected in 450 interviews in an attempt to understand a community phenomenon as a myth (DeWine et al., 1984). The task of training interviewers and managing a large research team in order to complete this study would discourage most researchers. The year-long effort to collect data also meant a longer commitment on the part of the research team. Albrecht and Ropp (1982) allude to the same issue: "Such a strategy (interpretive research) is clearly ambitious and means physical and economic demands on any research team" (p. 178).

In a second study (Ugbah, Brammer, Compton, Ray, & DeWine, 1985), the researchers observed individuals, interviewed workers, and the subjects completed more conventional research instruments to study innovation in organizations, change agents, and their communication style. Trying to collect qualitative and quantitative data at the same time was somewhat awkward. Interpretive data required that the researchers be present on site to observe and talk with employees. Quantitative data required that employees fill out rather conventional survey questionnaires. It was never clear if the interviews affected the subjects' responses on the questionnaires or if the responses to the questionnaire affected later interactions with subjects and observations of behavior.

In a third study (DeWine et al., 1985), a research team transcribed tape recordings of interviews conducted with teachers in an attempt to understand how females develop sources of power in male-dominated organizations. Once again, interpretive data as well as qualitative data were collected. Researchers observed teacher behavior in interviews, classrooms, and informal gatherings. In order to obtain a cross section of school districts, five different school systems were used. This sampling required a team of six researchers to manage the interview schedule. Making sense of the volume of transcriptions almost became overwhelming.

In the fourth study (Perotti, Lukens, & DeWine, 1985), two emerging organizations were studied for the early development of an organizational culture. Folk heroes, myths, and symbols were compared and predictions were made about the impact each developing culture might have on the success of the organization. We concluded that one organization would probably not succeed because it failed to understand the importance of its emerging culture. Actually, within two years, both organizations had folded. Instead of studying organizational culture, perhaps, a financial statement would have been a better predictor of success for either organization than the developing culture.

Finally, interpretive methods were used to further our understanding of the impact of technology on human communication systems (Compton, Hendricks, White, & DeWine, 1986). There were three other parts to the research project including aversion to computers and nonverbal dependency (White, Flint, & DeWine, 1986), message tracings with electronic mail (Porter, Reindl, & DeWine, 1986), and adequacy of information and the impact of technology (Compton, Ugbah, & DeWine, 1986). Subjects were invited to discuss their reactions to computers both in their personal lives and in the work environment. While we found the conclusions quite interesting, it is doubtful that the subjects were led to any new insights. In fact, top-level executives were uncomfortable with employees talking about how computers had changed their lives, and the executive officers of information technology were fearful that some might reveal culturally undesirable uses and effects of computer-mediated communication. The notion that Geertz (1973) promotes, that researchers should collect "thick descriptions" of interpretive data, was unrealistic in this case.

In comparison to more traditional research methods, the practical problems associated with interpretive methods seems to be focused on the extensive amount of time necessary to collect and analyze the data, the effort of managing larger research teams, the problems of collecting qualitative and quantitative data at the same time, and the struggle to help the subjects to understand the intent of such approaches. Of course, the difficulty of subjectively merging the research team's individual assessments of the data is an ever present problem. The question is, Are the results significantly engaging and useful to warrant resolving the difficulties of collecting the data? Are the arguments against traditional research methods sufficiently compelling to warrant their abandonment?

OUT WITH THE OLD?

Certainly social science research has been attacked before for its shortcomings. Many authors have argued that there is too large a dependence on cross-sectional studies with the use of single instruments measuring self-report perceptual data (Campbell & Fiske, 1959; Monge, Farace, Eisenberg, Miller, & White, 1984) and that too many studies in communication have been laboratory-experimental (Miller, 1983). The very instruments we use may indeed be flawed since many have not been tested for reliability and validity (DeWine & Pearson, 1985a, 1985b).

Some researchers have demonstrated that what we may conclude are causal relations between variables in traditional research efforts may in fact be causal reversals due to the manipulation of the variable itself (Farino, 1987; Staw, 1975). The Pilotta et al. article addresses an additional concern of many that we are confusing communication with social-psychological processes.

While these concerns are justified, some zealots have been carried away with their mission. Pilotta et al. suggest that any interest in structure results in a nonhumanistic view of organizations. "An interest in structure . . . has yielded an emphasis . . . [on the view] of employees as unmotivated, uncommitted, untrustworthy, and unreliable" (p. 313). They also insist that to study the interaction between individuals is to study psychology. They "tak[e] issue with the use of 'interaction between individuals' as the basis for the analysis of organizational *communication*" (p. 314). While I concur that some of the communication literature has focused more on personality character-istics and internal processes than the transactional nature of communication, I will not agree that the study of the interaction between individuals is the study of the psychology of the interaction. They go on to say that the organiza-tion "controls the *premises* of decision making. . . . [and that is] distinguish[ed] . . . from an individual's decision-making capacity" (p. 314), but gives us no clear idea of how one would go about studying the "decision premises" of an organization. Moreover, what makes that a communication study? Until we can more clearly articulate how these theoretical frameworks are put into practice, then, it appears that only Pilotta et al. can understand them. Instead, we are given "commandments" for doing interpretive research.

Commandments of Cultural Research
According to Pilotta, Widman, and Jasko

Thou shalt focus on the organization rather than on individuals within the organization. Exactly how does one go about studying the organization without starting with individuals? How would one study the "subtle means of control effected by decisional premises . . . the development of an organi-zational vocabulary, and the absorption of environmental uncertainty" (p. 314)? Pilotta et al.'s work would have been far more useful had they demonstrated rather than simply commanded.

Thou shalt follow these models. The Peters and Waterman (1982) and the Deal and Kennedy (1982) texts are the only examples of interpretive research cited in this article. There is very little documentation in either text that describes the process used to select "excellent" or "best-run" companies. The methods used to collect data and reach conclusions are a mystery. Are these the models we are to follow? The Putnam and Pecanowsky (1983) text at least gives us approaches to cultural research from a communication perspective. However, this text also lacks demonstrations of the method itself. Pacanowsky's "Small Town Cop" at the end of the text could be called a model, but the method seems uniquely suited to the author.

Weick (1979) claimed that traditional research covers only 20% of what is actually happening. Ironically, recent evidence suggests that Weick's model covers only about 20% of interaction behavior in a group process event (Rauschenberg, 1986). The purported models we have available for conducting interpretive research appear to be missing the mark altogether or are woefully inadequate.

Thou shalt call this culture. I have claimed elsewhere that culture research appears to be nothing more than organizational climate research with a "new wave" title (DeWine, 1986). In fact, Pilotta et al. make this connection as well: "Organizational culture in many respects represents a reformulation of variables previously grouped under the heading 'climate' by traditional organizational literature" (p. 316). What is it that makes organizational culture research unique? Deal and Kennedy (1982) suggest studying folk heroes and rituals that sound suspiciously like informal leaders and organizational procedures. I am not sure we have any clearer idea after reading the Pilotta et al. article. What does a "communication media code" look like in an organization? How do you recognize it when you see it? Before researchers can develop "commandments" for doing interpretive research, they have to be able to identify for the rest of us what it is they are studying.

THE WAY OF INTERPRETIVE METHODS

Pilotta et al. are not the first to support interpretive research for organizational communication. The interpretive approach to studying organizations has been heralded as "the way" to examine organizations. Bochner and Kreuger (1979) suggested that methods employed by "renegade" ethnomethodologists might be useful in establishing the contextual dimensions of communication. Numerous "renegade" authors have "proclaimed" the virtues of interpretive approaches to organizational communication (Brockriede, 1978; Deetz, 1982; Pacanowsky & O'Donnell-Trujillo, 1982; Putnam & Pacanowsky, 1983; Smircich, 1983). Weick (1979) charged that much of organizational research is method specific. "Both labs and surveys, when used alone, mislead us because they do not capture content effects" (p. 21). Denzin (1978) referred to the use of more than one method in the study of a phenomenon as "triangulation." Faules (1982) called for the use of multiple methods to study organizations and Jick (1979) maintained that such triangulation allows the researcher to "capture a more complete, holistic, and contextual portrayal of the unit(s) under study" (p. 603). While many researchers have called for interpretive approaches in conjunction with more traditional methods, few have actually attempted to use the methods they write about.

Albrecht and Ropp (1982) adopted the triangulation method, as did Tompkins and Cheney (1982) and Perotti, Lukens, and De Wine (1985). Perotti's (1986) conclusion, after an extensive use of various research methods, was that "the most heuristic outcomes of this study are judged to have emerged from the interpretive data generated through non-directive interviews" (p. 150). Even early efforts at communication audits revealed that the interview data provided a richness of understanding that was overlooked in the survey data (DeWine, James, & Walence, 1985). The difficulty is in trying to merge the two forms of data and in following the more abstract approaches to understanding organizations.

In Perotti's (1986) study, subjects were nominated by the chief executive officers of organizations as either "competent" or "noncompetent" communicators. Those individuals were interviewed and their communication behaviors observed. Signs and symbols used by executive officers helped reveal their definition of communication competence. A criterion reference test along with a self-report survey was also administered. Thus the researcher was attempting to follow the dictates of others in the workplace. It was not possible to "merge" the data. In fact, what resulted were two sets of results derived from two different methodological approaches.

Besides the difficulty of reconciling data collected under two or more different mind-sets is the problem of attempting to operationalize some of the "commandments" of the supporters of this approach. For example, exactly how would one go about operationalizing this view of organizations: "Organizations [should] be viewed as action systems integrated through the symbolic reproduction of generalized communication media" (Pilotta et al., p. 319) or "organizations can be conceived as self-interpreting configurations of meanings" (p. 324).

Certainly, in all of the previously cited cases of interpretative/cultural research conducted by myself and others, I think the researchers came away with a different understanding than would have been possible based only on quantitative data. Interpretive methods allow the researcher to enjoy a sense of the environment in which others work and to observe the subtleties and nuances of communication behavior in that organization. This type of data cannot be collected in a multiple response survey instrument. However, the data collected must ultimately be useful to the individuals working within that culture. This is what I find wrong with the Pilotta, Widman, and Jasko article. Statements like "theory, research, and analysis cannot be restricted to the plane of everyday experience, as though it might somehow be of greater scientific value to limit oneself to the view from the inside, in contradistinction to the researcher's customary 'outside' perspective" (p. 331) are not productive. Why isn't it important to understand everyday experience? I am a researcher because I want to understand my life better and function in my environment more effectively. If I can help others function better within their environments, then I suspect that we are fulfilling the mission of research.

A MODEL

How should we select the most appropriate approach to answer what we feel are significant and worthwhile questions? First, we need clearly articulated methods for studying organizational cultures. If researchers conduct in-depth interviews, "shadow" or observe employees, tape record conversations, and examine internal documents, are there clearly defined methods for analyzing that data from the communication discipline? Can researchers more clearly explain how one studies "organizations [as] self-interpreting configurations of meanings" (Pilotta et al., p. 324)? What is unique about the field notes of a communication ethnographer that will make this a communication-focused study rather than a social-psychological study?

Second, we need to generate more case examples. As Weick (1980) suggests, "First generate some work, then see what standards apply to it. When we have a prototypic case, we can then devise standards that are appropriate to this substance and medium" (p. 14).

Third, we should spend less time arguing the merits of various research paradigms and more time using them. As Miller and Sunnafrank (1984) suggested when analyzing applied and "pure" research, "There is no necessary disjunction between these two types of research" (p. 255). While there is a distinction between the worldviews of empirical and interpretive researchers, enough has been written on that distinction already. We should get on with the task of demonstrating what these approaches can yield in theory development, model building, and practical applications.

Finally, we need to develop a set of criteria for selecting research methods. In order to judge the usefulness of any research effort, Thomas and Tymon's (1982) criteria might be applied: descriptive relevance (Are we examining phenomena that the practitioner is likely to encounter in his or her organization?); goal relevance (Are the variables being examined those that organizational members want most to influence?); nonobviousness (Are we only studying the obvious?); and timeliness (Are our research results available to organizational members in time for them to use them to deal with problems?). Admittedly, these criteria reek of "applied research" with users who have been referred to as "abusers of the substantive knowledge and methods of inquiry produced by the scholarly community . . . snake oil salesmen who distort and twist knowledge for personal gain" rather than the images of "persons of unquestioned ability and impeccable ethics pursuing essential theoretical work" (Miller & Sunnafrank, 1984, p. 255). Obviously both images are off base. I would ask again, Are we writing for ourselves because we are infatuated with our own thoughts or are we studying organizational life to ultimately make that life more understandable for those who live it?

Interpretive research can be most useful when we are interested in the identification of specific causal linkages that were not identified by experimental methods, when we are engaged in the development of new theories, and when we want to find out what particular action means to the actors involved (Erickson, 1986). As Weick suggested (1980), "Anyone who drops case studies [or other forms of interpretive research] because of criticism by someone engaged in more experimental forms of inquiry forgoes the opportunity for productive work" (p. 181). And Spindler (1982) has pointed out:

> Inevitably, any movement that rapidly acquires many followers has some of the qualities of a fad, . . . it is not surprising that some work . . . is marked by obscurity of purpose, lax relationships between concepts and observation, indifferent or absent conceptual structure and theory, weak implementation of research method, confusion about whether there should be hypotheses and, if so, how they should be tested, confusion about whether quantitative methods can be relevant, unrealistic expectations about the virtues of ethnographic [research]. (pp. 1-2)

I refuse to let the Pilotta et al. essay discourage me. I do believe that interpretive research can "shed new light on old problems and ask new questions that will make some of the old problems obsolete. [interpretive research] cannot do this, however, if it is prematurely killed by the hostility inevitably directed at such more qualitative and more descriptive research methods" (Spindler, 1982, p. 4). It also will not survive with obtuse descriptions of research methods.

It is my belief that whatever research method is employed, the results should be useful to organizational members coping with the realities of life inside the organized anarchy we call an organization. We should use all research methods available to us. Unfortunately, the Pilotta, Widman, and Jasko essay does not move us toward a clearer understanding of methods for studying organizational culture or interpretive research. Instead of continually expressing the desire for interpretive approaches to understanding organizations, we should provide more models of what we mean, apply criteria of relevance to those models available to us, and be willing to place our meager attempts at interpretive research in the public arena. No one becomes more insightful without being challenged.

All research should be potentially capable of shedding light on real-world communication transactions. In the words of Poincare, "An accumulation of facts is no more a science than a heap of stones is a house" (cited in Weick, 1980, p. 185). I wonder how much of the house we have built during the last decades of organizational communication research?

REFERENCES

Albrecht, T. L., & Ropp, V. A. (1982). The study of network structuring in organizations through the use of method triangulation. *Western Journal of Speech Communication, 46,* 162-178.

Bochner, A., & Kelly, C. (1974). Interpersonal competence: Rationale, philosophy, and implementation of a conceptual framework. *Speech Teacher, 23,* 279-301.

Bochner, A. P., & Kreuger, D. L. (1979). Interpersonal communication theory and research: An overview of inscrutable epistemologies and muddled concepts. In D. Nimmo (Ed.), *Communication yearbook 3* (pp. 197-212). New Brunswick, NJ: Transaction.

Brockriede, W. (1978). The research process. *Western Journal of Speech Communication, 42,* 21-40.

Campbell, D., & Fiske, D. (1959). Convergent and discriminant validation by multitrait-multimethod matrix. *Psychological Bulletin, 56,* 81-104.

Compton, C., Hendricks, G., White, K., & DeWine, S. (1986, May). *Techno-sense: Interpretive methods of studying technological impacts on organizational communication.* Paper presented at the annual meeting of the International Communication Association, Chicago.

Compton, C., Ugbah, S., & DeWine, S. (1986, May). *New technology: The domino effect on information adequacy.* Paper presented at the annual meeting of the International Communication Association, Chicago.

Deal, T., & Kennedy, A. (1982). *Corporate culture.* Reading, MA: Addison-Wesley.

Deetz, S. (1982). Critical interpretive research in organizational communication. *Western Journal of Speech Communication, 46,* 131-149.

Denzin, N. K. (1978). *The research act: A theoretical introduction to sociological methods.* New York: McGraw-Hill.

DeWine, S. (1986, November). *Female leadership in male-dominated organizations.* Paper presented to the Association for Communication Administrators at the annual meeting of the Speech Communication Association, Chicago.

DeWine, S., Alspach, S., Branch, A., Labiano, A., Liston, S., & McDaniel, N. (1985, April). *Women and power in the male-dominated organization: An interpretive study.* Paper presented at the Interdisciplinary Conference on "Organizational Policy and Development," Louisville, KY.

DeWine, S., Brammer, C., Lukens, L., Rauschenberg, G., Shatto, M., & Walence, W. (1984, November). *The communication of organizational myths: Creating order out of chaos and confusion.* Paper presented at the annual meeting of the Speech Communication Association, Chicago.

DeWine, S., James, A., & Walence, W. (1985, May). *Validation of organizational communication audit instruments.* Paper presented at the annual meeting of the International Communication Association, Honolulu.

DeWine, S., & Pearson, J. (1985a, May). *State of the art: Self-report paper and pencil instruments reported in communication journals.* Paper presented at the annual meeting of the International Communication Association, Honolulu.

DeWine, S., & Pearson, J. (1985b, May). *The most frequently used self-report instruments in communication.* Paper presented at the annual meeting of the International Communication Association, Honolulu.

Dickens, M. (1983). Laws of experimental research. *Journal of Applied Communication Research, 11,* 69-73.

Erickson, F. (1986). Qualitative methods in research on teaching. In M. Wittrock (Ed.), *Handbook of research on teaching* (3rd ed.). New York: Macmillan.

Farino, G. (1987). *Reversal of causal order between organizational communication variables in a field-setting: A replication of Staw's (1975) laboratory study.* Unpublished thesis, Ohio University.

Faules, D. (1982). The use of multi-methods in the organizational setting. *Western Journal of Speech Communication, 46,* 150-161.

Geertz, C. (1973). *The interpretation of cultures.* New York: Basic Books.

Jick, T. D. (1979). Mixing qualitative and quantitative methods: Triangulation in action. *Administrative Science Quarterly, 24,* 602-610.

Miller, G. (1983). Taking stock of a discipline. *Journal of Communication, 33,* 31-41.

Miller, G., & Sunnafrank, M. J. (1984). Theoretical dimensions of applied communication research. *Quarterly Journal of Speech, 70,* 255-263.

Monge, P., Farace, R., Eisenberg, E., Miller, K., & White, L. (1984). The process of studying process in organizational communication. *Journal of Communication, 34,* 22-43.

Pacanowsky, M. E., & O'Donnell-Trujillo, N. (1982). Communication and organizational cultures. *Western Journal of Speech Communication, 46,* 115-130.

Perotti, V. (1986). *Communicative competence in the organization: Multiple methods toward a viable construct.* Unpublished doctoral dissertation, Ohio University.

Perotti, V., Lukens, L., & DeWine, S. (1985, May). *Management of cultures in emerging organizations: The comparison of two field studies.* Paper presented at the annual meeting of the International Communication Association, Honolulu.

Peters, T., & Waterman, R. (1982). *In search of excellence: Lessons from America's best-run companies.* New York: Warner.

Porter, M., Reindl, R., & DeWine, S. (1986, May). *Electronic mail vs. traditional methods of information dissemination.* Paper presented at the annual meeting of the International Communication Association, Chicago.

Putnam, L., & Pacanowsky, M. (1983). *Communication and organizations: An interpretive approach.* Newbury Park, CA: Sage.

Rauschenberg, G. (1986). *Reducing equivocality and assembling summaries: A Weickian analysis of the information-organizing processes of a North Central Association on-site visitation team.* Unpublished doctoral dissertation, Ohio University.

Smircich, L. (1983). Concepts of culture and organizational analysis. *Administrative Science Quarterly, 28,* 339-358.

Spindler, G. (1982). *Doing ethnography of schooling.* New York: Holt, Rinehart & Winston.

Staw, B. M. (1975). Attribution or the "causes" of performance: A general alternative interpretation of cross-sectional research on organizations. *Organizational Behavior and Human Performance, 13,* 414-432.

Thomas, K. W., & Tymon, W. G. (1982). Necessary properties of relevant research: Lessons from recent criticisms of the organizational sciences. *Academy of Management Review, 7,* 345-352.

Tompkins, P. K., & Cheney, G. E. (1982). *Unobtrusive control decision-making and communication in contemporary organizations.* Paper presented at the annual meeting of the Speech Communication Association, Louisville, KY.

Ugbah, S., Brammer, C., Compton, C., Ray, G., & DeWine, S. (1985, November). *Organizational mavericks and innovation: A triangulation study of culture.* Paper presented at the Speech Communication Association, Denver.

Weick, K. (1979). *The social psychology of organizing* (2nd ed.). Reading, MA: Addison-Wesley.

Weick, K. (1980). Blind spots in organizational theorizing. *Group and Organization Studies, 5,* 178-188.

White, K., Flint, L., & DeWine, S. (1986, May). *High-tech, low touch: Nonverbal dependency and technological aversion.* Paper presented at the annual meeting of the International Communication Association, Chicago.

9   Communication in the Empowering Organization

MICHAEL PACANOWSKY
University of Colorado, Boulder

In this ethnographic account, the concept of an empowering organization is developed through a description of the practices that distribute power and opportunity, provide open communication, integrative problem solving, and an environment of trust, and encourage high performance and self-responsibility. Returning to theory, the "rules of empowerment" are provided.

ON BEING A GOOD LATTICE PLAYER

At the end of May, at the end of my nine-month sabbatical, I was given a send-off farewell party in the main conference room of the Paper Mill East facility of W. L. Gore & Associates. The party included those associates, as they are always called at Gore, with whom I had the good fortune to work during my stay. There was coffee and punch. There was picture taking. And there were presents—one gray Gore-Tex® gym bag from the Paper Mill East corporate staff, and one black Gore-Tex® gym bag from the personnel associates from the various plants, an unplanned duplication of effort that caused some mild embarrassment until I commented that this resulted from the relatively unrestrained initiative typical of the Gore way of doing things that might be seen as a weakness to some, but was in fact a strength, as witnessed by the fact that I was walking away with *at least one* Gore-Tex® gym bag. (I had also been given a number of W. L. Gore & Associates pins, hats, and paraphernalia, so much so that decked out in all of them with the two gym bags hoisted up on my shoulders, someone was able to crack, "Looks like you've been to a sales convention.") And there was a cake.

In the upper-right-hand third of the cake, in brown icing, were evenly spaced horizontal and vertical lines that represented the crosshatching of a

AUTHOR'S NOTE: I wish to thank the associates of W. L. Gore & Associates with whom I have worked and talked. They have provided the grist for this chapter. I particularly want to thank Jim Buckley, John Giovale, Bob Gore, Sally Gore, Jim Lewis, Shanti Mehta, and Dave Pacanowsky—all of whom have in their various ways been my sponsors.

Correspondence and requests for reprints: Michael Pacanowsky, Department of Communication, University of Colorado, Boulder, CO 80309.

Communication Yearbook 11, pp. 356-379

lattice. Written in red icing were the words, "To Mike, A Good Lattice Player," a commendation of which I was proud.

W. L. Gore & Associates is a 28-year-old entrepreneurial dream founded by W. L. "Bill" Gore to exploit the properties of Teflon as an insulator for electronic wire. With the invention of Gore-Tex®—an expanded form of Teflon—in 1969 by his son Bob, W. L. Gore & Associates began diversifying its product lines into areas more familiar to more Americans. Vascular grafts made from Gore-Tex® have been used in over a million operations and have an unparalleled reputation in the medical community. And Gore-Tex® fabrics—used in everything from ski gloves to running suits to fashion boots to, yes, gym bags—have become popular items among both yuppies and those die-hard enthusiasts who require high-performance clothing and equipment.

But another "product," if you will, of W. L. Gore & Associates that is becoming more and more well known is the very organizational structure of the company itself. Dubbed by Bill Gore as "the lattice organization," the rather unique organizing characteristics of W. L. Gore & Associates has earned the company much coverage in local newspapers, a cover story in *Inc.*, a magazine for entrepreneurs, a spot in the *Wall Street Journal*'s weekly TV show, and coverage in *The New York Times Magazine*. W. L. Gore & Associates is listed in *The 100 Best Companies in America to Work For* (Levering, Moskowitz, & Katz, 1985), being in the top ten in terms of opportunity (making the high-tech Silicon Valley outfits seem like Marine boot camp, according to the book). In Tom Peters's new book, *Passion for Excellence* (Peters & Austin, 1985), W. L. Gore & Associates is highlighted as one of four organizational "gems" that Peters has uncovered. Perhaps most impressive, in John Naisbett's *Reinventing the Corporation* (Naisbett & Auberdene, 1985), Gore & Associates is introduced on the first page as the American corporation that has already gone the furthest toward "reinventing" what organizational life can be.

The "lattice organization" is a graphic descriptor much in use at Gore that permits and invites frequent contrasts to the traditional "pyramidal" organization. Where traditional organizations are organized pyramidally, with discrete lines of communication and authority moving upward and downward through a system broad at the base and narrow at the top, the lattice organization *looks like* a lattice, a regular crosshatching of lines, representing an unrestricted flow of communication with no overlap of lines of authority. As Bill Gore defines it, a lattice organization means "one-on-one communication" with whomever you need to talk to in order to get a job done, no fixed or assigned authority but leadership that evolves over time and that fluctuates with the specific problem at hand that most need attention, and tasks and functions that are organized through personally made commitments—not through job descriptions and organization charts.

There are numerous other buzzwords and catch phrases that characterize the Gore culture. The company objective (singular) is "to make money and have fun." Associates are guided by

The Four Principles: *Fairness*—Each of us will *try* to be fair in all our dealings. . . . *Freedom*—Each of us will allow, help, and encourage [other] Associates to grow in knowledge, skill, the scope of responsibility, and the range of activities. Authority . . . is not a power of command, only of leadership. *Commitment*—Each of us will make [our] own commitments—and keep them. *Waterline*—Each of us will consult with appropriate Associates who will share the responsibility of taking any action that has the potential of serious harm to the reputation, success, or survival of the Enterprise. The analogy is that our Enterprise is like a ship that we are all in together. Boring holes above the waterline is not serious, but below the waterline, holes could sink us.

At Gore, there are leaders and sponsors, not bosses, and the distinction is more than mere terminology. The uniqueness of the culture makes many associates feel that they work in a special place, and the practice of the culture has the effect of freeing up power, communication, and conceptions of organizational life. The result for many associates, as my own experience would confirm, was high morale, high initiative, responsible risk taking, and the ability to delight in getting things done. There was a decided change that came from being "a good lattice player."

In my own case, over the previous several years, I had been very interested in the notion of "corporate cultures" and especially in the ways that corporate cultures were made manifest in the everyday interactions between people (Pacanowsky & O'Donnell-Trujillo, 1982, 1983). Although we academic beagles on the trail of "corporate culture" were pointing to the rituals, oft-told stories, key symbols, and so on as the indicators of the cultural beliefs and values of organizations, we all knew that these highly visible cultural forms were just the tip of the iceberg, so to speak. The real weight of the culture lay in the less visible cultural forms—in the mundane ways people went about their everyday organizational activities. Besides, rituals, oft-told stories, and key symbols were largely under the control of management, and the interpretation a grunt on the loading dock might give of a story, say, might be very different from the one management might intend. So if I wanted to come to a richer understanding of a "corporate culture," I was going to have to do more than interview management on its stories and rituals. I was going to have to spend some time getting a view of everday activities.

So I went to work at W. L. Gore & Associates. I got in because my brother was a trusted associate of seven years' tenure, and in a company like Gore, who knows you and who will vouch for you is of extreme importance. (Family ties were common at Gore. Bill Gore told me that as many as 55% of the associates in the Delaware-Maryland area were related to one another.) I also got in because W. L. Gore & Associates had in the previous three years tripled in growth, going from about 1500 associates to 4500 associates. It was easy for them to see that they had, if not outright problems, at least opportunities for improving their communication practices.

I had had several previous "nonparticipant observer" research projects under my belt, and my previous working experiences were with a very bureaucratized aerospace company and with several universities—none of which provided familiar ground to what I came to experience at Gore. For the first four months, I wandered around in good researcher style, taking notes, asking questions, reading memos, newspaper clippings, and so on. Occasionally someone would invite me to a meeting and near the meeting's close would ask me, expectantly, "Well, how are we communicating?" I'd say what I thought, but would seldom give any feedback that would be specific enough that anybody could do anything different for having heard it.

And then somewhere in January, it all changed because problems had come up. Because Gore employees are known as associates the company's employee stock ownership program is called the Associate Stock Ownership Plan (ASOP). It is essentially the Gore retirement program, with the company annually contributing 15% of each associate's salary to the purchase of Gore stock. Back in December, the ASOP committee had made a change in the operating practice of the ASOP, and announced the change by memo. In an extraordinarily oral culture like Gore's, memos are seen to be either absolutely insignificant or enormously significant; the ASOP memo took on the latter image. The concern and confusion over the change in ASOP was coupled with some long-simmering concerns and confusions over just what the ASOP was. In Gore-like fashion, an ad hoc task force was put together to do a better job of communicating about ASOP. I was invited to be part of that task force.

At the first meeting of the task force, the proposal that seemed straightforward to most was that some of the members of the task force should get together with the ASOP committee to find out exactly what the ASOP committee wanted communicated; then the task force would go about preparing communications in various media to get the word out. Someone asked me what I thought. I said I thought that instead of asking the ASOP committee what it wanted to communicate, the task force ought to talk to associates first, to find out what they wanted to know. It was a simple enough idea, and the logic of it appealed immediately to all the members of the task force. Right then and there, the task force laid out a plan to hold several different focus group interviews with new associates, associates who had been around a while, and associates about to retire. It took about two weeks to get the focus groups together, gather up their questions, and then go to the ASOP committee. I had given some feedback that someone could act on.

From that first task force meeting until the end of my sabbatical, I enjoyed the role of participant observer. I worked with another task force to develop an orientation program at Gore in which we were trying to help new associates understand some of the subtleties of the Gore culture. We labored over an outline that was supposed to be the basis for a two-hour session. I ran the outline past Bill Gore, who looked at it and said, "I don't think you need any more input or revisions. You need to try it." We did; it didn't work—too long, and parts of it were too sophisticated for brand new associates. So the task force, without needing to consult with anyone else about it, decided to split the orientation program into two: One two-hour session for new associates to familiarize them with the Gore business and just the basics of the culture, and a second two-hour session designed for associates who had been around three to six months and for whom the more in-depth treatment of the culture was relevant and welcomed.

My efforts did not always lead to visible accomplishments, however. In my wandering-around phase, I spent some time with some of the leaders of the electronic products business. I learned a lot about how this very successful Gore business operated—especially how they epitomized team decision making in an environment of challenge and trust. I tried to take some of their wisdom and transport it to another division that was less successful and that was characterized by a lack of team decision making. In this attempt, I was not very successful, and although I was personally a bit humbled by my lack of impact, I believe most associates approved of my having at least tried. (This division now, thanks largely to some personnel changes of late, has come to embody much more of the team decision-making model.)

But probably the most rewarding experience for me came right at the very end of my sabbatical. Bob Gore had asked me to do a talk on communication and culture at Gore, and I had agreed. Having spent most of my time up until then with project leaders and marketing leaders, I decided I needed some other perspectives—from manufacturing operators and shop associates, as well as engineers and secretaries and sales associates. So I held my own focus groups, asking just two questions: What do you think of communication at Gore? and, What do you think of the Gore culture? I held 18 focus group interviews in nine plants. I gathered up my information, organized it, and reported it to a meeting of the business leaders and to the associates who had been in any of the focus groups.

The results of the focus groups showed that the associates really liked the way communication and culture were supposed to work at Gore and that most of them felt good about the way communication happened and the culture was practiced. But there was room for improvement. The associates in the focus groups gave me many examples of problems. I presented both the basic positive feelings, and the areas that needed improvement, and made some suggestions for change.

I was struck by the overall response of the business leaders. They listened intently. There was no defensiveness. As one of them said, "I've heard nearly everything you've said at least once before. But you've put it all together in one place for us, organized it, and laid it out in a way that we can't ignore." Someone else asked, "What are we going to do?" and then someone else said, not in a dismissive way, "I don't know that we have enough information, or the right kind of information, to do anything." The meeting broke up.

I returned to my office, and thought about the problem. Gore was a high-tech organization that made much of engineering precision. My anecdotes from focus group interviews lacked precision. How strong were the positive feelings, really? How extensive were the problems, really? More important, Gore was a highly decentralized organization, and unless I could provide decentralized information to the specific people who could do something about it, I couldn't have provided feedback that somebody could act on.

So I drafted a questionnaire. (Believe me, given my recent proselytizing for qualitative methods, I recognize the irony of this.) I showed it to my sponsor, who suggested I show it to Bob Gore, who suggested I show it to three or four other associates. I then enlisted the help of the personnel associates in each plant to administer the questionnaire. An associate in data processing helped with data analysis. Three weeks to the day after I had drafted the questionnaire, it had been approved and distributed to 1200 associates in 9 plants, the data had been analyzed, and the results had been reported to business leadership, who agreed to pass the results along to all associates in their plants. Results were broken down by plant and by work area within each plant, all reported against organizationwide means. I had provided a lot of feedback that could be acted on, and I had done it by being "a good lattice player."

GORE—THE CHARTER AND THE CULTURE

It seems to me that there is a useful distinction to be made between an organization's charter and an organization's culture. The charter is the *explicit*, organizationally sanctioned set of statements about a company, its vision of itself, what it does, why, and how. Hewlett-Packard's "HP way" is a classic example of an organizational charter. The culture of an organization is much broader than its charter; it is the totality of sense-making practices and resultant "sense made" of the organization. Ideally, the charter and the culture should be largely in sync with one another, although it is unreasonable to assume that organizational practices will never deviate from the charter. However, it is conceivable that an organization's charter could be very much out of sync with its culture, especially since having a "strong culture" (read: "strong charter") has recently become *de rigueur* for organizations. It is easy for organizations to hire a consultant and purchase a well-worded charter in today's enthusiasm for strong cultures.

W. L. Gore & Associates certainly has a well-developed and clearly articulated charter. Nearly every associate knows that the objective of the company is "to make money and have fun." Stories abound of Bill Gore walking into an associate's office at 4:30 and asking: "Did you have any fun today? Did you make any money today?" And the corporate objective is subject to both humor and criticism. I saw countless T-shirts, buttons, and posters that asked, "Are we having fun yet?" On the other hand, some associates object that "making money and having fun" doesn't seem businesslike enough. One influential associate told me, in utter disbelief, that someone had once seriously suggested that Gore buy the Chicago Cubs, because that would be a way to make money and have fun at the same time.

Even more well-known among the associates are the "Four Operating Principles—freedom, fairness, waterline, and commitment." There is rather constant disagreement about what these terms mean exactly, and whether or not specific situations manifest the practice of these principles. For one associate, an action becomes justifiable under the principle of "freedom." For another associate, that same action seems unjustifiable if it means not following through with a "commitment." For still another associate, the action may seem singularly irresponsible if the situation is clearly a "waterline" matter. For still another associate, regardless of how ill-advised the action may have been, the important question now is what will be a "fair" response.

For example, one associate may exercise his or her freedom to purchase a piece of equipment. Another associate may see that action as not following through on the team's commitment to try to control costs. Still another associate may agree that, for small purchases, individual responsibility is all that is called for, but in the case of this larger purchase, it is a waterline matter, and the entire team should have been consulted. Yet still another associate may agree that the purchase showed bad judgment, but the issue now is what response is fair to the offending associate *and* to the team.

In any case, all the discussion about what really constitutes "freedom" or "fairness" tends to keep the Four Principles alive, and the charter clearly sets an agenda for the practices of the culture.

Two other aspects of the Gore charter are important and universally known to associates: the lattice system of communication and the sponsor/leader system of authority. The "lattice," as it is typically called, refers to the practice of one-on-one communication on an "as needed" basis to get the job done. Associates typically do not ask permission of anyone to go to talk to someone else. There are no proper "channels" one needs to go through.

Although the lattice theoretically means that everyone can be linked to everyone else in a plantwide communication matrix, such a ponderous "comcon" (completely connected communication network) does not in fact exist. Keeping one's commitments does not require everyone to talk to everyone else, and patterns of communication evolve over time to form a structured network. Still, the network evolves in response to functional requirements, not by hierarchical fiat.

The lattice is a powerful and many-edged tool that needs to be wielded carefully and responsibly. And just as the lattice makes it possible for the newest of associates to ask Bob Gore a question, if that is required, it also makes it possible for Bob Gore to go directly to the newest associate if that is required. In some cases, such an interchange is marked with some trepidation on the part of the new associate. Bob Gore or a business leader or whoever is likely to be communicating *to get the job done*, and not just to exchange pleasantries.

In many different ways, Gore backs up its lattice preaching with practice. First, Gore tries to keep plants small—ideally 150 associates per plant and no more than 250—in order to give one-on-one communication a chance of being a reality. Second, Gore has invested in a mix of decentralized and centralized communication technologies—electronic voice mailboxes and plantwide paging systems—that make it easy for associates to contact one another. Through the voice mailbox system, a kind of interconnected set of answering machines, anyone can leave telephone messages directly with anyone else, without the need of intermediaries—typically secretaries—to type memos or take phone messages for someone who is out of the office. Through the plantwide paging systems, an associate in a plant can quickly locate another associate in the same plant or in another plant, even if that associate is not in his or her office. Third, it is a common leadership practice at Gore that should an associate go to his or her sponsor and mention a concern, question, complaint, suggestion, or piece of information relevant to another associate, the sponsor is most likely to say, "Have you brought that up with her [him] yet?" That is, the sponsor will encourage the associate to make the communication contact, rather than the sponsor becoming the intermediary between the two associates.

So strong is the value of one-on-one communication that many new start-up research projects look forward to getting big enough that they can move out of the established plants into isolated, cramped, and poorly furnished rental quarters where within-team communication is enhanced. In one particularly dedicated research team, the group got so large it outgrew its rental quarters and had to move into a newly built facility with magnificent front offices overlooking a pristine pine forest. The leaders of the team decided to forgo the windowed front offices for windowless offices in the interior of the plant so they could be closer to the manufacturing operators on the project.

An important consequence of the lattice—and particularly of the voice mailbox and paging systems—is that communication is not only direct, but rapid. For example, say three marketing associates in one plant are meeting and a question comes up about a manufacturing process. They call the process engineer on the phone. He is not in. They page him. He doesn't answer the page, but another associate does and reports that the process engineer has gone to a meeting in another plant. The marketing associates call there and put in a page. Soon, they reach the engineer, ask their question, and get back to their meeting. So heavily used is the paging system that the typical Gore plant has something of the quality of an airport—with the name of first this associate and then that being asked to punch a particular number on the nearest touch-tone phone. (Also like airports, the paging system quickly fades into background noise and is not particularly distracting; remarkably, however, associates are consistently able to pick out their own names from the background.)

Another example: A leader of a task force with representatives from six different plants needs to call a meeting. She accesses the voice mailbox system, suggests a Wednesday meeting, and sends the message to the six task force members with a few touches of the button. Within a few hours, by the end of the day at the latest, she will know if her Wednesday meeting time will work for everyone or not. In my own experience at Gore (and I was spending my time on various projects involving nine plants), I was invited to many meetings, and seldom were they scheduled more than a week in advance. More likely, they'd be scheduled one or two days in advance at most.

The second important structural feature of the Gore charter is the sponsor/leader system of authority. Sponsors are supposed to help associates grow in responsibility, guide them in making sound decisions, help them get access to the resources that will make it possible for them to get the job done, hold them accountable to their commitments, and act as their advocates to others in the organization.

Where sponsorship is an associate-to-associate relationship, leadership is a functional relationship. On the basis of competence displayed and acknowledged over time, some associates will become known as leaders—manufacturing leaders, personnel leaders, data-processing leaders, plant or business leaders. Leaders are often sponsors, and sponsors are sometimes leaders, but there is no exact correspondence between the two. There is therefore no organizational chart at Gore, and to try to construct one on the basis of who sponsors or leads whom would lead to a most perplexing crosshatch of lines. Many associates are sponsored by the leaders of the area in which they work. However, many associates are also cosponsored by several sponsors. An associate in one functional area or in one project may be sponsored or cosponsored by an associate in another area or project. In rare cases (but it is often thought of as the ideal to which all sponsorship relationships should aspire), sponsorship is transitive—that associate A sponsors associate B and associate B sponsors associate A.

Where did the "lattice" and "sponsors/leaders" come from? Gore legend has it that back in his preentrepreneurial days when he worked for DuPont, Bill Gore was amazed by how motivated everyone was when they worked on task forces and how motivation and accomplishment dropped off as the task forces were disbanded and people moved back into their niches in the hierarchy. Supposedly, Bill noticed that even in the hierarchy, the real work got done through the informal channels between people and the informal influence among them, rather than through the formal channels of the chain of command. Bill's insight was, if the work gets done through the informal system anyway, then free up the informal system as much as possible by doing away with the formal system. Thus the lattice and sponsors and leaders.

It is admittedly easy to be skeptical about how all this works. Usually, there is a presumption that somebody somewhere has to be calling the shots—an executive who determines ultimately who is going to do what when. Bob Gore, who is president of the company, has enormous personal—not positional—authority within Gore. The inventor of Gore-Tex®, he is very bright and quick. He has that all-important commodity at Gore, "credibility." (At Gore, *credibility* refers to a constellation of attributes, including technical competence, a track record of "good judgment," and a history of follow-through and accomplishment.) With his credibility and personal authority, Bob is able to influence, to a great extent, the directions the company moves in. Yet Bob is not so much an executive as he is a catalyst. I remember one important meeting that I attended that Bob led. The meeting lasted for four days. Most of the business leaders of the company attended. On the last day as the meeting was coming to a close, someone asked, "Well, what are we all supposed to do as a result of this meeting?" Bob quickly said, "I don't think we're *all* supposed to do any one thing. I know that I've come away from this meeting with three or four things I know I want to do, and I hope that everyone else has their own personal 'to dos' as well."

This notion of leadership as credible-catalyst-within-a-system-of-action, rather than leadership as hierarchical position, helps explain a number of things that happen at Gore that are absolutely contrary to what we would expect in a traditional company. For example, in a few plants, associates are allowed to choose their own sponsors, the presumption being that people will want to be sponsored by credible individuals who can best help them get their jobs done and succeed. One newly hired associate found himself in the unusual position after two weeks on the job of having his sponsor ask him to sponsor her! The sponsor could see that the new associate had some skills she lacked, and that he could help her get her job done more successfully than she was doing herself. Although associates are sometimes appointed by business leaders to be sponsors or leaders, more frequently associates evolve into these roles. It is not at all uncommon for an associate at Gore to say something like, "When did I become a sponsor? Well, officially it's been a year. But I was sort of sponsoring the people in my area for about a year before that, only I didn't realize it at first. Then some people asked me to be their sponsor, and it seemed like I was already doing it anyway, so it became official."

It is interesting that associates sometimes evolve out of positions of sponsorship and leadership. Again, it is not at all uncommon for an associate and a sponsor to agree that the sponsor relationship is not working out for either of them, and the associate goes off to seek another sponsor or another sponsor is recommended. Such a decision does not necessarily reflect badly on the associate or the sponsor. (However, if the associate can find no one who *wants* to sponsor him or her, that is a very bad sign.) Very infrequently, but it has happened, an entire team will decide it can no longer follow the team leader, and the team leader will be asked to look for a new set of commitments. Although at the time such a vote of no confidence is painful for all involved, Gore is not the kind of place that stigmatizes. Sometimes the associate who gets the vote of no confidence leaves Gore, but at other times such associates have quickly settled into new commitments where they can again make significant contributions. I will make one final observation here, although I will develop the point in greater detail later. This fluid authority structure that I've described might sound like a breeding ground for political gamesmanship of the highest order. I would claim, in fact, that Gore is a very political organization—given a definition of politics as an arena that recognizes legitimate conflict and its subsequent resolution within a system of open discourse. However, Gore is decidedly not a breeding ground for gamesmanship. This fact speaks in part to the integrity and maturity of the overwhelming majority of associates who simply do not act in that way.

These features of the Gore charter—freedom, fairness, commitment, waterline, lattice, sponsors, and leaders—all have consequential impact on the Gore culture and subsequently on the associates' experience of working at Gore. But singly or even lumped together, they do not give a very good picture of what the total culture is like; they do not provide a gestalt of what the experience of working there is like. I have found that in trying to describe the Gore culture to outsiders curious about Gore, as well as to associates who are interested in an outsider's perspective, I have taken to using three metaphors (similes, actually) that try to capture the culture in a gestalt image: Gore as a cluster of peasant villages, Gore as a very large improvisational jazz group, and Gore as factions in colonial America.

Gore as a Cluster of Peasant Villages

In its passion for decentralization, in its extraordinary orality, and in the way its communication patterns and leadership structures come into being through a process of evolution, Gore is like a cluster of peasant villages. In the eastern cluster (and here *cluster* is a Gore word), there are now 11 plants of between 100 and 250 associates all within a 15-mile radius of Newark, Delaware. In the Flagstaff cluster, there are six plants. Each plant has its own leadership, or village elders, and is remarkably independent of the other plants. Just as there is no formal communication channel within a peasant village, there is no formal communication channel within Gore. Still, patterns of communication evolve. Certain rituals pertain as to who should be brought in on what kinds of decisions and when. Gossip is important, even trusted if the source has credibility, and some associates play a crucial role in keeping the information flowing through the plant as they wander from area to area dropping this tidbit of news here, listening to that problem there. Occasionally, when there is an extremely important issue that needs to be aired, a mass meeting of all associates will be held, just as in the way that all the members of a village might be expected to turn out at the ringing of the church bell or some other such sign.

Leadership in the plants, like leadership in the village, tends to evolve. Sometimes it is because certain associates are particularly competent, sometimes because they are particularly credible, sometimes because they are particularly caring; whatever the reason, they find a following, and are brought in on major decisions. Their advice and blessings are sought.

Sometimes, when a plant is having problems it seems unable to solve on its own, Bob Gore will step in. In these cases, it is like the provincial governor appointing his own representative among the village elders. This move, of course, is sometimes grounds for some squawking among some of the village elders, and is sometimes grounds for much gossip within the village, and even between villages. But the newly appointed typically is soon adopted by the rest of the village, especially if needed relief is brought to the village's problems, and the process of evolution takes over once more.

The plants all have an ambivalence about how they are supposed to feel about what's going on in other plants, just as one village would have an ambivalence about what was going on in other villages. Because so many associates have relatives working in other facilities, there are a lot of blood ties that bind plants together and serve as extraordinarily quick and effective informal communication links between plants. The spirit of decentralization tends to make each plant feel it should just mind its own business. But, then, there is so much available information about what's going on elsewhere in the cluster, that it's hard not to be concerned about or intrigued by the rumors, gossip, and stories that come from elsewhere. Also, there is great curiosity as to whether the practices in one plant are the same as or different from the practices in other plants. Villagers wonder what the customs are in the villages across the river.

Other than the informal bloodlines that pass information between plants, the main carriers of information from one plant to another are the few members of the corporate staff, who often seem much like traveling merchants, priests, and beggars. Also, representatives from each plant who are members of the same guild (personnel, data processing, accounting, etc.) typically get together on a monthly basis to compare notes. (When I presented this model of the Gore culture to one of the sales leaders, he admitted first having trouble getting past the "peasant" part of the metaphor, but once he did, he had a ball trying to decide who in each "village" played the part of the "village idiot.")

Gore as a Large Improvisational Jazz Group

At one of the annual medical products sales meetings, one speaker was paying tribute to Bill Gore, saying that Gore was like one big symphony, and Bill was the orchestra conductor. My talk, scheduled next, was about the Gore culture as I saw it, and I began by saying that, without any disrespect meant toward Bill, I disagreed with the last characterization. Gore was hardly a symphony, I said, but was more like a 4500-member improvisational jazz group trying to make music in 25 different buildings at the same time. Each associate seemed busily engaged in making his or her own kind of music, hoping that he or she could find someone playing a compatible melody or rhythm. Once you found a fit, and once the music started getting good, you quickly found a whole lot of others joining in. Now this was not to say that, in each room, there wasn't a lot of counterpoint going on. There may even be occasions of dueling banjos. And there always seemed to be some lost souls wandering around playing out of sync with everyone else, but they were surprisingly tolerated. Occasionally, everything would seem to break down, and there wasn't music anymore, but just chaos and noise. Then, in time, a line would rise out of the cacophony, and there would be music again.

The real trick, of course, was to get the people in all the different 25 rooms to be playing something roughly the same, and under the circumstances, rough approximations were all that anyone hoped for. Given even those expectations, it was surprising how well they were met.

I concluded by saying that if you liked to improvise and you could fit in with a bunch of musicians who basically found their way as they played, you'd like Gore. But if you were the type who wanted a symphony conductor with a written musical score, Gore wouldn't be the place for you. I could tell by the laughter that my metaphor had—so to speak—struck a chord with the audience.

Gore as Factions in Colonial America

Not surprisingly, in a culture where freedom and independent thought are considered valuable, there is much variation in what associates think of the Gore charter. I imagine that there was great similarity in colonial America as the colonists contemplated independence from England. England represented the old ways, and America the new; just as, at Gore, other corporations represented the old ways, and Gore represented the new. Many comments about the Gore culture would be preceded with, "I worked for X company for 15 years before I came to Gore, and although this place isn't perfect, it sure is a hell of a lot better than what's been thought up before." A few associates, however, dispute the difference between Gore and elsewhere. (And there are even a few "Tories" who believe that Gore would be better off with a monarchy!)

But I think what is most similar to the colonial period is the attitudes and strengths of feelings that talk about what the Gore culture engenders. There is a sizable faction of Gore associates who, like a sizable faction of American colonists, believe that what this is all about is nothing short of the greatest experiment known to humankind—an experiment in freedom, equality, and other notable sentiments. There is again another sizable faction of Gore associates who, like a sizable faction of American colonists, are rather cynical about these starry ideals. What it's about, they'd say, is strictly economics. Where for the colonists, the issue might have been taxation without representation—and consequently higher taxes—at Gore the issue is likewise economic: How do we make more money and forget the ideals? And for another faction, the issue is to make the other two factions see that they're not adversaries—that ideals and practical economics are compatible with one another.

Gore is like colonial America also in that these debates are heated, and go on in public and private places. And also, I suspect, like in colonial America, at Gore, the debates are interspersed among a lot of hard work and attention to the practical necessities of getting the job done.

Coda on Culture:
One More View

There is a well-known story at Gore about an associate, Jack Dougherty, that was the lead in the *Inc.* article about W. L. Gore & Associates. Jack, fresh from an MBA program at William and Mary, came to work his first day and excitedly reported to Bill Gore and said, "Well, Bill, here I am. What am I supposed to do?" and Bill Gore said, "Well, Jack, why don't you look around and find something you want to do." And so Jack wandered around for a while and finally found a home for himself as marketer for the fledgling Gore-Tex® fabrics business. Jack became a very influential associate, opened a Hong Kong office, and has since returned to the states to be part of the leadership team in the fabrics division.

For some associates, this is a good Gore story because it speaks of the freedom and opportunity at Gore and what they hope to enjoy. For other associates, this is not a good Gore story because it makes Gore sound like it's not a real business. "I mean really," a typical response might go. "Most people we hire have a specific set of commitments on day one. Associates do not go wandering around looking for things to do." For still other associates, the story is neither good nor bad. It just doesn't square with their own experience. One operator told me a joke, and it was clearly a joke and not a complaint. "When I was hired, I was told to wander around until I found something that I liked. And so I started wandering around when I heard this deep voice behind me saying, 'You're getting warmer, you're getting warmer,' and then I stopped in front of the seam tape machine and then the voice said, 'That's it, you've found it, seam tape machine, second shift.' " The operator roared with laughter, as did the others in the group we were in. He quickly added that he loved working at Gore, but that Gore didn't always live up to the stories that were told about it.

One of the problems with writing about organizational culture is the tension that comes from trying to tell *a* good story and, at the same time, giving voice to contrasting experience and points of view. How do I represent "reality"? What is Gore "really" like? Which is more typical—Jack Dougherty's experience or the seam tape operator's experience? One associate will say, based on personal experience, that Gore is an organization that provides extraordinary freedom and opportunity. Another will say that operating a machine is operating a machine and no matter what company you work for you got to be there a certain time of day and work until another time of day. Another associate will chime in that at Gore, you're lucky because you probably won't have anybody breathing down your neck screaming at you to make quota or treating you in another hundred more subtle but no less demeaning ways. Moreover, the problem of representing a culture to others is no different than the problem of representing it to oneself. For a given associate, on one day, Gore *is indeed* a place of exceptional opportunity. For the same associate, on another day, the work is just as routine there as anywhere. Thus the problem: What is the main pattern, and what are the untangling threads? What I have presented as the story of the Gore culture has been admittedly influenced by my own experience in being a participant observer. I had the freedom to wander around, and the good fortune, consequently, to be involved in getting things done. And so, based on my own experience, I draw conclusions about what the main pattern is and what the untangling threats might be. I believe that the picture of the Gore culture that I have given is reasonably recognizable to most associates—that in fact I have drawn the main pattern. By and large, associates who have read drafts of this article agree with my presentation.

But what are the untangling threads? For whom doesn't the Gore culture work? Where does experience not fit? There is a general belief at Gore that individuals who need a lot of structure and guidance will not survive long. There is also a general recognition that associates who are "insecure" do not make very good sponsors, because they may be "threatened" by the accomplishments and potential of the associates they sponsor and thus may inhibit or obstruct their growth. My own observation is that Gore sometimes finds itself with a serious technical problem, and someone is hired from the outside to "fix it" fast. These people often employ rather autocratic means in attacking the problem, which are tolerated as long as everyone perceives a "crisis." Once the crisis is past, a "personnel" problem then sometimes develops. The new hire, having been recognized and rewarded for taking care of the technical problem, believes that the "Gore culture" is just fantasy, and continues in his or her autocratic ways. However, when the crisis has passed, other associates object to the autocratic ways, resist, and insist on the supremacy of the Gore ways of doing things. The effectiveness of the new hire is jeopardized, and confusion and bad feelings may result. In some cases, the new hire eventually leaves, and Gore loses his or her technical competence. In some cases, the new hire stays on, acts autocratically, and remains a source of friction. In most cases, the new hire "evolves" into an associate who comes to accommodate or even appreciate the Gore way of doing things.

Thus sometimes it's difficult to tell if what we're looking at is a loose thread or something that will be drawn back into the overall pattern. Consider, for example, the leader who acts like a boss, fails to keep commitments to the team, and loses credibility. He seems like a living counterexample to everything that the Gore culture stands for. But what is the solution? To have Bob Gore step in autocratically and fire him? Consider what has actually happened on a number of occasions—the team stops following the leader, the team relieves the leader of his or her commitments. Isn't this now an example of how the culture does work, rather than a counterexample?

In fact, at Gore there is among senior associates an abiding faith in what they call the "self-cleansing process of the lattice," by which they mean that, over time, culturally aberrant practices will be dealt with. There is some suspicion among some newer associates, however, that the self-cleansing process of the lattice may be rather slow or rather selective. A few sponsors seem to act like "bosses," a few associates seem to act more like "subordinates." The affected associate wants to know: Who will take care of the problem? Who will enforce the culture? My own answer, as tentative and unsatisfying as it may be, goes something like this: The Gore culture is not utopia, and its object is not to set up a perfect organization. Instead, it recognizes that there will inevitably be problems, mistakes, oversights, and conflicts. What the Gore culture does is increase the possibility that those who see problems, mistakes, oversights, and conflicts can do something about them. The issue is less Who will take care of the problem? and more What energy, skill, influence, and wisdom do *you* have to contribute to the solution? Sometimes we act, sometimes we must be patient, and sometimes—no doubt unfortunately—we must accept the reality that we live in an imperfect world and we lack the energy, skill, influence, and wisdom to solve some of the problems that confront us.

And so here is the picture of the Gore culture: the Gore charter—with its freedom, fairness, commitment, waterline, lattice, sponsor, leader; the images of Gore—as clusters of peasant villages, as a large improvisational jazz group, as factions in colonial America; the Gore experience—predominantly positive, yet variable, problematic, imperfect, pragmatic. Taken together, they give, I hope, some sense of the texture and feel of the place. But these still represent for me contexts, pictures of the background. The most striking memory about Gore that I have kept with me is a conversation that I overheard in one of the Gore lunchrooms between two associates—one the plant receptionist and the other the plant maintenance and security associate. Both were talking about why they liked working at Gore, and I doubt that they knew or cared that I was listening in. "I am thankful," said the one, "to be working in a place where I'm doing maintenance and security and anything else I want to tackle. It's not boring, but you know, it's more than that, it's that I feel I can honestly make a difference."

And the other replied, "And that's the way it is for me, too. And I'll keep working here as long as it stays fun and I feel I can make a difference."

That conversation was important to me because it alerted me to listen for particular things in conversations among associates. And after nine months of sabbatical, and the equivalent of another several months of consulting, I do not recall one case of an associate saying, "That's not my job," or "Don't ask me, I just work here." But I can think of case after case of associates saying the equivalent of "I think I can make a difference." To me, that is the most consequential feature of the Gore culture: that so many associates do not cower or dissemble or retreat or space out before some organizational monolith, but instead feel that they stand before their organization as an equal, as a partner, as an entity as capable of affecting their organization as of being affected by it. When I began my sabbatical, I was unprepared for such a vision of organizational life. Although my intellectual conception of organizational culture was evenhanded, and I talked about cultures being like webs that both enabled and constrained organizational members, my unsaid presumption was that in the real world, organizations did a lot more constraining than enabling. Certainly my own previous experience with organizations bore this out. I never felt more like a cog in the machinery than when I worked for a large aerospace company. And even in the university setting, where I felt a great deal of autonomy, I seldom felt that I could have an impact on the institutions in which I practiced my trade. And certainly as I read the literature, scholarly and popular, the constraints of organizational life became more and more apparent. So you can imagine my own surprise when I heard myself saying to a colleague, "Most organizations make you aware of the limitations placed on people by the organization, but at Gore, honest, I felt that what limitations there were were the limitations *of* people placed on people. By and large, the organization makes it possible for people to do their most." So, however interesting it might be to talk about the Gore charter, however clever it might be to say that Gore is the peasant village organization, or the improvisational jazz group organization, or the colonial America organization, however diffidently objective I might feel in pointing out flaws in the Gore way of doing things, what sticks with me the most and seems most consequential is the view of Gore as the empowering organization. And the question I have wrestled with of late is a simple one: Can I deduce the rules implicit or explicit in the Gore culture that make Gore an empowering organization? I now turn to my attempt to begin an answer to that question.

OPERATING RULES OF
THE EMPOWERING ORGANIZATION

I believe that Gore sustains an enabling or empowering culture by sometimes explicitly, sometimes intuitively, following six rules. I see these rules as a set, with no one of them "first" and none "dispensable." Moreover, I believe that, implemented as a set, they would be the basis for creating empowering organizational cultures elsewhere. They are as follows:

(1) Distribute power and opportunity widely. As a number of scholars have pointed out, "power" has two decidedly different connotations. Some have distinguished between "power over" and "power to" or between "power to dominate" and "power to accomplish" (Kanter, 1977). Ironically, organizational theorizing about authority began with the presumption that accomplishment was the outcome of domination—that you needed a power structure and clear chain of command in order to get things done. But revisionist thinking about contemporary American organizations shows that the two have become uncoupled, and that there is a preoccupation with domination and climbing the hierarchical ladder and a lack of attention to getting the job done. In fact, popular books such as *Power: How to Get It, How to Use It* (Korda, 1975) and *Games Mother Never Taught You* (Harragan, 1977) make it seem that the only issue alive in organizations is in getting power over others. No one seems to do any work anymore!

Although it is no doubt an exaggeration to conclude that the power to dominate and the power to accomplish are always unrelated, it is clear that at Gore the emphasis is on power to accomplish and that the power to dominate is minimized in many different ways. In part, the lack of an organizational chart helps keep people's eyes off of ladder climbing and status seeking. If there is no higher title to aspire to than "associate," there is little reason to expend energy in back-office politicking and impression management. Indeed, one of the most widely known stories in Gore and outside of Gore has to do with the lack of titles. A Flagstaff associate, Sarah Clifton, was a member of a women's professional club. As the other women had business cards to distribute indicating their lofty positions, and all she had was a card that said "Associate," she felt a certain discomfort. Her sponsor at the time, Peter Cooper, told her that she should just make up a lofty title for herself, that associates needed to be "associates" on the inside, but that they could take whatever title they wanted in dealing with people on the outside. So, as a joke, Peter had some business cards made up for Sarah that identified her as "Sarah Clifton, W. L. Gore & Associates, Supreme Commander."

While minimizing the focus on power to dominate, Gore supports the wide distribution of the power to accomplish. Because associates are bound by commitments rather than job descriptions, associates are more inclined to do what is necessary to get the job done (and take care of their commitments) rather than to be constrained by the definition of what it is their job description says they're supposed to do. In addition, associates have relatively free access to money (and the access becomes freer as the associate gets more "credibility") necessary to get the job done. Finally, the lattice gives the associates relatively free access to the information and knowledge of other associates that may be relevant to getting the job done.

The power to accomplish at Gore is intimately connected with the opportunities for accomplishment because it is the nature and magnitude of the opportunity that in large measure determines the resource power that an associate can bring to bear on a problem. Distributing opportunity widely means decentralizing the process by which important problems get attached to people. Rather than presume that problems ought to be attached to positions (which is what the organizational chart with its job descriptions would encourage), at Gore the presumption is that problems ought to be "owned" by those people interested enough, capable enough, and committed enough to do something about them. One consequence of widely distributing opportunities to work out problems is that, as associates successfully solve problems, they become visible as potential problem solvers for future problems, and they become models for other associates who now believe that indeed they too are capable of taking on problem-solving opportunities. Thus, by distributing opportunities widely (and giving people access to the resources to solve those problems), Gore makes it possible for associates to pursue accomplishment cooperatively, which increases the resources to take on additional problems.

(2) Maintain a full, open, and decentralized communication system. Such a communication system allows members to be informed about problems, opportunities, and resources so that they can make mature decisions about what to work on. Because such a communication system is decentralized, there is less danger of a monolithic "definition of organizational reality" that inhibits the organization from registering and responding to changes in the environment. Also, because such a communication system is decentralized, there is less of a tendency to have a "party line" mentality that members must adhere to, and more of a tendency for members to be actively involved in arguing for their perspectives, plans, and actions.

Additionally, if there is less need to "launder" information as it moves up the hierarchy, there is more opportunity for the organization systemically to maintain a more complex and equivocal view of its environment and of itself. Such a system presumes that people can indeed learn from dealing with equivocality, rather than being overwhelmed by it. Finally, such a system, coupled with a decentralized power structure, will likely mean that there will be more problem-solving information moving through the organization, and less energy spent on impression management and face management communication. Such a system presumes that people can learn from mistakes, for example, and mistakes do not need to be elaborately covered up or whitewashed.

At Gore, the lattice provides the communication system with remarkable openness and decentralization. The company newsletters reflect these qualities. They are staffed by associates who have other commitments, but who believe in the idea of company newsletters. Many of the articles are submissions by associates who are not in any way on the "staff" of the newsletter. The review process is not lengthy; the key issue in the review is not whether leadership is portrayed favorably, but whether there is anything legally questionable in any of the articles. As a result, the newsletters do not read like company propaganda. Although there are always some good news articles that tell of Gore successes and opportunities, that is not all that the newsletters print. The front page story in one recent newsletter was about an R&D project that, after several years of trying to develop a new medical product and on the verge of human testing, closed itself down because the quality of the product just wasn't as good as the team had wanted. In another newsletter, a group of associates concerned about AIDS drafted a statement, after meeting with state health officials, expressing their sentiments about how they felt Gore should deal with the situation should it arise among associates. The statement was an invitation for other associates to express their points of view or provide input so that all associates could make their opinions known in a dispassionate moment.

(3) Use integrative problem solving. Traditional management theory tends to encourage the use of localized or segmentalized problem solving (Kanter, 1983). Problem-solving responsibilities are assigned to the smallest functional unit. The presumption is that however much equivocality there is in a problem

that confronts an organization, as each functional unit deals with its piece of the problem, the equivocality will be proportionately reduced until all of the equivocality has been absorbed and the problem has been solved (Weick, 1979). However, reality often does not bear out traditional wisdom. At the very least, as Kanter has pointed out, localized or segmentalized problem solving encourages a past orientation to solving problems: Functional units confronting problems tend to ask, "What did we do last time this sort of thing came up?" Worse, functional units often engage in substantial expenditures of energy arguing over who has the problem, or who has caused the problem, with impression management rather than problem solving the typical response. And in some cases, as one subunit "solves" the problem from its point of view, its "solution" increases rather than decreases the equivocality that subsequent subunits have to deal with.

Integrative problem solving, which assigns problem-solving responsibilities among functional work units, is the classic task force approach to problem solving. To the extent that power and opportunity are genuinely distributed to task forces and to the extent that the task force has full and open access to information, then the task force approach permits the problem to be cast, not at local subunit definitions, but at a higher level of abstraction with greater initial equivocality. As Kanter points out, with integrative problem solving the past is less likely to be called upon as the source of solutions, and the unique configuration of people who make up the task force are freer to come up with an innovative solution. Because this innovative solution is addressed to a problem defined more equivocally and broadly by the task force than it would have been by a single functional unit, implementation throughout the organization is usually quicker and more effective. Finally, task forces make more people visible as problem solvers and encourage a "we" attitude among functional units rather than a "we/they" attitude between units.

Gore makes abundant use of task forces. The "waterline" principle, which encourages consultative decision making, encourages associates to think about involving others in defining and solving problems. The lack of an organizational chart keeps associates from too quickly deciding that the problem is "all mine" or "all theirs." And the presence of the lattice makes it very easy to invite a wide spectrum of associates in on tackling a perceived problem. Gore successfully uses task forces in dealing with a wide array of problems from manufacturing processes within a plant to benefits policy across the corporation.

(4) Practice challenge in an environment of trust. The premise here parallels the argument for the use of task forces: An individual will have the best chance of accomplishing something if problem definition and solution generation have been honed by competing perspectives. But challenge, to be most effective, must be offered in the spirit of help rather than in the spirit of one-upmanship. Thus a chain of presumptions is involved. Individuals with ideas or proposals will be more willing to expose the real strengths and weaknesses of their position, rather than overselling their position, because

they want real feedback and not just approval. Individuals challenging the position will do so, not to look good or smart or to score points, but to help expose hidden weaknesses and strengths. Action is taken and, whether it proves successful or not, all parties involved refrain from "I told you so's" and instead look to see what has been learned from the action and its consequence.

I came to see the strength of this rule at Gore from a discussion I had with two very successful sales leaders. They were describing for me how they conducted their business. What they kept going back to was the fact that in meetings, the most frequently used word was "bullshit." Regardless of who put the idea forward, or who was responding to it, there was no need to "salute" ideas. Yet at the same time, despite all the challenges, the presumption was that each person would not be paralyzed into inaction, but would do what seemed best to him or her as a result of the meeting and then would act.

(5) Reward and recognize people so as to encourage a high-performance ethic and self-responsibility. Reward here does not simply mean compensate people, and recognize does not simply mean institute "employee of the month" programs. Rather, include the idea that distributing power and opportunity is for many people reward and recognition. Thus reward and recognition (or power and opportunity) must be given to those who successfully attack problems and implement solutions that help get the job done. Problem-solving practices are best sustained by encouraging people to be responsible for themselves rather than constantly monitoring them. People should be expected, and should be held accountable by their peers, to do their best to understand what needs to be done, what they can uniquely and realistically contribute to getting it done, and what gives the greatest value for their effort.

At Gore, the greatest asset an associate has is his or her credibility, and the worst that can happen is for an associate to lose credibility. To lose credibility means that an associate is identified as being someone who won't perform, doesn't do what he or she promises, or who doesn't keep commitments. Such an individual is quickly identified as being a detriment to the team, and finds it increasingly difficult to find other associates who want to work with him or her. It isn't so much that the person is chastised or reprimanded, but rather, the flow of work moves around the person. He or she is left with no commitments to anyone—a sure sign that the person needs to find new commitments or to rethink his or her suitability to an organization like Gore.

(6) Become wise by living through, and learning from, organizational ambiguity, inconsistency, contradiction, and paradox. In organizations that follow rules 1 through 5, equivocality will be high and experience will have shown that the world is complex and many sided. In such organizations, technique and policy must give way to situated judgment. Individuals come to realize that they can never fully resolve the ambiguities and inconsistencies, but they can act and learn from their actions.

At Gore, the ambiguities and inconsistencies become dimensions to think about. For example, Gore believes in individual effort and in teamwork.

Which is more significant? Similarly, at Gore, the person with the greatest organizational perspective is paid attention to; so is the person closest to the problem. Who should be paid the most attention? At Gore, the presumption is that the best person to do a job is the person who can make good decisions or the person who is best at making decisions come to good ends. Who's the best person for a job? These inconsistencies cannot be resolved in the abstract, but only in specific situations. Gore's willingness to accept this state of affairs predisposes it to making people and not policy the mainstay of problem solving. Gore acts as though the old saw, "People are our most important resource," is true. And here, I believe, the innovation of the Gore style of organization has implications beyond its own success. It has implications for the future development of the American character.

ORGANIZATIONS, WORK, AND THE
EVOLUTION OF THE AMERICAN CHARACTER

When the Puritans stepped ashore in the new world, they brought with them a vision of work that tied each member of the community to all others by an injunction to be useful and that tied each member to God by a link between one's secular and general callings. The work ethic was more than a call to be diligent and frugal; it stamped work as a moral activity (Rodgers, 1974). But the work ethic of our Puritan forebears was conditioned by a socioeconomic system in which most people worked by themselves and for themselves, with seeable consequences for their communities. The industrialization of America has not lessened our rhetoric about the work ethic, but certainly has undermined the socioeconomic conditions that gave it rise. Modern corporate Americans have more concern for leisure than diligence, more concern for credit rating than frugality, and seem more coglike than useful. All of this would be an oppressive loss for us to bear, perhaps, were it not for the fact that we have also by and large lost our preoccupation with the morality of our work. Yuppies may claim that they have reenshrined American individualism and ambition, but the work ethic had moral and spiritual underpinnings that today's fast track is without.

Earl Shorris (1981) has written a black portrayal of modern corporate life that shows the consequences to people of the way we now organize ourselves. According to Shorris, we are impotent within the organizations we inhabit; the consequence of our impotence is an inability to relate to others, which subsequently individualizes us only by isolating us. Thus, feeling our aloneness rather than our individuality, we conform to the appearances of the mass of like beings. Our loyalties are not to one another, but to our organizations. And why are we impotent? Because in organizations, we are infantilized. We have little power, we are too fully aware of our replaceability and expendability; we are carefully fed information and misinformation; important things are kept secret; we get bread and circuses; our decisions count for little; rule is by nobody.

Shorris offers no clear-cut way to change this, but he offers a vision of what would need to be different. We would need to see ourselves truly as ends capable of beginnings rather than as means. We would need to be potent, capable of actions for which we can see the consequences. Only then can we be autonomous individuals rather than atomized individuals. Only then can we relate to collective others rather than conform to the appearances of the mass.

It seems to me that what Shorris has so dramatically portrayed is a vision of life in the disempowering organization. What Shorris has hinted at, and what we can try to envision with more specificity, is life in the empowering organization. In the disempowering organization, formalized rules and centralized planning are the mechanisms for achieving coordination and control. The initiation of action happens "out there," somewhere away from the individual, who experiences himself or herself as a cog in some larger wheel.

In the empowering organization, more emphasis would be put on creating a work environment where individuals could act responsibly. The initiation of action would happen "in here," as a consequence of human choice because the individual would have the power to make choices. For that action to be responsible, the individual would need to have information about what the consequences of that action was to the individual and to coworkers and to the organization.

The disempowering organization tends to encourage office politics, a careerist or cynic mentality, and obscene individualism clothed within an "other-oriented" personality. Incapable of directly initiating action, the individual gives up hope or tries to ferret out the clues behind the mysterious and incomplete information all around and thereby provide a way by which the flow of action can be foretold or perhaps even influenced. The cynic sees no possibility in relating to others; the careerist sees possibility in using others. Where one makes no waves and the other stands out, they both look out for themselves by carefully measuring the cues of others. The empowering organization would tend to encourage concern for accomplishment rather than for status. Power would be used to get the job done, rather than to stand over others. Being capable of initiating action, the individual could look at others as ends themselves—capable of initiating action and therefore as worthy collaborators. The disempowering organization considers work an amoral activity—a job's a job, somebody's got to do it, you're only following orders, you've got two kids to feed. The empowering organization would consider work a moral activity.

I do not know any truly disempowering organizations, nor do I want to claim that Gore is a completely empowering organization. But there is a telling exercise I have done in nearly every class I have taught since my sabbatical. "Write down what you consider to be the characteristics of a mature person," I say to the students. I then ask them what they've written and write their answers on the board. Usually the list looks something like this: responsible, cares about others, not afraid to admit mistakes, trusts others, confronts problems, knows own strengths and weaknesses, accepts the consequences of his or her own behavior. And then I write down a list of opposites: isn't responsible, doesn't care about others, hides mistakes, distrusts others, avoids problems, doesn't know own strengths and weaknesses, blames others for consequences of his or her behavior. And then I say, "This second list, this is the way too many people are in too many organizations today. And this first list, this is more like the way it is with people at Gore."

REFERENCES

Harragan, B. L. (1977). *Games mother never taught you.* New York: Warner.

Kanter, R. M. (1977). *Men and women of the corporation.* New York: Basic Books.

Kanter, R. M. (1983). *The change masters.* New York: Simon & Schuster.

Korda, M. (1975). *Power: How to get it, how to use it.* New York: Random House.

Levering, R., Moskewitz, M., & Katz, M. (1985). *The 100 best companies in America to work for.* Reading, MA: Addison-Wesley.

Naisbett, J., & Auberdene, P. (1985). *Reinventing the corporation.* New York: Warner.

Pacanowsky, M. E., & O'Donnell-Trujillo, N. (1982). Communication and organizational cultures. *Western Journal of Speech Communication, 46,* 115-130.

Pacanowsky, M. E., & O'Donnell-Trujillo, N. (1983). Organizational communication as cultural performance. *Communication Monographs, 50,* 126-147.

Peters, T., & Austin, N. (1985). *Passion for excellence.* New York: Random House.

Rodgers, D. T. (1974). *The work ethic in industrial America: 1850-1920.* Chicago: University of Chicago Press.

Shorris, E. (1981). *The oppressed middle.* Garden City, NY: Anchor Doubleday.

Weick, K. (1979). *The social psychology of organizing.* Reading, MA: Addison-Wesley.

Communication and Personal Control in Empowering Organizations

TERRANCE L. ALBRECHT
University of Washington

TO be "empowered" means that one comes to believe one can influence people and events in the organization to achieve desired ends (Greenberger & Strasser, 1986; Kanter, 1977). One is not merely at the mercy of external forces (political, economic, or social); rather, the individuals recognize ways they can directly intervene in the environment. This is fundamentally an interactional process, where a sense of personal control results from believing that it is one's *communication behavior* that can produce a desired impact on others (Parks, 1985).

My purpose in this commentary is to develop the concept of empowerment from the perspective of a personal control framework (see Abramson, Seligman, & Teasdale, 1978; Fisher, 1984; Wortman, 1976). The notion of control derives from a theoretically coherent and empirically rich literature base that has direct application to understanding the characteristics and consequences of empowering organizations. Pacanowsky has provided an intriguing and lively account of lattice playing at W. L. Gore & Associates, which appears to be a prototypical example of an empowering environment. His description converges with my own view that such organizations buttress members in ways that increase their opportunities to be self-directed and to bring energy and creativity to their jobs. The results are rewards not only for the individuals involved but for the organization as an enterprise.

AUTHOR'S NOTE: I would like to thank Annalee Luhman for helpful comments during the preparation of this article.

Correspondence and requests for reprints: Terrance L. Albrecht, Department of Speech Communication, University of Washington, Seattle, WA 98195.

Communication Yearbook 11, pp. 380-390

In this essay, I will first briefly explicate the notion of control and describe the structures and processes in the organization that determine such perceptions. This approach will then be used as a basis for my commentary on Pacanowsky's view of empowerment. The essay will conclude with a review of some implications of the link between personal control and communication processes in organizations.

BACKGROUND

Conceptual Foundations

Perceived control (as opposed to control stemming from explicit or implicit organizational sources such as bureaucracy, technology, hierarchy, or the force of implied premise building in decision making (see Bach & Bullis, 1986; Tompkins & Cheney, 1985) is an individual difference construct grounded in cognition. It is, straightforwardly, the individual's belief that his or her actions have desirable causal effects on the environment (Fisher, 1984, 1985; Greenberger & Strasser, 1986; see also Abramson & Alloy, 1980; Albrecht & Adelman, 1987; Alloy & Abramson, 1982). At the heart of one's realization that his or her actions have causal impact is the knowledge that it is one's *communication behavior* that elicits such effects (Miller & Steinberg, 1975).

The interactional/influence view of personal control was developed by Parks (1985), who argued that communicative competence is grounded in beliefs about the effects of one's communication. He argued that communicative competence is the ability to control or influence the environment through a hierarchy of levels and that the individual has an awareness of those causal patterns. The social influence perspective was also central to what Paulhus and Christie (1981) termed two (of three) "spheres" of control: the social or "interpersonal" realm and the "sociopolitical" or public sphere. Even in an earlier analysis of generalized organizational control, Tannenbaum (1968) equated the term with influence, defining it as "any process in which a person or group of persons or organization of persons determines, that is, intentionally affects, the behavior of another person, group or organization" (p. 5).

However, the present consideration of the term is much less broad. I am most concerned with the control experienced by individuals and the ways they are externally supported in the organization to achieve their desired goals and effects.

The concept of control has been treated along three continua. Locus of control refers to whether the individual believes his or her actions are the causes for effects on the surroundings (internal attribution) or that the cause is an external agent (external attribution). The stability/instability continuum is whether one perceives the causes as enduring across time. The global/specificity dimension is whether the causes are seen as broad or limited (Abramson et al., 1978; Parks, 1985; Rotter, 1966; see also Albrecht & Adelman, 1987).

People who have the strongest perceptions of personal efficacy are those who make internal attributions, believing that they affect people and events in ways that are enduring and global.

Manifestations of Control and Lack of Control

The outward signs of perceived influence or control in the organization are akin to those of power (Tannenbaum, 1968), including the individual's ability to generate behavioral options for self and others, obtain needed and timely information, have access to target others, make and act on decisions, and amass resources for task accomplishment. Believing one has control establishes momentum whereby the individual can be decisive and take initiative. Such actions are likely to be successful because the individual has the knowledge and support to take well-reasoned, calculated risks (see Kanter, 1982). Moreover, the organizational member is not victimized by bureaucratic inertia; he or she becomes a cause and a catalyst for important activity.

In contrast, *not* believing that one's communication strategies have desired outcomes on others likely constrains behavior and outlook. Without a sense of personal influence, the organization member is continuously on the receiving end of others' initiatives and directives, often creating deep dissatisfaction and stress, even leading to turnover. Workers or managers may lose motivation or develop physiological problems such as headaches and hypertension (see Greenberger & Strasser, 1986). They may also experience depression (Fisher, 1984), helplessness (Abramson et al., 1978; Miller & Norman, 1979; Parks, 1985), greater uncertainty and increased job stress (Albrecht & Adelman, 1984, 1987; Fisher, 1985; Sutton & Kahn, 1987), failure to recognize or engage in innovation (Greenberger & Strasser, 1986; Kanter, 1982, 1983), and may generally feel less accountable for their actions. Hall and Savery (1986) reported a correlation of .51 between bureaucratic interference and distress (p. 161) and argued that executives who undermine managers' decisions (particularly those of younger managers) produce excessive pressure, resentment, error rates, and embarrassment. Changing or overturning the decisions of middle managers strips them of control and confidence, negating their abilities to anticipate and follow through on critical projects for a sense of accomplishment and closure. This also hurts their future managerial effectiveness because failure to receive support from higher-ups can destroy their credibility with subordinates (see Pelz, 1952). Fisher (1985) argued that lack of control may have wider effects on the personal lives of workers, affecting family and other extraorganizational relationships.

The Illusion of Control

A major aspect of control is that perceptions of influence can often be illusions (Langer, 1975, 1983). The amount of influence one imagines wielding can be exaggerated and be lacking in objective evidence. Unwarranted judgments of personal influence are often due to idiosyncratic biases (Alloy & Abramson, 1979; Fisher, 1984).

Illusions of control can have positive and negative consequences for organizational members. Certainly, distorted views do spur action; the individual is able to maintain face while bolstering self-esteem and motivation (Albrecht & Adelman, 1987; Mechanic, 1974; Wortman, 1976). Conversely, overconfident judgments of personal influence may lead people to pursue tasks despite failure, making the consequences of futile efforts even more difficult (Langer, 1975; Wortman, 1976). Should undesirable outcomes occur, the individual may feel undue guilt and engage in dysfunctional self-blame (Wortman, 1976) and obsessive behavior (Langer, 1975; see also Albrecht & Adelman, 1987).

While the drawbacks of unfounded illusions should temper the inclination to distort one's self-image, inflated perceptions of accomplishment may be reinforcing, prompting individuals to take initiative in times of uncertainty or stress despite a sense of threat (Mechanic, 1974). It is this kind of risk taking among members throughout the system that produces beneficial change and development to help the organization adapt to environmental turbulence.

Individual and Organizational Determinants

Several factors leading to perceptions of personal control have been suggested in the literature. At the individual difference level, these factors include prior experience, persuasive skill, and general communication competence (Parks, 1985). Having a central or linking position in communication networks is also critical for gaining access to people and information. One has increased personal visibility and is in a position to manage the knowledge level of others (see Farace, Monge, & Russell, 1977). Persons in linking positions (unlike others) tend to see themselves at the center of work flow, have less frustration, and identify more strongly with their jobs, their superiors, and coworkers (Albrecht, 1979; Albrecht & Adelman, 1984). Important psychological characteristics that likely predispose individuals to control perceptions include self-esteem, need for autonomy, achievement motivation, and responsibility orientation (Fisher, 1985; Greenberger & Strasser, 1986).

Foremost among the organizational antecedents is the general adequacy of information channels running throughout the system (Sutton & Kahn, 1987). Adequate, relevant, and timely knowledge obviously enhances performance and reassures the individual that he or she is in the mainstream. The predictability of one's immediate superior and the extent to which that person passes along information also affects whether subordinates feel a sense of involvement and influence.

Control is also a result of the extent to which cause-effect patterns of work flow and performance evaluations are known, certain, and predictable (Albrecht, 1986; Albrecht & Adelman, 1987; Greenberger & Strasser, 1986;

Sutton & Kahn, 1987). The opposite experience is uncertainty about processes and performance/reward ratios, which can paralyze and confuse organization members, discouraging risk taking. Equally important is the feeling of job security and support from upper management. Personal control and confidence are seriously eroded by prevailing knowledge that company executives are uncommitted to avoiding layoffs and retraining the work force (Walton, 1985). The flexibility of rules and policies, whether employees have a true voice in decision making (Walton, 1985), the extent of job autonomy, feedback, and the freedom to modify one's job responsibilities (Greenberger & Strasser, 1986; Hall and Savery, 1986; Kanter, 1983) may all effect the amount of time and opportunity one has to make an impact on people, tasks, and system processes or structures.

Summary

Empowerment of individuals means that they possess the resources and communicative competence to make desired changes in the organization. Understanding that one can affect others (even if it is an admittedly exaggerated estimation of one's ability) is an impetus for action and risk taking. Knowledge that one has personal control in the workplace is created within the opportunities the manager or nonmanager has to test the causal impact of behaviors. Having sufficient job latitude to modify personal constraints and participating in company decision making activities are among the best situations for exercising personal influence.

PERSONAL CONTROL AND EMPOWERMENT

Commentary on Pacanowsky's Descriptors

In 1982, Robert Jackall wrote in the *Harvard Business Review* that modern American bureaucracies have reshaped workplace morality. Today's corporations, he argued, are institutions where the rules for success and reward change once one attains midlevel management. At that point, the manager faces a cause-effect dilemma. Reward is no longer tied to hard work but to the intangibles of organizational experience: a polished appearance, prestigious, powerful mentors, a commitment to conventional action, and a lack of expressed commitment to anything for which one could be blamed later. He emphasized that the pathways to success are no longer predictable for managers; rewards in bureaucratic work life are largely due to "luck":

> Managers have a sharply defined sense of the *capriciousness* of organizational life. Luck seems to be as good an explanation as any of why, after a certain point, some people succeed and others fail. The upshot is that many managers decide that they can do little to influence external events in their favor. One can, however, shamelessly streamline oneself, learn to wear all the right masks, and

get to know the right people. And then sit tight and wait for things to happen. (p. 125)

Jackall paints a picture in sharp contrast to the image of Gore & Associates created by Pacanowsky. The difference between the bureaucratic "maze" described by Jackall and the lattice structure described by Pacanowsky is the level of personal control or self-directed vigor possible in each situation. Jackall further accentuates the desecration of moral ethics that occurs in bureaucracies, stemming from the fact that the individual is disenfranchised in those situations. The lack of known cause-effect contingencies discourages the willingness of organization members to assume personal responsibility for their actions. In Pacanowsky's alternative structure, a moral imperative exists in which members appear to value their work and are personally accountable, because the people performing the work have value and are as committed to one another as they are to themselves.

Pacanowsky's essay is compelling for the thought-provoking arguments he raises in favor of the decentralized power arrangements of lattice organizations like Gore. However, this single case description beckons the deeper conceptual foundation of the control framework to help explain why organizations like Gore are successful. The first, most obvious value of the notion of control is for unifying Pacanowsky's six characteristics of empowerment (he calls them "rules" but I hesitate to apply that term given that several are yet to be rigorously tested beyond the observation at Gore). To review, they are:

(1) power and opportunity are widely distributed;
(2) full, open, and decentralized communication systems exist;
(3) integrative problem solving is used;
(4) challenges are practiced in environments of trust;
(5) people are rewarded and recognized in ways that encourage high performance and self-responsibility; and
(6) wisdom results from coping with and learning from organizational ambiguity, inconsistency, contradiction, and paradox.

In short, a sense of personal control develops among members of the organization when opportunities are afforded for the individual to attain rewards in sensible ways. This circumstance enables members to better predict reward contingencies and understand the requirements for success. Information and resources are adequate for reducing uncertainty, solving problems, and decision making, thereby maximizing one's influence capabilities. Even ambiguity and inconsistency enhance personal control if, in retrospect, the individual feels he or she was able to manage the ambiguity and learn from the experience for future benefit. Finally, ideas, not people, are challenged and openly debated. This encourages freer exchange of information and stimulates talk about new ideas (see Albrecht & Ropp, 1984).

The social/influence view of control as an approach to empowerment is incomplete without a consideration of three additional processes: inter-dependence, uncertainty, and strategic ambiguity. The balance between control and these aspects of communication helps to expand the conceptual framework advanced in this commentary:

Personal Control and Interdependence:
A Virtuous Circle

Though his arguments have much appeal, Pacanowsky takes an uncritical view of empowerment. Any consideration of system functioning needs an analysis of the upper limit on even beneficial structures and processes. Pacanowsky's dictum "distribute power and opportunity widely" should be tempered, remembering that too much of anything may be problematic for some sector of the organization. Clearly, widespread independent initiative by members throughout the enterprise may cripple the organization by disrupting coordination. Excessive differentiation and loose coupling can attenuate communication patterns, producing duplication of efforts, random, entropic patterns, lack of follow-up, and little shared meaning for threats and competition in the marketplace. (Indeed, Pacanowsky even described the duplicated gym bags he received as going away presents from different groups at Gore.) For example, a factor in the collapse of People's Express airline was the lack of a mechanism to forge interdependence among the numerous, dispersed, and heterogeneous members of the work force. Even though that firm's noble experiment included job trading for greater shared experience, the lack of coordinated supervision and blocked information channels resulted in inefficiency, waste, and expensive idleness. And as soon as workers perceived that the president was becoming more autocratic (i.e., controlling) in his efforts to recover losses, morale plummeted (Carley, 1986).

For the empowering organization to succeed there needs to be a "virtuous circle," or a beneficial deviation amplifying loop set in motion between personal control and interdependence (see Weick, 1979). Increases in personal control should lead to increases in interdependence and vice versa. Individual responsibility and reward are then continuously framed in terms of the larger social fabric of the organization. And the larger social linkage system then amplifies—rather than denies—individual achievement.

Weick (1974), however, argues that interdependence in social systems is largely psychological, so the caution is that such perceptions may fluctuate and be tenuous. But in organizations such as Gore the collective mind-set may be stronger because of the explicit recognition and affirmation by company members of their need to cooperate. The lattice structure is probably a very helpful mechanism for reinforcing the constant need to tie into the larger social network. Organizational members are structurally prevented from "drifting" into isolation. The lattice structure strengthens interdependence at a macro level by facilitating rapid information flow throughout the system to link people broadly. It is also tightened at a micro level by the action of dyadic sponsorship, particularly in cases of reciprocal sponsorship between partners. Reciprocity of support and assistance fosters a mutual sense of responsibility against the backdrop of the organization; such relationships have been found to be more enduring (Albrecht & Adelman, 1984).

Control and Uncertainty: A Self-Regulating Loop

Uncertainty is essentially the lack of attributional confidence about cause-effect patterns (Berger & Bradac, 1982; Berger & Calabrese, 1975; Parks, 1985). Unpredictability about one's circumstances is a deterrent to mastery, producing anxiety and a sense of helplessness (McFarlane, Norman, Streiner, & Roy, 1983; Sutton & Kahn, 1987). The need to reduce uncertainty about one's job, the setting, or other persons is actually strong in the workplace, to offset insecurity and distress. Providing more information, not less, is usually the optimal managerial strategy, especially during times of crisis or change (Miller & Monge, 1985; Sutton & Kahn, 1987).

Pacanowsky describes Gore as an organization where problems of uncertainty are minimal. The reduction of uncertainty appears to be a continuous process, given that decision making is widespread, information flows rapidly, and sensitive topics are considered openly (i.e., publicly, in the company newsletter). Members therefore have greater personal control because participation in decision making is one way that uncertainty is absorbed; those with the greatest influence are likely to be the persons who are most adept at coping with uncertainty and structuring issues for others (Hickson, Astley, Butler, & Wilson, 1981). Problems from uncertainty are also few in organizations where information is seen as a highly valued commodity, and hence sought after, rather than avoided, because new knowledge is not viewed as threatening.

But Pacanowsky does not explain how organizational members cope with the high volume of information that undoubtedly comes at them in a company like Gore. Kiesler (1986) points out that the more information managers receive, the more support they need to manage and respond to that information. So how are members supported in order that they gain personal control from information and not stress from sheer overload?

As Tichy and DeVanna (1986) noted, organizations need to be "designed either to reduce uncertainty or to absorb it" (p. 221). This development should begin during early socialization experiences. Selection and training programs should be structured to orient newcomers and help minimize their errors from a lack of reliable information. Infrastructure supports that are also useful for managing uncertainty include state-of-the-art communication technology, and administrative assistance. These are readily the most visible kinds of help, as are plentiful opportunities for project feedback and closure. And the concerted effort to routinize uncertainty-laden topics by systematic information storage and retrieval can further promote work efficiency (Farace, Taylor, & Stewart, 1978).

Personal Control and Strategic
Ambiguity: Variation and Unity

In contrast to the above discussion on uncertainty, Pacanowsky makes an insightful point in arguing that empowering organizations are those where people learn from ambiguity, inconsistency, and paradox (see his sixth characteristic). Flexibility is built in because "situated judgment" (his term) must be usually invoked over standard policy. Pacanowsky observes the situation ethic is empowering because it "predisposes [the organization] to making people and not policy the mainstay of problem solving" (p. 377).

Another way of looking at this is that the experience of ambiguity and inconsistency empowers organizational members in at least two ways, by increasing their coping thresholds and by uniting them despite their differences. First, these become opportunities for workers to resolve or at least cope with potentially difficult situations personally, enhancing feelings of efficacy. And learning new knowledge that can be stored for use in the future (see Weick, 1979) can provide longer-term benefits. Second, rather than being confronted with ambiguity or inconsistency and having to react to it, the individual may proactively use ambiguity as an influential communication strategy. By communicating in general terms about such topics as long-term goals and the mission of the organization, the manager is able to stir a common sense of identity among members of a diverse work force (Eisenberg, 1984). Recipients are then able to make freer personal interpretations of the behavioral implications of those statements. Varied personal responses may prompt action, unlocking possibilities for individual adaptation while maintaining a larger sense of unity with others in the organization (see Eisenberg, 1984). Corporate leaders obviously benefit from grass-roots induced change and evolution (rather than the dissension). In short, strategic ambiguity (as in the case of the "have fun and make money" premise at Gore) is an influence strategy that thwarts dissension while empowering organizational members to respond with their own creative choices.

CONCLUDING NOTE

Empowerment and the enhancement of personal control should be understood as processes that are probably most meaningful to individuals in retrospect (see Weick, 1979). That is, a person is probably best able to view himself or herself as having control after influence has been successfully exerted. Control is also a quality that has assured longevity when it is negotiated as an outcome of shared experiences among diverse organizational members over time. Saul Alinsky sharply asserted that equality is something that can never be "given" because to do so implies that it can also be taken away (National Film Board of Canada, 1968). Like equality, the ability to influence can be facilitated by other people, larger organizational structures and processes, but ultimately rests with the strength of the individual's self-directed actions and willingness to uphold responsibility.

REFERENCES

Abramson, L. Y., & Alloy, L. B. (1980). Judgment of contingency: Errors and their implications. In A. Baum & J. E. Singer (Eds.), *Advances in environmental psychology: Vol. 2. Applications of personal control* (pp. 111-130). Hillsdale, NJ: Lawrence Erlbaum.

Abramson, L. Y., Seligman, M., & Teasdale, J. D. (1978). Learned helplessness in humans: Critique and reformulation. *Journal of Abnormal Psychology, 87*, 49-74.

Albrecht, T. L. (1979). The role of communication in perceptions of organizational climate. In D. Nimmo (Ed.), *Communication yearbook 3* (pp. 343-357). New Brunswick, NJ: Transaction.

Albrecht, T. L. (1986, May). *Social support during early socialization experiences.* Paper presented at the annual meeting of the International Communication Association, Chicago.

Albrecht, T. L., & Adelman, M. B. (1984). Social support and life stress: New directions for communication research. *Human Communication Research, 11*, 3-32.

Albrecht, T. L., & Adelman, M. B. (1987). Communicating social support: A theoretical perspective on process and function. In T. L. Albrecht, M. B. Adelman, & Associates, *Communicating social support*. Newbury Park, CA: Sage.

Albrecht, T. L., & Ropp, V. A. (1984). Communicating about innovation in networks of three U.S. organizations. *Journal of Communication, 34*, 78-91.

Alloy, L. B., & Abramson, L. Y. (1979). Judgment of contingency in depressed and nondepressed students: Sadder but wiser? *Journal of Experimental Psychology, 42*, 441-485.

Alloy, L. B., & Abramson, L. Y. (1982). Learned helplessness, depression, and the illusion of control. *Journal of Personality and Social Psychology, 42*, 1114-1126.

Bach, B., & Bullis, C. (1986, November). *The relationship between organizational identification and network involvement: A preliminary investigation.* Paper presented at the annual meeting of the Speech Communication Association, Chicago.

Berger, C. R., & Bradac, J. J. (1982). *Language and social knowledge: Uncertainty in interpersonal relationships.* London: Edward Arnold.

Berger, C. R., & Calabrese, R. J. (1975). Some explorations in initial interaction and beyond: Toward a developmental theory of interpersonal communication. *Human Communication Research, 1*, 99-112.

Carley, W. M. (1986, June 25). People Express is a victim of its fast growth. *Wall Street Journal*, p. 6.

Eisenberg, E. M. (1984). Ambiguity as strategy in organizational communication. *Communication Monographs, 51*, 227-242.

Farace, R. V., Monge, P., & Russell, H. (1977). *Communicating and organizing.* Reading, MA: Addison-Wesley.

Farace, R. V., Taylor, J. A., & Stewart, J. (1978). Criteria for evaluation of organizational communication effectiveness: Review and synthesis. In B. Ruben (Ed.), *Communication yearbook 2* (pp. 271-292). New Brunswick, NJ: Transaction.

Fisher, S. (1984). *Stress and the perception of control.* Hillsdale, NJ: Lawrence Erlbaum.

Fisher, S. (1985). Control and blue collar work. In C. L. Cooper & M. J. Smith (Eds.), *Job stress and blue collar work* (pp. 19-50). London: John Wiley.

Greenberger, D. B., & Strasser, S. (1986). Development and application of a model of personal control in organizations. *Academy of Management Review, 11*, 164-177.

Hall, K., & Savery, L. K. (1986, January/February). Tight rein, more stress. *Harvard Business Review*, pp. 160-164.

Hickson, D. J., Astley, W. G., Butler, R. J., & Wilson, D. C. (1981). Organization as power. In L. L. Cummings & B. Staw (Eds.), *Research in organizational behavior* (Vol. 3, pp. 151-196). Greenwich, CT: JAI.

Jackall, R. (1982, September/October). Moral mazes: Bureaucracy and managerial work. *Harvard Business Review,* pp. 118-130.

Kanter, R. M. (1977). *Men and women of the corporation.* New York: Basic Books.

Kanter, R. M., (1982, July/August). The middle manager as innovator. *Harvard Business Review,* pp. 95-105.

Kanter, R. M. (1983). *The changemasters.* New York: Simon & Schuster.

Kiesler, S. (1986, January/February). The hidden messages in computer networks. *Harvard Business Review,* pp. 46-60.

Langer, E. J. (1975). The illusion of control. *Journal of Personality and Social Psychology, 32,* 311-328.

Langer, E. J. (1981). *The psychology of control.* Newbury Park, CA: Sage.

McFarlane, A. H., Norman, G. R., Streiner, D. L., & Roy, R. G. (1983). The process of social stress: Stable, reciprocal and mediating relationships. *Journal of Health and Social Behavior, 24,* 160-173.

Mechanic, D. (1974). Social structure and personal adaptation: Some neglected dimensions. In G. Coelho, D. Hamburg, & J. Adams (Eds.), *Coping and adaptation* (pp. 32-44). New York: Basic Books.

Miller, G. R., & Steinberg, M. (1975). *Between people: A new analysis of interpersonal communication.* Chicago: Science Research Associates.

Miller, I. W., & Norman, W. H. (1979). Learned helplessness in humans: A review and attribution-theory model. *Psychological Bulletin, 86,* 93-118.

Miller, K. I., & Monge, P. R. (1985). Social information and employee anxiety about organizational change. *Human Communication Research, 11,* 365-386.

National Film Board of Canada. (1968). *Encounter with Saul Alinsky, part 2: Rama Indian Reserve* [Film]. Wayne, NJ: Karol Media.

Parks, M. R. (1965). Interpersonal communication and the quest for personal competence. In M. L. Knapp & G. R. Miller (Eds.), *Handbook of interpersonal communication* (pp. 171-204). Newbury Park, CA: Sage.

Paulhus, D., & Christie, R. (1981). Spheres of control. In H. Lefcourt (Ed.), *Research with the locus of control construct* (Vol. 1, pp. 161-188). New York: Academic Press.

Pelz, D. C. (1952). Influence: A key to effective leadership in the first line supervisor. *Personnel, 29,* 3-11.

Rotter, J. B. (1966). Generalized expectancies for internal vs. external control of reinforcement. *Psychological Monographs, 80,* 609.

Sutton, R. I., & Kahn, R. L. (1987). Prediction, understanding, and control as antidotes to organizational stress. In J. W. Lorsch (Ed.), *Handbook of organizational behavior* (pp. 272-285). Englewood Cliffs, NJ: Prentice-Hall.

Tannenbaum, A. (1968). Control in organizations. In A. Tannenbaum (Ed.), *Control in organizations* (pp. 3-30). New York: McGraw-Hill.

Tichy, N. M., & DeVanna, M. A. (1986). *The transformational leader.* New York: John Wiley.

Tompkins, P. K., & Cheney, G. (1985). Communication and unobtrusive control in contemporary organizations. In R. D. McPhee & P. K. Tompkins (Eds.), *Organizational communication: Traditional themes and new directions* (pp. 179-210). Newbury Park, CA: Sage.

Walton, R. E. (1985, March/April). From control to commitment in the workplace. *Harvard Business Review,* pp. 77-84.

Weick, K. (1974). Middle range theories of social systems. *Behavioral Science, 19,* 357-367.

Weick, K. (1979). *The social psychology of organizing.* Reading, MA: Addison-Wesley.

Wortman, C. B. (1976). Causal attributions and personal control. In J. H. Harvey, W. J. Ickes, & R. F. Kidd (Eds.), *New directions in attribution research* (Vol. 1, pp. 23-52). Hillsdale, NJ: Lawrence Erlbaum.

"Empowering" as a Heuristic Concept in Organizational Communication

ERNEST G. BORMANN
University of Minnesota

MICHAEL Pacanowsky spent a sabbatical working for W. L. Gore & Associates and studying its communication. In a memoir about his study, Pacanowsky reports that his major insight was that the Gore organization is an "empowering" one.

In his chapter Pacanowsky poses the question, "Can I deduce the rules implicit or explicit in the Gore culture that makes Gore an empowering organization?"[1] In answering that question Pacanowsky deduces six general characteristics that, based on his experiences at Gore, he would generalize to other organizations. The six characteristics of an empowering organization are (1) a wide distribution of power, (2) a full, open, and decentralized communication system, (3) a use of integrative problem solving, (4) a climate of trust, (5) a strong reward and recognition system, and, (6) a wise use of ambiguity.

My major purpose will be not only to point out the strengths and weaknesses of the Pacanowsky article but to present a short interpretation from another of the multiple perspectives available on the issue. In trying to achieve this purpose, I will first develop my position on the issue of the Gore corporation as possessing an enabling culture that suggests six broader characteristics of enabling cultures in general. Second, from my position on this issue, I will address the way Pacanowsky provides evidence in support of his interpretation of the research material in his chapter.

Since Pacanowsky's basic question is designed to lead to generalizations about enabling cultures in organizations, his article raises the most important

Correspondence and requests for reprints: Ernest G. Bormann, Department of Speech Communication, University of Minnesota, Minneapolis, MN 55455.

Communication Yearbook 11, pp. 391-404

issue of the generalizability of interpretative studies of organizational communication.

The older tradition of rhetorical criticism and the newer school of interpretative studies in organizational communication have much in common (Putnam, 1982). The issue of generalization runs through many of the articles on methods in scholarly rhetorical criticism. The discussions of this issue among critics of rhetoric can serve to aid those of us making interpretive studies of organizations as we grapple with the question of generalizability.

Scholars of one school recommend that critics throw an idiosyncratic light on the discourse based upon their personal engagement with the material. The writing of criticism that concentrates on a singular engagement with a unique body of rhetoric functions much as imaginative literature does in enlarging the understanding by enabling the reader to participate empathetically and vicariously in a human experience.

The members of another school of criticism seek to make a direct contribution to communication theory by using their studies to develop generalizations. Hart (1986) has argued for such generalizations:

> In the situationally contingent world of human communication, there may exist few of what social scientists call "covering laws." But to the extent that we as public address scholars worship anecdotes we will be driven further and further away from such general understandings. (p. 286)

My position is based upon my case studies of small groups and organizations. Since 1959, scholars at the University of Minnesota have been making case studies of small task-oriented groups, and since 1968 these case studies have been expanded to include complex organizational simulations lasting for approximately three months. The case studies of simulated organizations were undertaken to find recurring patterns that could be generalized to other organizations. Reports of the early case studies (Bormann, 1975; Bormann, Pratt, & Putnam, 1978) have been supplemented by a number of additional case studies as yet unpublished. My position has been further amplified since 1970 by the development of the symbolic convergence theory (Bormann, 1983) as a way to make interpretive studies of organizational communication.

The theory grew out of fantasy theme analysis as a contemporary movement to develop a broad-based program of social, scientific, and humanistic studies in which a number of investigators use the same scholarly viewpoint and the same technical vocabulary. Such a research program allows comparisons to be made across a number of studies so investigators can draw generalizations with an eye to developing general theories about communication. Investigators using the symbolic convergence theory have increasingly drawn their research questions from previous studies and have been able to integrate their findings into the evolving symbolic convergence theory. A number of researchers (Cragen & Shields, 1981; Dotlich, 1980; Eyo, 1985;

Koval-Jarboe, 1986) have studied ongoing organizations using the symbolic convergence theory.

Before I turn to Pacanowsky's generalizations, however, I will briefly discuss his style of investigation and his presentation of materials. In an earlier work, Pacanowsky (1983) used the form of the nonfiction novel to report a study of a police organization using all the techniques of a novelist. In his chapter on the empowering organization, Pacanowsky uses a journalistic style filled with anecdotes and examples to present a nonfiction account of his work in making a study of W. L. Gore & Associates. Although he reports on several large data-gathering efforts involving the use of direct observations, focus groups, and large-scale surveys, Pacanowsky does not provide the reader with the typically in-depth discussion of the research procedures and findings that one often finds in a scholarly report. The interpretive approach to the study of organizational communication, which encourages case studies and participant observation, also encourages experimentation with alternative ways of presenting findings. There is a dynamic in the process that makes the techniques of imaginative literature attractive as a way to write up results in order to involve the reader in the experience of observing an organization's communicative culture.

The style of presentation of the opening two-thirds of Pacanowsky's article seems aimed at providing the reader with an opportunity imaginatively to take part in W. L. Gore & Associates' communicative culture. Undeniably the in-depth living in a culture of the participant observer can result in a thickly textured account of what it is like to be in such a symbolic environment. When the observers are scholars, such as Pacanowsky, trained in observational techniques and knowledgeable about organizational communication, the insights they can provide about a specific organization are both interesting and useful.

Pacanowsky's style of thinking and writing lead me to assume that his study was aimed at illuminating the case of the organizational culture of W. L. Gore & Associates. In the final portion of the article, however, Pacanowsky chooses to use the study as the basis for generalizing from one organization to a larger population of organizations. This latter move is, from my position, both the most interesting and the most problematic of the study. His style of presentation, to my mind, is more appropriate to illuminating the instance than it is to drawing generalizations.

Pacanowsky's use of the term *rules* is a problematic one. To begin with, a number of scholars (Cushman, 1977; Cushman & Pearce, 1974; Cushman & Whiting, 1972) have attempted to formulate an account of human communication using the concept of rules as a basic explanatory notion. Their definitions of the concept differ from Pacanowsky's.

In commonsense usage a "rule of thumb" is often a procedure or rule based on experience or practice rather than scientific knowledge. Pacanowsky's "operating rules of the empowering organization" seem more like rules of thumb than the rules of communication theorists. Suggestions to distribute power and opportunity widely and maintain a full, open, and decentralized communication system make good practical sense and could certainly serve experienced communication consultants who are trying to improve the communication in a similar organization. But, I read Pacanowsky as striving for something more important and widespread than ephemeral rules of thumb to aid North American organizational consultants who are working with brain industries in the late twentieth century.

Certainly Pacanowsky's study raises the important issue of what is the nature of those studies that can empower their members and create a high quality of life for them while they are at work. If his report can be cast into the technical terminology of the symbolic convergence theory, his generalizations can be related more directly to previous studies of the same and similar issues and thus shed additional light on the differences between enabling and disabling symbolic systems.

THE SYMBOLIC CONVERGENCE THEORY
AND PACANOWSKY'S FINDINGS

Similarity of Philosophical Assumptions

Pacanowsky's analysis and the symbolic convergence theory have much in common. Both Pacanowsky (Pacanowsky & O'Donnell-Trujillo, 1982) and I (Bormann, 1983) reflect the scholarly perspective, which emphasizes the importance of organizational communicative climates and how they are "made manifest in the everyday interactions between people" (p. 358). Further, I judge that we agree that the interpretive approach implies a new paradigm for communication that radically shifts a scholar's viewpoint from a corporate world in which there is an objective knowable "Truth" to one in which different culturally shared meanings provide alternative accounts of events. Thus different groups within the same organizational boundaries may interpret the same critical events in stories that portray them in diametrically opposed ways: "and the interpretation a grunt on the loading dock might give of a story, say, might be very different from the one management might intend" (p. 358).

Since Pacanowsky and I share the same paradigm and the same perspective on the importance of communication and culture in terms of organizing, it is possible to translate many of the key concepts that he uses into the technical terminology of the symbolic convergence theory.[2]

Translating Pacanowsky's Study
into Symbolic Convergence Concepts

The basic communicative dynamic of the theory is the sharing of group fantasies that brings about symbolic convergence for the participants. A dramatizing message (Bales, 1970) is one that contains one or more of the following: a pun or other word play, a double entendre, a figure of speech, an analogy, an anecdote, allegory, fable, or narrative.

Rhetorical fantasies may include fanciful and fictitious scripts of imaginary characters, but they often deal with nonfictitious events that have happened or are envisioned in the future. The symbolic convergence theory distinguishes between the ongoing unfolding of experience and the messages that discuss events in other than the here and now.

Investigators found that some dramatizing messages seemed to fall on deaf ears; the group members did not pay much attention to the comments. Some of the dramatizing, however, caused a symbolic explosion in the form of a chain reaction. As the members shared the fantasy, the tempo of the conversation would pick up. People grew excited, interrupted one another, laughed, showed emotion, and forgot their self-consciousness. The people who shared the fantasy did so with the appropriate responses. The result of people sharing dramatizing messages is a *group fantasy*. The content of the dramatizing message that sparks the fantasy chain is called a *fantasy theme*.

An investigator making an analysis of an organizational culture using the symbolic convergence theory should investigate the messages to find similar dramatizing material that appears in the group's communication in different contexts. Such repetition is evidence of symbolic convergence and the resultant messages are useful for further analysis. "Stories abound of Bill Gore walking into an associate's office at 4:30 and asking, 'Did you have any fun today? Did you make any money today?'" (p. 361).

Other evidence of the sharing of fantasies is furnished by cryptic allusions to symbolic common ground. Employees can use the inside cue to trigger a recollection of a previously shared fantasy with its associated emotion and meaning.

Pacanowsky reports that "the 'lattice organization' is a graphic descriptor" (p. 357) and "there are numerous other buzzwords and catch phrases that characterize the Gore culture" (p. 357). What Pacanowsky refers to as a graphic descriptor, and as buzzwords and catch phrases are inside cues. The inside cue, "lattice organization," is a reference to the entire organizational saga. Some of the other terms are inside cues to fantasy types such as the term *waterline*, which cues the archetypal fantasy of "the analogy . . . that our Enterprise is like a ship that we are all in together. Boring holes above the waterline is not serious, but below the waterline, holes could sink us" (p. 358).

The symbolic cue phenomenon makes possible the development of *fantasy types*, which are stock scenarios repeated again and again by the same characters or by similar characters. The many stories that Pacanowsky reports, for example, about Bill Gore walking into an associate's office and asking whether the person had fun today, all constitute a fantasy type.

People who dramatize a given theme or type in an appropriate tone and style are testifying to their participating in the fantasy. Of course, those who tell the story in an ironic way or in ridiculing fashion indicate an awareness of the fantasy type but not a sharing of it. Pacanowsky provides an example of someone who fails to share a dramatizing message as follows, "One influential associate told me, in utter disbelief, that someone had once seriously suggested that Gore buy the Chicago Cubs, because that would be a way to make money and have fun at the same time" (p. 361).

Differing Levels of Analysis

When small groups of people communicate on the job on a daily basis and begin to share fantasies identifying them as a separate group, whether formal or informal, and creating a sense of history and cohesiveness, they will have created a separate small group consciousness and culture (Bormann, 1975).

When a number of people within a communication subsystem, no matter what their official position or divisional membership, come to share a number of fantasies, inside cues, and fantasy types, they may come to share a rhetorical vision. A *rhetorical vision* is a unified putting together of the various scripts that gives the participants a broader view of things. Rhetorical visions are often integrated by a master analogy (McDonald, 1978), which structures the various elements together into a meaningful whole. When a rhetorical vision emerges, the participants in the vision come to form a *rhetorical community*.

The rhetorical communities may overlap, to a greater or lesser degree, a number of small group cultures in an organization. Such overlap creates commonalities that facilitate communicating with small group members who share a common rhetorical vision. Like small group cultures, however, rhetorical visions within the organizational context may be more or less antagonistic to one another and thus create a host of communication conflicts and difficulties. Pacanowsky's analysis does not make clear whether the difficulty in communication in W. L. Gore & Associates stems from communicating across the boundaries of small groups or rhetorical visions, but his description of the way associates respond to specific events in terms of the four operating principles is typical of the phenomenon.

> There is rather constant disagreement about what these terms mean exactly, and whether or not specific situations manifest the practice of these principles. For one associate, an action becomes justifiable under the principle of "freedom." For another associate, that same action seems unjustifiable if it means not following through with a "commitment." For still another associate, the action may seem singularly irresponsible if the situation is clearly a "waterline" matter. (p. 362)

Finally, all or most of the employees of an organization may share more or less of the organizational saga. A *saga* is a detailed narrative of the achievements and events in the life of a person, a group, or a community. The *organizational saga* (Baldridge, 1972; Clark, 1972) includes the shared group fantasies, the rhetorical visions, and the narratives of achievements, events, and the future dreams of the entire organization. The common symbolic ties that bind the participants to the organization are furnished by the saga.

The organizational saga answers such questions as, What kind of an organization are we? What kind of people are members of our organization? What do we do? What is our mission? What exploits of the past are we proud of? Why are we admirable? What great things do we plan to do in the future? Answers to these questions provide an explanation of our better nature and our strength. They often are the aspects of their symbolic ground that organizational members emphasize when they develop messages for outside consumption.

What I have been describing are the "front parlor" elements of the saga. Organizational sagas also included material relating to the less laudable features of the organization. Members usually talk about such matters in informal settings and under circumstances of interpersonal trust and disclosure. The researcher seeking to learn about the organizational saga should gather elements relating to both the front parlor and the back kitchen.

Pacanowsky gathered an extensive amount of data during his time as a participant observer at Gore & Associates using essentially the same sources as would be used by someone studying the organization from a symbolic convergence perspective. Had he used the perspective of the symbolic convergence theory (Cragen & Shields, 1981), he would have been able to organize his focus group interviews in such a fashion that he could have drawn clearer and more specific boundaries around the small group cultures and the rhetorical communities who shared rhetorical visions in the organization. (For an extension of this analysis, see Bormann, Kroll, Watters, & McFarland, 1984.) He would also have been able to describe the geography of the organizational saga in terms of how widely and where it was shared.

Using the symbolic convergence theory as an explanatory account enables the organizational communication scholar to search for the boundaries of rhetorical communities and to reveal the complex and complicated symbolic terrain of the typical business firm or religious or educational institution. Such analysis is a strong antidote to interpretations that select out of such complexity a cluster of ideas and suggest that this cluster represents the essence of an organization's communication and culture. One of the strengths of Pacanowsky's article is that he does not make the error of selecting out a limited subset of the communication, such as the lattice organization or the four operating principles, and assume that these represent the essence of an organization's communication and culture. For example, he also describes clearly cross-boundary communication difficulties relating to "the concern and confusion over the change in ASOP [Associate Stock Ownership Plan which] was coupled with some long-simmering concerns and confusions over just what the ASOP was" (p. 359).

Still, Pacanowsky's analysis is less precise than it could have been had he delineated more clearly the relationships among small groups, rhetorical visions, and the organizational saga. In his analysis of the inside cue phenomenon, which is a key step in drawing boundaries around shared consciousness, Pacanowsky notes some cues to the organizational saga (lattice organization) and the ship analogy, but the rest of his analysis tends to lump all other inside cues together without distinguishing whether they are cuing small group cultures or rhetorical visions. Making clear how the inside cue is functioning in the culture would add specificity to the analysis and facilitate cross-study comparisons.

SUPPORT FOR PACANOWSKY'S GENERALIZATION ABOUT INTEGRATIVE PROBLEM SOLVING

Our studies of simulated zero-history organizations provide support for Pacanowsky's generalization about integrative problem solving. We have also documented the relatively small impact that formal descriptions of how the organization is supposed to work have on the way it really works (Bormann, 1975; Bormann et al., 1978; Koval-Jarboe, 1986). A typical organizational explanation of problem solving indicates that decisions are examined by all relevant units at all levels and their findings reported upward to the appropriate levels of management. Upper management deliberates the question using the data generated by the lower levels. Upper management then makes a rational decision or solves the problem and communicates its conclusions to the appropriate units throughout all levels of the organization.

Our studies reveal that this model of organizational problem solving and decision making does not provide a good description of how organizations do their work (Bormann, 1975; Bormann et al., 1978; Koval-Jarboe, 1986). Indeed, at one point in these investigations I became cynical about formal structures and marveled that the organizations of our corporate culture succeeded in getting anything done at all. Further studies of problem solving revealed that there was much goodwill and desire to get the job done on the part of employees located throughout many organizations. This goodwill resulted in the people directly concerned going ahead and doing their jobs. When a problem needed to be solved, they solved it. Sometimes they reported their problem solving and decision making upward and sometimes they did not. People in upper management were generally given credit for, and were willing to accept responsibilities for, success even when they were not quite sure why the organization was succeeding or how their leadership or management or decision making had affected the ultimate success.

These findings sound very much like Pacanowsky's rule regarding integrative problem solving in that the concerned people solve the problems and the formal units discuss them often with a look back at the past and with typical conflict communication. Insofar as the formal structure is in line with the natural dynamics of organizational problem solving, one can expect an easier time of it for the people dealing with problem solving.

Additional Generalizations
Implied in Pacanowsky's Chapter

In my opinion, a careful reading of "Communication in the Empowering Organization" reveals implicit and explicit generalizations in addition to the six Pacanowsky highlights. Most important is the generalization, rephrased in symbolic convergence terms, that *for an empowering organization it is important that the organizational saga be shared by many of the members.*

Pacanowsky notes that "ideally, the charter and the culture should be largely in sync with one another, although it is unreasonable to assume that organizational practices will never deviate from the charter. However, it is conceivable that an organization's charter could be very much out of sync with its culture" (p. 361).

A major strength of the Pacanowsky article is the way he describes and analyzes the organizational saga of W. L. Gore & Associates. He recounts the founding fantasy type: "Gore legend has it that back in his preentrepreneurial days when he worked for DuPont, Bill Gore . . . " (p. 364). He notes how the persona of Bill Gore serves as a unifying symbol in the organizational saga. He discusses the dramas of lattice communication, and the meaning of the terms *associates/sponsors/leaders.* He describes the four basic principles and the emphasis on making money and having fun. He also explicitly or implicitly indicates that some elements of the organizational saga are widely shared by the employees and others are less widely shared. Pacanowsky refers to the formal elements of the saga as the organization's *charter.*

Pacanowsky's analysis indicates that the organizational saga serves to motivate positive organizing behaviors as well as to provide motives, values, and emotional interpretations of work-related events that are positive and satisfying for the participants. His explanatory account of how the saga results in fostering an empowering organization and how it enjoys a positive reciprocal relationship with the communication in the company is cogent, plausible, and enlightening.

Pacanowsky also indicates that there are elements within the organization who do not share the saga, who are characterized as having a "lack of team decision making" (p. 360). He contrasts a less successful division for which he served as communication consultant with the electronic products business, which was "very successful" in team decision making "in an environment of challenge and trust" (p. 360). He also points out, "Sometimes, when a plant is having problems it seems unable to solve on its own, Bill Gore will step in" (p. 366).

Some commitment to the organizational saga is important to the overall effectiveness and satisfaction that members experience in their communicative environment. When an investigator (Dotlich, 1981; Eyo, 1985; Koval-Jarboe, 1986) analyzes an organization and finds many battles and conflicts over policy, mission, decisions relating to future commitments, budget allocations, and hiring and firing of new people, the odds are that there are several large rhetorical communities in the organization committed to different organizational sagas. In such circumstances the consultant can also anticipate that organizational members will be attending many meetings to develop mission statements, future plans, ten-year projects, and to clarify the basic purposes and functions of units and divisions.

The Minnesota case studies of simulated organizations also provide support for the generalization that wide sharing of the organizational saga is important. In some of the simulations the members developed a culture that included established patterns of organizing and a strong feeling of commitment to the organization. In others, no such emergence of organizational cohesion emerged. In all of the simulations that succeeded in moving the feelings of cohesiveness generated in the small formal and informal groups to a level of organizational commitment, there was a group of members who developed and communicated an organizational saga.

Sometimes the members who promulgated a saga were part of the upper management of the simulations, but that was not always the case. The members of upper management were in the best position to develop a larger vision of the total effort and dramatize the "big picture" to the others, but if they did not do so, attempts were generally made by some other informal or formal group within the organization. When a substantial number of participants shared the organizational saga, the morale and effectiveness of the organization tended to increase, but not in all instances.

The widespread sharing of the organizational saga does not automatically result in an empowering organization. If the saga itself is a noncoping one, then having the saga in sync with other elements of the culture results in commitment to the organization, but not necessarily to organizational effectiveness or with member happiness.

The "we are in a ship or boat together and stay afloat by cooperating" is an often-used fantasy type in a cooperative organizational saga. Recently, the management of one simulated organization dramatized the fantasy type of the ship in their efforts to create a saga. When other units of the organization felt that things were not going as well as they should, they began to dramatize variations on the analogy. They portrayed the ship of their organization as becalmed, as a ship in need of a captain, as a ship going in circles. In this instance, the fantasy type of the ship failed to work as a way to create an empowering organization.

My position is that sharing the saga is a necessary but not sufficient requirement for building the empowering organization. What is required is the right kind of shared saga.

Another implied generalization in the Pacanowsky article that is not part of his six rules relates to the positive effects of the emergence of roles as compared to the assignment of formal positions in an empowering organization. The way the employees of W. L. Gore & Associates use terms like *sponsor* and *associate* and the patterns of leadership emergence documented by Pacanowsky are supported by the findings of the Minnesota case studies and other investigations. The use of a flat rather than hierarchical formal structure thus seems to encourage the empowering organization. Still it is my position that we are dealing with a communication system in most organizations and that gains do not take place without some unforeseen consequences.

The process of role emergence is never smooth. It is the case that the creation of ad hoc task forces to undertake projects encourages a flattened formal structure. Task forces also encourage the collection of necessary technical expertise in groups in which roles can emerge in a way that should assure that the available talent gravitates to the proper specializations. Still, there is a price to pay. In several of the simulations we have formed organizations that use the task force approach. When the members were able to allow roles, particularly leadership, to emerge and come to stability, the result was an increase in morale (fun) and task efficiency. However, creating and disbanding task forces always resulted in an uncertain social environment followed by a period of high primary and secondary social tensions, role confusions, and collisions. Having people shift roles is painful. Shifting people from one work group to another creates tension points. Shifting roles from associate to sponsor to leader creates further tension points. These upsetting incidents are not fun and take their toll on productivity. Such role upsets also encourage communication that includes secrecy, the hoarding of information, and the creation of distrust.

So the upside of providing a formal structure that allows a communication climate in which roles can emerge without much restriction based on formal positions and formal communication channels and networks is that such structures allow the natural dynamics of role emergence to have room to function. The downside is that continual role shifting results in periods of role instability and the danger that the communication culture shifts from a win-win or cooperative one to a win-lose or competitive one.

Small task-oriented groups and organizations provide contexts that on the surface would seem to encourage a cooperative value-added climate for communication. Cooperative climates encourage "*full, open, and decentralized*" communication, trust, reward, and recognition for participants (p. 374). The zero-sum contexts encourage communication characterized by secrecy, a lack of trust, misleading communication, jamming of the channels of communication, and bluster and bluff. While one might expect cooperative win-win communication to dominate in organizations, our research indicates that most communication climates in small groups and organizations turn out to be mixed-motive environments that may tip in either direction depending on the way the participants generate their culture.

The mixed-motive communication climate is often revealed by members casting blame, by assuming responsibility for the rewards of success and denying responsibility and casting blame for failure. Pacanowsky's discussion of these matters is in line with our findings, as is his distinction between political communication that is self-serving versus political communication that is empowering.

Role emergence, however, in the case studies of leaderless group discussions at Minnesota usually results in about one group in four creating a win-win cooperative communication environment, finding productive and stable roles for its members, generating high levels of cohesiveness and morale, and releasing much of the participant's energy to work on the task.

About one group in four will develop a win-lose competitive communication climate in which members are involved in long drawn-out and tension-producing role conflicts, generating little cohesiveness and dissipating much of their energy in interpersonal and task difficulties rather than working on the group's task goals.

About half the groups fall somewhere between the two extremes and are characterized by mixed-motive communication climates in which they find some role stability and some cohesiveness that allows the member to work with some productivity and create a moderate amount of esprit de corps.

Although Pacanowsky's study reveals the presence of the downside, it is also clear that W. L. Gore & Associates have developed a communication culture that has mitigated to a large extent the difficulties in the use of such an organizational structure while capitalizing on the pluses.

In many respects the formal organizational structure that Pacanowsky characterized as a cluster of peasant villages, or an improvisational jazz group, or like colonial America does seem to be well designed to fit the way roles, norms, leadership, and decisions emerge in the small groups and organizations that we have studied in our case studies at Minnesota. As such, his detailed case study of Gore & Associates provides the basis for some useful conjectures that, supplemented by other comparable studies, could provide generalizations about how to create empowering communication cultures for some larger class of organizations.

In addition, Pacanowsky's immersion in the culture of the company enables him to write an imaginative and convincing description of what it is like to live and work in an organizing climate where many people are indeed making money and having fun.

NOTES

1. Toulmin (1974) has pointed out a number of different definitions of rules and the implications of using alternative formulations as a way to understand human behavior. Constitutive and regulatory rules differ from organizational norms, and all three regularities differ from "rules of thumb."

2. It is very important when attempting to translate research reports into the language of fantasy theme analysis that the investigators are working within the same research paradigm. Symbolic convergence theory (Bormann, 1985b) uses a research paradigm that sees communi-

cation as epistemic and creating meanings and social knowledge by the process of sharing group fantasies.

REFERENCES

Baldridge, J. V. (1972). Organizational change: Institutional sagas, external challenges, and internal politics. In J. V. Baldridge & T. Deal (Eds.), *Managing changes in educational organizations* (pp. 123-144). Berkeley, CA: McCutcheon.

Bales, R. F. (1970). *Personality and interpersonal behavior.* New York: Holt, Rinehart & Winston.

Bormann, E. G. (1973). The Eagleton affair: A fantasy theme analysis. *Quarterly Journal of Speech, 59,* 143-159.

Bormann, E. G. (1975). *Discussion and group methods: Theory and practice* (2nd ed.). New York: Harper & Row.

Bormann, E. G. (1983). Symbolic convergence: Organizational communication and culture. In L. L. Putnam & M. E. Pacanowsky (Eds.), *Communication and organizations: An interpretive approach* (pp. 73-98). Newbury Park, CA: Sage.

Bormann, E. G. (1985a). *The force of fantasy: Restoring the American dream.* Carbondale: Southern Illinois University Press.

Bormann, E. G. (1985b). Symbolic convergence theory: A communication formulation. *Journal of Communication, 35,* 128-138.

Bormann, E. G., Kroll, B., Watters, K., & McFarland, D. (1984). Rhetorical visions of committed voters: Fantasy theme analysis of a large sample survey. *Critical Studies in Mass Communication, 1,* 287-310.

Bormann, E. G., Pratt, J., & Putnam, L. L. (1978). Power, authority, and sex: Male response to female leadership. *Communication Monographs, 45,* 19-155.

Clark, B. (1972). The organizational saga in higher education. *Administrative Science Quarterly, 17,* 178-184.

Cragan, J. F., & Shields, D. C. (1981). *Applied communication research: A dramatistic approach.* Prospect Heights, IL: Waveland.

Cushman, D. P. (1977). The rules perspective as a theoretical basis for the study of human communication. *Communication Quarterly, 25,* 30-45.

Cushman, D. P., & Pearce, W. B. (1977). Generality and necessity in three types of human communication theory: Special attention to rules theory. In B. Ruben (Ed.), *Communication yearbook 1* (pp. 173-182). New Brunswick, NJ: Transaction.

Cushman, D. P., & Whiting, G. C. (1972). An approach to communication theory: Toward consensus on rules. *Journal of Communication, 22,* 217-238.

Dotlich, D. L. (1980). *Worlds apart: Perception of opposite sex managers in three modern organizations.* Unpublished doctoral dissertation, University of Minnesota.

Eyo, B. (1985). *Quality circles, involvement teams, and participative management in modern business culture: A study of the rhetorical visions of line-unit managers, employees, and facilitators.* Unpublished doctoral dissertation, University of Minnesota.

Hart, R. P. (1986). Contemporary scholarship in public address: A research editorial. *Western Journal of Speech Communication, 50,* 281-295.

Henderson, B. (1975). *An evaluation of the October, 1972 rhetorical strategy of the White House when it chose to attack the* Washington Post *coverage of Watergate: A fantasy theme analysis of the rhetorical situation.* Unpublished doctoral dissertation, University of Minnesota.

Illka, R. J. (1977). Rhetorical dramatization in the development of American communism. *Quarterly Journal of Speech, 63,* 413-427.

Koval-Jarboe, P. (1986). *An analysis of organizational culture during change.* Unpublished doctoral dissertation, University of Minnesota.

Kroll, B. (1981). *Rhetoric and organizing: The Twin Cities' women's movement 1969-1976.* Unpublished doctoral dissertation, University of Minnesota.

McDonald, J. (1978). *Rhetorical movements based on metaphor with a case study of Christian Science and its rhetorical vision.* Unpublished doctoral dissertation, University of Minnesota.

Mohrmann, G. P. (1982). An essay on fantasy theme criticism. *Quarterly Journal of Speech, 68,* 109-132.

Pacanowsky, M. E. (1983). A small town cop: Communication in, out, and about a crisis. In L. L. Putnam & M. E. Pacanowsky (Eds.), *Communication and organizations: An interpretive approach* (pp. 73-98). Newbury Park, CA: Sage.

Pacanowsky, M. E., & O'Donnell-Trujillo, N. (1982). Communication and organizational cultures. *Western Journal of Speech Communication, 46,* 115-130.

Putnam, L. L. (1982). Paradigms for organizational communication research: An overview and synthesis. *Western Journal of Speech Communication, 46,* 192-206.

Toulmin, S. (1974). Rules and their relevance to human behavior. In T. Mischel (Ed.), *Understanding other persons* (pp. 9-30). Oxford: Basil Blackwell.

SECTION 5

CONVERSATIONS AND TEXTS

10 On Conversation: The Conversation Analytic Perspective

DON H. ZIMMERMAN
University of California, Santa Barbara

Conversation is an interactional activity exhibiting stable, orderly properties that are the analyzable achievements of the conversants. Conversational analysis is a set of qualitative procedures based on detailed observation to capture the discernible features of conversational exchange. This article discusses the underlying principles of these procedures and considers the nature of conversations governed by institutional membership and master identities.

CONVERSATION analysis developed primarily within the discipline of sociology. Not surprisingly, most of its practitioners consider their work to be essentially sociological in character. Schegloff (1987b), for example, has suggested that the organization of conversational interaction is a primordial form of social organization. Sacks, who set the initial course for this line of work, did not turn to the analysis of recorded conversational materials out of an interest in language per se, but rather to develop a rigorous approach to sociological inquiry. He was in search of materials that could be readily captured, examined in detail, and be available for repeated inspection (Heritage, 1984a; Sacks, 1963, 1984). An understanding of the sociological foundations of conversation analysis is therefore helpful in gaining an appreciation of the aims and methods of this approach and the issues it engages.

I should note, however, that many sociologists find the interests and procedures of conversation analysis rather curious. Until recently, conversation analysis has been reluctant to address questions that seem natural to most sociologists, for example, how attributes like race, class, and gender affect conversational interaction and what the relationship is between a particular institutional setting and the talk that occurs within it. Similarly,

Correspondence and requests for reprints: Don H. Zimmerman, Department of Sociology, University of California, Santa Barbara, CA 93106.

Communication Yearbook 11, pp. 406-432

students of communicative behavior might find conversation analysis resistive to many of its concerns, for example, the examination of differences in communicative competence related to success in achieving interactional goals, empathetic communication, self-disclosure, and the like. The methodological stance of the approach, involving the detailed, "qualitative" analysis of naturally occurring conversations, also runs counter to the quantitative emphasis in both sociology and communication and the reliance on experimental methods in the latter. Even those engaged in similar qualitative studies of language activities find certain aspects of the approach puzzling or objectionable, for example, the emphasis on local, sequential development of conversation to the neglect of more "global" social determinants; and the insistence on the use of actual rather than constructed data or the lack of explicit attention to the issues of inference and evidence (e.g., Jackson, 1986; McLaughlin, 1984; Sigman, Sullivan, & Wendell, in press).

The following questions naturally emerge. First, what is the focus of conversation analytic interest? Second, why does it assume a methodological posture seemingly at odds with the procedures generally favored in social science at large? And, third, given the apparent disregard of mainstream topics and methodology by conversation analysis, not only in its initiating discipline of sociology but also of communication, what alternative topics and methodology does it propose? To address these questions, I will examine some of the working principles of conversation analysis, and its methodological stance. Before undertaking a detailed discussion of the matters at hand, however, a brief overview of conversation analysis and its approach to the study of conversation will be useful here.

OVERVIEW

How might conversation analysis be characterized? First, it views conversation as a describable domain of interactional activity exhibiting stable, orderly properties that are the specific and analyzable achievements of speakers and hearers. Discovering the organization of this domain is the overriding concern of conversation analysis. For example, the machinery that provides for orderly interaction in this domain includes such things as the construction and allocation of turns at talk (Sacks, Schegloff, & Jefferson, 1974); procedures for the opening conversations and for establishing and aligning identities (Schegloff, 1968, 1979a; Schegloff & Sacks, 1973); the initiation and management of topics (Button & Casey, 1984, 1985; Jefferson, 1981; Maynard, 1980; Maynard & Zimmerman, 1984); the organization of repair activities addressed to a broad range of conversational "troubles" (Jefferson & Schegloff, 1975; Schegloff, Jefferson, & Sacks, 1977; Schegloff, 1979b, 1987a); preference organization—the structural allocation of preferred and dispreferred turn types in response to different activities, such as inviting, requesting, complimenting, and so on (Davidson, 1984; Pomerantz, 1975, 1978, 1984; Wooton, 1981); and closings, for example, achieving a coordinated exit from talk (Schegloff & Sacks, 1973; Button, 1987, in press). The list could be extended (see Heritage, 1985).

Viewed as activities in their own right, the processes of conversational interaction are examined in terms of their internal constraints as specimens of social interaction rather than as products of exogenous influences, for example, master identities such as race or gender, or the operation of institutional and organizational processes. Moreover, the constituent activities of this autonomous domain exhibit features that are produced and oriented to by participants as orderly and informative, and relied upon as a basis for further inference and action. Indeed, it is the fact that participants themselves locate these features (e.g., through behaviors subsequently addressed to them) that furnishes the warrant for regarding them as relevant to conversational activity in the first instance. From a conversation analytic perspective, participants' ability jointly to produce, recognize, and utilize these features constitutes their interactional and communicative competence.

The fundamental framework of conversation is sequential organization. Sequential organization encompasses the production and recognition of successive turns, for example, invitations and their subsequent acceptance or declination, or the initiation of repair by another in a next-turn when the prior speaker has not self-corrected. The course of conversational interaction is thus managed on a turn-by-turn basis, with the sequential environment providing the primary context for participants' understanding, appreciation, and use of what is being done and said in the talk (Schegloff, 1987b; Schegloff & Sacks, 1973).

The investigation of this autonomous, internally ordered domain requires close attention to the "minutiae" of interaction, with no order of detail exempt from organization, and hence from study. Conversation analysis holds itself analytically responsible for the particulars of interaction, and its formulations must be capable of recovering these details through close description of the methods by which interactants produce them. Data, then, consist of the features of naturally occurring conversation, that is, conversational encounters in which participants are free to employ the resources of conversational organization to deal with the interactional and situational contingencies of the exchange. Ordinarily this entails the study of conversations that occur as persons go about their everyday routines without the intervention of the researcher.

There are, at least, three issues worthy of additional comment embedded in this definition and description: the notion of achievement, the source of order in analysis, and the application of quantification. A short discussion of each follows.

On Achievement

Before undertaking this more extensive review, a brief comment on the notion of achievement (or, alternatively, accomplishment) will be helpful. The provenance of the term can be found in ethnomethodology (Garfinkel, 1967; see also Heritage, 1984a) where it is used to refer to the outcome of methodical, accountable work by members of society addressed to some task or tasks. In the case of conversation, that work consists of the *in situ* use of the general machinery of conversational organization to define, recognize, and manage the local and particular contingencies of interaction over the course of actual encounters.

If the conversational machinery is thought of as a set of rules or procedures, the achievement of an orderly sequence of talk in an actual conversation is the outcome of speakers and hearers working to discover and develop their applicability, usability, and accountability on that particular occasion of use. As Heritage (1984) has observed, by bringing a procedure into play, for example, by uttering an initial term of a greeting sequence in the presence of an intended recipient, this move itself becomes a feature of the occasion by altering it—a situation of interactional disengagemcnt now becomes one of potential engagement. The occurrence of the greeting item is now one of the situational contingencies for both the potential recipient, who is thrust into a "situation of choice"—to greet or not—and for the one issuing the greeting, who will now assess the recipient's subsequent conduct in terms of an expected reciprocation. If we assume there is a rule governing greetings—for example, if greeted, return the greeting—the situation would appear to be simple. However, the recipient of a greeting may not return it, and this absence of response also becomes a feature of the occasion, variously subject to interpretation in terms of the "rule" for greetings as a willful withholding of the rightly expected return greeting, that is, a snub, or as the unintended consequence of a faulty hearing aid, or some other good reason why the greeting was not returned (Heritage, 1984a; Schegloff, 1968). In either case, the intcractional episode is orderly, an order achieved by the use of the procedure to project, produce, recognize, modify, and interpret the situation.

Thus, while there is a procedural basis for achieving orderly conversational interaction, the availability of these procedures in and of themselves do not generate conversational order. Conversationalists are not—to adapt Garfinkel's phrase—procedural dopes who merely follow the rules of conversation the culture provides (1967; see also Heritage, 1984a). Rather, as procedures in use they reflexively fashion and engage the detailed opportunities and constraints of actual circumstances of talk and thus serve as a resource for permit speaker-hearers to achieve that order for one another, and hence, for the analyst.

The notion of achievement thus provides a stance toward the complexity and subtlety of conversation. While transcripts and tapes often furnish "clear cases" or ideal exemplars of conversational procedures in use, such data also exhibit circumstantial variations, that is, adaptations to the particulars of the instant conversation (e.g., Jefferson, 1980). The concept of achievement alerts us to such variants as possible outcomes of working with conversational procedures to constitute and work through actual occasions (see Schegloff, 1980) by which participants arrive at an analytically sensible and accountable course of talk.

Constructing Versus Discovering Order

The usual practice of social scientific inquiry is to develop theories and generate hypotheses based on idealized understandings of the subject matter (see Garfinkel, 1967; Heritage, 1984a), the latter conventionally designated as institutional or societal patterns of aggregate behavior. The identification and analysis of these patterns requires the simplification and reduction of social activities into manageable categories or variables—the construction, as it were, of a phenomenon—ostensibly extracting order from what is otherwise a confusing flux of particulars (see Garfinkel & Sacks, 1970). As Sacks (1984) has observed:

> The important theories in the social sciences have tended to view a society as a piece of machinery with relatively few orderly products, where, then, much of what else takes place is more or less random. . . . So we can have an image of a machine with a couple of holes in the front. It spews out some nice stuff from these holes, and at the back it spews out garbage. There is, then, a concern . . . for finding "good problems," that is, those data generated by the machine which are orderly, and then attempt to construct the apparatus necessary to give those results. (pp. 21-22)

At the level of societal or institutional patterns this constructed orderliness transcends everyday experience at the individual level, although it is thought that the echoes of social structure can be discerned in members' expressions of attitude or belief, and in their behaviors. The detail of everyday activity, however, is something to be sifted through, a kind of archaeological excavation clearing away the sediments that conceal the artifacts of real interest, the societal patterns of which particular, situated behaviors are partial and imperfect realizations. From this view, there is little sociological profit to be gained from the detailed study of everyday, mundane activities in their own right.

Moreover, the conventional wisdom of the profession does not consider that coming to terms with the particulars of the activities making up actual everyday interactions to be a respectable scientific project unless such details are aggregated and reduced to categories or variables subject to statistical manipulation. The notion that the production and recognition of that detailed conduct might be accounted for as the working through of social organization at the level of the most mundane and singular face-to-face interactions is similarly strange.

This end, however, is what conversation analysis undertook to accomplish. As for why the major focus fell on conversation, Sacks (1984) provides the following answer:

> It was not from any large interest in language or from some theoretical formulation of what should be studied that I started with tape-recorded conversations, but simply because I could get my hands on [them] and I could study [them] again and again, and also, consequentially, because others could look at what I studied and make what they could, if, for example, they wanted to be able to disagree with me. (p. 26)

Sacks's turn to the study of conversation, then, served to preserve the detail of social activity for intense examination that itself could be subject to interobserver inspection and review. The interactional detail he sought required close observation, careful description, and intensive analysis if the mechanisms that produce it were to be discovered.

Sacks's conception of the subject matter of sociology—the mundane or ordinary activities that make up human social interaction—is aligned with the views of both Garfinkel and Goffman, but distinctive for its focus on conversation. His emphasis on the analysis of conversation as an activity countered the abandonment of the detail of these everyday activities by sociological and other social scientific disciplines—their submergence in categories or scales undertaken in the interest in making social life more readily amenable to statistical analysis.

On Quantification

It is important, however, not to draw the wrong lesson from the reliance of conversation analysis on qualitative description instead of the conventionally required quantification. The fundamental issue is how and when quantitative analysis is appropriate. The aim of conversation analysis has been to discover and describe the "machinery" of conversation, that is, the resources for organizing interaction that members of society draw upon to manage their everyday activity. Once adequately described, such machinery may have both qualitatively assessable and quantitatively measurable consequences of interest.

Consider the Sacks et al. (1974) model of turn taking, which provides a representation of the mechanisms by which turns are constructed and allocated in conversation. Given that there are competing models of turn taking extant in the literature (see Wilson, Wiemann, & Zimmerman, 1984) how might such a model, derived from the close analysis of turn taking across many conversations, be evaluated?

Wilson and Zimmerman (1986) determined that the real-time operation of the option-cycle central to the turn allocation process in the Sacks et al. model should produce a distinctive periodic distribution of silences within and between turns if the model actually operates in the manner suggested. Testing for between-turn silences (which were more amenable to measurement by a computer algorithm), the predicted periodicity was observed. The fact that the model yielded a testable, quantitative hypothesis is not an occasion for irony, for the conversation analytic approach does not entail a principled rejection of quantitative approaches as such, but only of the unreflective application of quantitative techniques in a fashion that does not respect the nature of the subject matter. In fact, where distributional issues are relevant, or where it is necessary to demonstrate that particular consequences follow some verbal or rhetorical device, quantitative analysis is required (see, for example, Heritage & Greatbatch, 1986).

The foregoing (and rather condensed) formulation does not do full justice to conversation analytic work, nor does it address all the issues that emerge from this distinctive approach to the study of conversational activity. A more detailed review of the major working principles, both methodological and substantive, of the tradition is in order (see Heritage, 1984a, 1985; Hopper, Koch, & Mandelbaum, 1986; Levinson, 1983; West & Zimmerman, 1982).

SOME WORKING PRINCIPLES

My usage of *principles* here—they could as well be called *maxims*—is for economy of exposition. The principles referred to have emerged from attempts to address the data of conversation analysis, namely the tapes and transcripts of naturally occurring conversations or speech encounters—largely of the "mundane" (Heritage, 1984a) but also of the institutional variety. To formulate them as principles presents them as a framework or guide for analysis. They could as well stand as descriptive—at varying levels of generality—of the phenomenon to which conversation analysis is addressed and with which it must continue to come to terms.[1]

Specificity

It is convenient to start at the level of data. A very basic premise might be formulated (paralleling Heritage's discussion, 1984a) as a "specificity principle":

> Social activities must be dealt with, and be recoverable in their specific detail, so that any claimed finding can be assessed in strict reference to the data themselves.

The "detail" of concern here is, of course, the detail of a range of conversational features, not simply the words, phrases, or sentences. Included are the hesitations, cut-offs, restarts, silences, breathing noises, throat clearings, sniffles, laughter and laughterlike noises, prosody, and the like, not to mention the "nonverbal" behaviors available on video records that are usually closely integrated with the stream of activity captured on the audiotape (see Goodwin, 1981).

It is crucial to note that tapes of conversations are usually not collected for specific purposes, and consequently, transcripts are typically not produced with a specific problem in mind. This practice accords with the notion that an unmotivated consideration of such materials is a means for encountering otherwise unnoticed features of talk (Jefferson, 1985; Sacks, 1984), a view that runs counter to the notion that data collection and reduction should be hypothesis driven.

Transcription as Observation

While the analysis of conversational interaction starts with "member's knowledge" or intuition, the full scope of the phenomenon eludes intuition alone (see Heritage & Atkinson, 1984; Jefferson, 1985; Jefferson & Schenkein, 1978). Transcription is observation: the noticing and recording of events of talk that might otherwise elude analytic attention.

Jefferson (1985), for example, notes that there are transcripts in which laughter is often merely reported to occur, or is described in some fashion, for example "light laughter." While such a procedure may suffice for some purposes, it will prevent any detailed consideration of the possible inter-actional functions that laughter may serve.

What is needed is some characterization of the laughter itself, for example, the particles, in-breaths, and other sounds that make up a course of laughter, for example, "HUH HUH HE:H HE:H HA:H A:HH-hh" (Jefferson, 1979, p. 89). Even more important is laughter's placement relative to speech and other laughter. Consider an example from Jefferson (1985, pp. 28-29). In the original transcription, a laughter event is characterized as follows:

(GTS:I:1:14, 1965)
L: ((through bubbling laughter)) Playing with his organ yeah I thought the same thing!

A closer transcription provides more detail:

(GTS:I:2:33:r2, 1977)
L: heh huh .hh PLAYN(h)W(h)IZ O(h)R'N ya:h I thought the same

What the first transcription omits is the actual representation and placement of the "bubbling laughter," namely, as "break up" laugh particles within a particular utterance involving an off-color remark, PLAYN(h) W(h)IZ O(h)R'N. The immediately following "ya:h I thought the same," is laughter free. Notice how the characterization of the utterance in the second transcript differs from the first: the latter provides the unequivocal "playing with his organ," versus the more problematic "PLAYN(h) W(h) IZ O(h)R'N." What is obscured in the earlier transcript is not only the characterization of the laughter and its placement, but the consequent distortion of the utterance's production by virtue of that placement.

As Jefferson (1985) observes, "Once we have the specific placement of laughter as a possible phenomenon, we can begin to examine it as a methodic device" (p. 30). Unlike instances of "flooding out" in which laughter overwhelms speech (Jefferson, 1985; Goffman, 1961), this sequence of a laughter-infiltrated utterance followed by a laughter-free utterance suggests a role for laughter in producing utterances that deal with obscenities or improprieties. Jefferson (1985) suggests that laughter produced in this way distorts speech so as to call upon others to provide a hearing that may then implicate them in the recognition and appreciation of the obscene or indelicate remark.

Note that the first transcriber provided just such a hearing by transcribing L's utterance as she or he *understood it* rather than how it was *produced*. It is such understandings (which may or may not coincide with the understandings of the parties to the talk) that should be considered problematic and not rendered invisible by glossing the detail of actual speech, even when no particular warrant for preserving the detail is currently available.

In sum, plausible intuitions concerning what features of talk are important are not reliable guides for anticipating undiscovered features of conversational organization, or for selecting the correlative details to preserve in transcripts. Moreover, as the example above suggests, transcriber-supplied "understandings" of what has occurred may lead to the omission of important details, and the consequent loss of a phenomenon.

As a methodological principle, then, transcripts are prepared with as much detail as can be discerned and feasibly represented, which is essentially an archival task. Consequently, a given transcript will preserve more information than might be utilized in a given analysis. To the extent that the transcript does preserve many of the aspects of the actual production of the talk, it will also afford a critic access to a fuller context for assessing the adequacy of the analysis offered in a particular study.

The transcription system developed by Jefferson and variously modified (e.g., Atkinson & Heritage, 1984) represents an attempt to provide a scheme to record features of actual talk as heard by the transcriber. Phonetic transcription is not employed because most scholars outside of linguistics and phonetics are not familiar with it, and more important, such systems do not preserve the "production features" of talk, for example, stretches, cut-offs, laughter, stress, volume, and so on.

The transcribing conventions represent a cumulative commitment to capturing certain discernible features of conversational exchanges. They provide, for example, for the use of punctuation as intonational rather than grammatical markers ("?" indicating an upward or "interrogative" contour, "," indicating a sustained intonation, and "." indicating a falling or terminal contour). The onset of simultaneous speech is demarcated by a left bracket, its resolution by a right bracket. Conventions exist for perceived variations in the rate of speech production, for the elongation, clipping, or cutting off of speech, for loudness and softness, and so on. These conventions form a complicated code, for which reason transcripts are sometimes presented in "simplified" or "normalized" form when the nature of the particular analysis permits. Extended or adumbrated, they stand as explicit commitments to what is "there" to be heard.

Transcription, of course, involves a transformation of the target conversation. Clearly the conversationalists in question spoke rather than spelled and imparted melody not intonation markers to their speech. Transcripts are not conversation; by the same token, neither are the audio or video records. But both devices represent and preserve not only spoken words but the stream of minute and fleeting details of speech production and utterance placement many of which, while if not consciously produced and attended to by participants, contain potentially significant features that speaker-hearers tacitly employ to organize their conversational activities.

Thus the skillful use of transcribing conventions provides a way of representing what the transcriber hears, providing a record that any interested observer can compare against the source recording, and modify or abandon as the case may be. The usefulness of such conventions may be assessed in terms of what they enable the analyst—in conjunction with the source recordings—to say about the organization of conversation.

Scale

We have seen that there is no a priori basis for excluding any set of discriminable features from consideration (although, as a practical matter, no transcript preserves all the available information). Thus a corollary to the specificity principle (see Heritage, 1984a):

> No scale of detail, however fine, is exempt from interactional organization, and hence must be presumed to be orderly.

Note that the conversation analytic approach is founded, in part, on the further assumption (contrary to the conventional wisdom) that the field of data is not just capable of being ordered by analysis, but that it is in the first instance *ordered* by the methodical activities of the social actors themselves. What is distinctive about this formulation is that the details of social interaction are not treated as indicators of some abstract concept, nor are they treated as imperfect realizations of processes buffeted by random shocks. Instead, they are viewed as possible achievements of participants. Thus the observed features of talk are procedures systematically employed by participants to manage the contingencies of the interactional occasion, which includes, prominently, the course of the talk itself (Garfinkel & Sacks, 1972).

Organization

Thus there is a further premise that is based on the notion that interaction in all its aspects is indigenously achieved and thereby ordered and social in character. I will dub this the "organizational principle":

> Interaction (including conversational interaction) is a describable domain exhibiting stable, orderly properties that are specific and analyzable achievements of participants.

Heritage (1984a) observes that interaction in this domain is treated as "independent of the psychological or other characteristics of particular speakers" (p. 241). Indeed, one common practice among conversation analysts (related also to the premise of "local determination" to be discussed shortly) is to require detailed demonstration of any claim that factors exogenous to the organization of interaction per se figure in the management of conversation, a stricture that will be considered in more detail in our examination of three corollaries to the "organizational principle." These corollaries concern the autonomy, orientation, and appropriate data of the domain of interactional activities.

Autonomy

The autonomy corollary to the organization principle might go like this: *The domain of interactional activities is autonomous.*

This principle is in some respects similar to Goffman's (1983) notion of an "interaction order," which he characterized as being constituted by those features that uniquely come into play when individuals interact. The notion of autonomy would seem to imply a lack of articulation with other domains of human activity, for example, the institutional order. Goffman (1983), for example, suggests that the interaction order is at best only "loosely coupled" with the surrounding social order.[2]

I suggest that, as a working premise, the autonomy principle be viewed as a statement of an analytic strategy reflecting the fact that any activity, whatever its aims, cast of characters, and so forth, can be analyzed for specifically interactional features. Thus, for example, while a call to an emergency number engages the caller with a particular organization and its contingencies, it is also a telephone call, that is, a type of mediated interaction that presents a class of constraints (e.g., the identification and alignment of the parties to the call) operating across a variety of calls with quite disparate purposes and personnel (see Schegloff, 1979a; Zimmerman, 1984; see also Meehan, 1983). Whatever the institutional locale, interaction—including conversational interaction—will retain certain features by virtue of being interactional.

The "autonomy principle," then, does not necessarily imply that interaction is a realm of activity empirically disconnected from other institutional forms. Rather, it expresses a commitment to the investigation of social interaction as a distinctive domain with its own organization without presuming at the outset that its features directly reflect institutional or societal properties or processes.

This principle embodies a cautious stance regarding the issue of the connection between conversational interaction and the so-called larger contexts of social action. One tack has been to put aside such questions as either premature or unprofitable diversions from the central task, which is to discover and describe the organization of conversational interactions as such (Schegloff, 1987b). The latter aim is quite general in scope; to detail the mechanisms of conversation across settings, independent of social identities, societal institutions and indeed, across language and culture.

Let me emphasize that the search for general organizational forms in the interactional domain conceived as analytically autonomous is a fundamental task for conversation analysis. Moreover, it looks as if the available—but admittedly scant—empirical evidence favors the notion that such forms are remarkably stable across important social formations.

For example, Schegloff (1987b) has noted that the organization of repair activity in conversation appears remarkably constant across language, culture, and society. The variation that does exist is minor relative to what appears to be constant, and consists of adaptations to particular features of the language or culture in question (see also Besnier, 1982; Boden, 1983; Daden & McClaren, 1978, cited in Schegloff, 1987b; Moerman, 1977). Moreover, he insists that what is at issue here is human activity, the organization of which is aimed at rather general interactional exigencies. To the extent that it can be shown that there are such general exigencies, addressed by a stable, invariant organization of interaction, then the premises outlined above—and in particular the "organizational" and "autonomy principles"—will have proved to have indeed been valid characterizations of the phenomenon as well as useful guides for research to deepen and extend our knowledge of this domain.

Orientation to the Interactional Domain

An additional corollary to the organizational principle provides for the status of actions constrained by the organization of (conversational) inter-action:

> Participants are oriented to the stable, orderly features of the interactional domain as the basis of their further inference and action.

This corollary proposes that the stable, orderly properties of the domain are looked for, recognized, and appreciated by participants as the real and consequential circumstances of their action. It is worth emphasizing once again that it is not only that conversational materials are orderly, but that the orderliness is produced for participants by participants for their recognition and use (Schegloff & Sacks, 1973).

While it is the participants' own actions that effectively organize the domain, these actions involve interdependent, interactional sequences, and thus, while not wholly out of the hands of any given individual, they are not wholly in them, either (Heritage, 1984a). Each must recognize and take into account what type of act and hence what type of understanding of prior acts the other is doing. Indeed, it is this aspect of interactional dynamics that makes the features of this domain observable to the analyst as orderly features.

Thus the order found in conversational materials is not imposed by the analysts' use of a priori conceptual schemes or coding categories, but discovered. This is owed to the practices of conversationalists who orient to, analyze, and exhibit understanding of one another's activities in successive turns at talk. Order is not sought by soliciting participants' accounts of their conversational behavior, for what this elicits is their beliefs about ways of talking. It is found in the way they go about methodically solving problems and addressing issues posed by the situated, turn-by-turn management of conversational interaction.

Warranted inference. Sigman et al. (in press), however, have noted that the analysts' recourse to participants' displayed understanding of preceding conversational events itself requires the intuitive grasp—drawn from participation in the culture—of how such responses display the *particular* understanding being claimed. They suggest that the analyst should feel obligated to "defend the applicability of their cultural understandings to the particular transcripts and recoded events under study" (Sigman et al., in press, emphasis deleted). They propose using "non-text based sources" such as ethnographic materials, informant interviews, and explication of the materials by the respondents themselves as a means of warranting the analysts' inferences.

It strikes me that there are two related issues connected with the invocation of such nontext materials. First, the introduction of such materials must be done in a fashion that demonstrates that they were relevant to and consequential for the sequentially located production or *in situ* recognition of the conversational conduct they are used to analyze (see Schegloff, in press). Otherwise, one is faced with an indefinitely large set of "contextual" information that could be relevant but selection from which is justified by little more than surface plausibility. It may be true that participants hold certain attitudes or possess special knowledge or engage in particular activities, but how can these facts be connected to a particular conversation? In short, bringing more information into play does not in and of itself solve the problem of warranted inference in the analysis of talk.

The second issue also concerns the empirical control over inference. The claim that participants display particular understandings of conversational events is usually based on analyses of collections of comparable conversational materials in which similarly shaped and situated utterances can be shown to have similar consequences or to function in the manner claimed.

Heritage (1984b), for example, has pursued the function performed by the particle "oh" across a range of mundane conversations in which it appears reliably to mark "some kind of change in [a speaker's] locally current state of knowledge, information, orientation or awareness" (p. 299). "Oh" in part represents a participant's "analysis" of the particular import of a prior utterance, as one, perhaps designed to but nevertheless receipted as, prompting a "change of state" of some sort. What is entailed is not simply Heritage's intuition (or yours, or mine) but the pursuit of this particle in many conversations and through different sequential contexts (e.g., informings, counterinformings, other initiated repair, understanding checks, displays of understanding, and new topic beginnings). He observes that

> although it has been almost traditional to treat "oh" and related utterances (such as "yes," "un huh," "mm hm," etc.) as an undifferentiated collection of "back channels" or "signals of continued attention" . . . such treatments seriously underestimate the diversity and complexity of the tasks these objects are used to accomplish. . . . Within this collection, "oh" is unique in making a change-of-state proposal which is most commonly used to accept prior talk as informative. (Heritage, 1984b, p. 335)

To be sure, initial purchase on some phenomena may be gained on intuitive grounds, but this is merely the beginning. From this point on, the phenomenon is "worked up" by searching across many conversations, resulting in increasing empirical control and a more general understanding of the process that generates it. When applied to new cases (which, of course, could undercut the formulation and force its revision) such empirically grounded formulations furnish a warrant for the identification of particular conversational events. Indeed, the cumulative results of conversation analytic research should permit a detailed understanding of particular, singular conversations (Schegloff, 1987a).

Grounded critique. The development of empirically warranted inference beyond initial intuition also accounts for the insistence, noted by Jackson (1986), that any critique of analytical results within the tradition must itself be empirically grounded, that is, based on alternative analysis of appropriate materials. Disagreements concerning a given analysis must be based on either the demonstrable failure of the analysis to account adequately for the details of the exemplars presented or by providing additional data that the analysis should account for but does not. Jacobs (1986), working within the discourse analytic perspective, provides an example of an empirically based critique and reformulation of previous work (see also Schegloff, 1980). The validity of claims rests on their empirical support and not their plausibility or intuitive appeal.

This canon of procedure does not preclude criticism of research findings; instead, it subjects criticism to the same standard of evaluation as the work being criticized, namely, accountability to the data of actual conversation. Constructed or "remembered" counterexamples (see below) or the invocation of considerations external to the data of conversation carries little weight by this criterion. By honoring it, strong constraint is placed on the undisciplined use of intuition (what seems plausible or reasonable given what "anyone knows" about talk and interaction) and the speculative inferences that follow from it. It also encourages the habit of returning again and again to collections of conversational materials to determine the robustness of reported phenomena.

Appropriate Data

The third corollary to the organization principle addresses the question of what data are appropriate. If the domain of interaction is autonomously organized, then the appropriate data for analysis would be the naturally occurring interaction occurring within it. The logic here is straightforward: The object of study is the discovery and description of the workings of a form of social organization that, as a set of methodical procedures, enables interactants to manage complex and detailed streams of coordinated activity. It would seem to follow that the logical place to observe that organization is an occasion where talk and conduct are not contrived, channeled, or constrained for research purposes. Thus a "domain of data" principle:

> The data of conversation analysis should be drawn from the domain of naturally occurring talk and action.

Constructed examples. Some students of discourse (e.g., Jackson, 1986) argue that there is a role for contrived examples, including episodes of fully interactional speech exchange. The premise of this proposal—which is rooted in the linguistic tradition carried over by practitioners of discourse analysis (see Levinson, 1983)—seems to be that since the aim of analysis is to clarify and render explicit the intuitions of speaker-hearers, including analysts, the recourse to intuition to build examples is a legitimate tool for testing ideas and guiding research (Jackson, 1986; Sigman et al., in press; but see McLaughlin, 1984).

There are several objections to this proposal from the conversation analytic viewpoint. First, since the resources for organizing conversation are built to deal in detail with the specifics of various interactional circumstances, a constructed example built out of intuition alone is unlikely to reflect the subtlety of the operation of the conversational mechanisms as they operate on actual situations (recall here the discussion of achievement). While hypothetical examples may be plausible, this is a weak warrant for their bearing on the issue of how talk proceeds in actual situations. As I have argued above, this is an empirical question.

A closely related second objection is that while "intuition" (one's tacit understanding of the dynamics of conversational interaction) may provide initial access to the phenomenon, the possibility of processes operating out of the awareness and intuitive reach of participants must not be foreclosed in favor of getting on record the speaker-hearer's or analyst's intuitive (and possibly naive) notions of how talk is organized (Jefferson & Shenkein, 1978).

Indeed, if the analysis of conversation is to be anything more than an intuitive, interpretive exercise carried on through artfully posed opinions about what is going on in some segment of talk, or what is possible or plausible in interaction, then intuition and its offspring, interpretation, must be disciplined by reference to the details of actual episodes of conversational interaction. Thus while conversation analysts may occasionally have recourse to constructed examples for expositional convenience, their claims are based on the analysis of collections of conversational events, exemplars of which are presented to instantiate the mechanisms or procedures described in their work.

Laboratory conversation. In practice, much of the audio- and videotaped materials employed by conversation analysts consists of what might be termed casual or "mundane" conversation (see Heritage, 1984a). As a natural site for interaction, records of such conversations should furnish an ample basis for the study of the general organizational form of conversational interaction. There are a number of issues involved here, among them the question of how to regard talk situated in other circumstances, and most particularly, in the laboratory setting. The laboratory can furnish a useful setting for making technically superior recordings, whether audio or video.

If one brings subjects into a laboratory to record their verbal interaction, we might ask, Are such verbal encounters "conversations"? The answer is, It depends. I have already noted that Sacks et al. (1974) provide a definition of conversation as a species of speech-exchange system, namely, one in which turn size, turn order, and turn content are free to vary. If there are no prior constraints affecting the order, length, or content of turns at talk, then however unusual its auspices, the encounter falls within the definition of conversation as a speech exchange system. (There may be other constraints, for example, in their manner or starting and ending, and these must be taken into account in the analysis of the data.)

In the data collected by West (1978) and utilized by Maynard and Zimmerman's (1984) study of topic initiation, it could be observed that participants found the laboratory setting to be "strange" (and said so often). Moreover, the conversations were contrived, in a specific sense, that is, without the machinations of the researcher, they were highly unlikely to occur, and in that respect were not "naturally occurring" but rather "artificial," although the latter member-analytic term (see Atkinson, 1982) is in need of more careful scrutiny.

However, it does not seem likely that—granting that the occasion was unusual and even anxiety provoking—the participants had recourse to a different or freshly devised organization of conversation, and in particular, that they altered the usual way in which turn taking is managed. Their talk was fully interactional, that is, each addressed themselves to the other, to the other's talk, and each was thus presumably constrained in their own conduct by the other's actual or anticipated responses (see Schegloff, in press). The uniform way in which they dealt with their circumstances suggests that however "unnatural" the auspices of the talk and its physical setting, they (as dyads) independently and repeatedly employed common resources to produce talk that in significant ways was strikingly similar from trial to trial (see Maynard & Zimmerman, 1984).

The point here, of course, is that there can be a place for laboratory-generated talk within the conversation analytic paradigm. Space limitations preclude a full consideration here of the issues involved in the generation and analysis of this type of data other than to note that the laboratory paradigm must be carefully evaluated with respect to the constraints it places on subjects' verbal interactions (see McLaughlin, 1984).

Sequential Organization

The turn-by-turn character of conversational interaction yields yet another major working principle, that of "sequential organization":

The fundamental framework of conversation is sequential organization.

The concern for sequential organization is one of the most characteristic features of conversation analytic work. The structures of talk thus far identified by research in this tradition hinge, in one respect or another, on sequential processes.

Heritage (1984a) notes, for example:

Conversation analysis is . . . primarily concerned with the ways in which utterances accomplish particular actions by virtue of their placement and participation within sequences of action. It is sequences and turns-within-sequences which are thus the primary units of analysis. (p. 245)

Sequential organization, he suggests in a nice turn of phrase, provides for an "architecture of intersubjectivity" by which he means that such sequential objects as adjacency pairs, insofar as they provide a "reliable and accountable template for action [they furnish] . . . a reliable template for interpretation as well" (Heritage, 1984a, p. 254). The critical point is that for sequentially organized actions, a speaker's present turn displays a particular understanding of the prior turn.

In this fashion, a speaker can look to the next turn to find an analysis of what has just been said through the recipient's response to that talk. If the understanding does not align with that of the first speaker, the opportunity to address that issue would be afforded in the next turn after, which would permit the recipient to discover the discrepancy. It is worth reiterating in this regard that the notion of adjacency and other sequential forms as templates of both action and interpretation provides not only a basic organizational form for interaction but also, as we have already seen, a methodological resource for inquiry.

Local Determination

The principle of sequential organization furnishes the basics for spelling out another, closely tied working premise, the principle of "local determination:"

> The course of conversational interaction is managed on a turn-by-turn or local basis.

The principle of local determination specifies a particular type of contextual influence on interaction that Heritage (1984a) calls context shaped and context renewing. Context shaped means conversational actions cannot be understood without reliance on the preceding sequential context. Context renewing means that a present turn becomes part of the context for the turns that follow. This premise casts sequential organization in the role of providing the immediate frame within which action occurs, but also as it itself is shaped and developed by such action.

This emphasis on local determination appears to raise the question of when or whether factors exogenous to the particular interaction have a role to play in shaping the talk. This fairly intricate issue is the subject of the next section of this chapter.

ARTICULATING INTERACTIONAL
AND INSTITUTIONAL DOMAINS

Granted the importance of examining the conversational or interactional domain as an object of investigation in its own right, how might the organization of interaction be linked to other domains of social life? Consider the notion that there is a general organization for conversation. For every mechanism of conversational interaction identified, there corresponds an issue or set of issues to which the mechanism is addressed. The organization of closings, for example, provides for a means of suspending of the cycle of turn-taking options (Sacks et al., 1974) so that the relevance of further talk is foreclosed, a suspension that is interactionally achieved while affording opportunity for any participant to introduce new mentionables or reinstitute previous topics (Schegloff & Sacks, 1973). Issues such as these constitute the exigencies of conversation whenever and wherever it occurs.

If it is possible to entertain the notion of a broad set of such exigencies, there is no reason to rule out the possibility that the pursuit of some task or activity might confront issues generated by one or another institutional setting that the organization of talk as an integral component of that institutionally situated activity must address. For example, Atkinson (1982) suggests that

> the production of orderliness in multi-party setting is crucially dependent on practical solutions to . . . the problem of achieving and sustaining the shared attentiveness of co-present parties to a single sequence of actions. (p. 97)

The mechanism for turn-taking in everyday or "mundane" conversation systematically provides for locally controlled variation in turn size, turn order, and turn content (or type), as well as exhibiting a bias toward two-party talk in multiparty situations (Sacks et al., 1974). For certain kinds of occasions, such "free" variation may prove problematic in sustaining a specific focus of talk across multiple participants.

In such settings, which include courtrooms, faculty meetings, and other "formal" occasions upon which a number of people gather to conduct business of some sort, one can find rather systematic "modifications" of the turn system for mundane conversation, namely, in turn preallocation, turn-type preallocation, and turn mediation. Turn preallocation, as the phrase suggests, refers to the prior specification of the order in which interactants may speak; turn-type preallocation refers to what sort of turn may be produced by a given type of speaker; and turn mediation points to the practice of granting some designated participant special rights to determine who may speak when, what they may say, when they must stop, and so on (Atkinson, 1982).

Atkinson's (1982) general point here is that particular orders of interactional activity in a society may require the modification of the procedures employed in everyday talk because the conditions of interaction in institutional or organizational settings differ to some degree from those encountered in everyday conversation. The implication here, of course, is that the mechanisms of conversation—in this case, the speech exchange system—are responsive to a set of contingencies that are posed by particular settings that rely on talk as a means of action. Such contingencies might reasonably be expected to vary across settings, and hence, the organization of talk will also vary, although within the limits posed by the stable, underlying mechanisms of conversational interaction.

It is important to note that the variation immediately at issue here is variation in speech exchange systems of which conversation is the primordial form. Talk as a form of work in institutional settings may not be conversation per se but is instead a systematic variant of it, occasioned by the contingencies of the task in question (see Atkinson & Drew, 1979; Clayman, 1987; Greatbatch, 1985, in press; Heritage, 1984a).

Insofar as the speech exchange system in question is responsive to a set of contingencies that themselves could recur in a variety of social and cultural contexts, the variation in question has its primary site in the conditions or exigencies of interaction rather than in the particular society or institutional sector itself. That is, it is possible to conceive of rather different institutional settings in which "the problem of achieving and sustaining the shared attentiveness of co-present parties to a single sequence of actions" (Atkinson, 1982, p. 97) could arise, for example, courtrooms, classrooms, grand rounds, and so forth.

Finally, whatever the speech exchange system in question, once it is configured the principle that sequential organization furnishes the primary framework for interaction still pertains.

Variation in the character of speech exchange system is not the only way conversational interaction might be adapted to the purposes of a particular setting or social occasion. While the mechanisms of conversational organizations have been subjected to fine-grained description and analysis, the actual distribution of particular mechanisms or sequences has been little studied.

Additional study may show that such mechanisms may be differentially deployed in sharpened or modified form to constitute distinctive patterns of talk in particular settings. Part of this deployment could consist of contrasting deployments of sequences or events, for example, in the distribution of other-initiated to self-initiated repairs, which in "mundane" conversation is asserted to be structurally disposed to self-repair (Schegloff et al., 1977) but which might be altered under pressure of certain interactional exigencies, for example, asymmetrical distribution of pertinent knowledge as in lay-professional interaction (Schegloff et al., 1977; Mellinger, 1985).

The autonomous organization of talk as interaction can, then, be inspected for the ways in which it is adapted to tasks and activities directed beyond the realm of interaction per se (see Maynard & Wilson, 1980; Wilson, in press). The pursuit of studies of the internal organization of conversational interaction has yielded a growing literature describing the general mechanisms of talk, which furnishes the resource for the examination of the particular configurations and arrangements that constitute the scenes and settings of institutionally constrained activities (see Heritage, 1985). Workers in the field may of course differ on the gains to be had from focus on institutional talk as against a concentration on mundane conversation, or on what would constitute an adequate approach to the problem of talk in settings, but the autonomy principle does not foreclose such an extension.

LOCAL DETERMINATION AND
THE PROBLEM OF RELEVANCE

The concern of conversation analysis to identify the general organization of conversation anywhere and everywhere it occurs has not favored a focus on the master or situated identities of participants (e.g., gender, age, and race, on the one hand, and student, bus driver, telephone operator, on the other) and how these identities might bear upon the course of talk (but see Sacks, 1966; Schegloff, 1972). The conversation analytic stance requires that any claim that participants are acting under the auspices of some identity be demonstrated in the talk itself, thus ruling out distributional and correlational approaches.

One basis for this position lies in Sacks's (1966) formulation of the "relevance problem of categorization." Noting that any given individual could correctly be characterized in a number of different ways (e.g., woman, daughter, bank president, citizen, southerner), depending on setting and circumstance, empirical warrant must be established for the analyst's claim that a particular categorization is appropriate to some segment of behavior at issue (recall the requirement for consequentiality [Schegloff, 1987b] discussed above).

Note here that the relevance of "master" identities such as age, sex, race, and so on is "naturally" problematic, that is, is a source of practical concern for participants. Master identities—in contrast to situated identities, which are rendered relevant in specific settings—are potentially relevant anytime, anywhere. The emblems of identities like sex, age, and race are routinely and sanctionably available on virtually every occasion, and that participants sometimes take great steps to conceal the signs of such identity or fabricate alternative ones (see Garfinkel, 1967, on passing) is but one indication of the relevance of such identities to the conduct of social life.

The omnipresence of master identities poses the indigenous problem of determining when and in what way they become relevant for current activity. A particular individual may be the target of a range of behaviors, none of which is marked for its relevance to a given identity, but which may have been occasioned by it; that is, enacted in response or with regard to, for example, racial or sexual status. If the matter is topicalized, the party initiating this conduct may deny the asserted relevance, proposing instead that it was due to some other identity or circumstance, or was interpreted improperly. The source of the conduct, if the latter is rendered notable at all, is contentiously ambiguous. The matter is further complicated by the fact that the salient feature of the categorical identity may be derivative rather than direct, involving power or status relative to other identities, for example, male versus female, white versus black, and so on.

Thus the relevance to discourse of attributes such as race or sex may be intrinsically difficult to demonstrate in conversational terms as compared relative to discourse identities, which are integrally tied to the detail of conversational interaction. Indeed, it may be that at the level of master identities, their bearing on talk is artfully shielded from convenient demonstration, either by participants or analysts, by virtue of the ubiquity of the conversational conduct at issue. The only recourse, it seems, is distributional analysis, which can show that persons that can be categorized in a particular way are disproportionately subject to particular conversational fates. Such recourse is sometimes seen as compromising the rigorous standards of demonstration required by the conversation analytic approach.

In this light, the seeming neglect of this problem may be understood as a strategic decision that the best course for the progress of work in the area is to press the analysis of the organization of conversation as such without pursuing its linkages to master or situated identities and their influences on this form of interaction (see Schegloff, 1987b, in press). The attempt to trace such influences is seen as diverting attention from the prior task of understanding the mechanisms of conversation in their own terms, although the possibility of such exploration is neither denied nor foreclosed.

These considerations notwithstanding, it would be useful to examine the problem of establishing the relevance of external identities to specific spates of talk. As a case in point, let me briefly review work that my colleague Candace West and I have done attempting to relate the initiation of interruption to gender in conversation (West, 1978, 1982; Zimmerman & West, 1975; West & Zimmerman, 1983). In one study, we found that in conversations between acquainted persons recorded in a university community, males initiated nearly all the interruptions (96%). A laboratory study using previously unacquainted students conducted several years later found a similar, if less dramatic pattern, with males initiating three-quarters of the interruptions in five 10-minute conversations. In this work, we assumed that interruption, which asserts a claim to a turn over, against the right of a current speaker to complete it, constituted an exercise of dominance, or power.

The first issue of note is that the evidence for the relevance of speaker's sex to interruption is distributional in character, and founded on the identification of the sex category of speakers by the researchers. This is, in conventional terms, a standard procedure. Although, as Schegloff (1987b) points out, it may be the case that persons of a given sex initiate interruption more frequently than those of the other, focus on this fact ignores the possibly orderly process that might unfold from that point, that is, the resolution of the simultaneous speech occasioned by the interruption. He suggests that the process of resolution is not determined by the gender of the participants, but is rather under local control—the principle of local determination.

West (1978, 1982) examined the outcome of such a process subsequent to the initiation of interruption. Resolution of simultaneity is an interactive process involving competition for the turn space, including continuation by the recipient of their utterance, finishing the interrupted utterance in overlap, and dropping out by leaving the overlapped utterance incomplete (see Jefferson & Schegloff, 1975). When she examined the proportion of male and female recipients of interruption engaging in these behaviors, she found no differences (West, 1982). Thus, while males initiated more interruptions, the process of their resolution was gender neutral, a fact consistent with the notion of local determination. In terms of the "success" of the interruption in gaining the floor, males were proportionately no more likely to succeed than were females.

What is particularly interesting about this observation is that the process of resolution—an interactive sequence of move and countermove—is a response to an initial move that, on distributional grounds, appears linked to master identity. The outcome of the process, however, was subject to local, sequential constraints. Note, however, that because males initiated interruptions more frequently, they were, in absolute terms, more successful in gaining the floor. Nevertheless, the sex-relevant input is "passed through" the sex-neutral sequential organization of resolution to yield, in this case, a sex-relevant outcome (Wilson, 1985).

One avenue of approach to the "linkage" problem suggested by this example is the possibility that exogenous factors such as master identity enter into conversation as moves that initiate sequences. Interruptions, for example, may occasion the repair or resolution of the resulting simultaneity. Such initiations are likely candidates for exogenous influences to the extent that it is the case that they are not directly subject to prior, sequential constraints, although once undertaken, they become subject to them. This approach does not satisfy the requirement that the relevance of the proposed identity be demonstrated, but it does point to one class of locations in conversation where one might look for such evidence.

The preceding discussion was not intended to resolve the issues raised, but to indicate their nature, and the fact that there are different viewpoints concerning them. While the comprehensive description and analysis of the general organization of conversation remains an important task of conversation analysis, there nevertheless is room for consideration of how this organization is configured in different settings and with respect to different types of participants so that the distinctive activities of a society may be pursued at the most detailed and intricate level of experience.

CONCLUDING REMARKS

The foregoing discussion has highlighted some (but by no means all) of the working principles of conversation analysis. Taken together as both a product of and an outlook on the everyday practice of this craft, they are perhaps as much habitual ways of thinking about issues as they are theoretical precepts. The phenomena of concern to conversation analysis is conceived to be of such a nature that detailed qualitative rather than quantitative analysis is appropriate, but it was also suggested that quantitative techniques, thoughtfully applied, have a role to play. While the concern for "naturally occurring" conversation would seem to rule out contrived examples, elicitation techniques, and the laboratory as a site of research activity, with regard to the latter I argued that conversations occasioned by the researcher are hardly less natural than those freely entered into. They are simply different in that they reflect the peculiar conditions of interaction imposed by the experimental frame, which must be taken into account in the interpretation of the data.

The "autonomy principle" could be mistaken for a basis of skepticism concerning the possibility of relating the interactional realm to what is conventionaly talked about as social structure. In fact, it provides an analytic stance that, in discerning how talk is organized, provides the foundation for understanding the fundamental role in the organization of society. Similarly, the principle of local determination could subtly discourage a search for the circumstances under which exogenous factors like master identities influence the course of conversation, particularly given that the requirements for demonstrating their relevance are difficult and there is reluctance to make reference to distributional data.

But these matters constitute methodological issues for consideration and debate rather than settled matters. In short, the conversation analytic approach can be distinguished from other viewpoints on the study of conversation, communicative behavior, and social interaction, but the important point in recognizing those differences is to understand their basis, and recognize that the working assumptions outlined above are the starting point and not the destination, which is the detailed understanding of the fundamental structures of conversational interaction.

NOTES

1. I do not intend to define the boundaries of the approach, but rather to suggest guideposts to some of its central concerns. Although my comments have been strongly influenced by Heritage's (1984, 1985) treatment of similar matters, they represent my view of what should be emphasized. For other treatments of the conversation analytic approach, see the items by Heritage cited above; see also Hopper et al. (1986), Levinson (1983), and West and Zimmerman (1982).

2. He also considered the interaction order to be oriented to the preservation of ritual regard for the precincts of the self, an enclave of the sacred in a larger, secular context. Such concerns are peripheral to the conversation analytic emphasis on the sequential organization of interactional activity (but see Heritage, 1984).

REFERENCES

Atkinson, J. M. (1982). Understanding formality: Notes on the categorization and production of "formal" interaction. British *Journal of Sociology, 33*, 86-117.

Atkinson, J. M. (1984). *Our masters' voices: The language and body language of politics.* London: Methuen.

Atkinson, J. M., & Drew, P. (1979) *Order in the court: The organization of verbal interaction in judicial settings.* London: Macmillan.

Atkinson, J. M., & Heritage, J. C. (Eds.). (1984). *Structures of social action: Studies in conversation analysis.* Cambridge: Cambridge University Press.

Besnier, N. (1982). *Repairs and errors in Tuvaluan conversation.* Unpublished manuscript.

Boden, D. (1983, September). *Talk international: An analysis of conversational turn taking and related phenomena in seven Indo-European languages.* Paper presented at the annual meeting of the American Sociological Association, Detroit.

Button, G. (1987). Moving out of closings. In G. Button & J. Lee (Eds.), *Talk and social organization.* Avon: Multilingual Matters.

Button, G. (in press). Varieties of closings. In G. Psathas (Ed.), *Interactional competence.* New York: Lawrence Erlbaum.

Button, G., & Casey, N. (1984). Generating topic: The use of topic initial elicitors. In J. M. Atkinson & J. C. Heritage (Eds.), *Structures of social action: Studies in conversation analysis* (pp. 167-190). Cambridge: Cambridge University Press.

Button, G., & Casey, N. (1985). Topic nomination and topic pursuit. *Human Studies, 8*, 3-55.

Clayman, S. (1987). *Generating news: The interactional organization of news interviews.* Unpublished doctoral dissertation, University of California, Santa Barbara.

Davidson, J. (1984). Subsequent versions of invitations, offers, requests and proposals dealing with potential or actual rejection. In J. M. Atkinson & J. C. Heritage (Eds.), *Structures of social action: Studies in conversation analysis* (pp. 102-128). Cambridge: Cambridge University Press.

Garfinkel, H. (1967). *Studies in ethnomethodology.* Englewood Cliffs, NJ: Prentice-Hall.

Garfinkel, H., & Sacks, H. (1970). On formal structures of practical actions. In J. C. McKinney & E. A. Tiryakian (Eds.), *Theoretical sociology* (pp. 338-366). New York: Appleton-Century-Crofts.

Goffman, E. (1961). *Encounters.* Indianapolis: Bobbs-Merrill.

Goffman, E. (1983). The interaction order. *American Sociological Review, 48*(2), 1-17.

Goodwin, C. (1981). *Conversational organization: Interactions between speakers and hearers.* New York: Academic Press.

Greatbatch, D. (1985). *The social organization of news interview interaction.* Unpublished doctoral dissertation, University of Warwick, England.

Greatbatch, D. (in press). A turn taking system for British news interviews. *Language in Society.*

Heritage, J. C. (1984a). *Garfinkel and ethnomethodology.* Cambridge: Polity.

Heritage, J. C. (1984b). A change of state token and aspects of its sequential placement. In J. M. Atkinson & J. C. Heritage (Eds.), *Structures of social action: Studies in conversation analysis* (pp. 299-345). Cambridge: Cambridge University Press.

Heritage, J. C. (1985). Recent developments in conversation analysis. *Sociolinguistics, 15*, 1-18.

Heritage, J. C., & Atkinson, M. J. (1984). Introduction. In J. M. Atkinson & J. C. Heritage (Eds.), *Structures of social action: Studies in conversation analysis* (pp. 1-15). Cambridge: Cambridge University Press.

Heritage, J. C., & Greatbatch, D. (1986). Generating applause: A study of rhetoric and response at party political conferences. *American Journal of Sociology, 92*(1), 110-157.

Hopper, R., Koch, S., & Mandelbaum, J. (1986). Conversation analysis methods. In D. G. Ellis & W. A. Donahoe (Eds.), *Contemporary issues in language and discourse processes* (pp. 169-186). Hillsdale, NJ: Lawrence Erlbaum.

Jackson, S. (1986). Building a case for claims about discourse structure. In D. G. Ellis & W. A. Donahoe (Eds.), *Contemporary issues in language and discourse processes.* Hillsdale, NJ: Lawrence Erlbaum.

Jefferson, G. (1979). A technique for inviting laughter and its subsequent acceptance/declination. In G. Psathas (Ed.), *Everyday language: Studies in ethnomethodology* (pp. 79-96). New York: Irvington.

Jefferson, G. (1980). *Final report to the (British) Social Science Research Council on the analysis of conversations in which "troubles" and "anxieties" are expressed.* (Report No. HR 4805/2). London.

Jefferson, G. (1981). *"Caveat speaker": A preliminary exploration of shift implicative recipience in the articulation of topic.* Final report to the (British) Social Science Research Council. (mimeo) London.

Jefferson, G. (1985). An exercise in the transcription and analysis of laughter. In T. A. van Dijk (Ed.), *Handbook of discourse analysis* (Vol. 3, pp. 25-34). London: Academic Press.

Jefferson, G., & Schegloff, E. A. (1975, December). *Sketch: Some orderly aspects of overlap in natural conversation.* Paper presented at the annual meeting of the American Anthropological Association.

Jefferson, G., & Schenkein, J. (1978). Some sequential negotiations in conversation. In J. Schenkein (Ed.), *Studies in the organization of conversational interaction* (pp. 155-172). New York: Academic Press.

Levinson, S. C. (1983). *Pragmatics.* Cambridge: Cambridge University Press.

Maynard, D. (1980). Placement of topic changes in conversation. *Semiotica, 30,* 263-290.

Maynard, D., & Wilson, T. (1980). On the reification of social structure. In S. G. McNall (Ed.), *Current perspectives in social theory* (Vol. 1). Greenwich, CT: JAI.

Maynard, D., & Zimmerman, D. H. (1984). Topical talk, ritual and the social organization of relationships. *Social Psychology Quarterly, 47,* 301-316.

McLaughlin, M. L. (1984). *Conversation: How talk is organized.* Newbury Park, CA: Sage.

Meehan, A. T. (1983). *For the record: Organizational and interactional practices for producing police records for juveniles.* Unpublished doctoral dissertation, Boston University.

Mellinger, W. M. (1986, March). *Linking talk and social structure: Some observations on the study of repair in emergency calls.* Paper presented at the Talk and Social Structure Conference, University of California, Santa Barbara.

Moerman, M. (1977). The preference for self-correction in a Tai conversational corpus. *Language, 53,* 872-882.

Pomerantz, A. (1975). *Second assessments: A study of some features of agreements/disagreements.* Unpublished doctoral dissertation, University of California, Irvine.

Pomerantz, A. (1978). Complement responses: Notes on the cooperation of multiple constraints. In J. Schenkein (Ed.), *Studies in the organization of conversational interaction* (pp. 79-112). New York: Academic Press.

Pomerantz, A. (1984). Agreeing and disagreeing with assessments. In J. M. Atkinson & J. C. Heritage (Eds.), *Structures of social action: Studies in conversation analysis* (pp. 57-101). Cambridge: Cambridge University Press.

Sacks, H. (1963). Sociological description. *Berkeley Journal of Sociology, 8,* 1-16.

Sacks, H. (1966). *The search for help: No one to turn to.* Unpublished doctoral dissertation, University of California, Berkeley.

Sacks, H. (1984). Notes on methodology. In J. M. Atkinson & J. C. Heritage (Eds.), *Structures of social action: Studies in conversation analysis* (pp. 21-27). Cambridge: Cambridge University Press.

Sacks, H., Schegloff, E., & Jefferson, G. (1974). A simplest systematics for the organization of turn-taking for conversation. *Language, 50,* 696-735.

Schegloff, E. (1967). *The first five seconds.* Unpublished doctoral dissertation, University of California, Berkeley.

Schegloff, E. (1968). Sequencing in conversational openings. *American Anthropologist, 70,* 1075-1095.

Schegloff, E. (1972). Notes on a conversational practice: Formulating place. In D. Sudnow (Ed.), *Studies in social interaction* (pp. 75-119). New York: Free Press.

Schegloff, E. (1979a). Identification and recognition in telephone conversation openings. In G. Psathas (Ed.), *Everyday language: Studies in ethnomethodology* (pp. 23-78). New York: Irvington.

Schegloff, E. (1979b). The relevance of repair to syntax for conversation. In T. Givon (Ed.), *Syntax and semantics 12: Discourse and syntax* (pp. 261-288). New York: Academic Press.

Schegloff, E. (1980). Preliminaries to preliminaries: "Can I ask you a question?" *Sociological Inquiry, 50,* 104-152.

Schegloff, E. (1987a). Analyzing single actions and episodes: An exercise in conversation analysis. *Social Psychology Quarterly, 50,* 101-114.

Schegloff, E. (1987b). Between macro and micro: Contexts and other connections. In

J. Alexander, B. Giesen, R. Munch, & N. Smelser (Eds.), *The micro-macro link*. Berkeley: University of California Press.

Schegloff, E. (in press). *Reflections on talk and social structure*. In D. Boden & D. H. Zimmerman (Eds.), *Talk and social structure*. Cambridge: Polity.

Schegloff, E., Jefferson, G., & Sacks, H. (1977). The preference for self-correction in the organization of repair in conversation. *Language, 53*, 361-382.

Schegloff, E., & Sacks, H. (1973). Opening up closings. *Semiotica, 7*, 289-327.

Sigman, S. J., Sullivan, S. J., & Wendell, M. (in press). Conversational structure. In C. H. Tardy (Ed.), *Instrumentation in communication*. Norwood, NJ: Ablex.

West, C. (1978). *Communicating gender: A study of dominance and control in conversation*. Unpublished doctoral dissertation, University of California, Santa Barbara.

West, C. (1982). Why can't a woman be more like a man? *Work and Occupations, 9*, 5-29.

West, C., & Zimmerman, D. H. (1982). Conversation analysis. In K. R. Scherer & P. Ekman (Eds.), *Handbook of method in nonverbal behaviour research* (pp. 506-541). Cambridge: Cambridge University Press.

West, C., & Zimmerman, D. H. (1983). Small insults: A study of interruptions in cross-sex conversations between unacquainted persons. In B. Thorne, C. Kramerae, & N. Henley (Eds.), *Language, gender and society* (pp. 102-117). Rowley, MA: Newbury House.

Wilson, T. P. (1985, May). *Conversational analysis, interpersonal communication, and social organization*. Paper presented at the annual meeting of the International Communication Association, Honolulu.

Wilson, T. P. (in press). Social structure and sequential organization. In D. Boden & D. H. Zimmerman (Eds.), *Talk and social structure*. Cambridge: Polity.

Wilson, T. P., Wiemann, J., & Zimmerman, D. H. (1984). Models of turn-taking in conversational interaction. *Journal of Language and Social Interaction, 15*, 159-183.

Wilson, T. P., & Zimmerman, D. H. (1986). The structure of silence between turns in two-party conversation. *Discourse Processes, 9*, 375-390.

Wooton, A. (1981). The management of grantings and rejections by parents in request sequences. *Semiotica, 3*, 59-89.

Zimmerman, D. H. (1984). Talk and its occasion: The case of calling the police. In D. Schriffren (Ed.), *Meaning, form, and use in context: Linguistic applications* (pp. 210-228). Washington, DC: Georgetown University Press.

Zimmerman, D. H., & West, C. (1975). Sex roles, interruptions and silences in conversation. In B. Thorne & N. Henley (Eds.), *Language and sex: Difference and dominance* (pp. 105-129). Rowley, MA: Newbury House.

Evidence and Inference
in Conversation Analysis

SCOTT JACOBS
University of Oklahoma

C ONVERSATION analysis must be considered one of the most promising new directions available for the study of interpersonal communication. The work done by this research group over the past two decades has revolutionized the way in which we think about language use. Work in the areas of sociolinguistics (Labov & Fanshel, 1977), language development (Garvey, 1977), pragmatics (Levinson, 1983), and even cognitive science (Clark, 1979) has been influenced by the ideas of conversation analysis. Communication researchers would be well advised to consider both its methods and its findings carefully. Zimmerman provides a good explanation of what it is that conversation analysts think they are up to. It is an explanation that should go a long way toward clarifying some of the murkier aspects of the goals and rationale of this program of research.

In this commentary I want to expand upon one aspect of Zimmerman's exposition—the rationale for the methods used in conversation analytic research. In particular, I want to discuss an aspect of conversation analytic methods that I have elsewhere called the method of argument from example (Jacobs, 1986). Despite the confidence they have in their methods, conversation analysts have never really given much explicit attention to issues of inference and evidence—a point Zimmerman himself acknowledges. They have not paid much attention to basic questions such as the following: Just what kind of claims do conversation analysts think they are proving? What kind of a *burden of proof* does their approach impose upon them in order to make a *prima facie* case for some claim? What would an *un*convincing or

AUTHOR'S NOTE: I thank Sally Jackson, Barbara J. O'Keefe, and Daniel J. O'Keefe for useful comments and discussion ideas.

Correspondence and requests for reprints: Scott Jacobs, Department of Communication, University of Oklahoma, Norman, OK 73019.

Communication Yearbook 11, pp. 433-443

weakly documented case look like? For the most part, the "logic" behind the methods of analyzing data and of demonstrating claims remains unarticulated and uncodified. The result has been a great deal of misunderstanding concerning the nature of conversation analytic methods. And much of this misunderstanding revolves around the evidentiary role of examples.

In the following sections I hope to provide some basis for evaluating the degree to which any particular conversation analytic study meets the demands for proof imposed on it by its own overall theoretical framework. I also hope to dispel some of the more comprehensive doubts skeptics might entertain concerning the status of conversation analysis as a rigorous program of empirical research.

THE USE OF EXAMPLES IN
CONVERSATION ANALYSIS

Turn to any conversation analytic study and you will find one or more fragments of conversation prominently featured. What typically happens in the study is this: The analyst "works through" the details of these fragments to arrive at a particular characterization of features displayed. Then, on the basis of the characterization of these examples, some general categorical claim is made about the properties of conversational organization.

To anyone trained in the paradigm of experimental research, such analyses come off as nothing more than interesting speculation that happens to get illustrated concretely. How, one wants to ask, can one analyst's *intuitions* about *examples* of conversation count as empirical evidence for a general property of conversation? How do we objectively verify the existence of the features the analyst claims to see in the examples without obtaining judgments from respondents drawn from the community of language users at large? And don't empirical claims about conversational practices and interactional structures require *systematic* sampling and coding of observations?

Now, some might object at this point that I have not really accurately characterized conversation analytic methods. Conversation analysis, the objection might go, does not really employ a method of examples at all. Rather, it follows a kind of inductive logic based on broad-scale sampling of naturally occurring conversations and fine-grained analysis of the transcripts and taped records of those conversations with claims grounded in the close examination of the details of naturally occurring talk. And conversation analysts are at pains to point out this requirement when distinguishing their approach from the approach used by, say, speech act theorists (see Cole & Morgan, 1975) or cognitive scientists (see Schank & Abelson, 1977), who argue from hypothetical examples or other artificially constructed fragments of discourse (see Zimmerman's comments on this matter). Certainly no one should deny that, at least in part, the reader's confidence in the claims made in conversation analytic studies comes from the traditional warrants of qualitative study—that a broad, extensive data base has been obtained, that the data base is extracted from naturally occurring events, that close, careful observation has been conducted, that disconfirming cases have not been observed, and so on. And, as Zimmerman argues, the fact that analysts must confront naturally occurring conversation does "discipline" their intuitions and provide argumentative resources that are not available when using hypothetical examples.

But examples do more than just illustrate conclusions for which justification resides in analysis of broader collections of data. The conclusions are, in important ways, justified by *what the examples show*. The specific features intuited in the examples that are actually presented in the text ultimately provide the primary evidence for the existence of the asserted properties of conversation. And it is the cogency of the analysis that is given in the text of those examples presented in the text that, ultimately, makes a convincing or unconvincing case. So we need to examine how arguments from examples augments these other aspects of the methods of conversation analysis.

METHODOLOGY AND PROOF

There is a natural tendency in any discipline to equate empirical data and methodological procedures with the kind of data and rules of procedure that are traditionally used in the normal research paradigms of that discipline. We tend to forget that what makes data "empirical" and what makes rules and procedures "methodical" is their grounding in a broader rationale for producing justifiable knowledge claims. Jackson (1986) makes just this point, suggesting that "methodology is best seen as a way of generating arguments about empirical claims" (p. 133). She argues that specific design and analysis procedures should be seen "not as guarantors of correct conclusions, but as routinized solutions to argumentative problems" (p. 131).

From this viewpoint, methods can be seen as standardized ways of ruling out counterarguments to the validity of research designs. For example, random assignment of replications to treatment groups is a standard line of argument in anticipation of skeptical objections that group differences may be the result of differences in the individuals assigned to the groups rather than the result of treatment effects. Jackson points out that once it is seen that "the 'method' is in what has to be proven, not in any specific, concrete way of proving it" (p. 132) none of these design features becomes indispensable. She gives examples of how advances in research methodology show that, given sufficient ingenuity by the researcher, one may find that a standard line of argument can be replaced by some other form of argument.

Of course, the choice of any particular method always involves a more or less calculated trade-off between establishing certain kinds of claims and neglecting (or, rather, *presuming*) others. No method allows an equally strong defense against all possible sources of doubt. This is why methodology textbooks always caution the researcher to select the method best suited to answering the research question being posed. A choice of method reflects a judgment by the researcher concerning what types of claims can be most safely taken for granted, what types of claims are most problematic, and what types of evidence would most strongly support those claims that are problematic.

The methods of conversation analysis also have their own strengths and weaknesses, their own trade-offs. These trade-offs reflect the presumptions and concerns that grow out of the way in which conversation analysts view their subject matter. And they also reflect alternative ways of giving support to claims that have traditionally been established by other means.

USING EXAMPLES TO MAKE CLAIMS

Toward the end of providing a basis for evaluating the strength of the claims that can be supported by examples, let me suggest several rules of thumb and their rationales.

Patterns of Inference and Coherence

As Zimmerman points out, the goal of conversation analysis is to explain social order by describing the "machinery of conversation"—the practices and commonsense reasoning processes by which conversationalists display and recognize that order. For a conversation analyst, terms such as *order*, *orderliness*, and *organization* are closely related to terms such as *meaningfulness*, *interpretability*, and *recognizability*. Order is not exhibited in conversation simply, or even primarily, by regularities of patterning or by the frequent occurrence of some practice. Order is available to direct inspection of conversational materials because that order consists of the ways in which the utterances *make sense*. The direct inspection and analysis of transcripts and the subsequent display and analysis of selected examples in research reports allow the analyst (and the reader) to examine the detailed evidence for inferences, interpretations, and expectations and for the practices by which these are constructed and displayed in conversation. These details are recognizable and meaningful to natural language users as part of our communicative competence. And while conversation analysts may find regularities in the patterning of conversation, it is the meaning of any pattern that can be most strongly shown with examples.

For example, in fragment 1 below, we do not need to know how frequently compliments are received with downgraded evaluations to see that L's response to A's compliment is a downgrade that avoids either full agreement or disagreement with the compliment, nor do we need such knowledge to see that such a response is a systematic possibility provided by "the machinery of conversation."

(1) The referent is L's new bride

    A: She's a fox!

    L: Yeh, she's a pretty girl.

    A: Oh, she's *gorgeous!* (Pomerantz, 1978, p. 96)

Or, again, we do not need to know anything about the frequencies with which patterns like fragment 2 occur in order to see that a "collapsing" of sorts has occurred, that such a collapsing is based on an orientation to a possible upcoming request by A for some chocolate filbert, or that the building of "prerequests" like A's and preemptive replies like B's are systematic possibilities of language (see Jacobs & Jackson, 1983).

(2) A: What's chocolate filbert?

    B: We don't have any. (Sacks, 1967, lecture 9, p. 3)

The strongest use of examples, then, is not to support claims about behavioral regularities at all—though conversation analysts do find them and report them. The use of examples, I have in mind, supports claims about the structural possibilities and coherent configurations generated by conversational machinery. Here, conversation analysts work through the details of conversation fragments together with intuitions about those details to reflect the rules and procedures that generate the sense and order found in the examples.

On the other hand, claims about the relative frequency of occurrence or the situational variability of some conversational form can be supported only weakly by examples, if at all (see Jackson, 1986; Jacobs, 1986). Often, conversation analysts present examples that are prototypical in appearance in close conjunction with claims about observable regularities in conversational patterning. But the presentation of such examples does not justify any inference about the relative frequency or the relative distribution of occurrences of that type—no matter how casual the claim ("sometimes," "often," "usually") or how absolute ("always," "never"). Neither the fact that an example is prototypical in appearance nor the fact that it was recorded from naturally occurring conversation warrants the inference that examples of this type are typical in occurrence.

Of course, clear-cut examples can be used to remind readers of obvious regularities that anybody knows about and that, once pointed out, will be wholly uncontroversial. One hardly needs a quantitative demonstration of the claim that people usually reply to greetings in kind or that one way people sometimes lead into requests is with conventionalized formulas such as "Are you busy?" But caution is needed. The fact that we can readily recognize the function of a feature does not prove that we readily use the feature to perform that function. The warrant for our confidence in such claims rests in our confidence in the analyst's observations and in our own experience as participants in human life—and not in any properties apparent from the example itself. The display of the examples here serves at best as a secondary argument. With more controversial, counterintuitive claims the use of examples moves toward simple illustration of what the analyst claims to have seen in the process of examining transcripts. Here the warrant for the claim rests entirely in our confidence in the analyst's procedures for collecting and analyzing data.

Now, there is room for confusion on this distinction. Examples will often display expectations and interpretations of interactional features and patterns that are congruent with the assertion of a regularity. But we should not be confused about the evidentiary force of the examples. For instance, conversation analysts claim that there is a "structural preference" for agreement (see Pomerantz, 1978) or for affiliation (Heritage, 1984) in sequentially implicated replies. They claim to find in their observations of naturally occurring conversation that "structurally dispreferred" replies (e.g., rejections to invitations) are "routinely" designed to incorporate features such as delays; prefatory material; markers like "uh" or "well"; token agreements, appreciations, or apologies; hesitations; accounts; and mitigations, indirection, and qualifications of the actual reply (Heritage, 1984; Levinson, 1983). These features can be readily recognized in examples such as fragment 3.

(3) B: Uh if you'd care to come over and visit a little while this morning I'll give
           you a cup of coffee.

     A: hehh Well that's awfully sweet of you, I don't think I can make it this
           morning. hh uhm I'm running an ad in the paper and—and uh I have to
           stay near the phone. (Heritage, 1984, p. 266)

Clearly, the examples themselves do not show that such features regularly occur with disagreeable or disaffiliating replies, or that these features appear any less regularly with agreeable or affiliative replies. But such examples do demonstrate the existence of the preference as a *system of meaning* because readers can tacitly appreciate what the features displayed in the examples *mean*.

Paradigm Cases

Conversation analysts operate on the presumption that the describable features of conversation are intersubjectively available; that is, the features are a communicative achievement that can be reliably discerned by natural language users who are properly instructed in how to look. *Prima facie* evidence for the accessibility of any feature is the display of clear-cut, obvious cases that strongly resonate with the reader. Where such cases cannot be displayed, we should have strong doubts about the reliability of the observations. Where clear-cut cases are the subject of analysis, the call for respondent judgments or transcript coding seems least pressing. Schegloff's (1968) study of summonses, for example, makes reference to an informal classification of 500 observed cases. But the instances are so clear-cut that only the most dogmatic skeptic would demand a formal coding.

One might worry, however, that there is an inherent bias in dealing only with clear-cut cases, that the properties of less clearly defined cases may differ substantially from the properties of paradigm cases. Indeed, it would be surprising if cases that stood at the fuzzy boundaries of a conversational form did not differ! The fact that they are less apparent is a communicative property of such instances—a property that conversational participants themselves attend to (see Jacobs & Jackson, 1983). This circumstance should not be taken as a problem in the conceptual properties of the analyst's category system, but as an intrinsic property of natural language. Exhaustive coding is not likely to be a satisfactory solution to such worries, as coding presupposes reliable recognition procedures—and that is precisely what is absent in the cases in question. The best way to study such cases is not by force fitting them inside or outside the boundaries of some artificial category, but by encountering them in a way that preserves the details that give rise to vagueness and ambiguities in the first place.

Variety

The display of paradigm cases is the basic confirmatory evidence that some feature or pattern exists. But examples are used to do more than just point to a feature or pattern; they are used to justify a technical description of it. And to show that some particular technical description is correct, conversation analysts need to go beyond this confirmatory use of examples.

I think that the evidentiary power of examples can be best understood by first drawing a distinction between two ways of empirically corroborating claims—what Pepper (1942, pp. 47-51) has called "structural corroboration" and "multiplicative corroboration." These different types of corroboration represent two different "logics" of proof. Structural corroboration comes from the force of convergent evidence drawn from a variety of different kinds of observations. Here, our confidence in a claim is increased as a variety of different kinds of observations give us independent reasons for holding the claim. It is a desire for this kind of corroboration, for example, that lies behind the methodological principle that one should have independent reasons for postulating a theoretical construct to explain any particular type of observation.

Multiplicative corroboration comes from the force of the evidence of repeated observations. Thus our confidence in a claim is increased as that claim is supported by observations that are consistently made by the same individual on different occasions or by different individuals in similar circumstances. It should be apparent that traditional communication research has relied heavily upon multiplicative corroboration for most of its empirical claims—increasingly so as the technology of statistical inference provides ever more powerful procedures for the analysis of regularities in aggregate data. It is a desire for this kind of corroboration, for example, that lies behind calls for judgments by multiple respondents to support intuitions about the features of any particular example of conversation or behind calls for observations of multiple cases of conversation and for tabulations of their frequency relative to observations of other cases.

Examples, however, can provide a powerful form of structural corroboration—corroboration capable of answering many of the doubts that lead to calls for multiple corroboration while at the same time maintaining a faithfulness to the intricacy and context embeddedness of conversational patterning. Our confidence in any technical description of a conversational form or interactional pattern can be strengthened to the degree that it can be shown to be implicated in a variety of different types of cases. Rather than establishing the power of some principle of conversational organization by showing the frequent occurrence of some particular manifestation, showing a variety of different ways in which the principle is manifested can be used to argue for its pervasive implication throughout the conversational system. The display of a variety of different types of examples allows the analyst to argue that a wide range of different types of patterns and features of conversation would be unintelligible unless some particular principle were assumed to exist or some pattern were assumed to have the characteristics ascribed to it. And the greater the variety of types of examples that seem to implicate a claim, the greater our confidence in that claim.

Participant Accomplishments

Conversation analysts proceed under the assumption that the materials of conversation exhibit orderliness because those conversations have been methodically produced by the participants "so as to allow the display by the co-participants to each other of their orderliness, and to allow the participants to display to each other their analysis, appreciation and use of that orderliness" (Schegloff & Sacks, 1973, p. 290). In other words, conversational order is a communicative accomplishment. How, though, can we be sure that the intuitions of the analyst are in accordance with those of the participants? How can we be sure the analyst is not imposing idiosyncratic intuitions or has not constructed biased intuitions through the very process of artfully arranging comparisons among examples? Isn't the process of analyzing transcripts and taped records fundamentally different from the interpretive processes of participants who must encounter the talk as an unfolding, real-time phenomenon from within a system of practical relevancies?

In answer, conversation analysts go to features of the examples themselves for direct evidence of participant orientation to the pattern or principle in question. They assemble a kind of structural corroboration for their intuitions. At the level of the interpretation of particular observations (i.e., examples), there is a frequent emphasis on demonstrating the correctness of any particular interpretation by appealing to the convergence of a variety of details in the example that are consistent with the view that the participants themselves must be orienting to the pattern or feature described by the analyst. So, for example, in arguing for a structural preference for acceptances over rejections in reply to invitations, an analyst may point to the details of B's rejection in examples like fragment 3 as evidence that B is orienting to the dispreferred character of that rejection.

And many types of examples can be assembled as convergent evidence of participant orientations to the principles or patterns in question. So, in addition to finding convergent evidence within any example, the analyst may display examples where issuers of invitations preemptively withdraw an invitation or bolster it upon hearing the respondent pause, hesitate, or use disagreement markers or other filler material before formulating a reply. Or, again, the analyst may point to the use of "preinvitations" (e.g., "You doing anything tonight?") as a way of avoiding open rejection of invitations. Such examples provide independent reasons to believe that in any particular case the analyst is not simply imposing his or her view on the conversational materials. This is one of the real strengths of employing naturally occurring examples. They can be interrogated in a way that provides internal and external checks against decontextualized or artificially induced intuitions.

Now, as Zimmerman also admits, one can never be *sure* that one's intuitions match those of the participants. For, in pointing to such features as would suggest that the participants understand what is meant in the way that the analyst understands it, the analyst must once again use native intuitions (see Sigman, Sullivan, & Wendell, in press). All one can do is find further corroboration for one's interpretations—the problem of the hermeneutic circle. And certainly interviewing informants or providing evidence of membership in the community of language users who produce the conversations does enhance our confidence in the characterizations of the examples displayed. But the point to see is that, so long as the analyst exercises good sense with the materials confronted, the *presumption* of analyst (and reader) membership is reasonable, just as with the presumptions of other research techniques.

Critical Falsification

One may suspect that lurking in the use of examples described so far is a confirmationist bias. Obviously, the artful arrangement of examples can lead readers to arrive at intuitions and conclusions they might not otherwise hold. How do we know that the presentation of examples is not selectively biased to support the claims of the analyst?

All of the rules of thumb suggested above should increase our confidence that bias is not the case, but, obviously, we can never be *sure*. There are, however, two features of research that may increase our confidence that bias is not the case. First, our confidence in the claims of a study is strongest when the analyst gives us reason to believe that potential counterexamples to the claims and counterformulations of the data have been taken into account. In other words, does the analyst appear to have engaged in a self-consciously falsificationist search? Schegloff's (1968) study of telephone openings should serve as a model of this type of attitude. On the basis of a single deviation in a set of 500 observations, Schegloff reformulated an initially proposed rule.

Second, conversation analytic studies ultimately rest on the same principle of intersubjective testing as found with experimental research—can others replicate the findings in a variety of circumstances with a variety of materials? It should be seen that this replication is the responsibility of the research community as a whole and will be a function of the attitudes of that community toward public scrutiny and criticism. Any secure body of knowledge rests on a rather paradoxical characteristic: Our confidence in any line of research is greatest where we find studies being done that *dis*confirm prior claims and findings. It is only then that we can have any confidence that replications of prior studies have not routinely replicated the biases of prior research and that studies whose findings do stand the test of time do not stand for lack of critical scrutiny.

CONCLUSION

The rationality of any research enterprise is guaranteed not by some set of established procedures, but by a sensitivity to the nature of the claims being made, the burden of proof those claims impose, and the kind of evidence that can support those claims. Conversation analysis employs a methodology specially suited to meet the burden of proof imposed by the kinds of claims it makes. In particular, the method of arguing from examples adds a unique demonstrative potential to its methodology.

Traditions of qualitative research have often treated research methodology as though it were a process of personal discovery. Much attention is given to how to find out things. Little attention is given to how to prove what has been "discovered" once it is time for the analyst to write up the findings and present them in a publicly convincing fashion. Writing up one's findings is often treated simply as an exercise in informative reporting. Conversation analysis works with materials that can provide a decisive break from that tradition.

REFERENCES

Clark, H. H. (1979). Responding to indirect requests. *Cognitive Psychology, 11*, 430-477.
Cole, P., & Morgan, J. L. (1975). *Syntax and semantics: Vol. 3. Speech acts.* New York: Academic Press.

Garvey, C. (1977). The contingent query: A dependent act in conversation. In M. Lewis & L. A. Rosenblum (Eds.), *Interaction, conversation, and the development of language* (pp. 63-93). New York: John Wiley.

Heritage, J. (1984). *Garfinkel and ethnomethodology*. Cambridge: Polity.

Jackson, S. (1986). Building a case for claims about discourse structure. In D. G. Ellis & W. A. Donohue (Eds.), *Contemporary issues in language and discourse processes* (pp. 129-148). Hillsdale, NJ: Lawrence Erlbaum.

Jacobs, S. (1986). How to make an argument from examples in discourse analysis. In D. G. Ellis & W. A. Donohue (Eds.), *Contemporary issues in language and discourse processes* (pp. 149-168). Hillsdale, NJ: Lawrence Erlbaum.

Jacobs, S., & Jackson, S. (1983). Strategy and structure in conversational influence. *Communication Monographs, 50*, 285-304.

Labov, W., & Fanshel, D. (1977). *Therapeutic discourse: Psychotherapy as conversation*. New York: Academic Press.

Levinson, S. C. (1983). *Pragmatics*. Cambridge: Cambridge University Press.

Pepper, S. C. (1942). *World hypotheses: A study in evidence*. Berkeley: University of California Press.

Pomerantz, A. (1978). Compliment responses: Notes on the co-operation of multiple constraints in conversation. In J. Schenkein (Ed.), *Studies in the organization of conversational interaction* (pp. 79-112). New York: Academic Press.

Sacks, H. (1967, Fall). Lecture notes. School of Social Sciences, University of California, Irvine.

Schank, R., & Abelson, R. (1977). *Scripts, plans, goals and understanding: An inquiry into human knowledge structures*. Hillsdale, NJ: Lawrence Erlbaum.

Schegloff, E. A. (1968). Sequencing in conversational openings. *American Anthropologist, 70*, 1075-1095.

Schegloff, E. A., & Sacks, H. (1973). Opening up closings. *Semiotica, 7*, 289-327.

Sigman, S. J., Sullivan, S. J., & Wendell, M. (in press). Conversational structure. In C. H. Tardy (Ed.), *Instrumentation in communication*. Norwood, NJ: Ablex.

From Resource to Topic: Some Aims of Conversation Analysis

D. LAWRENCE WIEDER
University of Oklahoma

A persistent though sometimes subterranean theme of the conversation analysis literature concerns the place of tacit members' knowledge in the doing and in the results of conversation analysis. This topic is treated by Zimmerman under the headings of "warranted inference," "appropriate data," and "constructed examples," but there is considerably more that can be said about the matter. It is through concerns with this topic that conversation analysis is thematically as well as historically related to ethnomethodology. Further, it is in the way that conversation analysis treats tacit members' knowledge that it is methodologically unique among the social sciences, with the possible exception of linguistics, whose posture on tacit members' knowledge is similar to but, in crucial respects, also different from conversation analysis.

The topic arises in Zimmerman's exposition of conversation analysis, when he undertakes the clarification of the warrant for the claim that conversation analysts empirically *discover* the actual order in a conversation that is made available to the analyst substantially through the participants' display of understanding in their own turns at talk. Zimmerman confronts Sigman, Sullivan, and Wendell's (in press) contention that the analyst's recognition of what is displayed in a participant's "understanding of prior conversational events" requires the analyst to use his or her tacit members' knowledge to grasp intuitively the particular understandings being claimed as they are displayed in and through some specific utterances in a conversation. While acknowledging the use of tacit members' knowledge, Zimmerman insists that the intuitive employment of tacit members' knowledge

Correspondence and requests for reprints: D. Lawrence Wieder, Department of Communication, University of Oklahoma, Norman, OK 73019.

Communication Yearbook 11, pp. 444-454

must be [and is] disciplined by reference to the details of actual episodes of conversational interaction. Thus, . . . conversation analyst[s'] claims are based on the analysis of collections of conversational events, exemplars of which are presented to instantiate the mechanisms or procedures described in [the] work. (p. 421)

While this posture defends conversation analysis against criticism and misunderstanding, it leaves one other matter in need of further clarification: What is the place of tacit members' knowledge in the procedures of conversation analysis, and how is that knowledge implicated in the empirical status of conversation analytic findings?

TACIT MEMBERS' KNOWLEDGE IN
SOCIAL SCIENCE AND CONVERSATION ANALYSIS

Several years prior to Zimmerman's move from "classical" ethnomethodology to conversation analysis, Zimmerman and Pollner (1970) presented the view of the dependency of social scientific analysis upon tacit members' knowledge, a view that is based on the phenomenological studies of Schutz (1962) and their radical reformulation and extension by Garfinkel (1967).

[Social scientific] inquiry is addressed to phenomena recognized and described in common-sense ways (by reliance on the unanalyzed properties of natural language) [here, the authors cite Garfinkel, (1967: especially Chapter 1), Garfinkel and Sacks (1970), and Sacks (1963)], while at the same time such common-sense recognitions and descriptions are pressed into service as fundamentally unquestioned resources for analyzing the phenomena thus made available for study. Thus contemporary [social science] is characterized by a confounding of topic and resource. (Zimmerman & Pollner, p. 87)

Social science's profound embeddedness in and dependence on the employment of tacit members' knowledge (and that tacit members' "epistemology," the attitudes of daily life) was found in ethnomethodological studies to be the source of endless methodological difficulties and embarrassments. These range from problems in achieving literal description to the inability to demonstrate adequately the possibility of rationally mathematizing social science data and stating its findings in true logical form.

The tacit employment of commonsense recognitions and descriptions is vividly evident in the quantifying procedure of coding. Whenever the social scientist encounters the concrete particulars of social life (or ongoing communication) and then attempts to *describe* these particulars or to *reduce* or *transform* them into coded occurrences, commonsense or members' knowledge is unavoidably employed as a resource in the judgment that some particular doing or saying is an instance of, for example, "giving support"

(Bales, 1950) or is, for example, "disconfirming" or, more complexly, "one up" (Rogers & Farace, 1975).

The arguments and demonstrations concerning that conclusion are too complex and extensive to state here, but see Garfinkel (1959, 1967), Garfinkel and Sacks (1970), Cicourel (1964, 1968), as well as Zimmerman and Pollner (1970) and Sacks (1963), for some of the most prominent pre-1971 pieces of ethnomethodological work concerning this matter.[1]

The early works of Sacks (1963) can be read in the present context as articulating those problems concerning the philosophy and methodology of social science, the solution of which served as the initial motivations to develop conversation analysis. Sacks found it deeply puzzling that (1) social scientists could so easily take for granted that they understood what persons in a society were saying or doing, and by their saying, that (2) they could depict what they understood in the same language that they were depicting, (3) that no real effort was made to describe the language of the societal members in terms that could be coordinated with social science inquiry, and, of course, that (4) the language used to depict the speaking and other communicating of members was not itself described.

Until these tasks were seriously addressed, Sacks held that literal description for the social sciences would not be possible and that social scientific findings would be interwoven with and supported by an unspecified tacit members' knowledge that was simply taken for granted by social scientists in just the way that it is taken for granted by the lay members of the society.

It would be paradoxical if the current situation of conversation analysis vis-à-vis the use of tacit members' knowledge was no different than that of conventional social science as portrayed by Sacks (1963).

Early writings in conversation analysis, however, make their use of tacit members' knowledge as a resource for the analyst quite explicit. Along these lines, Speier (1972, pp. 413-414), referring to a particular conversation that he is about to analyze, writes:

> In coming to terms with the data, as is always the case, I must make continual reference to whatever information I have both from my own experience as a participant in the situation and as a transcriber of the tape, as well as to what anyone would find it necessary to employ as common-sense knowledge of the culture in order to make sense of the occasion in which this speech takes place. I do not maintain, however, that the reader is severely handicapped either because he was not a participant in the occasion or because he must rely on my say-so about it. I assume that the reader could do substantially the same conversation analysis as presented here, using the additional information I might supply. I am naturally aware of the problem of objectification that surrounds the use of such information, but I do not believe any defects that might exist on that score seriously prevent my generating some basic issues in conversation analysis. I believe these issues can be judged by the reader on his own with the data before him.

Acknowledging that one is using tacit members' knowledge in this way is a first step in altering one's methodological situation. That this change is the intent is clear in the explicit and positive references to the employment of commonsense or members' knowledge as a resource for the conversation analyst as in Turner (1970) and Sharrock and Turner (1978). Here the called-for use of members' knowledge contrasts with its ordinary use in the social sciences in several crucial respects. In attempting to grasp those features of an utterance that are available to the hearer of a speaker's utterance, the conversation analyst was to be *reflective* about the resources that he or she employed. The analyst was to inspect the sense that the utterance had for its implications for what the listener must know or suppose in order to see that sense. The analyst was to note that he or she, too, had access to just the same set of interpretive resources as those available to the participants. The analyst was to make some of these resources explicit in the analysis itself and was to rely on the reader to partake in the same members' knowledge that the analyst employed and make the same judgments based on it to furnish the rest. Indeed, Turner (1970) argues that

> the task of the analyst in analyzing naturally occurring scenes, is not to deny his [member's] competence in making sense of activities, but to *explicate* it. . . . [Such] explication provides for a cumulative enterprise, in that the uncovering of members' *procedures* for doing activities permits us both to replicate our original data and to generate new instances that fellow members will find recognizable. (p. 187)

That is, such an analysis is meant to be able to provide for the description and generation of all possible instances with and in full structural particulars—an aim that remains alive today but that now appears realizable only in the distant future.

While Turner's recommendations for the step-by-step procedures of conversation analysis and his focus upon the elucidation of member-recognized classes of activity (e.g., types of speech arts and types of members) have been substantially displaced by the current focus on uncovering various forms of sequential organization, the general relationship between tacit members' knowledge and the task of analysis remains the same. Showing how this is the case is the aim of the discussion to follow.

TACIT MEMBERS' KNOWLEDGE IN CONVERSATION ANALYTIC WORK

The potential interplay between a conversation as encountered by the analyst and the analyst's use of tacit members' knowledge in recognizing conversational events must be situated in the context of the current conversation analytic understanding of conversation as an available order. In Zimmerman's terms, the order found in conversational materials is there to be discovered because "interaction . . . is a describable domain exhibiting stable, orderly properties that are specific and analyzable achievements of parti-cipants" (p. 416). These orderly properties are produced not for analysts, but for participants by participants. In conducting their verbal activities competently, participants must behave in such a way that their conversational behavior is both recognizable to their coparticipants and makes evident (in some fashion displays) their recognition of the prior, current, or anticipated doings of their coparticipants (see Schegloff & Sacks, 1973; and Zimmerman, this volume). Inasmuch as the actions of each participant are constituents in interdependent, interactional sequences involving the actions of others, the resulting order cannot be traced to the actions or aims of a single participant. It is, then, a concerted achievement. But, since "each must recognize and take into account what type of act and hence what type of understanding of prior acts the other is doing" (p. 418) and since these recognitions or understandings can be displayed in the participant's next turn at talk and that talk will, at least, be consistent with these recognitions and understandings, the orderly features are made visible (and hence open to description) to the analyst, as well as to the participants.

As Zimmerman notes, the way in which the conversation analyst recognizes the orderly features that have been made available has been characterized by Sigman et al. (in press). Employing the same general line of argument that is to be found in "classical" ethnomethodology, Sigman et al. propose that the order that is made visible to fellow participants is visible to the analyst because he or she is also a competent interactional participant. The analyst is able to make "discoveries" by bringing his or her prior cultural experiences (an already possessed tacit familiarity with the phenomenon to be discovered) to bear upon the text. The discovery emerges as the product of an interaction between the tacit prefamiliarity and the textual particular.

Explicit Criteria

The relationship between an already-possessed, tacit prefamiliarity and a textual particular can be clarified and extended by casting it in those classic ethnomethodological terms of the documentary method of interpretation (see Garfinkel, 1967).

In these terms, the analyst approaches a text or tape with an unspecified member's background knowledge of conversational events. This background knowledge functions as a scheme of interpretation in recognizing conver-sational events for what they are within the conversation about to be taken as data. Some features of this background knowledge become activated in the recognition of some item in the text or tape. The item points to, and is interpreted in terms of, some now-thematized piece of tacit background knowledge. That tacitly employed member's background knowledge then functions as an essential resource in the doing of conversation analysis. Zimmerman acknowledges:

> To be sure, initial purchase on some phenomena may be gained on intuitive grounds, but this is merely the beginning. From this point on, the phenomenon is "worked up" by searching across many conversations, resulting in increasing empirical control and a more general understanding of the process that generates it. When applied to new cases . . . such empirically grounded formulations furnish a warrant for the identification of particular conversational events. (p. 419)

This sounds as if members' knowledge as a tacit resource (known intuitively) is replaced by an empirically grounded warrant—that the analyst somehow altogether dispenses with the employment of his or her member's background knowledge of conversational events and more general commonsense knowledge in locating and recognizing further particular conversational events as instances of the phenomenon under analysis.

Zimmerman, of course, knows that tacit members' knowledge is not altogether replaced and dispensed with, but says that it "must be disciplined by reference to the details of actual episodes of conversational interaction" (p. 421). Such a possible replacement of tacit members' knowledge with the full description of that knowledge in the form of explicit criteria has a surface appeal, for if it were possible, then some of the aims of Sacks (1963) and Turner (1970) would be fulfilled. Further, an empirical specification of a complete set of criteria that could be mechanically applied to transcripts could identify all instances of the phenomenon and only instances of the phenomenon. The analyst's and the reader's judgment, employing, as it does, tacit members' knowledge, would not come into play in such an operation except as an after-the-fact critique of the adequacy of the criteria.

Informed Exegesis

Clearly, conversation analysis does not single-mindedly pursue the generation of mechanically applicable criteria specifying its phenomena. In fact, its practitioners rarely focus on the criteria that would specify the lowest-level units of its analysis, which would specify "questions," "compliments," "requests," "summonses," "receipts," and so on for good reason, as will become apparent below. Further, they openly resist simple moves toward the specification of criteria *in the interest of being faithful to the phenomena* (see Shegloff, 1972).

Instead of generating criteria, the conversation analyst typically provides a step-by-step, informed exegesis of some conversational fragment that displays its organization and the understandings of specific conversational objects as they are displayed by conversational participants.

The claim that participants display particular understandings of conversational events is usually based on analyses of collections of comparable conversational materials in which similarly shaped and [similarly] situated utterances can be shown to have similar consequences or to function in the manner claimed. (Zimmerman, pp. 418-419)

It is at just these points that the analyst's use of tacit members' knowledge enters. The analyst's judgment (which the reader is invited to follow and affirm) that the utterances at hand are indeed *similarly* shaped and *similarly* situated and that they have *similar* consequences, or that they *function* in the same way, unavoidably rests in part upon the analyst's and the readers' tacit members' knowledge in grasping the particulars upon which the judgment is based. For example, tacit members' knowledge is unavoidably brought into play in the recognition that some particular pair of utterances function as a question and *its* answer. Seeing the "sequential implications" of the initial utterance and seeing that those implications are realized in the second utterance involves seeing *what* the "question" asks that is *answered* in the "answer." Although the analyst may reiterate the sense of this particular question and its answer (so that we may come to affirm the analyst's identification as our own), such a procedure does not replace tacit members' knowledge with an analytic description. In the very next instance of question and answer, the analyst and reader will once again have to rely upon their tacit members' knowlege in seeing both the questioning sense and the answering sense of the turns.

To the extent that a complete set of criteria cannot yet be articulated and employed in the certain recognition of an instance of some conversation analytic phenomenon (e.g., a question, or, better, a question-answer sequence), then the analyst's members' knowledge is still employed as a resource over the course of a "work-up" of many other conversations in which other instances of these phenomena are located, recognized, and analyzed.

Nonetheless, over the course of one or several analyses, something critical has occurred in making tacit members' knowledge explicit. Recurrent features that conversationalists attend to have surfaced, been analyzed, and have been located within the general structural organization of conversations, and these features, still augmented with members' knowledge, are used and displayed in judgments that two or more utterances are similarly shaped or situated, or have similar consequences or function.

Structural Location and Sequential Organization

Rather early in the development of conversation analysis, but after the quotations from Speier and from Turner, it became apparent that internal features of utterances (including syntax, lists of lexemes, paralinguistic features, and so forth) provided insufficient resources for conversationalist and analyst and that the sequential organization of a conversation and the structural locations within that sequential organization were deeply implicated in the sense of an utterance or utterance fragment within that conversation (see Schegloff, 1984).

Therefore, for the conversationalists (and following them, for the analysts as well) determining what an utterance is doing, saying, or meaning depends in the first instance, and as its first determining feature, on just where the conversationalists are in just this particular conversation organized in just the way that this one is. For example, what the utterance is doing, saying, or meaning is found in part by recognizing that their conversational coparticipant is in the middle of telling a story, or is near the end of giving a set of directions, or is beginning to offer an invitation. These locational matters are appreciated by conversationalists and analysts in the context of other sequential details concerning the location of the storytelling, direction giving, or invitation proffering within the conversation as it has developed up to that point.

Given the inadequacies of internal features, conversation analysts have insisted on the importance of sequential organization for determining the identity of utterances (i.e., that some particular utterance is a "question," "answer," "request," or "statement of agreement"). Paraphrasing Schegloff (1984, p. 34), every utterance occurs someplace within a sequence. Except for initial utterances, every utterance occurs after some other utterance or sequence of utterances, and its potential relationship to those just prior utterances is *always* relevant to its analysis by the conversationalists. Especially important for its analysis, comprehension, and treatment by conversationalists is the possibility that the utterance in question may have occurred in a structurally defined place within the conversation that, as a slot, has attached to it a set of features that may overwhelm its syntactic, prosodic, or other features.

The Explicit Use of Tacit Members' Knowledge

What, then, is the form of tacit members' knowledge that is rendered explicit over the course of conversation analysis and how is this "rendering explicit" situated within the analysis? Although conversation analytic work takes a variety of forms, the largest number of them begin with a piece of conversation that the analyst selects because it displays an organization or event that is especially worthy of analysis. The analyst then provides an exegesis of the conversational fragment or some part of it to show us, the readers, that the participants were involved in a specific form of conversational activity (see, especially, Schegloff, 1984). The analyst will use evidence that this activity is organized, in itself and in its placement vis-à-vis other utterances, to display an understanding of what is being done, that understanding being displayed to the speaker's coparticipant and to us as analysts and readers. The analyst is likely to introduce general findings, general analyses, and similar and/or contrasting data in showing what the participants were doing and in showing that it does or does not accord with prior analyses of similar materials. If successful, such an analysis strengthens and extends prior work.

The analyst may then go on to show *how* the participants were able to hear what was heard as well as *that* they heard what they heard. What was there in the utterance (i.e., internal to it), in its sequential-structural location, and in its being uttered by a participant occupying one particular conversational role (e.g., storyteller) rather than another, that enabled the coparticipants to achieve the specific hearing that had already been demonstrated in the analysis. Here, the analyst will perform a similar exegesis. He or she will ask if there are things that we already know about the particular activity that could inform the hearing. Are there more or less standardized ways of saying such things? Are they placed in particular places? Are there characteristic ways that they are related to prior utterances? Are there participants who, in terms of conversational roles, are especially entitled to perform certain actions and others who are especially obliged to respond to them? In treating questions of this order, the analyst again draws upon general findings, analyses, and specific materials from other conversations that are similar or contrastive. Again, prior analyses have been strengthened and extended by this particular analysis.

With each analysis that takes this form, prior findings and analysis, as well as tacit members' knowledge, are employed in locating, identifying, and describing an instance of conversational activity and in locating that activity's place within the overall organization of the conversation in which it takes place. While tacit members' knowledge still plays a crucial role, its employment has two distinctive features that markedly contrast with its use in traditional social sciences.

First, its operation is public. The affairs that occasion the employment of tacit members' knowledge and the products of that use, a recognition or a judgment, are displayed in their full particulars for the readers to encounter with "their" tacit members' knowledge and to serve as the object of "their" tacit-members'-knowledge-informed recognition or judgment. Indeed, it would defeat the purpose of the display of data and even of the analysis itself if the readers did not encounter the data in this way and affirm (or deny) for themselves the recognition or judgment that the analyst has also made. Thus the deployment of tacit members' knowledge in conversation analysis is public in a fashion that is similar to the public character of mathematical proofs or phenomenological analysis (Husserl, 1960; Zaner, 1970), where each reader is to work through the analysis for himself or herself and win the results as his or her own.

In conventional social science, many locations where tacit members' knowledge is permitted free and exclusive rein are out of sight of the reader. The coding of verbal data and its transformation into instances of a limited set of types requires the inventive exercise of tacit members' knowledge that, although we cannot judge the specifics for ourselves, we accept as a matter of the author's (or author's assistant's) competence, which is augmented by a report of a measure of reliability.

The use of tacit members' knowledge in conversation analysis also differs from its use in conventional social science, in that it is progressively displaced, bit by bit, by new discoveries that are brought to explicit description. Since tacit members' knowledge is a continuing topic, though not the sole topic, of conversation analysis, it progressively renders its judgments more transparent, more rational, and less dependent on unspecifiable resources. Since the parallel employment of tacit members' knowledge in the conventional social sciences is neither topicalized nor made a matter for public inspection, its dependence on unspecifiable resources (no matter how reasonable that employment is) remains without actual or even hoped for corrective.

The actual posture of conversation analysis toward the employment of commonsense or members' knowledge as a resource, then, is that it is an explicit, rather than tacit, resource that progressively becomes part of the descriptive findings of conversation analysis and then is analyzable as an explicit part of its own descriptive apparatus for describing and analyzing further conversations. The process of analysis is a continual making of the tacit explicit. That which is made explicit for the analyst is likewise something once tacit, now explicit, for the reader as well.

In this way, conversation analysis constantly works toward the realization of Sacks's (1963) rule for literal description: "Whatever we take as subject must be described; nothing we take as subject can appear as part of our descriptive apparatus unless it itself has been described" (p. 2).

Inasmuch as it takes descriptive and analytic work to convert members' knowledge from a resource to a pure topic, and topic alone, and that it takes steps to describe a "usage" so as to make that usage part of one's own descriptive apparatus, the radical shift in orientation toward commonsense or members' knowledge is not something that can be achieved in a single move. Whereas it is possible for the analyst to alter his or her attitude toward such knowledge—from tacit and ignoring employment to deliberate and reflective use—progressive and cumulative analyses are required in order to bring the phenomena to full explicitness and complete description. And such an analysis must be carried out without the guarantee that complete description is a real possibility.

On this point, however, Sacks (1963) reminded us that despite the long-held view within the social sciences that a literal description of concrete cases is impossible because no such description can, in principle, be complete, such a view has never been supported with a demonstration. Sacks argued that our ordinary social scientific descriptions appear to be impossible to bring to completion, because they are written in a language that has not itself been analyzed and that our descriptions "appeal to common experience" (p. 16), that is, to our tacit members' knowledge. But, as we see here, since the "purging" of conversation analysis' descriptive apparatus of not yet fully described components or terms is a progressive enterprise, the very possibility of complete description itself is contingent upon analyses that are yet to be done concerning problems that as of now are unknown. Conversation analysis will either finally be able to produce literal descriptions or will end up being the demonstration that complete description is indeed possible.

NOTES

1. Since much, if not most, ethnomethodological work treats this embeddedness and dependency, a complete reference here tends to become a complete bibliography of ethnomethodology. For one of the more complete bibliographies, which includes much post-1970 work, see Heritage (1984).

2. Of course, the analyst may have access to a tape recording of the conversation, which the reader does not have. This fact is "out of character" for the methodological posture of conversation analysis, which, I would assume, will be eliminated as soon as it is technically possible to provide sound recordings as parts of printed manuscripts.

REFERENCES

Bales, R. F. (1950). *Interaction process analysis.* Reading, MA: Addison-Wesley.

Cicourel, A. V. (1964). *Method and measurement in sociology.* New York: Free Press.

Cicourel, A. V. (1968). *The social organization of juvenile justice.* New York: John Wiley.

Garfinkel, H. (1959). Aspects of the problem of common-sense knowledge of social structure. In *Transactions of the fourth world congress of sociology, IV.* Milan and Stresa, Italy: Publisher.

Garfinkel, H. (1967). *Studies in ethnomethodology.* Englewood Cliffs, NJ: Prentice-Hall.

Garfinkel, H., & Sacks, H. (1970). On formal structures of practical actions. In J. C. McKinney & E. A. Tiryakian (Eds.), *Theoretical sociology* (pp. 338-366). New York: Appleton-Century-Crofts.

Heritage, J. C. (1984). *Garfinkel and ethnomethodology.* Cambridge: Polity.

Husserl, E. (1960). *Cartesian meditations* (D. Cairns, Trans.). The Hague: Martinus Nijhoff.

Rogers, L. E., & Farace, R. V. (1975). Analysis of relational communication in dyads: New measurement procedures. *Human Communication Research, 1,* 222-239.

Sacks, H. (1963). Sociological description. *Berkeley Journal of Sociology, 8,* 1-16.

Schegloff, E. A. (1972). Notes on conversational practice: Formulating place. In D. Sudnow (Ed.), *Studies in social interaction* (pp. 75-119). New York: Free Press.

Schegloff, E. A. (1984). On some questions and ambiguities in conversation. In J. M. Atkinson & J. Heritage (Eds.), *Structures of social action: Studies in conversation analysis* (pp. 28-52). New York: Cambridge University Press.

Schegloff, E. A., & Sacks, H. (1973). Opening up closings. *Semiotica, 7,* 289-327.

Schutz, A. J. (1962). *Collected papers I: The problem of social reality* (M. Natanson, Ed.). The Hague: Martinus Nijhoff.

Sharrock, W. W., & Turner, R. (1978). On a conversational environment for equivocality. In J. Schenkein (Ed.), *Studies in the organization of conversational interaction* (pp. 173-197). New York: Academic Press.

Sigman, S. J., Sullivan, S. J., & Wendell, M. (in press). Conversational structure. In C. H. Tardy (Ed.), *Instrumentation in communication.* Norwood, NJ: Ablex.

Speier, M. (1972). Some conversational problems for interactional analysis. In D. Sudnow (Ed.), *Studies in social interaction* (pp. 397-427). New York: Free Press.

Turner, R. (1970). Words, activities and utterances. In J. Douglas (Ed.), *Understanding everyday life* (pp. 169-187). Chicago: Aldine.

Zaner, R. M. (1970). *The way of phenomenology.* New York: Pegasus.

Zimmerman, D. H., & Pollner, M. (1970). The everyday world as a phenomenon. In J. Douglas (Ed.), *Understanding everyday life* (pp. 80-103). Chicago: Aldine.

11 On the Facts of the Text as the Basis of Human Communication Research

GEORGE CHENEY
PHILLIP K. TOMPKINS
University of Colorado, Boulder

The notion of "text" has emerged as an important and controversial frame for postmodern social inquiry (see, for example, the collection of essays in Baynes, Bohman, & McCarthy, 1987). While offering a particular angle on "textuality" and building on Kenneth Burke's (1954/1964) method of "indexing," this essay argues for the literal application of "the text" to human communication research. In this line of argument, the predicament of the (social) researcher, as well as that of the social actor, is seen as being one of "intertextuality." Such claims are advanced in the interest of bringing more closely together "humanistic" and "scientific" approaches to the study of human relations. The essay includes a critical-analytical illustration of Burkean indexing with respect to a historic document: the U.S. Catholic bishops' 1983 pastoral letter, *The Challenge of Peace*.

People usually think that the nonsymbolic realm is the clear one, while the symbolic realm is hazy. But if you agree that the words, or terms in a [text] are its "facts," then by the same token you see there is a sense in which we get our view of *deeds* as facts from our sense of *words* as facts, rather than vice versa. (Burke, 1954/1964, p. 147)

The only practice that is founded by the theory of the text is the text itself. (Barthes, 1981, p. 44, emphasis deleted)

In his provocative and wide-ranging essay in the recent *Handbook of Interpersonal Communication*, Arthur Bochner (1985) schematizes various

AUTHORS' NOTE: We wish to thank Professor Marshall Brown, Director of the Comparative Literature Program at the University of Colorado, for his careful reading of a previous draft of this chapter and for his suggestions incorporated herein.

Correspondence and requests for reprints: George Cheney and Phillip K. Tompkins, Department of Communication, University of Colorado, Boulder, CO 80309.

Communication Yearbook 11, pp. 455-481

understandings of and approaches to studying human communication. One of the varieties of "interpretive social science" in which Bochner sees great promise he calls *textualism*. As he explains, textualism stands at the confluence of the poststructuralist movement (e.g., Foucault, 1984) and current streams in literary criticism (e.g., deconstruction). One of the central insights of textualism—though it is expressed, understood, and translated in a variety of ways—is that, as Richard Rorty (1982) puts it, "all problems, topics, and distinctions are language-relative—the results of our having chosen to use a certain vocabulary, to play a certain language-game" (p. 140). Rorty (e.g., 1979) and other contemporary philosophers (e.g., Derrida, 1976) have sharply questioned the *representationalist* view of language (and other symbol systems), thus opening up the path for text interpretation to become, in Bochner's (1985) words, "a methodological paradigm for inquiry in the social sciences" (p. 43). This we take as our starting point (and our end point) in the text at hand.

Could it be that the current discussion of textuality has powerful application to all the activities of human communication research? If so, certain implications for the conduct and criticism of research can be articulated. This essay on method will (a) review several approaches to "the text"; (b) advance the claim of a particular understanding of textualism to the conduct of communication research; (c) explicate a consistent and systematic methodology—Burke's (1954/1964) "theory of the index"—appropriate to communication research; (d) offer an illustrative use of Burke's method to a text: the U.S. Catholic bishops' 1983 pastoral letter, *The Challenge of Peace*; and (e) conclude with a discussion of "textualistic" assumptions by which the humanistic and scientific approaches to human communication research can be drawn together into a more accommodating if not cooperative relationship.

APPROACHES TO THE TEXT

Clifford Geertz (1983), in his oft-quoted essay "Blurred Genres," recognizes three metaphors or analogies as contributing to the "refiguration of social thought": the notions of game, drama, and text. The third, Geertz argues, is the "broadest, . . . the most venturesome, and the least well developed." "Text," he continues, "is a dangerously unfocused term, and its application to social action, to people's behavior toward other people, involves a thorough-going conceptual wrench, a particularly outlandish bit of 'seeing as' " (p. 30). At the same time, however, Geertz sees much value in the metaphor of text for social investigation.

> The great virtue of the extension of the notion of text beyond things written on paper or carved into stone is that it trains attention on precisely this phenomenon: on how the inscription of action is brought about, what its

vehicles are and how they work, and on what the fixation of meaning from the flow of events—history from what happened, thought from thinking, culture from behavior—implies for sociological interpretation. To see social institutions, social customs, social changes as in some sense "readable" is to alter our whole sense of what such interpretation is and shift it toward modes of thought rather more familiar to the translator, the exegete, or the iconographer than to the test giver, the factor analyst, or the pollster. (p. 31)

Immediately, the reader is led to ask, How can Geertz (1983) both question and praise the textual metaphor as an analytical nexus in the study of human relations? Indeed, what is the meaning of this seeming ambivalence in Geertz's own text? For us, as students of human communication who draw from both humanistic and social scientific traditions, the answer is in recognizing the potent ambiguities surrounding the notions of text and textuality and in specifying our own use of them to advance human communication research.

As it has been promoted in texts of social inquiry of late, textualism has *at least* five identifiable but interrelated interpretations. (We make no claim that these are all possible approaches under this rubric.) First is the revival and reinterpretation of Nietzsche's (e.g., 1976) view of life-as-text. Nietzsche, whose late-nineteenth-century texts were long considered disturbing (for two very different reasons: links to fascism and the heavy reliance on an aphoristic style), sought to explain human relations with direct reference to the dimensions of literature. Taking perspective—on one's own behavior or that of another—was for Nietzsche fundamentally a matter of interpretation. Explains Granier (1985):

By introducing the notion of interpretation Nietzsche imposes a definition of Being as "text." Being is similar to a text that requires our exegesis, a task complicated by the fact that the text is obscure, often full of gaps, by the fact that several "readings" are possible and that certain fragments even remain undeciphered. (p. 192)

For the "philosopher" (a title extended to all those engaged in social inquiry), what Nietzsche recommends is "rigorous philology": the "art of reading well" in "the search for understanding" (Nietzsche, 1982). Though fraught with unresolvable but strategic ambiguities, Nietzsche's texts provide one inspiration for postmodern thought in philosophy and in literary criticism (see, for example, Derrida, 1976; Nehamas, 1985; Rorty, 1986). Rorty (1986), for example, explains Nietzsche's linkage of identity and textuality this way: "[In a] Nietzschean view, one which drops the reality-appearance distinction, to change how we talk is to change what, for our own purposes, we are" (p. 6).

A second historically grounded approach to textuality comes from the hermeneutic tradition. The hermeneutic impulse has undergone numerous transformations from its nineteenth-century orientation toward biblical interpretation. *Hermeneutic* means interpretation or interpretive understanding. It has been used for the understanding of both text (on its own terms) and context (as the range of contemporaneous meanings surrounding the text). At least two major branches of hermeneutic theory are noteworthy here, represented, respectively, by Dilthey (1976) and Gadamer (1977). In the first view, the interpreter's own context is considered to be a source of biases that *distort* understanding. The second view, in contrast, holds that the interpreter's interests are *productive* to understanding; individualized perspectives allow for new meanings to be expressed as each interpreter analyzes a text.

In allowing for multiple "readings" of social phenomena, Ricoeur (1979) poses this question: To what extent is the model of text interpretation appropriate to the human sciences in general? Ricoeur is most concerned about the process of *inscription* by which meanings become "fixated" in writing and therefore in texts literally conceived. This process, argues Ricoeur, must be fully appreciated by the social researcher if he or she is effectively to interpret social happenings. As Ricoeur (1979) asserts:

> Meaningful action is an object for science only under the condition of a kind of objectification which is equivalent to the fixation of a discourse by writing. . . . In the same way that interlocution is overcome in writing, interaction is overcome in numerous situations in which we treat action as a fixed text. (p. 80)

Thus, Ricoeur continues, "[action] constitutes a delineated pattern which has to be interpreted according to its inner connections" (p. 81). In this way, Ricoeur offers an analytic route in justifying wide usage of the model of text interpretation.

Calvin Schrag (1980) shares the hermeneutic impulse, but argues for an even broader view of textuality.

> The textual model of hermeneutical theory . . . needs to be broadened in such a manner as to incorporate into its scope the spoken word as well as the written word. It needs to be extended to include the sphere of perception and its comprehension of the world as well as the transmission of ideational contents. It demands an inclusion of the reading of nature as well as historically delivered texts. It is as much required for an understanding of the project of science as for an understanding of the various programs in the humanistic disciplines. Such a hermeneutic is avoidable if one is to achieve clarification of the interests and goals of any science of man. (p. 98)

For Schrag, textuality ought to be applied in a more radical, thoroughgoing manner so as to foster more authentic forms of social inquiry. "Hermeneutics, then has expanded beyond the analysis of literal texts; it now is considered applicable to all situations, events and phenomena that can be subjected to interpretation" (Foss, Foss, & Trapp, 1985, p. 221).

Radical too—especially when considered in historical context—is the application of the text advocated and adopted by Marcel Mauss (e.g., 1938/1985). Mauss saw some inconsistencies in the avowed positivism of his mentor, Emile Durkheim, and some of Durkheim's residual categories:

"anomie," for example. Rather than reject Durkheim's teachings, however, Mauss tried to transcend them by suggesting that we

> read our way into the phenomenon, entering into it mentally, deciphering it much as we would a text. When we speak of *reading* a text, instead of *observing*, this reflects an implicit understanding that it is not the words as physical entities that is important but their meaning. Similarly, instead of merely observing conduct in its externals, Mauss would have us decipher it. For Mauss this text of behavior is constituted specifically of the exchanges that we enact through our institutions, the systems of reciprocity and equivalence that are expressed in the ways we work, make and use tools, fight wars, secure wives, or rear children. The social fact is no longer an obdurate, concrete reality; instead it has become explicitly symbolic; it is a web, or language, of symbols with its own particular grammar and syntax, morphemes, and phonemes. (Brown, 1978, p. 150)

Herein we identify a third perspective on textuality. With Mauss (e.g., 1938/1985), "reading" is the primary task of the social researcher. Mauss views concepts (e.g., person, self, community) as "categories of the human mind." As such, concepts can take on different meanings in different "contexts," depending on historical period, culture, and situation. Using this line of analysis, Mauss considers how the very idea of person—as conceived in contemporary Western society—developed through a succession of texts. Textuality, from Mauss's perspective, is a way of directing our attention toward interpretation as the basic approach to social investigation, even to transhistorical analysis.

Of course, a fourth and popular usage of textuality is in the preoccupation with the text that characterizes much of structuralist and poststructuralist criticism. Harari (1979) captures the rationale for the trend with these words:

> Interpretation, in traditional literary criticism, was organized around the author, his [or her] thought, the influences that had affected him [or her], and so forth. (The signification given to a work always came from the outside; it was necessary only to define the point of view in order to be able to characterize the type of interpretation at work.) Structural analysis, however, bypasses the problems associated with the figure of the author as well as other criteria exterior to the text, and instead focuses its attention on the text, understood as a construct whose mode of functioning must be described. As a result, rather than talking about truth(s), it becomes necessary to speak about a work in terms of the validity and coherence of its language. "In itself," writes Barthes, "a language is not true or false, it is or is not valid." (p. 23)

(This preoccupation with text is also characteristic of "New Criticism," the movement that followed "traditional" literary criticism and was in turn followed by structuralism.)

The Harari quotation singles out Roland Barthes (1981) as the structuralist most closely identified with developing the concept of the text. This featuring of an author from among a movement of authors attempting to eliminate the author must surely be an unintended irony, but the characterization is nonetheless valid. In her introduction to a Barthes reader, Sontag speaks of the mandate supplied by "Barthes's notions of 'text' and 'textuality,' " and calls him the latest major participant in France's great national project: "the self as vocation, life as a reading of the self" (Sontag, 1983, p. xxxiii).

In his summarizing essay, "Theory of the Text," Barthes (1981) explains how "the text must not be confused with the work." While "[a] work is a finished object, something computable, which can occupy a physical space," writes Barthes, "the text is a methodological field" (p. 39). This point is central to Barthes's notion of textuality, and he elaborates it so: "One cannot . . . count up texts, at least not in any regular way: all one can say is that in such-and-such a work, there is, or there isn't, some text" (p. 39). Quoting his earlier essay, "From Work to Text" (Barthes, 1979), he makes the distinction clear this way: " 'The work is held in the hand, the text in language ' " (Barthes, 1981, p. 39). For Barthes, then, textuality refers to a domain of text production whereby the text goes on "working" through a potentially infinite *process of signification* (what Barthes calls "signifiance"). Thus Barthes moves textuality to a processual level and away from being seen as a mere "product."

In the radical deconstruction of Jacques Derrida (e.g., 1976) and his followers, the text is cleverly invoked to complicate the problem of "textual identity" even further: Words are detached from authors, meanings are inverted, everything is available for reading and rereading. Thus stated baldly is Derrida's (1976) slogan: "Il n'y a pas de hors-texte" (There is nothing outside the text) (p. 158). In deconstruction, "the denunciation of the concept of representation is *necessarily* based on the structuralist institution of the sign; it relies on structuralist premises in order, paradoxically, to show that structuralism has not fully pursued the implications of those premises" (Harari, 1979, p. 30). Hence, deconstruction is a brand of poststructuralism. When this approach is applied to literary criticism, textuality becomes a central problematic. One prominent Derridean, Geoffrey Hartman (1981), explains that "if predecessors are regarded as capable of interacting with successors through texts or reliques [relics], then they are, to that extent, contemporaries or consociates; and the concept of 'person' or 'individual' becomes 'socialized,' into a complicated blend of symbolic . . . properties" (p. xxv). In this way, the deconstructionist use of textuality both creates and manages ambiguities surrounding the very construction of text.

The literary notions of "intertext" and "intertextuality" also celebrate this predicament. Barthes (1981) explains that "any text is an intertext; other texts are present in it, at varying levels, in more or less recognisable forms: the texts of the previous and surrounding culture. Any text is a new tissue of past citations" (p. 39). For this reason, Barthes invokes the metaphor of the "network" for textual analysis, while crediting Julia Kristeva (e.g., 1984) for systematic exposition on intertextuality. Kristeva (1970) reveals the indissoluble connection between textuality and intertextuality when she writes: "We define the Text as a translinguistic apparatus which redistributes the order of the language by putting a communicative utterance, aiming to inform directly, in relation to different utterances, anterior to or synchronic with it" (p. 12; translated and cited in Barthes, 1981, p. 36).

A final meaning of text that we find in the "discourse-processing" investigations of psychology (and to a lesser extent in communication studies) merits attention here. The popular view of behavior as *scripted* relies indirectly on the textual metaphor. Schank and Abelson's (1977) now classic *Scripts, Plans, Goals, and Understanding* advances a view of human relations that focuses on the text as *an object to be comprehended* in the study of inference and patterned responses to situations; a "script" is, then, a "standard event sequence," a key structure through which the text is understood. Applying Schank and Abelson's work in our own field, Berger and Douglas (1982) have adopted the concept of script in their approach to interpersonal communication. Their assumption that "scripts are more properly viewed as *standardized episodes*—abstract summaries of *recurring* events"—leads them to the view that "scripts are not peopled by specific individuals but by generalized roles" (p. 44), calling to mind Goffman's (1959) dramaturgical perspective on human relations.

We offer this overview of approaches to textuality so as to con*text*ualize our own position better. The meanings of textuality discussed above are by no means exhaustive, but they do introduce our readers to the range of interpretations possible for the text as an analytic tool for social inquiry. Following Miller (1985), we recognize the need to speak of textualities and intertextualities. Given this plurality of concepts, it is not surprising that Geertz embraces textuality with both interest and dismay. We might say that he, along with Mauss, is concerned with the text-to-be-read. Gadamer and Ricoeur are more interested in the text-to-be-interpreted. Barthes, Derrida, and Kristeva focus on the text-to-be-constructed. Nietzsche examines life-as-text. And Schank and Abelson focus on the text-to-be-comprehended.[1] This review is to suggest the interrelationships of the various approaches to textuality, while at the same time highlighting their differences. Textuality, as an increasingly popular concept across the humanities and the social sciences, bridges (and often intermingles) meta-theoretical concerns of ontology and epistemology (see Rorty, 1979, 1982, 1986), theoretical issues such as the dimensions of written and spoken language (see Ricoeur, 1979), and methodological principles such as how to "read" social phenomena (see Mauss, 1938/1985). Baynes et al. (1987) express the shared spirit of many of these contemporary orientations this way: "The object of knowledge is always already preinterpreted, situated in a scheme, part of a text, outside which there are only other texts. On the other hand, the subject of knowledge belongs to the very world it wishes to interpret" (p. 5).

TEXTUALISM IN COMMUNICATION RESEARCH

Given this emphasis on the symbolic, we now ask the deceptively simple question, "How is it that we do human communication research?" Setting aside for a moment the process by which a person is socialized, educated, and trained to become a competent researcher and assuming the existence of researchers who are competent theoretically and methodologically, how is it possible for such persons to do research? We begin the answer not at the beginning but at the end points: "work" and "text." It is possible to begin an experiment, an observational or critical study, a survey, only by being able to imagine the final product and the possibilities of *communicating* the research—as work and text—to colleagues in the field. That is the meaning of the following quotation:

> Recently, James D. Watson and Frances Crick discussed on the BBC how they made their discovery of the molecular structure of DNA, a discovery which led them, along with Maurice Wilkins, to receive Nobel Prizes in 1962. In the course of their discussion they recalled the time when Maurice Wilkins had in his possession an X-ray photograph of DNA with the B form, which he was trying to keep Linus Pauling, Watson and Crick from seeing until he had a chance to exhaust his own study of the photograph. "But," Crick said, "he *had* eventually to make public the photograph because communication is the essence of science." (Garvey, 1979, p. ix)

Crick's remark that "communication is the essence of science" was slightly transformed by Garvey (1979) into the title of his book, *Communication: The Essence of Science*, the purpose of which "is to describe the communication structure of science" (p. ix). The foundation of that structure is, of course, a text: the journal article. The journal process provides a formal and public system of communication for scientists. It also establishes originality. "In other words, to be recognized as the originator of a contribution to science, one must document that he [or she] was the first to publish the contribution *and*, equally important, the first to recognize the significance of the contribution" (Garvey, 1979, pp. 69-70).

Thus we can regard the text as a *motive*. To contribute to science one must publish a text qua journal article. There is no other way; there is nothing outside such a text, although technological advances (e.g., computers) have altered the specific steps in the process by which scholarly works are produced. Nonetheless, there is a more profound sense in which this simple fact redoubles its support for our claim. To imagine the end point of research as a text is to constrain or force one to *conduct* research in such a way, and only that way, so as to reduce all facts, inferences, and proofs to the product of a research report. Nothing can be studied, no manipulations can be performed, no results can be gathered, no conclusions can be reached without the possibility of transcendence into a work with a text. To put it another way, the need to realize a text is a limiting factor *prior* to the conduct of research. In fact, before the final text can be composed, numerous subtexts dealing with theory, previous research, hypotheses or research questions, methods, results, interpretations, and conclusions must be composed or assembled, thus creating an intertext.

We thus state our central claim for this essay broadly: *Text is the locus of (social) inquiry*. We mean to apply this on two interrelated levels. The level of *communicating research* (discussed above) necessarily constrains the level of *representing the object* of investigation (discussed below). In unpacking the quotation used as the second epigraph for this paper, Barthes (1981) explains that textuality helps us to recognize that all steps in the research process engender texts. In this sense, he declares, "There are no more critics [or analysts], only writers" (p. 44). Textuality, as a methodological field, is the domain of all researchers in these distinct but fundamentally inseparable efforts.

The rhetorical critic, for example, must *transcribe* the politician's speech and the opponent's riposte before he or she can enter the critical intertext. "If an author comes to speak of a past text, he [sic] can only do so by himself producing a new text (by entering into the undifferentiated proliferation of the intertext)" (Barthes, 1981, p. 44). The same is true of the experimenter's oral "treatment" of subjects. All of our experiments, observations, questionnaires, interviews, coding schemes, and unobtrusive measures must yield *at some level* a text or set of subtexts. Nonverbal activity, for example, cannot be analyzed without being coded in a symbol system. And in interpreting even numerical data (which themselves are often derived from words), we create a new text. Even the strictest behaviorist must turn behavioral observations into words before they can be presented. Thus textual "production" and textual "interpretation" become intertwined in practice.

Of course, in concentrating on the text, we do not make the foolish mistake of assuming that *everything* is reported. Indeed, neither the lived experience of the social actor (the duree) nor the lived experience of the most scientific researcher can ever be communicated fully to colleagues. Instead, we say that consumers of research have access to nothing but *the* text—except for *other* texts; thus the true "recipe for analysis . . . is *writing itself*" (Barthes, 1981, p. 44).

The theory informing a research report is accessible most often as some kind of *prior* text. "Previous research" on a topic is a network of other texts. The same can be said for the details of statistical tests and computer programs. The research enterprise in communication, as in all other fields, is, then, an exercise in *intertextuality*; it must be, as Barthes (1981) argues, "situated in the infinite intercourse of codes, and not at the end-point of a 'personal' . . . activity of the author" (p. 45). By shifting the perspective slightly, we can now speak of researchers working with/within the interpersonal text of dyadic interaction and moving from there to the fields of group, organizational, even to societal and transsocietal texts. There is nothing outside the text if we are to conduct research and do criticism; textual production is required to discuss even things that *we commonly treat as outside the domain of the symbolic*: When we imagine, for example, that we are making *direct representation* of physical phenomena like the architecture and environment of a workplace in our reports. At the level of meta-research, literary/rhetorical criticism and summaries of empirical research are nothing more than texts *about* texts. And such meta-texts may themselves be recast at still another level of consideration.

From this standpoint, as Rorty (1979, 1982, 1986) argues so well, both the physical and the social sciences must confront the same intertextual predicament. Both types of inquiry are subject to their *terms* for things. To speak of human "essence" is to operate in a language-relative domain just as to speak of what some physical object *is* gives no "direct access" in the correspondence sense. All forms of inquiry, says Rorty (1982), share the burden of getting research texts to work for pragmatic results. What counts as knowledge in physics or sociology is the network of texts that is persuasive for the relevant audience.

In this attempt to redeem our claim that text is the locus of inquiry, we have treated the humanistic and scientific approaches to human communication, represented by criticism and empiricism, as equals under one umbrella. It is time now to acknowledge that at one level, empiricism has outstripped criticism in the sheer rigor of its analytic power by virtue of computer-assisted statistical techniques. In the next section, we explicate a little-known method of textual analysis developed in literary/rhetorical criticism, which can rival empiricism in its rigor and ironically outstrip it by at least one criterion. After explicating this method of humanistic research, it will remain for us to illustrate it and show how it can bring the two research approaches back together as parts of a larger text of human communication research.

BURKE'S THEORY OF THE INDEX

As Tompkins (1985) claims in reviewing the work of poststructuralist criticism in light of Kenneth Burke's (e.g., 1945/1969) insights, Burke's philosophy of language, his rhetoric, and his critical methods celebrated an informed "critical textualism" (our term) long before the current preoccupation with text emerged. Thus we locate Burke's own writings within the intertext on textuality. Put another way, we show how a Burkean perspective on method not only fits into the current discussion on text but also how it opens up possibilities for the social researcher both in communicating research and in representing the object of investigation.

One of Burke's least-cited works offers some of his most valuable comments on methodology for literary and social inquiry. In "Fact, Inference, and Proof in the Analysis of Literary Symbolism," Burke (1954/1964) cleverly outdoes positivism, points to a route toward validity and reliability in interpretation, and advances a strategy for analysis with applicability to any research "text." In this section, we draw on that and several other Burkean texts to outline and explicate Burke's method called "indexing" (see also Berthold, 1976). We do this by moving through a progression of propositions in order of increasing specificity.

(1) *All (social) inquiry yields texts.* Although we are accustomed to viewing *a text* as a coherent and defined body of written discourse, Burke made us aware, even before structuralism, that all commentary may be meaningfully considered "textually" (see also Tompkins, 1985). Acting first as a literary critic, Burke reminds us that one work's context can be read as other texts (Burke, 1941/1973, 1979). After all, there is no other way to treat "the surroundings" or the "referents" of a body of discourse but to describe it with other symbols. Burke (1984) put this critical point plainly at a conference in his honor: He responded to several participants' invocation of "the situation" as an explanatory device by saying, "But we need *words* to talk about *that situation*, or any situation."

Likewise, words (or other symbols) are required to refer to what's inside the head, whether the object of study is brain waves or images or worldviews. This is not to deny the existence or importance of things in the head, but simply to stress the necessary symbolization of those things by lay persons *and* by social scientists. Whether, for example, the constructs of constructivism (e.g., Delia, O'Keefe, & O'Keefe, 1982) are at base preverbal or subverbal is not at issue here; constructs are in any case *words* when they make their appearance in the texts elicited from research participants and in those produced about them. As language users, humans *both* put thoughts into words and put words into thoughts. Thus the role of language in lay and theoretical accounts of social phenomena must be acknowledged completely. Units of analysis such as the decisional premise, with explicit attention to verbalization and verbalizability, serve the authors well in this regard (e.g., Tompkins & Cheney, 1985).

From a view of research-as-text, it is, then, a logical step to consider the interrelations of various methods as intertextuality. For example, triangulation yields a research text written in at least two dialects of the same language. Such an approach displays a sensitivity to dialectic and helps us account for the multiple perspectives possible in a research situation. In this light, Burke (1945/1969) urges the critic (or analyst or researcher) to multiply *vocabularies*, and consequently perspectives, thereby reaching through a dialectical process a workably valid explanation, without falling into unresolvable relativism (see, e.g., Overington, 1977). This is reasonably consistent with the pragmatic, text-conscious position of Rorty (1982, 1986) discussed earlier.

(2) What is *fundamentally* true and verifiable for Burke is that *words are facts.* As he explains, "The ideal 'atomic fact' [in analysis or interpretation] is probably the individual word. We do not say that the [text] is 'nothing but' words. We do say that it is 'at least' words" (Burke, 1954/1964, p. 146). In making his case for words-as-facts, Burke makes two other moves as well. First, he deconstructs the "commonsensical" understanding of deeds-as-facts versus *mere* words; second, he undermines the traditional positivistic aim of a

neutral vocabulary of scientific description for a nonverbal world (Burke, 1954/1964, p. 147; see our first epigraph to this chapter).

As the creators and users of language, we can know its elements directly; for language is what lifts us out of nature, according to Burke. He urges us to realize "just how overwhelmingly much of what we mean by 'reality' has been built up for us through nothing but our symbol systems" (Burke, 1966, p. 5). Put another way, our symbol systems construct what we call the reality of a given situation, and words are the most taken-for-granted facts of those constructions. This view helps us to avoid what Burke (1966) calls a "naive verbal realism" (i.e., a denial of the factual status of words). Moreover, Burke is reminding us that words-as-action have *logical* priority: "Not—in the beginning was the word; but rather—in the beginning was the word-as-act" (Donoghue, 1984, p. 118).

(3) *The presence, absence, and arrangement of words in a text is a publicly accessible means of grounding analysis and interpretation.* Here we find an analog to the objective notion of validity: that our observations are representative of what we claim them to be. The *appearance* of a word in a text is an empirical certainty and is observable. Thus an observation *is what we say it is* when it is literally in the text; this becomes our validity check. Burke explains: "The *exact place* that [a] word has in a given verbal context *really is just what it is.* The other words that serve as modifiers for this one word . . . appear in *exactly their'given actual order*" (Burke, 1952, p. 62). The arrangement of words in a text is thus a factual territory from which one makes a map through inference. Any text is what it is prior to anything one might say *about* it. This proposition, when applied to a novel, or a presidential news conference, or a conversation, shows how indexing works with *a completeness of factual data* accessible to all other researchers in a way rarely achieved with the data used in behavioral research.

(4) *The specific associations or relationships between terms of a text are of three general types: equations, implications, and transformations. Equations* (or oppositions) bear most directly on what equals what (or what is opposed to what) in that a statement such as "War *is* evil" closely identifies the two terms and their related concepts. *Implications* are the suggestive "radiations" of a term; for example, how "order" spins off "hierarchy," "authority," "control," and the dialectical mate, "disorder." As Burke (1966) reminds us, "Many of [our] 'observations' are but implications of the particular terminology in which the observations are made" (p. 46). *Transformations* suggest "from what," "through what," "to what" developments such as "yesterday-today-tomorrow" or a syllogistic progression—such as "Who controls Berlin controls Germany; who controls Germany controls Europe; who controls Europe . . . " (Burke, 1979, p. 183). Of course, here we move a bit beyond our word-facts into the inferential realm; therefore, let us consider the nature of inference.

(5) *We make inferences when we comment upon what goes with what in a text, considering "the company a word keeps"* (Burke, 1941/1973, p. 35).

Following Burke, we maintain that " 'facts' are what [is] said or done, as interpreted in the strictest possible sense" (Burke, 1954/1964, p. 146). When we, in one fashion or another, move the discussion above the facts of our text, we forge into the realm of inference. Of course, one *can* make any judgment one likes about a literary work or any text, but—and this is the key—the "critic" ought to be held accountable to the factual text. Thus, for Burke, a guiding interpretive question becomes "how to operate with these 'facts,' how to use them as a means of keeping one's inferences under control, yet how to go beyond them, for purposes of inference, when seeking to characterize the motives and 'salient traits' of the [text], in its nature as a total symbolic structure" (Burke, 1954/1964, p. 145).

Inference, by this conception, the way we move beyond a "low" and unquestioned order of observations to a new or "higher" order of observations, with the latter of course emerging as another text. In this context, "reliability" has meaning both in terms of the consistency of inferential means by a single researcher and in terms of the consistency across inferences by multiple analysts. Each observer of a particular text may make unique inferences, but each should be held to the facts of the case.

(6) *From the "facts" of a text we make inferences, and from those inferences we construct "proofs."* For Burke, proof (an analog to what the typical social scientific study might label "results") is of two types. First, "while grounding itself in reference to the textual 'facts,' it must seek to make clear all elements of inference or interpretation it adds to these facts; and [second,] it must offer a rationale for its selections and interpretations" (Burke, 1954/1964, p. 147). In the ideal sense, Burke explains further, proof allows us to move from different facts to the same interpretation. Thus equations and oppositions can point to the same interpretation. Once one has articulated proof for a text, one should compare and contrast it with the conclusions of others, allowing the marketplace of ideas to determine which is the most persuasive. But in making such a judgment, the audience of peers should whenever possible return to the facts of the primary text.

(7) In returning to our hypothetical text, we summarize some of Burke's comments about *what to look for in discourse, what facts to select.* First, it is important to consider terms that recur in changing contexts. Such are often the keys to the symbolic structure of a text; thus we should isolate their equations, implications, and transformations. Second, one should note operational synonyms of a word, terms that are synonymous to it in the text under consideration. Third, names and titles are important as condensed symbols for the essences of things. Titles, for example, tell us not only *who people are* but also *how we should act* toward them. Fourth, the researcher should pay attention to beginnings and endings of sections, along with titles and subtitles of the text and its sections. These often represent attempts at "essentializing by entitlement" just as names do. Fifth, terms for order are noteworthy because of the human penchant for hierarchy. And so it is that a given text may make reference to social, physical, or spiritual pyramids. (Of

course, it is the linguistic pyramid, with its enabling and constraining powers, that makes the others possible.) (6) Terms of *scene* help us to place other elements of the text (e.g., agents) and also reveal something about the steps in the patterned development of the discourse. (7) One should observe all "striking terms" for acts, attitudes, ideas, images, and relationships. (8) Terms marking secrecy, privacy, mystery, marvel, power, silence, and guilt may be crucial in that they point to central concerns across cultures. (9) It is useful to note oppositions, what is posed against what; often such relationships suggest dialectical synthesis. (10) One should identify the term(s) at the mathematical *center* of a text (i.e., the "median"); these are often revealing as points in the discursive progression. (11) One should be sensitive to stylistic continuity and break points, along with the terms that contribute most to the shape of internal forms (Burke, 1954/1964, e.g., highlights the "furthest point of internality"). (12) It is interesting to isolate strategic points at which ambiguities are fostered—for example, when one key term is used to cover two seemingly diverse situations (Burke, 1945/1969). (13) Finally, it is helpful to note the *absence* of key terms in particular sections of a text; this absence often signals something important, as when silence in interaction must be labeled, creating a symbolic fact in the text. (Of course, while we may say quite "factually" that a word is not there, we must move to the level of verbal inference to give the "void" some meaning.)

ANALYSIS OF *THE CHALLENGE OF PEACE*

To illustrate the power and utility of Burke's (1954/1964) method, we have chosen a historic text, the U.S. Catholic bishops' 1983 pastoral letter, *The Challenge of Peace* (NCCB-USCC, 1983). The development of this document, spanning three years, marked the full-scale entry of the American Catholic hierarchy into the nuclear arms debate and became a revolutionary moment in the course of their corporate position toward Washington (see, e.g., Goldzwig & Cheney, 1984). As Harvey Cox (1984) observed:

> In 1982 [when the left-leaning second draft of the peace pastoral was issued] the role of the American Roman Catholic bishops in the formation of public policy . . . took a dramatic turn. Issuing a draft of a pastoral letter on war and peace that was highly critical of American nuclear weapons policy, the bishops served notice that Catholics were not interested merely in abortion or the institutional problems of parochial schools. (p. 18)

In developing the document, the National Conference of Catholic Bishops (NCCB) had to confront their own identities as individual bishops and as a corporate body (with over 300 members). They had to balance many competing interests both within the organization of the Catholic Church (e.g., the Vatican, theologians, peace activists, and conservative lay groups) and outside it (e.g., the Reagan administration, other religious groups, and the public at large). Finally, the bishops had to embrace complex rhetorical strategies in order to fashion a pastoral letter that would be both priestly and prophetic in addressing multiple audiences (U.S. Catholics, the Reagan administration, and the "nuclear" world) simultaneously.

These challenges are treated extensively in Cheney's (1985) study of the management of multiple identifications in the development of the peace pastoral. In that study he draws from 30 interviews, Church documents, and media accounts to explore the rhetorical, organizational, and identity-related aspects of the process. Here, we adapt the final part of that study, an analysis of the text of *The Challenge of Peace*, to illustrate Burke's (1954/1964) method. When helpful, we draw on other texts (e.g., interviews) for corroborating evidence; after all, the bishops can be seen, for our present purposes, as having been focal authors in a complex intertextual process.

As a literal written text, *The Challenge of Peace* involved more extensive preparation, received more careful scrutiny, and benefited from wider circulation than any document produced previously by the American Catholic hierarchy. To focus on *the* text is indeed revealing, both in terms of demonstrating Burke's method and in yielding rich interpretation.

Specifically, we present a partial Burkean indexing of *The Challenge of Peace*. We qualify the term *indexing* with the word *partial* because of the sheer length and complexity of the peace pastoral. A complex indexing of the content of the 339-paragraph document is beyond our scope. Thus, while we examined closely the entire letter, we restrict the analysis to certain key terms and interword relations in the document, *particularly those that surface in the commentary on the document* and in Cheney's larger study. In this way, we are able to demonstrate to the reader some of the potential of Burke's method, while also locating Burke's method within this larger discussion of textuality.

We begin the textual survey at the *center* of the document. Interestingly, the middle paragraph (the median, if you will) of the peace pastoral treats explicitly the nature of U.S. nuclear deterrence policy. Paragraph 165 [and from this point on all references to *The Challenge of Peace* (NCCB-USCC, 1983) are done by paragraph numbers within this text] begins with the words: "The evolution of deterrence policy strategy has passed through several stages of declaratory policy." The paragraph concludes with: "It is important to recognize that there has been substantial continuity in U.S. action policy in spite of real changes in declaratory policy." This placement is of much more than passing significance since eight of the interviewees highlighted *deterrence* as *the* most difficult moral and strategic challenge that faced the bishops. Moreover, the stress on *U.S. policy* supports several bishops' claim that the peace pastoral was targeted directly at the Reagan administration (among other audiences). And it is after this middle point in the text that the bishops adopt an *explicitly political* position (transforming their argument into specific secular terms), though they maintain what drafter Fr. Bryan Hehir told Cheney is "a centimeter of ambiguity."

In their treatment of deterrence, the bishops made careful distinctions, acknowledging that the policy has preserved "peace of a sort" but not the " 'genuine peace' required for a stable international life" (¶168). "Peace," of course, is *one of the most central terms* in the document, appearing in a variety of contexts and connections. Early in the document the bishops acknowledge their various usages of the term: the peace of "an individual's sense of well-being or security," "the cessation of armed hostility," "a right relationship with God," and "eschatological peace" (¶27). Moreover, the peace pastoral moves rather freely from one type of "peace" to another.

Not surprisingly, the term *peace* is often found in the *context* of the phrase "war and peace" (e.g., ¶s 5 and 12) or in its important reversal "peace and war" (which first appears, in ¶16, as a clear *transformation* of the usual order). It is interesting, too, that the term *peace* is not seen without *war* until ¶13, though *war* is introduced in the *first* paragraph of the document. (This occurrence represents foreshadowing of the "furthest point of internality," discussed below.) This order lends some support to the contention that the bishops, like most of us, find it easier to discuss war (or its absence) than a positive vision of peace (a "theology of peace" as the bishops call for, ¶23). Peace very often is treated as war's negation, although the phrase "war and peace" seems to put the two on equal footing.

Besides being linked to war, *peace* functions as *a terminological center in a whole cluster* of related words. Peace "is always seen as a gift from God and as fruit of God's saving activity" (¶32). "Peace is a special characteristic of [the] covenant," a covenant that binds "people to God in fidelity and obedience" (¶33). In the Old Testament, people were called to "make the peace which God has established visible through the love and the unity within their own communities" (¶53). Moreover, "the risen Lord's gift of peace is inextricably bound to the call to follow Jesus" (¶54). In this light, "we are called to our own peace and to the making of peace in our world" (¶55). And, at the same time, it must be recognized that "justice is always the foundation of peace" (¶60). Also, "true peace calls for 'reverence for life' " (¶284, subheading). Nevertheless, it is only "in the Kingdom of God [that] peace and justice will be fully realized" (¶60). "It is precisely because sin is part of history that the realization of the peace of the Kingdom is never permanent or total" (¶57). Finally, it is clear from a careful review that all of these usages of peace are echoed throughout the document.

Thus the term *peace* (which we traced throughout the document) is centrally located in a complex of terms within the bishops' letter. It is in a dialectical tension with *war*; it is a gift from God to his people; it is part of the convenant, *symbolized* by Christ; it is equated (and thus operationally synonymous) with *justice* and the dignity of *life*; it is indirectly linked to the notion of community; yet it is only fully realized in an eschatological sense. These interconnections and the terminological transcendence of peace can be depicted as shown in Figure 1. These terminological and ideational interrelationships are complex, nuanced, and profound. In exploiting the powerful

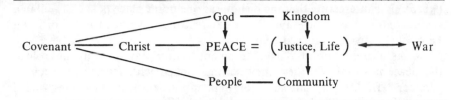

Figure 1. Terminological connections with peace.

ambiguities of peace as a "god-term," the bishops cross all of the terminological levels of *hierarchies* of which Burke (1954/1964) writes: words for the physical world, words for the social order, words for the supernatural, and (of course) words for words. These connections are made possible by multiple uses of the term *peace*, as suggested in the full title of the document: *The Challenge of Peace: God's Promise AND Our Response* (emphasis added).

A careful following of the term *peace* also leads us to *the furthest point of internality* in the peace pastoral. It is the beginning of the section titled "The Promotion of Peace" (¶200), where the bishops switch from an emphasis on "preventing and limiting the violence of war" to "the building of peace." In an interview with Cheney, Fr. Theodore Hesburgh, then president of Notre Dame, indicated that the "positive vision of peace," which frames the remainder of the letter, is one of the most important contributions of the bishops. Within the contexts of the letter and the official documents of the Catholic Church, this "proactive" posture toward "peace" is an important *transformation* of the term, especially because it involves explicit recognition of the traditions of pacifism and nonviolence.

Nuclear weapons and the possibility of nuclear war are posed as a global "threat" and as a "supreme crisis" throughout the letter (e.g., ¶s 1 and 4). These and other *scenic* terms emerge as a controlling, shaping force in the peace pastoral. Quoting the documents of the Second Vatican Council, the bishops introduce their entire discussion with these words: "The whole human race faces a moment of supreme crisis" (¶1). And the pastoral document concludes with an equally situational but more hopeful passage taken from the Book of Revelation: "Then I saw a new heaven and a new earth; for the first heaven and the first earth had passed away and the sea was no more. And I saw the holy city, new Jerusalem" (¶339). The bishops describe the international situation as one that urgently requires a response. The "moment of crisis," as they call it, brings us to recognize a "New Moment" with "new moral questions" (¶s 120 and 122). In this way, the bishops identify and isolate the present as a point in history generating unique or at least previously unseen judgments. The bishops see themselves as reading the "sign of the times" in the "increased awareness of the danger of the nuclear arms race" (¶125). As they explain: "At the center of the new evaluation of the nuclear arms race is a recognition of two elements: the destructive potential of nuclear weapons, and the stringent choices which the nuclear age poses for both politics and morals"

(¶126). (It is interesting that the bishops at one point place peace as well in a scenic context, when they say: "Peace is the setting in which moral choice can be most effectively exercised"; ¶67.)

Terms of *time*—"point," "age," "moment"—thus play an important role in the peace pastoral. Further, they become linked with fear terms such as "danger," "frightened," and the like. All people are portrayed as living "in [a] time of fear" (¶2). And it is within such a world that the bishops offer "an invitation and a challenge to Catholics in the United States to join with others in shaping the conscious choices and deliberate policies required in this 'moment of supreme crisis' " (¶4). In this "time of fear," the bishops "speak words of hope" (¶2).

Thus, while the bishops talk of the "progressive realization" of "the religious vision" (¶20) here on earth, they also highlight today as an especially important time for reflection and action. In this way, their stress on "timeliness" actually marks a contrast with their process notions of theology and ecclesiology. The terms of time and the metaphor of moment may become confining and actually subvert the ongoing purposes of the bishops should they become too closely wedded to them.

As indicated in responses to interview questions, the bishops see the United States as having a special, though not necessarily morally superior, place in an interdependent world. A close examination of the text supports this inference. Near the beginning of the peace pastoral, the bishops declare: "The nuclear threat transcends religious, cultural and national boundaries" (¶6). It is interesting to note that the other place the bishops use the term *transcendent* (or a form of it) is with the words "the transcendence of God" (¶15). This offers a further indication of the special terminological status of "nuclear threat" and its reinforcement of the idea of global interdependence. The bishops state:

> The truth that the globe is inhabited by a single family in which all have the same basic needs and all have a right to the goods of the earth is a fundamental principle of Catholic teaching which we believe to be of increasing importance today. In an interdependent world all need to affirm their common nature and destiny; such a perspective should inform our policy vision and negotiating posture in pursuit of peace today. (¶202)

This interdependence is linked to two bases: Catholic doctrine and political reality. The bishops first declare that "the fundamental premise of world order in Catholic teaching is a theological truth: the unity of the human family" (¶236). Then, a few paragraphs later, they argue:

> In the nuclear age, it is in the regulation of interstate conflicts and ultimately the replacement of military by negotiated solutions that the supreme importance and necessity of a moral as well as a political concept of the international common good can be grasped. (¶243)

Global unity, for the bishops, is both a moral imperative and a practical-political necessity.

Within this context, the United States is described as "one of the major nuclear nations" (¶2), as "the nation which was first to produce atomic weapons" (¶4), as a nation with a deterrence policy that requires "rethinking" (¶196), as a nation with a right "to defend itself" (¶221), as a country engaged in a "fragile" relationship and "global competition" with the Soviet Union (¶245), as a place where people enjoy "true freedom of religion, and access to a free press" (¶252), a country whose "capacity for leadership in multilateral institutions is very great" (¶265), and as comprising a people that must "express profound sorrow over the atomic bombing in 1945" in order "to repudiate future use of nuclear weapons or of conventional weapons in such military actions as would not fulfill just-war criteria" (¶302). In this way, the United States represents, in its preeminent position of power and freedom (and perhaps nuclear guilt), a vantage point from which to witness and foster true global interdependence.

Linked closely to the special responsibilities of the United States, but of a more embracing nature, are the special responsibilities of the Church. Just before the conclusion of the peace pastoral, the bishops hold: "The Church has a unique opportunity, precisely because of the strong constitutional protection of both religious freedom and freedom of speech and the press, to help call attention to the moral dimensions of public issues" (¶328). And just before that statement the bishops insist: "Nuclear weapons pose especially acute questions of conscience for American Catholics" (¶326). Thus the terms *American* and *Catholic* are seen as freely "interactive," but in that freedom, tension may emerge. In recognition of this possibility, the bishops continue: "As citizens we wish to affirm our loyalty to our country and its ideals, yet we are also citizens of the world who must be faithful to the universal principles proclaimed by the Church" (¶326). Finally, the bishops make even more clear the preeminence of Catholic allegiance when they explain: "As American Catholics, we are called to express our loyalty to the deepest values we cherish: peace, justice, and security for the entire human family. National goals and policies must be measured against this standard" (¶301). Thus the bishops affirm a partial *equation* of the terms *Church* and *world*, while also partially equating each of those with the United States. One element "left out" of the equations and held above is the Church as "universal" and transcendent with respect to the world and beyond it (e.g., ¶s 5, 6, and 57). "The Church" thus retains the privileged position. Here we are reminded of the irony that the bishops moved into the "mainstream" of American society (as accepted "corporate" advocates) while placing national allegiance in a secondary and subordinate position to Catholic commitments.

The Church is described as "a community of conscience, prayer and penance" (¶274, subheading). The bishops introduce the section with that title by saying: "We should like to spell out some of the implications of being a community of Jesus' disciples in a time when our nation is so heavily armed with nuclear weapons" (¶275). The *community* image is featured against the backdrop of the nuclear threat and the need to alter defense policies. The Church-as-community is linked to its roots and highlighted this way: "As believers we can identify rather easily with the early Church as a company of witnesses engaged in a difficult mission. To be disciples of Jesus requires that we continually go beyond where we now are"—more process terminology, to be sure. And the bishops conclude: "To obey the call of Jesus means separating ourselves from all attachments and affiliation that could prevent us from hearing and following our authentic vocation" (¶276). The Christian, the Catholic, must be prepared to "take a resolute stand against many commonly accepted axioms of the world" (¶277). Moreover, the bishops bemoan the fact that "convinced Christians are a minority in nearly every country of the world—including nominally Christian and Catholic nations" (¶276). Thus the Catholic and the broader Christian communities are exhorted to be involved in the affairs of the secular world at the same time that they are portrayed as being *against* or, at least, somewhat *alien* from it. This is a paradoxical and enormously challenging role within which to cast any social actor or group.

Importantly, the term *community* "spins out" in a number of other contexts as well. In a two-paragraph passage near the opening of the document, for example, the term appears *eight* times. It is used for "the wider civil community," "Christian[s], Jews, Moslems, [and] other religious communities," "the wider political community," and "the human community" (¶s 16 and 17). *Community* is therefore far from being a passive term in the peace pastoral; it is a desirable and handy label for describing *groups* in a vision of cohesiveness and interdependence. (The wider civil community is, after all, equated with "all people of good will," ¶16.) In this way, the bishops' rather comfortable usage of community to cover a whole range of human congregations may actually undermine their own portrayal of a Catholic-Christian community over and somewhat against the world.

The bishops see *themselves* as bridging the "community of the faithful" and the "wider political community." Not only do they specify their two audiences (in ¶s 16 and 17), but they also maintain:

> As bishops we believe that the nature of Catholic moral teaching, the principles of Catholic ecclesiology, and the demands of our pastoral ministry require that this letter speak both to Catholics in a specific way and to the wider political community regarding public policy. (¶19)

The bishops thus proclaim their self-awareness both as religious leaders and as advocates who would influence the political realm.

Most often, of course, the bishops speak *as* the collective body of U.S. bishops. And that is the context within which they use "we" in most instances. For example, the bishops say "As Catholic bishops *we* write this letter as an exercise of our teaching ministry" (¶3, in the official summary that precedes the text of the letter); "as bishops and pastors ministering in one of the major nuclear nations, *we* have encountered this terror in the minds and hearts of our people" (¶2); "as *we* locate ourselves in [the Catholic tradition on war and peace]" (¶7); "when making applications of these [moral] principles *we* realize . . . that prudential judgments are involved based on specific circumstances" (¶10); "*we* believe that the Church, a community of faith and social institution, has a proper, necessary, and distinctive part to play in the pursuit of peace" (¶21); "in this letter *we* wish to continue and develop the teaching on peace and war which *we* have previously made, and which reflects both the teaching of the universal Church and the insights and experience of the Catholic community of the United States" (¶64); "*we* see our role as moral teachers precisely in terms of helping to form public opinion with a clear determination to resist resort to nuclear war as an instrument of national policy" (¶139); "*we* do not perceive any situation in which the deliberate initiation of nuclear warfare, on however restricted a scale, can be morally justified" (¶150); "*we* believe there is much greater potential for response to these questions in the minds and hearts of Americans than has been reflected in U.S. policy" (¶262). (Emphasis is added in all of the above quotations.) In these ways, the bishops sought to make clear their identity as a national episcopal conference speaking to moral and political issues. This sense of "we-ness" was, to a significant extent, supported by their Collegeville, Minnesota, retreat of June 1982, held in the middle of the drafting process. Bishop James Malone, then vice-president of the NCCB, identified this meeting later for Cheney as a time when "the phrases 'role of the bishop,' 'the body of bishops,' 'I, Bishop Malone,' 'we, the bishops,' [called] up new images and prompted new intellectual and emotional responses."

It is of interest to note that there was a move on the part of one bishop, Auxiliary Patrick Ahern of New York, to change certain references to "we" and "us" in the document to designate "those of us who listened to the testimony." This effort at the Chicago meeting "failed resoundingly" (Castelli, 1983), thus indicating a desire on the part of the bishops to share equally and responsibly in their corporate "we." This idea was supported by the late Bishop Fulcher of Lafayette, Indiana, who told Cheney that "through an amazing process of conversion the peace pastoral came to be *owned* by all the bishops."

At the same time, however, the bishops broaden their "we-ness" in the letter to embrace persons beyond their own ranks. The bishops call themselves citizens: "A glory of the United States is the range of political freedoms its system permits us" (¶252). The bishops identify themselves with Christians generally: "We must probe the meaning of the moral choices which are ours as Christians" (¶67). The bishops equate themselves with the Church, in the same paragraph arguing for the Church's "unique opportunity . . . to help call attention to the moral dimensions of public issues" and citing one of their previous pastoral letters as an example of the fulfillment of this role (¶328). And the bishops see themselves as part of a world people under threat: "The 'new moment' in which we find ourselves sees the just-war teaching and nonviolence as distinct but interdependent methods of evaluating warfare" (¶120). In fact, this final example demonstrates just how the bishops "slide" from one "we" to another in a *hierarchy* of self-references. For while the "new moment" is invoked to embrace the greatest "we"—all humanity—the discussion of the Just War Theory and nonviolence invokes specifically (though not exclusively) Catholic traditions. In sum, the bishops are prone to refer to themselves most often as bishops; yet they also locate themselves within a larger Catholic Church, Christianity, the wider civil community, and the world order—as rhetorical strategy dictates.

The U.S. Catholic bishops' peace pastoral is about many things, as testified by a number of Cheney's interviewees when asked to indicate "the moral core of the letter" (what Burke, 1954/1964, calls "essentializing by entitlement"). What follow are a few of the elicited comments. Archbishop Thomas Kelly of Louisville: "No one can destroy human life." Milwaukee Auxiliary Bishop Richard Sklba (informal advisor to the bishops): "[The peace pastoral] put a laser beam on civil government, addressing its moral responsibility." Archbishop John Quinn of San Francisco (former president of the NCCB): "Raising the nuclear arms issue and embedding it firmly in a moral context." Cardinal Joseph Bernardin of Chicago (chairman of the bishops' drafting committee): "There should be no areas of life that escape moral scrutiny." Msgr. Daniel Hoye (general secretary of NCCB): "That we must reverse the trend, making a moral analysis of the arms race and saying 'no' to it." Professor Bruce Russett of Yale (principal consultant to the bishops' drafting committee): "That a radically intensive reflection on defense policies is necessary." Mr. Ed Doherty (member of staff for drafting committee): "There is virtually no use of nuclear weapons that could be morally justified." Bishop Leroy Matthiesen of Amarillo: "The statement by Pope John Paul II at Hiroshima that war has to be ruled out." Cardinal John Krol of Philadelphia: "The right of self-defense and how much force you can use in repelling an unjust aggressor." Fr. Richard Warner (representative to the drafting committee): "The value of human life, the dignity of human life." Sr. Juliana Casey (representative to the drafting committee): "It is twofold. First, there's a responsibility of the faithful and leaders to speak to issues of life and death. Second, and this is the *real* core—there's the principle that life is extremely valuable and cannot be handled lightly." Fr. Bryan Hehir (head of staff for drafting committee): "I'm not too sure. I wouldn't try to isolate it that way."

What should be clear, however one "essentializes" or sums up the peace pastoral, is that it says something important about who the bishops "were" (in terms of the intermingling of their perceptions of themselves and others' perceptions of them), how the bishops confronted frightfully complex organizational problems, and how they chose to foster specific connections in developing and articulating their rhetorical strategy. Clearly, the bishops— whether consciously or not—exploited *ambiguity* as a potent resource, using terms like *community*, *the new moment*, and *peace* as versatile symbolic tools to make their many chosen connections. In this way, their response to the situation may be fairly characterized as "structured ambiguity" (Varacalli, 1983; see also Castelli, 1983). As explained by Archbishop John Roach of St. Paul, "ambiguity" is "a legitimate, treasured part of the whole moral tradition of the Church" (as quoted in Briggs, 1982, p. A-14). Thus the bishops poised themselves in a number of positions simultaneously in their arduous effort to manage both issues and identities.

How well did the bishops do in "managing multiple identifications"? Fr. Andrew Greeley, sociologist and author, wrote Cheney in May 1984 saying: "My own feeling is that the Peace Pastoral will have no effect whatsoever." Greeley maintained that the bishops would be unable to balance competing interests and significantly affect the views of liberal, conservative, or moderate Catholics.

In an April 1985 article titled "Why the Peace Pastoral Did Not Bomb," Greeley unabashedly declared: "The American Bishops' pastoral on nuclear weapons appears to be the most successful intervention to change attitudes ever measured by social science." And he added: "This astonishing discovery raises fascinating questions about how church leadership should teach and about what American Catholics are really like." Obviously, in the 11 months between his letter to Cheney and the publication of his article, Greeley had dramatically *transformed* his prophecy. The reason he offers for the transformation is the result of surveys conducted by one of his own employing organizations, the National Opinion Research Center (NORC). One survey, taken just before the peace pastoral was signed in May 1983, reported that 32% of both Catholics and Protestants thought that "too much" money was being spent on arms. A year later, another NORC survey found 32% of Protestants responded in the same manner, but revealed a much higher figure for Catholics: 54%. According to Greeley, this shift represents "a change in attitude by perhaps 10 million Catholics."

HUMANISTIC AND
SCIENTIFIC STUDIES OF TEXT

We should be content if this essay succeeds no further than in encouraging colleagues in the humanities to experiment with the method of indexing (as we have) in the study of rhetorical and literary texts. We recognize, of course, that the "text" can obscure the processual development of communication phenomena. We do not see this limitation as peculiar to the approach we offer here but as inherent in reflection and commentary upon action (see, e.g., Schutz, 1967). Whenever one selects from and comments upon a portion of experience (or anticipated experience), he or she, in a sense, "freezes" the experience in time. Moreover, our terms of description goad us to reify, instantiate, and otherwise make firm those "elements" of experience to which we refer. And so, any "text" may lead the author, reader, or listener to downplay process and feature structure, though the two are complementary and essentially inseparable. To our knowledge, no rhetorical critic other than Burke has offered a method that can better account for process than treating the text as symbolic action. We should be content if other "textual analysts" would but adopt the method.

Our objectives were enlarged, however, by Burke's self-conscious use of such terms as *mathematical center*, *equation*, and *correlation*, acknowledging the possibility of the "statistical" analyses of texts in a variety of types of communication research. For example, indexing seems ideally suited for deriving key terms and thematic categories for content analyses. And if we want to know if certain "variables," say trust and openness, correlate in a particular organizational setting, why not look for places in the discourse of members where such terms and their "operational synonyms" co-occur? Further, by slight adaptation, indexing can be applied to such "texts" as film, audio- and videotape. For example, we saw the film *A Passage to India* after reading Burke's analysis of E. M. Forster's novel, in which he referred to the mathematical center of that text as the moment in which Dr. Aziz is formally charged with rape (Burke, 1966). Switching the unit of analysis from words to minutes it was observed that the arrest of Aziz occurred 30 minutes after the center of the film, indicating that film had compressed the last half of the novel into roughly one-third of its text. The material omitted in the adaptation explains why more film viewers than novel readers were baffled by Miss Quested's reversal at the trial.

In sum, Burke's "indexing" offers an epistemologically and methodologically sound basis for interpretation—of any kind. Burke's method fits within his larger epistemological framework, "Logology," because it starts with *empirical* considerations about symbolic activity (Burke, 1979, 1985); indexing engages us with the certainties of words-in-a-text, before allowing us "degrees of freedom" in our interpretations. In a manner analogous to the methods of quantitative-empirical research, indexing forces a scrupulous regard for "facts," the data base, while allowing an openness to theoretical sources of interpretation, an openness that is circumscribed by the forces of alternative hypotheses of greater explanatory power.

Indexing may be placed as well within Burke's overarching ontological framework, "Dramatism," because it helps us understand what people are doing (or saying) when they quite literally act (Burke, 1945/1969, 1976, 1985). With Burke's methodological principles as a guide, the larger body of human communication research, humanistic and empirical, can be seen as an intertextual inquiry by which to "come to terms" with the very "subjects" of our study.

In a manner parallel with that of social researchers, "lay persons" are embedded within networks of texts: Their discourse necessarily reveals points of contact with both known contemporaries and with persons who are gone or dead. In this sense, to say that one is loyal to a tradition, or shares a religious orientation with other worshippers, or has interests in common with fellow workers, is not fundamentally different from either an author's imitation of, or opposition to, or allusion to a predecessor; in each case individuals come to "terms" with/for their world and at the same time align their interests. Intertextuality is the predicament of all individuals as symbol users. The textual context of human relations mandates that the individual becomes "socialized" at the same time that the social becomes "individualized" (the latter occurring primarily through the adoption and adaptation of symbol systems).

In conclusion, it remains to situate our claims about the text on a continuum ranging from literality to metaphoricality. Our own position on this issue is to distinguish between text as epistemology or method and text as ontology or conceptual framework for understanding human communication. What we have said about the former is literal; what we have said about the latter is metaphorical. Nonetheless, the constraints of text-as-method on text-as-action are so powerful that *one is driven toward the literal text* in doing human communication research.

NOTE

1. We observe, of course, that the study of text comprehension, as it has emerged in psychology and communication, *interprets the literal text as an object of cognitive processing.* Van Dijk and Kintsch (1983), for example, describe "strategies" as a set of cognitive subprocesses by which information *in* a text is used. (See also Planalp, 1986, for an overview of discourse-processing work and its application in communication research.) Such an orientation distinguishes the discourse-processing view of "textuality" from the others we have offered.

REFERENCES

Barthes, R. (1979). From work to text. In J. V. Harari (Ed.), *Textual strategies: Perspectives in post-structuralist criticism* (pp. 73-81). Ithaca, NY: Cornell University Press.

Barthes, R. (1981). Theory of the text. In R. Young (Ed.), *Untying the text: A post-structuralist reader* (pp. 31-47). Boston: Routledge & Kegan Paul.

Baynes, K., Bohman, J., & McCarthy, T. (1987). General introduction: In K. Baynes, J. Bohman, & T. McCarthy (Eds.), *After philosophy: End or transformation?* (pp. 1-18). Cambridge: MIT Press.

Berger, C. R., & Douglas, W. (1982). Thought and talk: "Excuse me, but have I been talking to myself?" In F.E.X. Dance (Ed.), *Human communication theory: Comparative essays* (pp. 42-60). New York: Harper & Row.

Berthold, C. A. (1976). Kenneth Burke's cluster-agon method: Its development and an application. *Central States Speech Journal, 27*, 302-309.

Bochner, A. P. (1985). Perspectives on inquiry: Representation, conversation, and reflection. In M. L. Knapp & G. R. Miller (Eds.), *Handbook of interpersonal communication* (pp. 27-58). Newbury Park, CA: Sage.

Briggs, K. S. (1982, November 19). Bishops support letter on nuclear arms. *New York Times*, p. A-14, col. 3.

Brown, R. H. (1978). *A poetic for sociology.* Cambridge: Cambridge University Press.

Burke, K. (1952). "Ethan Brand": A preparatory investigation. *Hopkins Review, 5,* 45-65.

Burke, K. (1964). Fact, inference and proof in the analysis of literary symbolism. In S. E. Hyman (Ed.), *Terms for order by Kenneth Burke* (pp. 145-172). Bloomington: Indiana University Press. (Original work published 1954)

Burke, K. (1966). *Language as symbolic action: Essays on life, literature, and method.* Berkeley: University of California Press.

Burke, K. (1969). *A grammar of motives.* Berkeley: University of California Press. (Original work published 1945)

Burke, K. (1973). *The philosophy of literary form: Studies in symbolic action* (3rd ed.). Berkeley: University of California Press. (Original work published 1941)

Burke, K. (1976). Dramatism. In J. E. Combs & M. W. Mansfield (Eds.), *Drama in life: The uses of communication in society* (pp. 7-17). New York: Hastings House.

Burke, K. (1979). Theology and logology. *Kenyon Review: New Series, 1,* 151-185.

Burke, K. (1984, March). *Response to second general session.* Comments presented at the Burke Conference, Philadelphia.

Burke, K. (1985). Dramatism and logology. *Communication Quarterly, 33,* 89-93.

Castelli, J. (1983). *The bishops and the bomb: Waging peace in a nuclear age.* Garden City, NY: Doubleday.

Cheney, G. E. (1985). *Speaking of who "we" are: The development of the U.S. Catholic bishops' pastoral letter "The Challenge of Peace" as a case study in identity, organization, and rhetoric.* Unpublished doctoral dissertation, Purdue University.

Cox, H. (1984). *Religion in the secular city: Toward a postmodern theology.* New York: Simon & Schuster.

Delia, J. G., O'Keefe, B. J., & O'Keefe, D. J. (1982). The constructivist approach to communication. In F.E.X. Dance (Ed.), *Human communication theory: Comparative essays* (pp. 147-191). New York: Harper & Row.

Derrida, J. (1976). *Of grammatology* (G. C. Spivak, Trans.). Baltimore: Johns Hopkins University Press.

Dilthey, W. (1976). *Selected writings* (H. P. Rickman, Ed. and Trans.). Cambridge: Cambridge University Press.

Donoghue, D. (1984). *Ferocious alphabets.* New York: Columbia University Press.

Foss, S. K., Foss, K. A., & Trapp, R. (1985). *Contemporary perspectives on rhetoric.* Prospect Heights, IL: Waveland.

Foucault, M. (1984). *The Foucault reader* (P. Rabinow, ed.). New York: Pantheon.

Gadamer, H. G. (1977). *Philosophical hermeneutics* (D. E. Linge, Trans.). Berkeley: University of California Press.

Garvey, W. D. (1979). *Communication: The essence of science.* Oxford: Pergamon.

Geertz, C. (1983). *Local knowledge: Further essays in interpretive anthropology.* New York: Basic Books.

Goffman, E. (1959). *The presentation of self in everyday life.* Garden City, NY: Doubleday.

Goldzwig, S., & Cheney, G. (1984). The U.S. Catholic bishops on nuclear arms: Corporate advocacy, role redefinition, and rhetorical adaptation. *Central States Speech Journal, 35,* 8-23.

Granier, J. (1985). Perspectivism and interpretation. In D. B. Allison (Ed.), *The new Nietzsche* (pp. 190-200). Cambridge, MA: Harvard University Press.

Greeley, A. (1985, April 12). Why the peace pastoral did not bomb. *National Catholic Reporter,* p. 11, cols. 1-4.

Harari, J. V. (Ed.). (1979). Critical factions/critical fictions. In *Textual strategies: Perspectives in post-structuralist criticism* (pp. 17-72). Ithaca, NY: Cornell University Press.

Hartman, G. H. (1981). *Saving the text: Literature, Derrida, philosophy.* Baltimore: Johns Hopkins University Press.

Kristeva, J. (1970). *Le texte du roman: Approche semiologique d'une structure discursive transformationnelle.* The Hague: Mouton.

Kristeva, J. (1984). *Revolution in poetic language* (M. Waller, Trans.). New York: Columbia University Press.

Mauss, M. (1985). A category of the human mind: The notion of person; the notion of self. In M. Carrithers, S. Collons, & S. Lukes (Eds.), *The category of the person* (pp. 1-25). Cambridge: Cambridge University Press. (Original work published 1938)

Miller, O. (1985). Intertextual identity. In M. J. Valdes & O. Miller (Eds.), *Identity of the literary text* (pp. 19-40). Toronto: University of Toronto Press.

NCCB-USCC (1983). *The Challenge of peace: God's promise and our response.* Washington, NCCB-USCC.

Nehamas, A. (1985). *Nietzsche: Life as literature.* Cambridge, MA: Harvard University Press.

Nietzsche, F. (1976). *The portable Nietzsche* (W. Kaufman, Ed. and Trans.). Harmondsworth, England: Penguin.

Nietzsche, F. (1982). *Daybreak* (R. J. Hollingdale, Trans.). Cambridge: Cambridge University Press.

Overington, M. C. (1977). Kenneth Burke and the method of dramatism. *Theory and Society, 4,* 131-156.

Planalp, S. (1986). Scripts, story grammars, and causal schemas. In D. G. Ellis & W. A. Donohue (Eds.), *Contemporary issues in language and discourse processes* (pp. 111-125). Hillsdale, NJ: Lawrence Erlbaum.

Ricoeur, P. (1979). The model of the text: Meaningful action considered as a text. In P. Rabinow & W. M. Sullivan (Eds.), *Interpretive social science: A reader* (pp. 73-102). Berkeley: University of California Press.

Rorty, R. (1979). *Philosophy and the mirror of nature.* Princeton, NJ: Princeton University Press.

Rorty, R. (1982). *Consequences of pragmatism.* Minneapolis: University of Minnesota Press.

Rorty, R. (1986, April 17). The contingency of language. *London Review of Books,* pp. 3-6.

Schrag, C. O. (1980). *Radical reflection and the origin of the human sciences.* West Lafayette, IN: Purdue University Press.

Schutz, A. (1967). *The phenomenology of the social world.* Evanston, IL: Northwestern University Press.

Schank, R., & Abelson, R. (1977). *Scripts, plans, goals and understanding: An inquiry into human knowledge structures.* Hillsdale, NJ: Lawrence Erlbaum.

Sontag, S. (1983). Writing itself: On Roland Barthes. In S. Sontag (Ed.), *A Barthes reader* (pp. vii-xxxvi). New York: Hill & Wang.

Tompkins, P. K. (1985). On hegemony—"He gave it no name"—And critical structuralism in the work of Kenneth Burke. *Quarterly Journal of Speech, 71,* 119-131.

Tompkins, P. K., & Cheney, G. (1985). Communication and unobtrusive control in contemporary organizations. In R. D. McPhee & P. K. Tompkins (Eds.), *Organizational communication: Traditional themes and new directions* (pp. 179-210). Newbury Park, CA: Sage.

van Dijk, T. A., & Kintsch, W. (1983). *Strategies of discourse comprehension.* New York: Academic Press.

Varacalli, J. A. (1983). *Toward the establishment of liberal Catholicism in America.* Washington, DC: University Press of America.

On the Facts of the "Facts of the 'Text'"

ROBERT D. McPHEE
University of Wisconsin—Milwaukee

IT is a pleasure to respond to the chapter of Cheney and Tompkins. I think they offer valuable suggestions regarding the importance of the concept of "text" for communication research and Burke's method of indexing as a specific research approach.

I find it useful to separate two different subsets of remarks to be found in the work. First is the core, the account of the method of indexing and its illustrative application to *The Challenge of Peace.* Cheney and Tompkins pursue Burke's argument that the appearance and repetition of words in texts are, by the nature of writing, facts more solid and durable as bases for inference from experience than are any data available to us from "scientific observation." Cheney and Tompkins also show how a certain process of inference from texts, and proof of claims about texts, follows naturally from this sense of words as facts. Second is the periphery of contextualizing and interpretive comments about the method and its implications. The authors claim that the method of indexing resembles, and is in some ways superior to, standard social scientific methods, while also being inspired by and appropriate to the study of that recently controversial and remarkably Protean animal, the text.

My response itself is formed into four sections, each too brief for its matter. First, I take up several minor points raised by Cheney and Tompkins. I then discuss the relation between text and referent, in general agreeing with Cheney and Tompkins while questioning some of their formulations. Third, I take up the question of the nature of the text, and the relation between text and work drawn from the writings of Barthes. Finally, I make some suggestions about the status of the method articulated by Burke and formalized by Cheney and Tompkins.

Correspondence and requests for reprints: Robert D. McPhee, Department of Communication, University of Wisconsin, Milwaukee, WI 53201.

Communication Yearbook 11, pp. 482-493

NITPICKING

There are major issues to be addressed in Cheney and Tompkins's essay. Should we not discuss them immediately, without letting our attention be drawn to smaller matters? Perhaps so. But there are some of their peripheral, almost parenthetical themes, that are so provocative that I cannot remain silent about them. So I will speak out about them quickly, then move on to discuss the more central issues. (Or, in other words, here are either fish in a barrel or traps for the unwary.)

(1) *The journal article as the end point of research.* For Cheney and Tompkins, "end" has both its senses of the product or goal, which shapes, even motivates, the purposeful process of scientific activity, and the sole ultimate boundary point that separates yet connects the system of individual (or local) research with the larger social system of science. "To contribute to science one must publish a text qua journal article. There is no other way" (p. 462).

This is too pure a vision of science, almost that of only partially retrained English majors of the old school, believing that authors still live (Foucault, 1977). Even if we restrict our analysis to contemporary scientific research practice, we must be aware of other products. For instance, there are the data stocks, susceptible to reanalysis in ways that texts resist (as I shall argue further below). There are the innovations and improvements in methods, often inscribed in software, which—while able to be printed as a text—also has an existence as electromagnetic patterns that causally affect computer processes. There are graduate students, those products who themselves produce texts, who are unobtrusively molded as they cooperate with us in research, then dispatched to other universities. But they are not alone as students—there are our undergraduates, corrupted with the residua of knowledge they carry away from our courses, and our colleagues, corrupted in more informal face-to-face dealings.

A mere skip up a level of abstraction forces us to recognize that the organization of all this—professional associations, conferences, journals, universities, foundations—must be regarded as an emission of research processes, too, and as a series of further input-channels for scholarly deposits in the scientific filament. We may "mark our turf" more notably by reviewing and editing articles, by managing associations, by hiring job candidates, by distributing funding, than by writing even the most pungent and well-crafted articles. But, of course, the natural scientists have not been content with these, so to speak, small potatoes. Their discoveries are often interlarded with inventions, inscribed in patent applications and Nobel Prizes and in prototypes, technologies, productive organizations, commodities, pollution—modern life in the capitalist era is play and work in the by-products of scientific research, all of which exert their fertilizing influence on research and journal article writing. In thinking of the journal article as the product of science, we are tempted to consider science to be a self-feeding, perfectly efficient digestive system and to overlook the political relations among input, outcome, and social world.

(2) *Indexing and quantitative methods.* In noting the positive analogy between indexing and quantitative methods, and especially the firmer factual basis of the word than the experienced act or event (but see below), Cheney and Tompkins have completely overlooked the incommensurate aspects of the two methods. First, quantitative variables and indicators are ideally defined before observation proceeds, while the words to be indexed are chosen and arranged as reading proceeds. Second, quantitative scales are univocally meaningful across instances, while one possible interest during indexing is to observe the changes in meaning a term may undergo in different contexts. Third, quantitative methods require that observational outcomes—variable values—be shorn of unique contextual links before analysis, while Burke is mainly involved in analyzing just such linkages. Finally, as a result of the third point, concepts or variables in quantitative analysis are assumed to be independent and are independently manipulated in ways that words in a Burkean analysis are not. In short, quantitative methods have the extra strengths and weaknesses that come with a more total process of abstraction than the method of indexing, at its best, is wont to depend on.

(3) *Against words as facts.* Transcripts, articles, and other texts do seem given and factual to an extent that far surpasses the actuality of, say, observed interaction—indeed, to an extent that may delude us (Labov & Fanshel, 1977). Can anyone doubt that *Moby Dick* begins with "Call me Ishmael?" or that we should list this sentence in the index for both "call" and "Ishmael?" However, when we try to think of difficult examples, they sprout like dandelions. One large category would be the quasi facts—expressions that we might put into the index, but . . . For instance, in the index under "wine," we are told by Burke (1954) that we can list "wines," a variant grammatical form. But should we list "wined and dined," or "fruit of the vine" (twice, since "vine" is a homonym of *Wein*, the German word for wine), or "chablis," or "alcoholic beverage," or "whine" (especially if used as a pun), or "vineyard"? The connection between these words and "wine" is no less *factual* or potentially fecund than between it and "wines."

A second major category includes shaky facts—facts in textual *versions* that are open to questions based on privileged or other versions. What about words that appear in variant or corrupt texts, or in misprints of the sort reprinted in the *New Yorker*? Translations produce shaky versions of texts—the old version of *Remembrances of Things Past* supposedly averaged over one definite error per page. Equally shaky are transcripts, especially where talkovers or recording problems force the transcriber to guess or infer from context—and my experience indicates that such problems are frequent. A final sort of shaky fact is the word only partially articulated—"Max," the last word of a dying man in *Red Harvest*, turns out to be a partial utterance of "MacSwain," at least according to the last interpretation offered by the hero of the book (who lies repeatedly about such matters). Such shakiness may seem rare overall but surprisingly often affects our interpretations and actions (as in Wilson on Hamlet [1951] or in *Red Harvest*).

A final category of doubtful "facts" includes the illegitimate facts, drawn from texts whose status is open to question. One subcase here includes minority court opinions and speeches indicating the legislative intention of laws. Are the facts of these texts facts of law or not? Another example is the censored text—censored by dictatorial governments or, closer to home, by journal editors. I have had one article, not just cut, but completely rewritten by a journal editor. Should its words appear in future concordances of my work? What about words or statements in transcripts that are "repaired" by their speakers? Or the words of Heidegger or Derrida written "under erasure"—will the compulsion to index these lead us to violate ontological and epistemological principle?

I have more examples, but this aside threatens to take over my reply. The aside really has just one point. Our feeling of the "factuality" of words in a text is a product of specific scholasto-socio-econo-political conditions of practice, embedded in the publishing and printing industries. Even the slight deviations in these practices present in our culture give rise to questionable facts—what if our texts were revised on the spot by bards or computers?

(4) *Burke, text, and work.* More than to any other conception of text, Cheney and Tompkins refer to Barthes's distinction between "work" and "text." But a look at their description of the method of indexing leads us to apprehend that, apparently, indexing is suited to the examination of *works*, but not so well suited to *texts*.

To begin with, we must remember that Barthes (1977) sets up a vague distinction between works that are texts and works that are not: "many works of contemporary literature are in no way texts"; "in such-and-such a work there is, or isn't, some text" (p. 156); the concept of text is "a critical value, permitting an evaluation of works according to the degree of intensity of the 'significance' ["the text at work"] which is in them" (1981, pp. 39, 41). A text is a signifying practice, a production of the reader's infinite or perpetual play with the signifier, active and dynamic; it is "produced in the space of the relations between the reader and the written" (Young, 1981, p. 31). "The text cannot stop (for example on a library shelf): its constitutive movement is that of cutting across (in particular, it can cut across the work, several works)." Its "edges" and "seams are unpredictable" (Barthes, 1975, p. 36). So the suggestions, distilled from Burke by Cheney and Tompkins, that we "pay attention to the beginnings and endings of sections," that we "identify the term(s) at the mathematical *center* of the text," that we "be sensitive to stylistic continuity and break points" (p. 468), all seem unsuited to the specific nature of the text.

More important, the sciencelike enterprise of fact finding by indexing seems to reproduce the work so that it cannot be a text. Indexing of facts, leading to inferences, yields a higher-level commentary, a metadiscourse superior to the work that is its object. But this move violates Barthes's (1977) concept of text: "The destruction of metalanguage, or at least (since it may be necessary provisionally to resort to meta-language) its calling into doubt, is part of the theory [of the Text] itself" (p. 164). "The analysis of productivity cannot be reduced to a linguistic descriptions" (Barthes, 1981, p. 37), as the method of indexing seems to attempt. In short, it seems a method better suited to works that beg for New Critical close reading than to Barthean texts.

(5) *Against words as facts*. Here I offer a reading of the Burkean method of indexing complementary to that advanced by Cheney and Tompkins. My point is simply that Burke does not follow his own method very faithfully or rigorously (surely no surprise to readers of Burke).

When does he begin to deviate? On the second page of his essay, he notes the fact that Joyce's *Portrait of the Artist* "begins with a prior quotation from Ovid's *Metamorphoses*," then, a page later admits that this is a dubitable way to state the fact, not stressing the words themselves or their prior context. "Thus quickly and spontaneously we smuggle inferences, or interpretations, into our report of the 'factual' " (1954, pp. 284, 285). A page later, in his first actual example, Burke offers an index of two passages containing the word *swish*, then without even pausing to breathe, writes that "More remotely, the 'swish' might be said to *subsist* punwise in 'was wishing' "—the sort of fact that the more plodding social scientist might hesitate to note. A little later the notions of variant grammatical forms come in with the term (properly noted to rest on interpretation) *operational synonym* to infect the index.

Might a more self-disciplined Burke avoid these leaps toward remote facts? Here is his answer, with my emphasis of the remarkable phrase:

> As for "exile": unless we have missed some entries (and we may have!) the particular word does not appear elsewhere in this text. However, even assuming we are correct, a punctiliousness bordering on "*methodological suicide*" would be required to keep us from including, under the *principle* of "exile," Stephen's question, "Symbol of departure or loneliness" . . . And once we can equate "exile" with *aloneness* . . . , we open our inquiry almost to a frenzy of entries. (p. 293)

Methodological life itself forces Burke, with no grounding in fact, to mix facts in his index with far-reaching and questionable inferences.

(6) *Burke deconstructs facts*. But so far I have read Burke in the apparent spirit of Cheney and Tompkins. A somewhat different reading would lead us to doubt Burke's advocacy of an analogue to scientific method.

In the sections above, we have argued that a scientific indexing is not really analogous to quantitative method, that it frequently encounters problematic facts, that it is unable to capture the productivity of the Barthean text, and that it is obviously and avowedly transgressed by Burke. So it may come as no shock that we conclude that Burke is actually doing something else. Rather than advocate such an analogue, he proposes it only to undermine it. Rather than stick to the strict facts valorized by the method, he demonstrates how far facts must be stretched in the pursuit of interpretations. Rather than stick to modernist works, he demonstrates that the pursuit of facts in Joyce can initiate the boundlessly productive play of significance. Rather than purely transgress his method, for that matter, he indicates its place as a controlling moment and motive in critical discourse and in the hermeneutic circle. I have no space to demonstrate these claims.

We must remember when Burke's article was written. In 1954, the New Criticism, with their valorization of psychological science and close reading, was cresting. I think Burke tries in his article to exemplify an apotheostically data-driven approach to interpretation, and then to explode it.

Of course, this self-deconstructive argument in Burke, and his general ties to poststructuralism, is known to Cheney and Tompkins (see Tompkins, 1985). However, they pose a partial resistence to "my" argument that, against positivism, Burke proposes ambiguity as a resource. But this argument means that their text is a neat trap for unwary social scientists. Seeking to use Burke's method faithfully, the scientist may be drawn into a more self-conscious play of signifiers than the usual research practices demand, promote, or even allow.

But the fact that Burke can demonstrate a deconstructive play in his use of the method of indexing does not devalue it. On the contrary, it turns out to be a resource recognized and used by New Critics, poststructuralists, Burkean critics, and by Cheney and Tompkins, social scientists. Let us proceed from the standpoint of an enlightened social science to discuss the method of indexing and the correlative concept of textuality of social scientific evidence as a general base for social scientific understanding and research procedures. The next three sections bear on these topics.

TEXT IN WORLD

Our first major point in commenting on Cheney and Tompkins's essay must be to question somewhat their valorization and reification of the text. For them, and no doubt for all their readers, *The Challenge of Peace* is meaningful discourse, a locus of words, ideas, claims, arguments, and so on, and, when reflected on as Cheney and Tompkins do, a locus of "facts, inferences, and proofs." But another sort of reflection immediately reminds us that *The Challenge of Peace* is an object, a document, which is present, no doubt, in Cheney's and in Tompkins's libraries, but not in mine. More globally, it is a document characterized by certain distribution and sales figures, a document that seemingly changed many people's opinions. In short, it is a worldly object (or set of objects) as well as an instance of discourse. Said (1983) advocates this second view:

> Texts have ways of existing that even in their most rarefied form are always enmeshed in circumstance, time, place, and society—in short, they are in the world and hence worldly. Whether a text is preserved or put aside for a period,

whether it is on a library shelf or not, whether it is considered dangerous or not: These matters have to do with a text's being in the world, which is a more complicated matter than the process of reading. (p. 35)

The relationship between these two characterizations of *The Challenge of Peace* is complex and problematic. Its words are not just patterns of ink, the results of writing and printing institutions; they are also resources for understanding, inference, proof, and responses of various sorts. This distinction is roughly that offered by Giddens (1976, 1979, 1984) between system and structure. For Giddens, structure (linguistic, literary, or other rule and resource systems) is a property of a material social system, drawn on yet also constituted in its production and reproduction. This practical grounding and effectiveness is the necessary condition for words to have meaning, as Giddens (1979) argues using a famous example of Saussure's:

> The identity of the "Geneva to Paris train" cannot be specified independently of *the context in which the phrase is used*; and this context is not the system of differences themselves, such as Saussure mentions, but factors relating to their use *in practice*. Saussure implicitly assumes the practical standpoint of the traveler, or the time-tabling official, in giving the identity of the train; hence the "same" train may consist of quite distinct engines and carriages on two separate occasions. But these do not count as instances of the "same" train for a railway repair engineer, or a train-spotter. (p. 16)

Among the practical factors in meaning contexts are matters of power and of legitimate social norms, both of which help determine which meanings "count" as well formed, relevant, and acceptable. But for structuration, any analysis of such factors should concern production and reproduction *dually*, in what Giddens terms "the duality of structure." That is, analysis should make us aware both of how the activity of meaning draws on such practical factors and of how by involving them in meanings, a text helps sustain or transform the worldly distribution of such factors—helps reproduce the social system.

The consequences of ignoring this duality—of analyzing structure without attention to its dual status—are illustrated by Tibbetts and Johnson (1985) in their discussion of two approaches to the sociology of science—the text-oriented and the praxis-oriented approaches. They note that a focus solely on scientific discourse, as in several currently prominent works—on the words and accounts of scientists in the laboratory—is scant basis for a well-rounded account of scientific sense making, due to lack of grounding in the simultaneously theoretical and practical meanings of equipment, activities, and results that condition the very need for sense making. So even such sociological accounts, not just of meaning but of sense-making activities, are biased and partial.

But perhaps more important, a focus solely on discourse can lead us to ignore the relation of the discourse to the system of domination in the social world. This relation, often characterized by labels like "ideology" and "hegemony," is emphasized by Said in various books, and by Giddens (1981) in his emphasis on the power of surveillance and information as bases of current social order. Olson (1977) argues that the very development from utterance to text, whether by children or by civilizations, brings a redistribution of mental energy from memory to analysis, and of discursive organization from mnemonic device to deep meaning-structure and logical argument. And in an example closer to home, it is possible that different sorts of texts— conversation transcripts versus published books—involve varying textual resources and have varying relations with the more general Western form of life.

Now the method of indexing tends toward ignoring the place of the text in the processes of the world. In urging interpretive reliance solely on textual facts, it even boasts of being purely internally oriented, and derogates facts about the production and reproduction of signification, legitimation, and domination in the text.

Cheney and Tompkins's practice in their example, however, generally and laudably resists this tendency. Their text, *The Challenge of Peace*, is surely a worldly one, not least in the intention of its authors. And they mix internal textual analysis with interview materials, survey results, and so on that they treat realistically as meta-commentaries on their main text, not as an intertextual dialogue. We must laud their structurational impulses, however unacknowledged. But in one crucial respect, their analysis still accords a privileged status to the text: The analysis of its words—the use of indexing— still controls the organization of the discussion and the selection of material from interviews and other sources. For instance, they cite interview material indicating conflicts of purpose and interpretation among the bishops about the text. Perhaps, rather than letting the index dictate the organization of the analysis, the text might have been examined as a compromise product from the group of bishops, with attention directed to uncovering aporias and other indications of conflict and compromise, with the index helping to suggest evidence. The appropriateness of this focus on the words of the text will be discussed in my concluding section.

So what is an acceptable paradigm for the study of discursive objects or texts? A useful provisional model is suggested by Thompson (1984) for the study of ideology. He proposes three thematically distinct phases. First is social analysis of the discursive context at three levels: the context of action and interaction, involving aims, location in social space and time, and constraints; the institutional context; and the context of macro-structural elements constraining institutional structuration. Second is discursive analysis of the narrative, argumentative, and syntactic structures of discourse; it is in this phase that indexing might make uniquely valuable contributions. The last phase is that of interpretation, with special attention to the "ideological reference" of the discourse. This model, while not unflawed, helps ensure attention to the world-text relation.

In conclusion, the method of indexing tempts us to regard it as complete or primary, at least as outlined by Burke and by Cheney and Tompkins. Before we follow that primrose path, we should make sure that it leads to the strait gate to structurational analysis, over Burke to Giddens.

TEXT AND REFERENT

To quote Derrida's "there is nothing outside the text" is to suggest a totalizing view of textual analysis in social science that has been suggested by such scholars as Paul Ricoeur. Since there is nothing outside the text, the object of social scientific study and research must be the text and nothing else. Only in a text is evanescent human action fixed and preserved for reflective study and as evidence for hypotheses and theories. The necessary result is that methods of textual interpretation are the initial and controlling methods of social science, and that texts and readings are the central objects of study in a solely hermeneutic discipline.

This conclusion has a great deal of attraction for qualitatively oriented researchers and does have considerable heuristic value, leading us to revise some of our more mechanical research activities. Moreover, it has been argued for, convincingly, by poststructuralists, who show that meaning is not a matter of pure *reference* to some conceptual or objective referent outside of but represented in discourse. Rather, it is the outcome of differences produced in the free play of signifiers in discourse. So in this respect, we must think of discourse as a closed system. A text can refer only to itself or other texts. A different reason has been articulated by Ricoeur (1981), who claims that action and text are similar in important respects: Action, to be studied by science, must have its meaning "fixed," and a text is the only medium for fixation that can *refer* to the action in any sense (in other bases, the action record is important or relevant *in* a world but does not refer *to* a world). And a text "interrupts" reference, creating an "autonomous" "world of the text," which it actually refers to (or "opens up" as its own product).

Moreover, several of Cheney and Tompkins's statements suggest that they agree with this stand. They state that "all of our experiments, observations, questionnaires, interviews, coding schemes, and unobtrusive measures must yield *at some level* a text or set of subtexts. Nonverbal activity, for example, cannot be analyzed without being coded in a symbol system" (p. 463). And, "there is no other way to treat 'the surroundings' or the 'referents' of a body of discourse but to describe it with other symbols" (p. 465).

But overall, I find misleading the suggestion that texts are *the* object of social scientific concern. Although representation and reference as general grounds of meaning have been rightly rejected, representation and especially reference may still be *possible*, though logically subordinate to and dependent on meaningful practice. As Wittgenstein argues, reference and even ostensive definition are possible; they simply are not basic. This argument preserves a place for a nontextual order of reality in our form of life, as well as for a reference relation, derivative and complex, between "text" and "reality."

As for Ricoeur's argument about the textuality of human action, it seems deficient in three respects. First, Thompson (1984) notes that Ricoeur's argument depends on attributing speech-act properties, autonomy, and so on to action, which are actually properties of action-descriptions. Such descriptions are inevitably plural, contested, *and context-infected*. Second, there are clearly various media for the preservation of human action. One is the natural order of causal results of actions. Atomic tests and Agent Orange retain not just importance and relevance, but current causal impact in human experience. And Bullock (1987) has recently argued that photographs must be understood as fossils or tracks that have an important nonsymbolic place in human experience. Another locus of perdurance of human action is the institution—I would say that organizations are a good example. They involve, in Smith's (1984) terms, textually *mediated* social interactions, but they are not texts. Such media involve chains of events that change constantly but have enough continuity to allow repeated study. But third, even if texts were the only medium for the fixation of actions, it would not follow that texts are the *object* of social inquiry. We can study a text with a special interest in its explicit referent, in what it is about. That referent or object, "pointed to" by the text, is never *captured* in it. The object (or a chain of effects, as above) is a methodological and fallible guarantee that more texts about the same object, with equally primary status, are possible, and it distinguishes such texts from secondary commentaries and interpretations. In Barthean terms, the discipline of social science demands that certain texts be regarded and treated as *works* (whatever the virtue of another mode of treatment).

But the main line of Cheney and Tompkins's argument is actually to resist concluding that objects of social scientific analysis are in essence textual. Their stand is much more sensitive: that the process of research itself is a process of writing, of strategically transforming the experience, practices, and results of research into a text. The text alone is available to the *consumer* of science, but that limit does not apply to the scientist at work. But I would urge caution about considering the text as a cybernetic goal controlling research. We should be true to our object more than to our product. Surely, it is apparent that the journal article is a deeply flawed medium for the communication of social science research, and that we should follow proper procedures even if we cannot fully report their results.

Cheney and Tompkins's analysis of *The Challenge of Peace* is in easy accord with the stand just articulated. The avowed focus of analysis is a text, which by any standards deserves interpretive scrutiny of the kind they bring to it. And they are clearly involved in such scrutinizing, analytic research, employing secondary material instrumentally in developing a metatext. That is, their aim is not to produce the kind of intertextual field that a poststructuralist procedure would produce, equating in status text and commentary. My point is merely that these procedures, while both legitimate and revealing at times, are not the only or even the best choices when approaching a matrix of quantitative data or field notes.

STATUS OF THE METHOD OF INDEXING

Up to now, our analysis has led to two general conclusions. First, texts are dually system and structure; the method of indexing is relevant only within a more general approach that recognizes that duality. Second, indexing is usually not the primary method of social scientific research, since the texts and other materials of research are oriented toward some object that replaces the index in guiding and organizing the analysis. Still, this leaves a definite and important place for the method of indexing, both as a predominant method where the object of social scientific interest is a text to be interpreted and as an important method for the critical elucidation and penetration of research materials. One final question set remains about the status of the method of indexing, as applied even within those limits: Is it a general method of interpretation, a hammer to be used whenever we approach a text? How reliable are the conclusions, the inferences, and proofs that follow from it? How routinely and even mechanically are we able and justified to apply it? How firm is the ground of its facts for references and proofs?

Now to begin with, Burke and Cheney and Tompkins make explicit claims about the method that they also deny, explicitly and in their example. We have already discussed the ease with which Burke goes from repeated words to weaker facts and inferences. Moreover, we must recognize, as Burke does explicitly, that the method depends from the very beginning on the choice of words indexed, and less apparently on the choice of boundaries of the work. And of course, for social scientific uses, the text the method is applied to is usually composed of inferences about the object of study. That is, there is an inescapable need for interpretation prior to the method. There remains little doubt that the method of indexing is probable, leading to neither univocal nor indubitable conclusions.

Moreover, we must be conscious of the reflexivity of all human endeavors, especially of the rules for understanding discourse. If Burke's method becomes well known and generally accepted, authors will begin to violate and mock it intentionally. An obvious early move would be a Gricean resort to implicature (e.g., Grice, 1975)—deviant ties created by the text's "facts" in order to convey some variant meaning. Of course, such a move would force us to use the method of indexing, and then go beyond it—just such moves might characterize Barthean "texts."

In sum, to the boundaries on the method of indexing due to the dual nature of the text and the intentional nature of the social scientific genre must be added a recognition of its contingency and dependence on a more general and nonmethodical interpretive practice. All these limiting clauses may seem to constrict severely the importance we should assign to the method. I would not agree with such an impression—one need only think of the widespread use of some version of the method to be struck by its value.

REFERENCES

Barthes, R. (1975). *The pleasure of the text* (R. Miller, Trans.). New York: Hill & Wang.
Barthes, R. (1977). From work to text. In *Image-music-text* (pp. 155-164; S. Heath, Trans.). New York: Hill & Wang.
Barthes, R. (1981). Theory of the text. In R. Young (Ed.), *Untying the text: A post-structuralist reader* (pp. 31-47). Boston: Routledge & Kegan Paul.
Bullock, M. (1987). *The hanging gardens of Babylon*. Seminar presented at the Center for Twentieth Century Studies, University of Wisconsin—Milwaukee.
Burke, K. (1954). Fact, inference, and proof in the analysis of literary symbolism. In L. Bryson, L. Finkelstein, R. MacIver, & R. McKeon (Eds.), *Symbols and values: An initial study*. New York: Cooper Square.
Foucault, M. (1977). What is an author? In D. Bouchard (Ed.), *Language, counter-memory, practice* (pp. 113-138). Ithaca, NY: Cornell University Press.
Giddens, A. (1976). *New rules of sociological method*. New York: Basic Books.
Giddens, A. (1979). *Central problems in social theory*. Berkeley: University of California Press.
Giddens, A. (1981). *A contemporary critique of historical materialism* (Vol. 1). Berkeley: University of California Press.
Giddens, A. (1984). *The constitution of society*. Berkeley: University of California Press.
Grice, H. P. (1975). Logic and conversation. In P. Cole & J. L. Morgan (Eds.), *Syntax and semantics: Vol. 3. Speech acts*. New York: Academic Press.
Labov, W., & Fanshel, D. (1977). *Therapeutic discourse: Psychotherapy as conversation*. New York: Academic Press.
Olson, D. R. (1977). From utterance to text: The bias of language in speech and writing. *Harvard Educational Review, 47*, 257-281.
Ricoeur, P. (1981). *Hermeneutics and the human sciences* (J. B. Thompson, Ed. and Trans.). New York: Cambridge University Press.
Said, E. (1983). *The world, the text, and the critic*. Cambridge, MA: Harvard University Press.
Smith, D. (1984). Textually mediated social organization. *International Social Science Journal, 26*, 59-74.
Thompson, J. (1984). *Studies in the theory of ideology*. New York: Cambridge University Press.
Tibbetts, P., & Johnson, P. (1985). The discourse and *praxis* models in recent reconstructions of scientific knowledge generation. *Social Studies of Science, 15*, 739-749.
Tompkins, P. K. (1985). On hegemony—"He gave it no name"—And critical structuralism in the work of Kenneth Burke. *Quarterly Journal of Speech, 71*, 119-131.
Wilson, J. D. (1951). *What happens in "Hamlet"* (2nd ed.). New York: Publisher.
Young, R. (1981). Introduction to "Theory of the text." In R. Young (Ed.), *Untying the text: A post-structuralist reader* (pp. 31-32). Boston: Routledge & Kegan Paul.

Constructing "Texts" and Making Inferences: Some Reflections on Textual Reality in Human Communication Research

MARY S. STRINE
University of Utah, Salt Lake City

Texts are places where power and weakness become visible and discussable, where learning and ignorance manifest themselves, where the structures that enable and constrain our thoughts and actions become palpable.

(Scholes, 1985, p. xi)

Diverse, often competing, notions of "text" and "textuality" are at the forefront of current theoretical debate in the human sciences. Each notion carries with it a particular constellation of assumptions about the nature and function of textuality in human culture and promotes particular interpretive methods that inform and animate the research process. The sustaining authority of each notion of text rests on the quality of research that it inspires and the interpretive insights that it yields. Cheney and Tompkins put forth a compelling case for Burkean "indexing," rooted in Burke's theory of dramatism and symbolic action, as an alternative approach to the interpretation and analysis of textual phenomena. They provide a detailed explanation of indexing procedures as well as a powerful demonstration of the insights that indexing a communication "text" might generate through their illustrative analysis of the U.S. Catholic bishops' 1983 pastoral letter, *The Challenge of Peace*.

Correspondence and requests for reprints: Mary S. Strine, Department of Communication, University of Utah, Salt Lake City, UT 84112.

Communication Yearbook 11, pp. 494-500

For Cheney and Tompkins, as for Burke, the construction of the text is not at issue. Rather, the communication text is given as a unified symbolic structure. The "facts" or words of the text cohere as symbolic action; "indexing," then, provides a rigorous method for analyzing the textual arrangement of words as "facts." As Cheney and Tompkins explain, the text is "a factual territory from which one makes a map through inferences" (p. 466). They support this construal of the communication text as a coherent symbolic structure by claiming that some sort of textual objectification or reification is a necessary phase in all interpretive effort (see also Ricoeur, 1981):

> We recognize, of course, that the "text" can obscure the processual development of communication phenomena. We do not see this limitation as peculiar to the approach we offer here but as inherent in reflection and commentary upon action. . . . Whenever one selects from and comments upon a portion of experience (or anticipated experience), he or she, in a sense, "freezes" the experience in time. Moreover, our terms of description goad us to reify, instantiate, and otherwise make firm those "elements" of experience to which we refer. (p. 477)

However, for some researchers in the human sciences, including communication, the construction of the cultural "text" is itself problematic, both epistemologically and politically. Some ethnographic researchers have become agonizingly reflexive in their attempts to represent textually the lived reality of others and have begun to incorporate indications of their own emergent uncertainties and misgivings about the interpretive process within the ethnographies that they produce. The resultant scholarly "texts" are less coherent symbolic structures than frequently ruptured and self-questioning displays of open-ended textuality (see Clifford, 1983, 1986). My purpose in this commentary is to extend the important discussion of the text in human communication research begun by Cheney and Tompkins in a direction that addresses these concerns.

The conception of text most appropriate for the line of discussion that I want to pursue is that of Roland Barthes. In two key essays, "From Work to Text" and "Theory of the Text," Barthes focuses on the essential differences between what is traditionally understood as a "work" and the poststructuralist notion of text. Works are concrete, culturally determinate and stable objects; when perceived as works communication phenomena are approached as naturally cohesive, inherently meaningful entities to be interpreted and analyzed. Whereas texts are interwoven tissues of always potential meanings and values. They are, in Barthes's terms, "methodological fields." When perceived as "texts" communication phenomena are approached as discourses, sites of signifying practice or forms of social productivity to be encountered in the researcher's construction of meaning (Barthes, 1979, 1981). Jameson (1981) sums up the wide-ranging, transformative significance of the shift from work to text within the human sciences as follows:

This [textual] "revolution," essentially antiempiricist, drives the wedge of the concept of a "text" into the traditional disciplines by extrapolating the notion of "discourse" or "writing" onto objects previously thought to be "realities" or objects in the real world, such as the various levels or instances of a social formation: political power, social class, institutions, and events themselves. When properly used, the concept of the "text" does not . . . "reduce" these realities to small and manageable written documents of one kind or another, but rather liberates us from the empiricist object—whether institution, event, or individual work—by displacing our attention to its *constitution* as an object and its *relationship* to the other objects thus constituted. (pp. 296-297)

Emphasis on the intertextuality of human culture unavoidably complicates the researcher's relationship to the social phenomena or works that he or she is investigating. Epistemological problems of textual reality construction have raised major concerns among "fieldwork" researchers in the human sciences regarding the validity of the knowledge claims inherent in the scholarly texts that they produce. Clifford (1986) puts this issue in terms that apply in some sense to all aspects of human communication research:

If "culture" is not an object to be described, neither is it a unified corpus of symbols and meanings that can be definitively interpreted. Culture is contested, temporal, and emergent. Representation and explanation—both by insiders and outsiders—is implicated in this emergence. The specification of discourses [that follow from this awareness] . . . is thus more than a matter of making carefully limited claims. It is thoroughly historicist and self-reflexive. (p. 19)

Efforts to engage these problems of scholarly investigation and representation directly have given rise to a new wave of anthropological research (known variously as "processual anthropology," "poststructural anthropology," "interpretive anthropology," and "symbolic anthropology") emphasizing the situated, experiential nature of the researcher's understanding and have led to a move away from conventional forms of research publication, such as the "research report," toward more experimental forms of scholarly discourse (see Turner & Bruner, 1986; Clifford, 1986).

In a similar vein, critical scholars sensitized to the intertextual bases of human culture have begun to focus on the power relations inherent in textual reality construction, including those authoritative texts produced by researchers and critical scholars. For example, Bryan Green (1983) provides a trenchant analysis of the ways in which the "texts" of social scientific reports on poverty effectively shaped public knowledge about and subsequent policy toward the poor in nineteenth-century England. And Edward Said (1983) offers an incisive explanation for the broad sociopolitical ramifications of the essay as the primary textual form that criticism takes in modern culture. For Green, Said, and others, texts are fundamentally "a system of forces institutionalized by the reigning culture at some human cost to its various components" (Said, 1983, p. 53). The aim of criticism from this perspective is both oppositional and reconstructive; critical texts stand opposed to the reifying, dogmatizing tendencies in culture by revealing the affiliative network of intertextual relations that sustain certain cultural texts in positions of prominence and power. Said argues that critical discourse must maintain a resonant, if precarious, position between culture and the critical system being employed:

> Criticism in short is always situated; it is skeptical, secular, reflectively open to its own failings. This is by no means to say that it is value-free. Quite the contrary, for the inevitable trajectory of critical consciousness is to arrive at some acute sense of what political, social, and human values are entailed in the reading, production, and transmission of every text. To stand between culture and system is therefore to stand *close to* . . . a concrete reality about which political, moral, and social judgements have to be made and, if not only made, then exposed and demystified. (p. 26; see also Belsey, 1980)

The reflexive concerns about textual reality construction expressed by the social scientists and critics discussed here achieve a unifying focus, if not a resolution, within the dialogical theory of the Russian semiotician Mikhail Bakhtin and his Circle. Bakhtin's theory provides an especially rich potential for communication researchers because it grounds the notions of cultural text and textuality in a concrete operation of speech genres involving the communicative interactions of historically situated, mutually responsive subjects. Newcomb (1984) and Fiske (1986), for example, have suggested innovative ways in which dialogical theory might enrich the study of how meanings emerge in the relation between actual audiences and their mass-mediated experiences.

The relationship between Bakhtin's dialogical theory (Bakhtin, 1986, pp. 60-102) and the concept of text can be summarized as follows: The fundamental unit or fact of the text is not the word or the sentence but the living communicative utterance. Because each utterance necessarily implicates a speaker, an addressee, and the focus or theme of the address, texts comprising one or more utterances are not inherently meaningful but are sites where different voices actively struggle for meaning. Relatively stable types of utterances (e.g., research reports, novels, political campaign speeches, situation comedies, and so forth) within each sphere of cultural discourse (e.g., academic research, literature, politics, prime-time television, and so forth) constitute textual forms or speech genres. Culture consists of the aggregation of textual forms or speech genres in use during a particular historical period. Gary Saul Morson (1986), a leading Bakhtin scholar, explains the historical and social nature of speech genres, and by extension that of textuality, in these terms: "Speech genres temporarily crystallize a network of relations between or among interlocutors—their respective power and status, their presumed purposes in communicating, their characterization of the subject of discourse, and their relation to other conversations" (p. 89).

When viewed from the perspective of dialogical theory, all forms of scholarly representation, whether social scientific or critical, are inherently dialogized and the problem of textual reality construction appears in a new light. As Bakhtin (1986) explains,

> The transcription of thinking in the human sciences is always the transcription of a special kind of dialogue: the complex interrelations between the *text* (the object of study and reflection) and the created, framing *context* (questioning, refuting, and so forth) in which the scholar's cognizing and evaluating thought takes place. This is the meeting of two texts—of the ready-made and the reactive text being created—and, consequently, the meeting of two subjects and two authors. (pp. 106-107)

My foregoing overview of alternative poststructuralist and dialogical perspectives on text and textuality provide a pretext for engaging Cheney and Tompkins once more on the issue of textual reality construction in communication research. Cheney and Tompkins briefly acknowledge that "textual 'production' and textual 'interpretation' become intertwined in practice" (p. 463), however, they are not inclined to regard this intermixture as a problem because of the *inter*textual affiliations that constrain the research enterprise. They note that the anticipated textual form of research representation influences the research process from the outset and that the academic community to which the research is addressed determines which forms of textual representation count as knowledge. The scientific "resarch report" is the textual model of scholarly representation on which Cheney and Tompkins's understanding of the "larger text of communication research" turns:

> To imagine the end point of research as a text is to constrain or force one to *conduct* research in such a way, and only that way, so as to reduce all facts, inferences, and proofs to the product of a research report. Nothing can be studied, no manipulations can be performed, no results can be gathered, no conclusions can be reached without the possibility of transcendence into a work with a text. To put it another way, the need to realize a text is a limiting factor *prior* to the conduct of research. In fact, before the final text can be composed, numerous subtexts dealing with theory, previous research, hypotheses or research questions, methods, results, interpretations, and conclusions must be composed or assembled, thus creating an intertext. (pp. 462-463)

The generic features of the "research report" described in this quotation—discrete subtexts representing theory, previous research, hypotheses or research questions, methods, results, interpretations, conclusions—distance the researcher from the process of inquiry and objectify the communication phenomena to be analyzed in order to make "positive" knowledge claims.

Cheney and Tompkins propose to broaden the range of textual forms of research representation through their conception of the research text as composite intertext, however, they fall short of that objective. Cheney and Tompkins's argument in support of Burkean indexing as a unifying method for social scientific and humanistic research in communication rests soundly on a positivist understanding of what facts and texts are. But to say that indexing as a method for analyzing the facts of the text parallels computer-assisted statistical techniques in rigor is still too constraining. Within such an epistemology, much that is insightful and valuable in past and current critical texts can be depreciated or severed from the intertext of communication research altogether.

If, however, the alternative conceptions of text and textuality discussed above have efficacy, then the vitality of communication as a research discipline requires a more heterodox view of what constitutes a legitimate research text and what the "larger text of communication research" might entail. Within this view, the purpose of scholarly representation would not be simply the accumulation of positive knowledge *about* communication phenomena—though this collection is an undeniably important goal that such methods as Burkean indexing could effectively serve. An added, perhaps equally important, aim would be the production of research texts as "answerable representations" (see Biolastosky, 1986), texts that invigorate and extend the "larger text of communication research" by inviting response from other textual perspectives thereby contributing to an open and unending disciplinary dialogue (see Strine & Pacanowsky, 1985).

REFERENCES

Bakhtin, M. M. (1986). *Speech genres and other late essays* (V. W. McGee, Trans.). Austin: University of Texas Press.

Barthes, R. (1979). From work to text. In J. V. Harari (Ed.), *Textual strategies: Perspectives in post-structuralist criticism* (pp. 73-81). Ithaca, NY: Cornell University Press.

Barthes, R. (1981). Theory of the text. In R. Young (Ed.), *Untying the text: A post-structuralist reader* (pp. 31-47). Boston: Routledge & Kegan Paul.

Belsey, C. (1980). *Critical practice*. New York: Methuen.

Bialostosky, D. H. (1986). Dialogics as an art of discourse in literary criticism. *Publications of the Modern Language Association, 101*, 788-797.

Clifford, J. (1983). On ethnographic authority. *Representations, 1*(2), 118-146.

Clifford, J. (1986). Introduction: Partial truths. In J. Clifford & G. E. Marcus (Eds.), *Writing culture: The poetics and politics of ethnography* (pp. 1-26). Berkeley: University of California Press.

Fiske, J. (1986). Television: Polysemy and popularity. *Critical Studies in Mass Communication, 3*, 391-408.

Green, B. S. (1983). *Knowing the poor: A case-study in textual reality construction*. Boston: Routledge & Kegan Paul.

Jameson, F. (1981). *The political unconscious: Narrative as a socially symbolic act*. Ithaca, NY: Cornell University Press.

Morson, G. S. (Ed.). (1986). *Bakhtin: Essays and dialogues on his work.* Chicago: University of Chicago Press.

Newcomb, H. (1984). On dialogic aspects of mass communication. *Critical Studies in Mass Communication, 1*, 34-50.

Ricoeur, P. (1971). The model of the text: Meaningful action considered as a text. *Social Research, 38*, 529-562.

Said, E. W. (1983). *The world, the text, and the critic.* Cambridge, MA: Harvard University Press.

Scholes, R. (1985). *Textual power: Literary theory and the teaching of English.* New Haven, CT: Yale University Press.

Strine, M. S., & Pacanowsky, M. (1985). How to read interpretive accounts of organizational life: Narrative bases of textual authority. *Southern Speech Communication Journal, 50*, 283-297.

Turner, V. W., & Bruner, E. M. (Eds.). (1986). *The anthropology of experience.* Urbana: University of Illinois Press.

SECTION 6

PUBLIC OPINION
AND AGENDA-SETTING

12 Communication Perspectives in Public Opinion: Traditions and Innovations

ALEX S. EDELSTEIN
University of Washington, Seattle

This article takes the position that the reality of public opinion arises in communication processes and that the search—albeit with limited success—for behavioral effects has diverted researchers from recognizing the presence of strong "communication effects." This article reviews the major perspectives in public opinion research and reconsiders their findings from a communication effects perspective.

THERE are as many definitions of public opinion as there are disciplinary points of view. Political scientists see public opinion in terms of the distribution of power and the management of societies. Sociologists theorize about collective forces at work. This review will take a communication perspective to public opinion. It will center on research traditions that address the *perception* that public opinion exists and that this perception is gained by observing and communicating. If we accept as reality that perceptions of the reality of public opinion exist, then we may ask how people gain those perceptions and how they act upon them.

Lippmann (1922) spoke of perceptions and cognitions as "pictures in our minds" and described how those pictures were constructed, for example, by the use of stereotypes. Allport (1937) saw public opinion as an elusive form of public consciousness, but he was critical of the tendency of scholars and journalists alike to "personify" public opinion as if it were a collective person, an entity unto itself; public opinion, unless actually communicated, could only express an aggregate of individual opinions. It depended for its character as a collective force upon an awareness on the part of individuals that other individuals held opinions directed at the same object; this process invoked perception, cognition, and communication.

Correspondence and requests for reprints: Alex S. Edelstein, School of Communications, University of Washington, Seattle, WA 98195.

Communication Yearbook 11, pp. 502-533

Boorstin (1971a), writing as an intellectual and historian of mass communication, also adopted the concept of perception in describing *Democracy and Its Discontents*. Public opinion was, he said, whatever people thought it was. Lemert (1981), writing from the perspective of mass communication, described public opinion as the perception that public opinion exists. And Noelle-Neumann (1979), reviewing public opinion in the "classical tradition," asserted that seventeenth- and eighteenth-century philosophers such as John Locke, David Hume, and Jean-Jacques Rousseau dealt in their own terms with a "climate of opinion" that was perceived by the society and affected behavior. Glynn (1984a) most recently observed that researchers increasingly have considered perceptions of others' opinions to be an important focus of study.

The larger question is the extent to which we may focus our attention on communication aspects of public opinion. One way is to look beyond such "limited behavioral effects" approaches as agenda setting to the implications the approach carries for "communication effects." We need to move from cognitions and cognitive structures, primarily as mechanisms for making voting choices, to a consideration of cognitive steps as anchoring points for communication in the formation and expression of opinions. Viewed in terms of steps, cognitions represent additional potential for observing communication. In each of the six perspectives of opinion research that follow, we will look for the implications of *communication* and *mass communication* for public opinion and attempt, as well, to point to directions in the field and to new parameters for research. Those perspectives are as follows:

(1) *Limited behavioral effects.* The limited effects perspective includes agenda-setting, the "third person effect," and the normative function of media. Agenda-setting has ascribed limited behavioral effects to media in "ordering" attention to the salience of opinion objects, rather than giving the content of those objects. A more recent "third-person effect" hypothesis described by Davison (1983) also suggests a limited behavioral effect in that the individual chooses a course of action only after weighing the implications of the behavior of others. This consequence is an indirect behavioral effect in that the individual acts not on the basis of media content itself, but on perceptions of how others, who are directly affected, might act. The "normative function" media described by Glynn (1985) is a limited behavioral effects model in that it specifies one explicit media function in calling attention to the importance of normative opinion. "Normativeness" does, however, specify a "meaning" function, which agenda-setting does not.

In each of these examples, it may be possible to observe strong communication effects in what otherwise has been regarded as a limited behavioral effect. We would expect the processes of observing, learning, and interacting to determine the salience of opinion objects, the perceptions of others, or the assessment and expression of normativeness to have a high potential for communication effects.

(2) *A dependency model of mass communication.* Advanced by Ball-Rokeach and DeFleur (1976), the "dependency model" explains broader mass media effects in sociological theory as expressions of larger and formative societal forces that work toward social change and reflect social and community conflicts. Other communication and opinion effects are not specified by the model, but recent efforts have been made to address these parameters.

Rather than a broadly conceived "condition of dependency," Blumer (1971) sees in a sociological perspective the mass media functioning in an integrative role, publicizing and "legitimizing" social change and conflicts. The media facilitate public consciousness and thus permit formation and expression of public opinion.

(3) *The social-psychological context.* Avoiding cognitive explanations for behavior, notions of "the climate of opinion" and "pluralistic ignorance" invoke social-psychological constructs such as "fear of isolation," "projection," and the "looking-glass self" as explanations for communication and opinion behavior. Each psychological construct carries implications for the accuracy of perceptions of opinions and willingness to express opinions.

(4) *From evaluative to cognitive coorientation.* Orientations and coorientation to opinion objects may address "cognitive" as well as "affective" aspects of problems or issues. Cognitive approaches raise the question as to whether evaluative studies of coorientation might not be confounding different aspects of the same opinion object. As Edelstein, Ito, and Kepplinger (1988) point out, individuals may be cooriented cognitively to different aspects of the same problem or to the same aspects of different problems. They may also coorient to "subissues" of a problem.

(5) *Opinion structures and processes.* Cognitive structures (in the individual) and social structures (that show the organization of the society) reflect, at the levels of the individual and the society, changes in perceptions, cognitions, or evaluations of objects. These changes may be mapped in terms of the communication that occurs as a consequence of those processes. Edelstein et al. (1988) put forward a "communication-step theory" based upon "cognitions" held at each "step" of the emergence of a problem.

(6) *A constructivist approach to methodology.* Moving to the issue of research method, questionnaire formats vary in their potentialities for permitting the observation of communication. Poll questions structure communication by providing opinion objects and means of evaluating them. Questions that limit the definition of the opinion object and relevant values also limit communication. Swanson (1981) and others have proposed a "constructivist" approach that permits the respondent to "construct" more of his or her own realities and enhance potentialities for referencing exchanges of information and communication.

These summaries serve to introduce the traditions. We may now address the implications of each approach in more detail.

THE LIMITED EFFECT HYPOTHESIS

The pioneering research of McCombs (1981) has been characterized as a "limited behavioral effects" approach; the individual is not told *what* to think but what to think *about*. The consequences of agenda setting need not be limited communication, however; the critical question is not the cognitive discrimination itself, but the communication that occurs as a consequence.

Thus far we have failed to specify opinion and communication processes that might be linked to the demands for "thinking about" as contrasted with "thinking." Is the amount and quality of opinion formation and attendant communication related to the degree of salience of an opinion object? There is reason for thinking that salient objects that are "placed on agendas" to be "thought about" may make strong demands upon the individual for communication. We need to specify and observe the conditions under which the communication of opinions is most likely to occur.

Observing Complex Cognitions

Observation of more complex cognitions may also enhance communication effects. Benton and Frazier (1976), following the suggestion of Palmgreen, Kline, and Clarke (1974), asked agenda-setting questions about the status of issues. The rationale was that salience was associated not only with the object, itself, but with information-processing steps taken to deal with that object, that is, a "uses" approach that assumes a more active audience. The two investigators looked at what they called the agenda-setting function for levels of information. The three levels included (1) the nominal category of the issue; (2) subissues, causes, and proposed solutions; and (3) the criteria or bases for dealing with the issues.

The approach was rewarded: It was found that newspapers set opinion agendas for newspaper users at levels 2 and 3, but television failed to reach these "levels." It was apparant at these levels that respondents were operating on the basis of more information than could be attributed to media. Permitting a respondent to talk about various parameters of a problem, as well as being able to visualize the criteria that were brought to bear upon them, provided degrees of freedom for communication and reports of opinion behavior.

Edelstein (1980, 1981, 1983, 1985) and Edelstein et al. (1987) tested a similar although larger matrix of cognitive parameters in an analysis of the opinion behaviors of university students in four countries. They observed that students perceived and exchanged opinions about their awareness of the consequences, causes, and solutions to social problems. These cognitive foci also lent themselves to analysis as "stages" or "steps" in the emergence of a social problem. While Benton and Frazier (1976) posed questions as to which media set what kinds of "subissues" agendas, Edelstein et al. (1987) asked what *cognitive* agendas were set for communication. The cognitive parameters were defined in structural terms as the consequences, causes, and/or solutions to problems.

Salience Effects in Agenda-Setting

The impact of cognition upon opinions and communication is stressed by Weaver (1984) in calling attention to the communication implications of what have been assumed to be purely cognitive "salience" effects in agenda-setting. He notes the distinction made by Carter (1965) between cognitions of opinion objects and the means of evaluating them, but observes that evaluation is embedded implicitly in cognition. When the media fasten attention upon criteria that express values, the media convey those values in what otherwise might be construed as a purely "cognitive" agenda-setting process. Also, the amount of attention given to the opinion object tends to give it an evaluative dimension either of favorableness or unfavorableness. This effect is paralleled by a so-called priming effect; that is, the cognitions of the opinion object and relevant criteria "prime" the opinion pump of the public by associational thinking. Publics link old problems and issues to those most recently placed on the agenda and hence form a far more complex opinion than would be proposed by a simpler agenda-setting formulation. Weaver's position is that there is a substantial "evaluative" effect attached to any conferring of salience; hence "thinking about" needs to be constructed as a substantial focus for the study of communication and public opinion. Weaver cautions, however, that the direction of influence may often run from the public to the media rather than the other way around.

Beyond cognition, agenda effects must be attributed to techniques of media presentation rather than to the sheer volume of content over time. Thus we need to relate structural factors that govern media functioning and the technologies that are employed. Psychographic and demographic factors such as life space, predispositions, and interpersonal communication account, as well, for the attention that publics give to media agendas. In these terms, Weaver (1984) asks if agenda-setting affects individuals or collectivities, and occurs with single issues or sets of issues. It may be less accurate to speak of media influencing individuals' agendas as influencing the distribution of the top one or two issues among representative groups of voters or the public:

> Even though this is not as dramatic an effect as some advocates of agenda-setting might hope for, it is still an important phenomenon, for it suggests that the relative amount of emphasis on various issues by the media determine the size of the various groups of individuals in a given community or society who are most concerned about these same issues. (p. 683)

Weaver has proposed that fresh insights demand a revision of Katz's often cited (1966) model of stages in the formation of public opinion. To Katz's initial steps of "salience, discussion, formation of alternative solutions, and final mobilization of public opinion for a collective decision," Weaver would add an enhanced definition of salience as well as "priming" related to attitudes and opinions.

Normative Functions as "Limited" Functions

Like agenda-setting, Glynn's work (1985) on the "normative functions" of media suggests a possible amplification of mass communication effects upon the formation and expression of public opinion. While the approach is "limited" in that it specifies only one effect, that effect is far from limited in its implications. The Glynn-McLeod formulation sees the mass media as establishing social and behavioral boundaries for behavior. In that construction of the situation, the media define and redefine opinion parameters as responses to audience predispositions and societal forces. The media do not themselves create those parameters; rather, they produce "normative bounding" effects.

Perhaps the most interesting aspects of "boundedness" occurred in the finding that the more the public used mass media—and particularly opinion-oriented contents—the less discrepancy occurred between their own opinions and their perceptions of the opinions of others. The causal relations are not established; hence, Weaver's suggestion that the direction of influence might be as much from audiences to media as from media to audiences. The greater significance of this relationship, from the standpoint of public opinion, is that by reflecting normative values the media make it easier for active publics to find a common basis for communication. The audience to media directionality also seems to explain the finding that fewer opinion discrepancies were perceived by readers of editorials and viewers of talk and call-in shows on television. Printed commentary and broadcast discussion also produced a greater sense of similarity between perceptions of one's own and the opinions of others than did other content types. But television commentary and editorializing was perceived as less two way in its character; audiences saw substantial differences in opinions held by themselves and by others. Those who read letters to the editor were also more likely to perceive differences between themselves and others; thus readers of letters to the editor were more critics than followers. This empirical articulation of individual differences contrasts with more broadly stated "normative" theories advanced by critical theorists and even by Noelle-Neumann (1973, 1974, 1976, 1977, 1984a) in her construction of a media-bounded society.

Cultivating Normativeness

Gerbner's "cultivation" hypothesis (see Gerbner & Gross, 1976) sees the media driven by structural and technological forces, actively propounding normative and thus reactionary values. Gerbner (1977) claims that the message systems of a culture not only inform but form common images or mental pictures; they not only entertain but create publics for entertainment and opinions. They provide the boundary conditions and overall patterns within which the processes of behavior go on. Analysis must begin with insights into institutions and their functioning. The relevant message systems cultivate the terms upon which they present subjects and aspects of life; thus communication effects (and public opinion) are not primarily what they make us "do," but what they contribute to the meaning of what is done.

Cook et al. (1983), on the other hand, see normativeness in terms of more complex relations among government elites, the media, and the public. The media produce content that has an impact upon the public, whose policy priorities are thereby changed (by this agenda-setting behavioral effect); this change influences policymakers, who in numerous instances gain their understanding of public opinion through the media to make policy or programmatic changes. The authors emphasize, however, that the more significant agenda setting may be the interaction and mutuality of elites and media in which the more distant public is also served.

Thus we see three contrasting definitions of role of the media and the individual in defining "normative opinion boundaries" for their publics. The Glynn-McLeod position is the most "scientific" and assumes the most active audience; the structural position, which incorporates the cultivation hypothesis, is "critical" in defining audiences as more passive and media most active, while the system concept is integrative in according the media a capacity not only for representing boundedness but as partners with elites in creating it. Our interest must lie in how each of those approaches influences the processes of communication and public opinion. In adopting one approach or the other, our communication and public opinion questions will be bounded by the assumptions implicit in each approach.

The Third Party Effect

To the extent that he describes "indirect" rather than "direct" effects, Davison (1983) takes a "limited" effect position with his intriguing "third person" hypothesis. He cites a situation in which both adversaries judge a media report as biased. The third party effect comes into play when the third party does not perceive bias but perceives that the adversaries so define the situation. Thus a calculated response is required that takes biases into account.

Recognizing that others are perceiving, the third person observes that there must be some *reasons* for the perceptions. The reward is not social; the rationalization is cognitive. The third party may act in any of a variety of ways that permits him or her to cope with the presumed actions of others. Davison takes essentially a cognitive approach; and sees bias as infecting and even corrupting public communication.

Glynn and McLeod (1985a) provide support for the Davison thesis in discussing "public opinion about public opinion." They asked respondents if they believed in public opinion and felt themselves to be influenced by it. Some 52% said they were not themselves influenced but that others were influenced. Regardless of whether or not they felt themselves to be influenced, they believed that others were influenced. While the most perceived-influence-on-self was associated with lower education and income, political conservatism, and low levels of informational media use, mass media were not the operating mechanisms. People tended to see others as more influenced by public opinion regardless of the source of their own opinions.

Posing Communication Questions

Davison's work poses several communication questions, some of which Glynn and McLeod begin to answer: (1) Why are the exaggerated expectations about the effects of communication and public opinion—upon others, rather than upon ourselves—so common? (2) Do these distortions occur in all kinds of public opinion and persuasive communication situations or only in certain kinds? As an example, distortions are more common as a function of mass media presentation than in personal encounters, where validation may be more immediate and inclusive. (3) Is it possible that we do not overestimate effects upon others but, rather, underestimate them upon ourselves?

TOWARD A DEPENDENCY MODEL
OF MASS COMMUNICATION EFFECTS

In her various explications of what she considers to be "powerful media" (summarized by Donsbach and Stevenson, 1984), Noelle-Neumann advances a concept of how the media exert their influence in two terms: (1) the observational biases of the media and (2) the consequent constraints upon audiences. Her thesis is that in situations of morally defined conflict, the media reduce the pluralism of information and opinions to values consonant with the biases of journalists and the internal media processes that permit their portrayal. A negative and reductionist agenda-setting effect occurs in which the media construct a moral agenda that crowds out competing values. This internally supportive and consonant view is presented as a majority view on a given subject. It may not, however, represent an objective appraisal of the distribution of attitudes or opinions on that issue. As a consequence, the media constrain the diversity of ideas and information and diminish the cognitive and opinion functioning of their audiences. This reduction in turn contributes to the readiness of individuals to speak up or to remain silent. By lending their voices to limited viewpoints, the media enhance the communication potential of certain groups and limit the potential of others. Thus

Noelle-Neumann views with alarm and sees a direct rather than an indirect pattern of media effects upon the opinion agenda that society may propose.

A Sociological View

Ball-Rokeach and DeFleur (1976) seem to agree, but not for the same reasons: Classic sociology leads us to treat both media and audiences as integral parts of a larger social system. Media and audiences thus would respond to the same social forces and look to each other for a definition of those realities. Social realities portrayed by the media ensue both from their connection to societal structures and from their interaction with audiences.

Ball-Rokeach and DeFleur see the mass media as gaining influence because of the emergence of more complex social systems; the more complexity and the more change in the social order, the less the more remote aspects of it may be perceived and thus the greater dependency upon the media. Fewer and fewer people may be aware, at first hand, of what is occurring beyond their own place in the structure. This lack suggests that opinions that are situationally based, rather than value or knowledge oriented, are more influenced by the media.

Ball-Rokeach (1985) and others have tested dependency theory at the level of the individual; the individual exercises selectivity in exposure to media content but also demonstrates "structural media dependency." Becker and Whitney (1980) formulated reliance/exposure as "dependency" and produced empirical evidence of its relevance. Miller and Reese (1982) isolated the reliance and exposure variables and confirmed Ball-Rokeach's expectations: What they predicted for media in general held for specific media, and dependency on a medium enhanced the opportunity for that medium to demonstrate effects. While the individual is relatively "independent" in making "quasi-statistical" judgments about opinion, she or he is nonetheless dependent on the media for definitions of the situation. Thus dependency is expressed empirically as a relation between the individual's goals and the extent to which they are contingent upon the resources of the media system. In these terms, dependency may change with changes in goals and the capacities of the media system. We may infer that opinions, as a part of the problem-solving process, express desired goals toward which individuals work but also create the risk of media dependency.

Constraints Upon the Media

Noelle-Neumann has held internal media structures to be responsible for constraints upon audiences, but she has not detailed the ways in which those structures create their own dependencies. It might help to distinguish dependencies as structural and functional in the sociological sense, and social-psychological and cognitive in the behavioral sense. External structures in most cases define events for the media. The internal structures of the media determine whether and how these events will be pictured and evaluated. The media alone cannot determine the public agenda; power is conferred upon them within their capacities to act. The media bring intellectual and other resources to bear upon social problems, but they amplify more than define both those problems and public opinion about those problems. It might be said as well that governmental actors, economic and social elites, interest groups, and intellectuals are similarly bounded by their own needs and capabilities.

The capacity of the American journalist (contrasted, perhaps, by journalists in other political cultures) to "distort" the news is limited by technologies (e.g., film, video, print, and voice), by administrative and bureaucratic controls, by limitations of time and space, and by the characteristics of news, for news is as much a product of its boundaries as of its goals. A vibrant literature describes the constraints upon news: They are structural, systemic, social, and technique oriented, artistic and creative, ego motivated, illusionary, symbolic, and even "logical."

THE SOCIOLOGICAL-PSYCHOLOGICAL CONTEXT

Noelle-Neumann (1973, 1974, 1976, 1977, 1979, 1984a) has advanced perceptual approaches to public opinion that rest upon perceptual, cognitive, and sociological-psychological theories. Her "quasi-statistical" concept in which individuals assess the direction of opinion change and optimize their utilities is perceptual and cognitive. The "climate of opinion" and "spiral of silence" offer both cognitive and social-psychological explanations for behavior. The climate of opinion is the more purely cognitive of the two. The cognitive orientation is reflected in the requirements for detecting the opinion climate. As summarized by Glynn and McLeod (1984, p. 46) detection demands that the individual perceive "accurately": (1) the distribution of opinions held by others; (2) shifts in support for various positions; (3) evaluations of the strength and commitments of those holding views; (4) the urgency of the situation; and (5) the prospects for success of the parties to the debate.

The climate of opinion is integral to the spiral of silence in that the individual holding a differing opinion fears "isolation" as a consequence of his or her perceptions of that "climate." The sources of those perceptions include the social environment, communication, and "signs" in the mass media that corroborate one another.

By advancing the perceptual approach, Noelle-Neumann has opened the door further to development of communication theory in public opinion. Donsbach and Stevenson (1984) point out that her macro theory combines theories of society, communication, and social psychology. Nevertheless, Glynn and McLeod (1984) point to the difficulties of treating public opinion, the spiral of silence, and mass media influences at the same time; each must be examined independently of the other if the particulars as well as the generality of the theories are to be established.

The Perceptual Approach

Noelle-Neumann's work consistently accords perception and communication a central role. Mass media play a dominant role in creating climates of opinion, and perceptions of voting outcomes and the flow of opinion are more predictive than expressed voting preferences at a single point in time, a finding confirmed by Glynn and McLeod (1984). Those who sense (perceive) ultimate victory, despite the objectively determined "balance" of voting preferences, are more willing to express publicly their preferences and thus be perceived by others to be stronger. The minority, acknowledging the situation, retires gradually into silence. Members acknowledge that interdependency in society is an indispensable means of "social control," again because the individual recognizes the threat of isolation if she or he fails to take prevailing values into account. Noelle-Neumann (1979) makes explicit the communicating of opinions:

> Today we can *show* it, we can prove it: Man has an organ to perceive opinion, the gift to perceive with great subtlety the development of opinions in his environment. We can ask questions (of anonymous subjects) about almost every matter of common interest . . . Their replies mirror the actual changes of opinions as measured by public opinion research; not as uncertain suggestions, but on the contrary . . . with (the most minute) decreases and (notably) increases . . . in the opinion climate. (p. 147)

She asks, almost rhetorically:

> Where do people learn that a few per cent of the population have changed their opinion—that, at this very moment, they are thinking more in one or the other direction?

> *How* exactly this communication system works we do not yet know; but from the sensitivity of reactions, we can realize what an unbelievable energy people spend on making these observations. [They seek] to avert an evil greater than that caused by the strain of observing one's environment—the danger of isolating oneself with a losing opinion that is about to go out of fashion. (p. 148)

Noelle-Neumann presents a scenario in which individuals become aware of change and possible danger in the environment; she centers attention upon the "communication sphere," which is controversial and contains a potential to isolate. By unspecified means of observation and communication, the individual perceives herself or himself to be in the majority or the minority; if the latter, she or he becomes unsure and withholds dangerous views. Those who perceive themselves to be in the majority speak up more freely, while the minority becomes more cautious; thus the spiral of communication, on the one hand, and the spiral of silence, on the other. From this thesis Noelle-Neumann articulates her definition of public opinion: "Public opinions are those in the sphere of controversy that one can express in public without isolating oneself" (p. 150).

None of these aspects of the theory has gone unchallenged as seen in the work of Katz, 1981; Taylor, 1982; Donsbach and Stevenson, 1984; Salmon and Kline, 1984; Glynn and McLeod, 1981, 1982, 1984, 1985a, 1985b; Merten, 1984; as well as Noelle-Neumann, 1984a.

The Question of Accuracy

The question of accuracy of perceptions of the "opinion climate" (rather than the extent of perceptual activity) has often been raised. This question in turn has led to questions about the sources of those (accurate or inaccurate) perceptions, including mass media. Lippmann (1922) commented about elements of time and space:

> In putting together our public opinions, not only do we have to picture more space than we can see with our eyes, and more time than we can feel, but we have to describe and judge more people, more actions, more things than we can ever count, or vividly imagine. We have to summarize and generalize. We have to pick out samples, and treat them as typical. (p. 148)

The accuracy question is raised most critically by Fields and Schuman (1976). Fields and Schuman point out that in social communication some cues are unmistakable, but in other situations one's beliefs about what other people think may be inaccurate because direct information is absent. Where such inaccuracy is systematic in direction, and collective rather than idiosyncratic, the consequences of action predicted on those beliefs might be profound. Referring to studies of pluralistic ignorance, Fields and Schuman concluded that biased perceptions permitted people to operate in an unreal world. More representative attitudes assessed in surveys often were not manifested in subsequent behavior because individuals believed that significant others would be displeased. So, it was not actual beliefs that were critical but "beliefs about beliefs." Comparing expectations of beliefs about the beliefs of neighbors and of more remote city residents, Fields and Schuman found a "conservative bias"; that is, people thought both their neighbors and others were more conservative on black-white child play relations than they themselves were. Other data suggested that the differences they had observed could not be explained by a "halo effect," that is, people deliberately misstating their positions as more liberal (or conservative). These findings held for other racial and civil liberty issues as well.

The Looking-Glass Self

In addition to the scanning of the environment through a "transparent glass," as the Noelle-Neumann thesis seems to imply, other evidence suggests that individuals mirror self-opinions, the so-called looking-glass effect. Glynn and McLeod (1985b) are helpful in showing how some conditions encourage looking-glass perceptions, while others do not. In nonsensitive areas, looking-glass perceptions prevailed; in sensitive situations, the individual was more likely to disown an unpopular position. Thus we need to specify conditions where accuracy or inaccuracy in perceptions are most likely to occur.

Fields and Schuman evidently accept the need to state more formally the communication implications of psychological states such as the looking-glass self, the spiral of silence, and the "disowning" hypothesis. For themselves, they are only able to say that people "appear" to look out into the world and "somehow" see their own opinions reflected. Glynn and McLeod have proposed a number of requirements, similar in many respects to Noelle-Neumann's (1984) response to criticisms of her theories, for data gathering that would permit hypothesis-testing about communication:

(1) Demonstrate that changes in perceptions of support for various positions lead to changing rates of interpersonal communication.
(2) Trace these changes in the climate of opinion to their origins in media coverage or interpersonal communication.
(3) Show that declining communication was due to fear of isolation. Alternative explanations would have to be ruled out.
(4) Show that changing degrees of expression of opinions were functionally related to changing levels of support.
(5) Demonstrate that changes in support were manifested by changing perceptions of the climate of opinion. While correlations have been shown, causal direction has been ambiguous.

An operational question is addressed to the special treatment accorded to Noelle-Neumann's so-called hard-core groups—who have been separated from samples. Hard-core individuals are those who are so committed to their cause as to resist communication and influence. Although they found results that Noelle-Neumann had predicted (i.e., that hard-core groups were more likely to use interpersonal communication rather than mass communication for verification of opinions, as contrasted to other than hard-core groups), they questioned, on grounds of the inclusiveness of the theory, the propriety of dropping them from the collective analysis. That is, does the theory apply to "society" or only to certain entities within it? If the latter, more entities should be specified and predictions made as to the communication and opinion behaviors of each entity.

Glynn and McLeod (1984) also discovered that hard-core opinion holders were more interested in the political campaign but, surprisingly, were less knowledgeable. While they were more likely to discuss the campaign, they felt that the discussion had less influence on their voting decisions, and they were less likely to perceive the climate of opinion as a factor in their choice. With respect to interpersonal communication, Glynn and McLeod again found a degree of support for the Noelle-Neumann theory. Other than the hard-core group, those who perceived themselves as losing support tended to communicate less, although not significantly so.

The two researchers found different effects upon perceptions for those persons who preferred television or newspapers. There was, however, only anecdotal evidence that both newspaper and television coverages were consistent with the perceptions of their users and that they changed together over time; a more adequate research design—including content analysis—would have been needed to test the relevant propositions.

Glynn and McLeod also found some degree of support for Noelle-Neumann's "quasi-statistical" thesis—the proposal that individuals could "scan" the horizon and detect shifts in the direction of support for an opinion. And they found that perceptions of public opinion appeared to be relatively independent from the individual's own position. As another partial source of support for the theory, the two investigators found that one's own preferences for a candidate increased or decreased toward the direction of the percentage of the perceived outcome for the candidates; in fact, the respondents' perceived outcomes began to approximate actual national poll data. The causal connections were not clear however. The authors suggest that perceptions of opinion should be studied in relation to poll data and alternative behavioral and communication responses should be explored. Behavior alternatives could be viewed in positive as well as negative terms: One could, other than retreating to isolation, pursue the promise of limited rewards for one's efforts or work harder to forestall or ward off adversity. Further, under some conditions, a minority may affect a majority. Glynn and McLeod experience their most discomfort in the lack of specification and explication of concepts. They find the theory and results "tantalizing" and the implications for communication and public opinion to be important, but they urge that the theory and data should not be accepted as ends in themselves but as steps in a process.

Restating Situational Perspectives

Fields and Schuman restate the need for situational analysis by asserting that the perceptual approach should be stated in terms of particular conditions rather than proposed as a general theory. They point to situations where the real distribution of opinions did affect perceptions. One example was the period of change in opinion to a less interventionist foreign policy for Vietnam. Both perception of opinions and opinions themselves became less interventionist over the 15-year period, giving rise to the inference that the open public debate over Vietnam changed opinions and altered perceptions about those opinions.

On the interracial playmate study noted above, changes in perceptions followed actual changes in opinion. Curiously, while conservatives on this issue became less confident (presumably as a consequence of observed liberalizing tendencies), the minority liberals (whose numbers were growing) did not become as confident as they might have been that others shared their views. This evidence of perceptions of change implicitly support Noelle-Neumann's notion of quasi-statistical theory, but Fields and Schuman do not see potential for absolute accuracy of perceptions by publics:

> The fact that we need to specify three different forces to account for perceptions of public beliefs, and for none of them can we claim a full understanding of the underlying processes involved, testifies to the complexity of this area. Certainly any assumption that perceptions of the attitudes and expectations of others is a simple and transparent step in the total process of social and normative influence is untenable. (pp. 446-447)

We might raise some empirical questions at this juncture. At what point in a perceived shift of influence does the spiral of silence begin to operate? How much of a majority or minority must there be? Are there graduated and related changes in perceptions and behaviors? How much more support would produce how much more accuracy of perceptions of direction of change? What are the most efficacious sources of communication for a majority that is losing power and a minority that is gaining it? What kinds and how many "signs" must occur in the environment before one might hope for perceptual clarity?

In their empirical test of the "accuracy" hypothesis, Tichenor and Wackman (1973) found that only one in three respondents correctly estimated majority opinion. They questioned the extent to which media provided information about the real state of public opinion and how well media performed this function when they actually did so. In expressing surprise as to those results, Noelle-Neumann has countered that her own findings, and those of Hart (1981) are much lower, pointing also to the relevance of the research of Donsbach and Stevenson (1984) in undertaking cross-cultural comparisons.

The Relevance of Groups

Another major challenge directed to the spiral of silence by Salmon and Kline (1984) contends that individuals are influenced (through mass communication) more by reference groups than by anonymous publics in coping with any fear of isolation that they might experience. The empirical question is what kinds of reference groups and what kinds of anonymous publics contribute most to the spheres of communication in which fear of isolation is played out? Of some relevance to the questions raised by Salmon and Kline are the findings by Glynn (1986a) that neighbors were more accurate in their perceptions of the opinions of other neighbors than those "in the city" who were more remote. Size of the social unit was an important perceptual criterion and, remindful of Davison (1958), casting the neighborhood as the unit for certain areas of public opinion formation was essential. Glynn proposes that social conditions be specified under which individuals act on the basis of perceptions of others' opinions as opposed to their own or stated opinions. She notes that the more social sanctions that are attached to behaviors, the more likely the individual will conform to perceptions of the other; while the more public the alternative behaviors, the more useful the perceptions of public behavior and the greater the power of the individual to make independent choices. When social norms proscribe certain opinions, it is less likely that the individual will seek group support for that behavior. Glynn proposes panel studies to investigate changes in one's own opinions and perceptions of others' opinions across a range of opinion objects and under a variety of social influences. Exploring the relationships between interpersonal mass communication and the expression of opinions with respect to sensitive issues, Glynn (1986b) reported a number of additional findings that have implications for social and group effects.

Interpersonal communication was more used by those who saw their environment as cohesive and similar, and mass media were more used by those who saw environments as less cohesive and similar. Those who did not use much interpersonal or mass communication perceived others as having different (usually more conservative) opinions than their own, whereas those who used a great deal of interpersonal and mass communication saw others as having opinions similar to their own. Those who used a great deal of mass media but little interpersonal communication tended to see the opinions of others as different (usually more liberal) than their own, while more interpersonal communication left opinions fairly intact, possibly a looking-glass self that tended to impose upon one's neighbors the views that the mass media projected. Thus Glynn concluded again that perceptions were important in the public opinion process and in relation to public opinion itself, but that this was far from a simple proposition, individually or "normatively" speaking.

The Linkage with Pluralistic Ignorance

The linkages between the concepts of climate of opinion, spiral of silence, looking-glass self, projective biases, disowning behavior, and pluralistic ignorance are as important as their differences. All rest on cognitive and perceptual bases and imply social-psychological processes. Pluralistic ignorance may be traced to research traditions occurring earlier than the climate of opinion or spiral of silence, but the latter concepts are stated more explicitly in communication terms.

One needs to look to Breed and Kitsanes (1961) to find explicit references to communication as a concomitant of pluralistic ignorance, which was more pronounced in large groups because there was less communication. Cognitive reorientation, therefore, was slower to develop. Communication implications are present in findings that those who are less bigoted (and probably more educated) more accurately "guess" the distribution of opinions about segregation values. In a similar study, less educated church members grossly underestimated liberal views among their membership, implying that observing and communicating were occurring less. It may seem difficult to argue that more communication variables should be built into studies of pluralistic ignorance. What cognitive and communication activities might be associated with ignorance? Yet there are conceptual links to the spiral of silence that need be explored.

O'Gorman (1975, 1979, 1980) and O'Gorman and Geary (1976) have worked extensively with the concept of pluralistic ignorance, but Taylor (1982) broadened the conceptual basis by seeing a functional equivalence between it and the spiral of silence. He discerned that pluralistic ignorance was brought about by misguided (and outdated) perceptions of majority opinion. These misconceptions addressed conflicts of values but favored older, existing beliefs, implying minimal communication.

In his 1975 study, O'Gorman found a pervasive tendency among white adults to perceive greatly exaggerated white support for racial segregation in their communities. This error in perception was strongly associated with whites' own racial values and their stated preferences for desegregation, continued segregation, or some compromise position. The study revealed a strong conservative bias—that is, the preservation of older biases. In essence, this bias characterized both northerners and southerners: Those who shared the same racial views imputed those views to the majority. O'Gorman's 1979 study went on to test the proposition that values (such as segregationism) should provide a more accurate prediction of perceptions of racial bias than place in the social structure; while blacks as a class might perceive that there were fewer segregationists among whites than would whites themselves, the more powerful predictor would be that blacks and whites who shared the same values, regardless of age, sex, and education, would also hold the same perceptions. O'Gorman concluded that while blacks and whites occupied different racial *statuses*, it was not until they shared the same racial *values* that they made similar cognitive judgments of other blacks and whites around them.

The distinction between values and statuses proposes a shifting paradigm that would require a variety of communication and mass media uses to form and express relevant opinions. Consider those who share statuses and values, those who share neither, and those who share one but not the other. What would be the communication and opinion behaviors with respect to sources of value; the utility of interpersonal, group, and media sources; and cognitive mapping in relation to the uses and evaluation of sources of knowledge and opinions? Additionally, the social-psychological formulations of looking-glass self, pluralistic ignorance, and the spiral of silence need to be sorted out and counterposed for their communication implications. While all imply errors in perception, they are different in kind. Although the looking-glass effect implies that we see ourselves rather than others, it does not imply the narrowness of vision or the social environments that characterize pluralistic ignorance.

The spiral of silence suggests an individual who, rather than seeing his or her own views pictured in a mirror, sees instead a majority view that forces him or her into a growing isolation or alienation. Different manners of observation and communication should occur in situations of perceived majority agreement and isolation. Does perceived isolation reduce inter-personal and mass communication and affect opinion holding? Are there similar or different outcomes for pluralistic ignorance? To address the cultural question implicit in Noelle-Neumann's findings, we need to undertake comparative studies to determine the generality of these concepts. To borrow a metaphor from Glynn and McLeod, we need to learn how well theories and concepts travel if we are to gain a true approximation of the universality of behaviors and the sources of differences.

FROM EVALUATIVE TO COGNITIVE COORIENTATION

The idea of "evaluative coorientation" is that one individual perceives another person (or public opinion) as sharing opinions. In the cognitive mode, coorientation represents a focus of attention: People perceive that they and others are or are not talking about the same opinion object.

The coorientation approach addresses, as one of its most significant concerns, a major problem inherent in assumptions made by the social-psychologically oriented theories of climate of opinion, spiral of silence, pluralistic ignorance, and looking-glass self. That is the question of accuracy: To what extent may individuals achieve a reliable "quasi-statistical" appraisal of the perceptions of others?

In studies of accuracy of perceptions, Grunig and Stamm (1971) distin-guished between cognition and affect. Individuals described the orientations of those who were guided by social values, on the one hand, and economic determinism, on the other. Each "orientation" perceived that it communicated much more with people who shared their orientations. Stamm, Bowes, and Bowes (1973) found both accuracies and inaccuracies in mutual perceptions of youth and adults. Although there was no conclusive "generation gap," adults did misperceive the opinions of students, but accurately judged the perceptions of adults.

Studies of coorientation have been extended to perceptions of public opinion. Tichenor and Wackman (1973) and Bowes and Stamm (1975) examined public policy issues in local communities. They compared the accuracy of mutual perceptions of groups such as journalists, community leaders, governmental officials, and publics. They asked who most accurately perceived the opinions of others. By comparing perceived and actual favorability of these groups toward local issues, they were able to identify gaps in public opinion. An important aspect of those studies was the relationship of mass media use to coorientation.

The Tichenor and Wackman study is relevant to a number of conditions specified by the climate of opinion. It speaks to a "definition of the situation," the selectivity processes of actors and audiences, an atmosphere of social conflict, "distribution of opinions," and the extent to which individuals asserted they actually had attempted to ascertain majority opinion. The best predictor of this behavior was not mass media use, although it was correlated, but talking with others. Posed against this is the finding by Atwood, Sohn, and Sohn (1978) of relationships between reading about local and national affairs and topics that readers discussed with others. There was something that could be called "community discussion," which was influenced by the content of the local newspaper. Consistent with the hypothesis of the looking-glass self-hypothesis those who most supported official actions most believed that other people supported the actions, and most of those who attempted to estimate majority opinion thought other people held the same view as themselves.

Tichenor and Wackman also concluded that although knowledge and support for public officials were high for the heaviest media users (with newspapers more efficacious than television), it was apparent that the media had not informed publics adequately about public opinion. Their study was confined to a rural-urban location which was not necessarily typical, but they ventured that other than through the publication of public opinion polls, the media did not fully or systematically "distribute" opinions, and that studies were required to assess this need and to satisfy it.

Although each of the coorientation studies implied cognitive as well as evaluative elements of behavior, none took up purely cognitive considerations. Edelstein et al. (1987), however, took a purely cognitive approach to their study of student cognitions and opinions. Students from Germany, Hong Kong, Japan, and the United States described the cognitive foci of their own opinions, their perceptions of the foci of "public opinion," their own foci of opinion in their communication with others, and what they perceived others said to them. By matching up their own views with their perceptions of public opinion and their perceived to-and-from communication with others, measures of cognitive coorientation were derived. The analysis illustrated structural, cultural, and situational factors at work. The structural element, the universality of university students, produced similarities across cultures. Cultural and situational factors accounted for differences.

German students were much more likely than the Japanese to talk about consequences of problems. One reason was that German students were very participative and observed consequences of problems from that vantage point. Japanese students were least participative, and they felt themselves to be more isolated as a social class; thus they focused their discussion least on the consequences of problems. American students were most tuned into solutions, reflective of a political culture that demands solutions. Hong Kong students cited local problems such as housing, population, and transportation, which were amenable to solutions. German students were least oriented to solutions because of their status as protestors of the status quo. They and Japanese students pointed most to problem causes.

Taking each of the relationships with respect to cognitive coorientation, we found a surprising degree of perceived cognitive coorientation by students vis-à-vis publics in all four countries. The most striking perceptions of coorientation with publics were with respect to the less complex aspects of consequences and solutions to problems. Causes are perhaps more complex and thus elusive. Although our data show only perceived coorientation by students vis-à-vis publics, and not public perceptions of coorientations to students, the figures for student perceptions are remarkably high and probably would be greater than that perceived by publics. It should be noted that Stamm et al. (1973) found that students perceived public opinions more accurately than publics perceived student opinions.

These cognitive parameters—consequences, causes, and solutions—are implicit in questions asked of general population samples. Noelle-Neumann and Kepplinger (1978) classified opinions in a local community as pertaining to the consequences and solutions to problems. Theberge (1982) found that television coverage emphasized causes and solutions to the energy crisis; but no coorientational measures were used. A review of polls in the Roper Center Archives on the oil crises revealed that a variety of polling questions tapped consequences, causes, and/or solutions as foci of public opinion.

Different problems lend themselves to different patterns of attention. Concern about AIDS has moved quickly from causal aspects to the growing consequences and the need for solutions. There is little cohesive opinion or discussion about the causes of child abuse or the solutions to this social problem; we are still assessing the nature and consequences of the problem. Publics were able to form as many opinions about the causes as the consequences of the Iran-Contra affair and Watergate, but the solutions were (are) much more obscure. Emphasis upon aspects of problems may reflect a stage in the life of the problem—is it an old problem or a new one, is it amenable to solution, and so forth. Public orientations to problems nonetheless may be maintained independently of the objective life of the problem; some of our students were oriented to causes, no matter what the problem, and not to solutions or to consequences. They were thus able to communicate as easily about one problem as another, coorienting to process as well as to content.

We may then ask: (1) What are the communication and opinion implications when media, pollsters, and publics focus upon different aspects of the same problem and/or the same aspects of different problems? (2) Are there classes of problems, or stages of problems, where the foci of opinions are upon consequences, solutions, or causes? (3) Are there different degrees of actual and perceived accuracy in coorientation related to different aspects of problems?

OPINION STRUCTURES AND PROCESSES

Structure is of course only a concept, and it must meet certain tests before it can be useful. The parameters must be limited, conceptually coherent, and the boundaries must be clear. Given valid structures, we may employ them in ways that justify the definitional efforts that are made in rationalizing them. One way in which structural differentiation justifies itself is by enabling us to observe processes at work. These processes reflect a systematic and purposeful interplay of those forces that are born of structures and express their underlying dynamics.

Research traditions in coorientation do not appear, at first glance, to advance concepts involving the relationships between structure and process. The evaluative components of opinions—agreeing and disagreeing, liking and disliking, and so on—are more limitless than finite, as are the conceptual breadth and variety of attributes. Cognitive parameters are more limited and the boundaries are more clear; cognitive parameters are more conceptually coherent and order is implied, contributing to the idea of system as well as structure.

A Communication-Step Approach

The four-culture student study by Edelstein et al. (1987) postulated a "communication-step" process of public opinion. Students could be seen as shifting their attention over time to more complex aspects of a social problem. The first and most simple step, in terms of focus and communication about a problem, would center upon its impact upon the individual or perceived effects upon the society, that is, consequences. The second and third steps would focus upon the more complex phenomena of causes or solutions. The frequency of the responses suggests the tenability of a hypothesis of that kind. The greatest number of references were to consequences of problems, then solutions, and finally causes. Some students took all the steps while others took only some of them.

Sociologists have theorized about the systematic emergence of public opinion and communication related to social problems, whether it be an energy crisis, a drug abuse crisis, child abuse, AIDS, or poverty. Each problem is postulated to go through steps or stages as society collectively attempts to cope with it. Different social actors and institutions become key participants at each of these "stages." As the energy crisis obtruded, one could observe government officials taking cognizance, publics and interest groups on the attack, energy producers and distributors defending themselves, and the media amplifying the situation. Zygmunt (1986) believes that the process of emergence of a social problem is so predictable as to parallel, in many ways, the growth of social movements.

Undertaking a review of major social movements in America, Kielbowicz and Scherer (1986) observed that while communication and mass communication were important at all stages of a social movement, the media were "indispensable" at the first stage of emergence of a problem. Their "steps" included the creation of a general consciousness of some shared problem, moves by activists to coalesce their efforts into an organization to mobilize support, and use of the media to synthesize seemingly fragmented elements into a perceptible whole giving the appearance of a widespread phenomenon. The media accomplished this appearance by publicizing concrete dramatic events such as protests and demonstrations and giving them spatial as well as temporal relevance. Media were needed to maintain the visibility of the movement.

An examination of news reporting itself reveals quickly that the most often cited news sources in stories about social problems are public officials. Lippmann would say that media use public officials because they have authority rather than expertise. Experts contradict one another and therefore confuse publics. Social critics speak to a small audience.

The Blumer Step-Theory

Blumer (1971) used the term *emergence* to describe the initial stage of society's recognition of a social problem. Various actors play a variety of roles at this initial stage, depending primarily upon the nature of the problem. Neither Blumer nor similar theorists have been explicit about the functions of the mass media in the opinion process at this first (or any) stage, beyond, presumably, pointing to a problem, its consequences, and perhaps its causes and possible solutions. Blumer's further steps in the resolution of a social problem—legitimation, mobilization, an official plan of action, and imple- mentation—also accord the media a general publicizing role, but more explicit functioning needs to be outlined. What functions might media play at each stage of the process?

We might look, as well, at the media role in social mobilization—as in Lemert's (1981) "mobilizing information"—and examine the functions of media in problem solving and in subsequent public approval or disapproval of implementation of a solution. Ross and Staines (1972) are much more specific as to the role of the media. Describing the transformation of "private troubles" into a social problem (as perceived by individuals or groups), they confer a legitimizing function on the media, while issue-salience is measured by public opinion polls, media coverage, and the intensity of responses of nonmedia elites. The two sociologists see government officials and the media as the principal actors in the definition of issue consciousness. The media role is to provide visibility and confer legitimacy; they accomplish this role by selection processes, remindful of Noelle-Neumann's function of limiting agendas for discussion. Ross and Staines see government-media relations also as efforts to control one another, but they are more sanguine than Noelle- Neumann and see opportunities for complementariness that often are seized. Thus leadership policies are viewed in terms of media potential.

Schoenfeld, Meier, and Griffin (1979) describe the "constructing of a social problem" concerning the environment. Social critics defined the problem, interest groups staged "earth days" and other dramatic programs, and government took action. The media at first found it difficult to translate familiar ideas such as conservation and reclamation into concepts of a cosmic and finite earth. It was difficult to bring media performance into line with cosmic thinking. Thus the media played a limited role in the emergence phase of the problem; they were taken by surprise at the mobilization stage; and they were left to record actions that were taken at the problem-solving stage. The agenda was set for the media by other actors.

Zygmunt's (1986) transactionist analysis of Blumer's thinking carries communication implications for collective behavior and public opinion. Like Blumer, Zygmunt speaks of the "emergent" nature of problems as collective behavior, the interactional processes as representing a variety of forms of communication, and the emergence of consensus as an ongoing process that represents a need for additional communication. To pursue the communication and public opinion implications of the emergence and resolution of social problems is a task that is almost heroic in its proportions. But rich opportunities for research and theory lie in this direction.

A CONSTRUCTIVIST
APPROACH TO METHODOLOGY

The constructivist approach to methodology proposed by Swanson (1981) seeks to better observe *communication* aspects of public opinion. The lesson to draw from this approach is that when polling results are for public consumption, methodological decisions are *communication* decisions. Each research decision point rests on whether we are enhancing or constraining communication in both the collection and dissemination of information. While evaluations of open- and close-ended questions by Schuman (1979) and his recent commentary on public opinion research (1986) help us to understand methodologically inspired decisions, those decisions were not formulated as *communication* questions. The problem was more narrowly formulated: From the standpoint of efficacy—validity and reliability—should open- or close-ended questions be asked? The specific concern was not that of enhancing communication.

It is only a conceptual step from a methodological question to a communication question. That is the constructivist's intent—to utilize methodologies that will maximize the exchange of information and communication. If we reason with Schuman (1979), we would ask open-ended questions at the first stage of the "emergence" of a problem. At that stage the problem is not well enough along for us to assume that communication might easily take place. Respondents should be permitted to construct situations as much as possible in their own terms so that meanings might be more easily conveyed.

Opinion research during the war in Vietnam created many problems of communication. All polls used the same methodological approach and similar questions produced similar outcomes. Close-ended questions constrained respondents by the limits placed on alternatives and the values that were associated with them. These questions yielded a picture of the public "supporting" the war and gave the president polls to prove he was right. Motivated by the "false pictures" produced by those polls, researchers at Stanford University (Verba et al., 1967) shifted to a more "constructivist" format for their questioning. It offered a greater range of alternatives and values for judging them. More information was presented and more information was exchanged. Respondents could, by fitting a range of values to the several alternatives that were posed to them, construct to some extent different pictures of reality. But the approach stopped short of solving the problem it sought to address and produced, actually, some anomalous findings.

Edelstein (1973) extended this approach by allowing respondents to supply their own alternatives and values, permitting additional "constructing" of reality. He suggested that close-ended questions had created two kinds of errors of "construction":

> *(1) Solution-errors* occurred when the respondent was asked to "agree" or "disagree" with or to "support" or "reject" alternatives with which s/he previously was unfamiliar and which s/he had not evaluated previously.

> *(2) Evaluation-errors* occurred when the respondent might be familiar with the solution that had been proposed, and might have a rationale for accepting or rejecting it, but that rationale was not contained in the pollster's statement. Hence the respondent "evaluated" alternatives on the basis of unfamiliar criteria. (p. 87)

Both errors produced communication gaps. While these limitations might be accepted by policymakers, the construction failed to stimulate meaningful communication. In Thurstone's (1929) long-stated terms, the Vietnam questions required the respondents to bring their resources to bear upon the pollster's definition of the situation; questions were not asked in a way that permitted them to function in their everyday world.

This admonition applies to a host of circumstances. In terms of the structural parameters that we introduced in describing cognitive coorientation, if pollster's questions address one aspect of a problem (the nature of the problems, the consequences, the causes, or solutions) when the respondent is attuned to another, gaps in communication occur. If a question incorporates two or more aspects, a double-barreledness results and communication is confounded.

As noted by Benton and Frazier (1976) earlier, Mitchell (1980) points out that important problems have many aspects or foci of attention that are substantive, having to do with particulars of the problem, as well as its structure. He notes that the nuclear energy debate has centered on at least six major issues, if not more. He cites such so-called subissues as nuclear waste transporting and disposal, reprocessing, emissions, proliferation, access to information and loss of political control, and even meltdowns, as was threatened at Three Mile Island and occurred at Chernobyl. Different publics are more or less interested in and capable of addressing each of these subissues; pollsters, on the other hand, are not willing or able to address all the salient aspects of a problem.

Some aspects of problems tax the analytical capabilities of respondents. In the Vietnam study, we asked respondents who said that they "could not decide" how the war should be brought to an end "why" they could not decide. They answered that "it was too difficult to decide," "it was not up to them to decide," they had "too much information," "not enough information," and/or the "wrong information." They said that "if they decided they would have to defend their decisions," that they didn't have "confidence" in their decisions, and that people, in any case, didn't listen to them. Given the opportunity to so respond to nuclear issues, we might encounter similar problems.

Gallup (1980), Bogart (1972), and Noelle-Neumann (1980), nonetheless, have made articulate cases for the communication potential of public opinion polls. Gallup believed that the polls were more informative and reliable than government itself. Others, of course, have characterized the polls as "multiplying ignorance." Noelle-Neumann (1980) comments that poor polls misinform leaders, and, consequently, leaders do not lead, but follow. Greater substance and more effective communication might occur if we took a more constructivist approach to polling.

Beyond the questions of the limitations of polling and the competence of respondents, there is the problem of a clarity of meaning. Many questions create ambiguities or may actually mislead, as Lang and Lang (1983) discuss with respect to the Watergate "impeachment" question. Despite the focus of questions on impeachment, the more comprehensible issue was the removal or resignation of President Nixon, for the implications of impeachment were not clear. Lang and Lang (1962) also express a constructivist's concerns as they describe viewer behavior of "The Great Debates" as looking for "signs" that they could relate to the candidate's ability to perform, to his fitness for a political role, and to his "quality" as a human being. Miller and McKuen (1979) come to a similar conclusion.

Stamm (1985) has sought in methodological ways to enhance the communication potential of questions on voting choices. Although attributional studies do contribute something to the communication process, they do not require as active an intervention by the respondent as if she or he were asked to engage in the construction of ideas. Stamm's research requires the respondents to "imagine" situations and to deal with a more "processual" concept of image. The respondent is required not only to provide attributes for candidates but is asked to offer an intepretation of them. Thus the respondent goes beyond the candidate-attribute relation to associate it with other objects, events, and/or conditions.

Swanson, Stamm, and others believe that potentialities for enhancing political communication would be increased if researchers would seek interpretation of images; what is meaningful about an image is not merely its attributes but the connections and/or associations that can be made. Reeves, Chaffee, and Tims (1982) urged a study of "processing mechanisms" as a way of understanding what was being communicated. Carter (1978) makes a distinction between learning about candidates and issues and constructing or "imagining" them.

Bogart (1972) sees the polls in more complex and interactive terms; they are mechanisms by which the public becomes sensitized to itself and by which journalists and political leaders appraise the public's sense of things. This view reflects a condition of mutual dependency in which the quality of the mechanisms determines the effectiveness of public communication.

To determine perceptions of polling efficacy, several studies of media and public attitudes were commissioned for the American Association for Public Opinion Research. Answering the question, "Is there a crisis of confidence about polls?" Kohut (1986) found a close division of opinions as to whether the polls were better at forecasting the vote than explaining it. There was a division of opinion on whether the polls enhanced or interfered with the electoral process. One implicit communication question yielded the result that over a 50-year period, more people had heard of polls but only 41% followed them even occasionally.

Roper (1986) said about 75% thought that polls worked in the public interest, 56% felt that they were almost always or usually accurate and honest, but only 28% thought that polls accurately reflected the views of the nation. In turn, respondents thought that all or most polls "told the truth." These studies are helpful but inconclusive. More constructivist approaches need to be developed that are within the capabilities of pollsters and the competence of respondents. At this point, we must conclude that the ability of the polls to keep people "in touch" is limited and, in fact, elusive.

DISCUSSION

In reviewing the literature of a field one becomes as sharply conscious of what has not been identified as what one is able to observe amidst the prominence of published works. If one is fortunate, one might gain an overall perspective that transcends a simple aggregation of research findings.

In reviewing the research that bears upon communication aspects of public opinion, one is forced to the conclusion that despite the exceptions that have been taken to the formulation of such concepts as the climate of opinion and the spiral of silence, they nonetheless represent our most singular efforts to address *communication* dimensions of public opinion. Although the outcomes have fallen short of first aspirations for the theories, this shortfall is an inevitable outcome of any ambitious undertaking. We need to remind ourselves of the long road to theory.

One of our tasks now is to reconcile, through specification, the various social, cognitive, and social-psychological conditions that have been advanced. We may, as an example, extend efforts to link Gerbner's cultivation analysis and Ball-Rokeach's social dependency theory to the climate of opinion and normative theories. We need more of the relevant and carefully conceived empirical work exemplified by Glynn and McLeod to gain a better comprehension of communication and opinion linkages between mass media and their audiences and the bases for their shared conceptions of public opinion and society.

Some efforts to establish conceptual links may be seen. One example is that between the spiral of silence and pluralistic ignorance. The common bases for communication, however—if those exist—have not been explored. There are implications for equivalence in the properties of the looking-glass self and pluralistic ignorance, as well as the climate of opinion. The third person and quasi-statistical hypotheses also are relevant to one another in their underlying assumptions of accuracy of perceptions of relevant climates of opinion. These concepts may be part of a more inclusive theory that embraces multivariable linkages. We need to observe and compare relevant mass media and communication behaviors that contribute to or are a consequence of these psychological and cognitive states.

A clearer conceptual linkage is afforded by the relation between established traditions of coorientation research into affective relations and the proposals for studies of cognitive variables. We also ask what affective orientations are likely to occur with what cognitive orientations: Is more or less affect demonstrated in relation to the nature of problems, consequences, causes, or solutions?

Weaver (1980, 1984) has shown us how agenda-setting research, which previously had been confined largely to methodological questions, could be lifted out of that context to permit us to view more broadly conceived significant "communication effects." The constructivist view of methodology and communication engages in similar thinking. By its approach, constructivism seeks to enhance methodological potential by observing the communication of public opinion. It is a burden, as Glynn and McLeod suggest, to innovate methodologically at a time when theory in our field is elusive. Yet that very absence of theory might rationalize our risk taking; we need to devote effort to exploring, to experimenting, and to creativity. Such efforts would not be wasted and are indeed in the spirit of the theory that we have reviewed.

This review has neglected far more than it has addressed. Fortunately, Paletz will be commenting about interest group communication in the tradition of his field (see Paletz & Entman, 1981). We bypassed most of the work in political communication because it recently has been addressed so thoroughly by Chaffee and Hocheimer (1985) and Glynn and McLeod (1984). We might have talked about diffusion, rumor, letters to the editor, and institutional, organizational, and ideological values in mass communication, but we could not do so. Tichenor, fortunately, has added to our appreciation of communication and community. Thus it can be seen that this review article is a piece of the pie, not the pie itself.

REFERENCES

Allport, F. (1937). Toward a science of public opinion. *Public Opinion Quarterly, 1*, 7-23.

Asch, S. (1953). Effects of group pressure upon the modification and distortion of judgements. In D. Cartwright & A. Zander (Eds.), *Group dynamics: Research and theory* (pp. 151-162). Evanston, IL: Row, Peterson & Camp.

Atwood, L. E., Sohn, A. B., & Sohn, H. (1978). Daily newspaper contributions to community discussion. *Journalism Quarterly, 55*, 570-576.

Ball-Rokeach, S. J. (1985). The origins of individual media-system dependency: A sociological framework. *Communication Research, 12*, 485-510.

Ball-Rokeach, S. J., & DeFleur, M. (1976). A dependency model of mass media effects. *Communication Research, 3*, 3-21.

Becker, L. B., & Whitney, D. C. (1980). Effects of media dependencies: Audience assessment of government. *Communication Research, 7*, 95-121.

Benton, M., & Frazier, J. P. (1976). The agenda-setting function of the mass media at three levels of "information-holding." *Communication Research, 3*, 261-274.

Blumer, H. (1971). Social problems as collective behavior. *Social Problems, 18*, 298-306.

Bogart, L. (1972). *Silent politics: Polls and the awareness of public opinion.* New York: Wiley-Interscience.

Boorstin, D. (1971a). *Democracy and its discontents.* New York: Vintage.

Boorstin, D. (1971b). *The image: A guide to pseudo events in America.* New York: Altheneum.

Bowes, J., & Stamm, K. S. (1975). Evaluating communication with public agencies. *Public Relations Review, 1*, 23-28.

Breed, W., & Kitsanes, T. (1961). Pluralistic ignorance in the process of opinion formation. *Public Opinion Quarterly, 25*, 382-392.

Carter, R. F. (1962). Some effects of the debates. In S. Kraus (Ed.), *The great debates.* Bloomington: Indiana University Press.

Carter, R. F. (1965). Communication and affective relations. *Journalism Quarterly, 42*, 203-212.

Carter, R. F. (1978). A very peculiar horserace. In G. Bishop, R. Meadow, & M. Jackson-Beeck (Eds.), *The presidential debates: Media, electoral and policy perspectives.* New York: Praeger.

Chaffee, S. H., & Hocheimer, J. L. (1985). The beginnings of political communication research in the United States: Origins of the "limited effects model." In M. Gurevitch & M. R. Levy (Eds.), *Mass communication review yearbook 5.* Newbury Park, CA: Sage.

Converse, P. E. (1964). The nature of belief systems in mass publics. *International Yearbook of Political Behavior Research, 5*, 206-262.

Cook, F. L., Tyler, T. R., Goetz, E. G., Gordon, M. T., Protess, D., Leff, D. R., & Molotch, H. L. (1983). Media and agenda setting: Effects on the public, interest group leaders, policy makers, and policy. *Public Opinion Quarterly, 47*, 16-35.

Davison, W. P. (1958). The public opinion process. *Public Opinion Quarterly, 22,* 91-106.
Davison, W. P. (1983). The third-person effect in communication. *Public Opinion Quarterly, 47,* 1-15.
Donohue, G., Tichenor, P. J., & Olien, C. N. (1982). Gatekeeping: Mass media systems and information control. In F. G. Kline & P. Clark (Eds.), *Current perspectives in mass communication research.* Newbury Park, CA: Sage.
Donsbach, W., & Stevenson, R. L. (1984, May). *Challenges, problems, and empirical evidence of the theory of the spiral of silence.* Paper presented at the annual meeting of the International Communication Association, San Francisco.
Edelstein, A. (1973). Decision-making and mass communication: A conceptual and method-ological approach to public opinion. In P. Clarke (Ed.), *New models for communication research* (Vol. 2). Newbury Park, CA: Sage.
Edelstein, A. (1980). Continuing the search for validity in public opinion about social problems and social decision making. In H. Baier, H. M. Kepplinger, & K. Reumann (Eds.), *Public opinion and social change.* Frankfurt: Westdeutscher Verlag.
Edelstein, A. (1981). A problem oriented reconceptualization of public opinion. *Journal of Communication Inquiry, 6,* 97-117.
Edelstein, A. (1983). Konzept fur eine vergleichende kommunikations foreschung: Eine kritsche perspecktive. *Rundfunk und Fernsehen, 1,* 12-23.
Edelstein, A. (1985). Problematic situations and mass communication: A comparative analysis of public opinion. In H. Bortis & L. Bosshart (Eds.), *Technological change in economy and society.* Freiburg, Switzerland: Universitatsverlag Freiburg.
Edelstein, A., Ito, Y., & Kepplinger, H. M. (1988). *International communication and comparative behavior.* Unpublished manuscript.
Fields, J. M., & Schuman, H. (1976). Public beliefs about the beliefs of the public. *Public Opinion Quarterly, 40,* 427-448.
Gallup, G. (1980). Polling: The state of the art. In *Ethics, morality, and the media: Reflections on American culture.* New York: Hastings House.
Galtung, J., & Ruge, M. H. (1965). The structure of foreign news: The presentation of the Congo, Cuba and Cyprus crisis in four Norwegian newspapers. *Journal of International Peace Research, 1,* 64-90.
Gerbner, G. (1977). Comparative cultural indicators. In G. Gerbner (Ed.), *Mass media policies in changing cultures.* New York: John Wiley.
Gerbner, G., & Gross, L. (1976). Living with television. *Journal of Communication, 26,* 173-199.
Gerbner, G., Gross, L., Beeck, M. J., Jeffries-Fox, S., & Signorielli, N. (1978). Cultural indicators: Violence profile No. 11. *Journal of Communication, 28,* 176-207.
Gerbner, G., Gross, L., Morgan, M., & Signorielli, N. (1980). The mainstreaming of America: Violence profile 11. *Journal of Communication, 30,* 10-29.
Glynn, C. J. (1984a). *Alternative concepts of public opinion.* Paper presented at the annual meeting of the American Association for Public Opinion Research, Delevan, WI.
Glynn, C. J. (1984b). *The communication of public opinion.* Paper presented at the annual meeting of the Association for Education in Journalism and Mass Communication, Norman, OK.
Glynn, C. J. (1985, May). *Mass communication and the development of "normative opinions."* Paper presented at the annual meeting of the International Communication Association, Honolulu.
Glynn, C. J. (1986). *Perceptions of others' opinions as a component of public opinion.* Paper presented at the annual meeting of the American Association of Public Opinion Research.
Glynn, C. J. & McLeod, J. (1981). Implications of the spiral of silence theory for communication and public opinion research. In D. D. Nimmo & K. R. Sanders (Eds.), *Handbook of political communication.* Newbury Park, CA: Sage.

Glynn, C. J., & McLeod, J. (1982). Public opinion, communication processes, and voting decisions. In M. Burgoon (Ed.), *Communication yearbook 6*. Newbury Park, CA: Sage.

Glynn, C. J., & McLeod, J. (1984). Public opinion du jure: Its impact on communication and voting behavior. *Public Opinion Quarterly, 48*, 731-740.

Glynn, C. J., & McLeod, J. (1985a). *Public opinion about public opinion*. Paper presented at the annual meeting of the American Association for Public Opinion Research, McAfee, NJ.

Glynn, C. J., & McLeod, J. (1985b). The spiral of silence ten years later: An examination and evaluation. In *Political communication yearbook 2*. Carbondale: Southern Illinois University Press.

Grunig, J. E., & Stamm, K. R. (1971). Communication and coorientation of collectives. *American Behavioral Scientist, 16*, 567-593.

Hart, H. (1981). *People's perceptions of public opinions*. Paper presented at the annual meeting of the International Society of Political Psychology.

James, B. A. (1983). Radical humanist perspective for communication inquiry. In R. N. Bostrom (Ed.), *Communication yearbook 7* (pp. 858-866). Newbury Park, CA: Sage.

Katz, E. (1966). Attitude formation and public opinion. *Annals of the American Academy of Political and Social Science, 367*, 150-162.

Katz, E. (1981). Publicity and pluralistic ignorance: Notes on the "spiral of silence." In H. Baier & H. Kepplinger (Eds.), *Public opinion and social change*. Opladen, Germany: Westdeutscher Verlag.

Kielbowicz, R. B., & Scherer, C. (1986). The role of the press in the dynamics of social movements. In G. Lang & K. Lang (Eds.), *Research in social movements, conflicts and change*. Greenwich, CT: JAI.

Kohut, A. (1986). Is there a crisis of confidence? Rating the polls: The views of media elites and the general public. *Public Opinion Quarterly, 50*, 1-9.

Lang, G., & Lang, K. (1983). *The battle for public opinion*. New York: Columbia University Press.

Lang, K., & Lang, G. (1962). Reactions of viewers. In S. Kraus (Ed.), *The great debates*. Bloomington: Indiana University Press.

Lemert, J. (1981). *Does mass communication change public opinion, after all?* Chicago: Nelson-Hall.

Lippmann, W. (1922). *Public opinion*. New York: Harcourt Brace.

MacKuen, M. G. (1981). Social communication and the mass policy agenda. In M. B. MacKuen & S. L. Coombs (Eds.), *Political communication*. Newbury Park, CA: Sage.

McCombs, M. E. (1981). The agenda-setting approach. In D. D. Nimmo & K. R. Sanders (Eds.), *Handbook of political communication*. Newbury Park, CA: Sage.

Merten, L. (1984). Some silence in the spiral of silence. In K. R. Sanders, L. L. Kaid, & D. D. Nimmo (Eds.), *Political communication yearbook 1*. Carbondale: Southern Illinois University Press.

Miller, A., & MacKuen, M. G. (1979). Learning about the candidates: The 1976 presidential debates. *Public Opinion Quarterly, 43*, 326-346.

Miller, M. M., & Reese, S. D. (1982). Media dependency as interaction: Effects of exposure and reliance on political activity and efficacy. *Communication Research, 9*, 227-248.

Mitchell, R. C. (1980). Polling on nuclear power: A critique of the polls after Three-Mile Island. In A. H. Cantril (Ed.), *Polling on the issues*. Cabin John, MD: Seven Locks.

Nimmo, D. D., & Sanders, K. (Eds.). (1981). *Handbook of political communication*. Newbury Park, CA: Sage.

Noelle-Neumann, E. (1973). Return to the concept of powerful mass media. *Studies of Broadcasting, 9*, 67-112.

Noelle-Neumann, E. (1974). The spiral of silence: A theory of public opinion. *Journal of Communication, 24*, 43-51.

Noelle-Neumann, E. (1976). *Mass media and the climate of opinion*. Paper presented at the annual meeting of the International Association for Mass Communication Research, University of Leicester, England.

Noelle-Neumann, E. (1977). Turbulences in the climate of opinion: Methodological applications of the spiral of silence theory. *Public Opinion Quarterly, 41*, 143-158.

Noelle-Neumann, E. (1979). Public opinion and the classical tradition: A re-evaluation. *Public Opinion Quarterly, 43*, 143-156.

Noelle-Neumann, E. (1980). Public opinion polls and democratic theory: The role of opinion polls in a democratic system. Paper submitted to the Seminar Sobre Inquestas Electorales, Informacion y Comportamiento Electoral, Madrid.

Noelle-Neumann, E. (1984a). The spiral of silence: A response. In K. R. Sanders, L. L. Kaid, & D. D. Nimmo (Eds.), *Political communication yearbook 1* (pp. 66-94). Carbondale: Southern Illinois University Press.

Noelle-Neumann, E. (1984b). *The spiral of silence: Public opinion, our social skin*. Chicago: University of Chicago Press.

Noelle-Neumann, E., & Kepplinger, H. M. (1978). *Communication in the community: A report on the German section of an international research project*. Institut fur Publizistik de Universitat Mainz, Germany.

O'Gorman, H. J. (1975). Pluralistic ignorance and white estimates of white support for racial segregation. *Public Opinion Quarterly, 39*, 313-330.

O'Gorman, H. J. (1979). White and black perceptions of racial values. *Public Opinion Quarterly, 43*, 48-59.

O'Gorman, H. J. (1980). False consciousness of kind: Pluralistic ignorance among the aged. *Research on Aging, 2*, 105-128.

O'Gorman, H. J., & Garry, S. L. (1976). Pluralistic ignorance: A replication and extension. *Public Opinion Quarterly, 40*, 449-458.

Paletz, D. L., & Entman, R. M. (1981). *Media, power, politics*. New York: Free Press.

Palmgreen, P., Kline, F. G., & Clarke, P. (1974, May). *Message discrimination and information-holding about political affairs: A comparison of local and national news*. Paper presented at the annual meeting of the International Communication Association, New Orleans.

Reeves, B., Chaffee, S., & Tims, A. (1982). Social cognition and mass communication research. In F. Poloff & C. Berger (Eds.), *Social cognition and communication*. Newbury Park, CA: Sage.

Richman, A. (1979). The polls: Public attitudes toward the energy crisis. *Public Opinion Quarterly, 43*, 576-585.

Roper, B. W. (1986). Evaluating polls with poll data. *Public Opinion Quarterly, 50*, 10-16.

Ross, R., & Staines, G. L. (1972). The politics of analyzing social problems. *Social Problems, 20*, 18-40.

Salmon, C. T., & Kline, F. G. (1984). The spiral of silence ten years later: An examination and evaluation. In K. A. Sanders, L. L. Kaid, & D. D. Nimmo (Eds.), *Political communication yearbook 1* (pp. 3-31). Carbondale: Southern Illinois University Press.

Schleifer, S. (1986). Trends in attitudes toward and participation in survey research. *Public Opinion Quarterly, 50*, 17-26.

Schoenfeld, A. C., Meier, R. F., & Griffin, R. J. (1979). Constructing a social problem: The press and the environment. *Social Problems, 27*, 38-61.

Schuman, H. (1979). The open and closed question. *American Sociological Review, 44*, 692-712.

Schuman, H. (1986). Ordinary questions, survey questions and policy questions. *Public Opinion Quarterly, 50*, 422-442.

Schuman, H., & Presser, H. (1981). *Questions and answers in attitude surveys*. New York: Academic Press.

Spector, M., & Kitsuse, J. I. (1973). Social problems: A re-formulation. *Social Problems, 21*, 145-159.

Spector, M., & Kitsuse, J. I. (1977). *Constructing Social Problems*. Menlo Park, CA: Cummings.

Stamm, K. (1985). *Effects of the Bush/Ferraro debate on candidate characterization*. Paper presented at the annual meeting of the Association for Education in Journalism, Gainesville, FL.

Stamm, K., Bowes, J., & Bowes, B. (1973). Generation gap as a communication problem: A co-orientational analysis. *Journalism Quarterly, 50*, 629-637.

Stamm, K., & Grunig, J. (1977). Communication situations and cognitive strategies in resolving environmental issues. *Journalism Quarterly, 54*, 713-720.

Swanson, D. L. (1981). A constructivist approach. In D. D. Nimmo & K. R. Sanders (Eds.), *Handbook of political communication.* Newbury Park, CA: Sage.

Taylor, D. G. (1982). Pluralistic ignorance and the spiral of silence: A formal analysis. *Public Opinion Quarterly, 46*, 311-335.

Theberge, L. J. (1982). *TV coverage of the oil crises: How well was the public served? Vol. 1. A qualitative analysis.* Washington, DC: Media Institute.

Thurstone, L. L., & Chave, E. J. (1929). *The measurement of attitude.* Chicago: University of Chicago Press.

Tichenor, P. J., & Wackman, D. B. (1973). Mass media and community public opinion. *American Behavioral Scientist, 16*, 593-606.

Verba, S., Brody, R. A., Parker, E. B., Nie, N. H., Polsby, N. W., Ekman, P., & Black, G. S. (1967). Public opinion and the war in Vietnam. *American Political Science Review, 61*, 317-333.

Weaver, D. (1980). Audience need for orientation and media effects. *Communication Research, 7*, 361-376.

Weaver, D. (1984). Media agenda-setting and public opinion: Is there a link? In R. N. Bostrom (Ed.), *Communication yearbook, 8.* Newbury Park, CA: Sage.

Zygmunt, J. F. (1986). Collective behavior as a phase of societal life: Blumer's emergent views and their implications. In G. Lang & K. Lang (Eds.), *Research in social movements, conflict and change.* Greenwich, CT: JAI.

Interest Groups and Public Opinion

DAVID L. PALETZ
JOHN BOINEY
Duke University

P ROFESSOR Edelstein's essay offers observations and insights about the relationships between interest groups and public opinion. For obvious reasons, his emphases are on the traditions and innovations of the communications perspective.

In our commentary, therefore, we shall draw on the theoretical and case study literature to adumbrate, discuss, illustrate, and, of necessity, speculate about interest groups and public opinion in the United States. Starting with the nature of interest groups themselves, we then look at their relations with the public at large, the media, and government. To conclude, we raise the larger, disturbing issue that emerges from our discussion and analysis.

INTEREST GROUPS

Interest group is a slippery term, requiring definition. David Truman's (1951) is useful: "any group that, on the basis of one or more shared attitudes, makes certain claims upon other groups in the society for the establishment, maintenance, or enhancement of forms of behavior that are implied by the shared attitudes" (p. 33). Explicitly or implicitly excluded by this definition are government agencies, even though they often strive mightily to influence public opinion, and unorganized political participation.

So defined, interest groups abound. They can be variously categorized in terms of subjects of interest (agriculture, women's rights, business, morality, environment), types of people represented (dairy farmers, Vietnam veterans,

Correspondence and requests for reprints: David L. Paletz, Department of Political Science, Duke University, Durham, NC 27706.

Communication Yearbook 11, pp. 534-546

college professors), as material or ideological, private or public, and so on. They can be distinguished on the bases of size, resources (especially financial), internal unity and cohesion, quality and quantity of staff, leadership skills and effectiveness, strategies employed, priorities, and number and types of goals (some are single, others multi-issue).

Three Elements

All the above factors have some bearing on whether, to what extent, and with what success or failure, a group interacts with public opinion. But three additional elements require special consideration.

First, is the relevance of public affairs and government to the group's activities. Many organizations are designed specifically to make claims on the political system. Others, for example, the American Political Science Association, only do so when governmental policies (e.g., cutbacks in funding for social science research) impinge on the group and its members.

The members themselves are the second element. They pay dues to belong to the organization. Group membership may be based on any combination of incentives. The most important are "material," tangible rewards such as money and services; "specific solidary," meaning intangible rewards limited to certain members of the group; "collective solidary," intangible rewards created by the act of associating together and thus open to every group member; and "purposive" incentives derived from feelings of satisfaction in having contributed to the deserving cause espoused by the group (Moe, 1980; Wilson, 1973).

Depending on the incentives, members are more or less loyal to the group and deferential to its leadership. But even the most devout member's allegiance is not guaranteed, it must often be molded and reinforced. Thus the first recipients of opinion-influencing material from the group are members themselves. It comes through publications (magazines, brochures, newsletters), in speeches, at conventions, and during elections for the group's officers. Considerable effort is often expended to ensure (or at least give the impression) that members are considered and consulted—that the group represents them (Berry, 1977).

One likely effect of this membership cultivation is that such phenomena as the spiral of silence discussed by Edelstein may apply most effectively to the group members, especially those belonging to ideological organizations.

It is not entirely clear, however, that interest groups always or even often represent their members' opinions. Members may lack relevant views, especially when they join the group for tangible rather than purposive reasons. The membership may be divided in its views. Leaders may assume they know the members' opinions without consulting them. Or the consultation mechanism may be inadequate (if, indeed, an effective means exists). Moreover, leaders sometimes purport to represent their group's opinions even on subjects about which the members have been neither polled nor consulted and in which most of the members may be quite disinterested.

As a result, leaders often enjoy considerable leeway in taking positions and speaking for their groups. But journalists and policymakers may then be emboldened to discount the leaders' claims to represent cohesive bodies of opinion whose preferences should not be ignored.

We shall have more to say about representation, our third element, when we consider the relations of interest groups with the media and with policymakers. But first, we discuss groups' interactions with the opinions of their nonmembers, the overwhelming bulk of the public.

THE PUBLIC

Engaged in a constant struggle for influence, interest groups ignore the views of the mass of the public at their risk, sometimes even at their peril. Ideally, from a group's point of view, the climate of opinion is favorable, the group's concerns are part of the public's issue agenda, the public accepts the group's diagnosis of the causes and consequences of these issues, adopts its proposed policy solutions, and pressures government for their establishment.

Successful cultivation of public opinion also reduces the likelihood of policies inimical to the group's interests being proposed, rendering their chances of enactment remote. Witness how the life insurance industry built up such an appealing image in the public mind that it became very difficult for states effectively to regulate—let alone curb—its enormous power (Orren, 1974).

Certainly not every group needs to go public. Some organizations eschew publicity, preferring to operate away from any glare of public attention or scrutiny. The Business Roundtable, whose elite members have easy access to policymakers, is one example. Other groups may fear that bringing an issue to the attention of more people could backfire by mobilizing the opposition (Schlozman & Tierney, 1986). More common, groups may want to woo the public, but lack the requisite unity and strong direction, resources, skills, and contacts (Key, 1961).

Groups have a particular incentive to go public when they are unable to receive a favorable hearing in the corridors, antechambers, and hideaway rooms of power for their policy concerns and proposals. Doing so can expand the visibility and intensity of feeling about the issues (Schattschneider, 1960). Indeed, a group's only alternative may be to take its case to the public. When state legislatures speedily began ratifying the Equal Rights Amendment, its opponents launched a major campaign to stimulate public pressure on state legislatures to reject ratification. They mobilized sufficient strength in enough key states to keep the minimum number of states from ratifying, despite a countercampaign from groups supporting the ERA (Boles, 1979).

Without a model of how public opinion is formed, however, it is difficult to comprehend the process and measure the effects of interest groups' attempts to influence public opinion. Unfortunately, as Edelstein demonstrates, a viable model does not exist.

Lance Bennett's psychological approach might be useful, even if incomplete. Bennett (1975) claims that, in forming an opinion, the average person is affected by her or his cognitive or analytical style, and by "strategies of political definition common to the culture" (p. 47). Individuals attempt to place the people, events, and so on that they encounter into some kind of context and fit them into their cognitive framework. The better educated may have a more sophisticated cognitive style, enabling them to deal more easily with complex information. The bulk of the population, however, with rudimentary cognitive or analytical styles, are vulnerable to having their opinions shaped, even determined, by the "culturally familiar paradigms of stories, accounts, and scenarios" (Bennett, 1975, p. 49).

Bennett's approach might be integrated with W. Russell Neuman's division of Americans into three publics: 5% political activists, 20% apoliticals, and those who form a kind of middle stratum (Neuman, 1986). The activists would have sophisticated cognitive styles and be resistant to "cultural strategies of political definition." The apoliticals, without cognitive style, could be vulnerable to dubious definitions, but are usually insulated by their disinterest in public affairs and politics.

It is the middle mass, who "keep track of the most important issues with modest effort, but . . . lack the background information and rich vocabulary necessary for the quick and convenient processing of large amounts of political information" (Neuman, 1986, p. 172), whose limited cognitive styles may make them susceptible to the propounders of political definitions, to political activists and to interest group leaders with their particular visions and versions of the world.

Not to exaggerate, people are not always empty vessels waiting to be filled by interest groups' views. Many individuals have preexisting opinions, attitudes, and values of varying intensity. Selective exposure, perception, and retention may also be at work. In certain instances, people may even be classifiable as fellow travelers, potential sympathizers, neutral, independent, or hostile, depending on their prior actual and inchoate sentiments about a group and its objectives (Truman, 1951).

If a group's activities are successful, public opinion mounts on its behalf and can bring pressure on government for responsive action. Odegard (1928) chronicled how the Anti-Saloon League succeeded in stimulating public support for its goals by couching its arguments in general, widely accepted terms. Saloons were portrayed as the perverters of children, enemy of the home, the black hole of the working man's hard earned dollar, and the vanguard of economic ruin.

Accounting in part for the League's success, it was capitalizing on many years of public opinion molding by temperance organizations and it ran an emotionally resonant campaign appealing to and fomenting people's quite understandable fears.

THE MASS MEDIA

Interest groups may be able to promulgate their views, assert their definitions of events through many agencies—schools, churches, and the workplace. But nowadays if they are to reach the bulk of the activist and mass public, then the media are central. By media, we mean television and radio, newspapers, mass and specialized publications.

Paid Announcements

Interest groups can reach the public by purchasing media time and space. The promotion may be indirect: Businesses advertise to sell their products, but in the process they boost their images and may even extol the virtues of capitalism. More overtly, major corporations like Exxon and Xerox "sponsor" programs on public television, perhaps fostering the climate of opinion that their operations and profit making should be undisturbed by government.

The image-making and policy pronouncement may be explicit: Mobil Oil has run a series of advertisements in such elite-readership organs as the *New York Times*, *Washington Post*, and *New York Review of Books* with the continuing theme of "the need for free market solutions to questions of public policy" (Berry, 1984, p. 140).

At the other extreme, sponsorship may be concealed. The "Calorie Control Council" paying for newspaper advertisements attacking the Food and Drug Administration's proposed ban on saccharin was actually composed of manufacturers and processors of dietary products (see also Paletz, Pearson, & Willis, 1977).

One of the most effective campaigns was successfully staged by the American Medical Association during the late 1940s against President Truman's proposal for national health insurance. It included advertisements, press conferences, and supposedly neutral experts who spoke on radio shows and wrote newspaper articles decrying "socialized" medicine. The campaign actually coined and popularized that loaded term as a substitute for "national health insurance"—on the accurate assumption that anything smacking of socialism exudes negative vibrations in the United States (Key, 1964).

The AMA's example was rare, and in 1961 Key described the impact of the propaganda campaigns of most private groups on the general public as "almost infinitesimal" (p. 515).

That judgment may no longer apply. The last 25 years have witnessed the growth of television abetted by technological developments (satellites, cable), the loosening of governmental restrictions on and regulations of the media (especially television), and the proliferation of public relations practitioners with ever more sophisticated techniques.

As one example stemming from these changes, consider the ability of some religious organizations to spread their views before the mass public. These so-called televangelists produce their own television programs that air throughout the United States (and in many other countries). Whether their styles are arm-waving passionate, comfortably conversational, or emotionally self-revelatory, these preachers are masters of the medium, supported by sophisticated professionals. They frequently take positions, either explicitly or obliquely, on public policies and issues of the day. It may be that the effects of these messages are limited and that the evangelists are preaching mainly to the converted. But their audiences, vulnerable to strategies of political definition, deferring to the "divinely inspired" views of televangelists, may be particularly susceptible to these opinions, which they might not otherwise encounter. Many certainly show their trust through financial donations.

News Coverage

Since expensive, paid advertising campaigns are beyond the resources of most groups, their public images are largely determined by the free news coverage they receive.

How groups are depicted by the news media, then, can be a major determinant of the public's opinions and impressions about, and responses and reactions to, interest groups. Our own research, moreover, indicates that media news coverage is drastically and dramatically different depending upon the group portrayed. Certain groups are scorned as pariahs, some ignored, others indulged. For a favored few, the media serves as a conduit, transmitting whatever news and views the group's leaders care to provide.

There are two sides to this explanation. One is made up of journalism's organizational processes and daily routines, imperatives, norms, and news definitions. These include reporters' propensity to go in packs, rely on official sources, and their lack of time for detailed investigation of noncontroversial events. Perhaps most important is their reliance for encapsulating events on certain stock frames based on cultural assumptions, values, and beliefs so pervasive and accepted that they are not perceived by journalists or politicians or the public as interpretive frames at all, but as objective facts (Paletz & Entman, 1981).

The other side consists of the resources and skills, the understanding of press practices and interest, and the media manipulating techniques and tactics that the leaders and staff of interest groups are able to employ in their relations with the press.

Before we turn to actual cases, it would be useful to know whether, indeed, the news has any effect on public opinion. Unfortunately, there is a dearth of research. The most ambitious study, although imaginative and heuristic, is a flawed attempt by Page, Shapiro, and Dempsey (1987) to assess the impact of network television news on aggregate changes in U.S. citizens' policy preferences. They argue plausibly that new information can have such effects if it "is (1) actually received, (2) understood, (3) clearly relevant to evaluating policies, (4) discrepant with past beliefs, and (5) credible" (p. 24). Their approach entailed collecting data from

> many pairs of identically repeated policy preference questions that were asked of national survey samples of U.S. citizens; coding TV news content from broadcasts aired in between (and just before) each pair of surveys; and predicting or explaining variations in the extent and direction of opinion change by variations in media content. (p. 25)

As far as we can discern, this approach does not permit the researchers to test their arguments about effects. They offer no evidence that the people whose opinions changed met the five conditions of receiving, understanding the material, and so on, or that members of the sample watched television network news at all. Indeed, the actual data are limited to 80 cases. And, while the before-after questions for each policy are identical, the individuals polled in each survey are different. Consequently, we do not know who changed or why, nor do we have any data about other possible effects such as reinforcement.

Despite, or perhaps because of, these methodological deficiencies, the study's conclusions are intriguing. News commentary (statements by commentators and reporters) had a strong impact. This effect may have occurred, the authors suggest, because it reflected "the positions of many journalists or other elites who communicate through additional channels besides TV news or even a widespread elite consensus in the country" (Page et al., 1987, p. 35). Of course, news commentators are a vanishing breed on network news, with most of the individuals mentioned in the study having departed. Nor is overt editorializing from news anchors or reporters much apparent these days—if it ever was.

Among the other sources who have a substantial impact on public opinion change are experts, popular presidents, and certain public interest groups. In contrast, "groups and individuals representing various special interests, taken together, tend to have a negative effect on public opinion" (Page et al., 1987, p. 37). These include demonstrators and protestors (against the war in Vietnam), and groups such as business corporations and organized labor pushing selfish or parochial interests. Also in disrepute are blacks, women, and the poor.

Marginal Groups

In our view, the ways these groups were depicted on the news explains in great part their particular effects on public opinion. Let us therefore consider the coverage respectively of marginal groups and the more successful Common Cause.

Least successful in eliciting favorable coverage are marginal groups. There are two often overlapping types: ideological and economic. On the edge of

American politics, of interest to few people, with little obvious impact on society, marginal groups rarely make conventional news. Their policy objectives are not widely shared. Their credibility is low, their prestige lower. They are off reporters' beats and lack the resources to package any news they do make in usable form for journalists. Their leaders have few if any "exclusive" stories to offer the press and are often naive about the constraints and imperatives under which reporters operate.

To achieve coverage, fringe groups must impinge on institutions regularly covered by reporters, either by becoming a subject of concern or by forcibly intruding themselves. Alternatively, they can appeal to media interests by doing something—anything—newsworthy. Dramatic gestures, marches, boycotts, sit-ins, demonstrations, confrontations, strikes, and riots are newsworthy and visual. As long as there is no surfeit of such activities and they remain novel, the media will tend to cover them, particularly, if the activities expose injustice and exploitation and can be tied to an existing news peg. Nevertheless, the coverage is usually negative (Goldenberg, 1975, on the effective struggles of resource-poor groups to obtain coverage; Gitlin, 1980, on destructive portrayals of Students for a Democratic Society; and Paletz, Ayanian, and Fozzard, 1982, on negative depictions of "terrorism").

The coverage is negative because it is usually the behavior—the demonstration, the confrontation, the violence—not the underlying policy objectives that take precedence in press coverage. In addition, when the groups' leaders are afforded access to the mass media they are almost invariably subject to rebuttal. The reporter or host or narrator usually poses as a disinterested compiler, siding with neither extreme. In so doing, he or she frames the issue from a conventional perspective, thereby defining the views and objectives of the contending groups as extremist. (For a discussion of the civil rights movement of the 1960s as an exception to this treatment, see Paletz & Entman, 1981; or Garrow, 1978.)

It is possible to produce favorable media coverage. Manheim and Albritten (1984) document how the governments of South Korea, the Philippines, Yugoslavia, Argentina, Indonesia, and Rhodesia succeeded in improving portrayals of their countries in the *New York Times* after they hired American professional public relations consultants. Mexico expressly declined to contract for such services; its image did not improve.

For our purposes, however, the *New York Times's* coverage of Common Cause during the 1970s provides a classic case of positive coverage (Paletz & Entman, 1981).

On the one hand, Common Cause possessed legitimacy and credibility through its founder, John W. Gardner, and from the number and social standing of its members. In turn, the group's media-conscious staff knew how to obtain coverage by creating events, giving them visibility, emphasizing their newsworthy details, and structuring them into a story for the press. They continually issued timely news releases, editorial memoranda, research reports, testimonies, and speeches packaged for media consumption and publication, hand-delivering them to key reporters. Important themes were emphasized and repeated.

Common Cause worked to obtain extensive and favorable coverage from the *New York Times*. The *Times* bestowed that coverage because the material provided fit into its concept of news (big names, derelictions and malfeasance, personalized symbols). Common Cause also gathered and pried out information about campaign finances that journalists wanted but lacked the time and resources to obtain. Shared values is another explanation: in particular, reporters accepted the desirability of Common Cause's goals of a more "accessible," "accountable," "effective," and "responsive" government.

Consequently, existing members of Common Cause were given reasons to stay with the group, new members were attracted, and the organization's distinctive area of competence were reaffirmed. Most important, the *Times'* coverage enabled Common Cause to imprint upon public opinion and public officials its definition of the woes of American politics and its prescriptions for those woes.

Marginal groups and Common Cause are almost ideal types for comparing coverage types. Obviously media coverage of most groups falls between these extremes: sometimes favorable, sometimes unfavorable, varying over time, changing in amount and, less likely, differing appreciably between media (television and newspapers) and, even rarer, between organs in a medium (the CBS and NBS evening news shows).

The public's opinion of a group is influenced by more factors than media coverage of the group itself. Groups may benefit or suffer from news stories about events in which they are peripheral or uninvolved (e.g., the relation between assassination attempts on presidents and the National Rifle Association); or stories about allied organizations (the depredations of one prescription drug company harm the reputation of other drug firms and the industry as a whole).

Even when an interest group and the media cooperate to their mutual benefit, the results may not fulfill their expectations. In an illuminating essay, Harvey Molotch and his co-authors (Molotch, Protess, & Gordon, 1987) recount how Chicago's Better Government Association worked through investigative journalists in an effort to influence public policy. They show how a chain leading logically from the association to policy consequences often broke at key places. Thus the association's research did not necessarily lead to journalistic investigation, nor the investigations to publication, nor publication to public opinion changes, nor inevitably on to policy initiatives by policymakers, nor invariably to policy consequences. Molotch et al. (1987) document how the process often stopped at one or another of the links, how the chain was (and is) in no sense inexorable. Nonetheless, it is clear that interest groups and media can be a formidable pair, influencing public opinion to mutual advantage.

GOVERNMENT

The interest group-government connection influences public opinion (and is influenced by it) in complex, little recognized and underresearched ways. We will briefly discuss three aspects: the interactions of groups with political parties, candidates, and office holders.

Political Parties

Interest group representatives testify before the platform committees of the political parties' national presidential nominating conventions. This testimony itself can attract media coverage. If the platform incorporates group positions, perhaps because a block of delegates belongs to the interest group, then there is a reasonable chance that the party's presidential candidate will endorse the proposals during the subsequent campaign and, if elected, will recommend their enactment into law (Fishel, 1986). If only part of the scenario transpires, the group's views will be brought, at least momentarily, before the public; if it all occurs, public opinion is likely to show the views becoming both more visible and more favored.

Candidates

Many groups are intimately involved in election campaigns. Endorsing candidates is one technique. The assumption is that many of the group's members and some nonmembers who share or respect its purposes will follow the recommendation. In this sense, the group delivers public opinion, in the tangible form of votes, to its past and (it hopes) future friends in public office. But a group's endorsement does not necessarily result in such votes even from members. They may lack a deep commitment to the group's goals, be unwilling to follow their leaders' recommendations without persuasive arguments, and have reasons for voting for other candidates. Worse, some group endorsements, from the Ku Klux Klan for example, hurt rather than help a candidate's electoral chances.

Giving funds and other kinds of support directly and through Political Action Committees (PACs) is more common. There are more than 4000 PACs. It is estimated they will contribute as much as $155 million in 1987, not a presidential election year. One major objective is to facilitate or ensure the election of candidates sympathetic to the group's interests and objectives. A side benefit is that these candidates may sometimes expound issues and issue positions during the campaign that are shared by the group, perhaps influencing public opinion in the group's favor.

There is a risk of political isolation if the candidates supported by the group lose. There is little incentive for the unsupported winners to work for the group's goals. On the other hand, today's defeated are often tomorrow's victors. Besides, they are still politicians, and do not casually reject the possibilities of cooperation and compromise, of gaining a modicum of financial and political support from some of their former antagonists.

In many constituencies challengers have little chance of success. One expedient is for groups to give to incumbents who do not particularly favor their views with the hope for access and, optimistically, an occasional vote for their objectives.

Office Holders

Political elites can guide, sometimes even direct, public opinion. Thus achieving enactment of its policy preference by policymakers can be a way for a group to attract attention and affect public opinion. But just as groups vary in their ability to attract media coverage, so they differ in their influence in the policy process. Eldersveld (1958) has devised a sixfold typology that is still useful:

1. Penetration into formal policy roles;
2. maintenance of close political support and referral relationships;
3. unchallengeable veto status;
4. attention, representative, and pressure relationships;
5. potential reprisal relationship;
6. rejection by power structure, agitational and resistance role. (p. 187)

Obviously the interest groups that have penetrated into formal policy roles are the most likely to succeed in the policy competition. Others rely more on direct lobbying, testimony at hearings, instituting court cases. These tactics may attract media and public attention. Of course, favorable public opinion will not necessarily ensue; much depends on the group's demands, governmental responses, and media depictions.

Interest group leaders may not only seek to influence public opinion through policymakers, they can try to influence officeholders, especially elected officials, by conveying the impression that they represent concerned or aroused members. They inspire letter-writing and telegram campaigns, and have influential constituents contact the legislators. These "inspired" expressions of opinion may certainly be genuine but they are often not as widespread or intense as they seem, and policymakers tend to discount them and minimize their effects.

Polls lessen the need of public officials to rely on, let alone believe, the claims of group leaders and activists to represent their members' opinions. As one example, the Nixon administration was emboldened to impose wage and price controls over the intense opposition of organized labor because polls showed that rank and file workers did not share their leaders' views (Ginsberg, 1986).

The media can contribute to this undermining of group leaders' claims of representation by frequently sponsoring, devising, and reporting public opinion polls. However, as Paletz et al. (1980) document, most of the polls whose results the media publish or air do not deal meaningfully with policy issues.

CONCLUSIONS

We have documented and speculated about the ways interest groups try with varying success to influence public opinion. We know that public opinion influences public policy (Page & Shapiro, 1983). It is logical to conclude, then, that interest groups influence public policy not only directly through penetration into formal policy roles, lobbying and other involvement with policymakers, but also indirectly through their effects on public opinion. Thus the public issues with which government deals are often those propounded by powerful interest groups and amplified by the media. For, as Schattschneider (1960) observed in one of his more felicitous insights, "all forms of political organization have a bias in favor of the exploitation of some kinds of conflicts and the suppression of others" (p. 71).

The beneficiaries of this "bias" would appear to be "upper-status individuals—those with high levels of education, prestigious jobs, and high incomes—[who] are much more likely to be members of organizations than lower status individuals" (Schlozman & Tierney, 1986, p. 60).

We could conclude dolorously that interest groups are manipulating a largely ignorant public to endorse the interests of the rich and powerful. But caution may be more appropriate. For it is not entirely obvious that interest groups in the aggregate necessarily articulate views and objectives primarily benefiting the material interests of the well-to-do. Many groups, sustained by upper-status members, espouse the public interest (a notoriously tricky term to be sure). Nor are we convinced by our survey of the literature (see also Bauer, Pool, & Dexter, 1963) that interest groups yet dominate either public policy or public opinion.

REFERENCES

Bauer, R. A., Pool, I. S., & Dexter, L. A. (1963). *American business and public policy: The politics of foreign trade.* New York: Atherton.

Bennett, W. L. (1975). *The political mind and the political environment.* Lexington, MA: D. C. Heath.

Bennett, W. L. (1980). *Public opinion in American politics.* New York: Harcourt Brace Jovanovich.

Berry, J. M. (1977). *Lobbying for the people: The political behavior of public interest groups.* Princeton, NJ: Princeton University Press.

Berry, J. M. (1984). *The interest group society.* Boston: Little, Brown.

Boles, J. K. (1979). *The politics of the Equal Rights Amendment.* New York: Longman.

Edelman, M. (1964). *The symbolic uses of politics.* Urbana: University of Illinois Press.

Eldersveld, S. J. (1958). United States. In H. W. Ehrmann (Ed.), *Interest groups on four continents* (pp. 173-196). Pittsburgh: University of Pittsburgh Press.

Fishel, J. (1986). *Presidents and promises*. Washington, DC: Congressional Quarterly Press.

Garrow, D. J. (1978). *Protest at Selma: Martin Luther King and the Voting Rights Act of 1965*. New Haven, CT: Yale University Press.

Ginsberg, B. (1986). *The captive public*. New York: Basic Books.

Gitlin, T. (1980). *The whole world is watching*. Berkeley: University of California Press.

Goldenberg, E. N. (1975). *Making the papers*. Lexington, MA: D. C. Heath.

Key, V. O., Jr. (1961). *Public opinion and American democracy*. New York: Knopf.

Key, V. O., Jr. (1964). *Politics, parties, and pressure groups* (5th ed.). New York: Crowell.

Manheim, J. B., & Albritton, R. B. (1984). Changing national images: International public relations and media agenda setting. *American Political Science Review, 78*, 641-657.

Moe, T. M. (1980). *The organization of interests: Incentives and the internal dynamics of political interest groups*. Chicago: University of Chicago Press.

Molotch, H. L., Protess, D. L., & Gordon, M. T. (1987). The media-policy connection: Ecologies of news. In D. L. Paletz (Ed.), *Political communication research: Approaches, studies, assessments* (pp. 26-48). Norwood, NJ: Ablex.

Neuman, W. R. (1986). *The paradox of mass politics*. Cambridge, MA: Harvard University Press.

Odegard, P. H. (1928). *Pressure politics: The story of the Anti-Saloon League*. New York: Columbia University Press.

Orren, K. (1974). *Corporate power social change: The politics of the life insurance industry*. Baltimore: Johns Hopkins University Press.

Page, B. I., & Shapiro, R. Y. (1983). Effects of public opinion on policy. *American Political Science Review, 77*, 175-190.

Page, B. I., Shapiro, R. Y., & Dempsey, G. R. (1987). What moves public opinion? *American Political Science Review, 81*, 24-43.

Paletz, D. L., Ayanian, J. Z., & Fozzard, P. A. (1982). Terrorism on TV news: The IRA, the FALN, and the Red Brigades. In W. C. Adams (Ed.), *Television coverage of international affairs* (pp. 143-165). Norwood, NJ: Ablex.

Paletz, D. L., & Entman, R. M. (1981). *Media power politics*. New York: Free Press.

Paletz, D. L., Pearson, R. E., & Willis, D. L. (1977). *Politics in public service advertising on television*. New York: Praeger.

Paletz, D. L., Short, J. V., Baker, H., Campbell, B. C., Cooper, R. J., & Oeslander, R. (1980). Polls in the media: Content, credibility, and consequences. *Public Opinion Quarterly, 44*, 495-513.

Schattschneider, E. E. (1960). *The semi-sovereign people*. Hinsdale, IL: Dryden.

Schlozman, K. L., & Tierney, J. T. (1986). *Organized interests and American democracy*. New York: Harper & Row.

Truman, D. B. (1951). *The governmental process: Political interests and public opinion*. New York: Knopf.

Walker, J. L. (1983). The origins and maintenance of interest groups in America. *American Political Science Review, 77*, 390-406.

Wilson, J. Q. (1973). *Political organizations*. New York: Basic Books.

Commentary on Edelstein

Public Opinion and the Construction of Social Reality

PHILLIP J. TICHENOR
University of Minnesota, Minneapolis

A central theme of Edelstein's review is that public opinion consists in considerable measure of what people believe others think. Whether the dominant process is called a "third person effect," a "spiral of silence," "group pressure," "coorientation" or "the rule of the mob," judgments and decisions take into account what "the public" is presumed to believe.

A closely related theme in this review is that polling and reporting of poll results are part of a process of construction of social reality. In much of the literature, this question has been confined to the question of so-called bandwagon effects of polling on voter behavior. While those effects may be minimal, judging from a variety of studies, there is a continuing question about the impact of polling and poll reporting on perceptions, behaviors, and social processes other than those measurable in voter turnout.

Three questions worthy of extensive study seem to be suggested by Edelstein's review: (1) What are the social conditions affecting "third person" perceptions? (2) What are the consequences of "third person" perceptions for future behavior, of citizens and leadership groups? (3) What are the agenda-setting consequences of polling and poll reporting?

PUBLIC OPINION AND SOCIAL CONTROL

In approaching these questions, it is well to note that the study of public opinion is essentially a study of social control. Lippman pointed out that "public opinions" are opinions about how others should manage their affairs,

Correspondence and requests for reprints: Phillip J. Tichenor, School of Journalism and Mass Communication, University of Minnesota, Minneapolis, MN 55455.

Communication Yearbook 11, pp. 547-554

that is, about the rules under which management of human affairs should occur. Opinion polls about abortion, tax regulations, seat-belt laws, anti-smoking legislation, capital punishment, affirmative action, rights of minorities, or censorship of media make this control dimension highly explicit.

It is difficult to recall a poll that does not have a social control dimension, even though the relevance in some cases may be indirect. A poll measuring beliefs about life in the hereafter or existence of extraterrestrial intelligence may, at first glance, seem devoid of control implications. The control aspects of such a poll become apparent in the context. Belief in external existence is generally tied to beliefs about behaviors during wordly existence that increase or decrease the likelihood of such salvation. Belief in extraterrestrial life may have similar implications, and it will no doubt be interpreted as support for a particular course of action such as doing research in outer space.

Study of public opinion requires an emphasis on *publics* that are formed around interests that may conflict with interests of other publics. The analytical problem is generally to identify the group interests that account for a given complex of opinions. The recurring emphasis on conformity theories stands as recognition of this point, although the group basis of opinion is not always made as explicit as it is in Namenwirth, Miller, and Weber (1981). They demonstrated that *organizations* are seen by people as having opinions, a finding that may have major implications. How do perceptions of those organizational opinions affect actions of members and constituents? The organizational opinions emerge from seats of power, and linkages within the system enforce those opinions.

Early social theorists saw the social control implications of public opinion as constraints on individual choice and creative thought. E. A. Ross (1920) offered an extensive analysis of how social suggestion could bring about the same social control results as punishments and rewards. Much of the literature of that period emphasized "crowd" behavior, in terms of the mechanisms by which individuals were pressured to conform to predilections of a particular group. Whether the action being analyzed was that of a labor union on strike, a suffrage group at the gates of Parliament, farmers protesting railroad shipping rates, or lynch mobs in the American South, the focus was on behavior that individuals would presumably not conduct on their own, or isolated from the group setting.

It is quite reasonable to view Noelle-Neumann's "spiral of silence" theory as a current version of conformity theory. Her notion that fear of isolation leads to less likelihood that a person will express an opinion is a fundamental hypothesis about social control. It seems entirely consistent with the early writers' concerns about crowd control of individual behavior.

Social Conditions Affecting
"Third Person" Perceptions

The "third person" effect as described by Davison (1983) appears to imply a group conformity theory, although in a more complex way than stated in earlier literature. The assumption is not that individuals immediately take on the views that others are perceived to hold, but that the assumed views of others are taken into account. As Edelstein points out, the assumption is that individuals perceive the majority as being influenced by communications that the individual himself or herself rejects. Thus a statement often heard is that "the opinion polls don't affect me, but they have a powerful affect on the public." It's an interesting question whether individuals overestimate effects on others rather than underestimate impact on themselves, as Davison asks. An even more basic issue is the consequences of these third person perceptions for subsequent behavior, and how the consequences vary according to social setting.

This third person idea seems, on the surface, to be contrary to certain other perspectives, such as the "looking-glass" or projection theories reviewed by Edelstein. In some cases, we see our own views reflected in the world around us. In others, we tend to see media affecting third persons and not ourselves, much as we may reject certain positions that we believe are common in the population. Belief in racial prejudice is often mentioned as an example that a majority of members in a community may accept the idea of minority group members living in their own neighborhoods but believe that most others would prefer to keep such persons out.

One might ask whether there are certain conditions that lead to looking-glass effects and others that produce a third person or rejection response. A determining factor would in principle be the interest group with which individuals identify, and the phenomenon may be reminiscent of the familiar "assimilation-contrast" problem posed two and a half decades ago by Sherif, Sherif, and Nebersall (1965). It might be suggested that the belief in gullible others is basically a contrast effect, since it implies rejecting those who are not considered part of the respondent's interest group. On the other hand, those who are seen as part of the same interest group may be seen as having more similar opinions and as more resistant to media content that goes against group beliefs. The greater the solidarity of a group, the more likely that projection effects would occur for the membership and the greater the rejection, or perceived contrast, with members outside the group.

Some questions need to be asked about how media content, theoretically, would affect perceptions of self versus other opinions. Consider the finding by Glynn that newspaper readers saw fewer discrepancies between their own opinions and others than did television viewers. The underlying process here may be closely tied to the social power of the groups. Those who follow printed as well as broadcast news tend to have higher socioeconomic status and identify with more influential segments of society. Those who confine their news behavior to television news alone tend to have lower socioeconomic status and may quite accurately perceive themselves as less influential. If that is the case, it would follow that such persons would perceive discrepancies between themselves and, at least, certain others. Such discrepancies are more likely to be seen by those who recognize that the views of their reference groups are not shared by the power structure.

It is also worthy of study to determine whether the third person effect is culturally bound, and more characteristic of some social structures than of others. Is denial of persuasive effects on one's self tied to the feelings of rugged individualism and self-sufficiency that are often found to be characteristic of northern groups in the United States? Is belief in third person impact the flip side of persuasibility, which the Yale researchers of three decades also claimed to be a general personality trait? That is, are less persuasible groups more likely to perceive third person effects?

Consequences of Third Person Perceptions

Assuming that the belief in third person effects is widely held, what are its consequences for individuals and leaders? Are those with strong third person effect beliefs more likely to think or behave in some related way? And what form would those related behaviors take? Might they be mimicking, complementary, or offsetting behaviors? If one believes that Sylvester Stallone's portrayals make others more aggressive, does one then become paranoid toward those who enjoy Rambo and similar movies? The "cultivation" perspective of Gerbner and Gross (1978) would lead us to hypothesize that such is the case.

It might be well to consider different forms of third person effects, and which social groups are perceived as experiencing these effects. Suppose one is studying the perceptions that community leaders have of the impact of a campaign to legalize abortion. It would seem reasonable to establish hypotheses according to which group the perceptions are about. Is it a group with higher status than the leadership group, or with lower status? Presumably a group will shape its behavior in different ways, depending upon status of the third person group. One might expect a group to behave in terms of what it sees more powerful groups as expecting, and to treat less powerful groups in terms of what those groups *should* be doing. Judging from the early literature on social comparison processes, one might expect groups to look up the status hierarchy for guides to their own behavior, but look down in specifying restrictions to maintain conformity with the norms of the dominant group.

Raising such questions might also move public opinion research into the study of "cooptive" behavior, with particular relevance for organizational management generally and for journalists in particular. One cooptive situation of potential interest is the circumstance in which the actor sees a more powerful group, such as organizational leadership, having a sharply different view than does the actor. Since the leadership sets the rules and has control, the actor complies. What are the consequences for the actor's outlook as this process repeats itself? Two decades ago, dissonance theorists would have argued that it is a matter of perception of choice. If the individual sees no possibility to modify the decision, there is—in effect—no discomfort with the decision and therefore no substantial change. "What else could I do?

I had no choice," the individual says, and complies without conversion, as Kelman (1961) contended.

A great deal might be learned by studying the long-run effects of such compliance in circumstances familiar to journalists. More than 30 years ago, Kerrick, Anderson, and Swales (1964) conducted an experiment in which student reporters wrote editorials that were either in agreement with or contrary to the reporters' own views. The findings suggested that the strongest editorials were written by journalists whose own opinions were contrary to media policy. In a more recent study, Kosicki, Dunwoody, and Beam (1985) studied prize-seeking behavior among a sample of reporters, and found that the stronger predictor of entering contests was not self-attitudes about prizes, but what the reporters saw their organizations as favoring. A reporter submitted entries into competition not in terms of what he or she thought to be professionally proper, but according to what "the newspaper wants." Similarly, St. Dizier (1986) found that editors of chain newspapers differed more from their owners in political views than did editors of nonchain papers. On presidential elections, this means that chain-paper editors were more likely than nonchain-paper editors to be "living with" an endorsement that went against the strain of their own convictions.

These are third person situations in the sense that the actor is constrained to make regular decisions in terms of an organizational power with which he or she may not agree. When the journalist sees a story breaking, the question is not the self-impact that the journalist perceives, but how the reporter perceives the management of the paper as reacting. Over a period of time, one would expect the journalist to adopt the third person perception or to leave the organization. Since there are various constraints on leaving, cooptation is often the more likely result.

This claim is not that total conversion to the organization's views or leaving it are the only alternatives. There may be numerous situations in which professionals remain in organizations whose policies they reject but cannot counteract. It then becomes problematic whether their independence is organizationally reinforced or whether a process of organizational isolation occurs, leading to alienation of the dissaffected individuals. Such was the apparent outcome in a newspaper organization studied by Stark (1962), where there were wide cleavages in philosophy between the newsroom and management. Out-of-town reporters served in an uneasy truce with the publisher with whom they disagreed, and compensated in maladaptive ways that led to low morale.

AGENDA-SETTING CONSEQUENCES OF POLLING AND POLL REPORTING

The questions of media capacity for setting public agendas, and where media agendas come from, are fundamental for social control. While the literature points to a variety of conditions under which agenda-setting correlations will or will not be found, there is little doubt that the effect may occur and there is more evidence for media effect on the general public than the reverse. What this says is not that media make agenda decisions in an interest-group vacuum, but that they respond more to some interest groups than to others. Their agendas are those of the dominant forces in society, principally agencies of government and business, as numerous analyses suggest.

A question that Edelstein explores in some detail in his literature review is whether agenda-setting should be seen as a "limited" or "powerful" effect. He notes the emphasis in much of the literature upon the notion from Cohen (1963) that media are successful in telling the public not what to think but what to think about. Interesting as this frequently cited notion is, one can question the idea from social psychology that an "opinion object" occurs in communication separately from "criteria." All communication occurs within a cultural context and as Tuchman (1978), Fishman (1980), and other analysts of news reporting point out, judgments are implicit throughout the reporting enterprise. Indeed, as Edelstein's review indicates, Benton and Frazier (1976) found that both "causal" agendas and "criteria" agendas in the media were correlated with public agendas. These findings are consistent with the "cultivation theory," which sees media dramatic content as telling audiences what is right, what is wrong, who is strong, who is weak, and who wins and who loses. This view is clearly one of powerful media effects and yet it evidently does not treat media as independent agents.

Public opinion polling may be seen as a special case of agenda setting. Polling the population on a selected topic and then reporting the results presumably works toward maintaining the salience of those issues. Consider the case of a citizen group conducting a telephone poll asking local people whether they favor or oppose building a new prison on the edge of town. The newspaper report of that poll the next day is like any other agenda-setting media content, in that it reinforces the perception that the prison is a high-priority local issue. Opinion poll reporting on abortion, AIDS, gun control, or the hostage situation have similar consequences. It would be difficult to conclude from years of research that media reporting about public issues has widespread agenda-setting effects and then argue that poll reporting has no consequences.

One might raise here the longstanding question about the alleged "bandwagon" effects of public opinion polling. Public opinion polling has various ramifications for political behavior, ranging from support for the campaign organization to intelligence that provides a basis for exploiting the weakness of an adversary. Beniger (1976), in his analysis of election-year polling, found no relationship between results of a given poll and results of the next one. He interpreted this finding as the absence of a bandwagon effect. At the same time, he did find a correlation between the results of preference polls before primary elections and the results of those primaries. His results as a whole suggest that polling is very much part of the political campaign process and may be highly instrumental to outcomes of that process.

While this claim is not to attribute initial causation to poll reporting, the polls do serve as basic resources and weapons of political warfare. The consequences are not all of one type or all in one direction. There might be bandwagon consequences in some cases and underdog effects in others. The latter case is illustrated by a midwestern senatorial election a few years ago, when a popular "straw poll" found the incumbent far behind the challenger in popular support with several weeks to go in the campaign. The incumbent had a private poll showing the incumbent leading by a thin margin, but chose not to report those results. One interpretation is that by thinking they were behind, the incumbent's party workers were motivated to overcome their complacency and work harder to win. Overconfidence may indeed be a problem in politics as well as in athletic competition, and underdog strategies are well known in both professions.

AN AGENDA FOR PUBLIC OPINION RESEARCH?

Edelstein's review of the public opinion literature portrays the field as moving well beyond the question of simple one-way effects. Public opinion is formed, maintained, and expressed in a social situation, which must be taken into account in analysis. In recognizing the process involved, Edelstein has contributed immeasurably to setting an agenda for future research.

REFERENCES

Beniser, J. (1976). Winning the presidential nomination: National polls and state primary elections. *Public Opinion Quarterly, 40*, 22-38.

Benton, M., & Frazier, J. P. (1976). The agenda-setting function of the mass media at three levels of "information-holding." *Communication Research, 3*, 261-274.

Cohen, B. C. (1963). *The press and foreign policy*. Princeton, NJ: Princeton University Press.

Davison, W. P. (1983). The third-person effect in communication. *Public Opinion Quarterly, 47*, 1-15.

Gerbner, G., & Gross, L. (1978). Living with television: The violence profile. *Journal of Communication, 26*(2): 172-199.

Kelman, H. C. (1961). Processes of public opinion. *Public Opinion Quarterly, 25*, 57-78.

Kerrick, J. S., Anderson, T. E., & Swales, L. B. (1964). Balance and writer's attitude in news stories and editorials. *Journalism Quarterly, 41*, 207-215.

Kosicki, G. M., Dunwoody, S., & Beam, R. A. (1985, August). *Individual and organizational predictors of journalistic prize-seeking*. Paper presented at the annual meeting of the Association for Education in Journalism and Mass Communication, Memphis, TN.

Namenworth, J. Z., Miller, R. L., & Weber, R. P. (1981). Organizations have opinions: A redefinition of publics. *Public Opinion Quarterly, 45*, 463-476.

Ross, E. A. (1920). *Social control*. New York: Macmillan.

Sherif, M., Sherif, C., & Nebergall, R. (1965). *Attitudes and attitude change: The social judgment approach.* Philadelphia: Saunders.

St. Dizier, B. (1986). Autonomy on the editorial page: A comparison of chain-owned and independent newspapers. *Newspaper Research Journal, 8,* 63-68.

Stark, R. (1962). Policy and the pros: An organizational analysis of a metropolitan newspaper. *Berkeley Journal of Sociology, 7,* 11-32.

Tuchman, G. (1978). *Making news.* New York: Free Press.

13 Agenda-Setting Research: Where Has It Been, Where Is It Going?

EVERETT M. ROGERS
JAMES W. DEARING
Annenberg School of Communications
University of Southern California

Understanding the processes of influence in societies has intrigued generations of scholars. One method of studying such influence in modern democracy is to investigate mass media, public, and policy *agendas*, defined as issues or events that are viewed at a point in time as ranked in a hierarchy of importance. Research by communication scholars and other social scientists has typically conceptualized either the mass media agenda, the public agenda, or the policy agenda as a dependent variable in order to explain how it is influenced by other factors. This chapter (1) analyzes past research on agenda-setting in order to learn where this research literature is deficient and where it is sufficient and (2) synthesizes this research literature with a view toward learning important theoretical and methodological lessons for future agenda-setting research.

Public sentiment is everything. With public sentiment, nothing can fail. Without it, nothing can succeed. Consequently, he who moulds public sentiment goes deeper than he who enacts statutes and pronounces decisions. (U.S. President Abraham Lincoln, quoted in Rivers, 1970, p. 53)

Appreciation for the power of public opinion and the influence wielded by the press has continued since Lincoln's comment. Such concerns address the processes of influence by which American democracy functions. As Lincoln's comment shows, in the mid-1800s the earlier notion of classical democracy, whereby a government responds directly to the wishes of its public, with the

AUTHORS' NOTE: This chapter was originally presented as a paper at the meetings of the American Association for Public Opinion Research, St. Petersburg, FL, May 15-18, 1986. We wish to thank William H. Dutton, associate professor, and Michael D. Cozzens, doctoral candidate, both of the Annenberg School of Communications, University of Southern California, and Maxwell E. McCombs, Department of Journalism, University of Texas, Austin, for their thoughtful comments.

Correspondence and requests for reprints: Everett M. Rogers, Annenberg School of Communications, University of Southern California, Los Angeles, CA 90089-0281.

Communication Yearbook 11, pp. 555-594

mass media serving as a go-between, was being questioned. Later, political analysts like Key and Lippmann provided a new view of the democratic process: Elected political elites decide upon policies for the public, and the public can make itself heard through political parties, which serve to link policymakers with their constituents.

Many scholars now see omnipotent mass media systems as the mechanism linking the public with political policymakers. The media have usurped the linking function of political parties in the United States, creating what can now be thought of as a "media democracy" (Linsky, 1986). One method for understanding modern democracy is to concentrate upon mass media, public, and policy *agendas*, defined as issues or events that are viewed at a point in time as ranked in a hierarchy of importance. Agenda research, concerned with investigating and explaining societal influence, has two main research traditions that have often been referred to as (1) *agenda-setting*, a process through which the mass media communicate the relative importance of various issues and events to the public (an approach mainly pursued by mass communication researchers), and (2) *agenda-building*, a process through which the policy agendas of political elites are influenced by a variety of factors, including media agendas and public agendas. The agenda-setting tradition is concerned with how the media agenda influences the public agenda, while the agenda-building tradition studies how the public agenda and other factors, and occasionally the media agenda, influence the policy agenda.

AN OVERVIEW

In the present chapter, we prefer to utilize the terminology of *media agenda-setting*, *public agenda-setting*, and *policy agenda-setting*. We refer to the entire process that includes these three components as the *agenda-setting process* (Figure 1). We call the first research tradition *media* agenda-setting because its main dependent variable is the mass media news agenda. We call the second research tradition *public* agenda-setting because its main dependent variable is the content and order of topics in the public agenda. We call the third research tradition *policy* agenda-setting because the distinctive aspect of this tradition is its concern with policy as, in part, a response to both the media agenda and the public agenda.

The present chapter has two objectives: (1) to analyze past research on agenda-setting in order to learn where the work reported in this literature is deficient and where it is robust; and (2) to synthesize this research literature with a view toward learning important and methodological lessons for future agenda-setting research.

Although recent years have seen an outpouring of research publications about agenda-setting, this research front has numerous critics. For example, Iyengar and Kinder (1987) state:

Although research on agenda-setting has proliferated over the last decade, so far, unfortunately, the results add up to rather little. With a few important exceptions, agenda-setting research has been theoretically naive, methodologically primitive, both confused and confusing. . . . Agenda-setting may be an apt metaphor, but it is no theory.

Other analysts have described the triviality of research questions and findings. Such criticisms imply a present need for an academic stock-taking of agenda-setting research.

Media Agenda-Setting

The issue of the homogenization of the news into a set of topics addressed by all members of the news media was raised early by the Hutchins Report (Commission on Freedom of the Press, 1947). This set of topics was recognized as the media agenda. The question of who sets the media agenda and the implications of that influence for society were initially explored by Lazarsfeld and Merton (1948). Lazarsfeld and Merton conceived of the media issue agenda as a result of the influence that powerful groups, notably organized business, exerted as a subtle form of social control. "Big business finances the production and distribution of mass media. And, all intent aside,

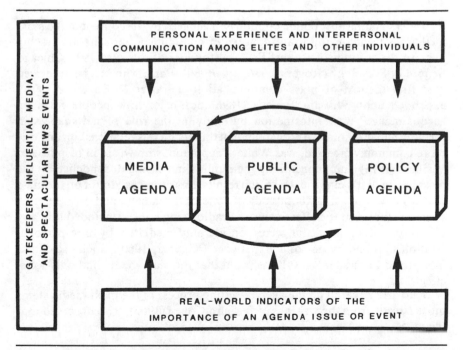

Figure 1. Three main components of the agenda-setting process: media agenda, public agenda, and policy agenda.

he who pays the piper generally calls the tune" (Lazarsfeld & Merton, 1948, reprinted in Schramm, 1975, p. 503). Similarly, Qualter (1985) argued that a commercially sponsored mass media system is operated by those in the ruling class of society; therefore, the media cannot be expected to question the socioeconomic structure of that society seriously. Ball-Rokeach (1985) suggested analyzing the structural dependency organizing the relationship between the political system and the media, which she describes as "cooperation based on mutuality of central dependencies" (pp. 491-492).

The mass media softly but firmly present the perspective of the ruling class to their audiences. The result is consent and support (Schudson, 1986). This result is not a conscious objective of the media. Qualter (1985) stated:

> The media are far from being the sinister manipulators of the popular mind suggested by some conspiracy theories. Their major functions seem to be to support the system, to uphold conformity, to provide reassurance, and to protect the members of society from excessively disturbing, distracting, or dysfunctional information. (pp. x-xi)

These media functions are perpetuated through recruitment and the socialization of media elites, editors, and journalists. In this way, the traditions, practices, and values of media professionals shape the news agenda.

The Public Agenda

Understanding how public opinion is influenced by the content of the mass media has been an important concern of communication scholars tracing back to the writings of Robert E. Park, founder of the 1915-1935 Chicago School of Sociology (Rogers, 1986, pp. 76-80). Park, who has been termed "the first theorist of mass communication" (Frazier & Gaziano, 1979), expanded upon William James's (1896) notion of how people form an "acquaintance" with information by studying the role of newspapers in forming public opinion. Another seminal thinker on this relationship, and one more commonly credited, was Walter Lippmann, who wrote in response to Wallas's (1914) claim concerning the public's increasing dependence on the mass media. Early empirical research results, however, cast doubt on the mass media's power to bring about audience effects. Lazarsfeld and Stanton, in a series of studies on the effectiveness of radio campaigns, concluded that any effects of the mass media were considerably mediated by interpersonal relationships and by personal experience (Klapper, 1960). Social scientists interpreted Lazarsfeld's results as proof that the mass media had only weak effects.

Scholarly research on the agenda-setting process of the mass media stems most directly from the writings of Bernard Cohen (1963), who observed that the press

> may not be successful much of the time in telling people *what to think*, but it is stunningly successful in telling its readers *what to think about*.... The world will

look different to different people, depending . . . on the map that is drawn for them by writers, editors, and publishers of the papers they read. (p. 13; emphasis added)

Cohen thus expressed the metaphor that stimulated both traditions of agenda-setting research described later in this chapter.

The Policy Agenda

Of direct importance to assumptions about democratic societies is the relationship of public opinion to policy elites' decisions and actions. Agenda-setting researchers who conceptualize policy information as a dependent variable want to know whether the agenda items that are salient to individuals in the public also become salient to policymakers. Occasionally, policy agenda-setting researchers investigate the extent to which the media agenda influences the policy agenda.

David Hume (1739/1896) was one of the first to propose a theory of government founded upon, and responsible to, widespread opinion. Hume extended the work of John Locke, who had posited several laws of human nature. The contribution of Hume was his theoretical development of the democratic society, the idea that widespread, supportive opinion alone was the justification by which a government is in power.

Early assessments reflecting on Hume's principle were optimistic (Dewey, 1927). Gradually, however, such optimism was replaced by skepticism, as empirical researchers began looking for evidence of a responsive government. Gabriel Almond (1950) was one of the first scholars of politics to attempt to understand the growing body of survey data and the course of foreign policy. Almond's pioneering emphasis, however, did little to explain how a transfer of opinion from public to policymakers (if indeed there was a transfer) happened. An explanatory mechanism of a policymaker-to-public transfer suggested by Katz and Lazarsfeld (1955) was a "two-step flow" of communication, whereby opinions in a society are first circulated by the media and then passed on via opinion leaders by interpersonal communication. This concept was expanded to a "four-step flow" by James Rosenau (1961) in his book *Public Opinion and Foreign Policy*. Rosenau played an important role in orienting policy research toward issue salience and agenda-setting: "We know practically nothing about why it is that some situations abroad never become the subject of public discussion, whereas others take hold and soon acquire the status of national issues" (Rosenau, 1961, pp. 4-5). Rosenau served another important function for later policy agenda-setting research by concentrating on the mass media and their relationships with policymakers.

Cohen's reviews (1973/1983) of the evidence supporting the hypothesis that foreign policymakers are responsive to public opinion concluded, "Our knowledge is partial, unsystematic, disconnected and discontinuous" (p. 4). "We are left with the unsatisfactory conclusion that public opinion is important in the policy-making process, although we cannot say with confidence how, why or when" (p. 7).

Two Dominant Traditions

Table 1 shows the chronology of 153 publications about agenda-setting, organized by two research traditions of (1) public agenda-setting by the mass media and (2) policy agenda-setting.[1] The distinct tradition of inquiry into media agendas is not reviewed in this article.[2] The research tradition on policy agenda-setting started earlier than the public agenda-setting effort, but has led to fewer research publications (51 versus 102). As detailed in a later section of the present chapter, the policy agenda-setting scholars tended mainly to be political scientists, with some sociologists. The central research question for these scholars is "How does a public issue get on the policy agenda?" rather than "How do the mass media put an agenda item on the public agenda?" So the two research traditions shown in Table 12.1 are both centrally concerned with the agenda-setting process, but investigate how two different agendas are set. The dependent variable for public agenda-setting scholars (the public agenda) becomes one of the important independent variables of study for the policy agenda-setting scholars. Despite these contrasting intellectual orientations, one might expect that the two research traditions would at least indicate awareness of each other's work by citing it in their publications. Our analysis of the citations made in both traditions indicates that cross-citation is common for policy agenda-setting scholars but rare for public agenda-setting scholars.

Why are scholars so fascinated by agenda-setting? The main reason for interest by mass communication scholars is because agenda-setting research appeared to offer an alternative approach to the scholarly search for direct media effects, which had seldom been found in early mass communication research. Many of the agenda-setting publications by mass communication researchers stated or implied their main justification as an attempt to overcome the limited-effects findings of past communication research. Here are typical statements, drawn from the justification section of agenda-setting research publications:

(1) "The ability of the mass media to change attitudes has frequently been challenged. However, recent studies suggest that, if nothing else, the mass media set agendas for discussion" (Gormley, 1975, p. 304).

(2) "Since the publication of McCombs and Shaw's original statement of this [agenda-setting] thesis, scholars have continued to question the prevailing wisdom that the media have little, if any, influence on voters" (Tardy, Gaughan, Hemphill, & Crockett, 1981, p. 624).

(3) "Its initial empirical exploration was fortuitously timed. It came at that time in the history of mass communication research when disenchantment both with attitudes and opinions as dependent variables, and with the limited effects model as an adequate intellectual summary, was leading scholars to look elsewhere" (McCombs, 1981a, p. 121).

TABLE 1
Growth of Public Agenda-Setting and Policy Agenda-Setting
Research Traditions

Public Agenda-Setting		Policy Agenda-Setting	
Year	Authors	Year	Authors
	1922 Lippmann		
	Park		
	1927 Lasswell		
	1948 Lazarsfeld		
	& Merton		
	1950 Almond		
	1952 Davis		
	1961 Rosenau		
	1963 Cohen ———→	1963	Miller & Stokes
		1965	Cohen
		1967	Cohen
		1970	Cohen
		1971	Cobb & Elder
			Crenson
1972 McCombs & Shaw		1972	Cobb & Elder
			Downs
			Peterson
			Weber & Schaffer
1973 Bowers		1973	Cohen
Funkhouser			
Funkhouser			
1974 McLeod and others		1974	Eyestone
Molotch & Lester			
1975 Becker and others		1975	Gormley
Bloj			
Chaffee & Izcaray			
Hubbard and others			
Siune & Borre			
Tipton and others			
Weaver and others			
1976 Becker & McLeod		1976	Beniger
Benton & Frazier			Carey
McCombs			Cobb and others
McCombs & Masel-Walters			Erikson
McCombs & Shaw			McClure & Patterson
Westley			Stimson

Continued

TABLE 1   Continued

| *Public Agenda Setting* | | *Policy Agenda Setting* | |
Year	Authors	Year	Authors
1977	Auh	1977	Walker
	Becker		
	Bowers		
	Chaffee & Wilson		
	Junck and others		
	Kaid and others		
	McCombs		
	McCombs & Shaw		
	McCombs & Shaw		
	Mullins		
	Palmgren & Clarke		
	Shaw		
	Shaw		
	Shaw		
	Shaw & Clemmer		
	Weaver		
	Williams & Larsen		
1978	Sohn	1978	Beniger
	Swanson & Swanson		Erikson
	Williams & Semlak		Lambeth
	Williams & Semlak		Miller
	Zucker		
1979	Becker and others	1979	Hibbs
	Iyengar		Miller and others
	Kipplinger & Roth		Monroe
	Shaw		
	Winter		
1980	Gilberg and others	1980	Erbring and others
	Smith		Soderlund and others
1981	Atwood	1981	Cobb & Elder
	DeGeorge		Lang & Lang
	Eyal		Mansback & Vasquez
	Eyal and others		
	McCombs		
	McCombs		
	Mackuen		
	Mackuen & Coombs		
	Mazur		
	Stone & McCombs		
	Sutherland & Galloway		
	Tardy and others		
	Watt & van den Berg		
	Weaver and others		
	Winter		
	Winter & Eyal		

TABLE 1   Continued

Public Agenda-Setting		Policy Agenda-Setting	
Year	Authors	Year	Authors
1982	Becker Blood Caspi Gadir Winter and others	1982	Black & Snow Iyengar and others Rabinowitz and others
1983	Asp Grunig & Ipes Ramaprasad Williams and others	1983	Beniger Cook and others Lang & Lang Page & Shapiro
1984	Einsiedel and others Iyenger and others Weaver	1984	Beniger Kingdon Manheim
1985	Atwater and others Kraus McCombs & Weaver Neuman & Fryling Protess and others Salwen	1985	Behr & Iyengar Fryling Iyengar & Kinder Neuman
1986	Adams Anokwa & Salwen Boyer Gaddy & Tanjong Hezel and others Iyengar & Kinder Kepplinger and others McCombs & Gilbert Megwa & Brenner Pritchard Salwen Wanta Wright	1986	Leff and others Linsky Linsky and others Manheim
1987	Barkin & Gurevitch Chaffee Lowery & DeFleur Miller O'Keefe & Reid-Nash Shoemaker and others Smith	1987	Iyengar & Kinder

ANALYSIS OF THE
PUBLIC AGENDA-SETTING LITERATURE

The basic conception of agenda-setting was a theoretical idea without much basis in empirical research until the study by McCombs and Shaw (1972) of the media's role in the 1968 presidential campaign. A sample of 100 undecided voters, as "presumably those most open or susceptible to campaign information," were identified and personally interviewed during a three-week period in September-October 1968. These voters' public agenda of campaign issues was measured by aggregating their responses to a survey question: "What are you *most* concerned about these days? That is, regardless of what politicians say, what are the two or three *main* things that you think the government *should* concentrate on doing something about?" (p. 178n). The number of mentions of each of five main campaign issues was utilized to index the public agenda (see Table 2).

McCombs and Shaw concluded from their analyses that the mass media set the campaign agenda for the public, or, in other words, that the media agenda influenced the public agenda. Presumably the public agenda was important in a presidential election because it would determine who one voted for, although McCombs and Shaw did not investigate this consequence of the public agenda.

What was McCombs and Shaw's special contribution? Their methodologies for measuring the two conceptual variables were not new; both content analysis of mass media messages and surveys of public opinion about an issue were common in mass communication research. Neither was McCombs and Shaw's contribution in linking the two methodologies to test the degree of agenda-setting that occurred (Chaffee, 1987). Twenty years earlier, F. James Davis (1952) had combined content analysis, survey research, and real-world variables in testing the public agenda-setting hypothesis. McCombs and Shaw's contribution was in clearly laying out the hypothesis, referring to the process as "agenda-setting," and in following through with further research.

Agenda-setting was conceptualized by McCombs and Shaw as a *process* (even though they examined it cross-sectionally), and this characterization would help lead later communication scholars to include data gathering over time in their analyses of agenda-setting. The additional dimension of time encouraged mass communication scholars to focus on agenda-setting as a process rather than just on questions of media effects (or at least on questions of effects over time). The rise of the agenda-setting paradigm led communication scholars back to the study of public opinion formation, a topic that had increasingly been neglected.

Why Public Agenda-Setting?

The historical content of mass communication research at the time that agenda-setting research began undoubtedly affected how this research issue was conceptualized, which research methodologies were chosen to investigate the process of agenda-setting, and how the resulting research findings were interpreted and shaped to fit with the dominant intellectual concerns of the emerging field of communication science. The influence of these early beginnings of agenda-setting research has cast a long shadow over the scholarly nature of this research front.

TABLE 2
The Public Agenda and the Media Agenda of
Five Main Campaign Issues in the 1968
Chapel Hill Study of the Agenda-Setting Process

Public Agenda (in rank-order, as indicated in a survey of 100 undecided voters)		*Media Agenda (indexed as the number of news articles, editorials, or broadcast stories in nine mass media)*	*Media Agenda (in rank-order)*
1st	Foreign policy	56	1st
2nd	Law and order	33	2nd
3rd	Fiscal policy	11	4th (tie)
4th	Public welfare	11	4th (tie)
5th	Civil rights	11	4th (tie)
—	Other	84	—
Total		206	

SOURCE: Data from McCombs and Shaw (1972).

In 1968, at the time that the McCombs and Shaw (1972) data were gathered, mass communication research had recently changed from being mainly a temporary pursuit of social psychologists (like Kurt Lewin and Carl Hovland), political scientists (like Harold Lasswell), and sociologists (like Paul Lazarsfeld), to becoming predominantly the full-time concern of the new breed of Ph.D.s that were emerging from schools of communication (Rogers, 1986, pp. 96-110). Until about 1960, when doctoral degrees began to be awarded in mass communication, many social scientists were attracted to the study of communication, and while many tarried, few stayed (to paraphrase a remark by Wilbur Schramm). The new communication scholars typically had predoctoral experience in journalism or broadcasting, followed by social science training emphasizing the work of Lewin, Hovland, Lasswell, and Lazarsfeld, plus courses in statistical methods and quantitative research methods. The new breed "knew" from their personal backgrounds that the mass media had effects, even though the scientific findings of the field's four founders generally indicated only minimal effects of the media. This paradox between past professional beliefs versus scientific results sent the new communication scholars off in search of evidence of strong media effects. The broad historical context of mass communication research at the time in which the McCombs/Shaw paradigm was launched therefore helps explain why agenda-setting research became so popular with mass communication scholars.[3]

Distinguishing Issues from Events

What is an *agenda*? It is a list of issues and events that are viewed at a point in time as ranked in a hierarchy of importance. The items on agendas of past study included (1) such *issues* as the war in Vietnam, Watergate, an auto safety law, unemployment, abortion, and drug abuse and (2) such *events* as the Sahel drought, earthquakes, and other natural disasters.

What is an issue? As Lang and Lang (1981) noted: "Without a clear definition, the concept of agenda-setting becomes so all-embracing as to be rendered practically meaningless" (p. 450). A rather wide range of issues have been studied in past agenda-setting research, and little care has been given to defining exactly what an issue is. Most typically, however, public agenda-setting scholars (e.g., McCombs & Shaw, 1972), have investigated general issues like inflation and the war in Vietnam rather than specific news events or media events like a hurricane or a nuclear power plant disaster.

An important step toward pruning the conceptual thicket of what constitutes an agenda item was taken by Shaw (1977), who distinguished between (1) *events*, defined as discrete happenings that are limited by space and time, and (2) *issues*, defined as involving cumulative news coverage of a series of related events that fit together in a broad category. Thus the drug-related deaths of Len Bias and Don Rogers, two young athletes, in 1986 were news events that helped put the issue of drug abuse higher on the national agenda, even though such "real-world" indicators of the drug problem as the total number of drug users in the U.S. population had remained fairly constant for several years. Our perspective is that events are specific components of issues. Both have been investigated in public agenda-setting research (McCombs, 1976), although we conclude that issues have been more often studied than events. The distinction is often difficult to make due to the conceptual confusion in the past regarding just what an issue and an event are. Further, the mass media often fit a news event into a broad category of a larger issue, as they seek to give the event meaning for their audience. For example, a news event like the 1986 *Challenger* explosion was interpreted by the U.S. media into the more general issue of NASA incompetence and the need for higher funding for the U.S. space program (American Association for the Advancement of Science, 1986; Miller, 1987). Similarly, a news event like the 1986 Chernobyl nuclear power plant was interpreted by the U.S. media into the issue of the closed nature of Soviet society (and, yet more broadly, into the issue of U.S./Soviet international conflict).

Is it necessary for an issue to involve contention? Political science scholars in the policy agenda-setting tradition generally think so. For example, Eyestone (1974) stated: "An issue arises when a public with a problem seeks or demands governmental action, and there is public disagreement over the best solution to the problem" (p. 3). Similarly, Cobb and Elder (1971) stated: "An issue is a conflict between two or more identifiable groups over procedural or substantive matters relating to the distribution of positions or resources" (p. 82).

Further scholarly effort should be given to classifying the issues and events that are studied in agenda-setting research. Certainly, a rapid-onset news event like the 1986 U.S. bombing of Libya is markedly different from a slow-onset natural disaster issue like the 1984 Ethiopian drought. A high-salience, short-duration issue like the 1985 TWA hijacking is different from such low-salience issues as the ups and downs of U.S. unemployment or from such long-duration issues as Japanese-U.S. trade conflict in that an agenda item (such as in the case of an election issue) may influence the agenda-setting process, as Auh (1977) demonstrated.

Finally, agenda-setting research should recognize more clearly that each agenda item influences other items on the media agenda and on the public agenda. Today's top news story crowds out yesterday's. The salience of an item on the agenda is "not just an absolute but to some extent a relative matter" (Lang & Lang, 1981, p. 453). Issues compete for attention. Unfortunately, agenda-setting researchers have tended to treat each issue on an agenda as if it were *not* dependent on the other items, which is a serious oversimplification. "Some issues . . . very rarely share space on the same agenda, while others quite regularly travel together" (Crenson, 1971, p. 163). One can appreciate the measurement and conceptual difficulties resulting from such interrelationships of agenda items.

Adding the Public Attitudes Link

Several studies raise the possibility that the mass media may be doing more than just setting the public agenda. Weaver, Graber, McCombs, and Eyal (1981), in a study of the 1976 presidential election, concluded that the mass media affected *voter evaluations*, as well as cognitive images of candidates. Davidson and Parker (1972) found a positive correlation between mass media exposure and public support for members of the U.S. Congress. Mazur (1981) found negative correlations between amount of mass media coverage and U.S. public support for fluoridation and for nuclear power:

> Detailed studies of a few technical controversies suggest that there is at least one simple effect of media coverage on attitudes which works in a reliable manner. When media coverage of a controversy increases, public opposition to the technology in question (as measured by opinion polls) increases; when media coverage wanes, public opposition falls off. (p. 109)

Can we then say that the mass media can change public attitudes, as well as public cognitions (like the public agenda)? Becker and McLeod (1976) proposed a model that suggested that public cognitions (the public agenda) could be a direct effect of the mass media agenda, or an indirect effect of mass media semantic content, mediated by public attitudes. Public attitudes, they suggested, could result either directly from mass media semantic content or indirectly from the media agenda, mediated by public cognitions.

A recent analysis of 12 field experiments on television news concluded that public judgments as well as cognitions may result from mass media agenda-setting. Iyengar and Kinder (1987) concluded that television coverage of U.S. presidential performance not only heightened viewer cognizance of the issues, but also set the standards (by highlighting some issues at the expense of others) by which presidential performance was then judged. The concept employed by Iyengar and Kinder (1987) to explain this power of the media is *priming,* defined by Fiske and Taylor (1984, p. 231) as the effects of prior context on the interpretation and retrieval of information. Iyengar and Kinder (1987) use the concept of priming to mean the changes in the standards that underlie the public's political evaluations. Iyengar and Kinder (1987) see priming as "a possibility at once more subtle and consequential than agenda-setting." They found considerable support for both public agenda-setting and priming hypotheses in their field experiments.

Priming, especially in its broader definition by Fiske and Taylor (1984), addresses the importance of both the mass media agenda and mass media semantic content in affecting public attitudes. If the mass media agenda "primes" readers and viewers by giving salience to certain events, these events are not merely made more salient to the audience. The mass media prime focuses on specific issues raised by a news event in the journalistic search for explanation. This selectivity forces those issues, not just the event, to the forefront of mass media coverage and of, perhaps, personal consideration. Moreover, these "event-issues" are prominently publicized by the media, not in an impartial way, but rather with positive or negative valences. Mass communicators may be "telling it like it is," but issues raised by the event retain their media intensity through positive or negative semantic content. An issue will not move through the priming sequence if it has not aroused public interest. As Downs (1972) observed, "A problem must be dramatic and exciting to maintain public interest because news is 'consumed' by much of the American public (and by publics everywhere) largely as a form of entertainment" (p. 42). Thus priming acts upon public attitude formation both through heavy media coverage (media agenda-setting), by showing people that the issue is important, and, in "successful" event-issues, by demonstrating a kind of entertainment value (semantic content).

Other Influences of the Public Agenda

The mass media are not the only influences on the public agenda, which is one reason the correlation of the mass media with the public's agenda of items is less than perfect. "Social processes other than mass communication also affect the public's judgment of an issue or person as important. For one thing, people talk to one another about social issues, and these conversations may play an important part in their judgments" (Wright, 1986, p. 155). In fact, McLeod, Becker, and Byrnes (1974) found that mass media content had a greater effect in forming the news agendas of individuals who participated in conversations about the topics on the media agenda, than for individuals who did not have such interpersonal communication. This finding is entirely consistent with the conclusions from research on the diffusion of innovations, where an individual's exposure to mass media channels often creates awareness of new ideas, but then interpersonal channels are necessary to persuade the individual to adopt the innovation.

Most scholars of agenda-setting seem to take a contingent view of the process: Agenda-setting does not operate *everywhere*, on *everyone*, and *always* (McCombs, 1976). Why might an individual's agenda *not* be influenced by the mass media agenda?

Low media credibility. A particular individual may regard the media in general, or the particular medium to which the individual is exposed, as low in *credibility* (defined as the degree to which a communication source or channel is perceived by an individual as trustworthy and competent). For instance, a Wall Street lawyer may regard the *National Enquirer* as less credible regarding international news than the *New York Times*; so when the lawyer reads a headline in the *Enquirer* about a new Soviet disarmament proposal, the medium's salience for this news item likely will not be accepted. The individual is informed about the news item by the media, but is not convinced that the item is important.

Conflicting evidence from personal experience or other communication channels about the salience of the issue or news event. Perhaps an individual hears the president of the United States pronounce in a televised address that America is experiencing a drug crisis, but this individual has recently heard CBS News's Dan Rather state that the number of U.S. drug users has remained constant for several years. Such conflicting statements in the media represent content about the drug issue, but are unlikely to raise that issue on the public agenda.

The individual holds different news values than those reflected by the mass medium or media. The individual's reaction to a newspaper headline might be to think, "How could they regard *that* as important news?"

An important step toward understanding why individuals have different issue agendas was taken by McCombs and Weaver (1973) by introducing the notion of a *need for orientation.* Any individual, when issue relevance is high and uncertainty is high, has a high need for orientation. This need leads to greater media exposure, which in turn leads to greater agenda-setting effects. Nevertheless, as McCombs and Weaver (1985) noted, "Such a limited three-part model is far from the full picture of the mass communication process" (p. 102). Future research should seek to understand more clearly the individual cognitive processes that are involved in the agenda-setting process at the individual level.

Assessing Causality

Agenda-setting research has generally found a positive association between the amount of mass media content devoted to an item and the development of a place on the public agenda for that item. The next step in establishing a causal relationship between the media agenda and the public agenda was to seek evidence for the expected time order; if the public agenda preceded media content, the latter could hardly cause the former. The expected time order of the two conceptual variables has been found in several post hoc studies.

Funkhouser (1973a, 1973b) advanced the field of agenda-setting research by investigating a longer time period than in other studies; he utilized years as units of analysis for eight issues that emerged on the public agenda in the United States during the 1960s. The rank-order of these issues on the public agenda corresponded to their degree of mass media coverage.

Such media coverage did not correspond to the "real-world" severity of the agenda item; for example, in the case of drug abuse, mass media coverage began its decline well before the social problem began to become less serious, as indicated by "objective" indicators obtained from extramedia sources. When the mass media coverage of the issue and the real-world severity of the agenda item differed, the public agenda followed the degree of media coverage more closely. Overall, Funkhouser's analysis supported the media agenda moving toward public agenda relationship, although this support was limited to the particular era and issues that he studied (MacKuen, 1981, p. 24).

Real-world indicators are possible confounders of the media agenda moving toward public agenda relationships. A few studies support this view; for example, MacKuen (1981) found a direct influence of real-world indicators on the public agenda, without this relationship going through the media agenda. In contrast, Funkhouser (1973) generally found strong associations between the media agenda and the public agenda, and weaker associations between real-world indicators and either the media agenda or the public agenda.

Unfortunately, relatively few agenda-setting scholars have included real-world indicators in their analysis. We recommend (1) that future agenda-setting research should include real-world indicators of the importance of an agenda item and (2) that research designs should be used in future research that allow for control of possible spurious variables that might confound the media-agenda-moving-toward-public-agenda-moving-toward-policy-agenda relationship. If these two methodological guidelines were followed, progress could be made toward determining the necessary and sufficient conditions under which these relationships hold, and when they do not.

In only a few agenda-setting investigations were the researchers able to control the independent variable of the media agenda as it influenced the public agenda (the dependent variable). An example is a field experiment conducted by Iyengar, Peters, and Kinder (1982), in which families were paid to watch only special television news programs created by the investigators. When national defense was stressed in the television news programs constructed by the investigators, this issue became more salient to the families in the field experiment. A similar agenda-setting "effect" was achieved for the topic of pollution in a second field experiment, and for inflation in a third.

Causality rests on a third factor (in addition to covariance and time order), the degree to which media content has a "forcing quality" on public opinion. Forcing quality is a theoretical matter, rather than an issue solely for empirical exploration.

Further, there is undoubtedly a two-way, mutually dependent relationship between the public agenda and the media agenda in the agenda-setting process. Media gatekeepers have a general idea of the news interests of their audience, and this perceived priority of news interests is directly reflected in the news values with which media personnel decide the media agenda. A few studies, for example, Erbring, Goldenberg, and Miller (1980), have found a two-way relationship between the media agenda and the public agenda. This influencing of the media agenda by the public agenda is a gradual, long-term process through which generalized news values are created. In contrast, the influence of the media agenda on the public agenda for a specific news item is a more direct, immediate cause-effect relationship, especially when the public lacks alternatives (such as personal experience) that might influence their agenda. However, for general agenda issues like inflation, Watergate, and unemployment, where their priority on the public agenda is built up in a slow, accretionary process over many months or years, the nature of the media agenda moving toward public agenda relationship may be very gradual and indirect. Certainly there must be differences from agenda item to agenda item as to how rapidly they climb the public agenda.

If our present reasoning is correct, it is inappropriate to expect a one-way causal relationship of the media agenda on the public agenda, although it might seem to be evidenced when scholars investigate short-term effects of the mass media in communicating a news event. More realistically, both the media agenda and the public agenda are probably mutual causes of each other. Obviously, then, it is a futile oversimplification (in a theoretical sense) to search for agenda-setting *effects* (that is, results of causes) of the mass media agenda. Thus the original reason for scholarly interest in agenda-setting (resulting from the limited-effects model of the mass media) is somewhat misplaced.

Since there is a great deal of variance in the agenda items studied, some items probably can be expected to demonstrate linear, rather than circular, causality. In quick-onset major events, where there typically is little previous public concern, the causal direction is *only* from the media agenda to the public agenda. Unidirectional causality should occur for agenda items that Zucker (1978, p. 227) termed "unobtrusive," that is, events giving rise to issues with which people ordinarily have no direct experience. The less direct experience one has with an agenda issue, the more one must rely upon the mass media for information and an interpretation of the agenda issue. Zucker (1978) found that for unobtrusive issues, salience on the media agenda led to public agenda salience for that item. In the case of obtrusive issues, with which people had greater familiarity, salience on the public agenda led to salience on the media agenda. Zucker's results were confirmed by Eyal (1979), who used factor analysis to categorize agenda items as obtrusive and unobtrusive (Zucker had categorized issues on the basis of his own judgment).

Agenda-Setting as a Process

Presumably, by definition, agenda-setting is a process (a series of events and activities happening through time). However, many past investigations of agenda-setting have depended entirely on one-shot data collection and cross-sectional data analysis, a type of research design particularly unsuited for investigating process. To determine whether the mass media agenda precedes the public agenda, these two variables can hardly be studied at one point in time.

Why has the agenda-setting process often been investigated by mass communication scholars as if it were a nonprocess? Because agenda-setting has been generally treated as one part of the general quest by mass communication scholars for media effects. The overwhelming research orientation of mass communication researchers on effects has structured theory and research mainly in one direction (Rogers, 1986). In the case of public agenda-setting studies, this effects orientation led away from overtime research designs, particularly in the very early research on this topic.

Later studies of the agenda-setting process (1) gathered data on the media agenda and the public agenda at two points in time, and then utilized cross-lagged correlational analysis to gain understanding of process, (2) traced agenda-setting over a wider range of years (e.g., Funkhouser, 1973a, 1973b, discussed previously), and (3) manipulated the media agenda in a field experiment approach (e.g., Iyengar et al., 1982, discussed previously). The methodological progression in agenda-setting research has been from one-shot, cross-sectional studies, to more sophisticated research designs that allow more precise exploration of agenda-setting as process. With the strengthening of research designs, the agenda-setting process has stood out more clearly.

What is the optimum time period in which mass media messages about an issue should preceed the measurement of the public agenda about that issue? Salwen (1985) has pointed out that "even though most agenda-setting researchers have implicitly accepted the notion that audience issue salience is a function of media presentation over time, few researchers have tackled the problem concerning the *amount of time* required for the media to make an issue or a set of issues salient among the mass media audience" (p. 30). Gandy (1982) has argued, "Some kinds of issues or events move easily to the public agenda, others take more time, and the theoretical base of agenda-setting research is incapable of predicting just what that optimal lag should be" (p. 7). Stone (1975) and Winter (1979), who tested several different time lags in order to identify the optimum timing for media content to influence the public agenda, however, report the optimal timing to be about two to four months (Eyal et al., 1981, pp. 214-215). Shoemaker, Wanta, and Leggett (1987), using hierarchical regression analysis found support for optimal time lags of both one and four months.

Salwen, in response to his own challenge (1986), content analyzed three Michigan newspapers for 33 weeks as to their coverage of seven environmental issues, such as disposal of wastes, quality of water, and noise pollution. The public agenda was measured by about 300 telephone interviews conducted in three waves. The week-by-week media agenda had its first effect on the public agenda after the accumulation of five to seven weeks of media coverage of an environmental issue; the peak relationship of the media agenda to the public agenda occurred after eight to ten weeks of media coverage; thereafter the correlations declined with the passage of time. "By simply keeping an issue 'alive' by reporting about it for some duration the media may transmit to the public more than just information, but also a subtle message concerning the legitimacy of such an issue" (Salwen, 1986). The rise, peak, and fall of the media agenda's influence on the public agenda, Salwen (1986) argued, might be parallel to the S-curve found for the diffusion of innovations (Rogers, 1983). Only gradually does a media item spread among members of the public, creating awareness of that topic. Eventually, after two or three months, enough media coverage had accumulated for the issue to rise to high priority on the public agenda, and thereafter the issue dropped slowly on the public agenda with further media coverage decreasing more rapidly (hence the low correlation between the media agenda and the public agenda at this final stage in the agenda-setting process).

Disaggregation of the Units of Analysis

The varied research approaches that were followed in studies of agenda-setting led to findings that lacked a high degree of integration, so their meta-research is thus more difficult. One reviewer of public agenda-setting research by mass communication scholars concluded: "Past research lacks uniformity in design. Many of the studies share few, and often only incidental, common denominators. . . . Research on agenda-setting branches off, uncontrolled, in many directions" (Eyal, 1981, p. 231). So despite the general acceptance of the McCombs-Shaw paradigm for investigating public agenda-setting, many specific variations on a theme (such as in the type of agenda items studied, the particular media that are content analyzed, or the unit of analysis) are represented in the research literature on this topic. Perhaps an even greater variability in future research on public agenda-setting is needed. One such direction for further variability concerns disaggregation.

Many of the public agenda-setting studies, particularly the early investigations in this research tradition, were highly aggregate in their data analysis. All members of a public were pooled in computing the relative salience of various agenda items, as if individual differences in item rankings and in exposure to the media agenda either did not exist or else were unimportant. Certainly, the public agenda is not a homogeneous aggregate, and some scholars of agenda-setting (e.g., McLeod et al., 1974) began to measure and investigate individual differences in the priority accorded an agenda item. Media access and exposure are, of course, determinants of individual differences in the priority given to various news events. How could extensive coverage of the law-and-order issue in the *Raleigh Times* possibly affect a resident of Chapel Hill who does not subscribe to this newspaper? Or affect an individual who reads only comics and the sports section?

The McCombs and Shaw (1972) study aggregated the data on both the media agenda and the public agenda into just five issue categories, one of which—foreign policy—included 10% of the media content dealing with the 1968 presidential campaign. What if a greater number of more precise agenda categories, say 20 or 120, had been utilized? Less information would have been discarded in the aggregating of both individuals' responses (about the public agenda) and the mass media content. Unfortunately, "the strength of the correlations between public and media agendas varies with the number of categories or items arranged in any list of priorities—the longer the list, the lower the correlation" (Gandy, 1982, p. 6). And, unfortunately, the fewer the number of agenda items studied, the less useful the findings because of their highly aggregated nature.

One means of data disaggregation in the early research on agenda-setting would have been to use individual respondents, rather than campaign issues, as the unit of analysis. After all, the process of agenda-setting presumably occurs (or does not occur) for an individual who is exposed to the media agenda and then forms his or her own agenda. McCombs and Shaw (1972) called for such an individual-level analysis in future research on agenda-setting, but they did not perform such an investigation with their own data. Within two years, however, McLeod, Becker, and Byrnes (1974) reported an agenda-setting study in which individual differences were pursued. Several later studies of agenda-setting have investigated individual differences.

The problem of aggregated numbers is also important for focusing our attention on the subjectivity of audience members. Subjectivity, which acknowledges the different backgrounds and experiences that each person uses to interpret mass media messages, suggests that the public must be disaggregated by attributes as much as is feasible. Someone who has been "sensitized" to an issue previous to mass media coverage of that issue will likely respond differently from someone who has not been exposed. People seek out and attend to those messages that have relevancy for them.

McCombs (1981a) stated: "Agenda-setting is not a universal influence affecting all issues among all persons at all times." Researchers can investigate differences (1) among *agenda items* (as in the early agenda-setting research), (2) among *individuals* (who rate an issue high or low on their personal agenda), and (3) over *time*. We can also look at media differences in agenda-setting, such as television versus newspapers, as has been done by McCombs (1977) and several other scholars.

A general trend in agenda-setting studies across the 15 years of our analysis is toward disaggregation of the units of analysis, so as to allow a wider range of research approaches to be utilized.

Wider Variability Across Agenda Items

The relative influence of the mass media in setting the public agenda for an agenda item depends greatly on whether the event is (1) of major importance or not and (2) a rapid-onset type versus a gradual, slowly developing topic. In a major, quick-onset news event, the importance of the news event is immediately apparent. Almost at once the news event jumps to the top of the media agenda and remains there for some time. The public usually has no other communication channels (such as personal experience) through which to learn of these news events. So the mass media would be expected to place the news event high on the public agenda quickly.

In the case of a relatively slow-onset news issue like a drought, the media often play an important role in "creating" the issue. Typically, the mass media discover the slowly developing news event through a particularly spectacular message about it, which serves as a "triggering device" (Cobb & Elder, 1983, p. 85) in setting the media agenda. In the case of the Ethiopian drought, a film report of a refugee camp at Korem by Mohamed Amin was shown by the BBC and then by NBC in October 1984. Immediately, other U.S. mass media began to feature this disaster as a major news issue, and rather quickly the public considered the Ethiopia drought an important issue. Relief activities by the U.S. government and by rock musicians (who attracted massive financial support from the public) soon followed. In this case, the mass media helped to "create" the news event, set the public agenda, and facilitate amelioration of suffering in Ethiopia through fund raising.

Much public agenda-setting research, especially the studies reported in the 1970s, involved a rather narrow range of political issues. This primary emphasis on political issues is understandable, in the sense that a great many media news events *are* political in nature. But much other news content is not directly political in nature, and these news events should also be included in agenda-setting research, in order to determine the generalizability of public agenda-setting across various types of media content. Wanta (1986), for example, studied the public agenda-setting role of dominant news photographs.

What role does commercial advertising play in the agenda-setting process? For some agenda items, advertising must be very important. For example, the tremendous advertising campaigns for microcomputers in the 1980s by Apple, IBM, and other manufacturers certainly must have raised the American public's consciousness of computers. In recent years, microcomputers represented one of the most advertised products on U.S. television. Despite the obviously important role of advertising as an agenda-setter for certain issues, advertising's role in the agenda-setting process has received very little attention by communication scholars other than that given to political campaign spots. Exceptions are Sutherland and Galloway (1981) and Hauser (1986), who investigated how a consumer's agenda of products is affected by advertising.

In a sense, one of the strongest pieces of evidence of the media's agenda-setting influence may consist of the fact that issues and events that are completely ignored by the mass media do not register on the public agenda. As McCombs (1976) noted: "This basic, primitive notion of agenda-setting is a truism. If the media tell us nothing about a topic or event, then in most cases it simply will not exist on our personal agenda or in our life space" (p. 3). Unfortunately, it is extremely difficult or impossible for scholars to investigate such a "non-agenda-setting" process because of the problem of identifying news events or issues that are not reported by the mass media, which by definition cannot be measured by a content analysis of the media.

Nevertheless, there may be an implication for future communication research in the idea of non-agenda-setting. Most of the issues and events investigated in past agenda-setting research are of very high salience. For example, such election issues as civil rights, unemployment, Vietnam, and inflation have been studied, along with such news events as Watergate. These blockbusters are hardly typical of the full range of media content. Future scholars of the agenda-setting process should include issues and events that receive much less media attention (ranging down to those that are hardly mentioned in the media) and that may only barely register on the public agenda. Such research poses special measurement difficulties for its investigators, as it approaches the non-agenda-setting process, but it may provide improved understanding of just how limited our present knowledge of agenda-setting is. Perhaps public agenda-setting by the mass media only occurs in the case of transfixing issues and blockbuster events that receive very heavy media attention over an extended period of time. In any event, it is certainly dangerous to extrapolate intuitively from the present findings about agenda-setting for high-salience issues and events to those of much less salience.

Salwen (1986) chose noise pollution as one of his seven environmental issues of study because it received very little media attention. He found it to be low on the public agenda, as expected in light of its low priority on the media agenda. By including a low-salience agenda item, this scholar was uniquely able to obtain further evidence of public agenda-setting by the mass media. We recommend that a wider variability across agenda items should be incorporated in future agenda-setting research.

CRITIQUE OF THE
POLICY AGENDA LITERATURE

Scholars investigating policy agendas have concentrated on how a political issue gets on the agenda of a city, state, or national government. Often a case study approach is followed in an attempt to reconstruct the main events and decisions in the process of political policy determination. An example is Crenson's (1971) investigation of how the issue of air pollution got on the policy agenda of two cities, Gary and East Chicago.

Concomitant with interest in the public opinion-policy relationship has been interest in the influence that the mass media agenda has on U.S. foreign policy. As Cohen (1965) stated:

> The press functions in the political process like the bloodstream in the human body, enabling the [foreign policy] process that we are familiar with today to continue on, by linking up all the widely-scattered parts, putting them in touch with one another, and supplying them with political and intellectual nourishment. (p. 196)

In recent years, scholars often incorporate the media agenda, along with other variables, in research on policy agenda-setting. For example, Lang and Lang (1983, pp. 58-59) found that Watergate was an issue that required months of news coverage before it got onto the public agenda. Then, finally, Watergate became an agenda issue for action by U.S. governmental officials. In this particular case of policy agenda-setting, public agenda-setting by the mass media led to government action, and then policy formation.

Further exploitation of both the public opinion moving toward policymaker and mass media moving toward policymaker relationships was advanced by Cohen (1963), who concentrated on the agendas of elites responsible for foreign policy. Yet public opinion as a meaningful determinant of elite agendas was not clearly established in the way that communication scholars were able to replicate the media agenda moving toward public agenda link (e.g., stricter federal laws regulating campaign financing). So there may be various longer-range consequences of the mass media agenda than just forming the public agenda. But the main point of the Lang and Lang analysis of the agenda-building process for Watergate is that the mass media were only one element, along with government and the public, involved in a process through which the elements reciprocally influenced each other. Such multiple agenda-setting for an issue, with complex feedback and two-way interaction of the main components in the agenda-setting process, probably occurs in many cases. The media's influence upon policymakers might be expected to be greater for quick-onset issues when the media have priority access to information; alternatively, when policy elites control the information sources, they might be expected to set the media agenda.

An example of policy agenda-setting research that illustrates the impact of policy elite agendas upon media agendas is Walker's (1977) study of setting the agenda in the U.S. Senate. He commented:

> Once a new problem begins to attract attention and is debated seriously by other senators, it takes on a heightened significance in the mass media, and its sponsors, beyond the satisfaction of advancing the public interest as they see it, also receive important political rewards that come from greatly increased national exposure. (p. 426)

Walker (1977) investigated the policy agenda-setting process for the auto safety legislation enacted by the U.S. Senate in 1966. Important prerequisites to this policy decision were (1) four or five years of increasing traffic fatality rates in the early 1960s, following 15 years of decreasing rates; (2) safety research that showed the potential of designing safer autos and adding seat belts, rather than trying just to improve driver performance; and (3) an activist senator, Abraham Ribicoff, who launched a subcommittee hearing, hired Ralph Nader, and proposed legislation that was to lead to an unprecedented expansion of the federal government's activities to protect the safety of its citizens.

Walker (1977) plotted (1) the annual number of traffic deaths per million miles driven, and (2) the annual number of column inches on traffic safety in the *New York Times*, for a 20-year period including the passage of the 1966 auto safety law. A massive upsurge of the *New York Times* content on safety occurred in 1966, with such coverage continuing at a high level thereafter. Walker (1977) concluded: "The newspaper was reacting to events, not stimulating the controversy or providing leadership" (p. 435). A similar time order, with mass media content reacting to policymakers' attention to an issue rather than leading it, was reported by Walker (1977) for two other safety policies: (1) the 1969 Coal Mine Health and Safety Act, and (2) the 1970 Occupational Health and Safety Act. Note, however, that Walker's investigation did not include a measure of public opinion toward traffic safety (that is, the public agenda), a variable that might have considerably enriched his analysis. Other studies in the agenda-building research tradition have generally included measures of the public agenda over time (Beniger, 1984).

An illustration of the influence of the media agenda on the public agenda, and then on the agenda of policymakers, is provided by Cook et al. (1983). A single issue, fraud and abuse in home health care, was investigated through pre-post interviews with a sample of Chicago citizens in a field experimental design (with individuals randomly assigned to watch a television news program dealing with the issue of study versus another television program). The television broadcast on the home health care problem set the public agenda. In addition, a small sample of government policymakers (city and state officials in agencies relevant to the home health care issue) were also interviewed after the TV broadcast; the results indicated that the news program also set the public policymakers' agenda. Further support is provided by Leff, Protess, and Brooks (1986), Gormley (1975), and other studies of policy agenda-setting.

In a recent study of mass media impact upon federal policymaking, Linsky (1986) concluded that the media are far more important than had previously been suggested. Out of 500 former government officials surveyed and 20 federal policymakers interviewed, 96% said that the media had an impact on federal policy. A majority considered the impact to be substantial. Linsky (1986) concluded that the media can speed up the decision-making process by positive issue coverage, as well as slow down the process by negative coverage.

Policy agenda-setting researchers typically operationalize public opinion by gathering survey or poll data, and then correlate this public agenda measure with the policy positions or actions of elites. The correlations assume that policymakers are influenced by surveys of public opinion. As Cohen (1983) noted, this assumption is often not borne out. In interviews with U.S. State Department policymakers, Cohen showed that public opinion is "sensed" through personal intuition and experience, not by utilizing public poll data. Statements by policymakers such as "I have reservations about computer methods of assessing opinions," and "You can't run a government on IBM machines," led Cohen (1983, pp. 67-68) to conclude that primary sources of "sensing" public opinion for policymakers in the U.S. State Department are interpersonal networks of colleagues and mass media reporters, and media news stories. According to Cohen (1983), State Department policymakers consider the media agenda to be the public agenda. Therefore, while public opinion poll results over time might be valuable as "objective" public agenda measures, the media agenda is considered by policymakers to be a better indicator of the public agenda.

We conclude our review of policy agenda-setting research with three generalizations: (1) The public agenda, once set by, or reflected by, the media agenda, influences the policy agenda of elite decision makers, and, in some cases, policy implementation; (2) the media agenda seems to have direct, sometimes strong, influence upon the policy agenda of elite decision makers, and, in some cases, policy implementation; and (3) for some issues, the policy agenda seems to have a direct, sometimes strong, influence upon the media agenda.

DISCUSSION AND CONCLUSIONS

In this final section, we shall (1) summarize our conclusions in the form of lessons learned about the agenda-setting process, (2) integrate agenda-setting more closely with other mass communication theories, and (3) state our suggestions for future directions for agenda-setting research and theory.

Lessons Learned

What are the main theoretical and methodological lessons learned from the past 15 years of research on the agenda-setting process?

(1) The mass media influence the public agenda. This proposition, implied by the Cohen (1963) metaphor, has been generally supported by evidence from most public agenda-setting investigations, which cover a very wide range of agenda items, types of publics, and points in time.

(2) An understanding of media agenda-setting is a necessary prerequisite to comprehending how the mass media agenda influences the public agenda.

(3) The public agenda, once set by, or reflected by, the media agenda, influences the policy agenda of elite decision makers, and, in some cases, policy implementation.

(4) The media agenda seems to have direct, sometimes strong, influence upon the policy agenda of elite decision makers, and, in some cases, policy implementation.

(5) For some issues the policy agenda seems to have a direct, sometimes strong, influence upon the media agenda.

(6) The methodological progression in agenda-setting research has been from one-shot, cross-sectional studies to more sophisticated research designs that allow more precise exploration of agenda-setting as a process.

(7) A general trend in agenda-setting studies across the more than 15 years of their history is toward disaggregation of the units of analysis, so as to allow (1) a wider range of research approaches to be utilized and (2) a more precise understanding of the process of agenda-setting.

(8) Scholars in the two main research traditions on the agenda-setting process, especially those studying public agenda-setting, need to become more fully aware of each others' research and theory, so that agenda-setting research can become more of an integrated whole (our analysis of the citations by the two research traditions shows there is little intellectual interchange in this direction).

Relating Agenda-Setting to Mass Communication Theories

McQuail and Windhal (1981), in their book about mass communication models, concluded: "It would seem that agenda-setting theory has a number of boundaries with other approaches, and that these boundaries are not clearly marked. It has affinities with the position of Noelle-Neumann [1984, the spiral of silence], the uses and gratifications approach, and the news diffusion model." (One could add bandwagon research, as well.) The authors of the present chapter feel that the intellectual boundaries that have been placed around the scholarly field of agenda-setting research should be broken down so that conceptual and methodological ideas could be exchanged with other fields of mass communication theory and research. Here we suggest some of the more obvious interfaces that could then be exploited in future work.

If the agenda-setting process is influenced by the public's needs and interests, then the uses and gratifications research tradition is obviously related to agenda-setting (Shaw, 1979). On the other hand, if an agenda item is selected by mass media professionals and then featured in their media, leading to its climb on the public agenda, the needs of individual members of the public are less important in the agenda-setting process. Uses and gratifications on how the media agenda is set is a relatively underdeveloped research topic, so it might seem difficult at present to evaluate how applicable the uses and gratifications approach might to be agenda-setting: If an individual's needs for information about some topic do not match with the media agenda for that topic (however the media agenda is set), the mass media will have little influence in setting the public agenda for that particular agenda item, for that individual.

Both uses and gratifications and the theory of media-system dependency (Ball-Rokeach, 1985) posit an active audience member, rather than the general view of a passive audience member implied in agenda-setting research. *Media-system dependency* is defined as the degree to which an individual relies on a particular mass medium or a class of mass media to obtain information to fulfill that individual's goals. Media-system dependency is relevant to agenda-setting in a similar sense to the way in which uses and gratifications research is relevant: The media will only transfer an issue agenda to those individuals whose goals are similar to that which the media offers. The lesson for agenda-setting research? Differentiate not only the audience (to individuals) but also the media agenda, by events and issues. Without disaggregation, media impact will be diluted or omnipotent, when in fact it probably varies from individual to individual and from agenda item to agenda item. The general trends in agenda-setting research design, encouragingly, have been in this very direction of disaggregation. Further sensitivity to disaggregating units of analyses will help deepen our understanding of the agenda-setting process. The goal, in other words, is what Przeworski and Teune (1970) call "thick analysis."

The agenda-setting notion has been applied, we believe usefully, to better understand the role of mass media, public opinion, and policymakers in society. The concept also has potential applicability to other types of social systems than just societies. For example, an agenda-setting process must occur in an organization, and, in fact, must be fundamental to understanding how change occurs in an organization. In the past decade, a small set of organizational investigations have utilized the agenda-setting concept to understand how an organization begins the process of adopting (or rejecting) an innovation. Strictly speaking, agenda-setting is continuously under way in every organization, as organizational problems, which may create a perceived need for an innovation, are identified and defined, and then the environment is searched for potential solutions (including innovations) that may help solve the high-priority problems (Rogers, 1983, p. 363). Sometimes, awareness of an innovation by one or several individuals in an organization may create a need that otherwise would not exist. Following the agenda-setting step in the innovation process in organizations, the problem from the organization's agenda is matched with some innovation, and then the innovation is implemented (that is, put into use).

On the basis of his study of legislative processes in the U.S. Senate, Walker (1977) concluded: "Those who manage to shape the legislature agenda are able to magnify their influence many times over by determining the focus of attention and energy in the entire political process" (p. 445). The agenda-setting role in an organization (or any other system) is a tremendously powerful one. Thus study of the agenda-setting process in any system—including society—is, in a broader sense, research on the process of power.

The agenda-setting approach may similarly be a useful method for investigating foreign policy behavior, a dependent variable of longtime interest to scholars of international relations. Power, after all, has remained a central concept in most theories of international relations. Moreover, foreign policy analysis has suffered from a theoretical impasse that has caused at least one international relations scholar to question whether foreign policy analysis is now "a discredited pseudo-science" (Smith, 1986). The policy agenda-setting approach, applied widely to the study of local, state, and national issues, may likewise prove fruitful at the level of international policy analysis. This approach is similar to Rosenau's (1980) conception of international politics as four "issue areas" representing vertical political systems. This emphasis on issues and agendas is further developed by Rosenau (1987) and by Mansbach and Vasquez (1981), who move from studying the issue of power to the power of issues.

Other communication theories could well be related to agenda-setting research: persuasion (Reardon, 1987), the diffusion of innovations (Rogers, 1983), pseudoevents, pluralistic ignorance, and bandwagon effects. But such discussions are beyond our present scope.

Future Directions for Agenda-Setting Research and Theory

At the beginning of this chapter, we quoted Iyengar and Kinder (1987) as stating that "agenda-setting may be an apt metaphor, but it is no theory." This might seem like a rather gloomy assessment, given the 15 years of research activities that have occurred since the McCombs and Shaw (1972) study. Why haven't agenda-setting researchers contributed to greater theoretic progress (assuming that Professors Iyengar and Kinder might be at least partly correct in their pessimistic assessment)? One fundamental reason is because much greater effort by agenda-setting scholars has been devoted to conducting empirical investigations than to furthering theoretical development. The research activity has generally moved toward improved measurement of media agendas, public agendas, and policy agendas; toward more adequately capturing the over-time processual aspects of agenda-setting; and toward better statistical and other analytical techniques for controlling possibly spurious relationships linking the three concepts of media agendas, public agendas, and policy agendas. However, we feel there has been a very incomplete "digestion" of the growing set of research findings about agenda-setting into a theory of agenda-setting. Here is a research front in which the empirical building blocks of theoretic advance have been going relatively unutilized. Agenda-setting research needs a thorough meta-research analysis much more than it needs a 154th empirical study.

A three-by-three matrix is one way of looking at the "holes" in research on the media agenda, the public agenda, and the policy agenda. Nine possible relationships exist: the media's influence upon itself, the public, and policymakers; the public's influence upon itself, the media, and policymakers; and policymakers' influence upon themselves, the media, and the public. Most agenda-setting studies have appeared in the three cells that represent the media to public, media to policy, and public to policy agenda relationships. Although research conceptualizing the policy agenda as a dependent variable is increasing, studies treating the policy agenda as an independent variable are exceedingly rare. Such analyses have been suggested: Cohen (1983), in his investigation of the U.S. State Department, noted that what policymakers release to the media as "public relations" is often reinterpreted by those same policymakers when it is published as "feedback from the public" about the policy issue in question (p. 178). Such conceptualization reveals more empty than full matrix cells.

Underrepresented are studies treating the mass media as a dependent variable. Especially if centered on issues for which optimum governmental influence would be hypothesized—as in the case of fast-breaking events when governmental sources disclose little information, or gradual, accretionary issues upon which governmental sources are vital—knowledge of the antecedents to the media agenda could contribute to our insight regarding the mass media in modern society.

Some research designs, particularly recent longitudinal studies, cover several of the squares of the agenda matrix simultaneously. Similarly, studies that deliberately approach their place of the agenda matrix to seek explication of contingency conditions *within* a cell, and, in addition, draw conclusions that serve to explain the relationships *between* cells deserve attention. The former specifies the conditions under which that influence will be consistent, while the latter seeks generalizations that inform us about crucial interactions in society.

Recommendations

We now turn to a series of specific recommendations for future research on the agenda-setting process.

(1) *Improvements are needed in measuring public agendas.* Depending on a single survey question to assess such an important concept in agenda-setting research, and one that is so complex, amounts to resting a very large research superstructure on a single, rather thin need. Certainly the exact wording of the question asked respondents about the nature of their priorities, is crucial. For example, Gandy (1982) noted:

> Black people, who have tended to set themselves apart from, and in opposition to the policies and concerns of the Reagan administration, would give one response to the question: "What are the most important problems facing the government today?", and quite another to the question, "What are the most important problems facing black people today?" (p. 6)

A triangulation approach to measuring public agendas, in which two or more different operations are utilized to measure the concept, will be an improvement over just the single, open-ended question that has been used in most past research.

(2) *Future research should seek to understand more clearly the cognitive processes that are involved in the individual-level agenda-setting process.*

(3) *Future agenda-setting research should include real-world indicators of the importance of an agenda item* (for example, the number of drug users in the United States, or the number of deaths due to AIDS). Rosengren (1974, 1977, 1983) makes a good case for the inclusion of "objective indicators," as do Gaddy and Tanbjong (1986). Real-world indicators of the importance of an agenda item may be one useful predictor of the media agenda, but they do not explain much variance in the priorities of items on the media agenda in research to date (Adams, 1986).

(4) *Future investigations should use research designs that allow for control of possible spurious variables that might confound the media-agenda-moving-toward-public-agenda-moving-toward-policy-agenda relationship.*

(5) *Future agenda-setting research should be carried out in a wider range of nations.* At present, research on the agenda-setting process has been conducted in 12 nations (Salwen, 1985). Most of these countries have been democratic societies in the First World (i.e., the United States, Denmark, Canada, and Australia); there have been too few agenda-setting studies in developing nations (Anokwa & Salwen, 1986; Chaffee & Izcaray, 1975). Does the agenda-setting process operate in approximately similar ways in a military dictatorship in the Third World, such as Korea, Chile, or Libya, or in a socialist nation, such as Cuba or Russia? The parochial history of agenda-setting research deprives us of learning to what extent the media agenda, public agenda, and policy agenda in other societies differ from, or resemble, those found in the United States. Future research in other countries, preferably in a comparative design, could contribute toward our understanding of how the mass media, via public opinion, influence society as well as interaction between policymakers and the media.

(6) *A wider variability across agenda issues (and nonissues) should be incorporated in future agenda-setting research.* Thoughtful criticisms have called for structural analyses of the mass media industry (Gitlin, 1978). Other observers have described the proliferation of direct media effects studies at the intellectual expense of studying the *process* of media-society dynamics (Rogers, 1986). We now have two rich traditions of relatively short-term agenda-setting studies, yet little empirical research on describing long-range media socialization of individuals such as the indoctrination of "worldviews." Study of such longer-term impacts of the mass media can benefit from past research and theory on such short-term indirect effects as agenda-setting. The scope of inquiry on the agenda-setting process should be lengthened in time, so as to determine how adequately the conceptual framework for agenda-setting summarized in this chapter will apply to that set of public agenda items (like U.S.-Soviet conflict, world population, and domestic unemployment) that seem to remain on the U.S. public agenda year after year.

(7) *Future agenda-setting research should include analyses of the media agenda, in addition to studying policy and public agenda-setting. The* impressive research traditions of agenda-setting strongly suggest that the

topic should be given broad theoretical inclusion in mass communication textbooks. Yet our review of Curran, Gurevitch, and Woollacott (1979), DeFleur and Dennis (1985), Dominick (1983), Emery and Smythe (1986), and Pember (1983) shows that this inclusion is not the case. All five texts present the basic notion of the agenda-setting process and typically review one or two agenda-setting studies. The coverage, however, is only two or three pages in each textbook. One might conclude from these texts that agenda-setting is not important for understanding how the mass media affect society. We suggest that the theory, method, and contingencies of agenda-setting should receive far more attention in mass communication texts.

As pointed out elsewhere in this chapter, initial interest in research on the public agenda-setting process was stimulated by scholars who were questioning the limited direct effects of the mass media, and who thus searched for indirect effects. This expectation now seems to have been fulfilled: The media do indeed have important indirect effects in setting the public agenda. But how could the mass media have relatively few direct effects, and at the same time have strong indirect effects in setting the public's agenda? McQuail and Windahl (1981) stated:

> This hypothesis [agenda-setting] would seem to have escaped the doubts which early empirical research cast on almost any notion of powerful mass media effects, mainly because it deals primarily with learning and not with attitude change or directly with opinion change. (p. 62)

In other words, individuals learn information from the mass media about which agenda items are more important than others; this task is accomplished by the mass media, even though research shows these media are much less capable of directly changing attitudes and opinions. These general research results from agenda-setting research make sense in an intuitive way. Therefore, the theory of McCombs and Shaw (1972) that proposes the media agenda would influence the public agenda, drawn from the Cohen (1963) metaphor, has been largely supported by some 102 studies in the public agenda-setting tradition.

Here we see the main intellectual significance of agenda-setting research. No scholarly issue has been so important to the field of mass communication research as that of the research for media effects. The actual issue driving the mass communication field for the past 30 years or so has been this one: Why can't we find evidence for mass media effects? Agenda-setting research is viewed as important by many mass communication scholars because it has established that the media *do* have an indirect effect, public agenda-setting. This conclusion contains the germ of a lead for future research: Mass communication scholars should investigate indirect media effects on individual knowledge, rather than direct media effects on attitude and behavior change. Obviously, there are many other potential types of indirect media effects on knowledge than just agenda-setting.

We have called for the closer integration of the two research traditions on agenda-setting. Scholars concentrating on public agenda-setting should ask themselves, "So what?" To answer this question, they must become concerned with the policy agenda. Likewise, policy agenda-setting scholars should look not just to the media agenda, but also to factors that determine the public agenda. In short, future research on components of agenda-setting should realize that an integrated research approach can better lead to theoretical understanding of the processes of influence in societies.

NOTES

1. In order for a research publication to be included in our synthesis of studies listed in Table 1, it was necessary for it to focus on variables related to one of three concepts: (1) the media agenda, usually measured by a content analysis of the mass media, (2) the public agenda, usually measured by an audience survey, and (3) the policy agenda, as might be indexed by interviews with public officials, from legislative records, and so on. We did not consider it necessary for the author(s) of a research publication included in Table 1 (1) to use the term *agenda-setting* in the title (for example, Miller et al., 1979), or (2) to cite other publications on agenda-setting. We do not include convention papers in our literature synthesis unless they were presented so recently that they could not yet have been published in a scientific journal. Our categorization of the publications in Table 1 into the two research traditions is based mainly on what we considered their main dependent variable to be (public agenda-setting versus policy agenda-setting), although this distinction was not very clear-cut for several publications). Moreover, a number of the later publications measured both public and policy agendas.

2. The tradition of inquiry into media agendas, though it has exhibited neither the continuity nor the quantity of work that characterizes the other two traditions, is nevertheless important for understanding processes of societal influence. In a forthcoming work, the present authors consider the effects of various factors upon media agendas, including structural dependency, gatekeepers, and particularly influential mass media, real-world indicators of the importance of an agenda item, and spectacular news events that act as powerful symbols to affect the media agenda for the issue of AIDS in the United States.

3. There are other possible reasons for the rapid take-off of the invisible college of public agenda-setting scholars: For example, a number of these scholars might have independently invented the idea of agenda-setting research at about the same time. At least one such case occurred when G. Ray Funkhouser (1973a, 1973b) reported his research on public agenda-setting during the 1960s; he was unaware of the McCombs/Shaw paradigm until his research was in the publication stage. We conclude, however, that not much other independent investigation of the agenda-setting process occurred on the basis of the frequent citations to McCombs and Shaw by the public agenda-setting research tradition. It is true that the policy agenda-setting research tradition was growing up almost without knowledge of the McCombs/Shaw paradigm, although this parallel tradition was inspired by the same metaphor. An equally intriguing question is why the publication by Davis (1952) went virtually unnoticed.

REFERENCES

Adams, W. C. (1986). Whose lives count? TV coverage of natural disasters. *Journal of Communication, 36,* 113-122.
Almond, G. A. (1950). *The American people and foreign policy.* New York: Harcourt Brace.
American Association for the Advancement of Science. (1986). *Media coverage of the shuttle disaster: A critical look.* Washington, DC: Author.

Anokwa, K., & Salwen, M. B. (1986). *Newspaper agenda-setting among elites and non-elites in Ghana.* Paper presented at the annual meeting of the International Division of the Association for Education in Journalism and Mass Communication, Norman, OK.

Asp, K. (1983). The struggle for the agenda: Party agenda, media agenda, and voter agenda in the 1979 Swedish election campaign. *Communication Research, 10*(3), 333-355.

Atwater, T., Salwen, M. B., & Anderson, R. B. (1985). Media agenda-setting with environmental issues. *Journalism Quartery, 62*(2), 393-397.

Atwood, L. E. (1981). From press release to voting reasons: Tracing the agenda in a congressional campaign. In D. Nimmo (Ed.), *Communication yearbook 4.* New Brunswick, NJ: Transaction.

Auh, T. S. (1977). *Issue conflict and mass media agenda-setting.* Unpublished doctoral dissertation, Indiana University, Bloomington.

Ball-Rokeach, S. J. (1985). The origins of individual media-system dependency: A sociological framework. *Communication Research, 12,* 485-510.

Ball-Rokeach, S. J., & Cantor, M. G. (Eds.). (1986). *Media, audience, and social structure.* Newbury Park, CA: Sage.

Barkin, S. M., & Gurevitch, M. (1987). Out of work and on the air: Television news of unemployment. *Critical Studies in Mass Communication, 4,* 1-20.

Bauer, R. A., de Sola Pool, I., & Dexter, L. A. (1963). *American business and public policy: The politics of foreign trade.* New York: Atherton.

Becker, L. B. (1977). The impact of issue saliences. In D. L. Shaw & M. E. McCombs (Eds.), *The emergence of American public issues: The agenda-setting function of the press* (pp. 121-131). St. Paul, MN: West.

Becker, L. B. (1982). The mass media and citizen assessment of issue importance: A reflection on agenda-setting research. In D. C. Whitney, E. Wartella, & S. Windahl (Eds.), *Mass communication review yearbook 3* (pp. 521-536). Newbury Park, CA: Sage.

Becker, L. B., McCombs, M. E., & McLeod, J. M. (1975). The development of political cognitions. In S. H. Chaffee (Ed.), *Political communication: Issues and strategies for research* (pp. 21-63). Newbury Park, CA: Sage.

Becker, L. B., & McLeod, J. M. (1976). Political consequences of agenda-setting. *Mass Communication Research, 3,* 8-15.

Becker, L. B., Weaver, D. H., Graber, D. A., & McCombs, M. E. (1979). Influence on public agendas. In S. Kraus (Ed.), *The great debates: Carter vs. Ford 1976* (pp. 418-428). Bloomington: Indiana University Press.

Behr, R. L., & Iyengar, S. (1985). Television news, real-world cues, and changes in the public agenda. *Public Opinion Quarterly, 49,* 38-57.

Beniger, J. R. (1976). Winning the presidential nomination: National polls and state primary elections, 1936-1972. *Public Opinion Quarterly, 40,* 22-38.

Beniger, J. R. (1978). Media content as social indicators: The Greenfield Index of agenda-setting. *Communication Research, 5,* 437-453.

Beniger, J. R. (1983). *Trafficking in drug users: Professional exchange networks in the control of deviance.* New York: Cambridge University Press.

Beniger, J. R. (1984). Mass media, contraceptive behavior, and abortion: Toward a comprehensive model of subjective social change. In C. F. Turner & E. Martin (Eds.), *Surveying subjective phenomena* (Vol. 2, pp. 475-500). New York: Russell Sage Foundation.

Benton, M., & Frazier, P. J. (1976). The agenda setting function of the mass media at three levels of "information holding." *Communication Research, 3*(3), 261-274.

Black, E. R., & Snow, P. (1982). The political agendas of three newspapers and city governments. *Canadian Journal of Communication, 8,* 11-25.

Bloj, A. G. (1975). Into the wild blue yonder: Behavioral implications of agenda setting for air travel. In M. E. McCombs & G. Stone (Eds.), *Studies in agenda setting.* Syracuse, NY: Syracuse University, Newhouse Communications Research Center.

Blood, W. (1982). Agenda setting: A review of the theory. *Media Information Australia, 26,* 3-12.

Bowers, T. A. (1973). Newspaper political advertising and the agenda-setting function. *Journalism Quarterly, 50,* 552-556.

Bowers, T. A. (1977). Candidate advertising: The agenda is the message. In D. L. Shaw & M. E. McCombs (Eds.), *The emergence of American public issues: The agenda-setting function of the press* (pp. 53-67). St. Paul, MN: West.

Boyer, P. J. (1986). Famine in Ethiopia: The TV accident that exploded. In M. Emery & T. C. Smythe (Ed), *Readings in mass communication: Concepts and issues in the mass media.* Dubuque, IA: Brown.

Carey, J. (1976). How media shape campaigns. *Journal of Communication, 26*, 50-57.

Caspi, D. (1962). The agenda-setting function of the Israeli press. *Knowledge: Creation, Diffusion, Utilization, 3*(3), 401-414.

Chaffee, S. H. (1987). Assumptions and issues in communication science. In C. Berger & S. Chaffee (Ed.), *Handbook of communication science.* Newbury Park, CA: Sage.

Chaffee, S. H., & Izcaray, F. (1975). Mass communication functions in a media-rich developing society. In S. H. Chaffee (Ed.), *Political communication: Issues and strategies for research* (pp. 367-395). Newbury Park, CA: Sage.

Chaffee, S. H., & Wilson, D. G. (1977). Media rich, media poor: Two studies of diversity in agenda-holding. *Journalism Quarterly, 54*, 466-476.

Cobb, R. W., & Elder, C. D. (1971). The politics of agenda-building: An alternative perspective for modern democratic theory. *Journal of Politics, 33*, 892-915.

Cobb, R. W., & Elder, C. D. (1981). Communication and public policy. In D. D. Nimmo & K. R. Sanders (Eds.), *Handbook of political communication* (pp. 391-416). Newbury Park, CA: Sage.

Cobb, R. W., & Elder, C. D. (1983). *Participation in American politics: The dynamics of agenda-building* (2nd ed.). Baltimore: Johns Hopkins University Press.

Cobb, R. W., Ross, J., & Ross, M. H. (1976). Agenda building as a comparative political process. *American Political Science Review, 70*, 126-138.

Cohen, B. C. (1963). *The press and foreign policy.* Princeton, NJ: Princeton University Press.

Cohen, B. C. (1965). *Foreign policy in American government.* Boston: Little, Brown.

Cohen, B. C. (1967). Mass communication and foreign policy. In J. N. Rosenau (Ed.), *Domestic sources of foreign policy.* New York: Free Press.

Cohen, B. C. (1970). The relationship between public opinion and foreign policy maker. In M. Small (Ed.), *Public opinion and historians.* Detroit: Wayne State University Press.

Cohen, B. C. (1983). *The public's impact on foreign policy.* Lanham, MD: University Press of America. (Original work published 1973)

Commission on Freedom of the Press. (1947). *A free and responsible press.* Chicago: University of Chicago Press.

Cook, F. L., Tyler, T. R., Goetz, E. G., Gordon, M. T., Protess, D., Leff, D. R., & Molotch, H. L. (1983). Media and agenda-setting: Effects on the public, interest group leaders, policy makers, and policy. *Public Opinion Quarterly, 47*, 16-35.

Crenson, M. A. (1971). *The un-politics of air pollution: A study of non-decision making in two cities.* Baltimore: Johns Hopkins University Press.

Curran, J., Gurevitch, M., & Woollacott, J. (Eds.). (1979). *Mass communication and society.* Newbury Park, CA: Sage.

Davidson, R., & Parker, G. (1972). Positive support for political institutions: The case of Congress. *Western Politics Quarterly, 25*, 600-612.

Davis, F. J. (1952). Crime news in Colorado newspapers. *American Journal of Sociology, 57*, 325-330.

DeFleur, M. L., & Dennis, E. E. (1985). *Understanding mass communication* (2nd ed.). Boston: Houghton Mifflin.

DeGeorge, W. F. (1981). Conceptualization and measurement of audience agenda. In G. C. Wilhoit & H. DeBock (Eds.), *Mass communication review yearbook 2* (pp. 291-222). Newbury Park, CA: Sage.

Dewey, J. (1927). *The public and its problems.* New York: Henry Holt.

Dominick, J. R. (1983). *The dynamics of mass communication.* Reading, MA: Addison-Wesley.

Downs, A. (1972). Up and down with ecology: The issue-attention cycle. *Public Interest, 28,* 38-50.

Einsiedel, E. F., Salomone, K. L., & Schneider, F. P. (1984). Crime: Effects of media exposure and personal experience on issue salience. *Journalism Quarterly, 61,* 131-136.

Emery, M., & Smythe, T. C. (1986). *Readings in mass communication: Concepts and issues in the mass media* (6th ed.). Dubuque, IA: Brown.

Erbring, L., Goldenberg, E. N., & Miller, A. H. (1980). Front-page news and real-world cues: A new look at agenda-setting by the media. *American Journal of Political Science, 24,* 16-49.

Erikson, R. S. (1976). The relationship between public opinion and state policy: A new look based on some forgotten data. *American Journal of Political Science, 20,* 25-36.

Erikson, R. S. (1978). Constituency opinion and congressional behavior: A reexamination of the Miller-Stokes representation data. *American Journal of Political Science, 22,* 511-535.

Eyal, C. H. (1979). *Time-frame in agenda-setting research: A study of the conceptual and methodological factors affecting the time frame context of the agenda-setting process.* Unpublished doctoral dissertation, Syracuse University, Syracuse, NY.

Eyal, C. H. (1981). The roles of newspapers and television in agenda-setting. In G. C. Wilhoit & H. DeBock (Eds.), *Mass communication review yearbook 2* (pp. 225-234). Newbury Park, CA: Sage.

Eyal, C. H., Winter, J. P., & DeGeorge, W. F. (1981). The concept of time frame in agenda-setting. In G. C. Wilhoit (Ed.), *Mass communication review yearbook 2* (pp. 212-218). Newbury Park, CA: Sage.

Eyestone, R. (1974). *From social issues to public policy.* New York: John Wiley.

Fiske, S. T., & Taylor, S. E. (1984). *Social cognition.* Reading, MA: Addison-Wesley.

Frazier, P. J., & Gaziano, C. (1979). *Robert E. Park's theory of news, public opinion and social control.* Lexington, KY: Journalism Monographs.

Fryling, A. (1985). *Setting the congressional agenda: Public opinion in a media age.* Unpublished doctoral dissertation, Massachusetts Institute of Technology.

Funkhouser, G. R. (1973a). The issues of the sixties: An exploratory study in the dynamics of public opinion. *Public Opinion Quarterly, 37,* 62-75.

Funkhouser, G. R. (1973b). Trends in media coverage of the issues of the sixties. *Journalism Quarterly, 50,* 533-538.

Gaddy, G. D., & Tanjong, E. (1986). Earthquake coverage by the Western press. *Journal of Communication, 36,* 105-112.

Gadir, S. (1982). Media agenda-setting in Australia: The rise and fall of public issues. *Media Information Australia, 26,* 13-23.

Gandy, O. H., Jr. (1982). *Beyond agenda setting: Information subsidies and public policy.* Norwood, NJ: Ablex.

Gilberg, S., Eyal, C., McCombs, M., & Nicholas, D. (1980). The State of the Union Address and the press agenda. *Journalism Quarterly, 57*(4), 584-588.

Gitlin, T. (1978). Media sociology: The dominant paradigm. *Theory and Society, 6,* 205-253.

Gormley, W. T., Jr. (1975). Newspaper agendas and political elites. *Journalism Quarterly, 52,* 304-308.

Grunig, J. E., & Ipes, D. A. (1983). The anatomy of a campaign against drunk driving. *Public Relations Review, 9,* 36-52.

Hauser, J. R. (1986). Agendas and consumer choice. *Journal of Marketing Research, 23,* 199-212.

Hezel, R. T., Andregg, C., & Lange-Chapman, D. (1986). *The agenda-setting function of TV movies: Newspaper coverage of TV movie social issues.* Paper presented at the annual meeting of the Association for Education in Journalism and Mass Communication, Norman, OK.

Hibbs, D. A., Jr. (1979). The mass public and macroeconomic performance: The dynamics of public opinion toward unemployment and inflation. *American Journal of Political Science, 23*(4), 705-731.

Hubbard, J. C., DeFleur, M. L., & DeFleur, L. B. (1975). Mass media influences on public conceptions of social problems. *Social Problems, 23,* 22-34.

Hume, D. (1896). *A treatise of human nature.* Oxford: Clarendon. (Original work published 1739)

Iyengar, S. (1979). Television news and issue salience: A re-examination of the agenda-setting hypothesis. *American Politics Quarterly, 7,* 395-416.

Iyengar, S., & Kinder, D. R. (1985). Psychological accounts of media agenda setting. In S. Kraus & R. Perloff (Eds.), *Mass media and political thought* (pp. 117-140). Newbury Park, CA: Sage.

Iyengar, S., & Kinder, D. R. (1986). More than meets the eye: TV news, priming, and public evaluations of the president. In G. Comstock (Ed.), *Public communication and behavior* (Vol. 1). New York: Academic Press.

Iyengar, S., & Kinder, D. R. (1987). *News that matters: Agenda-setting and priming in a television age.* Chicago: University of Chicago Press.

Iyengar, S., Peters, M. P., & Kinder, D. R. (1982). Experimental demonstrations of the "not-so-minimal" consequences of televison news programs. *American Political Science Review, 76,* 848-858.

Iyengar, S., Peters, M. P., Kinder, D. R., & Krosnick, J. A. (1984). The evening news and presidential evaluations. *Journal of Personality and Social Psychology, 46,* 778-787.

James, W. (1896). *The principles of psychology.* New York: Henry Holt.

Junack, M. E., McCombs, M. E., & Shaw, D. L. (1977). Using polls and content analysis to study an election. In D. L. Shaw & M. E. McCombs (Eds.), *The emergence of American public issues: The agenda-setting function of the press* (pp. 157-169). St. Paul, MN: West.

Kaid, L. L., Hale, K., & Williams, J. (1977). Media agenda setting of a specific political event. *Journalism Quarterly, 54,* 584-587.

Katz, E., & Lazarsfeld, P. F. (1955). *Personal influence.* New York: Free Press.

Kepplinger, H. M., Donsbach, W., Brosius, H., & Staab, J. (1986). *Media tenor and public opinion: A longitudinal study of media coverage and public opinion on Chancellor Kohl.* Paper presented to the Joint World Association for Public Opinion Research/American Association for Public Opinion Research Conference, St. Petersburg, FL.

Kepplinger, H. M., & Roth, H. (1979). Creating a crisis: German mass media and oil supply in 1973-74. *Public Opinion Quarterly, 43,* 285-296.

Kingdon, J. W. (1984). *Agendas, alternatives, and public policies.* Boston: Little, Brown.

Klapper, J. T. (1960). *The effects of mass communication.* New York: Free Press.

Kraus, S. (1985). The studies and the world outside. In S. Kraus & R. M. Perloff (Eds.), *Mass media and political thought.* Newbury Park, CA: Sage.

Lambeth, E. B. (1978, Spring). Perceived influence of the press on energy policy making. *Journalism Quarterly, 72,* 11-18.

Lang, G. E., & Lang, K. (1981). Watergate: An exploration of the agenda-building process. In G. C. Wilhoit & H. DeBock (Eds.), *Mass communication review yearbook 2* (pp. 447-468). Newbury Park, CA: Sage.

Lang, G. E., & Lang, K. (1983). *The battle for public opinion: The president, the press, and the polls during Watergate.* New York: Columbia University Press.

Lasswell, H. D. (1927). *Propoganda technique in the World War.* New York: Knopf.

Lazarsfeld, P. F., & Merton, R. K. (1948). Mass communication, popular taste, and organized social action [Reprinted in W. Schramm (Ed.), *Mass communication* (2nd ed.)]. Urbana: University of Illinois Press.

Leff, D. R., Protess, D. L., & Brooks, S. C. (1986). Cruisading journalism: Changing public attitudes and policy-making agenda. *Public Opinion Quarterly, 50,* 300-315.

Linsky, M. (1986). *Impact: How the press affects federal policymaking.* New York: W. W. Norton.

Linsky, M., Moore, J., O'Donnell, W., & Whitman, D. (1986). *How the press affects federal policy making: Six case studies.* New York: W. W. Norton.

Lippmann, W. (1922). *Public opinion.* New York: Harcourt Brace.

Lowery, S., & DeFleur, M. L. (1987). *Milestones in mass communication research: Media effects* (2nd ed.). New York: Longman.

MacKuen, M. B. (1981). Social communication and the mass policy agenda. In M. B. MacKuen

& S. L. Coombs (Eds.), *More than news: Media power in public affairs* (pp. 19-144). Newbury Park, CA: Sage.

MacKuen, M. B., & Coombs, S. L. (1981). *More than news: Media power in public affairs.* Newbury Park, CA: Sage.

Manheim, J. B. (1986). A model of agenda dynamics. In M. L. McLaughlin (Ed.), *Communication yearbook 10* (pp. 499-516). Newbury Park, CA: Sage.

Manheim, J. B., & Albritton, R. B. (1984). Changing national images: International public relations and media agenda setting. *American Political Science Review, 73,* 641-647.

Mansbach, R. W., & Vasquez, J. A. (1981). *In search of theory.* New York: Columbia University Press.

Mazur, A. (1981). Media coverage and public opinion on scientific controversies. *Journal of Communication, 31,* 106-115.

McClure, R. D., & Patterson, T. E. (1976). Print vs. network news. *Journal of Communication, 26,* 23-28.

McCombs, M. E. (1976). Agenda-setting research: A bibliographic essay. *Political Communication Review, 1,* 1-7.

McCombs, M. E. (1977). Newspapers versus television: Mass communication effects across time. In D. L. Shaw & M. E. McCombs (Eds.), *The emergence of American political issues: The agenda-setting function of the press* (pp. 89-105). St. Paul, MN: West.

McCombs, M. E. (1981a). The agenda-setting approach. In D. D. Nimmo & K. R. Sanders (Eds.), *Mass communication review yearbook 2* (pp. 219-224). Newbury Park, CA: Sage.

McCombs, M. E. (1981b). Setting the agenda for agenda-setting research: An assessment of the priority, ideas and problems. In G. C. Wilhoit & H. DeBock (Eds.), *Mass communication review yearbook 2* (pp. 219-224). Newbury Park, CA: Sage.

McCombs, M. E., & Gilbert, S. (1986). News influences on our pictures of the world. In J. Bryant & D. Zillman (Eds.), *Perspectives on media effects* (pp. 1-15). Hillsdale, NJ: Lawrence Erlbaum.

McCombs, M. E., & Masel-Waters, L. (1976). Agenda-setting: A perspective on mass communication. *Mass Communication Review, 3,* 3-7.

McCombs, M. E., & Shaw, D. L. (1972). The agenda-setting function of mass media. *Public Opinion Quarterly, 36,* 176-184.

McCombs, M. E., & Shaw, D. L. (1976). Structuring the "unseen environment." *Journal of Communication, 26,* 18-22.

McCombs, M. E., & Shaw, D. L. (1977a). Agenda-setting and the political process. In D. L. Shaw & M. E. McCombs (Eds.), *The emergence of American political issues: The agenda-setting function of the press* (pp. 149-156). St. Paul, MN: West.

McCombs, M. E., & Shaw, D. L. (1977b). The agenda-setting function of the press. In D. L. Shaw & M. E. McCombs (Eds.), *The emergence of American political issues: The agenda-setting function of the press* (pp. 1-18). St. Paul, MN: West.

McCombs, M. E., & Weaver, D. H. (1973, May). *Voters' need for orientation and use of mass communication.* Paper presented at the annual meeting of the International Communication Association, Montreal.

McCombs, M. E., & Weaver, D. H. (1985). Toward a merger of gratifications and agenda-setting research. In K. E. Rosengren, L. A. Wenner, & P. Palmgreen (Eds.), *Media gratification research* (pp. 95-108). Newbury Park, CA: Sage.

McLeod, J. M., Becker, L. B., & Byrnes, J. E. (1974). Another look at the agenda setting function of the press. *Communication Research, 1,* 131-166.

McQuail, D., & Windahl, S. (1981). *Communication models for the study of mass communication.* New York: Longman.

Megwa, E. R., & Brenner, D. J. (1986, May). *Toward a paradigm of media agenda-setting effects: Agenda-setting as process.* Paper presented to Political Communications Division at the annual meeting of the International Communication Association, Chicago.

Miller, A. H., Goldenberg, E. N., & Erbring, L. (1979). Type-set politics: Impact of newspapers on public confidence. *American Political Science Review, 73,* 67-84.

Miller, J. D. (1987). *The impact of the Challenger accident on public attitudes toward the space program* (Report to the National Science Foundation). Northern Illinois University, Public Opinion Laboratory.

Miller, S. H. (1978). *Reporters and congressmen: Living in symbiosis* (No. 53). Lexington, KY: Journalism Monographs.

Miller, W. E., & Stokes, D. E. (1963). The politics of agenda-building: An alternative perspective for modern democratic theory. *Journal of Politics, 33*, 892-915.

Molotch, H., & Lester, M. (1974). News as purposive behavior: On the strategic use of routine events, accidents, and scandals. *American Sociological Review, 39*, 101-112.

Monroe, A. D. (1979). Consistency between public preferences and national policy decisions. *American Politics Quarterly, 7*(1), 3-19.

Mullins, L. E. (1977). Agenda-setting and the young voter. In D. L. Shaw & M. E. McCombs (Eds.), *The emergence of American political issues: The agenda-setting function of the press* (pp. 133-148). St. Paul, MN: West.

Neumann, W. R. (1985). *The threshold of public attention.* Paper presented at the annual meeting of the American Political Science Association, New Orleans.

Neumann, W. R., & Fryling, A. C. (1985). Patterns of political cognition: An exploration of the public mind. In S. Kraus & R. M. Perloff (Eds.), *Mass media and political thought* (pp. 223-240). Newbury Park, CA: Sage.

Noelle-Neumann, E. (1984). *The spiral of silence: Public opinion—our social skin.* Chicago: University of Chicago Press.

O'Keefe, G. J., & Reid-Nash, K. (1987). Crime news and real-world blues. *Communication Research, 14*, 147-163.

Page, B. I., & Shapiro, R. Y. (1983). Effects of public opinion on policy. *American Political Science Review, 77*, 175-190.

Palmgreen, P., & Clark, P. (1977). Agenda-setting with local and national issues. *Communication Research, 4*, 435-452.

Park, R. E. (1922). *The immigrant press and its control.* New York: Harper.

Pember, D. R. (1983). *Mass media in America* (4th ed.). Chicago: SRA.

Peterson, S. (1972). Events, mass opinion, and elite attitudes. In R. L. Merritt (Ed.), *Communication in international politics* (pp. 252-271). Urbana: University of Illinois Press.

Pritchard, D. (1986). Homicide and bargained justice: The agenda-setting effect of crime news on prosecutors. *Public Opinion Quarterly, 49*, 19-37.

Protess, D. L., Leff, D. R., Brooks, S. C., & Gordon, M. T. (1985). Uncovering rape: The watchdog press and the limits of agenda setting. *Public Opinion Quarterly, 49*, 19-37.

Przeworski, A., & Teune, H. (1970). *The logic of comparative social inquiry.* New York: John Wiley.

Qualter, T. H. (1985). *Opinion control in the democracies.* New York: St. Martin's.

Rabinowitz, G., Prothro, J. W., & Jacoby, W. (1982). Salience as a factor in the impact of issues on candidate evaluation. *Journal of Politics, 44*, 41-63.

Ramaprasad, J. (1983). Agenda-setting: Is not a 1984 or is a 1984 view. *Gazette, 32*, 119-135.

Reardon, K. K. (1987). *Where minds meet.* Belmont, CA: Wadsworth.

Rivers, W. L. (1970). Appraising press coverage of politics. In R. W. Lee (Ed.), *Politics and the press.* Washington, DC: Acropolis.

Rogers, E. M. (1983). *Diffusion of innovations.* New York: Free Press.

Rogers, E. M. (1986). *Communication technology.* New York: Free Press.

Rosenau, J. N. (1961). *Public opinion and foreign policy.* New York: Random House.

Rosenau, J. N. (Ed.). (1980). Pre-theories and theories of foreign policy. In *The scientific study of foreign policy* (rev. ed., pp. 115-169). New York: Free Press.

Rosenau, J. N. (1987). *Patterned chaos in global life: Structure and process in the two worlds of world politics.* Unpublished manuscript, University of Southern California, Institute for Transnational Studies.

Rosengren, K. E. (1974). International news: Methods, data and theory. *Journal of Peace Research, 11*, 145-156.

Rosengren, K. E. (1977). Four types of tables. *Journal of Communication, 27,* 67-75.

Rosengren, K. E. (1983). Communication research: One paradigm, or four? *Journal of Communication, 33,* 185-207.

Salwen, M. B. (1985). *An agenda for agenda-setting research: Problems in the paradigm.* Paper presented at the annual meeting of the Speech Communication Association of Puerto Rico, San Juan.

Salwen, M. B. (1986, May). *Time in agenda-setting: The accumulation of media coverage on audience issue salience.* Paper presented at the annual meeting of the International Communication Association, Chicago.

Schudson, M. (1986). The menu of media research. In S. J. Ball-Rokeach & M. G. Cantor (Eds.), *Media audience and social structure* (pp. 43-48). Newbury Park, CA: Sage.

Shaw, D. L. (1977). The press agenda in a community setting. In D. L. Shaw & M. E. McCombs (Eds.), *The emergence of American public issues: The agenda-setting function of the press* (pp. 19-31). St. Paul, MN: West.

Shaw, D. L., & Clemmer, C. L. (1977). News and the public response. In D. L. Shaw & M. E. McCombs (Eds.), *The emergence of American public issues: The agenda-setting function of the press* (pp. 33-51). St. Paul, MN: West.

Shaw, D. L., & McCombs, M. E. (Eds.). (1977). *The emergence of American political issues: The agenda-setting function of the press.* St. Paul, MN: West.

Shaw, E. F. (1977). The interpersonal agenda. In D. L. Shaw & M. E. McCombs (Eds.), *The emergence of American public issues: The agenda-setting function of the press* (pp. 69-87). St. Paul, MN: West.

Shaw, E. F. (1977). The agenda-setting hypothesis reconsidered: Interpersonal factors. *Gazette, 23,* 230-240.

Shaw, E. F. (1979). Agenda-setting and mass communication theory. *Gazette, 25*(2), 96-105.

Shoemaker, P. J., Wanta, W., & Leggett, D. (1987, May). *Drug coverage and public opinion, 1972-1986.* Paper presented at the annual meeting of the American Association for Public Opinion Research, Hershey, PA.

Siune, K., & Borre, O. (1975). Setting the agenda for a Danish election. *Journal of Communication, 25*(1): 65-73.

Smith, K. A. (1987). *Newspaper coverage and public concern about community issues: A time-series analysis.* Lexington, KY: Journalism Monographs.

Smith, S. (1986). Theories of foreign policy: An historical overview. *Review of International Studies, 12,* 13-29.

Smith, T. W. (1980). America's most important problem: A trend analysis, 1946-1976. *Public Opinion Quarterly, 44,* 164-180.

Soderlund, W. C., Wagenberg, R. H., Briggs, E. D., & Nelson, R. C. (1980). Regional and linguistic agenda-setting in Canada: A study of newspaper coverage of issues affecting political integration in 1976. *Canadian Journal of Political Science, 13*(2), 348-356.

Sohn, A. B. (1978). A longitudinal analysis of local non-political agenda-setting effects. *Journalism Quarterly, 55,* 325-333.

Stimson, J. A. (1976). Public support of American presidents: A cyclical model. *Public Opinion Quarterly, 40,* 1-21.

Stone, G. C., & McCombs, M. E. (1981). Tracing the time lag in agenda setting. *Journalism Quarterly, 58,* 51-55.

Sutherland, H., & Galloway, J. (1981). Role of advertising: Persuasion or agenda setting. *Journalism Quarterly, 58,* 51-55.

Swanson, L. L., & Swanson, D. L. (1978). The agenda-setting function of the first Ford-Carter debate. *Communication Monographs, 45,* 330-353.

Tardy, C. H., Gaughan, B. J., Hemphill, M. R., & Crockett, N. (1981). Media agendas and political participation. *Journalism Quarterly, 58,* 624-627.

Tipton, L., Hanley, R., & Basehart, J. (1975). Media agenda-setting in city and state election campaigns. *Journalism Quarterly, 52,* 15-22.

Walker, J. L. (1977). Setting the agenda in the U.S. Senate: A theory of problem selection. *British Journal of Political Science, 7,* 433-445.

Wallas, G. (1914). *The great society.* New York: Macmillan.

Wanta, W. (1986). *The agenda-setting effects of dominant photographs.* Paper presented at the annual meeting of the Association for Education in Journalism and Mass Communication, Norman, OK.

Watt, J. H., Jr., & van den Berg, S. (1981). How time dependency influences media effects in a community controversy. *Journalism Quarterly, 58*(1), 43-50.

Weaver, D. H. (1977). Political issues and voter need for orientation. In D. L. Shaw & M. E. McCombs (Eds.), *The emergence of American public issues: The agenda-setting function of the press* (pp. 107-119). St. Paul, MN: West.

Weaver, D. (1984). Media agenda-setting and public opinion: Is there a link? In R. N. Bostrom (Ed.), *Communication yearbook 8* (pp. 680-691). Newbury Park, CA: Sage.

Weaver, D., Graber, D. A., McCombs, M. E., & Eyal, C. H. (1981). *Media agenda-setting in a presidential election: Issues, images, and interest.* New York: Praeger.

Weaver, D., McCombs, M. E., & Spellman, C. (1975). Watergate and the media: A case study of agenda-setting. *American Politics Quarterly, 3,* 458-472.

Weber, R. E., & Shaffer, W. R. (1972). Public opinion and American state policy-making. *Midwest Journal of Political Science, 16,* 683-699.

Westly, B. H. (1976). What makes a change? *Journal of Communication, 26,* 43-47.

Williams, W., Jr., & Larsen, D. C. (1977). Agenda-setting in an off-election year. *Journalism Quarterly, 54,* 744-749.

Williams, W., Jr., & Semlak, W. D. (1978a). Structural effects of TV coverage on political agendas. In G. Gerbner (Ed.), *Journal of Communication, 28*(4), 114-119.

Williams, W., Jr., & Semlak, W. D. (1978b). Campaign '76: Agenda setting during the New Hampshire Primary. *Journal of Broadcasting, 22,* 531-540.

Williams, W., Jr., Shapiro, M., & Cutbirth, C. (1983). The impact of campaign agendas on perceptions of issues in 1980 campaign. *Journalism Quarterly, 60,* 226-231.

Winter, J. P. (1981). Contingent conditions on the agenda-setting process. *Mass communication review yearbook 2* (pp. 235-243). Newbury Park, CA: Sage.

Winter, J. P., & Eyal, C. H. (1981). Agenda setting for the civil rights issue. *Public Opinion Quarterly, 45,* 376-383.

Winter, J. P., Eyal, C. H., & Rogers, A. H. (1982). Issue-specific agenda-setting: The whole as less than the sum of the parts. *Canadian Journal of Communication, 8,* 8-10.

Wright, C. R. (1986). *Mass communication: A sociological perspective* (3rd ed.). New York: Random House.

Zucker, H. G. (1978). The variable nature of new media influence. In B. D. Rubin (Ed.), *Communication yearbook 2* (pp. 225-245). New Brunswick, NJ: Transaction.

New Directions of Agenda-Setting Research

SHANTO IYENGAR

University of California at Los Angeles

A S Professors Rogers and Dearing have so ably demonstrated, there can no longer be serious doubt over the ability of the mass media to influence the political agenda. The agenda-setting effect has proven to be quite robust, spanning a variety of issues, media channels, and target audiences. In my role as commentator, I would like to outline a set of research questions their chapter raises and, where appropriate, describe the results of research bearing on these questions.

CONSEQUENCES OF AGENDA-SETTING FOR PUBLIC OPINION AND VOTING

The influence of news coverage of public issues is not limited to individuals' judgments about issue importance. An important consequence of agenda-setting concerns the relative weight accorded issue beliefs and opinions when individuals evaluate political leaders or choose between candidates. When issues move up the public agenda, considerations bearing on these issues exert a stronger impact on evaluations of the incumbent president and on voting preferences. News coverage of unemployment, for instance, not only boosts the salience of unemployment, but also makes individuals' evaluations of the president and their candidate preferences more sensitive to beliefs and opinions concerning unemployment. How well individuals rate President Reagan's performance in dealing with unemployment, for example, becomes a stronger determinant of his overall popularity under conditions of heavy unemployment news coverage. Similarly, assessments of the state of the economy and the candidates' positions on economic

Correspondence and requests for reprints: Shanto Iyengar, Department of Political Science, University of California, Los Angeles, CA 90024.

Communication Yearbook 11, pp. 595-602

issues have a stronger impact on voting decisions when the economy is featured prominently in the media agenda (for details on these and similar results, see Behr, 1985; Iyengar & Kinder, 1986, 1987).

This phenomenon is certainly well known to politicians. Witness their strenuous efforts to control "media spin"—the terms in which they are covered by the media (for further discussion, see Arterton, 1984; Kernell, 1986). By associating themselves with "good news" and distancing themselves from "bad news," they strive to reap the political benefits of agenda-setting. In sum, agenda-setting spills over to political attitudes and voting by altering the criteria underlying attitudes and voting choices.

DIRECTION OF CAUSALITY AND RELATED QUESTIONS

Rogers and Dearing point out (quite correctly, in my judgment) that agenda-setting research suffers from serious methodological limitations, most of which concern the validity of the inference that media agendas determine audience agendas. The reverse possibility cannot be ruled out, namely, that what plays in Peoria and elsewhere will eventually make its way into the national media agenda. The diffusion of econometric and other simultaneous-equation techniques across the behavioral sciences enables agenda-setting researchers to test more effectively for the precise direction of the causal flow. For instance, in Behr and Iyengar (1985), we were able to test and reject the hypothesis that public concern dictated television news coverage for the issues of energy and unemployment. In the area of inflation, however, we uncovered slim (but statistically significant, nonetheless) evidence that the level of public concern influenced (positively) the amount of inflation coverage. The Behr and Iyengar study thus reveals that media agenda-setting may entail reciprocal effects, with media coverage and public concern feeding on each other. Obviously, estimates of the strength of media agenda-setting will be inflated unless they are purged of such a feedback effect.

A second methodological problem facing agenda-setting research concerns disentangling the effects of news coverage from the effects of direct experience. Rogers and Dearing note that media are but one of several potential determinants of the public's agenda. Several issues, most notably those in the economic realm, can be felt directly. The unemployed worker may not need news coverage of unemployment to convince him or her that unemployment is a significant national problem. Analogously, one whose home has been burglarized may regard crime as a significant problem quite independently of the level of crime news. Personal experience is, in short, an important source of political agendas. Moreover, personal experience may make individuals more or less receptive to the media agenda. In their pioneering paper, Erbring, Goldenberg, and Miller (1980) showed that agenda-setting was in fact an interactive effect, jointly produced by news coverage and audience sensitivities. Individuals with direct experience of some issue are the first to respond to news coverage, with others responding more sluggishly. Measures of direct experience with political issues must thus be incorporated into analyses of media agenda setting.

In one set of experiments, Donald Kinder and I explicitly tested for interaction between audience members' personal experience with national issues and television news coverage of these issues. News coverage of unemployment was provided to unemployed and employed subjects; news coverage of racial discrimination was shown to blacks and whites; and news coverage of the financial instability of the social security fund was shown to retired and young subjects. The results revealed a significant interaction between personal experience and news coverage in the case of social security and racial discrimination, with elderly and black viewers being considerably more likely to alter their judgments in response to news coverage of "their" issue. The picture for unemployment was more complex since we ran two experiments on this particular issue. The first of the two was run during a time of relatively low unemployment (in 1981), while the second coincided with the peak of the 1982 recession (July). The results from the first study did include a significant interaction effect in the expected direction (that is, unemployed viewers were more susceptible to agenda-setting) but the second study showed quite the reverse. We surmised that this deviation was due to the fact that by July 1982 there were very few Americans left (most of whom were employed) who did not consider unemployment to be among the most important problems facing the nation. On balance, our results quite clearly support Erbring's model in that the strength of media agenda-setting was conditioned by personal experiences.

Finally, and related to the subject of personal experience, I wholeheartedly agree with the authors' prescription that estimates of media agenda-setting control for indicators of real-world developments. As unemployment worsens, more and more people are affected by the issue and apt to encounter the issue be it in the form of interpersonal communication or direct experience. At the same time, as unemployment worsens, news coverage of unemployment is likely to increase. As editors and other journalistic "gatekeepers" are prone to assert, the media merely mirror reality. Be this as it may, the agenda-setting researcher must be concerned with the possibility of spurious results: the possibility that what he or she takes for an agenda-setting effect is nothing more than the media and the public responding in concert to real-world events. Unless indicators of "reality" are incorporated, agenda-setting effects are bound to be confounded with the effects of direct experience.

Surprisingly (given the importance of this issue), very few researchers have taken the trouble to add indicators of the actual magnitude or scope of issues to indicators of news coverage. These studies (Behr & Iyengar, 1985; MacKuen, 1981) demonstrate that indeed there are unmediated influences on the public agenda and that news coverage is to a significant degree determined by actual conditions and trends concerning public issues. In the Behr and

Iyengar study, for example, a 6% increase in the price of energy drove television news coverage of energy upward by 21 stories over a 60-day period. Similarly, changes in the unemployment rate (in either direction) significantly affected television news coverage of unemployment as well as the proportion of the public naming unemployment as among the three most important problems facing the nation. In fact, in the case of unemployment, Behr and Iyengar found that once the effects of real-world developments were taken into account, television news had *no effect* on public concern for unemployment (see Behr & Iyengar, 1985).

PSYCHOLOGICAL MEDIATORS OF AGENDA-SETTING

My next set of concerns deal with the how and why of media influence. This is tantamount to delineating a theory of public agenda-setting. Naturally I cannot in the space of this commentary do full justice to the myriad factors that might condition the impact of media news presentations on the audience's political agenda (for an authoritative discussion of these conditional relationships, see McGuire, 1985). I will focus instead on three potential mediating mechanisms—counterargument/yielding, assessments of source credibility, and the arousal of affect.

Individuals do not register incoming information passively. Instead, they interpret, elaborate upon, and evaluate information within an existing network of knowledge, attitudes, and beliefs. The evaluative component of this process is crucial: To the degree individuals take issue with the news or can call up information that challenges news items, agenda-setting is weakened. In sum, the greater the level of counterarguing, the weaker the impact of news presentations (for a general overview of counterargument and its importance to persuasion, see Petty & Cacioppo, 1981).

Counterargument requires effort and motivation. Since many people pay only casual and intermittent attention to media public affairs presentations, and have a limited store of political knowledge to call upon, alternative mediators of agenda-setting must be considered. Instead of carefully deliberating over the content of news stories, the typical viewer may instead resort to various shortcuts for deciding whether issues covered in the news are indeed important.

One such shortcut is source credibility. That more credible sources are in fact more persuasive has been documented in endless experiments (see McGuire, 1985). In the particular case of agenda-setting, television newscasts may be particularly effective because so many Americans consider television news the most authoritative and accurate source of public affairs information (see Bower, 1985).

In addition to counterargument and assessments of source credibility, the impact of media presentations may also be mediated by the degree to which these presentations provoke emotional responses. Television may be an effective agent of agenda-setting because viewers can "feel" the issues covered in the news. The vividness of television as a medium and the tendency of the networks to personalize news items may elicit strong emotions, especially since politics is an area of "hot cognition."

Affect may by itself contribute to individuals' perceptions of issue importance. Merely feeling anger, sadness, or fear while watching news coverage of unemployment may cause an upward shift in perceptions of the importance of unemployment (for evidence that affect can independently shape cognitions, see Zajonc, 1984). Alternatively, affect may conribute indirectly by directing attention to the triggering stimulus—news coverage of some issue. Viewers angered by a news story describing the plight of an unemployed worker find their attention drawn to unemployment, and as a consequence may attribute more importance to that problem at the expense of others. (The relationship between affect and attention is discussed in Clarke, 1984; the role of focused attention in social judgment is discussed in McArthur, 1981.)

In a series of experiments designed to assess the agenda-setting impact of television news programs, Kinder and I tracked the relative contributions of counterargument, source credibility, and affect to viewers' judgments of issue importance (for details, see Iyengar & Kinder, 1985). Basically we found that source credibility was the most consistent mediator. Viewers who gave the networks high marks on credibility were generally more influenced than those who felt otherwise. We also found that viewers more prone to emotional responses tended to be more susceptible to agenda-setting, but this effect was not robust. Finally, we found only limited evidence in favor of the counterargument hypothesis. The power of television to set the public agenda cannot be attributed to viewers' favorable evaluations of the content of television news coverage. Agenda-setting is instead mediated by viewers' assessments of source credibility and their emotional responses to news coverage.

LIMITATIONS TO AGENDA-SETTING

While the agenda-setting effect has proven robust, it would be erroneous to assume that media influence on public agendas is limitless. In the first place, virtually every study dealing with a national audience has shown that media coverage of some *national* issue boosts concern for that issue. The point is that all these issues could *plausibly* be considered significant, given that they have the potential to affect large numbers of people, and thereby society as a whole. Were the media to attempt to build up public concern for manifestly local or particularistic issues, it is doubtful that many Americans would respond by including these issues in their political agendas. Watching or reading news of unemployment is one thing, watching or reading about political corruption in New York City is quite another.

A second limitation concerns the *specificity* of the agenda-setting effect. In general, news coverage of some issue raises the importance audience members accord that issue *and that issue alone*. In the course of our experimental research, Kinder and I searched in vain for traces of spillover in agenda-setting whereby news coverage of some issue would also increase concern for related issues. The specificity of agenda-setting may be a product of the way in which most Americans think about politics—innocent of abstract, overarching ideological frameworks that might link national issues to each other.

Finally, it must be remembered that citizens have resources of their own with which to counteract media influence. As I have already noted, individuals with the ability to counterargue with public affairs presentations can effectively resist agenda-setting.

BROADER RAMIFICATIONS OF AGENDA-SETTING

I began this commentary by suggesting that researchers move beyond searching for agenda-setting and attempt to document the attitudinal or other consequences of changes in the public agenda. In this concluding section, I will raise my sights further and consider the consequences of agenda-setting for the governmental process, thus addressing what Rogers and Dearing have called the "policy agenda" literature.

The most likely consequence of media agenda-setting at the governmental level concerns the policymaking priorities of political elites. The critical question is whether those issues at the top of the public agenda also make their way onto decision makers' agendas (see Kingdon, 1984, for an extended analysis of the general question). Needless to say, this is no easy question. Congruence between what transpires in Washington and what citizens say are the most important national problems may occur not because the latter influences the former, but because policymakers "lead" public opinion. It is not possible in the scope of this chapter to deal with the finer points of the agenda-building concept. It suffices to note that there is now a sufficient body of evidence to warrant the conclusion that policymakers do march to the drumbeat (admittedly with something lacking military precision) of public concern. In a recent analysis, for instance, Page and Shapiro (1983) found significant correspondence between changes in public opinion and the direction of governmental policy between 1935 and 1979, particularly when opinions were strong and when changes in public opinion were clear-cut.

A further aspect of agenda-building concerns the power of the president. Scholars of the presidency have shown that the president's power stems partly from his public popularity (Kernell, 1986; Neustadt, 1960). A president with high popularity is more apt to get his way in Washington. This phenomenon has not been lost to presidents, all of whom (in the posttelevision era) have arduously cultivated favorable media coverage. As Lloyd Cutler, President Carter's special counsel, recollected on leaving his post:

I was surprised by how much the substantive decisions in the White House are affected by press deadlines, and, in particular by the evening television news. So that if something happened, let us say, on a Monday, or somebody strongly criticized the President or one of his programs, everything stopped! Whatever you'd been working on as the great priority of the next morning you had to put aside in order to reach a decision about how the President would respond in time for the evening television news. (*New York Times*, 1983, p. B4).

Finally, it can be argued that the media contribute to agenda-building in government by influencing the outcome of elections. As I have already noted, one of the significant consequences of the agenda-setting effect is the altering of weights people assign to issues when they choose between candidates, a phenomenon that can affect who wins or loses. By stressing economic issues at the expense of foreign policy, media coverage may influence the composition of Congress, and hence the course of governmental policy (for further discussion, see Iyengar & Kinder, 1987, chap. 11).

To sum up, media agenda-setting has important implications for the governmental process. By influencing what American citizens' regard as important problems, the media also influence the policymaking agenda, presidential power, and electoral outcomes.

In concluding, it is clear that agenda-setting research has come a long way since the pioneering insights of Walter Lippman and the empirical research initiated by Max McCombs and his colleagues. At present, less research is needed on establishing the agenda-setting effect. As I have tried to suggest, researchers must now confront a new generation of research questions concerning the responsiveness of media agendas to real-world developments, the political consequences of agenda-setting, and the psychological dynamics of media influence.

REFERENCES

Arterton, F. C. (1984). *Media politics: The news strategies of presidential campaigns.* Lexington, MA: D. C. Heath.

Behr, R. L. (1985). *The effects of media on voters' considerations in presidential and congressional elections.* Unpublished doctoral dissertation, Department of Political Science, Yale University.

Behr, R. L., & Iyengar, S. (1985). Television news, real-world cues, and changes in the public agenda. *Public Opinion Quarterly, 49*, 38-57.

Bower, R. T. (1985). *The changing television audience in America.* New York: Columbia University Press.

Clarke, M. (1984). A role for arousal in the link between feeling states, judgments, and behavior. In M. Clarke & S. Fiske (Eds.), *Affect and cognition: The seventeenth Carnegie Symposium on Cognition.* Hillsdale, NJ: Lawrence Erlbaum.

Erbring, L., Goldenberg, E., & Miller, A. (1980). Front-page news and real-world cues: A new look at agenda-setting. *American Journal of Political Science, 24*, 16-49.

Iyengar, S., & Kinder, D. R. (1985). Psychological accounts of media agenda-setting. In S. Kraus & R. Perloff (Eds.), *Mass media and political thought.* Newbury Park, CA: Sage.

Iyengar, S., & Kinder, D. R. (1986). More than meets the eye: Television news, priming, and presidential evaluations. In G. Comstock (Ed.), *Public communication and behavior* (Vol. 1). New York: Academic Press.

Iyengar, S., & Kinder, D. R. (1987). *News that matters: Television and American opinion.* Chicago: University of Chicago Press.

Kernell, S. (1986). *Going public.* Washington, DC: Congressional Quarterly Press.

Kingdon, J. (1984). *Agendas, alternatives, and public policies.* Boston: Little, Brown.

MacKuen, M. (1981). Social communication and the mass policy agenda. In M. MacKuen & S. Coombs (Eds.), *More than news: Media power in public affairs.* Newbury Park, CA: Sage.

McArthur, L. Z. (1981). What grabs you? The role of attention in impression formation and causal attributions. In E. Higgins et al. (Eds.), *Social cognition: The Ontario Symposium.* Hillsdale, NJ: Lawrence Erlbaum.

McGuire, W. J. (1985). Attitudes and attitude change. In G. Lindzey & E. Aronson (Eds.), *Handbook of social psychology.* New York: Random House.

Neustadt, R. (1960). *Presidential power: The politics of leadership.* New York: John Wiley.

New York Times. (1983, July 6). Interview with Lloyd Cutler.

Page, B., & Shapiro, R. (1983). Effects of public opinion on policy. *American Political Science Review, 77,* 175-190.

Petty, R., & Cacioppo, J. (1981). *Attitudes and persuasion: Classic and contemporary approaches.* Dubuque, IA: W. Brown.

Zajonc, R. (1984). The interaction of affect and cognition. In K. Scherer & P. Ekman (Eds.), *Approaches to emotion.* Hillsdale, NJ: Lawrence Erlbaum.

Feeling the Elephant:
Some Observations on
Agenda-Setting Research

DAVID L. SWANSON
University of Illinois, Urbana-Champaign

I N the mass communication research literature, the term *agenda-setting* is most often associated with the various lines of work based on McCombs and Shaw's (1972) agenda-setting hypothesis concerning how the prominence that news media give to an issue affects the public's perception of the issue's importance. Rogers and Dearing survey a wider terrain, encompassing not only studies of media effects on individuals' agendas but also the extent to which public policy responds to media and individuals' agendas.

Perhaps the principal advantage of Rogers and Dearing's more expansive conception of the domain is that their conception encourages us to frame agenda studies in terms of some fundamental questions about the role of mass media in society. To what extent do the media influence or mirror the public's concerns? In what ways do the public's concerns influence the priorities of policymakers? Do policy elites treat the media's priorities as a surrogate for the opinions of the public? If the media have some power to influence both public and policy agendas, how—and how responsibly—is this power exercised? We sometimes lose sight of such questions when we situate ourselves, as researchers must, within the tight boundaries of particular theoretical views, methodological practices, and narrowly drawn research questions. Yet, these are the sorts of questions that remind us of why mass communication is worth studying.

This short essay offers a view of how agenda studies can—and cannot—help us find better answers to the fundamental questions that the Rogers and Dearing perspective poses. Taking that survey as its point of departure, the

Correspondence and requests for reprints: David L. Swanson, Department of Speech Communication, University of Illinois, Urbana-Champaign, Urbana, IL 61801.

Communication Yearbook 11, pp. 603-619

essay first calls attention to some distinctions and differences in agenda studies that must be recognized as we consider where this research might go in the future. A slightly different way of organizing the literature is proposed and a few approaches that have especially important implications for the future of agenda studies are discussed in somewhat more detail than Rogers and Dearing offer. Second, the possibility of bringing the diffuse agenda literature into more of "an integrative whole," as Rogers and Dearing urge, is critically assessed. Finally, an alternative path for agenda studies is sketched that offers greater likelihood of accomplishing what is wanted.

THE ELEPHANT AND THE
JUNGLE OF AGENDA STUDIES

The universe of agenda studies as described by Rogers and Dearing calls to mind the ancient tale of the blind men who tried to figure out what an elephant is by touching the beast. Without their realizing it, each man felt of a different part of the animal—tusk, ear, flank, leg, tail. Thus Ali thought the elephant to be like a spear, Bul like a fan, Con like a wall, Dor like a tree stump, and Eri like a rope. Depending on where one grabs hold, agenda studies, like the elephant, can seem to be several quite different beasts.

Rogers and Dearing have ably mapped many strands of agenda research. Without further confusing an already bewildering literature, it is useful to supplement their survey by making a few additional distinctions between approaches and calling attention to some varieties of research they do not stress. The following look at some features of the terrain of agenda studies will help us better judge where this research profitably might go in the future.

Setting the Public's Agenda

Of the literatures reviewed by Rogers and Dearing, that devoted to testing the basic public- or personal-level agenda-setting hypothesis is by far the most elaborate and diffuse. The one consistent attribute of this literature is inconsistency of conceptualization, method, and result. The relative priorities or agendas of the public have been determined alternately using aggregate data summed across individuals (e.g., Siune & Borre, 1975) and individual-level data (e.g., McLeod, Becker, & Byrnes, 1974). Media agendas have been measured by examining the prominence given to coverage of a single event or issue (e.g., Kaid, Hale, & Williams, 1977) or a group of issues (e.g., Williams & Larsen, 1977), by a single media outlet (e.g., Becker & McCombs, 1978) or a group of outlets (e.g., McClure & Patterson, 1976) during a short (e.g., Swanson & Swanson, 1978) or long period of time (e.g., Neuman & Fryling, 1985). Researchers have sought to gauge the relationship of these two agendas either cross-sectionally (e.g., McCombs & Shaw, 1972) or over time (e.g., Funkhouser, 1973).

In order to know what to make of this research, it is useful to identify the major approaches that scholars have pursued. Three approaches in particular should be noted: ad hoc studies, which have no explicit theoretical grounding and present empirical tests of the basic hypothesis; studies based on need for orientation, which elaborate a particular individual-level cognitive explanation of agenda-setting; and studies based on psychological responses to exposure, which test a variety of individual-level psychological explanations of agenda-setting.

Ad Hoc Studies

Most studies of media effects on public or personal agendas are of this sort. For the most part, their conceptual framework is simply a statement of the basic hypothesis. Operational definitions of media and public agendas and suspicions about additional variables that might mediate agenda-setting are derived in an ad hoc way, leading to great variation in research questions and practices. In the past few years, many researchers, perhaps in response to the fairly large number of studies that have failed to find a main agenda-setting effect (Becker, 1982), have concentrated on discovering contingent conditions that encourage or inhibit public- or individual-level agenda-setting (e.g., differences between media as in McClure & Patterson, 1976; availability of alternative views of topic importance from nonmedia sources such as interpersonal discussions as in Atwood, Sohn, & Sohn, 1976; demographic attributes of individuals as in McLeod et al., 1974; individuals' predispositions concerning topics in the news as in McClure & Patterson, 1976; attributes of topics such as whether they are directly experienced or known about only through mass media as in Eyal, Winter, & DeGeorge, 1979; preference for one or another medium as a source of news as in Williams & Larsen, 1977).

The diversity in ad hoc studies has made comparisons difficult and frustrated reviewers' attempts to gauge what has and has not been proved (Kinder & Sears, 1985; Kraus & Davis, 1976; Roberts & Bachen, 1981; Roberts & Maccoby, 1985), leading Rogers and Dearing to protest that theoretical development is what is needed, not another empirical study. Although these studies have yielded mixed and discrepant results, in general, research has been more successful in demonstrating agenda-setting when studies have been conducted over time rather than cross-sectionally, when "issues" constituting an agenda have been defined at higher levels of generality, with individuals who are exposed to comparatively large doses of news, especially from newspapers, and when personal agendas have been determined from individual-level rather than aggregate data. There is counterevidence for each of these generalizations, however, and the only conclusion that can be drawn with great confidence is that, as Rogers and Dearing stress, continuing to approach agenda-setting as a purely empirical, rather than conceptual question is not likely to clarify matters.

Studies Based on Need for Orientation

The agenda-setting hypothesis originally proposed by McCombs and Shaw (1972) did not assert that media agendas affected all persons equally. Those researchers focused their initial study only on the issue agendas of undecided voters, because such persons were thought to be most susceptible to agenda-setting by the media (McCombs & Weaver, 1985), and called for subsequent research to move from the aggregate agenda level to the individual level and to social psychological explanations of individual differences (McCombs & Shaw, 1972). A psychological construct, need for orientation, was proposed by McCombs and Weaver in 1973 as explaining media agenda-setting effects on individuals and has generated a more or less sytematic program of research on individual cognitive bases of agenda-setting.

Derived from Tolman's (1932) theory of cognitive mapping, need for orientation was conceived as a cognitive utilitarian motivation growing out of each person's "need to be familiar with his surroundings," to "strive to 'map' his world, to fill in enough detail to orient himself" (McCombs & Weaver, 1973, p. 3). Need for orientation to public affairs and current events was thought to lead to media use, which in turn was thought to lead to agenda-setting; the higher the need for orientation, the greater the level of exposure to orientational (news and public affairs) content in mass media and the more pronounced the agenda-setting effect. Following Jones and Gerard (1967), need for orientation was conceived as consisting of two lower-order components, the personal relevance of the subject and the degree of one's uncertainty about the subject. The two components were combined to produce three levels of need for orientation, as depicted in Figure 1.

Conceptualization of need for orientation has changed over time. Finding in a study of the 1976 presidential election that respondents' levels of relevance and certainty were reciprocally related, Weaver (1978) proposed the typology shown in Figure 2 in which moderate need for orientation results either from low relevance and high uncertainty or high relevance and low uncertainty. Although the two different conditions depicted in Figure 2 as producing a moderate level of need for orientation are conceptually and qualitatively different, apparently no attempt has yet been made to determine whether these two conditions lead to different patterns of exposure or of agenda-setting effects.

Procedures measuring need for orientation also have changed over time. Originally (McCombs & Weaver, 1973), relevance was ascertained by combining responses to measures of interest in the campaign, amount of discussion about specific political issues, and amount of discussion about politics in general; uncertainty was gauged by consistency of the respondent's voting record over the last four presidential elections, strength of party identification, and degree of certainty reported about the respondent's choice of a presidential candidate. Weaver (1978) reduced the measurement of relevance to a single 4-point scale reflecting degree of interest in the campaign. Uncertainty was measured alternately by a single voting intention scale (those with a definite voting choice were "low" in uncertainty; all others were "high") or a measure of political party affiliation (those with no party preference were "high" in uncertainty; all others were "low").

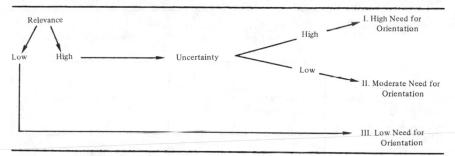

Figure 1. Original conception of levels of need for orientation. *Source:* McCombs and Weaver (1973).

Studies based on the need for orientation construct have been moderately successful, although, as with the ad hoc agenda-setting studies, results seem to raise more questions than they answer. Studies using aggregated agendas (e.g., McCombs & Weaver, 1973; Weaver, 1977; Weaver, Graber, McCombs, & Eyal, 1981) have found that higher levels of need for orientation lead to higher levels of exposure to political information in mass media and to increased agenda-setting effects, especially for newspapers and somewhat less so for television news. When analyses have been based on individual rather than aggregated agendas, however, the results have been somewhat different. Schoenbach and Weaver (1983, 1985) found greatest agenda-setting effects at moderate levels of need for orientation; those with low interest and high uncertainty were most susceptible to agenda-setting effects. McLeod et al. (1974) also found agenda-setting effects to be strongest among less interested and more uncertain voters. Such indications that the association of agenda-setting and individual-level need for orientation is nonlinear have prompted rethinking of what motives might be tapped by measures of need for orientation, most often in the form of exploring the ways need for orientation might relate to more specific cognitive and other motives for informational media use (e.g., McCombs & Weaver, 1985).

A second question raised in need-for-orientation (as well as ad hoc) research concerns discrepant findings about the agenda-setting effects of media coverage of obtrusive issues (topics with which people have direct personal experience) and unobtrusive issues (topics for which media may be people's only source of information). Some studies (e.g., Weaver et al., 1981) have found greater agenda-setting effects for unobtrusive topics than for obtrusive topics; Iyengar and Kinder (1985), in contrast, found agenda-setting effects for television news treatments of a problem to be greatest among viewers who were personally affected by the problem. These results illustrate some of the ambiguity in the need for orientation construct. On the one hand, the construct might predict that uncertainty would be highest for unobtrusive topics, since people have no direct experience with such topics, so unobtrusive topics should produce more agenda-setting. On the other hand, personal

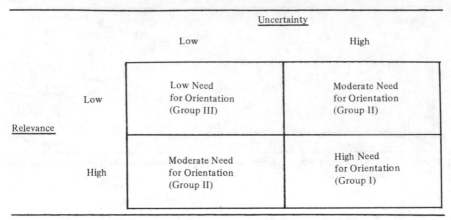

Figure 2. Revised conceptions of levels of need for orientation. *Source:* Weaver (1978).

relevance should be highest for topics with which people have direct experience (such as, in Iyengar and Kinder's study, news about civil rights for black viewers, unemployment for unemployed viewers, and social security for elderly viewers), so coverage of obtrusive topics should produce more agenda-setting.

The need for refinement of the need-for-orientation construct may be reflected also in the results mentioned earlier showing greatest agenda-setting at moderate levels of need for orientation. By extrapolation, Iyengar & Kinder's "most affected" groups might be expected to feel high relevance but low uncertainty about their respective topics, hence moderate need for orientation. These subjects would fall in the lower left quadrant of Weaver's (1978) fourfold typology (Figure 2) and should be distinguished from persons who arrive at moderate need for orientation via low relevance but high uncertainty. The present conceptualization of need for orientation offers no basis for making differential predictions concerning the two different combinations of relevance and uncertainty that lead to moderate need for orientation.

Studies Based on Psychological Responses to Exposure

Iyengar and his coworkers (Iyengar & Kinder, 1985; Iyengar, Kinder, Peters, & Krosnick, 1984; Iyengar, Peters, & Kinder, 1982) have conducted a number of experiments in which, by inserting into network television newscasts stories from previous broadcasts, the researchers, have manipulated the relative prominence the newscasts gave to various topics. Observing changes in subjects' assessments of the relative importance of the manipulated topics over a week's viewing of the newscasts, the researchers confirmed both the general agenda-setting influence of television news and the existence of significant individual differences between viewers in the strength of the agenda-setting effect.

In the Iyengar et al. (1982) study individual differences were explained in terms of covert evaluations that the news stories triggered in viewers. Viewers who, when asked to report their thoughts, reactions, or feelings about the manipulated stories, offered greater numbers of negative responses in the form of counterarguments showed less agenda-setting. These viewers also were more interested in, knowledgeable about, attentive to, and active in politics. But, the counterarguing explanation fared less well in the 1985 study (Iyengar & Kinder) when pitted against alternative accounts based on affective response to the stories and assessments of the credibility of network news. The counterarguing hypothesis received the weakest support, affective response received stronger support, and the most compelling evidence favored the influence of source credibility judgments. Given the high degree of trust most viewers accord network television newscasts, the 1985 results suggest that agenda-setting is mediated more by emotional reactions to stories than by cognitive responses.

When these findings are set against the backdrop of ad hoc and need-for-orientation-based agenda-setting studies, two considerations that must be kept in mind become clear. First, studies taking those other approaches have found with some consistency that, compared to television, newspapers exert stronger agenda-setting effects. The results of Iyengar and his coworkers concerning television viewing thus provide fairly impressive evidence of agenda-setting. Second, the advocates of need for orientation assert that their construct's value stems from its ability in natural settings to predict both levels of exposure to news and agenda-setting effects. By controlling exposure, the experimenters have posed a somewhat different question than that asked by field researchers—namely, at a given level of exposure, what accounts for individual differences in the magnitude of agenda-setting? While it is tempting to find in one approach solutions to puzzles raised in the other (e.g., does high need for orientation lead to less agenda-setting than moderate need for orientation because persons who rank high have the qualities that lead to counterarguing?), such reasoning should be restrained by the very significant differences between the settings and questions that characterize each approach.

The Media Agenda and the Public Agenda

Questions about the effects of media agendas on public or personal agendas have been pursued largely in public agenda-setting studies. Included in that diffuse body of research are studies that explore such topics as differential agenda-setting effects of various media (e.g., McClure & Patterson, 1976; Patterson & McClure, 1976; Shaw & Clemmer, 1977; Whitney & Becker, 1982), influence on agenda-setting of interaction of attributes of topic and medium (e.g., Palmgreen & Clarke, 1977), length of time over which media coverage of an issue has its greatest, cumulative agenda-setting effect (e.g.,

Winter & Eyal, 1981), and the extent to which different media exert their greatest agenda-setting effects at different stages in the evolution of a political campaign (e.g., McCombs, 1977).

Over-time comparisons of aggregate media agendas to aggregate public agendas may provide indications of whether the two agendas vary together, suggesting that they both reflect the influence of real-world cues (Iyengar, 1979). As with most other facets of agenda-setting research, empirical findings on this question are discrepant. Charting media and public agendas over periods of a decade or more, Funkhouser (1973) and MacKuen (1981) found that, with some exceptions, public concern for problems reflects changes over time in the attention paid to those problems by media. Over an eight-year period, however, Neuman and Fryling (1985) found media and public agendas varied together on six issues, public agendas led media agendas on two issues, and public and media agendas varied independently on two other issues. The researchers characterized this pattern as "interactive feedback" reflecting mutual causality between media and public agendas. Iyengar (1979) determined that changes in network television news agendas over a two-year period were not accompanied by corresponding changes in the agendas of the news audience and, although there was some degree of convergence between the two agendas, the direction of causality was unclear. Despite these inconsistencies, the weight of the evidence suggests to some reviewers (e.g., Roberts & Maccoby, 1985) that media agendas seem to lead and exert causal influence on the public agenda, "for at least some issues under some conditions" (p. 564).

The Process of Setting Media Priorities

Considerable research has been conducted in recent years that, while not oriented explicitly to agenda-setting, reveals much about the process by which news editors and their coworkers decide how much prominence to give to various topics that might be covered in the news. Some of this research has probed the professional practices and conventions that guide "news judgment" (e.g., Gans, 1979; Tuchman, 1978), the process by which events are judged to be newsworthy and decisions are made about how, and how prominently, to report events. Among other things, this process has been found to include the use of particular interpretive frames to decide what is news and how a particular event can best be translated into a "story" (see, e.g., Nimmo & Combs, 1983; Swanson, 1977). Such frames, which are thought to reflect requirements of the audience and the medium, have been shown to produce news stories that challenge established institutions and authority as well as support them (e.g., Nimmo & Combs, 1985).

Another useful approach to the process by which media agendas are formed examines the relationship between news professionals and the officials who are their major source of information. The mutual dependency linking news media and government has often been noted (e.g., Ball-Rokeach, 1985). Blumler and Gurevitch (1981) have proposed a conception that goes beyond the simpler adversary and exchange models in which media-government relationships are usually formulated. Their conception recognizes that the relationship is governed by an emergent shared culture that constrains both parties while allowing each to pursue its own (different) interests to an extent that is sufficient for the relationship to be successful. Like the use of common interpretive frames in news, the management of press-politician dependency also typically leads to news coverage that supports established institutions, but that is not always the case nor a goal of news practices per se. It is too simple to describe news as selling "the perspective of the ruling class" (Rogers & Dearing, p. 558) without recognizing the concrete practices that indirectly lead to that result or the many tensions and exceptions that such a characterization glosses over. Although not "agenda research," studies such as these have provided our most detailed understanding of the process by which media agendas are formed and of some of the most important attributes of the content of news stories.

Setting the Policy Agenda

There are, as Rogers and Dearing's survey makes clear, few connections between studies of how public policy agendas are formed and acted upon and research on media and public or personal agendas. To understand why this should be so, it is important to recognize that the relationship of public policy to media and personal agendas is of a different sort than the relationship that we imagine links media and personal agendas. That is, while agenda researchers look for a straightforward causal relationship between media and public agendas (mediated by various contingent conditions), the relationship of both agendas to public policy is quite complex.

The premise that public policy, among other things, should be responsive in some way to "public opinion" does not lead to the conclusion that there should be a direct or substantial relationship between the public agenda and the making of public policy. Without rehearsing the serious debates over what we should understand "public opinion" to be (see Nimmo, 1978; Zukin, 1981), most usages of the term make reference to the content or substance of citizens' views about issues of the day. The public's agenda does not reveal what persons think about topics in the news, only that some of those topics are perceived to be important. Nor does the aggregated public agenda reflect the judgments of diverse subgroups or publics to which policymaking is, or should be, responsive.

The public agenda is one source of limited information about the public's concerns. It reflects one facet of aggregated public opinion, which in turn is one of several touchstones (e.g., election results, individual and mass expressions of views, organized advocacy of group interests) policymakers may consult to determine the views of citizens. When we realize that policymaking is produced through a process of negotiations among policy elites who represent divergent interests and work within numerous constraints and that the process of making public policy is highly variable and sensitive to numerous contextual influences, the relationship we should expect to find between public agendas and policymaking becomes further complicated (see Cobb & Elder, 1981). Perhaps this complexity is why, although wishing to encourage the integration of policy and public agenda research, Rogers and Dearing are unable to offer much specific guidance concerning how we should proceed.

Translated to the domain of policymaking, the concept of public agenda-setting does suggest one straightforward empirical question we might ask: To what extent do the agendas of policy elites reflect or lead citizens' agendas? However, pursuing even this question is made difficult by ambiguity concerning what constitutes the agenda of policy elites. Is this agenda to be found in policy actions (e.g., legislation), or elites' private views (similar to individuals' rankings of issues), or elites' public discourse (e.g., election campaign speeches and other persuasive messages)? Some agenda-setting researchers have examined congruence between politicians' agendas displayed in campaign discourse and voters' agendas either over the course of a campaign (e.g., Siune & Borre, 1975) or in terms of a specific agenda display such as a campaign debate (e.g., Swanson & Swanson, 1978). In general, such studies have found some degree of congruence between politicians' and voters' agendas as well as circumstances in which politicians might be viewed as leading voters' agendas, at least to a limited extent.

Evidence reviewed by Rogers and Dearing offers better reasons to assume that media agendas relate to the perceptions and actions of policy elites in fairly straightforward ways, both by reflecting the emphases that elites give to topics or issues and by serving as one source of information elites may consider in forming impressions of what the public is concerned about (see also Cobb & Elder, 1981; Nimmo, 1978). As those reviewers make clear, both relationships are predictably and fortunately imperfect.

PUTTING THE PARTS TOGETHER:
INTEGRATING AGENDA STUDIES?

The main argument of Rogers and Dearing's survey seems to be that we need to integrate and bring theoretical coherence to public, media, and policy agenda research. While doing so might offer several advantages, as Rogers and Dearing note, there are also reasons to be skeptical of the effort. The closer we get to the details of agenda research, the less appealing the prospect of integration becomes.

The Limited Scope of "Agenda"

One reason for caution is the limited scope of the concept of "agenda." As we have seen, the public's agenda tells us comparatively little about the contents of citizens' views. Similarly, the media agenda is uninformative about the content of news coverage of topics or issues. It seems obvious that if we wish to understand fully how the media influence the public's views or the actions of policymakers, then we must go beyond agendas and consider the content of persons' opinions and of news stories. Yet, the concept of agenda-setting, even in its most precise theoretical formulation as presented by McCombs and his coworkers (e.g., McCombs & Shaw, 1972, 1977; Shaw, 1977), contains no resources that can be extended straightforwardly to encompass media content or media effects other than the awareness and salience of topics.

Attempts to relate the concept of agenda to attitudes and to the content of news stories have enjoyed only limited success. McCombs and Shaw (McCombs, 1981; McCombs & Shaw, 1977) have proposed that we conceive of news stories as presenting not only topics but also agendas of attributes of those topics. This approach was taken by Becker & McCombs (1978), who sought to relate changes in respondents' "candidate agendas" (judgments of which Democratic candidate for the nomination was leading) and descriptions of candidates ("attribute agendas") to attributes of candidates given in media coverage of the 1976 presidential primary campaigns. In so doing, the meaning of "agenda" was altered (i.e., saying that Carter is leading the race is not quite the same as saying that Carter is in some sense the "most important" candidate) so that it is not clear what is being measured. Moreover, the notion of attributes (e.g., a Southerner, a former governor) invites infinite regress in coding the content of a news story (are attributes propositions of fact, nouns, relationships—is Fawn Hall an attribute of Oliver North, who is an attribute of the Iran arms scandal?) and still leaves us some distance away from persons' attitudes and even their agendas. Learning that the phrase "soon may resume testing nuclear weapons" is an attribute of "the Soviets" may or may not affect one's judgment about the threat of nuclear war and may or may not change one's attitude toward the Soviets. In effect, this approach shifts attention from personal agendas to learning the content of news stories (or, more properly, recalling information about a topic in the same attributional categories represented in the news stories). Proceeding in this way does not so much extend agenda-setting research as supplant it with a quite different approach that connects to a long tradition of studies of learning from mass media (concerning, for example, political socialization) without telling us much about personal agendas or how they are formed.

A different approach is offered by Iyengar et al.'s (1982) conception of priming, which holds that the public's judgment of a president's overall performance (and, to a lesser extent, competence) may be affected by the relative prominence news media give to stories that may seem to reflect presidential performance. The process that may explain this effect concerns the accessibility of information in making judgments. This process has been the subject of considerable research (see the review by Higgins & King, 1981) in the study of social cognition. While we cannot adequately understand media agenda-setting or policy decisions by reference to information accessibility phenomena, there may be a useful way of linking a kind of media content (stories reflecting presidential performance) to a certain sort of attitude (judgment of overall presidential performance and competence). This approach leaves us some distance from dealing with the details of typical media content and with the contents of persons' opinions on matters of public interest, however.

Thus it appears that efforts to broaden the scope of the concept of agenda may lead to changing the concept's meaning and converting agenda-setting into an instance of some other, more general phenomenon or process (e.g., learning information from mass media or effects of information accessibility on social cognition) that carries us far from agenda-setting. This may be the inevitable result of attempting to broaden a concept that proposes an empirical fact, not a theory, and lacks resources to support extending that fact to related facts.

Problems of Translation Between Levels

To be successful, an integration of agenda research of the sort Rogers and Dearing urge presumably would need to be based on a substantive conception of how agendas are formed that could guide investigation at each level of agenda-setting—public, media, and policy—and bring needed theoretical and methodological consistency to the conduct of research. While the prospect of a general framework is appealing, the possibility is diminished by problems encountered in translating conceptions of agenda-setting between levels or types of agendas.

At the personal or public level of agenda-setting, as we have seen, most research has been conducted in an ad hoc fashion with no explicit theoretical grounding (stating the agenda-setting hypothesis serves as a surrogate for a theoretical conception in many of these studies). The only theoretical conception that has generated a program of systematic research is built upon the idea of need for orientation (McCombs & Weaver, 1973; Schoenbach & Weaver, 1985; Weaver, 1977, 1978). In this view, persons who regard a topic or issue as personally salient or relevant and who are uncertain about the topic or issue may become motivated to acquire information about the topic or issue through the mass media, leading to the agenda-setting effect. While there are reasons to believe that the concept of need for orientation needs refinement, it is our most likely candidate for a theory of individual-level agenda-setting.

Need for orientation is of no help in understanding the process by which media agendas are set. The most useful accounts of how media priorities are determined point to the influence of especially prestigious news outlets and organizations, the emergent culture and routine interactions governing reporters' relationships with official news sources, and the interpretive frames used to transform events into news "stories." Judgments of personal salience and uncertainty do not figure in constructing the news agenda.

While we have no theoretical account of agenda-setting at the level of public policy (and some uncertainty about what such an account might look like or explain), it is clear from what we have seen that theoretical conceptions used to explain personal and media agenda-setting offer little help in understanding the formation of policy agendas. Here too it seems likely that distinct processes not found at the personal or media level are at work. Theoretical accounts that offer adequate explanations at one level do not translate to the other level.

Problems of translation suggest that each level of agenda-setting is likely to be best understood by theoretical conceptions that are specific to that level. There does not appear to be a single, underlying process of agenda-setting on which a general integrative framework might be based. As a result, a general framework could have only topical, not theoretical, coherence. Such a framework might describe agenda-setting phenomena at each level (although the very meaning of "agenda" is different at each level) and, perhaps, invoke level-specific local theories as explanations. The theoretical and methodological coherence and consistency that are so needed in agenda research could be achieved only within levels of agenda-setting, not across levels. And, greater theoretical coherence and methodological consistency would result not from having a general framework but from taking seriously local theories of the sort that at least some researchers presently work with.

Thus while the desire to answer fundamental questions about the role of media in representative political systems and pluralistic societies and to bring theoretical coherence and methodological consistency to agenda research is understandable, seeking a general framework does not seem to be an effective way to accomplish what is wanted. The limited scope of the concept of agenda prevents us from answering fully the major questions, and creating an integrative framework will not overcome problems of translation or bring to the research the qualities that are desired. The parts of this animal simply do not fit together. Instead, they seem to be parts of several different beasts.

AN ALTERNATIVE TO A GENERAL
FRAMEWORK: BETTER PARTS

That a general integrative framework is no solution to whatever we might think ails agenda research should not cause pessimism. Indeed, recognizing that the solution does not lie in a general framework helps to clarify the nature of the task confronting those who wish to bring consistency and coherence to agenda research. For the present, the prudent course seems to be pursuing systematic programs of research within levels of agenda-setting based on level-specific theories. The following very brief discussion points out how some of the most interesting questions raised in agenda studies can be addressed in research based on local theories and argues against the assumption that we need agenda research per se in order to learn about agenda-related matters.

The closest approximation we have to a theoretical account of media effects on individuals' agendas is based on the idea of need for orientation. As we have seen, perhaps the most interesting questions raised by research concerning this construct have to do with curiosities concerning moderate levels of need for orientation (e.g., whether there is theoretical justification for the empirical distinction made by Weaver, 1978, and others; why greatest agenda-setting effects should occur at moderate levels of need for orientation). Dealing with these questions requires careful conceptual analysis. It is crucial to recognize, for instance, that changes noted earlier in the measurement of need for orientation have effectively altered the meaning of the concept: Relevance has become simply "interest" in a campaign; uncertainty has come to reflect such various matters as having a party preference or having made a voting choice in an impending election (Weaver, 1978) and feeling "sufficiently informed" about issues in an election (Schoenbach & Weaver, 1985).

While we are uncertain about what "uncertainty" refers to in the context of election campaigns, given the diversity of methods used to determine it or what it might refer to outside the campaign context, it it clear that "interest" encompasses a range of quite different motives that might lead persons to follow news coverage of a political campaign (see, e.g., Blumler, 1979). Some of these motives are cognitive utilitarian (e.g., surveillance), while others are not (e.g., diversion). The current method of ascertaining need for orientation thus combines a (presumably) cognitive utilitarian incentive to attend to media (uncertainty) with an index of general interest, which may reflect motives that are unrelated to cognitive utilitarian goals. It is not surprising that predictions based on the assumption that need for orientation measures cognitive utilitarian motives for media use (McCombs & Weaver, 1972) have not been confirmed consistently in recent research (e.g., the nonlinear association of need for orientation with agenda-setting found in McLeod et al., 1974, and Schoenbach & Weaver, 1983, 1985).

We need to consider what is revealed in measures of need for orientation. One promising avenue is illustrated by Weaver's (1980) examination of how need for orientation and specific gratifications sought from media use influence the association between using media for political information and levels of political knowledge. Proceeding in this way does not produce "agenda research," though it can clarify the construct that is our best explanation of individual-level agenda-setting effects.

Similarly, the process by which media agendas are formed seems to be best revealed not through, say, comparisons of "real-world" objective indicators of the significance of events and the prominence given those events in news agendas but rather through direct investigation of the professional conventions and interpretive practices that lead to judging events as newsworthy and determining the kind and prominence of coverage they should be given.

Attempting to find answers to the questions raised by agenda studies in programs of research based on local theories, including research that is not "agenda research" per se, may offer ways around some difficulties that seem to be inherent in agenda research. For example, the agenda-setting hypothesis does not include any recognition that individual interpretive processes may bend and shape media messages in ways that channel the messages' effects, yet this vital component of an adequate understanding of the influence of mass communication can be incorporated if agenda-setting is studied as an instance of more general processes, such as those that link gratification-seeking to media exposure and effects (see Blumler, Gurevitch, & Katz, 1985). Studying the learning of information presented in news stories directly rather than as an indirect indicator of "attribute agenda-setting" can reveal some cognitive effects of exposure to news without the definitional frustrations created by determining whether what is learned is an attribute, a topic, an event, or an issue (and, therefore, "agenda information"). Such wrangling does not help us better understand mass communication's effects but is made necessary by trying to force those effects into the framework of agenda research.

The most promising future for agenda-related research seems to be one that capitalizes on the valuable contributions of agenda research (such as raising some critical questions about media and society and identifying particular kinds of effects) but does not assume that in order to study the issues raised in agenda studies we need "agenda research." The approaches that may best answer the questions raised in Rogers and Dearing's survey may lead us away from agendas as a construct for organizing research but closer to more penetrating and comprehensive understandings of the process of mass communication.

REFERENCES

Atwood, L. E., Sohn, A., & Sohn, H. (1976). *Community discussion and newspaper content.* Paper presented at the meeting of the Association for Education in Journalism, College Park, MD.

Ball-Rokeach, S. J. (1985). The origins of individual media-system dependency: A sociological framework. *Communication Research, 12,* 485-510.

Becker, L. B. (1982). The mass media and citizen assessment of issue importance: A reflection on agenda-setting research. In D. C. Whitney & E. Wartella (Eds.), *Mass communication review yearbook 3* (pp. 521-536). Newbury Park, CA: Sage.

Becker, L. B., & McCombs, M. E. (1978). The role of the press in determining voter reactions to presidential primaries. *Human Communication Research, 4,* 301-307.

Blumler, J. G. (1979). The role of theory in uses and gratifications studies. *Communication Research, 6,* 9-36.

Blumler, J. G., & Gurevitch, M. (1981). Politicians and the press: An essay on role relationships. In D. D. Nimmo & K. R. Sanders (Eds.), *Handbook of political communication* (pp. 467-493). Newbury Park, CA: Sage.

Blumler, J. G., Gurevitch, M., & Katz, E. (1985). Reaching out: A future for gratifications research. In K. E. Rosengren, L. A. Wenner, & E. Katz (Eds.), *Media gratifications research: Current perspectives* (pp. 255-273). Newbury Park, CA: Sage.

Cobb, R. W., & Elder, C. D. (1981). Communication and public policy. In D. D. Nimmo & K. R. Sanders (Eds.), *Handbook of political communication* (pp. 391-416). Newbury Park, CA: Sage.

Cohen, B. (1963). *The press and foreign policy.* Princeton, NJ: Princeton University Press.

Eyal, C. H., Winter, J. P., & DeGeorge, W. F. (1979). *Time frame for agenda-setting.* Paper presented at the meeting of the American Association of Public Opinion Research, Buck Hills Fall, PA.

Funkhouser, G. R. (1973). The issues of the sixties: An exploratory study in the dynamics of public opinion. *Public Opinion Quarterly, 37,* 62-75.

Gans, H. J. (1979). *Deciding what's news: A study of CBS Evening News, NBC Nightly News, Newsweek and Time.* New York: Vintage.

Higgins, E. T., & King, G. (1981). Accessibility of social constructs: Information-processing consequences of individual and contextual variability. In N. Cantor & J. Kihlstrom (Eds.), *Personality, cognition, and social interaction* (pp. 69-121). Hillsdale, NJ: Lawrence Erlbaum.

Iyengar, S. (1979). Television news and issue salience: A reexamination of the agenda-setting hypothesis. *American Politics Quarterly, 7,* 395-416.

Iyengar, S., & Kinder, D. R. (1985). Psychological accounts of agenda-setting. In S. Kraus & R. M. Perloff (Eds.), *Mass media and political thought* (pp. 117-140). Newbury Park, CA: Sage.

Iyengar, S., Kinder, D. R., Peters, M. D., & Krosnick, J. A. (1984). The evening news and presidential evaluations. *Journal of Personality and Social Psychology, 46,* 778-787.

Iyengar, S., Peters, M. D., & Kinder, D. R. (1982). Experimental demonstrations of the "not-so-minimal" consequences of television news programs. *American Political Science Review, 76,* 848-858.

Jones, E. E., & Gerard, H. B. (1967). *Foundations of social psychology.* New York: John Wiley.

Kaid, L. L., Hale, K., & Williams, J. A. (1977). Media agenda setting of a specific political event. *Journalism Quarterly, 54,* 584-587.

Kinder, D. R., & Sears, D. O. (1985). Public opinion and political action. In G. Lindzey & E. Aronson (Eds.), *The handbook of social psychology* (3rd ed., Vol. 2, pp. 659-741). New York: Random House.

Kraus, S., & Davis, D. (1976). *The effects of mass communication on political behavior.* University Park: Pennsylvania State University Press.

MacKuen, M. B. (1981). Social communication and the mass policy agenda. In M. B. MacKuen & S. L. Coombs (Eds.), *More than news: Media power in public affairs* (pp. 19-144). Newbury Park, CA: Sage.

McClure, R. D., & Patterson, T. E. (1976). Print vs. network news. *Journal of Communication, 26*(2), 23-28.

McCombs, M. E. (1977). Newspapers versus television: Mass communication effects across time. In D. L. Shaw & M. E. McCombs (Eds.), *The emergence of American political issues* (pp. 89-105). St. Paul, MN: West.

McCombs, M. E. (1981). The agenda-setting approach. In D. D. Nimmo & K. R. Sanders (Eds.), *Handbook of political communication* (pp. 121-140). Newbury Park, CA: Sage.

McCombs, M. E., & Shaw, D. L. (1972). The agenda-setting function of mass media. *Public Opinion Quarterly, 36,* 176-187.

McCombs, M. E., & Shaw, D. L. (1977). The agenda-setting function of the press. In D. L. Shaw & M. E. McCombs (Eds.), *The emergence of American political issues* (pp. 1-18). St. Paul, MN: West.

McCombs, M., & Weaver, D. (1973, April). *Voters' need for orientation and use of mass communication.* Paper presented at the annual meeting of the International Communication Association, Montreal.

McCombs, M. E., & Weaver, D. H. (1985). Toward a merger of gratifications and agenda-setting research. In K. E. Rosengren, L. A. Wenner, & P. Palmgreen (Eds.), *Media gratifications research: Current perspectives* (pp. 95-108). Newbury Park, CA: Sage.

McLeod, J. M., Becker, L. B., & Byrnes, J. E. (1974). Another look at the agenda-setting function of the press. *Communication Research, 1,* 131-166.

Neuman, W. R., & Fryling, A. C. (1985). Patterns of political cognition: An exploration of the public mind. In S. Kraus & R. M. Perloff (Eds.), *Mass media and political thought* (pp. 223-240). Newbury Park, CA: Sage.

Nimmo, D. (1978). *Political communication and public opinion in America.* Santa Monica, CA: Goodyear.

Nimmo, D., & Combs, J. E. (1983). *Mediated political realities.* New York: Longman.

Nimmo, D., & Combs, J. E. (1985). *Nightly horrors: Crisis coverage in television network news.* Knoxville: University of Tennessee Press.

Palmgreen, P., & Clarke, P. (1977). Agenda-setting with local and national issues. *Communication Research, 4,* 435-452.

Patterson, T. E., & McClure, R. D. (1976). *The unseeing eye: The myth of television power in national politics.* New York: Putnam.

Roberts, D. F., & Bachen, C. M. (1981). Mass communication effects. *Annual Review of Psychology, 32,* 307-356.

Roberts, D. F., & Maccoby, N. (1985). Effects of mass communication. In G. Lindzey & E. Aronson (Eds.), *The handbook of social psychology* (3rd ed., Vol. 2, pp. 539-598). New York: Random House.

Schoenbach, K., & Weaver, D. H. (1983, May). *Cognitive bonding and need for orientation during political campaigns.* Paper presented at the annual meeting of the International Communication Association, Dallas.

Schoenbach, K., & Weaver, D. H. (1985). Finding the unexpected: Cognitive bonding in a political campaign. In S. Kraus & R. M. Perloff (Eds.), *Mass media and political thought* (pp. 157-176). Newbury Park, CA: Sage.

Shaw, D. L., & Clemmer, C. L. (1977). News and the public response. In D. L. Shaw & M. E. McCombs (Eds.), *The emergence of American political issues* (pp. 33-51). St. Paul, MN: West.

Siune, K., & Borre, O. (1975). Setting the agenda for a Danish election. *Journal of Communication, 26*(1), 65-73.

Swanson, D. L. (1977). And that's the way it was? Television covers the 1976 presidential campaign. *Quarterly Journal of Speech, 63,* 239-248.

Swanson, L. L., & Swanson, D. L. (1978). The agenda-setting function of the first Ford-Carter debate. *Communication Monographs, 45,* 347-353.

Tolman, E. C. (1932). *Purposive behavior in animals and men.* New York: Appleton-Century.

Tuchman, G. (1978). *Making news: A study in the construction of reality.* New York: Macmillan.

Weaver, D. H. (1977). Political issues and voter need for orientation. In D. L. Shaw & M. E. McCombs (Eds.), *The emergence of American political issues* (pp. 107-119). St. Paul, MN: West.

Weaver, D. (1978, April). *Need for orientation, media uses and gratifications, and media effects.* Paper presented at the annual meeting of the International Communication Association, Chicago.

Weaver, D. H. (1980). Audience need for orientation and media effects. *Communication Research, 7,* 361-376.

Weaver, D. H., Graber, D. A., McCombs, M. E., & Eyal, C. H. (1981). *Media agenda-setting in a presidential election.* New York: Praeger.

Whitney, D. C., & Becker, L. B. (1982). "Keeping the gates" for the gatekeepers: The effects of wire news. *Journalism Quarterly, 59,* 60-65.

Williams, W., & Larsen, D. C. (1977). Agenda-setting in an off-election year. *Journalism Quarterly, 54,* 744-749.

Winter, J. P., & Eyal, C. H. (1981). Agenda setting for the civil rights issue. *Public Opinion Quarterly, 45,* 376-383.

Zukin, C. (1981). Mass communication and public opinion. In D. D. Nimmo & K. R. Sanders (Eds.), *Handbook of political communication* (pp. 359-390). Newbury Park, CA: Sage.

SUBJECT INDEX

ABOUT THE EDITOR

JAMES A. ANDERSON (Ph.D., University of Iowa, 1965) is Professor of Communication at the University of Utah. His scholarly writing concerns the relationship between theory and method in science, an area he most recently explored in *Communication Research: Issues and Methods* (1987). His research interests focus on the communication structures and practices of social action routines, political campaigns, media literacy, and family ethnographies.

ABOUT THE AUTHORS

TERRANCE L. ALBRECHT (Ph.D., Michigan State University, 1978) is Associate Professor of Speech Communication at the University of Washington. Her work has appeared in several journals in communication and allied disciplines and she is coauthor of *Communicating Social Support.* Her current research involves a large-scale study of supervisory support and performance outcomes of health care personnel in Northwest regional hospitals. In addition, she has continuing research interests in the role of personal relationships in fostering the innovation process, with current studies in a clinical setting, a large school district, and a manufacturing organization.

ROBERT C. ALLEN (Ph.D., University of Iowa, 1977) is Associate Professor of Radio, Television, and Motion Pictures and Associate Dean of the College of Arts and Sciences at the University of North Carolina at Chapel Hill. His books include *Speaking of Soap Operas* (1985) and *Film History: Theory and Practice* (1985), the latter coauthored with Douglas Gomery. He is the editor of *Channels of Discourse: Television and Contemporary Criticism* (1987). His most recent research, which he pursued while a Fellow at the National Humanities Center in 1986-87, concerns nineteenth-century American popular entertainment.

DAVID L. ALTHEIDE (Ph.D., University of California, San Diego, 1974) is Professor in the School of Justice Studies at Arizona State University, where he also serves as Field Research Director in the Center for Urban Studies. His award-winning books (*Creating Reality* and *Media Power*) and other research reports have delineated the nature and social consequences of mass communication content and formats for social control. Now completing a study of the relevance of TV formats for dispute resolution, he has also begun work on an analysis of the role of the mass media in peace and war.

FRANK A. BIOCCA (Ph.D., Wisconsin—Madison, 1988) is Assistant Professor of Journalism and Acting Director of the Center for Research in Journalism and Mass Communication at the University of North Carolina at Chapel Hill. His current research includes a series of experimental studies on the structural and syntactic properties of television. He is also studying the cognition and psychosemiotics of political advertising under a grant from the Gannett Foundation.

JOHN BOINEY (A.B., Dartmouth College, 1985) is currently enrolled in the Ph.D. program at Duke University, where his research interests are the U.S. presidency and the role of the mass media in the U.S. political system.

ERNEST G. BORMANN (Ph.D., University of Iowa, 1953), Professor in the Department of Speech-Communication at the University of Minnesota—Minneapolis, is currently conducting an international study of the predisposition to share fantasies in West Germany, the Netherlands, Great Britain, and the United States. The ultimate goal of the program is to develop an artificial imagination computer capability. His publications include numerous articles as well as *Communication Theory* (1980) and *The Force of Fantasy: Restoring the American Dream* (1985).

GEORGE CHENEY (Ph.D., Purdue University, 1985) is Assistant Professor of Communication at the University of Colorado at Boulder. His primary areas of interest in research and teaching include organizational communication, communication theory, and rhetorical theory and criticism, with a special emphasis on how the relationship of the individual to society is shaped and expressed in the organizational setting. He has published in a number of scholarly journals and edited volumes and has received a dissertation award from the Speech Communication Association. He is at work on a book offering an integrative perspective on human identity, social organization, and rhetorical process.

JAMES W. DEARING (B.A., California State University, Sacramento, 1985) is a doctoral candidate at the Annenberg School of Communications, University of Southern California. His primary research interests include studying patterns of influence among mass media, policymakers, and public opinion in international contexts, as well as studying areas of high technology growth in Japan and the United States and the processes of technology transfer within those areas.

STANLEY DEETZ (Ph.D., Ohio University, 1973) is Associate Professor and Chair of the Department of Communication at Rutgers University. He is author of *Managing Interpersonal Communication* and has published widely on interpersonal and organizational communication. Currently his work focuses on the application of European critical philosophies to the study of cultural forms in business and governmental organizations.

CAREN J. DEMING (Ph.D., University of Michigan, 1976) is Professor and Head of the Department of Media Arts at the University of Arizona. Her primary research interests are television criticism and contemporary feminist theory. Publications representative of her work have appeared in *Critical Studies in Mass Communication, Journal of Broadcasting and Electronic Media,* and Journal of Popular Culture. She is the editor of *Media in Society: Readings in Mass Communication*, with Samuel L. Becker.

SUE DeWINE (Ph.D., Indiana University, 1977) is Professor of Organizational Communication in the School of Interpersonal Communication at Ohio University in Athens, Ohio. She is former chair of the Organizational

Communication Division of the International Communication Association, has served as Associate Editor for a variety of professional journals and as Editor of the *Ohio Speech Communication Journal,* and is coauthor of four books and many published articles in communication, psychology, business, and consulting journals. Her research interests include computer-mediated communication and human communication systems, instrumentation and research methods, training evaluation and organizational development, female leaders, conflict, and power.

ALEX S. EDELSTEIN (Ph.D., University of Minnesota, 1958) is Professor of Communication at the University of Washington. He recently served as the Hosa Bunka Chair Professor of Communication at the Institute for Communication Research, Keio University, in Tokyo, where he continued his research and teaching in the communication processes of public opinion.

GARY GUMPERT (Ph.D., Wayne State University, 1963) is Chair and Professor of Communication Arts and Sciences at Queens College of the City University of New York. His major interests include the relationship of interpersonal communication and media, media grammars, and the nature of stereotyping. His latest publications include *Talking Tombstones and Other Tales of the Media Age* (1987) and *Intermedia: Interpersonal Communication in a Media World* (1986), coedited with Robert Cathcart.

BARRIE GUNTER (Ph.D., North East London Polytechnic, 1980) is Head of Research at the Independent Broadcasting Authority in London, UK. His primary research interests include the impact of television violence, memory and comprehension of broadcast news, and the influence of television on social beliefs and attitudes. He has written nine books and has published over 100 papers on various mass communications and psychological research topics.

SHANTO IYENGAR (Ph.D., University of Iowa, 1973) is Associate Professor of Political Science and Director of the Media Research Laboratory at the State University of New York at Stony Brook. He has taught at Kansas State University and Yale University. His current research, which is supported by the National Science Foundation, is directed at the role of the media in framing political issues. He is coauthor of *News That Matters: Television and the Shaping of American Opinion* (University of Chicago Press, 1987). His research has appeared in numerous journals, including *American Political Science Review, American Journal of Political Science, Comparative Political Studies, Journal of Personality and Social Psychology,* and *Public Opinion Quarterly.*

SCOTT JACOBS (Ph.D., University of Illinois, 1982) is Assistant Professor of Communication at the University of Oklahoma. He has research interests in discourse analysis, argumentation, and communication theory.

SUSAN A. JASKO (M.A., Ohio State University, 1985) is a doctoral candidate at Ohio State. She has worked and consulted for large public and private organizations. She specializes in qualitative research applications. Her research interests include complex organizations, cultural models, gender bias in social research, cognitive science, and language.

GARY L. KREPS (Ph.D., University of Southern California, 1979) is Associate Professor of Communication Studies, Northern Illinois University. His research interests include the role of information and communication processes in health care and human organization. He has held faculty positions at Rutgers, Indiana, and Purdue universities, and served as Senior Research Fellow at the National Cancer Institute, helping to frame national policy for cancer information dissemination. His books include *Organizational Communication* (1986), and *Health Communication* (with Barbara C. Thornton, 1984). His publications include numerous articles and chapters concerning communication, health care, management, information science, and education.

THOMAS R. LINDLOF (Ph.D., University of Texas at Austin, 1980) is Associate Professor of Telecommunications at the University of Kentucky. His research interests include children and media socialization, the interpretive dimensions of mediated communication, and the utilization of telecommunications in families, subcultures, and institutions. His publications have appeared in several volumes and journals, including *Communication Research, Communication Yearbook,* and *Journal of Broadcasting & Electronic Media*. Research from a study he recently completed of the forms of family accommodation of VCR-augmented television will appear in the forthcoming volumes *World Families Watching Television* (J. Lull, Ed.) and *Television and the American Family* (J. Bryan, Ed.). He is the editor of *Natural Audiences*, the first collection of ethnographies of media use to appear in the United States.

ROBERT D. McPHEE (Ph.D., Michigan State University, 1978) is Associate Professor of Communication at the University of Wisconsin—Milwaukee. He was recently a Fellow of the Center for Twentieth Century Studies at the same institution. His scholarly interests include organizational communication, communication/social theory, and research methods. He has been known to produce articles (especially replies to people such as Cheney and Tompkins) that have occasional remarks written with tongue irresistibly drawn into cheek.

EILEEN R. MEEHAN (Ph.D., University of Illinois, 1983) is Assistant Professor in the Department of Communication Studies at the University of Iowa. Her research focuses on the political economy of the entertainment/information industries, particularly on the constraining influence of market structure and technological innovation on the selection, assemblage, and distribution of cultural commodities. Her work has appeared in *Critical Studies in Mass Communication; Media, Culture, and Society; Studies in Communication and Society; Journal of Broadcasting and Electronic Media*; and *Journal of Communication Inquiry*. She is a founding member of Communication Perspectives and the Union for Democratic Communication, for which she currently serves as national coordinator.

TIMOTHY P. MEYER (Ph.D., Ohio University, 1970) is the Ben J. and Joyce Rosenberg Professor of Communication and the Arts at the University of Wisconsin—Green Bay. His current interests include research on the impact of mediated communication, advertising, and methodology. His latest coauthored book, *Advertising Research Methods,* combines these interests. His decade-long effort to produce an ethnographically based, mediated communication effects text with J. A. Anderson continues.

MICHAEL PACANOWSKY (Ph.D., Stanford University, 1979) is Associate Professor of Communication at the University of Colorado at Boulder.

DAVID L. PALETZ (Ph.D., University of California, Los Angeles, 1970) is Professor of Political Science at Duke University, and Chairman of the Political Communication Research Group of the International Association for Mass Communication Research. He coauthored *Media Power Politics* (Free Press, 1983), and edited *Political Communication Research* (Ablex, 1987). He is currently working on an extensive comparative study of press coverage throughout the world of the U.S. invasion of Grenada, of the shooting down by the Soviet Union of KAL Flight 007, and of false nuclear alerts.

LOYD S. PETTEGREW (Ph.D., University of Michigan, 1977) is Associate Professor of Communication and Director of the Center for Organizational Communication Research and Service at the University of South Florida. His interests are in organizational communication and the communication processes of health care.

JOSEPH J. PILOTTA (Ph.D., Ohio University, interpersonal communication; Ph.D., University of Toronto, sociology, 1981) is Associate Professor of Communication at Ohio State University. His expertise is in the area of contemporary European social theory, phenomenology and its influence and application to communication theory, methodology, and social issues. His research is in the areas of intercultural communication, technology transfer, community development, and empowerment research. He has edited several books, most recently, *The Underside of High-Tech* (Greenwood Press) and *Practical Reasoning in Human Affairs* (Reidel). He is currently director of two major research projects, the Urban Consortium for Human Services Development and Intercultural Communication for International Trade.

KATHLEEN KELLEY REARDON (Ph.D., University of Massachusetts, 1978) is Associate Professor of Business Communication at the University of Southern California. She holds a joint position in the Department of Preventive Medicine. Her research focuses on interpersonal communication and persuasion, particularly in health settings. She has published three books; *Persuasion: Theory and Context* (Sage), *Gift-Giving Around the World* (Passepartout Travel Publishers), and *Where Minds Meet* (Wadsworth). She has also published in communication, business, and health journals.

EVERETT M. ROGERS (Ph.D., Iowa State University, 1957) is the Walter H. Annenberg Professor of Communication and Associate Dean for Doctoral Studies at the Annenberg School of Communications at the University of Southern California. For the past 34 years, he has been conducting research on the diffusion of innovations, and has authored a series of books on this topic, the most recent of which is *Diffusion of Innovations* (1983). Rogers is currently collaborating with James Dearing, his coauthor in the present volume, in research on the agenda-setting process.

ROBERT P. SNOW (Ph.D., University of Minnesota, 1967) is Associate Professor in the Department of Sociology at Arizona State University. He has pioneered a cultural perspective in understanding the role of the mass media in social life. In addition to *Media Culture,* he also coauthored *Media Logic* (with David Altheide). His recent work focuses on formats for emotional control and presentation.

MARY S. STRINE (Ph.D., University of Washington, 1972) is Associate Professor of Communication at the University of Utah. She has published widely in the area of interpretive and critical studies. Her recent articles on modern critical theory, the rhetoric of cultural forms, and the relationship between American literature and culture have appeared in various national and regional journals as well as in special book-length collections. Her current research focuses on the communicative practices of interpretive communities and on the cultural authority of aesthetic forms of communication. She has served or is currently serving on the editorial boards of *Quarterly Journal of Speech, Critical Studies in Mass Communication, Literature in Performance, Western Journal of Speech Communication*, and *Liberal and Fine Arts Review.*

DAVID L. SWANSON (Ph.D., University of Kansas, 1971) is Associate Professor and Associate Head of Speech Communication, University of Illinois at Urbana-Champaign. His research concerns political communication, the effects of mass communication, and the critical analysis of public discourse. His previous work on these topics has appeared in such journals as *Human Communication Research, Communication Monographs, Quarterly Journal of Speech, Communication Research,* and *Journal of Broadcasting &*

Electronic Media, as well as several edited volumes. He is coeditor of the forthcoming second edition of the *Handbook of Political Communication.*

PHILLIP J. TICHENOR (Ph.D., Stanford University, 1965) is Professor and specialist in Mass Communication Theory and Research in the School of Journalism and Mass Communication at the University of Minnesota. His areas of interest include mass media in the community setting, flow of scientific and technological information, and the knowledge gap phenomenon. He is coauthor, with G. A. Donohue and C. N. Olien, of *Community Conflict and the Press* (Sage, 1980).

PHILLIP K. TOMPKINS (Ph.D., Purdue University, 1962) was Professor of Communication and Associate Dean of the School of Humanities, Social Science, and Education at Purdue University before joining the faculty of the University of Colorado as a Professor of Communication in 1986. His interests include the sensory nature of ordinary language, communication and control at the organizational level, and hegemony at the societal level. He recently presented a paper on the Aviation Safety Reporting System at a conference on natural and technological hazards sponsored by the National Science Foundation. He has written articles and reviews for *Communication Monographs*, the *Quarterly Journal of Speech,* the *James Joyce Quarterly, Esquire,* the *Journal of Communication*, and others. He is the author of *Communication: Traditional Themes and New Directions.* He is currently the President-Elect of the International Communication Association.

TIMOTHY WIDMAN (Ohio State University) holds a degree in philosophy, and specializes in applications of current continental social theory to communication research regarding complex social organizations, international communication, and technology transfer. He directs an award-winning international television producers' consortium and produces minority business programs for Columbus public-access television. Currently, he is completing his doctoral dissertation on postcritical phenomenology and social research.

D. LAWRENCE WIEDER (Ph.D., University of California, Los Angeles, 1969) is currently Associate Professor of Communication at the University of Oklahoma. His current research concerns child-child and child-adult interaction in a preschool setting and indirect modes of speaking in officials' reports of error. He has published numerous research articles and chapters, and is author of *Language and Social Reality: The Telling of the Convict Code* (1974).

DON H. ZIMMERMAN (Ph.D., University of California, Los Angeles, 1966) is a Professor of Sociology and Communication Studies at the University of California, Santa Barbara. His current work involves the analysis of audio- and videotape recordings of communications in an emergency dispatch center, including calls from the public as well as interactions between dispatchers. His most recent publication on emergency telephone calls (coauthored with Marilyn Whalen) appeared in *Social Psychology Quarterly*.